Emily Post's
E T I Q U E T T E
The Blue Book of Social Usage

Published by Funk & Wagnalls Company, Inc.
for the EMILY POST INSTITUTE, INC.

Etiquette: The Blue Book of Social Usage
Children Are People
The Emily Post Cook Book

THE BLUE BOOK OF SOCIAL USAGE

Emily Post's
ETIQUETTE

REVISED BY *Elizabeth L. Post*

FUNK & WAGNALLS
A *Division* of READER'S DIGEST BOOKS, INC.
New York

EMILY POST'S ETIQUETTE
Library of Congress Catalogue Card Number 65–15320
Copyright under the Articles of the Copyright Convention
of the Pan-American Republics and the United States
Composed, printed, and bound in the United States of America

PREFACE

to the Eleventh Edition

When my husband and I became engaged, one of the first things he wanted to do was to take me to Edgartown, Massachusetts, and introduce me to his grandmother, Emily Post. In spite of his reassurances, and obvious devotion to her, I had all the natural reservations about meeting the famous First Lady of Etiquette, and I was a very nervous young lady when we arrived at her lovely island home that day in June, 1944. And I remained nervous for at least five minutes! In that space of time, I found that the supposedly unapproachable authority on all our manners and behavior was the sweetest, most natural, warmhearted, unaffected person I had ever met. From that day on, we were as close as two people separated by a span of some years can be, and I was never once made uncomfortable or self-conscious in her presence. That, to me, is the proof of the value of etiquette. To practice perfect manners without appearing to be "stiff" and at the same time to let those about you feel that *they* are equally well-mannered is a goal that can be achieved only by making consideration and unselfishness an integral part of your behavior.

My husband and I, and our children, spent a great deal of time with "Grandmama," as we always called her, and the children loved her as much as we did. Even they felt the gracious atmosphere that radiated from her and were almost invariably at their best in her presence, not because they had to be, but because they wanted to be.

We often discussed etiquette in those years, both the subject itself and the book she wrote about it. Emily Post was thoroughly aware of the changing pattern of modern living and made a point of keeping in constant touch with the changes both through her correspondence with readers and through the activities of the members of her own family. Furthermore, she fully realized that the time would come when etiquette would necessarily be affected by these changes. She herself eliminated and changed parts of her original work in frequent revisions over the years, and she foresaw that one day still other parts would no longer be applicable. And, conversely, she recognized that new aspects of modern life, nonexistent then and therefore unmentioned in earlier editions, would need to be considered.

As a result, Emily Post founded—in 1946—the Emily Post Institute. The purpose of the Institute was, and is, to perpetuate the traditions of gracious living by making available the most recent information on etiquette today. The staff of the Institute worked closely with Mrs. Post herself, and she actively supervised all phases of the work until her recent death. She insisted from the beginning that I take an active part, and it is for this reason that I have undertaken this revision of *Etiquette*.

All of us connected with this project have constantly kept in mind the need to maintain the high standards set by Emily Post, although in the less formal life that most of us lead today, some of the rules may seem more stringent than ever. If we have succeeded in making this revision of her book a useful, readable, and practical guide on all questions of etiquette for young and old alike, then we will know that we have carried on the work started by Emily Post as she would have wished.

ELIZABETH L. POST

CONTENTS

Part *TWO*

CORRESPONDENCE

the Check—Tipping—A Host's Responsibilities—Women Dining
Out—Restaurant Courtesy

13
The opera, the theater, and other indoor entertainments « 110

The Opera—The Theater—The Movies—Circuses, Ice Shows, and
Rodeos

14
Outdoor events « 117

At a Professional Match—At College and School Matches—At a
Public Beach—Parks and Playgrounds

15
Appearing on television and radio « 121

Dressing for Television—Your Voice and Manner

16
Conducting meetings « 123

Meetings of Large Organizations—Meetings Held in the Home

Part FOUR

ADVICE FOR TRAVELERS

17
Planning your trip « 127

Reservations—Leaving Your Home in Order—Travel Documents

Part *FIVE*

FORMAL ENTERTAINING

Part SIX

INFORMAL ENTERTAINING

Part *SEVEN*

SPECIAL OCCASIONS

Part *EIGHT*

WEDDINGS

and How Big?—The Invitations—The Wedding List—Choosing the Bride's Attendants—Choosing the Best Man and Ushers—Another Word About Attendants—Planning the Church Service—Planning the "Wedding Breakfast"—The Wedding Cake—The Flowers—Other Decorations and Accessories—Music for Church and Reception—The Wedding Pictures—Wedding Presents and Other Gifts

Part TEN

CARDS AND CALLS

Part *ELEVEN*

Part *TWELVE*

Part THIRTEEN

ON HOW TO DRESS

Part FOURTEEN

THE WELL-APPOINTED HOUSE

Emily Post's
E T I Q U E T T E
The Blue Book of Social Usage

Part ONE

THE ART OF CONVERSATION

1

Introductions, greetings, and farewells

Many times, the few words that we are called upon to say as we meet someone, whatever our feelings about him, and whether or not we ever expect to see him again, can create an impression with far-reaching consequences. This also applies to our manner of leaving a group, be they our best friends or our merest acquaintances. As a result, the forms that are used on such occasions may be of more importance than their brevity and simplicity suggest. An automatic familiarity with them leaves our minds and energies free for the more complicated arts of conversation and gracious listening.

THE UNBREAKABLE RULES OF INTRODUCTION

Rules for introductions have become much less rigid in recent years, but although there is considerable variation in identifying those being introduced and in the phrases used, certain rules must be followed.

First, a younger person is presented to an older person, but, second, a gentleman is always presented to a lady, even though she is no older than eighteen. Third, no woman is ever presented to a man, with the following exceptions: (1) to the President of the United States; (2) to the recognized heads of other countries; (3) to members of a royal family; (4) to cardinals and other high church dignitaries.

THE USUAL FORMS OF INTRODUCTION

The simplest introduction, suitable not only on informal occasions but whenever two individuals are introduced, is the mere pronouncing of two names: "Mrs. Woodman—Mrs. Norman."

A man is also introduced "Mrs. Woodman—Mr. Norman." A mother introducing a man to her married daughter would say, "Mr. Brown, I would like to introduce you to my daughter Mary Smartlington."

It is certainly discourteous to speak of one's husband as "Mr. Smith" or one's daughter as "Miss Smith." But if one's daughter has a different name, the name can be said with a pause between that makes a parenthesis. "My daughter (pause, and then), Mrs. Smartlington."

The same pause can be used when introducing a stepparent and an acquaintance. In order to avoid confusion if your names are likely to be thought the same, you say, "Mrs. Brown—my stepfather," and after a pause add, "Mr. Jones." This is reallly much more pleasant and more approving of him than saying, "Mrs. Brown—my mother's husband."

Although the name of a stranger or of the older or more notable person is properly said first, this is not really too important—except that a woman's name should be said before a man's, unless the preposition "to" is used before the lady's name. For instance, if you find yourself saying Mr. Norman's name first, it is quite simple to make this slip polite by saying, "Mr. Norman, may I introduce you to Mrs. Maddox?" Or, with greater friendliness, "Mr. Norman, I should like to introduce you to Mrs. Maddox."

Formally, a man introduces another man to his wife: "Mr. Brown, may I present you to my wife?" Or if this seems to you to imply that you are asking Mr. Brown's permission to present him to your wife, you can say, "Mr. Brown, I should like to introduce you to my wife."

To an old friend, a husband would say, "Jim, I want you to meet my wife" (on no account "the wife"!). Then he adds, as though in parentheses, "Mary, Jim Buyer" or "Mr. Buyer." Or if they are all young, he probably says, "Mary, this is Bob Ace," because he is really introducing his friend, not to Mrs. Jones, but to Mary.

A lady introduces her husband to friends and talks about him as "John" and to acquaintances as "my husband." The two names of safety are "my husband" and "my wife," because they are proper no matter to whom you are talking. With others than friends and acquaintances and in business situations, "Mr. Brown" and "Mrs. Brown" are quite correct.
» *See the further discussion of names of safety in Chapter 2.*

It might be emphasized that an introduction prefaced by the phrase "This is," when said with an enthusiastic inflection, can express a warmth and charm that other introductions lack. This feeling was once illustrated in London *Punch* by a drawing of a small boy approaching his mother, holding an abashed small girl by the hand, and radiantly exclaiming, "Mummy! THIS IS HER!" In the same way, a child would introduce a beloved teacher enthusiastically, "Mother, *this* is Miss Brown," or, on the other hand, exclaim, "Miss Brown, *this* is my mother!"—in the sense of "Behold! this is she—my mother."

INTRODUCING RELATIVES-IN-LAW

A lady formally introduces her son's wife to acquaintances as "My daughter-in-law," but with friends she uses the less formal form, "Mary, Dick's wife." To the acquaintance, "my daughter-in-law" depends for its warmth on the tone of voice in which it is spoken. And this is, of course, an extremely important point in all introductions. By tone alone, the same words can convey every shade of feeling from cool indifference to adoration.

While the intention of introducing a parent-in-law as simply "Father" or "Mother" is well meant, it may be confusing. It is better to say, "This is my mother-in-law" or, if you prefer, "my husband's mother." When introducing other relatives-in-law, say "my husband's sister" and "my brother John's wife" (or "Jim's sister" and "John's wife" to one who knows who Jim and John are). These identifications are more clearly understood than "My sister-in-law."

TEEN-AGERS AND YOUNG ADULTS

Informality is equally suitable to young adults and teen-agers. Muriel Manners, for example, taking a friend to the country club, greets a group of friends with "Hello, everybody. This is Sally Stranger." Everyone then calls Sally by her first name, and further introductions may be made in the same way by those she has just met: "Sally Stranger, Lucy and Bob Gilding." Or "Lucy, this is Sally Stranger," and then to Sally, "That is Bob Gilding, and that is Tom Brown," for a man is always introduced to a girl.

If Muriel were not really a friend of Sarah Stranger, but found herself responsible for making the introductions, she would introduce her—and her own friends as well—by their titles of Mrs., Miss, or Mr., quite as formally as her mother would. The stranger, by the way, must wait to be called by her first name before calling others by theirs. A younger person never calls an older person by his or her first name unless he is asked to, and whether older people choose to have those who are younger call them by their first names is for them to decide. This informal practice is, however, becoming increasingly popular.

OTHER PERMISSIBLE FORMS

There are many other forms of introduction that might be called conversational introductions. For example: "Mrs. Parker, do you know Mrs. Norman?" "Mrs. Parker, you know Mrs. Robinson, don't you?"

Or you may say, "Mrs. Robinson, have you met Mrs. Parker?" or, to attract her attention, "Mary! you have met Mrs. Parker, haven't you?—Mrs. Robinson."

At times, a few words of explanation make the introduction of a stranger pleasantly smooth. "Mrs. Worldly—Miss Jenkins. She writes as Grace Gotham." Or, "Mr. Neighbor, I should like you to meet Mr. Tennis. He has just won the tournament at Forest Hills." Such well-meant explanations can be overdone, however, for you may create the effect of trying to impress one acquaintance with the importance of another.

FORMS TO AVOID

Never say, "Mr. Jones, shake hands with Mr. Smith," or "Mrs. Jones, I want to make you acquainted with Mrs. Smith." And, in introducing one person to another, do not call one of them "my friend." You may say "my aunt" or "my sister" or "my cousin," but to pick out one person as "my friend" is bad manners, for it implies that the other person is not.

If you are introducing someone to another who is a very special friend, you may say, "Mrs. Smith, I want you to meet Mrs. Jones." But in no circumstances say, "Mrs. Smith, meet Mrs. Jones." This last phrase lacks friendliness and courtesy.

Do not repeat "Mrs. Jones—Mrs. Smith. Mrs. Smith—Mrs. Jones." To say each name once is enough, except when one is foreign or difficult to pronounce. In this event, repeating the name a second time, and slowly, is helpful.

Some people dislike being asked their names. To say "What is your name?" is abrupt and unflattering. If giving your own name doesn't elicit the information, you can almost always find a third person later and ask, "Who was the lady with the gray feather in her hat?" The next time you see her, you will be able to say, "How do you do, Mrs. Green?"

FORMAL AND CEREMONIAL FORMS OF INTRODUCTION

The most ceremonious introduction possible is: "Mrs. Distinguished, may I present Mr. Traveler?" or "Mrs. Young, may I present Professor Gray?"

Present is somewhat more formal than *introduce*, but "may I introduce" is equally proper.

TO THE PRESIDENT OF THE UNITED STATES

The correct introduction of either a man or woman is: "Mr. President, I have the honor to present Mrs. [or Mr.] Williams." Or "Mrs.

Williams of Chicago," or whatever, if further identification is really necessary.

Both men and women respond in the same way. That is, Mrs. Williams bows. If the President offers his hand, Mrs. Williams gives him hers. She does not offer hers should he fail to make this gesture of courtesy—as is most unlikely.

TO A REIGNING SOVEREIGN

Because the formality of having one's name put on a presentation list has been gone through beforehand, at the actual presentation the "accepted" name is repeated from one functionary to another and nothing is said to the king or queen except "Mrs. [or Mr.] Williams."

Mrs. Williams curtsies, and, if the king offers to shake hands, she curtsies again as she gives him her hand. If by any chance she has any objection to curtsying, she must not ask to be presented to the sovereign. Mr. Williams follows the same procedure, bowing instead of curtsying.

On less formal occasions, a woman is presented to any member of a reigning family, "Your Royal Highness [or whatever the title], may I present Mrs. Williams?"

TO CHURCH DIGNITARIES

To a cardinal, one says, "Your Eminence [or in England, Your Grace], may I present Mrs. Williams?"

One who is not a Catholic behaves exactly as he would to a king, but a Roman Catholic drops on the right knee, places the right hand, palm down, under the cardinal's extended hand, and kisses his ring.

A woman is always presented to archbishops, bishops, monsignors, and priests. Mrs. Williams would reply to these introductions by saying to the archbishop or bishop, "How do you do, Your Excellency?" and to the monsignor, "How do you do, Monsignor Ryan?" She would speak to a priest as "Father Kelly" or simply "Father."

TO OTHER DISTINGUISHED PERSONS

With the exception of heads of state and high church dignitaries, who are discussed in the paragraphs above, these persons are all presented *to* women by their proper titles. For example, a foreign ambassador is presented, "Your Excellency, may I present you to Mrs. Williams?"—or a senator, "Mrs. Williams, may I present Senator Davis?" A senator is always "Senator Davis" even when he is no longer in office. But the President of the United States, once out of office, becomes "Mister."

Former governors and former ambassadors are both properly "The Honorable." On ceremonial occasions, you would present "The Honorable John Jones, former governor of the State of Blank." Among friends, of course, "The Honorable John Jones" may be introduced simply as "Mr. Jones."

Doctors and judges are always introduced and addressed by their titles. Protestant clergymen are "Mister" unless they hold the title of doctor, dean, or canon, in which case the surname is added to the proper title. A Catholic priest, however, is "Father Kelly," whatever his other titles may be.

If when you are introduced to an eminent person, the one making the introduction has not spoken clearly or has not used a title (as he should have), the safest thing for you to say is "How do you do?" If the conversation continues and the person's title is still not mentioned, it is acceptable to address any gentleman as "Sir." In fact, to avoid repetition of long titles like "Your Royal Highness" or "Mr. President," it is preferable to say "Ma'am" or "Sir" occasionally.

» *For a chart of titles to be used in addressing and introducing important persons, see Chapter 7.*

WHEN TO INTRODUCE

One occasion that always requires introductions is the presentation of everyone to a guest of honor. If you arrive after the receiving line has dispersed, you must look for this guest and present yourself, because it is the height of rudeness to go to an entertainment given in honor of someone and fail to greet him.

RECEIVING LINES

If the party is a very big one for a stranger, the hostess receives, standing with the special guest. People are presented to her as they arrive: "Mrs. Eminent, this is Mrs. Neighbor." She offers her hand. At a smaller, friendly party given for someone who is not a stranger to the majority of the guests, she does not receive with the hostess, but sits or stands in a convenient place so that others can go up and talk with her.

Even at large balls and semipublic receptions, the receiving line should be limited to four whenever possible. Although one thinks of a receiving line as being composed entirely of women, there are many occasions when men also are included, and sometimes men receive alone.

GUESTS AND FRIENDS UNKNOWN TO HOSTESS

When you are taking a house guest with you to a party and your guest is not known in your neighborhood, it is necessary to remember to introduce him or her to all you closely encounter. This does not mean that you should make a grand tour of the room—but do remember that unless your guest is notable, it is unfair to your hostess to expect her to look after *your* guest and to have a stranger's name at the tip of her tongue in order to introduce him to her other guests.

A guest (either man or woman) in a box at the opera, at a horse show, race track, or in any similar place introduces to his host and hostess anyone who comes to speak to him, unless other people block the space between so that an introduction would be awkward.

FORMAL DINNERS

At a formal dinner, the host should see that every gentleman either knows or is presented to the lady he is to take in to dinner, but at a very large dinner, this is not always practical. The gentleman who does not know Mrs. James Jones, whose name is in his "dinner envelope," is expected to find out who she is and ask to be introduced to her. But if even this is difficult, it is entirely correct for him to go up to her, bow slightly, and say, "Mrs. Jones? I'm Henry Smith, and I believe that I am to have the pleasure of taking you in to dinner."

Strangers sitting next to each other at table usually introduce themselves. A gentleman says, "I'm Arthur Robinson," and an older lady replies, "I'm Mrs. Hunter Jones," or a younger one says, "I'm Mary Brown," and perhaps adds, "Bob Brown's wife." If her husband is at the dinner, she may continue, "He is sitting across the table on the right of the lady in the red dress."

When a young woman finds herself next to an unknown man at a dinner party, she may talk to him without telling him her name. But if he introduces himself to her as "John Blank," she says, "I'm Mary Smith," possibly adding, "I'm one of the Smiths who live on Maple Street." She would be thought very prissy should she say, "I'm Miss Smith."

At a dinner with place cards, one may show one's card and say, "This is my name. What's yours?" while looking toward the stranger's card. This gesture is helpful particularly if your name is unusual or difficult to understand.

It is an unbreakable rule that all people who find themselves seated together at any table accept the obligation of talking, with or without a formal introduction. To sit side by side without speaking is one of the greatest discourtesies a guest can show a hostess.

ONE PERSON TO A GROUP

On formal occasions, when a great many people are present, one person is not introduced to each and every person there. An arrival may be introduced to one or two people, or he may be left to talk with those nearby without exchanging names.

But at a small lunch, for instance, let us suppose you are the hostess. Your position is not necessarily by the door, but it is toward it. Mrs. King is sitting quite close to you, and so is Mrs. Lawrence. Miss Robinson and Miss Brown are much farther away. Mrs. Jones enters. You take a few steps forward and shake hands with her, then stand aside, as it were, to see whether Mrs. Jones goes to speak to anyone. If she apparently knows no one, you say, "Mrs. King—Mrs. Jones." Mrs. King, if she is young, rises, shakes hands with Mrs. Jones, and then sits down. If Mrs. King is about the same age as Mrs. Jones, she merely extends her hand and does not rise. Having said "Mrs. Jones" once, you do not repeat it immediately, but turning to the other lady sitting nearby, you say, "Mrs. Lawrence." You can, if you choose, look across the room and continue, "Miss Robinson, Miss Brown—Mrs. Jones." The two nod but do not rise.

It is much more practical to name those already present before naming the new arrival. Naturally, Mrs. Jones is paying attention, but one who is chatting may need to hear her own name before she hears the name of the new arrival.

Typical of many hospitable hostesses who give very large parties is the practice of leading a guest, particularly a stranger, on a tour around the room to make sure that he—or more especially she—is introduced to everyone. Unfortunately, this well-meant tour is often a failure. The poor stranger is hopelessly confused by too many names, and the good intentions of the hostess are often interrupted by the arrival of other guests.

The best procedure is to seat a stranger with a nearby group, introducing her to them. Even if the hostess overlooks these introductions or is interrupted, the stranger will not be marooned because in a friend's house people *always* talk with those seated near them. The good hostess will, of course, make every effort to see that all her guests are introduced during the course of any party of moderate size.

At a very big lunch, when a newcomer does not at once join someone he knows, the hostess places him or her next to one or more earlier arrivals. Although it is polite to introduce strangers to those who will be seated together while dining, it is not really necessary because they quite properly introduce themselves at the table. In the living room before and after the meal, a guest falls naturally into conversation with those she or he is next to without the giving or asking of names.

INTRODUCING ONESELF

At all informal gatherings, the roof of a friend serves as an introduction, but at a very large party (a dance or a wedding reception, for example) it is not necessary to speak with those whom you do not know, unless you and another guest find yourselves apart from the others. In such a case, you might make a casual remark about the beauty of the bride or a comment on the weather. Then, if you wish to continue the conversation, you should introduce yourself with an identifying remark: "I am Sally's cousin," or "I am a neighbor of the groom." Whether to talk or not usually depends on mutual willingness.

There are many occasions when you have a good reason for knowing someone, and then it is quite proper to introduce yourself. For instance, you would say, "Mrs. Worldly, aren't you a friend of my mother? I am Jane, Mrs. John Smith's daughter." Mrs. Worldly says, "Yes, indeed, I am. I am so glad you spoke to me."

But if a strange man says, "Aren't you Muriel Manners?" Muriel says, "Yes," and waits for his explanation. Then if the stranger continues, "I think my sister Millicent—Brown—is a friend of yours," Muriel offers her hand and, smiling, asks, "Are you George or Alec?"

"I'm Alec." Whereupon Muriel probably says, "Well, Alec, I *am* glad to meet you at last."

But unless he is the brother of a friend, or a particular friend of a friend, a man should say, "Are you Miss Manners? I am Arthur Jones. I met you at a dinner at Mrs. Worldly's last winter." Whereupon Muriel would greet him with the usual, "How d'you do, Mr. Jones?"

» *For further information on announcing oneself, especially in business situations, see Chapter 2.*

WHEN NOT TO INTRODUCE

We all know at least one of those introduction enthusiasts who cannot let one person pass another without insisting that they stop to be introduced. At a small "get-together," this is quite all right, but at a large tea or wedding reception, or at any general gathering, repeating never-to-be-remembered names is a mistake unless there is some special reason for doing so. For instance, a friend might be chagrined should he have missed meeting a celebrity or a person in whom he has an especial interest.

On any occasion, a newly arriving visitor is not introduced to someone who is taking leave. Nor is an animated conversation between two persons interrupted—very especially one between a young woman and man—to introduce a third, who then joins them without encouragement! It should be unnecessary to write this injunction, but it is a definite and needed protest against the all-too-many elderly men and women who cannot observe a girl and a man obviously enjoying a conversation without breaking into it.

CONVERSATION WITHOUT INTRODUCTION

Sometimes it happens that in talking to one person you want to include another in your conversation without making an introduction. For instance, suppose you are talking in your yard to a landscape gardener and a friend joins you. You greet your friend and then casually include her by saying, "Mr. Smith is suggesting that I dig up these daisies and put in delphiniums." Whether your friend gives an opinion about the change in color of your flower bed or not, she has been made part of your conversation.

There are other occasions when a half-way introduction seems most appropriate. Suppose, for example, you wish to make a domestic employee known to a guest. "Olga, would you please take Mrs. Jones's bag to her room?" Or you might say to your guest, "Mary, this is Hilda, who will be glad to take your bag for you."

Even in formal households, loved and respected servants, especially those who have been with a family for many years, are often introduced to close friends. For example, a young man might say to his new fiancée, "Mary, this is Lizzy Smith, who brought me up," and to Lizzy, "Lizzy, I know you will love Mary as much as I do."

In many homes today, one domestic is employed who helps in so many ways that she becomes more than a "maid" and is often known as a "mother's helper." These wonderful people frequently become almost a member of the family and rightfully expect to be treated as such. Therefore, out of consideration for their feelings, the thoughtful employer introduces them to guests, especially to house guests. The hostess might say, "Mary, this is Sally Jones, whom we couldn't manage without. Sally, this is my friend, Mrs. Charles." If Sally is on hand to take wraps from dinner guests, she may be introduced in the same way. An older woman, especially one whose employers are a young couple, may be called and introduced as "Mrs. Jones."

WHAT TO DO WHEN INTRODUCED

WHAT TO SAY

In answering an introduction, adding the name of the person whom you have met after saying "How do you do?" is the warmest, and therefore most polite, response. In the case of an older person or one of stature, it also adds a note of respect. Repeating the name is a great help, too, in committing it to memory.

If you have not heard the new name clearly, it is perfectly correct to say simply, "How do you do?" It may be said gladly or casually, and it may be varied in pronunciation or emphasis, depending on the degree of warmth you wish to convey. In any event, when Mrs. Worldly has been introduced to Mr. Struthers and replies, "How do you do, Mr. Struthers?" he nods and need not say anything more, although he may say, "I'm very glad to meet you."

One should never say, "I am pleased to make your acquaintance," a stilted response that has, fortunately, almost died out. On an occasion when you meet someone whom you have heard much about and have long wanted to meet, you may of course say, "Oh, I am so *glad* to meet you," and then go on to say, "John Brown speaks of you all the time" or whatever may be the reason for your special interest.

WHEN TO SHAKE HANDS

Gentlemen always shake hands when they are introduced to each other even if they have to cross a room to do so. Ladies may do as they wish. Boys and girls both follow the example of their fathers and shake hands when introduced, but not when greeting their friends—except at a formal party when they shake hands with both hostess and host.

When a gentleman is introduced to a lady, she generally smiles, nods, and says, "How do you do?" Strictly speaking, it is her place to offer her hand or not, as she chooses; but if he should extend his hand, she as a matter of course gives him hers. Nothing could be ruder than to treat any spontaneous friendliness curtly. In general, it is the place of a gentleman to whom another is being introduced to offer his hand first, but usually the gesture is simultaneous.

As to whether or not one shakes hands on parting, there is no fixed rule. One is more likely to shake hands with someone whom one finds sympathetic than with one who is the contrary. Nearly all rules of etiquette are elastic, but there is a wide distance between rudeness and reserve. You can be courteously polite and at the same time reserved to someone who does not appeal to you, or you can be welcoming and friendly to another whom you like on sight.

THE PERSONALITY OF A HANDSHAKE

A handshake may create a feeling of liking or of irritation between two strangers. Who does not dislike a "boneless" hand extended as though it were a spray of seaweed or a boiled fish? It is equally annoying to have one's hand clutched aloft in exaggerated manner, or shaken violently, as though it were being used to clean a spot out of the atmosphere. What woman does not wince at the viselike grasp that cuts her rings into her flesh and temporarily paralyzes her every finger?

The proper handshake is made briefly, but there should be a feeling of strength and warmth in the clasp, and one should at the same time look into the countenance of the person whose hand one takes. In giving her hand to a foreigner, a married woman always relaxes her arm and fingers, as it is still customary in some Latin countries for him to lift her hand to his lips. (Except in the movies, the hand of an unmarried girl is not kissed.) But by a relaxed hand is not meant a wet rag; a hand should have life even though it be passive.

To a good friend a woman gives a much firmer, warmer clasp than she does to a mere acquaintance. Younger women usually shake the hand of the older; otherwise, women merely clasp hands, give them a dropping movement rather than a shake, and let go.

WHEN TO RISE

On formal occasions, the hostess always stands at the door and the host nearby. Both shake hands with every arrival. On informal occasions, they both rise and go forward to greet each guest. The children in the family should rise for every grown person who enters the room (and to receive another child) and stand until the older person is seated. Grown as well as half-grown members of the family other than the host and hostess rise to greet guests, but do not necessarily shake hands.

A woman guest does not stand when being introduced to someone at a distance, nor when shaking hands with anyone, unless that person is very much older.

Should an old lady enter the room in which many other ladies are seated, only the members of the family rise, since seven or eight all getting up at once would produce an effect not so much of politeness as of confusion.

Every gentleman stands as long as his hostess or any other lady near him does. Nor does he sit if any other gentleman with whom he is talking remains standing.

Furthermore, a man always rises when a woman comes into a room. In public places, men do not jump up for every strange woman who happens to approach, but if any woman addresses a remark to him, he stands as he answers her.

When a woman goes to a man's office on business, he should stand up to receive her, offer her a chair, and should not sit down until after she is seated. When she rises to leave, he must get up instantly, stand for as long as she remains, and then go with her as far as the door, which he holds open for her.

In a restaurant, when a lady greets him, a gentleman merely makes the gesture of rising slightly from his chair and nodding. » *For additional details, see Chapter 12, "In restaurants."*

THE YOUNG GREET THE OLD

It is very rude for young people not to go and shake hands with an older person of their acquaintance whom they meet away from home, especially a host or hostess to whose house they have often gone. It is not at all necessary for either young women or young men to linger and enter into a long conversation, unless the older person detains them, which he should not do beyond the briefest minute. The one excuse for passing by as quickly as possible is when the older person is a clinging questioner who won't let any approach of friendliness end without asking for a complete report on the health and occupation of every relative and friend of one who merely wished to bid a polite "Good evening" to one of the "family friends."

NAME "BLACK-OUTS"

When you are talking with someone whose name you are struggling to remember and are joined by a friend who looks inquiringly from you to the nameless person—perhaps even asks you, "Won't you introduce me?"—you are obviously helpless to do anything further than introduce your friend to the stranger by saying to the latter, "Oh, don't you know Mrs. Neighbor?"

Everyone is satisfied when the stranger is so tactful and understanding as to announce her own name. If she says nothing, however, and Mrs. Neighbor makes matters worse by saying, "You didn't tell me your friend's name," the situation reaches the depth of embarrassment. The only solution is to be completely frank, admit you haven't heard or do not remember the name, and, throwing yourself on their mercy, ask them to complete the introduction themselves.

When meeting someone who may have forgotten you, you should never say, "You don't remember me, do you?" and then give no further help. Unless the person you speak to greets you by name, you should say at once, "I'm Mrs. Brown or Mary Brown [and then if this does not bring a sign of recognition], we met at the Roberts'."

INFORMAL GREETINGS

"Hello" is the universal form of greeting in America. It is acceptable in any situation except after a formal introduction. Even comparative strangers say "Hello" in passing, and among young people it is considered friendly after a first-name introduction. "Sally, I'd like you to meet Joan," and Sally says, "Hello, Joan, I'm glad to meet you."

Even more informal is the widely-used "Hi." Although it should never be said in answer to an introduction, at any other time it is a friendly greeting for young and old alike.

In the business world, "Good morning" is the usual greeting before the lunch hour. After lunch, "Good afternoon" is proper, but because it sounds somewhat stilted, it has largely been replaced by "Hello" and a smile.

"Good afternoon" is used, however, as a phrase of dismissal, indicating that an interview is ended, a class dismissed, etc. Among friends or business acquaintances who know each other personally, "Good-by" or "Good night" is said on parting.

GREETINGS IN PUBLIC

In Europe a gentleman bows to a lady first; in the United States a lady is supposed to greet a gentleman first, but today few people observe this formality. Because the custom of "bowing" has long since become a tipping, or slight raising, of the hat on the part of the man, and a nod and smile on the part of the woman, nothing more is necessary when one passes a casual acquaintance.

In theaters, restaurants, shops, or almost any public place, people speak to acquaintances as long as the greeting does not create a situation that may disturb others around them, as it would in the middle of a movie. If they are too far apart to speak without shouting, they simply smile and wave.

Unless one has a good memory for people, it is always better to nod to someone whose face is familiar than to run the risk of ignoring an acquaintance. It is often difficult to recognize people whom one has met when they are wearing a different type of dress or hat—sports clothes or evening dress, for instance.

But the habit that causes most unintended rudeness is absent-mindedness. Absorbed in their own thoughts, the unmindful do not hear the voice or see the motions made by someone trying to speak to them. They pass a friend unaware of his proximity. It may be annoying to be passed by an "unseeing" acquaintance, but one should be careful not to confuse absent-minded unseeingness with intentional slight; often it is you who have changed in appearance.

Except at a wedding, people do not greet each other in church. At weddings, people do speak softly to friends sitting near them. It would be shocking, however, to enter a church and hear an undignified and unceremonious babel of voices. Ordinarily, if a friend happens to catch your eye, you may perhaps smile, but never actually nod or speak. If you go to a church not your own and a stranger offers you a seat in his pew, you should, of course, almost soundlessly say, "Thank you." But you do not greet anyone until you are out in the vestibule or on the church steps, when you naturally speak to your friends as you encounter them.

THE ANSWER TO "HOW ARE YOU?"

The trait of character that more than any other produces good manners is tact. To one who is a chronic invalid or is in great sorrow or anxiety, a gay "Hello, Mrs. Jones! How *are* you? You look fine!" while kindly meant, is really tactless, since to answer truthfully would make the situation emotional. In such a case, she can only reply, "All right, thank you." She may be feeling that everything is all wrong, but to let go and tell the truth would open the floodgates disastrously. "All right, thank you" is an impersonal and therefore strong bulwark against further comment or explanation.

Normally, "Fine, thank you" or "Very well, thank you" is the correct and conventional answer to "How are you?" unless there is reason to believe that the person asking really wants to know the state of one's health.

THE INTENTIONAL "CUT"

For one person to look directly at another and not acknowledge the other's greeting is a breach of civility. One must therefore be careful not to confuse poor sight or a forgetful memory with an intentional cut. Anyone whose eyes are not sharp or who is not quick of memory can all too easily fail to recognize good friends as well as newly made acquaintances. This does not excuse the bad memory, but it explains the unintended rudeness.

A "cut" is different. It is a direct stare of blank denial, not only insulting to its victim but embarrassing to every witness. Happily it is virtually unknown in polite society.

TAKING LEAVE

When a visitor is ready to leave, he or she merely stands. To one with whom he has been talking, the visitor says, "Good-by. I hope I shall see you again soon," or "I've enjoyed talking to you so much," or, simply, "I'm glad to have met you." Naturally a woman is less effusive in what she says to a man than in what she may say to another woman. And yet she may very well comment enthusiastically on a particular opinion or on some outstanding work he has done. Whatever pleasant remark one person makes, the other answers, "Thank you. You have been very good to listen to me." Or a woman replies to another who hopes to see her again, "I hope so, too," or merely, "Thank you."

In taking leave of a group of strangers—it makes no difference whether you have been introduced or merely included in their conversation—you nod and smile a "Good-by" to any who happen to be looking at you, but you do not attempt to attract the attention of those who are unaware that you are leaving.

When leaving a party early, you find your hostess and say good-by, but you try not to attract more attention than necessary to your going. It might suggest leaving to others and so lead to the premature breaking up of the party.

2

Names and titles

A century ago it was not unusual for a wife to refer to her husband as "Mr. Jones" and to call him "Mr. Jones" when she was speaking to him, even in private. The use of first names was restricted to children, brothers and sisters, close cousins, a very few lifelong friends (of the same sex, of course), and perhaps (but only before their wedding day) by a girl and her fiancé. Ridiculous as these customs now sound, the pendulum seems to have swung too far in the other direction. First names, titles of respect, and descriptive phrases for members of the family have become a hodgepodge of informality and confusion.

THE USE OF FIRST NAMES

In general, first names should indicate that people have met more than once, despite the fact that today they are often used by strangers who have just been introduced. If, however, later in the first meeting one person finds another unusually attractive or if they have common interests or friends, it is perfectly correct for one to say, "Please call me Sally," thus showing a wish to expand the new acquaintance. Furthermore, at any informal party in the home of friends, it is customary to use first names after having responded correctly to the introductions. If you don't, you will be thought stiff and unfriendly. » *For what to do when introduced, see Chapter 1.*

We all know countless people of middle age and older who seem to think that being called "Sally" or "Jack" by Doris Debutante and Bobby Freshman will take them back to the same age level. It may be true that "Sally" or "Jack" does suggest a camaraderie that "Mrs. Autumn" or "Mr. Sere" does not. But one wonders how Mrs. Autumn would feel should she overhear those she supposed were accepting her as their contemporary say, "Here comes Old Sal!" If she and Mr. Sere prefer to be "Sally" and "Jack," however, no one else has a right to object.

Certainly when an older person calls a younger person by his first name, the younger is not to take it as an invitation to respond with a first name unless very specifically invited to do so.

CHILDREN AND OLDER PEOPLE

PARENTS

Unfortunately, in America today, respect for older people is not so prevalent as it was a few generations ago. One of the areas in which parents should insist on respect is in the manner in which they permit their children to address them. *It is a flagrant violation of good manners for children to call their natural parents by their first names.*

STEPPARENTS

The question of what children should call their stepparents is a difficult one, because the circumstances are so variable, and the answer can depend only on what seems to be best in each case.

The most important thing, however, is that children should *never* be forced to call a stepparent "Mother" or "Father" or any nickname having that meaning, especially if their own parent is living. If they *choose* to do so, it is a compliment to the stepparent and should be encouraged.

If a child goes to live with a stepparent at a very young age, and if his own parent is dead or if the child is not and probably will never be acquainted with that parent, then he would consider his stepparent as his own and say "Mother" or "Father." This is especially true if he has stepbrothers or stepsisters whom he hears using those names. However, if the child is older when one parent remarries the situation is quite different. If he has known the stepparent for some time, he may call him (or her) by a nickname or even by his first name. Actually, a nickname seems to be the best solution if one can be found that is appropriate and not a derivative of "Mother" or "Father."

NAMES FOR PARENTS-IN-LAW

The question of what a bride is to call her parents-in-law has no definite answer, and the choice of names is purely personal. In unusually formal families, one hears "Mr." and "Mrs.," which to most of us sound very uncaring. Usually, and more naturally, parents-in-law are called by names that mean mother and father, but are not the names that the bride uses for her own parents. Or perhaps they are called "Mr." and "Mrs." until a grandchild's nicknames—"Mimi" and "Pompy," for example—gradually become theirs.

The ban against "Mother" and "Father" results from consideration for one's own parents. Very few mothers or fathers would be happy to hear their own special names bestowed elsewhere.

Curiously enough, the less intimate relationships of aunts, uncles, and even grandparents never come into question, because with the exception of his parents, the bride calls all her husband's relatives exactly what he does, and he in turn does the same in speaking of hers.

OTHER ADULTS

A child or young person may call an older person by his first name only when that person has specifically asked that he do so. There are numerous reasons why close family friends may choose to be so informal, and as long as the child understands that it is done only at the request of the grown-up, it is quite acceptable.

Some adults, for example, dislike being called "Aunt," "Uncle," or "Cousin." In other cases, really intimate friends are devoted to the children and feel that "Mr. [or "Mrs.] Surname" does not express the relationship. Sometimes not wanting to be called by their first names, these friends or relatives suggest nicknames for themselves. Otherwise, a child addresses all friends of his parents as "Mr. [or "Mrs.] Surname."

REFERRING TO HER HUSBAND OR HIS WIFE

Usually—and correctly—a lady says "my husband" when speaking of him to an acquaintance. But to a friend or to the friend of a friend, she speaks of him as "John." This usage does not, however, give anyone else the privilege of calling him "John" unless asked to do so.

In the same way, Mr. Worldly speaks of "Edith" to intimate masculine friends and to every woman whom they both know socially, whether they themselves call her "Edith" or "Mrs. Worldly." But to a man not an intimate friend and to a woman who is a stranger, he speaks of her as "my wife." In most business situations, if he has occasion to speak of her at all, he would say, "Mrs. Worldly thinks, or says, thus or so. . . ." Thus, when the Duke of Edinburgh, accompanying Queen Elizabeth II, was hailed by a former shipmate in the British Navy, he correctly introduced him to "my wife."

NAME OF SAFETY

The so-called "name of safety" used by every well-bred man, woman, or child when speaking to a stranger about any member of the family is "my wife," "my husband," "my daughter," "my mother," or, as necessary, "my sister Alice," "my son George." No matter to whom these merely descriptive names are said, they can't be wrong. On the other hand, should Mrs. Jansen, whom you have met socially, speak of her husband as "Mr. Jansen," she would be very rude.

WHEN NOT TO REFER BY FIRST NAME

In speaking about other people, "Mr.," "Mrs.," or "Miss" is used if the person with whom you are talking is not acquainted with the one to whom you refer. It is improper to speak of absent friends by their first names unless you have referred to them often enough so that the person to whom you are talking recognizes them readily and feels that he or she knows them. For example, to your close friend to whom you had often spoken of your college roommate you might say, "We are so delighted— Jane Stuart is coming East to visit us next month." But speaking of someone you may have mentioned only once or twice, a word of identification is necessary. "Yesterday I ran into that nice Mrs. Brown whom Jim and I met on the cruise last year."

ANNOUNCING ONESELF

ARRIVING AT THE DOOR

When an adult member of the family comes to the door in answer to your ring, you should never call yourself "Mr." or "Mrs." or "Miss," but announce yourself as "John Grant" or "Sally Smythe" and explain the purpose of your visit. If he obviously does not recognize you, you should further identify yourself by a sentence or two: "I'm a friend of Jim's at the office" or "Susan and I met at the Barry's cocktail party" or whatever seems appropriate.

If a child answers the door, you say, "I'm Mr. Grant" or "Mrs. Smythe" and "Would you please call your Mother for me, if she is at home?"

If the door is answered by a maid who does not know you and if you are not expected, you announce yourself as "Mr. John Grant." If you are expected, you merely say, "Mr. Grant." You do the same when giving your name to the announcer at a party.

THE BUSINESSMAN ANNOUNCES HIMSELF

When you enter an unfamiliar office, best form is to say to the receptionist, "Good morning. My name is Rodger Sailscurve. I have a 10 o'clock appointment with Mr. Byre." At this point, offer your business card. Some firms keep a card or other record of each visitor; in any case, it helps the receptionist give your name correctly to the secretary of the person you wish to see.

If you do not have a specific appointment, it is helpful to give a little information about your business. "Good afternoon, I am Rodger Sailscurve of the Schmid Corporation. I would like to see Mr. Byre about our line of lubricants."

ON THE TELEPHONE

» *Introducing oneself on the telephone is described in Chapter 62.*

USE OF TITLE OF DOCTOR

When the title "Doctor" indicates a degree required for the practice of a profession, as in medicine, surgery, or dentistry, it is used instead of "Mister" at all times.

But when the title is an earned or honorary one indicating that a man or woman has received a degree in such a faculty as divinity, law, philosophy, or literature, it is used mainly in professional work. In private life, he may continue to call himself "Mister." In any event, he usually uses "Mr." or no title at all on visiting cards and in club or social directories. His friends and acquaintances may wish to call him "Doctor" in courtesy.

NAMES LEGALLY CHANGED

Whatever the reason for changing the name by which one has been known, social and business associates should be notified of the change if embarrassing situations are to be avoided. The quickest and simplest way of telling them is to send out formal announcements in this form:

Mrs. and Mrs. John Original-Name
Announce that by Permission of the Court
They and Their Children
Have Taken the Family Name of
Miller

3

Words and how we use them

The quality of our speech is of prime importance because the measure of our cultivation is made evident the moment we begin to talk. Nothing so instantly reveals our background, training, self-discipline, and education as the words we choose and the way we pronounce them. Well-educated people, for example, invariably use certain expressions and appear to avoid others instinctively; when a stranger uses an avoided one, he proclaims a lack of information in much the same way that someone does when he fails to respond with the correct password.

To use English of distinction is not too difficult. The dictionary is meticulous in its definitions, and grammar determines each word's use. These matters can be learned by anyone who cares enough to try. Furthermore, whenever necessary, the dictionary labels words as preferred, archaic, colloquial, popular, slang, or vulgar. The shades of meaning of a word, however, may vary from one locale to another, and there are, of course, local or regional dialects and accents. Usually, to speak as the cultivated element in one's home town speaks is sufficient for all social and domestic purposes. Be sure, though, not to confuse the cultivated with the caricature—the "lady" with the comic-strip society manner who says "Pardon *me*" and talks of "desiring a new gown" and "attending" this and that with her "escort" and who prates of "cult-your." The offense of pretentiousness is committed more often perhaps by women than by men, who are usually more natural and direct.

Of course, there are certain exceptional people, virtually uneducated and almost illiterate, who can seemingly overcome all handicaps. They may say "He don't want to" and "I done it," proving their lack of grammatical training, but at the same time their exceptional characters make them respected by everyone who knows them, because they are what they seem and nothing more. Far better this extreme than the extreme of pretentiousness. A genuine, sincere, kindly American man or woman can go anywhere and be welcomed by everyone, provided that he be a person of some natural talent, ability, wit, or grace. One finds him all over the world, neither aping the manners of others nor treading on the sensibilities of those less fortunate than himself.

PRONUNCIATION

Traits of speech that are typical of whole sections of the country, or accents that have been inherited from foreign-born parents are not to be confused with crude pronunciations that have their origins in illiteracy or carelessness.

REGIONAL AND FOREIGN ACCENTS

A gentleman of Irish blood may have a brogue as rich as plum cake. Another person may speak in a soft Southern drawl, or a flat New England tone, or a rolling Western style. The Boston accent is very crisp and is considered by some the best English spoken in America. On occasion the vowels are flattened in a way that suggests London, but not quite. In the South, there is much softness, with "I" turned to "Ah" and a slight tendency toward a drawl. Chicago calls itself "Chicawgo" and eats "chawklut." Philadelphia's "haow" and "caow" for "how" and "cow" and its "mee" for "my" are quite as tenaciously preserved as the "water-r" and "thot" of the West. All these variations merely indicate the part of the country we are from. "Water," pronounced as though it were the watt of electric measure—watter—came, so it is said, from German settlers who pronounced it like "Wasser." "Bot" and "thot" sound ugly to those who pronounce "bought" and "thought" with lips shaped like an "O." But it is very possible that "bought" and "thought" sound ugly to the others, just as "lowng" and "strowng" sound ugly to the English, who always say "lahng" and "strahng."

N'Yawk is supposed to say "yeh" and "Omurica" and "Thuh spoim erl wuz berled" (the sperm oil was boiled). Perhaps five percent of it does, but as a whole the city has no distinguishing accent, because it is a composite of many tongues and many accents. The speech of Boston may be the best, but the pronunciation of New York may be considered the generally accepted speech of Americans, and it is likely to become even more widely recognized by virtue of its dissemination by the radio and television networks.

This is not to say that the regional variations are in any way unacceptable. To some, the speech of others may sound too flat, too soft, too harsh, too refined, too clipped or slow or drawling, but it does not sound uncultivated. Only to those involved in making public speeches, either to the nation at large or to representatives of several areas of the country—perhaps as a candidate for federal office or as a delegate to a national convention—might a markedly local accent be a handicap and then only because it might connote to the listeners a mind limited to that particular locality and uninformed about the broader issues.

As a general rule, therefore, when you look up the pronunciation of a word in your dictionary, you need not be concerned because you may say the "ou" as in "out" or the "a" as in "add" in a way quite unlike that of a Bostonian, say, or a San Franciscan. As long as the sound you produce is natural to you and consistent with your general speech pattern and your region's, you are quite correct—for *you*.

CARELESS AND IGNORANT PRONUNCIATION

Given a good dictionary and the willingness to use it, anyone can pronounce common English words properly. Too many errors are the result of nothing more or less than slovenliness. They are totally unnecessary and only mark the one who makes them as ignorant or uncaring about the impression he makes on others. Such differences as those between "wash" and "wawsh" or "cahn't" and "can't" are of small importance. But one who considers himself able to qualify as an educated person should know better than to commit such errors as "cherce" for "choice," "the ay′ ter" for "theater," and "Feb u ary" for "February."

THE USE AND MEANING OF WORDS

REGIONAL EXPRESSIONS

Like pronunciation, words themselves vary from one section of the United States to another. In one town, the local grocer will put your purchases in a "bag"; in another, he provides a "sack." An expression common in Dallas might as well be Greek when the Texan uses it in Vermont. No one can be expected to know each and every one of these regional words and phrases, certainly—and very often we do not recognize our own special usages. But we ought to be aware that such differences exist, especially when we find ourselves in another part of the country or talking with a visitor from another city. To ignore them can suggest a rudeness that may not be intended, but to talk with apparent unconcern for the listener's understanding—and hence his feelings—is hardly polite. Or if you are the listener, do not hesitate to ask for clarification of such a phrase or word. Otherwise, the conversation may slip away into misunderstanding and confusion for no good reason.

SLANG

The *Standard College Dictionary* defines the word "slang" as follows: "Language, words, or phrases of a vigorous, colorful, facetious, or taboo nature, invented for specific occasions or uses, or derived from the unconventional use of the standard vocabulary." The vocabulary of slang, although usually ephemeral, may achieve wide use, and in the evolution of language, many words originally slang have been adopted by good writers and speakers and have ultimately taken their place as accepted English.

The fact that slang is apt and forceful makes its use irresistible. Naturally, coarse or profane words are unacceptable, but "cool" (meaning attractive or pleasant), "doll" (an attractive girl), and "hood" (a tough boy) are words in such common use that their exclusion from any but the most formal conversation would be absurd.

Slang, to be an asset to your conversation, must be fresh and applicable or it is as unappetizing as cold gravy. Moreover, using slang is like underscoring written words; to be effective, it must be sparingly done. It is all too easy to fall into the habit of using too much or depending on it to express ideas that it cannot adequately convey.

FOREIGN WORDS

Sprinkling foreign words indiscriminately through your speech does not show great education or culture, but an occasional word, used in its proper sense, adds color and interest to English speech and writing. In fact, there are many foreign words that have become an accepted part of our language and, therefore, should be familiar in meaning and pronunciation to all of us.

There are so many foreigners living in the United States, and our paths cross so often, that it is easy to increase one's knowledge of their languages. We have Italian grocers, German bakers, French waiters—to name only a few—all of whom are delighted if you show an interest in their language, how it sounds and what it means.

COMMON FRENCH WORDS

Among modern languages, French is the one from which we have borrowed the greatest number of words, and some, like "amateur," "fiancée," and "hors d'oeuvre," are used so frequently that it is essential to know how to pronounce them correctly.

The French (and Italian) terms used on menus in many of our restaurants are too numerous to learn all at once. Many good cookbooks contain glossaries of these terms and provide an excellent source of reference. In any case, the waiter or headwaiter is always available to explain the dish to you if there is no translation on the menu, and one may always make a note of the words for future study.

WORDS AND PHRASES TO AVOID

Among educated people, no one "arises," or "retires," or "resides" in a "residence." One gets up, takes a bath, goes to bed, and lives in a house. In other words, everything that is simple and direct is better form than the cumbersome and pretentious.

Never say	*Say instead*
I desire to purchase	I would like to buy
Request (suitable for third-person invitations or official communications)	Ask (the proper word under usual circumstances)
He expressed a desire to make your acquaintance	He said he would like to meet you
I presume	I suppose
Converse	Talk
A song entitled (unless used in legal sense)	A song called
I will ascertain	I will find out
Residence (except in printing or engraving)	House
Mansion	Big house
Realtor (except as a technical term)	Real estate agent
Make you acquainted with	(See Introductions, Chapter 1)
Pardon *me*!	I beg your pardon, or, Excuse *me*! or, I'm sorry!
Lovely food	Good food or delicious food
Elegant	Beautiful, lovely, tasteful
Formals	Formal clothes, evening clothes
Boy (when over twenty-one years of age)	Man
Gentleman friend	"A man who is a friend of mine"
Lady friend	"A woman who is a friend of mine"
Drapes	Curtains are hung at a window; hangings or draperies as decoration for walls
Consensus of opinion	Consensus ("consensus of opinion" is redundant, as the word means "collective opinion")
An invite	An invitation
The wife	My wife

Folks	Family
Allow me	Let me
Limb	Arm or leg

Many other expressions are provincial; as offenses they are small, but one who seeks purity of speech should, if possible, avoid them. They include such homey terms as:

Reckon, guess, calculate, *or* figure, *meaning* think.

Visiting with, *meaning* talking with.

WORDS CONFUSED AND MISUSED

Lady and gentleman. These once beautiful words have become so discredited by misappropriation that those to whom they most accurately apply have substituted for them the words man and woman, even putting man first.

However, an understanding of the true meaning of "lady" and "gentleman" is essential to an understanding of the true meaning of good manners. To say a "man" does thus or so has no meaning other than the mental and physical limitations of every male human being. But to say no man cheats at cards or strikes a woman in the face or to say no woman tries to attract the attention of strange men would not be true. Each of these statements is true of a gentleman and of a lady but not necessarily so of a man or a woman.

In practice, these words, though necessary in a book such as this, are very rarely used in ordinary conversation.

Home versus house. In its true meaning, the word "home" is the sentiment, the atmosphere, the spirit, the personality, the hospitality that the house in which you dwell expresses. "Home" is not a synonym for "house." A house is built of wood or brick or stone. You can love your home, work for your home, be at home, or have or do whatever you please at home. You can also eat home cooking, do home designing and home sewing (meaning food cooked in your kitchen and designing or sewing done by yourself or done under your roof); but if you are sensitive to tradition, you never put a piece of furniture in "the home" unless you mean a charitable institution. You would say, "Our home was an old Georgian house," but not "We had a Georgian home."

Formal and informal. "Formal" is a synonym for "ceremonial." A formal party is always conducted according to rules of ritualistic or established forms of ceremony.

In certain houses—Mrs. Worldly's, for instance—formality is inevitable no matter how informal may be her "will you dine informally" invitation.

On the other hand, the Kindharts can invite a hundred guests, half of them strangers, and at the same time achieve a party that has nothing formal about it. In short, the ordinary pleasant social intercourse between friends and neighbors should, it is to be hoped, never be characterized as formal.

While the word "formal" itself denotes the extreme degree of correctness, its exact opposite is illustrated by the following dialogue, which took place between one of yesterday's distinguished gentlemen and his ought-to-be-equally-distinguished grandson. The two were sitting together at a fashionable beach club, when George called out to a passing friend, "Hey, Jim! D'you know—are we going formal tonight?"

Jim answered, "Yeah—guesso!"

Grandfather looked at George's shorts, bare feet, and open collar. "Tell me," he said, "what is meant by 'going formal'?"

The boy shrugged and then half sheepishly replied, "I don't know. I guess it means we've got to put on ties and the girls'll wear skirts."

Precious. When not referring to a gem, but when used as a term of endearment, "precious," is one of the loveliest words in the language. It should for this reason be used only when meaning most beloved, most cherished. A house or a dress is not precious.

In contrast, this word can be used to express irony. When a completely spoiled child has become a neighborhood menace, the neighbors properly speak of him with cutting irony as "his mother's 'precious' son."

Gracious. Although the word "gracious" is one of the most beautiful in our language, it does imply an unavoidable flavor of condescension, and it is therefore most suitably applied to an elderly person who is bending down, as it were, from an earlier period of time rather than from an assumed position of superiority. Obviously, it is not suitably said of a very young person who would better be called friendly, lovely, responsive, or charming. "Your gracious invitation" does not mean "your kind invitation."

Party. In general speech, "party" is correctly used to describe a social gathering, but never in referring to a person. "Do come and bring your guests or friends," never "you and your party." The word probably crept in as a synonym for "person" because of legal usage.

The Man of Distinction. The man of distinction is a very real loss to the vocabulary of this book because he is now concentrating his attention on a tall glass. A very distinguished man implies definite achievement as well as an impressive personality.

CULTIVATING AGREEABLE SPEECH

INCREASING VOCABULARY

Irritating speech is like a badly tuned car engine, for no matter how shiny the chrome, each knock and thump disconcerts the listener. He hears the "er-er-and-er," shares the frantic search for a word, the effort with which each word is pronounced, and never even hears the thoughts the speaker is trying so desperately to convey.

There is no better way to cultivate taste in words than by constantly reading books of proven literary standing. But it must not be forgotten that there can be a vast difference between literary standing and popularity and that many that appear on the best-seller lists have no literary merit whatever.

In recommending the reading of two English authors—Rebecca West and Winston Churchill—as sources of flawless English, it must not be taken as implying that we ourselves have none of our own. But it is true that Winston Churchill's war memoirs have a value of "matter" as well as "manner" of writing English that sets a high standard. And Rebecca West's is of definite advantage to those who are interested in finding an example of English at its *best*.

There is no better way to cultivate both vocabulary and a perfect pronunciation, apart from association with cultivated people, than by getting a small pronouncing dictionary and reading it word by word, marking and studying any that you use frequently and mispronounce or those you wish to learn. Choose a book and read it aloud to yourself, looking up any words you come across that are not familiar to you, and learn the meaning as well as the correct pronunciation. After you can pronounce the words in the book, read it aloud again, this time trying to speak naturally as though you were talking with a friend.

There are available many excellent books containing vocabulary-building instructions, with exercises to help you increase your knowledge of words and test your achievement. The consciousness of these exercises may make you stilted in conversation at first, but by using your new vocabulary constantly this tendency can be overcome with ease.

A postscript of encouragement, however, is that plain speech, which is natural and therefore gives an impression of sincerity, is much more pleasing and friend-making than the self-conscious use of a broad vocabulary that is not really natural to the speaker.

THE CHARMING SPEAKER

The often-heard but not too polite expression "You know she is a lady as soon as she opens her mouth" is not an exaggeration. The first requirement for charm of speech is a pleasing voice. A few singing lessons—even though you have no gift for music and will never sing a note—are of inestimable value in teaching you to place your speaking voice and in teaching you to breathe. A low voice—low in pitch, not in range—is always more pleasing than one forced up against the ceiling and apparently let out through a steam vent in the roof. On the other hand, a voice uttered with so little strength that it threatens to be extinguished or so low as to be heard only with effort is even more trying. Making yourself heard is chiefly a matter of enunciation; if you breathe properly and pronounce distinctly, a low voice carries well and delights a sensitive ear. Socially and in a business office, it is annoying to have to ask a "mumbler" to repeat. Few people with loud voices have any idea that their screaming is not only ear-splitting but in extremely bad form, since it attracts the attention of everyone within shouting radius.

As a nation we do not talk so much too fast as too loud. Tens of thousands twang and slur and shout and burr. Many of us drawl and many others race tongues and breath at full speed, but the speed of our speech does not matter so much. It is pitch of voice that is important, along with pronunciation and enunciation, both of which are essential to the comfort of the listener.

But the outstanding attribute of the charming speech is brevity. The speech that bores, exhausts, and exasperates is one that goes on and on and on with complete disregard of the increasing lethargy of its enforced listeners. Of course, if you are giving a course of lectures or have been asked to give a half-hour- or even an hour-long talk, your primary concern will be not brevity but content. In this case, you must be sure not to dwell at excessive length on any one point. The long speech that entertains is the one that informs and keeps its listeners interested in the subject.

» *See also Chapter 4, "Public speaking."*

Public speaking

Many excellent books have been published on the subject of parliamentary procedure, and in many of our high schools, students are required to take courses in this subject and also in public speaking. This chapter is not directed to experienced speakers, nor those who have to run formal meetings frequently, but to the thousands of private citizens, housewives or storekeepers, who may be called upon to speak at a club meeting, a PTA meeting, or a testimonial dinner. If we are not accustomed to speaking in public, it is likely to be a terrifying experience, but there are many hints that, if thought about in advance, can be a great help in making the occasion a success.

INTRODUCING A SPEAKER

Perhaps more often than women, men are called upon to serve as masters of ceremonies or chairmen at dinners and are expected to introduce the speakers. When the appointed time comes, if he is on a stage or platform, the chairman rises, steps forward, and taps firmly on the speaker's podium or table to attract attention. If he is at a dinner table, he simply rises and the people near him immediately stop talking; this should be enough to bring quiet to the rest of the hall.

An introductory speech should be extremely brief in order not to divert time or attention from the main speaker. A few sentences to identify him are all that is necessary. If he is very well known, you might open your introduction by saying, "Our speaker tonight is Mr. Jim Jones. I know that it is not necessary for me to tell you about him as we have all read of his exploits in Africa. We are most fortunate in having persuaded him to fit this evening with us into his busy schedule, and it gives me great pleasure to introduce—Mr. Jones."

If the speaker is less famous, a few more remarks might be added to explain his background and the reason for his speaking to your organization. But beware of overdoing it, and confine your talk to two or three minutes at the most.

Having made the introduction, sit down quietly until the speech is over. Then you should rise, shake hands, and thank the speaker for his time, his effort, and his excellent speech. » *See also Chapter 16, "Conducting meetings."*

PREPARING YOUR SPEECH

The greatest asset to a successful speech is having it well prepared and rehearsed in advance. It may be long or short, serious or humorous, but the confidence that is gained from knowing that your material is good and your presentation smooth is worth hours of preparation and practice. This does not mean that your speech should be rattled off like a memory exercise, and certainly it should never sound as if it were being read.

After writing the speech, notes should be made (if it is long enough to warrant them) in large clear print on index cards or a small pad. These notes should be only an outline of the speech—simply a reminder in case you lose the train of thought. The speech should be rehearsed several times, first in front of a mirror and then, if possible, before members of your family or friends. This will help you feel less strange when you stand before a larger audience. It is a good idea to try to express a thought in several different ways while you practice, as this tends to make your speech sound less "rehearsed" and more as if you were thinking about what you are saying.

OPENING WORDS

There is a set formula for opening a speech, and it is helpful to an inexperienced speaker because he hears the sound of his voice for a second or two while repeating exact phrases that he has committed to memory. He must turn to the chairman first and, calling him by name, thank him for his introduction. He then starts out by greeting any distinguished persons present and finally the audience. "Mr. Chairman, Sena-

tor Brown, and fellow members of Delta Psi, good evening." Or "Mr.
President, Distinguished Guests, Ladies and Gentlemen."

Some speakers start by giving the audience a suggestion of the points
they will cover in their speech. Others start with an amusing story or a
pertinent quotation to introduce the subject. It is wise not to make too
important a point in the opening paragraphs because the audience may
take a few minutes to settle down to listen. Also, most speakers "warm"
to their subject and will make their salient points more forcefully after
they have overcome any initial nervousness.

USE OF HUMOR AND PROPS

Everyone enjoys listening to a speaker who tells an amusing story
well, but it must have some connection with the subject being discussed.
There is nothing worse than a poor attempt at humor, which fails
either in the choice of the story itself or in its presentation. This distracts
the audience and leaves them searching for the point rather than listening to the speaker. Jokes, anecdotes, and quotations are all useful means
of giving your talk variety and interest. But remember that the audience
wants to hear what YOU have to say and not just a collection of other
peoples' thoughts and actions.

If your subject permits the use of illustrations or slides, by all means
take advantage of this. Not only does it make your preparation easier
(although you still must rehearse, using the slides and perfecting the
timing and mechanical details), but the attention of an audience is held
more firmly when it is seeing as well as hearing.

THE IMPORTANCE OF YOUR VOICE

Closely rivaling in importance your material and preparation is the
quality of your voice. A low-pitched voice is vastly more attractive than
a high one, but it must be loud enough so that the audience need not
strain to hear. Speak slowly rather than fast (between 90 and 130 words,
or half a typed page a minute), but vary the tempo or you will sound
monotonous. A certain amount of variation in pitch is desirable, especially in telling a joke or story, and some words should be stressed for
emphasis. All this is a matter of practice, and you should think of these
points, as well as the content of your speech, while rehearsing.

If a microphone is to be used, try to arrive early enough to test it
with your own voice. If this is not possible, make certain that someone
has proved it to be working properly and try to watch the chairman while
he is introducing you to see how close he stands, how loudly he speaks,
and how he adjusts the height. Most people have a tendency to speak
much too loudly into a microphone and to hold onto the stand, causing
interference. If you have advance notice that a microphone is to be used,
it is almost essential to practice speaking with one beforehand.

THE DANGER OF RAMBLING

The most serious fault of the inexperienced speaker is a tendency to go on and on for too long. Almost invariably, at meetings where a number of people are allotted five or ten minutes to speak, they must be cut off long before they have made their points. When you have been told, or have decided for yourself, the length of the speech, you must plan your remarks to fit that time limit and stick to your plan. The use of notes helps you stay with the subject, but the extemporaneous speaker is in real danger of rambling too long on each thought as it occurs to him.

The most successful speakers say what they have to say concisely and simply, without pretentious language or repetition. When your point is made, go on to the next one—it is not necessary to make it in three other ways. Your audience will go away thinking you a wonderful speaker if you end your speech before they become restless and while they are still hoping that you have more to say.

IN CLOSING

When you have said all that you have to say, or your time is up, a brief summary of the speech prepares the audience for the ending. Sometimes an entertaining story in conclusion will leave them with a pleasant memory, and some speakers like to close by thanking the audience for their attention. Whatever way you choose to end, do not let yourself fade away, but make your closing remarks firmly and without apology.

WHEN CALLED ON UNEXPECTEDLY

If it happens that you are called on unexpectedly to "say a few words," it is in very poor taste to contradict, out of embarrassment, the speech of the chairman who graciously introduces you. To say "I'm afraid the chairman has greatly exaggerated my abilities" is a very natural impulse of modesty, but actually, not only is it discourteous to the chairman, but all too seldom does it ring true.

If your knees begin to shake and you feel incapable of uttering a sensible word, you must acknowledge the chairman's introduction at least briefly by some such words as "I'm sorry, I'm not a speaker but I do wish to thank you all for [attending *or* supporting our cause *or* whatever the occasion may call for]," and sit down. But if you are able to speak, you should smile and think (whether or not you actually say it) "How nice of you to say that!" and make at least a few remarks. Try to think of what you are saying, rather than the impression you are making. Remember that the speech that charms is the one that ends to its listeners' regret. Even one who is kept speaking by the enthusiasm of the audience is wise to stop while applause is at its highest.

THE PROBLEM OF YOUR HANDS

One of the greatest problems for a public speaker is what to do with his hands. If you are standing at a podium on a stage, you are fortunate, because you may grasp the side edges with your hands and keep them there, moving them only to turn the pages of your notes or to make an occasional gesture. At a dinner table you may press your hands against the table, but only if it is high enough so that you need not bend over. Avoid the temptation to pick up a piece of silver or finger your napkin or glass. And wherever you are speaking, if you are a man, be sure that you do not have loose change or keys in your pockets. It is a perfectly natural gesture for a man to put his hand in his pocket, but if it results in rattling or jingling it is most distracting to the audience.

If you are using slides in connection with your talk, be sure there is a pointer available. Not only is it practical for pointing out details in the pictures, but it also serves as a prop for you to grasp during the rest of your speech.

If there is no support of any kind available, you must do your best to keep your hands reasonably still, clasping them before you or behind your back or simply letting them hang at your sides. Gestures are important and add emphasis to your speech, but avoid repetition of the same movement again and again. Do not throw your arms about or move around with sufficient abandon to divert your listener's attention from what you are saying.

DRESSING FOR SPEAKING ENGAGEMENTS

The keynote of a woman's costume for speaking in public is simplicity. If the occasion is an afternoon meeting, a neat suit or a simple dress, long sleeved and high necked in winter or short sleeved in summer, is suitable. Jewelry in the daytime should be confined to simple earrings, a necklace, and a bracelet, which must not jangle. A small hat or a veil should be chosen, although younger women often prefer not to wear hats.

At an evening meeting, a slightly more elaborate dress or a cocktail suit is appropriate.

For a dinner speaking engagement, the woman speaker should find out what the other women to be present will wear and dress accordingly. The variety of costume might range from a simple cocktail dress to a short dinner dress or a long evening dress, depending on the formality of the occasion. In all cases, however, the dress should not have a very low neckline and should not be ruffled or elaborate in design. A veil or small hat may be worn with a cocktail dress or suit. Jewelry for evening naturally may be more elaborate than that worn in the daytime, but it should not be brilliant enough or in such quantity as to attract attention or criticism.

Wear shoes that go with the rest of your costume, but be sure that they are very comfortable, especially if the speech is a long one.

If you happen to be appearing on television, it is well to ask the producer of the show what type of clothing you should wear. » *See also Chapter 15.*

A man speaking in the daytime wears a business suit with a conservative tie. In the evening he may wear anything from a business suit to "white tie and tails." For a dinner engagement, he must find out what the other men at the speaker's table will wear and dress in the same way. If he is speaking from a stage or if he knows for certain that his audience will be informally dressed, then he should wear a tuxedo. If the men in the audience are to wear tuxedos, he may do the same or, if he wishes, wear a white tie and tails. But he must always be as formally, or more formally, dressed than his audience.

The good conversationalist

Ideal conversation is an exchange of thought and not, as many of those who worry most about their shortcomings believe, an eloquent exhibition of wit or oratory. Fortunately for most of us, it is not necessary to have any special gift of cleverness to be a person with whom others are delighted to talk.

Conversation should be a matter of equal give and take, but unhappily it is too frequently all "take." The voluble talker or chatterer rides his own hobby straight through the hours without giving anyone else a chance to do other than await the turn that never comes. Once in a while —a very long while—one meets a brilliant person whose talk is a delight.

But as a rule the man who has been led to believe that he is a brilliant talker has also been led to make himself a pest. He is the authority on all subjects. No conversation is possible between others whose ears are within reach of his insistent voice. There is a simple rule by which, if one is voluble, one can at least refrain from being a pest or a bore. And the rule is merely to stop and think.

BE CALM! THERE IS NOTHING TO FEAR

If you are one of those who dread meeting strangers because you are afraid you won't be able to think of anything to say, you might do well to remember that most of the faults of conversation are committed not by those who talk little, but by those who talk too much. A bore is almost always one whose voice is never still. A tactless person invariably rushes in with what ought never to be said.

On the other hand, those who have great difficulty in carrying on a conversation are usually those who for some reason are terrified of silence. This terror is very like the terror of sinking felt by those who are learning to swim. It is not just the first stroke that overwhelms them, but the thought of all the strokes that must follow.

The endless effort to keep on thinking of further remarks is dismaying, and the result is that the frightened talker hears not a word said to him because he is so desperately trying to think of what to say next. So the practical rule for continuing a conversation is the same as that for swimming: "Don't panic. Don't splash violently. Just take it calmly."

To change the simile, the old sign at the railroad crossings—STOP, LOOK, LISTEN—is excellent advice in many circumstances other than when waiting to cross the tracks. In conversation, "Stop" means not to rush recklessly forward; "Look" means pay attention to the expression of the person with whom you are talking; and "Listen"—meaning exactly that—is the best advice possible, because the person whom most people love to sit next to is a sympathetic listener who makes others want to talk. It must, of course, be remembered that a sympathetic listener really listens. To hold a fixed expression of sympathy and let your mind wander elsewhere won't do at all.

"THINK BEFORE YOU SPEAK"

Nearly all the faults or mistakes in conversation are caused by not thinking, that is, by lack of consideration. One of the primary rules for behavior in company applies particularly to conversation. Try to do and say only that which will be agreeable to others. But alas! There are many people who really should know better, people who would be perfectly capable of intelligent understanding if they did not let their brains remain asleep, if they were not too lazy to be considerate. They go night after night to dinner parties, day after day to other social gatherings, and absent-mindedly chatter about this or that without ever taking the trouble to think what they are saying and to whom they are saying it! Would a young mother describe a dozen cunning tricks and sayings of the baby to a bachelor who has been helplessly sitting next to her at dinner if she *thought*? A more considerate woman would understand that only a very dear friend would care for more than an *hors d'oeuvre* of the subject.

The older mother is even worse, unless something occurs to make her wake up and realize that she not only bores her hearers but prejudices everyone against her children by the unrestraint of her own praise. The daughter who is ceaselessly lauded as the most captivating and beautiful girl in the world seems uninteresting and plain to weary listeners. In the same way, the magnificent son is handicapped by a mother's or a father's pride and love in exact proportion to their displayed intensity. That great love has seldom perfect wisdom is one of the great tragedies in the drama of life. In the case of the overloving wife or mother, someone should love *her* enough to make her stop and think that her lavish praise is not merely boring her friends but handicapping unfairly those for whom she would gladly lay down her life—and yet few would have the courage to point out this fact to her.

But hers is not the only fault, and the rest of us are just as unlikely to have anyone to instruct or remind us about thoughtless and inconsiderate talk. Only by careful listening to our own words and considerate attention to the reactions of our listeners can we discover our personal infelicities. The burden of thinking before speaking is our own.

PLEASANT TALK

HUMOR: RAREST OF GIFTS

If you know anyone who is gay, beguiling, and amusing, you will, if you are wise, do everything you can to make him prefer your house and your table to any other, for where he is, the successful party is also. What he says is of no moment. It is the twist he gives to it, the intonation, the personality he puts into his quip or retort or observation that delights his hearers. To him the ordinary rules do not apply.

Bob Hope could tell a group of people that it had rained today and would probably rain tomorrow and make everyone burst into laughter—or tears, if he chose—according to the way it was said. But the forced wit is a bore, and the ordinary rest of us, if we would be thought sympathetic, intelligent, or agreeable, must "go fishing."

FISHING FOR TOPICS

In talking to a person whom you have just met and about whom you are in complete ignorance, there is really nothing to do but try one topic after another just as a fisherman searches for the right fly. You "try for nibbles" by asking a few questions: "Are you fond of the theater?" If the answer is "Yes, very," you can talk theater. When the subject runs down, you try another. Or perhaps you take your turn and talk of something you have been doing or thinking about—planting a garden, planning a journey, contemplating a job, or similar safe and neutral topics. Do not snatch at a period of silence. Let it go for a little while. Conversation is not a race that must be continued at breakneck pace.

MY NAME IS BETSY JAMES

Introducing oneself is sometimes the most practical way to begin a conversation with a stranger seated next to you at a party. "I'm Betsy James. That's my husband sitting opposite you. We live in the country and raise show cattle and dahlias, but we come to town very often in the winter to hear music." The one spoken to is very likely to reply that he lives in the city, knows nothing about music or flowers or cattle, but his favorite occupations are golf and fishing. Probably after this you talk fishing, and this leads to other things. If these topics fade out, he perhaps asks about cattle and what one must know to take prizes. It's really very simple.

Or if you are a woman talking to a man, another helpful gambit is to ask advice. "We are planning to drive through the South. Do you know the roads?" Or "I'm thinking of buying a television set. Which make do you think is best?" In fact, it is safe to ask his opinion on almost anything. Politics, sports, the stock market, the current fad—anything. Or if you are a man talking to a young woman, ask her what she thinks about life, love, work, amusement, romance, almost any question about the relative values of the things people do or think or try for. If she is an older woman, she will probably talk to *you!*

FORBIDDEN GROUND

AVOIDING SORE SUBJECTS

Certain subjects, even though you are very sure of the ground upon which you are standing, had best be shunned: for example, criticism of a religious creed or disagreement with another's political conviction. Also, since few can parry an opponent's thrusts with good temper as well as skill, be careful not to let amiable discussion turn into argument. The tactful person keeps his prejudices to himself, and even when involved in a discussion he says, "It seems to me thus and so." One who is well bred never says, "That's not so!" If he finds another's opinion unreasonable, he tries to find a more pleasant subject as soon as possible.

If you care too intensely about a subject, it is dangerous to allow yourself to say anything. That is, if you can only lecture about your fixed point of view, then you should never mention the subject except as a platform speaker. But if, on the other hand, you are able to listen with an open mind, the chances are that you need put no barriers whatever on any topic.

At the present moment Mrs. Oldname and Mrs. Kindhart, really the most devoted of neighbors, are so violently opposed to each other on a certain political question that their neighbors have made a rule to which both have amiably agreed: the first person who mentions the forbidden topic must pay a fine.

After all, a conversation between two people is very simple. You find a topic on which you agree—one topic that is pleasant to both. Then you stumble on another about which you don't agree. Careful here! Much better withdraw unless you can argue without bitterness or bigotry. Argument between cool-headed, skillful opponents is a delightful, amusing game, but very, very dangerous for those who may become hot-headed and ill-tempered.

THE TACTLESS BLUNDER

Inner or sacred thoughts and feelings are ruthlessly laid bare by such remarks as "Oh, but your son's lameness is getting much worse!" "I suppose you feel lonely since the death of your daughter?" "Are you really going to be divorced?" These examples sound unbelievable, yet each of these crude remarks has actually been made on occasion by persons of supposed education who had not a semblance of excuse for their cruelty.

Commonplace examples of tactlessness include the means-to-be-agreeable elderly man who says to an old acquaintance, "Twenty years ago you were the prettiest girl in Philadelphia." Or in the pleasantest tone of voice to one whose only son has just married, "Why is it, do you suppose, that young wives always dislike their mothers-in-law?"

If you desire to be sought after, you must not talk about the unattractiveness of old age to the elderly, about the joys of dancing and skating to the lame, or about the advantages of ancestry to the self-made. It is needlessly unkind to ridicule or criticize others, especially for what they can't help. To say "She looks as though her mother had been scared by a white mouse" may make your listeners laugh at a girl who is very blond, shy, and pale, but it is a cheap trick and not worth the taking.

A young girl who admired her own facile adjectives said to a casual acquaintance, "How *can* you go about with that squint-eyed girl!" "Because," answered the young man whom she had hoped to impress, "she is my sister."

It is scarcely necessary to say that one whose tactless remarks ride rough-shod over the feelings of others is not welcomed by many.

PERSONAL REMARKS

Although personal remarks are likely to be in bad form, it is proper to say and always pleasant to hear something appreciative about something one has done. "Your speech was splendid!" "Such a delicious dinner you gave us," "I've never seen such beautiful flowers," "You always know how to make a room inviting." But it is certainly bad taste to comment on physical attributes: "What a lovely nose you have and what an enchanting mouth."

And never, never comment on or ask about expense or other money matters. "What a lovely dress! How much did it cost?" is the height of rudeness.

UNPLEASANT TYPES

THE BORE

It has been said of the bore that he is "one who talks about himself when you want to talk about yourself"! This is superficially true, but a bore might more accurately be described as one who insists on telling you at length something that you don't want to hear about at all. He insists that you hear him out to the bitter end in spite of your plainly shown boredom.

There are certain delightful people who refuse to be bored. Their attitude is that no subject need ever be utterly uninteresting, so long as it is discussed for the first time. Repetition alone is deadly dull. Besides, what is the matter with trying to be agreeable yourself? But not too agreeable. It has been truly said: "Be polite to bores and so shall you have bores always round about you." There is no reason why you should be bored when you can be interested. But when you find yourself sitting in the hedgerow with nothing but weeds, there is no reason for shutting your eyes and seeing nothing, instead of finding what beauty you may in the weeds. Cynically, life is too short to waste in drawing blanks; therefore, it is up to you to find as many pictures to put on your blank pages as you possibly can!

THE WAILER

One of the fundamental and common-sense rules of all conversation is that one must talk about things that will be interesting and agreeable to the listener. It seems unbelievable, therefore, that so many people use as the staples of their conversational subject matter misfortunes, sickness, and other unpleasantness. Don't dilate on your own problems. Your audience has them, too, and won't be entertained by yours. Only your nearest and dearest care how many times you have been in the operating room.

THE CUTTING WIT

In great danger of making enemies is the man or woman of brilliant wit. Sharp wit tends to produce a feeling of mistrust even while it stimulates. Furthermore, the applause that follows every witty sally becomes in time breath to the nostrils, and perfectly well-intentioned people who mean to say nothing unkind in the flash of a second "see a point" and in the next second score it with no more power to resist than a drug addict has to refuse a dose put into his hand.

The mimic is a joy to his present company, but eccentric mannerisms are much easier to imitate than charm of personality, and the subjects of the habitual mimic are all too likely to become enemies.

"I'D SAY IT TO HER FACE"

A good resolve to make and keep, if you would also keep your friends, is never to speak of anyone without, in imagination, having him or her overhear what you say. One often hears the exclamation "I would say it to her face!" Be very sure that this is true, and not a braggart's phrase, and then—nine times out of ten—think better of it and refrain. Preaching is all very well in a textbook, schoolroom, or pulpit, but it has no place in society. Society is supposed to be a pleasant place; telling people disagreeable things to their faces or talking behind their backs is not a pleasant occupation.

THE KNOW-IT-ALL

Why a man, because he has millions, should assume that they confer omniscience in all branches of knowledge is something that may be left to the psychologist or psychiatrist to answer, but most people thrown into contact with millionaires will agree that an attitude of infallibility is typical of a fair majority.

A professor who has devoted his life to a subject modestly makes a statement. "You are all wrong," says the man of millions. "It is this way. . . ." Because he can pay for anything he fancies, he considers himself an accredited expert as well as a potential owner. Topics about which he has a smattering of knowledge he simply appropriates; his prejudices are, in his opinion, expert criticism, his taste impeccable, his judgment infallible. The world was created for his sole pleasure. But to the rest of us, who also have to live in it with as much comfort as we can, such persons are certainly elephants at large in the garden. Sometimes we can induce them to pass through gently, but they are just as likely at any moment to pull up our fences and push the house itself over on our defenseless heads.

There are countless others, of course, often the richest of all, who are authoritative in all they profess, who are human, helpful, and respecters of the garden enclosure of others. And in the same way, there are know-it-alls of limited means, just as offensive and as much to be avoided.

FOR THOSE WHO TALK TOO MUCH

The faults of commission are far more serious than those of omission; regrets are seldom for what you left unsaid. "Better to keep your mouth closed and be thought a fool than open it and remove all doubts."

Don't pretend to know more than you do. To say that you have read a book and then give evidence that you have understood nothing of what you have read proves you a half-wit. No person of real intelligence hesitates to say, "I don't know."

Above all, stop and *think* what you are saying. This is really the most important rule. If you stop, you can't chatter or flounder ceaselessly;

and if you *think*, you will find a topic and a manner of presenting your topic so that your neighbor will be stimulated rather than bored.

FUNDAMENTALS TO REMEMBER

People who talk too easily are likely to talk too much and at times imprudently. And those who have vivid imaginations are often unreliable in their statements. On the other hand, the "man of silence," who never speaks except when he has something worthwhile to say, tends to wear well among his intimates, but he is not likely to add much to the gaiety of a party. In conversation, as in most things, the popular "middle road" is best. Be neither too silent nor too glib. Know when to listen to others, but know also when it is your turn to carry the conversation.

Try not to repeat yourself, either by telling the same story again and again or by going back over details of your narrative that seemed especially to interest or amuse your hearer. Many things are of interest when told briefly and for the first time; nothing interests when too long dwelt upon or told a second time.

When someone is talking to you, it is inconsiderate to keep repeating, "What did you say?" Those who are deaf are often obliged to ask that a sentence be repeated, for otherwise their irrelevant answers would make them appear half-witted. People who are hard of hearing should use a hearing aid. It makes life more comfortable for them, and friends do not have to shout at them. But countless persons with perfectly good hearing say "What?" from force of habit or inattention.

Remember that the sympathetic listener is the delight of delights. The person who is seemingly eager for your news or enthralled with your conversation, who looks at you with a kindling of the face and gives you spontaneous and undivided attention, is the one to whom the "orchid" for the art of conversation would undoubtedly be awarded.

Part TWO

CORRESPONDENCE

The appearance and style
of your letters

The letter you write, whether you realize it or not, is always a mirror that reflects your appearance, taste, and character. A sloppy letter—the writing running up and down hill, badly worded, badly spelled, paper and envelope unmatched, even possibly a blot—proclaims the sort of person who might have uncombed hair, run-down heels, or a run in her stockings; so too, a neat, precise, evenly written note portrays a person of those happy characteristics. Therefore, while it cannot be said that one may read a person's future in his handwriting, it is true that if a young man wants a wife in whose daily life he is always sure to find the finished task, the tidy mind, and the organized housekeeping, he may be quite safe in selecting her from those whose letters are well-written, even, and neat. The businessman picks his secretary not only because her neat and efficient letters are a credit to him every time he signs one but also because they indicate that she herself is well-organized and tidy.

Excellent secretaries have an advantage over most of us in that they have usually had good training in the preparation of business correspondence. And, of course, the mechanical nature of the typewriter it-

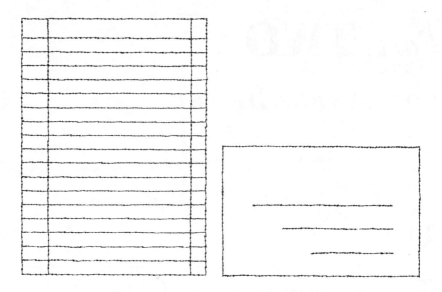

self simplifies such matters as the evenness of margins and the regular spacing of lines and words. Writing letters by hand is more difficult, but some people are fortunate in being able to make graceful letters easily, to space their words evenly, and to put them on a page so that the picture is pleasing. Others are discouraged at the outset because their fingers are clumsy and their efforts childlike. But no matter how badly formed each individual letter may be, the page as a whole will look fairly well if the writing is consistent throughout. Avoid such exaggerated styles of writing as dotting "i" with a circle, however, for no amount of attention to other matters can compensate for such childish habits!

You can make yourself write neatly and legibly. You can—with the help of a dictionary if need be—spell correctly. You can be sure that you understand the meaning of every word you use. If it is difficult for you to write in a straight line, use the lined guide that comes with some stationery, or make one yourself; if you find it impossible to keep an even margin, draw a perpendicular line at the left of the guide so that you can start each new line of writing on it. A guide line one-half inch from the right edge of your paper to tell you where to stop each line will also help. You can also make a guide to slip under the envelope. Far better to use a guide than to send envelopes and pages of writing that slide uphill and down, in uncontrolled disorder, so that the recipient must all but stand on his head to read it.

On many occasions, of course, it is perfectly correct to avoid these calligraphic complications by using the typewriter yourself. All business letters—from home as well as office—should be typed if you have access to a machine, and long letters to friends certainly may be if you wish.

Some forms of correspondence must always be written by hand, and the following rules are unbreakable:

Never type an invitation, an acceptance, or a regret.

Never type letters of congratulations or thanks.

Never type letters or notes of condolence.

STATIONERY

Suitability should be considered in choosing your stationery, just as in choosing a piece of furniture for your house. For a handwriting that is habitually large, pick a paper of a larger size than you would choose for writing that is small. The shape of paper should also depend somewhat upon the spacing of the lines typical of the writer, and whether a wide or narrow margin is used. Low, spread-out writing looks better on a square sheet of paper; tall, pointed writing looks better on paper that is high and narrow.

Whether the paper is rough or smooth is entirely a matter of personal choice—but let the quality be good and the shape and color conservative. Paper should never be ruled, or highly scented, or oddly shaped, nor should it have elaborate or striking ornamentation.

Many people have correspondence cards or a smaller size of their regular paper cut to the size of their envelopes for notes. Others use the same size for all correspondence, but leave a wider margin on top and bottom as well as on left and right in writing notes.

The flap of the envelope should be plain and the point neither skimpy nor unduly long. If the flap is square instead of pointed, it may be allowed greater length without being eccentric. When the paper is thin, envelopes with colored linings are used so that the writing cannot be read through the envelope. And the monogram or address may be stamped on the paper in a color to match the lining. Young girls may use quite gay envelope linings, and the device on the paper may be gay to correspond, but it must not be so large or loud as to be ostentatious. Oblong envelopes are excellent for business, but those more nearly square are smartest for personal use.

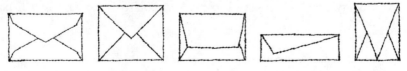

Acceptable form   Bad form

Linings for Christmas-card envelopes may be as gay as the ornaments that decorate a Christmas tree. This is the time one may go "overboard." But unrestrained masses of red and gold, swirls of purple and green or other striking colors, are abominations at any other time.

Metal-edged paper is not good form. Deckle-edge paper is widely used, but for most of us it is not so appropriate as clean-cut edges.

PAPER FOR A MAN

Writing paper for a man should always be conservative. Plain white or cream, gray or granite paper, medium size or larger, and stamped with his address, his initials, or, for social correspondence, his crest, if he has one, is suitable. The color of the engraving (or printing) should be black, gray, or navy blue. Writing ink should be black or blue-black.

A very practical paper for a man's nonsocial correspondence is a single sheet 7 or 7¼ inches by 10 or 10½ inches marked in plain block letter in navy blue at the top. His name without title, his address, and his telephone number—all three appear. This paper can be used for type-writing or handwriting and is folded in threes to fit into a 7¼ or 7½ by 4-inch envelope. For his social correspondence, he uses paper of the same color and size, but he may use initials in block letters if he wishes, or a crest if he has one. Good stationers supply correctly sized paper and envelopes that match.

PAPER FOR A WOMAN

White, cream, all blues, grays, and, more recently, greens are in best taste. Paper should be of small or medium size, single or double sheets, plain or with colored border, as long as it is stamped with either a mono-gram, initials, address, or both, in color to match the border. Writing ink should be black or blue, but green may be used, if that is the color of your paper.

A married woman's name is written "Mrs. William Frost," not "Mrs. Mary Frost" or "Mary Frost." An unmarried woman uses "Miss" only on the envelope.

PAPER FOR EVERYONE IN THE FAMILY

A paper suitable for the use of all the members of a family has the address engraved or printed in plain letters at the top of the first page. Frequently the telephone number is put in small letters under the ad-dress, or in the upper left-hand corner under a small telephone device, with the address in the center—a great convenience in the present day of telephoning.

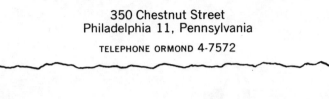

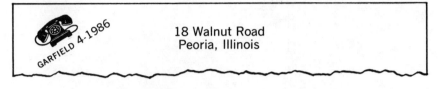

FOR THE YOUNG CORRESPONDENT

A girl's name—either Elizabeth in full or Betty—embossed in color is popular for all personal correspondence of a young girl. But it should not be used by an older woman. If her first name is not distinctive, the young girl may wish to use her surname also. Also available for very young ladies are attractive papers with designs in the left-hand top corners or along the left or top borders, usually flowers, birds, or perhaps a kitten or puppy. They may or may not have a monogram, too, and the style of the picture varies with the age of the girl. The paper illustrated below would be suitable for a young teen-ager.

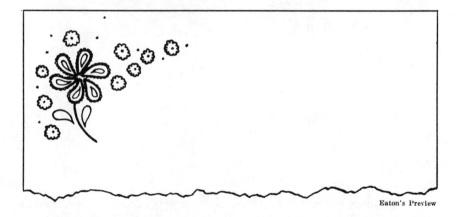

Eaton's Preview

Many stationers also sell paper for young children, girls or boys. It is lined, usually has an illustration of animals, toys, or something from a familiar story or nursery rhyme, and may come in a variety of shapes. It is designed to amuse the young child and make him consider letter writing a pleasure rather than a chore.

Eaton's Tall Letters

NOTE PAPER

For short notes, for acceptances or regrets, and for invitations, a supply of fold-over note paper, half the size of a single sheet of lady's writing paper, is invaluable. It may be of any color appropriate to the household and engraved or printed with initials or with the owner's name and address, and possibly with the telephone number. If not marked with initials or a name, it is useful for every feminine member of the family.

PAPER FOR COUNTRY HOUSES

Paper for a country house may be brighter in color and less rigid in form than personal paper or that for a city address. If the telephone exchange, mailing address, and station or airport are different, a row of little symbols often is stamped or printed in the left-hand corner.

STIRLINGTON, NEW YORK

RINGWOOD, NEW JERSEY

SLOATSBURG, NEW YORK
611-394-6161

Houses with easily illustrated names often have them pictured. BIRDCAGE, for instance, may have a bright blue paper with a red bird-case suggestive of lacquer; the BANDBOX, a fantastically decorated milliner's box on oyster-gray paper, the envelope lining of black and gray pin-stripes; and the DOLL'S HOUSE might use the outline of a doll's house in grass green on green-bordered white paper, and white envelopes lined with grass green. Each of these devices loses its charm unless it is as small as the outline of a cherry pit, and the paper itself should not be of a large size.

If the house is located on winding roads off the main highway, a simple line-drawn map is very helpful to visitors who come by car.

OFFICIAL WRITING PAPER

An ambassador or minister has the coat of arms of his country—in gold, usually—stamped at the top of writing paper and on cards of invitation for official or formal use. For his personal use and for the use of all who live at the embassy or the legation, note paper is engraved merely

AMERICAN EMBASSY

LONDON

The letter paper of a governor is stamped

EXECUTIVE MANSION

COLUMBUS

OHIO

and is usually surmounted by the coat of arms of the state. The letter paper used for social correspondence by a governor's family as well as himself is engraved EXECUTIVE MANSION. But EXECUTIVE OFFICE is often chosen as the heading for official letters.

This same paper, but without the coat of arms, may be used by his family if the address is also that of their home. Otherwise their paper is engraved with their personal address.

It should be unnecessary to add that the wife of a senator has no right to use stationery headed THE SENATE, nor may the wife of a representative write on paper engraved HOUSE OF REPRESENTATIVES.

MOURNING PAPER

Few people use mourning paper at all, and plain white paper has almost replaced that with a black border. A heavy border (from ⅜ to ½ inch) is unknown in the United States today. One fourth of an inch is considered deepest mourning, and 3/16, 1/16, or 1/32 of an inch is generally used.

PRINTING AS WELL AS ENGRAVING

Some years ago, the paper used by a lady was either engraved (diestamped) or left plain. This was the era when the mystery of the typewriter was still the special province of the professional stenographer. Today the writing equipment of a busy man or woman is almost as certain to include a typewriter as it is to employ modern pens in place of quills. The convenience of paper upon which one's full name and address are printed has become indispensable to everyone who must write many letters. Therefore, a small supply of engraved paper at unavoidably higher cost and probably used only for formal letters is augmented by a larger supply of printed paper for informal social correspondence and for business letters.

CRESTS

Because heraldry, with its origins in the Middle Ages, is not an institution in America, the use of a coat of arms is as much a foreign custom as the speaking of an alien tongue. But when an old family has used their family arms continuously since the days when they brought the device—and their right to it as certified by the colleges of heraldry—from Europe, its use is proper, but somewhat conspicuous, at the present time.

It must be remembered, however, that the crest is the exclusive property of male members of a family, although it may be used jointly by husband and wife on some occasions. Its appearance on the paper of a widow or a spinster is as absurd as it would be to put "Esquire" at the end of her name. Surprisingly few Americans, however, seem to be aware of this heraldic rule. A widow has no right to use her husband's crest on her letter paper. Properly she may use the device on the shield of his coat of arms, transferred to a diamond-shaped device called a lozenge. She may also, if she chooses, divide the lozenge perpendicularly into two parts and crowd the device from her husband's shield into the left half and the device from her father's shield into the right half. A spinster uses her paternal arms on a lozenge without crest or motto.

THE MECHANICS OF THE LETTER ITSELF

SEQUENCE OF PAGES

Folded stationery may cause problems about the proper order in which to use the pages. If a letter is longer than one page but shorter than three, it is customary to use the first page and third, as this leaves the fourth page blank and prevents the writing from showing through the envelope. For longer letters, one may write first, second, third, fourth, in regular order; or first and fourth, then, opening the sheet and turning it sideways, write across the two inside pages as one. The sequence is not important.

Certain people have the habit of repeating the last word on a page at the top of the next. It is undoubtedly a good idea, derived from old manuscripts, but it does make a stuttering impression upon a reader not accustomed to it.

On fold-over or informal note paper, when the address is at the top and there is nothing in the center, the letter or note begins on the first page and follows into the center pages. The paper is opened flat and written on vertically as if it were a single page. If there is an initial or name in the center of the front page, the note begins at the top of the opened center pages if it is long enough to cover more than half, and on the lower half if it is to be only a few words.

YOUR HOME ADDRESS AND THE DATE

If your stationery is not marked with your address, it is only courteous to let your correspondent know what it is for his convenience in replying. The upper right side of the first page of your letter is the usual place, but sometimes, especially on a short note, it may be put at the far left, just below the level of your signature. In either case the date goes below the address.

Sincerely,

Mary Swenson
(Mrs. John Swenson)

45 Barton St.
Racine, Wisconsin
May 5, 1966

When your address is already engraved or printed on the stationery, the date is placed in about the same way—at the upper right-hand side of the first page of a letter, or at the end and to the far left of the signature of a note. Your correspondent will find it easier to read May 9, 1965, than 5-9-65. The latter is often confusing because it is not known whether the sequence is month-day-year or day-month-year, a growing usage of European origin.

At the end of a note, "Thursday" is sufficient unless the note is an invitation for more than a week ahead, in which case you write, as in a letter, "January 9." The year is not essential for it can hardly be expected that a year will be required for a letter's delivery.

RECIPIENT'S ADDRESS

The correct form for business letters demands that the address of the receiver be put at the left, below the level of the date and directly above the salutation, exactly as it appears on the envelope.

```
                June 7, 1966

Mr. James Johnson
Smith, Johnson & Co.
20 Broadway
New York 4, New York

Dear Mr. Johnson:
```

```
                              June 7, 1966

        Smith, Johnson & Co.
        20 Broadway
        New York 4, New York

        Dear Sirs:
```

Personal letters and notes, however, never have the address of the receiver anywhere except on the envelope itself.

THE SALUTATION

For business letters, the salutation "Dear Sir" or "Sirs" is a better form than "Gentlemen." When writing to a firm or organization composed of women, the salutation is "Dear Madams." Never write "Mesdames," any more than you would write "Messieurs" instead of "Sirs."

An impersonal business letter to a woman begins

Mrs. Richard Worldly
4892 Third Avenue
New York 94, New York

Dear Madam:

A personal business letter, meaning a letter from a business or professional man to a customer or client he knows personally, begins

Mrs. Richard Worldly
4892 Third Avenue
New York 94, New York

My dear Mrs. Worldly:

The most formal beginning of a social letter is "My dear Mrs. Smith." Increasingly intimate are "Dear Mrs. Smith," "Dear Sarah," "Dear Sally," "Sally dear," "Dearest Sally," and "Sally darling." In this area, your own feeling must be your guide, although it is perhaps better to err on the side of formality when you are not absolutely certain of your recipient's feeling.

Except in the most intimate correspondence, a man is always addressed "Dear Bob," when something less formal than "Dear Mr. Smith" is suitable.

Forms used in addressing distinguished persons or those in special categories are discussed elsewhere. » *See Chapter 7.*

THE CLOSING

It is too bad that, for personal letters and notes, the English language does not permit the charming and graceful closing of all letters in the French manner, those little flowers of compliment that leave such a pleasant fragrance after reading. But ever since the eighteenth century, English-speaking people have been busy pruning away all ornament of expression; even the last remaining graces—"kindest regards," "with kindest remembrances"—are fast disappearing, leaving us little but an abrupt "Sincerely yours."

The best ending to a formal social note is "Sincerely," "Sincerely yours," "Very sincerely," or "Very sincerely yours."

"I remain, dear madam," is no longer in use, but "Believe me" is still correct when a degree of formality is to be expressed in the close of a note.

> Believe me
> Very sincerely yours,
> *or*
> Believe me, my dear Mrs. Worldly,
> Most sincerely yours,

The second is an English form, and although it seems somewhat affected today, it is used by quite a number of Americans.

The close of a business letter should be "Yours truly" or "Yours very truly." "Respectfully" is used only by a tradesman to a customer or by an employee to an employer, never by a person of equal position. No lady should ever sign a letter "Respectfully," except as part of the long, formal "have the honor to remain" close of a letter to the President of the United States or to a bishop or a mother superior.

Appropriate for a man is "Faithfully" or "Faithfully yours" when he is writing to a woman or for any uncommercial correspondence, such as a letter to the President of the United States, a member of the Cabinet, an ambassador, a clergyman, etc.

The intimate closings are many. "Affectionately yours," "Affectionately," "Devotedly," "Love," and "With much love" are an increasing scale of intimacy.

"As always" is useful to some one with whom you may not be on intimate terms, especially when you have not seen them for some time.

"Sincerely" in formal notes and "Affectionately" or "Love" in intimate notes are the most used in the present day. Between the first and last two there is a blank; in English we have no expression to fit sentiment more friendly than the first and yet less intimate than the others. "Cordially" was coined no doubt to fill this need, but it sounds a bit condescending. However, it has become quite widely used.

"Yours in haste" or "Hastily yours," while not bad form, is rather carelessly rude unless for some reason your communication indicates real and necessary haste.

"Gratefully" is used only when a benefit has been received, as to a lawyer who has skillfully handled a case, to a surgeon who has saved a life dear to you, to a friend who has gone to unusual trouble to do you a favor.

In an ordinary letter of thanks, the signature is "Sincerely," "Affectionately," "Devotedly"—whatever your usual close may be.

The phrases that a man might devise to close a letter to his betrothed or his wife are limited only by the extent of his imagination, and they are too personal to be set down in this, or any, book.

Forms used in letters to distinguished persons or those in special categories are discussed elsewhere. » *See Chapter 7.*

THE SIGNATURE

In America, it is not customary for a man to discard any of his names, so John Hunter Titherington Smith, finding his name too much of a penful for letters and documents, chooses J. H. T. Smith instead, or perhaps at the end of personal letters, John H. T. Smith. Of course, if he is writing a business associate with whom he is on terms of close personal acquaintance, he may sign simply "Jack" over the typed "J.H.T. Smith." Mail is addressed to him in the typed form (or the printed form, if the letterhead carries his full name).

A married woman should always sign a letter to a stranger, a bank, a business firm, etc., with her legal name. If her stationery is marked with her full married name and address, her signature—Mary Jones Mathews —needs no further explanation. But if it is not, she should give her married name (to which the reply will be sent) in one of several ways. When she writes by hand, she adds her married name in parentheses, beneath her signature, or to the left of it, thus:

> Very truly yours,
> Mary Jones Mathews
> (Mrs. John Mathews)

When the letter is typed, her married name is typed beneath the space left for her signature, and in this case, it is not necessarily enclosed in parentheses.

> Very truly yours,
> Mary Jones Mathews
> Mrs. John Mathews

The only times when a woman actually uses "Mrs." in her signature are these: in a hotel register, on a business telegram, or on an order letter to a tradesman. And then it must be "Mrs. John Smith." To a servant in her own employ it is "Mrs. Smith."

To acquaintances who may not know which Mrs. Mathews she may happen to be, she signs her name this way:

> Sincerely,
> Mary Mathews
> (Mrs. John Mathews)

An unmarried woman uses much the same form in a typed letter:

> Sincerely,
> Mary Mathews
> Miss Mary Mathews

When she writes by hand, she may use this style:

> Sincerely,
> (Miss) Mary Mathews

Those who fear to sign their names "Mary Smith" because they think someone might then feel privileged to call them "Mary" can write clearly beneath their signature, "Kindly reply to Mrs. John Smith." And they may moreover sign their name "M. J. Smith" instead of "Mary Jones Smith."

And a final warning about the signature: Avoid a flourishing, illegible one. While the reader may be able to decipher a word in a sentence because of the meaning of the whole, if he does not know from whom the letter comes, he cannot possibly make sense of a scrawl that resembles a doctor's prescription!

FOLDING A LETTER

To fold a letter in such a way that the recipient shall be able to read the contents without having to turn the paper is giving too much importance to nothing. It is sufficient that the paper be folded neatly—once, of course, for the envelope that is as deep as half the length of the paper, and twice for the envelope that is a third as deep. The paper that must be folded into thirds is used only as personal stationery for men or for business purposes. Women's social letter paper should fold only once and fit into its envelope. Note paper is the same size as the envelope and goes into it flat with only the original fold.

THE OUTSIDE ADDRESSES

Write the name and address on the envelope as precisely and as legibly as you can. If your writing is poor, print. Remember that the post office has enough to do deciphering the letters of the unlettered without being asked to do unnecessary work for you!

When you are writing to someone who lives in an American city with a postal zone, or zip code, write it on the envelope as it is an essential part of the address. Zone numbers are used in many foreign cities, too, and are an integral part of the address.

Formerly the address was always written with each line indented a few spaces:

> *Mr. Harvey S. Simpson*
> *4 Hillside Lane*
> *Clinton*
> *Ohio*

but many people now prefer a straight margin on the left:

> *Mr. Harvey S. Simpson*
> *4 Hillside Lane*
> *Clinton*
> *Ohio*

CORRECT USE OF "ESQ."

The use of "Esq." has virtually gone out of general use in the United States—except among the conservative members of the older generation and among lawyers and justices of the peace. Its correct use, furthermore, is confusing. For example, formally engraved invitations are always addressed to Mr. Stanley Smith on both invitation and envelope. Written invitations, as well as all other personal letters, may be addressed to Stanley Smith, Esq.

A WIDOW AND HER HUSBAND'S NAME

No note or social letter should ever be addressed to a married woman—even if she is a widow—as Mrs. Mary Town. Correctly and properly a widow keeps her husband's name, always. If her son's wife should have the same name, she becomes Mrs. James Town, senior, or simply

Mrs. Town, if there is no other in her community with the same name.

A divorced woman takes her own surname in place of her ex-husband's Christian name. Supposing her to have been Mary Simpson before her marriage, she calls herself Mrs. Simpson Johnson.

DAUGHTERS, SONS, AND CHILDREN

Formerly, the eldest daughter was correctly Miss Taylor; her younger sister, Miss Jane Taylor. Today this right to Miss Taylor is considered rather suggestive of a spinster of uncertain age. Miss Alice Taylor and Miss Jane Taylor are invariably used.

Envelopes to children are addressed to Miss Katherine Taylor, and to Robert Taylor, the latter with no title. Little boys under 10 years of age may, however, be addressed as "Master."

Do not write The Messrs. Brown in addressing a father and son. The Messrs. Brown is correct only for unmarried brothers.

"PERSONAL" AND "PLEASE FORWARD"

If you are writing to someone at his home address, you will properly assume that no one else will open the letter, and it is rude to write "Personal" on it. But if you are writing a social note to a friend's business address, it is entirely correct. "Please Forward" is correct if you know only a former address but not the current one.

RETURN ADDRESS

It has always been customary to place a return address at the top left-hand corner on the face of a business envelope. When it was necessary to use one on a personal letter, it was put on the flap. Whatever the real reason for making this distinction, it did separate the two types of letters in our mail.

Today (in response to requests made by the United States Post Office) it is considered permissible and even advisable to put any return address on the face of the envelope. If handwritten, it should be very small. Remember also that zone numbers and zip codes are a part of the return address.

UNSEALED LETTERS

Best form dictates that any letter given to a person (other than a commercial messenger) for delivery by hand be unsealed. Customarily the person carrying it seals it immediately, in the presence of the writer, but this is not obligatory.

Exceptions may be made, of course, should there be a heavy or particularly valuable enclosure that might slip out after the time of writing, but in this case, it is polite to explain why the envelope has been sealed.

7

Addressing important persons

At one time or another nearly every one of us either meets or has to write a letter to someone of importance, perhaps a senator or a judge, a clergyman or a professor, and we certainly do not want to be thought ignorant because we address him or her improperly. Neither can we remember all the proper forms of address for all the personages we might ever need to speak to or write to. The chart in this chapter has been prepared to cover as many as possible of the situations likely to occur in the ordinary course of events—and some not so ordinary.

Special attention has been given to the official and formal occasion, for naturally Governor Marvin's friends continue to call him Joe at purely friendly functions, and their wives continue to address their dinner and luncheon invitations to the Governor's wife. Indeed, no matter how important the personage or what your degree of acquaintance with him, Mrs. Joseph L. Marvin receives the invitations just as she did before her husband entered public life. Only when a wedding or other formal invitation would in any case be sent to both husband and wife is it necessary to use the special forms included below in the "Social Correspondence" column.

"The Honorable" is an expression that may cause confusion because its British usage is so different from ours. Federal custom here bestows the title "Honorable," first officially and then by courtesy for life, on the following: the President, Vice President, United States Senators, United States Congressmen, members of the cabinet, all federal judges, ministers plenipotentiary, ambassadors, and governors of all states. But this title is not used by the person himself on his visiting card or letterhead or in his signature. The people of the state address their state senators as "The Honorable Lawrence Hamilton, State Senator," as a courtesy title only.

Best usage dictates that "The Honorable" (spelled out in full) appear on a separate line, as shown in the chart in this chapter, and that his wife, when she is included, have a line to herself below his name and slightly indented.

We refer to our country briefly and casually as "America," but when we address anyone elsewhere in the Western Hemisphere, our good manners should remind us that we have no monopoly on the name. Thus, although it is customary in both Europe and Asia to speak of or write to the American Embassy or the American Legation, it should not be done in Latin America or Canada. The address on a letter to one of our government representatives there always specifies "the United States of America." The same applies to any letter to our Ambassador to the United Nations; in all other ways, he is addressed and spoken to as are our ambassadors to foreign powers.

Representatives of other countries who are living in the United States present no particular problems as the ways of addressing them are firmly fixed by governmental protocol. But whether their wives are addressed as Mrs., Madame, Señora, or some other title depends upon the usage of her particular country. In many instances, she uses whatever she would in her own country (that is, the wife of the Mexican ambassador is Señora Ortega), but sometimes, especially when hers is a difficult or little known language, she uses Mrs. or Madame.

In this age of international travel, we may very well find ourselves in need of information about the important personages of countries other than our own. Customs vary, of course, and no general rules can be made for the more than one hundred nations in the world. But should you find yourself about to leave for Ghana or Japan or Finland, there are many sources of help. Try the consulate nearest you or the embassy in Washington or the mission to the United Nations in New York. Information officers from all over the world stand ready to help you and eager to facilitate your communication with their homelands.

Personage	ENVELOPE ADDRESS	SOCIAL CORRESPONDENCE	INFORMAL BEGINNING OF LETTER
THE PRESIDENT	The President The White House Washington, D.C.	The President and Mrs. Washington The White House Washington, D.C.	My dear Mr. President:
THE VICE PRESIDENT	The Vice President United States Senate Washington, D.C.	The Vice President and Mrs. Hope Home address	My dear Mr. Vice President:
CHIEF JUSTICE, SUPREME COURT	The Chief Justice The Supreme Court Washington, D.C.	The Chief Justice and Mrs. Page Home address	My dear Mr. Chief Justice:
ASSOCIATE JUSTICE, SUPREME COURT	Mr. Justice Katsaros The Supreme Court Washington, D.C.	Mr. Justice Katsaros and Mrs. Katsaros Home address	My dear Mr. Justice Katsaros:
CABINET MEMBER	The Honorable Gary George Gussin The Secretary of the Treasury or The Attorney General or The Postmaster General Washington, D.C.	The Honorable The Secretary of the Treasury and Mrs. Gussin Home address or (for a woman cabinet member) Mr. and Mrs. Henry Leo Woods	My dear Mr. Secretary: or My dear Mr. Attorney General or My dear Mr. Postmaster Gene or Madam Secretary:
FORMER PRESIDENT	The Honorable Alfred Edward Work Office address	The Honorable Alfred Edward Work and Mrs. Work Home address	My dear Mr. Work:
UNITED STATES SENATOR	The Honorable John Wandzilak United States Senate Washington, D.C.	The Honorable John Wandzilak and Mrs. Wandzilak Home address or (for a woman senator) Mr. and Mrs. John Row Doe	My dear Senator Wandzilak:
THE SPEAKER OF THE HOUSE OF REPRESENTATIVES	The Honorable Walter James Grevesmuhl The Speaker of the House of Representatives Washington, D.C.	The Speaker and Mrs. Grevesmuhl Home address	My dear Mr. Speaker:
MEMBER OF THE UNITED STATES HOUSE OF REPRESENTATIVES	The Honorable Henry Cobb Wellcome United States House of Representatives Washington, D.C.	The Honorable Henry Cobb Wellcome and Mrs. Wellcome Home address or (for a woman member) Mr. and Mrs. John Knox Jones	My dear Mr. Wellcome:
AMBASSADOR OF THE UNITED STATES	The Honorable John Wilson Smith The Ambassador of the United States American Embassy London, England	The Honorable John Wilson Smith and Mrs. Smith Home address or (for a woman ambassador) Mr. and Mrs. Leeds Walker Home address	My dear Mr. Ambassador: or My dear Madam Ambassador:

FORMAL BEGINNING OF LETTER	INFORMAL CLOSE OF LETTER	FORMAL CLOSE OF LETTER	IN CONVERSATION	TITLE OF INTRODUCTION
r:	Very respectfully yours,	I have the honor to remain, Most respectfully yours,	Mr. President *or* Sir	*Only the name of the person being introduced is spoken*
r:	Sincerely yours, *or* Faithfully yours,	Very truly yours,	Mr. Vice President *or* Sir	The Vice President
r:	*Same as above*	*Same as above*	Mr. Chief Justice *or* Sir	The Chief Justice
r:	Sincerely yours,	*Same as above*	Mr. Justice *or* Mr. Justice Katsaros *or* Sir	Mr. Justice Katsaros
r: *or* ear Sir: *or* Madam:	*Same as above*	*Same as above*	Mr. Secretary *or* Mr. Attorney General *or* Mr. Postmaster General *or* Sir *or* Madam Secretary	The Secretary of the Treasury *or* The Attorney General *or* The Postmaster General
r:	*Same as above*	*Same as above*	Mr. Work *or* Sir	The Honorable Alfred Edward Work
r: *or* Madam:	*Same as above*	*Same as above*	Senator *or* Senator Wandzilak *or* Sir *or* Madam	Senator Wandzilak of Alaska
r:	*Same as above*	*Same as above*	Mr. Speaker *or* Sir	The Speaker of the House of Representatives
r: *or* Madam:	*Same as above*	*Same as above*	Mr. Wellcome *or* Mrs. Jones *or* Sir *or* Madam	Representative Wellcome of Nebraska
r: *or* Madam:	*Same as above*	*Same as above*	Mr. Ambassador *or* Madam Ambassador *or* Sir *or* Madam	The American Ambassador *or (if necessary)* Our Ambassador to England

Personage	ENVELOPE ADDRESS	SOCIAL CORRESPONDENCE	INFORMAL BEGINNING OF LETTER

MINISTER PLENIPOTENTIARY OF THE UNITED STATES	The Honorable
	James Lee Row
	The Minister of the United States
	American Legation
	Oslo, Norway
		The Honorable
		James Lee Row
		   and Mrs. Row
		Home address
		   or (for a woman minister)
		Mr. and Mrs. Arthur Johnson
		Home address
			My dear Mr. Minister:
			_or_
			My dear Madam Minister:

CONSUL OF THE UNITED STATES	Mr. John Smith American Consul Rue de Quelque Chose Paris, France	Mr. and Mrs. John Smith Home address	Dear Mr. Smith:
AMBASSADOR OF A FOREIGN COUNTRY	His Excellency Juan Luis Ortega The Ambassador of Mexico Washington, D.C.	His Excellency The Ambassador of Mexico and Señora Ortega Home address	My dear Mr. Ambassador:
MINISTER OF A FOREIGN COUNTRY	The Honorable Carluh Matti The Minister of Kezeah Washington, D.C.	The Honorable Carluh Matti and Mrs. Matti Home address	My dear Mr. Minister:
GOVERNOR OF A STATE	The Honorable Joseph L. Marvin Governor of Idaho Boise, Idaho	The Honorable Joseph L. Marvin and Mrs. Marvin Home address	Dear Governor Marvin:

State Senators and Representatives are addressed like U.S. Senators and Representatives, with appropriate addresses

MAYOR	His [or Her] Honor the Mayor
	City Hall
	Easton, Maryland
		His Honor the Mayor
		   and Mrs. Lake
		Home address
		   or (for a woman mayor)
		Mr. and Mrs. L. T. Wayne
		Home address
			Dear Mayor Lake:

JUDGE	The Honorable Carson Little Justice, Appellate Division Supreme Court of the State of New York Albany, New York	The Honorable Carson Little and Mrs. Little Home address	Dear Judge Little:
BISHOP, PROTESTANT	The Right Reverend John S. Bowman Bishop of Rhode Island Providence, Rhode Island	The Right Reverend John S. Bowman and Mrs. Bowman Home address	My dear Bishop Bowman:

CLERGYMAN, PROTESTANT	The Reverend David Dekker
	Address of his church
	   or (if he holds the degree)
	The Reverend David Dekker, D.D.
	Address of his church
		The Reverend David Dekker
		   and Mrs. Dekker
		Home address
			Dear Mr. [or Doctor] Dekk

RABBI	Rabbi Paul Aaron Fine Address of his synagogue _or (if he holds the degree)_ Paul Aaron Fine, D.D. Address of his synagogue	Rabbi [or Doctor] and Mrs. Paul Aaron Fine Home address	Dear Rabbi [or Doctor] Fir

	INFORMAL CLOSE OF LETTER	FORMAL CLOSE OF LETTER	IN CONVERSATION	TITLE OF INTRODUCTION
or am:	*Same as above*	*Same as above*	Mr. Row *or* Mrs. Johnson	Mr. Row, the American Minister *or (if necessary)* Mrs. Johnson, the American Minister to Denmark
or ear Sir:	*Same as above*	Sincerely yours,	Mr. Smith	Mr. Smith
lency:	Sincerely yours, *or* Faithfully yours,	Very truly yours,	Mr. Ambassador *or* Excellency *or* Sir	The Ambassador of Mexico
	Sincerely yours,	*Same as above*	Mr. Minister *or* Sir	The Minister of Kezeah
	Same as above	*Same as above*	Governor Marvin *or* Sir	The Governor *or (if necessary)* The Governor of Idaho
or am:	Sincerely yours,	Very truly yours,	Mr. Mayor *or* Madam Mayor	Mayor Lake
	Same as above	*Same as above*	Mr. Justice	The Honorable Carson Little, Judge of the Appellate Division of the Supreme Court
Reverend Sir:	Faithfully yours, *or* Sincerely yours,	Respectfully yours,	Bishop Bowman	Bishop Bowman
or ear Sir:	Sincerely yours,	Sincerely yours, *or* Faithfully yours,	Mr. [*or* Doctor] Dekker	Mr. [*or* Doctor] Dekker
Sir:	*Same as above*	Sincerely yours,	Rabbi [*or* Doctor] Fine	Rabbi [*or* Doctor] Fine

Personage	ENVELOPE ADDRESS	SOCIAL CORRESPONDENCE	INFORMAL BEGINNING OF LETTER
THE POPE	His Holiness Pope Paul VI *or* His Holiness the Pope Vatican City		
CARDINAL	His Eminence Alberto Cardinal Vezzetti Archbishop of Baltimore Baltimore, Maryland		
ARCHBISHOP, ROMAN CATHOLIC	The Most Reverend Preston Lowen Archbishop of San Francisco San Francisco, California		Most Reverend and dear Sir:
BISHOP, ROMAN CATHOLIC	The Most Reverend Matthew S. Borden Address of his church		My dear Bishop Borden:
MONSIGNOR	The Right Reverend Monsignor Ryan Address of his church		Reverend and dear Monsigno Ryan:
PRIEST	The Reverend John Matthews [*and the initials of his order*] Address of his church		Dear Father Matthews:
MEMBER OF RELIGIOUS ORDER	Sister Angelica [*and initials of order*] *or* Brother James [*and initials*] Address		Dear Sister Angelica: *or* Dear Brother James:
UNIVERSITY PROFESSOR	Professor Robert Knowles Office address *or (if he holds the degree)* Dr. Robert Knowles *or* Mr. Robert Knowles	Professor [*or Doctor or Mr.*] and Mrs. Robert Knowles Home address	Dear Professor [*or Doctor or* Knowles:
PHYSICIAN	William L. Barnes, M.D. Office address	Doctor and Mrs. William L. Barnes Home address	Dear Doctor Barnes:

...AL ...NING ...TTER	INFORMAL CLOSE OF LETTER	FORMAL CLOSE OF LETTER	IN CONVERSATION	TITLE OF INTRODUCTION
...Holiness:		Your Holiness' most humble servant,	*See Chapter 21*	*See Chapter 21*
...Eminence:		I have the honor to remain, Your Eminence's humble servant,	Your Eminence	*One is presented to* His Eminence, Cardinal Vezzetti
...Excellency: ... ...Reverend Sir:	*Same as formal close*	I have the honor to remain, Your Excellency's humble servant,	Your Excellency	*One is presented to* The Most Reverend, The Archbishop of San Francisco
...Reverend Sir:	Faithfully yours,	I have the honor to remain, Your obedient servant,	Your Excellency	Bishop Borden
...Reverend dear ...nsignor Ryan:	Respectfully yours,	Respectfully yours,	Monsignor Ryan	Monsignor Ryan
...nd Father:	Faithfully yours,	I remain, Reverend Father, Yours faithfully,	Father *or* Father Matthews *or* Your Reverence	The Reverend Father Matthews
...ar Sister: ... ...ar Brother:	Faithfully yours,	Respectfully yours,	Sister Angelica *or* Brother James	Sister Angelica, [*or* Brother James,] may I present Mrs. Jones
...ir:	Sincerely yours,	Very truly yours,	Professor [*or* Doctor] Knowles (*within the college*) Mr. Knowles (*elsewhere*)	Professor [*or* Doctor] Knowles
...ir:	*Same as above*	*Same as above*	Doctor Barnes	Doctor Barnes

8

The contents of business letters

Business letters written from business offices depend so thoroughly on the nature of the concern that little can be said beyond an injunction to be clear, concise, and to the point. A rambling effusion never does the job of a well-organized and brief communication. Know exactly what you want to say and give considerable thought to the initial statement of your most important point, and you cannot go far astray. And by all means, when you have said what you intended to say, stop. A meandering last paragraph influences no one in your favor.

Business letters written by a customer or client differ very little from those sent out from a business house. They too should always be as brief and explicit as possible. For example:

May 17, 1964

H. J. Paint & Co.
22 Branch St.
New York 7, N. Y.

Dear Sir:

    Your estimate for painting my dining room, living room, and entry is satisfactory, and you may proceed with the work as soon as possible.

Very truly yours,
Ida Town
(Mrs. James Town)

TO A STORE

An order letter to a store should contain precisely this information:
1. name or description of article
2. quantity, size, color
3. price
4. how paid for (C.O.D., check enclosed, or charge account)
5. how sent, when necessary
6. address and date.

May 3, 1965

Brown, Green, and Company
Evanston, Illinois

Dear Sirs:

Please forward by Railway Express C.O.D. to
                    Mrs. J. B. Greatlake
                    20 Lakeshore Drive
                    Chicago, Illinois
1 chair (No. 4433 in your catalogue), price $59.50
1 quilt (No. 1746) in rose color, price $22.00

Yours truly,
A. K. *Greatlake*

TO A HOTEL OR A RESORT

101 PARK AVENUE
NEW YORK

May 22, 1965

Proprietor of Ocean House
Beach Haven, Maine

Dear Sir:

I would like to know what accommodation you can offer me for the month of August. I require one double room with bath for my husband and myself, a single room for my daughter, and a single room for my son, with baths if possible.

Your hotel was recommended to me by Mrs. Arthur Norman.

If you will send me your folder, describing facilities and prices, I will let you know my decision promptly.

Very truly yours,
Mary Newhouse
(Mrs. John Newhouse)

TO AN "ANSWER COLUMN"

When you write to an "answer column," it is obvious that briefly and clearly put questions, easily and quickly read and briefly answered, will be the ones given consideration—of necessity because of the obviously limited time that can be given to the reading of each one of scores of letters. In other words, several pages of illegible handwriting requiring a half-hour to decipher and answer cannot be chosen instead of twenty short, clearly typed letters. It is not a question of don't want to, but of can't, on the part of the columnist, and this you should keep in mind as you sit down to write.

LETTERS OF INTRODUCTION

The letter that will introduce one business acquaintance to another or possibly to a personal friend is considered elsewhere because of the wide range from the extremely formal to the very casual, depending upon the particular circumstances. » *See Chapter 9.*

THE LETTER OF RECOMMENDATION

A letter of recommendation for membership in a club is addressed to the secretary and should be somewhat in this form:

To the Secretary of the Town Club.
My dear Mrs. Brown,
> *Mrs. Walter Smith, whose name is posted for membership, is a very old friend of mine.*
> *She is a person of great charm and intelligence and when you meet her I am sure you will agree with me in thinking that she will be a valuable addition to the club.*

> *Very sincerely,*
> *Ina Jackson*

» *For other letters pertaining to clubs, see Chapter 65.*

LETTERS OF RESIGNATION

A letter of resignation should be concise, but always polite. It should touch briefly on the reason for the resignation, but whatever that may be, it should never in any way give any indication of rancor or ill-feeling on the part of either the firm or the individual. Resignations are almost always discussed in person in any case and rarely come as a surprise, so there is no need to do more than write a letter that will serve as a permanent record.

Mr. Henry Farthing
Associated Household Wares
14 Kent Place
Cincinnatti, Ohio

Dear Mr. Farthing,

It is with great regret that I feel that I must tender my resignation from the firm. In recent weeks my health has been very poor, and my doctor has indicated that I must retire from business if I wish to recover completely.

Our long association has been a most happy one for me, and I leave you all with sincere gratitude and best wishes for the continued success of the firm.

Sincerely,
Foster Hayes

In the case of an unpleasant parting, the letter should not reveal any signs of vituperation and should attempt to alleviate bitterness.

Dear Mr. Farthing,

It is with regret that I feel that I must tender my resignation. An opportunity has been offered me to take a position which will allow me more time with my family, and I feel that I should accept it.

I truly believe a younger man will be better able to fulfill the requirements of my rather strenuous position with your company. However, I leave Associated with the highest regard for you and the other members of the firm.

Sincerely,
Robert Pugh

» *For letters of resignation from a club, see Chapter 65.*

REFERENCES FOR EMPLOYEES

Although the written recommendation that is given to an employee carries very little weight compared to the slip used by some employment agencies, where either "yes" or "no" has to be answered to a list of specific and important questions, one is nevertheless put in a trying position when reporting on an unsatisfactory servant.

Either a poor reference must be given—possibly preventing the employee from earning his or her living—or one has to write what is not true. Consequently it has become the custom to say what one truthfully can of good and to leave out the qualifications that are lacking, except in the case, for example, of a careless nurse, where evasion would border on the criminal. It is not necessary to say of a cook that her soufflé never rises more than an inch or that her steak is always overdone.

This evasion solves the poor recommendation problem pretty well; but as a result, the good servant suffers unless one is very careful. In writing for a very worthy employee, therefore, it is of the utmost importance in fairness to him or her to put in every mark of merit that you can think of, remembering that omission implies demerit in each trait of character not mentioned. All good references should include honesty, sobriety, capability, and a reason, other than their unsatisfactoriness, for their leaving. Especial attention should be given to the recommendation for a baby's nurse, which cannot be too conscientiously written.

It is not necessary to begin a recommendation with "To whom it may concern" or "This is to certify." The form can be very simple.

For example, a good reference:

Two Hundred Maple Square

Selma Johnson has been in my employ as cook for two years and a half.

I have found her honest, sober, industrious, neat in her person as well as her work, of amiable disposition, and a very good cook.

She is leaving—to my great regret—because I am closing my house.

I shall be very glad to answer personally any inquiries about her.

Josephine Smith
(Mrs. Walter Smith)

February 17, 1965

AN ENGRAVED CARD OF THANKS

An engraved card of thanks is proper only when sent by a public official to acknowledge the overwhelming number of congratulatory messages he must inevitably receive from strangers when he has carried an election or otherwise been honored by his state or country. Thus it falls into the category of business communications rather than personal letters.

Executive Mansion is the established name of the house in which a governor lives; but if he prefers, all official letters may be sent from the Executive Office. A recent and excellent example follows:

Executive Mansion

My dear [name inserted by hand]

I warmly appreciate your kind message of congratulation, which has given me a great deal of pleasure, and sincerely wish that it were possible for me to acknowledge it in a less formal manner.

Faithfully,
[signed by hand]

9

Personal letters

The practice of general letter writing today is shrinking to such an extent that the letter threatens to become a telegram, a telephone message, or just a postcard. Since the events of the day are communicated by newspapers, radio, and television with far greater accuracy, detail, and dispatch than ever they could be by the single efforts of a Voltaire himself, the circulation of general news—which formed the chief reason for letters of the stagecoach and sailing-vessel days—has no part in the hurried correspondence of the twentieth century. Still, people *do* write letters, and there are some who possess the divinely flexible gift for a fresh turn of phrase with which to express a delightful keenness of observation. It may be, too, that in other days the average writing was no better than the average of today, for, not unnaturally, the letters of the unusually gifted are the ones that have been preserved for us over the years.

THE LETTER EVERYONE LOVES TO RECEIVE

The letter we all love to receive is one that carries so much of the writer's personality that he or she seems to be sitting beside us, looking at us directly, and talking just as naturally as if we were together, instead of by proxy in ink-made characters on mere paper. To achieve this happy feeling of *talking* through a letter, one must employ certain devices in order to detract from the stilted quality of the written word. Here are a few specific suggestions that may help to make your letters reflect your personality.

It is quite correct to type a personal letter, but only if the writer is proficient enough so that the number of errors and erasures does not distract the reader.

The clever use of punctuation can add interest and variety, much as the change in tone of a speaker's voice can. Underlining a word or using an exclamation point after a phrase or sentence gives emphasis where you want it. A dash is effective instead of writing out a longer, possibly more grammatical phrase. "We went to a dance last night—what a party!" is more colorful than "We went to a dance last night and it was a great party."

In a personal letter, phrases typical of your speech should be used and not artificially replaced by more formal language. A young person who commonly uses the expression "a real doll" would sound most unnatural and self-conscious if she wrote "she is a lovely girl."

Occasionally inserting the name of the person to whom you are writing gives your letter an added touch of familiarity and affection. "And, Helen, guess what we are going to do this summer!" makes Helen feel as though it will be of special interest to *her*.

The use of contractions is another means of making your writing natural. You would probably never say "I do not know" for "I don't know" or "I am so glad" for "I'm so glad," so why write it that way?

And, finally, don't stop too long to think of *how* to say it. Decide what you want to say, and then write it as quickly as possible; that way, it will come out as if you were truly talking to your friend.

LETTERS THAT SHOULDN'T BE WRITTEN

LETTERS OF GLOOMY APPREHENSION

Even in so personal a matter as the letter to an absent member of one's immediate family, remember not to write needlessly of misfortune or unhappiness. To hear how ill or unhappy those we love are is to have our own distress intensified by the number of miles that separate us from them.

The chronic calamity writers seem to wait until the skies are darkest and then, rushing to their desks, luxuriate in pouring out all their troubles and most especially their fears of trouble-to-come on paper to their friends.

"My little Betty ["my little" makes it so much more pathetic than saying merely "Betty"] has been feeling miserable for several days. I am worried to death about her, as there are so many sudden cases of polio. The doctor says the symptoms are not alarming, but doctors see so much of illness that they don't seem to appreciate what anxiety means to a mother," etc., etc.

Another writes: "The times seem to be getting worse and worse. I always said we would have to go through a long night before any chance of daylight. You can mark my words, the night is hardly more than begun."

THE DANGEROUS LETTER

Every day the mails carry letters that are truly H-bombs should their contents be exploded by falling into wrong hands. Every day letters that should never have been written are put in evidence in courtrooms and many of them cannot, in any way, be excused. Often silly girls and foolish women write things that sound to a jury, for example, quite different from what was innocently, but stupidly, intended.

Remember this above all: Never write a letter to anyone—no matter whom—that would embarrass you were you to see it in a newspaper above your signature. Not that this means *you*, but thousands upon thousands of women, inspired by every known emotion, have poured words on paper, and few of the many made public have had charm or beauty.

However, if you are a young girl—or even a not-so-young woman—and are determined to write a letter to a man that contains any possibility of emotion, then at least put it away overnight in order to reread it and make sure that you have said nothing that may sound different from what you intended to say.

The point to remember, then, is that written words have permanency, and thoughts carelessly put on paper can, when not destroyed by accident, exist for hundreds of years.

A FEW MORE WARNINGS

The light jesting tone that saves a quip from offense cannot be expressed in writing, and remarks, spoken remarks that would amuse, can pique and even insult their subject when written. Without the interpretation of the voice, gaiety becomes levity, raillery becomes accusation. Moreover, words that should be of a passing moment are made to stand forever.

Anger in a letter carries with it the effect of solidified fury. The words spoken in reproof melt with the breath of the speaker once the cause is forgiven; the written words on the page fix them everlastingly. Admonitions from parents to their children may very properly be put on paper—they are meant to endure and be remembered—but momentary annoyance should never be more than briefly expressed. There is no better way of insuring against his letters being read than for a parent to get into the habit of writing in an irritable or faultfinding tone to his children.

One of the fundamental rules for the behavior of any man who has the faintest pretension to being a gentleman is that he never writes a letter that can be construed, even by a lawyer, as damaging to any woman's good name.

One point cannot be overstressed: Letters written under strong emotion should be held for twenty-four hours and reread before being sent—and then probably torn into small pieces and not sent at all.

THE DIFFICULTY IN BEGINNING

For most people—when they are faced with a wordless sheet of paper and wonder how in the world they will ever fill it—the difficult parts of a letter are the beginning and the closing. The instruction of a professor of English—"Begin at the beginning of what you have to say, go on until you have finished, and then stop"—is just about as much help as was the instruction of the celebrated artist who proclaimed, "You simply take a little of the right color of paint and put it on the right spot." Let us see if I can give a few more helpful suggestions.

Even one who loves the very sight of your handwriting could not be expected to find pleasure in a letter beginning "I know I ought to have written sooner, but I haven't had anything to write about." Or one saying "I suppose you have been thinking me very neglectful, but you know how I hate to write letters." Yet such sentences are written time and again by persons who are utterly unconscious that they are really expressing an unfriendly thought.

Suppose you merely change the wording of the above sentences, so that, instead of slamming the door in your friend's face, you hold it open. "Do you think I have forgotten you entirely? You don't know, Ann, how many letters I have planned to write you." Or "Time and time again I have wanted to write you but each moment that I saved for myself was always interrupted by—*something*."

One of the difficulties frequently encountered in beginning a letter is that the answer has been so long delayed that it must be begun with an apology—at best an unhappy beginning. These examples, however, show how even an opening apology may be attractive rather than repellent. If you take the trouble to write a letter, you have remembered someone in a friendly way; otherwise you would not be writing at all.

It is easy enough to begin a letter if it is to be an answer to one that has just been received. The news contained in it is fresh and the impulse to reply needs no prodding. Nothing can be simpler than to say, "We were all overjoyed to hear from you this morning," or "Your letter was the most welcome thing the postman has brought for ages," or "It was more than good to have news of you this morning," or "Your letter from Capri brought all the allure of Italy back to me," or "You can't imagine, Ann, how glad I was to see an envelope with your writing this morning."

And then you take up the various subjects in Ann's letter, which should certainly launch you without difficulty upon topics of your own.

Remember to answer any of her specific questions. It is certainly not only unflattering to be given the impression that you read them hurriedly, but often very upsetting to have long-awaited information one has asked for completely overlooked.

ON ENDING A LETTER

Just as the beginning of a letter should give the reader an impression of greeting, so should its ending express friendly or affectionate leave-taking. Nothing can be worse than to seem to scratch helplessly around in the air for an idea that will effect your escape. "Well, I guess you've read enough of this" and "You're probably bored by now so I'd better close" are stupid.

When you leave the house of a member of your family, you don't have to think up any special sentence in order to say good-by. Leave-taking in a letter is the same. In personal letters to friends, it is not necessary to use the standard forms of closing.

Will write again in a day or two.

Martin

Lunch was announced half a page ago! So good-by, darling, for today.

Nancy

Counting the hours 'til next weekend!

Betsy

THE NOTE OF APOLOGY

The note of apology should offer some real excuse for breaking an engagement. Although you may have telephoned or sent a telegram, a note should follow.

BROADLAWNS

Dear Mrs. Town,

I do deeply apologize for my seeming rudeness in having to send the telegram about Monday night.

When I accepted your invitation, I stupidly forgot entirely that Monday was a holiday and that all my own guests, naturally, were not leaving until Tuesday morning; Arthur and I could not therefore go out by ourselves and leave them!

We were disappointed and hope that you know how sorry we were not to be with you.

Very sincerely,
Ethel Norman

Tuesday morning

Occasionally, an unfortunate incident occurs, which, although it may have been entirely beyond our control, requires that we send another type of note of apology.

Dear Mrs. Neighbor,

My little boy has just told me that our chickens got into your flower beds and did a great deal of damage.

The chicken netting is being built higher at this moment, and they will not be able to damage anything again. I shall send you some plants to replace those that were ruined, although I know that ones newly planted cannot compensate for those you have lost. I can only ask you to accept my contrite apologies.

Sincerely yours,
Katherine Pennybacker

THANK-YOU LETTERS

In the following examples of letters that are intimate and from young persons, such expressions as "divine," "awfully," "too wonderful" are purposely inserted, because to change all those enthusiasms into "pleased with," "very," "most kind" would be to change the validity of the "real" letters into stilted and self-conscious utterances at variance with anything ever written by young men and women. Even the letters of older persons, although they are more restrained than those of youth, avoid anything suggesting smugness or affectation.

LETTERS OF THANKS FOR WEDDING PRESENTS

All wedding presents are sent to the bride, but she generally words her letters of thanks as though the gifts belonged equally to the groom, especially so if they have been sent by friends of his. She might write something like this:

Dear Mrs. Beck,

To think of your sending us all this wonderful glass! It is simply divine! Jim and I both thank you a thousand times!

The presents are, of course, to be shown on the day of the wedding, but do come in Tuesday morning for a cup of coffee and an earlier view.

Thanking you again, and with love from us both,

Affectionately,

Joan

More formally, the bride-to-be might write:

Dear Mrs. King,

It was more than thoughtful of you and Mr. King to send us such a lovely clock. Thank you very, very much.

Looking forward to seeing you on the tenth,

Very sincerely,
Joan McCord

Sometimes, as in the example above, thanks to the husband is definitely expressed in writing to the wife. Usually, however, "you" is understood to mean "you both."

Dear Mrs. Potter,

All my life I have wanted a piece of jade, but I have never imagined a cigarette box quite so beautiful as the one you have sent me. It was wonderfully sweet of you, and I thank you more than I can tell you.

Affectionately,
Joan McCord

For a present received after the wedding, she could say, for example,

Dear Mrs. Chatterton,

The mirror you sent us is going over our living room mantel just as soon as we can hang it up! It is exactly what we most needed, and we both thank you ever so much.

Please come in soon to see how becoming it will be to the room.

Yours affectionately,
Mary Smith Smartlington

THANKS FOR CHRISTMAS AND OTHER PRESENTS

Dearest Lucy,

It was wonderful of you to send us the gorgeous armchair. Jack says I'll never get a chance to sit in it if he gets there first. In fact, Lucy, we both thank you ever and ever so much.

With much love,
Sally

Dear Kate,

I am fascinated with my utility box—it is too unusual for words! You are the cleverest one anyway for finding what no one else can—and everyone wants. I don't know how you do it! And you certainly were sweet to think of me. Thank you ever so much.

Love,
Ethel

THANKS FOR A BABY PRESENT

Dear Mrs. Kindhart,

Of course it had to be from you because no one else can knit like you! The sweater you made the baby is the prettiest thing I have ever

seen, and it is perfectly adorable on her! Thank you, Mrs. Kindhart, for your goodness to

> *Your affectionate*
> *Sally*

Dear Mrs. Cooper,

Thank you ever so much for the lovely blanket you sent the baby. It is by far the prettiest one he has, and so soft and warm that it keeps him cozy on the coldest days!

Do come in and see him, won't you? We both love visitors, any day between 4 and 5:30!

> *Affectionately always,*
> *Lucy*

LETTERS OF INVITATION AND ACCEPTANCE

The letters or notes that you write asking someone to share a meal or a weekend with you are properly invitations, and therefore you will find a complete discussion of them and the answers to them in Chapters 53 and 55.

BREAD-AND-BUTTER LETTERS

When you have been staying overnight, or for a longer time, at someone's house, it is absolutely necessary that you write a letter of thanks to your hostess within a few days after the visit.

Bread-and-butter letters, as they are called, are the stumbling blocks of visitors. Why they are so difficult for nearly everyone is hard to determine, unless it is that they are often written to persons with whom you are on formal terms, and the letter should be somewhat informal in tone. Very likely you have been visiting a friend and must write to her mother, whom you scarcely know; perhaps you have been included in a large and rather formal house party and the hostess is an acquaintance rather than a friend; or perhaps you are a bride and have been on a first visit to relatives or old friends of your husband, but strangers, until now, to you.

As an example of the first, when you have been visiting a girl friend and must write a letter to her mother, you begin "Dear Mrs. Town" at the top of a page, and nothing in the forbidding memory of Mrs. Town encourages you to go further. It would be easy enough to write to Pauline, the daughter. Very well, write to Pauline then—on an odd piece of paper, in pencil—about what a good time you had, how nice it was to be with her. Then copy the note you composed to Pauline on the page beginning "Dear Mrs. Town." You have only to add "Love to Pauline, and thank you again for asking me," end it "Very sincerely" or better "Affectionately"—and there you are!

Don't be afraid that your note is too informal; older people are always pleased with any friendly and spontaneous expressions from the young. Never think, because you cannot write a letter easily, that it is better not to write at all. The most awkward note imaginable is better than none— for to write none is the depth of rudeness, whereas the awkward note merely fails to delight.

AFTER A HOUSE-PARTY WEEKEND

Dear Franny,

Again I realize that there is no house to which I always go with so much pleasure, and leave on Monday morning with so much regret, as yours.

Your party over this last weekend was simply wonderful! And thank you ever so much for having included me.

With much love to you all,
Betty

Dear Mrs. Oldname,

Thank you more than I can tell you for a wonderful week.

I enjoyed every minute of it and think you were very kind to include me in such a delightful house party.

Very sincerely,
John Huntington Smith

FROM A BRIDE TO HER NEW RELATIVES-IN-LAW

A letter that was written by a bride after paying a first visit to her husband's aunt and uncle won her, at a stroke, the love of the whole family. This is the letter:

Dear Aunt Abigail,

Now that it is all over, I have a confession to make! Do you know that when Dick drove me up to your front door and I saw you and Uncle Bob standing on the top step—I was simply paralyzed with fright!

"Suppose they don't like me" was all that I could think. Of course, I knew you love Dick, but that only made it worse. How awful, if you couldn't like—me! The reason I stumbled coming up the steps was because my knees were actually knocking together! And then you were both so perfectly adorable to me and made me feel as though I had always been your niece—and not just the wife of your nephew.

I loved every minute of our being with you, just as much as Dick did, and we hope you are going to let us come again soon.

With best love from us both,
Your affectionate niece,
Eloise

This type of letter would not have served perhaps if Dick's aunt had been a forbidding and austere woman; but even such a one would be far more likely to take a new niece to her heart if the new niece herself gave evidence of having one.

AFTER VISITING A CLOSE FRIEND

Dear Ellen,

It was hideously dull and stuffy in town this morning after the fresh coolness of Strandholm. A back alley-way is not an alluring outlook after the beauty of your place.

It was so good being with you and I enjoyed every moment.

With love,
Caroline

Dearest Bett,

We both had a wonderful time!

You were very good to ask us so soon again, and we thank you very, very much.

Yours,
Mary

TO AN ACQUAINTANCE

After a visit to a formal acquaintance or when someone has shown you especial hospitality in a city where you are a stranger:

My dear Mrs. Duluth,

It was more than good of you to give my husband and me so much of your time. We enjoyed and appreciated all your kindness to us more than we can say.

We hope that you and Mr. Duluth may be coming East before long and that we may then have the pleasure of seeing you at Strandholm.

In the meanwhile, thanking you for your generous hospitality, and with kindest regards to you both, in which my husband joins,

Very sincerely yours,
Katherine Hill Starkweather

LETTERS OF CONGRATULATION

ON AN ENGAGEMENT

Dear Stella,

While we are not altogether surprised, we are both delighted to hear the good news. Ted's family and ours are very close, as you know, and we have always been especially devoted to him. He is one of the finest—and now luckiest—of young men, and we send you both every good wish for all possible happiness.

> *Affectionately,*
> Nancy Jackson

Dear Ted,

Just a line to tell you how glad we all are to hear of your happiness. Stella is everything that is lovely, and, of course, from our point of view, we don't think her exactly unfortunate either! Every good wish that imagination can think of goes to you from your old friends,

> Arthur and Nancy Jackson

Dear Bob,

So you've landed her! Wonderful! I know how crazy you've always been about her—and she's worth being crazy about.

In short, I think it's great, and send every wish for happiness to you both.

> George

LETTER FROM MOTHER TO SON'S FIANCÉE

When it is impossible for a mother to pay the conventional visit upon her son's new fiancée, a letter should be written to her. The general outline is:

Dear Mary,

John has just told us of his great happiness, which, of course, brings joy to us. Our one distress is that we are so far away [or whatever else] that we cannot immediately welcome you in person.

We do, however, send you our love and the hope that we shall meet very soon.

> *Sincerely and affectionately,*
> Martha Jones

ON THE BIRTH OF A BABY

Dear Sue,

We were so delighted to hear the news of Jonathan Junior's birth. Congratulations to all three of you! I can just see big John bursting his buttons with pride.

May I come to see you and the baby the first time that I am in town? I will call and let you know when that will be.

> *Much love,*
> Helen

OTHER LETTERS OF CONGRATULATION

Dear Mrs. Steele,

We are so glad to hear the good news of David's success; it was a very splendid accomplishment and we are all so proud of him and happy for you. Please give him our love and congratulations and with full measure of both to you.

Affectionately,
Mildred Bowen

Dear Michael,

We all rejoice with you in the confirmation of your appointment. The state needs just such men as you—if we had more of your sort, the ordinary citizen would have less to worry about. Our best congratulations!

James Bowen

THE LETTER OF INTRODUCTION

A letter of business introduction can be much more freely given than a letter of social introduction. For the former it is necessary merely that the persons introduced have business interests in common—which are more easily determined than social compatibility, the necessary requisite for the latter. It is, of course, proper to give your personal representative a letter of introduction to anyone to whom you send him.

On the subject of letters of social introduction there is one chief rule:

Never *ask* for such letters of introduction, and be very sparing in your offers to write them.

Seemingly few persons realize that a letter of social introduction is actually a draft for payment on demand. The form might as well be "The bearer of this has (because of it) the right to demand your interest, your time, your hospitality—liberally and at once, no matter what your inclination may be."

Therefore, it is far better to refuse in the beginning than to hedge and end by committing the greater error of inconveniencing a valued friend or acquaintance.

When you have a friend who is going to a city where you have other friends and when you believe that it will be a mutual pleasure for them to meet, a letter of introduction is proper and very easy to write. But sent to a casual acquaintance—no matter how attractive or distinguished the person to be introduced—it is a gross presumption.

THE MORE FORMAL NOTE OF INTRODUCTION

Dear Mrs. Miller:

Julian Gibbs is going to Buffalo on January tenth to deliver a lecture on his Polar expedition, and I am giving him this note of introduction to you. He is a very great friend of ours, and I think that perhaps you and Mr. Miller will enjoy meeting him as much as I know he would enjoy knowing you.

With kindest regards, in which Arthur joins,

Very sincerely,
Ethel Norman

If Mr. Norman were introducing one man to another, he would give his card to the visitor, inscribed as follows:

```
Introducing Julian Gibbs

    Mr. Arthur Lees Norman
```

Mr. Norman would also send a private letter by mail, telling his friend that Mr. Gibbs is coming.

Dear Jack,
I am giving Julian Gibbs a card of introduction to you when he goes to Buffalo on the tenth to lecture. He is delightfully entertaining and a great friend of ours. I feel sure that Mrs. Miller would enjoy meeting him. If you can conveniently ask him to your house, I know he would appreciate it; if not, perhaps you could put him up for a day or two at a club or arrange for a reservation in a good hotel.

Faithfully,
Arthur Norman

INFORMAL LETTER OF INTRODUCTION

My dear Ruth,
I am giving this letter to George Perrin, a great friend of ours, who is going to be in Chicago the week of January seventh.
I want very much to have him meet you and hope that this will find you in town.

Affectionately,
Louise Hill

At the same time a second and private letter of information is written and sent by mail.

My dear Ruth,
I have sent you a letter introducing George Perrin. He is young, about thirty-five or so, good-looking, very good company, and an altogether likable person.
He has only one flaw. He does not play cards, which is not im-

portant; but, knowing how much you play, it is only fair to him, as well as to you, to ask you to invite him to something other than a card party.

I know you will like him; and I hope you will be able to get together.

Affectionately,
Louise Hill

PROCEDURE ON ARRIVAL

A letter of introduction is always handed you unsealed. It is correct for you to seal it at once in the presence of its author. You thank your friend for having written it and go on your trip.

If you are a man and your introduction is to a lady, you go to her house soon after you arrive in her city and, if the door is opened by a maid, leave the letter with your card, if you have one, at her door, without asking to see her. If she herself opens the door, you introduce yourself and give her your letter of introduction. She should—unless prevented by illness—at once invite you to cocktails, lunch, or dinner, or at least name an hour when she would like you to come to see her.

If your letter is to a man, you mail it to his house, unless the letter is a business one. In the latter case, you go to his office and send in your business card and the letter. Meanwhile, you wait in the reception room until he has read the letter and calls you into his office.

If you are a woman, you mail your letter of social introduction and do nothing further until you receive an acknowledgment from the recipient. But the obligation of a written introduction is such that only illness or mourning can excuse her not asking you to her house—either formally or informally.

When a man receives a letter introducing another man, he calls the person introduced on the telephone and asks how he may be of service to him. If he does not invite the newcomer to his house, he may arrange a hotel reservation or ask him to lunch or dinner at a restaurant, as the circumstances seem to warrant. But it is absolutely necessary that he show this stranger what courtesy he can.

THE INDIRECT LETTER OF INTRODUCTION

When the Newcomers go to live in Strangetown, an indirect letter of introduction is better than a direct one. By indirect is meant a letter written by Mrs. Neighbor at home to a friend of hers in Strangetown. As already explained, a letter of introduction presented by Mrs. Newcomer to Mrs. Oldhouse puts Mrs. Oldhouse in a position where she must do something for the Newcomers, no matter how inconvenient or distasteful it may be. Her neglect of them can be construed as nothing less than a repudiation of friendship for the writer of the letter and an unforgivable rudeness to the Newcomers.

If, on the other hand, Mrs. Neighbor merely writes to Mrs. Oldhouse, "My friends, the Newcomers, are going to live in your neighborhood," the former is free to make advances only insofar as she feels inclined.

Mrs. Newcomer, knowing nothing about this letter and expecting nothing in the way of hospitality, is far more likely to be pleased when Mrs. Oldhouse calls on her—and to feel that it is because she is liked for herself—than when she is invited to whatever it may be because Mrs. Neighbor made the invitation obligatory. A letter of introduction is usually an inconvenience and on occasions a very real burden. If you are ill or in mourning—the only excuses possible—you must send a note explaining your lack of hospitality, and even then, if possible, send a deputy. Your husband, or your sister, or even your nearest friend goes to explain and insofar as possible to take your place.

A transient visitor is soon gone again and your obligation quickly ended; but when someone comes to live in the neighborhood permanently, it is obvious that a letter of introduction involves you in a sponsorship that can conceivably become irksome and even embarrassing.

With the indirect letter, you and the Newcomers have the same opportunity to know each other well, if you like each other, but you are bound only by inclination.

THE LETTER OF CONDOLENCE

Intimate letters of condolence to those close to you are like love letters in that they are too sacred and too personal to follow a set form. One rule, and one only, should guide you in writing such letters. Say what you truly feel. Say that and nothing else. Sit down at your desk; let your thoughts be with the person you are writing to.

Don't dwell on the details of illness or the manner of death; don't quote endlessly from the poets and Scripture. Remember that eyes filmed with tears and an aching heart cannot follow rhetorical lengths of writing. The more nearly a note can express a handclasp, a thought of sympathy, above all a genuine love or appreciation for the one who has gone, the greater comfort it brings.

Write as simply as possible and let your heart speak as truly but as briefly as you can. Forget, if you can, that you are using written words. Think merely how you feel—then put your feelings on paper—that is all.

Suppose it is the death of a man who has left a place in the whole community that will be difficult, if not impossible, to fill, and you think of all he stood for that was fine and helpful to others and how much and sorely he will be missed. All you can think of is "Dear Steve—what a prince he was! I don't think anything will ever be the same again without him." Say just that! Ask if there is anything you can do at any time to be of service to his people. There is nothing more to be said. A line into which you have unconsciously put a little of the genuine feeling that you had for Steve is worth pages of eloquence.

A letter of condolence may be abrupt, badly constructed, ungrammatical—never mind. Grace of expression counts for nothing; sincerity alone is of value. The letters from friends and associates, expressing genuine affection for a man's personality or admiration for his character and irreplaceable ability, are the only ones that share a widow's or a mother's grief.

An occasional letter from one who has suffered an undeniably equal loss, who in sincerity writes words of encouragement and assurance that in time the pain will grow less instead of greater, is of genuine help. But such a letter must never be written by anyone whose own suffering has not been equally devastating. Glibly listed qualities that did not exist are as meaningless as attributes of true greatness entirely overlooked.

As has just been said, a letter of condolence must, above everything, express a genuine sentiment. A few examples are included here merely as suggestive guides for those at a loss to construct a short but appropriate message.

My dear Mrs. Neighbor,

We are so very shocked to hear of the sorrow that has come to you.

If there is anything that either my husband or I can do, I earnestly hope that you will ask someone to call upon us.

Alice Rivington Blake

My dear Mrs. Neighbor,

I know how little words written on a page can possibly mean to you at such a time. But I must at least tell you that you are in our thoughts and in our hearts, and if there is anything that we can do for you, please send us a message—whatever it may be.

With deepest sympathy,
Mary Newling

LETTER WHERE DEATH WAS RELEASE

The letter to one whose loss is for the best is difficult in that you want to express sympathy but cannot feel sad that one who has long suffered has found release. The expression of sympathy in this case should not be for the present death, but for the illness or whatever it was that befell long ago. The grief for a paralyzed mother is for the stroke that cut her down many years before, and your sympathy, though you may not have realized it, is for that. You might write: "Your sorrow during all these years—and now—is in my heart; and all my thoughts and sympathy are with you."

10

Greeting cards

Birthday and anniversary cards and all other messages of friendship are charming evidences of good wishes from family and friends. The wide variety of these cards, either comical or sentimental, now available makes the choosing and sending of them a pleasure rather than a chore.

But a word of warning is unfortunately in order. The very fact that such cards are pleasant and easy to use may on occasion lead to their abuse. Elderly Aunt Margaret may be delighted with her birthday card only if you take the trouble to add a little note in your own handwriting expressing something of your own feelings about the day or giving her a bit of family news. A printed message, however charming, cannot always make up for the lack of personal attention, and she may feel that troubling to write only your name indicates neglect or rudeness on your part. Consider the recipient not only when you choose the card, but when you sign and send it. » *See also Chapter 42, on the proper (and improper) use of "Thank you for your sympathy" cards.*

CHRISTMAS CARDS

At one particular season of the year, the greeting card becomes very important to most of us, and there is virtually no limit to the list of those to whom one may send Christmas cards, beginning with dearest friends and ending with the slightest acquaintances. However, the custom that has arisen in many communities of sending a card to every one with whom you have a nodding acquaintance is ridiculous and certainly contrary to the spirit of Christmas. In many areas it has become a contest to see who can receive the most cards—each person who sent a card the previous year must be sent one, plus all the new acquaintances made during the intervening months. Even the tradespeople in some towns send cards to their customers, which, unless there is a personal relationship, can be for no other reason than to bolster their business. These masses of cards are proudly displayed—on mantels, stair railings, pianos, hanging on the walls, and even from the ceiling! Surely the idea of a heartfelt greeting and sincere wish for a happy holiday cannot go with each and every one of these messages!

Christmas cards should be sent to those whom you really wish to greet, but who are not quite close enough to you to exchange gifts, to those good friends you may not have seen for some time, and most of all to those who do not live near you and with whom your Christmas card may be your only communication. In this last case, a card that is always appreciated is the picture of your children, a new home, etc. It need not be elaborate—a snapshot pasted on red paper, with "Merry Christmas" in green ink, is sufficient, although film stores and stationers do make these cards up to order in attractive folders, with or without a printed message.

CARDS TO BUSINESS ACQUAINTANCES

When it is company policy to send a Christmas card to a client, it is preferable to send it, addressed to the man at his business address, in the name of the company—"The Hollister Hardware Company wishes you a Merry Christmas and a Happy New Year"—rather than sending a card to his home in the name of the president or other officer. But if the client is known to the executive socially as well as through business, it may be addressed to husband and wife, even though she may not be known to him personally. It should be signed, however, by the executive—not by him and his wife. This also applies to people working with you, or for you, in your own company.

ENGRAVED CARDS

Very few people send engraved cards today unless they are prominent in public life or hold an official position. These cards are very simple—they may contain the message and no more, or they may have a little decoration, perhaps a straight gold border or a simple design of holly leaves around the edge. The title is included in the signature and the message usually reads, "Mr. and Mrs. Christopher Holly send you their best wishes for a Merry Christmas and a Happy New Year," or "Governor and Mrs. Herbert Black wish you a Merry Christmas and a Joyous New Year."

An important point to be made is that engraving of names on Christmas cards (as opposed to printing) naturally follows the rules for the engraving of names on visiting cards. For example, a woman's name should never be engraved without the title of Mrs. or Miss, although a man's card may be left without a title.

IS HUSBAND'S OR WIFE'S NAME WRITTEN FIRST?

When the cards are sent by husband and wife, the one who writes the names courteously writes his or her own name last. To very close friends, the last name need not be written; to others, it should be included. When cards are printed, there is no rule about whether the husband's or the wife's name shall be first, but the last name is always used. Mary and John seems more polite to Mary, but John and Mary does, of course, follow the conventional Mr. and Mrs. form. However, when children's names are included, the father's name comes first—always. For example: John and Mary and John Jr. Sometimes, by the way, a baby's arrival at any time during the year is announced by adding his name on the Christmas cards—John and Mary and their new son Timothy. Cards sent to intimate friends, by a family having several children, might be from The John Smiths—all Five, or from the Smiths—John, Mary, Johnny, Marie, and Tim. There is of course no rule about anything so informal as this.

On the printed cards sent by a widow and her grown son together, or a widower and his grown daughter, the name of the parent would be on one line and that of the son or daughter on the line below. Or if written by hand, the parent's name would come first: Henry Brown and Mary, or to those who call the parent by the first name, Henry and Mary, each signing his or her name.

Engaged people often send cards together to their intimate friends with their first names either written by hand or printed to match the rest of the printing on an informal card.

COLORED INKS FOR GAILY COLORED CARDS

Although red and orange ink are still rejected for social correspondence, there is no objection to signing cards in red or other colored ink to match the wording on a gaily informal Christmas card. Also Christmas envelope linings can be as vividly colorful as you please. You should paste return address stickers or write your address on envelopes going to people whose address you are not certain about or to any you think may not know your own address. The Christmas seals sold to help support the fight against tuberculosis and for other worthy causes look gay on the back of the envelope. They should be applied to the tip of the flap or to the center of a square flap.

A CARD FOR THE WHOLE FAMILY

When a card is intended for the whole family and one dislikes the ambiguousness of Mr. and Mrs. Brightmeadow and Family, it is best to address the envelope to Mr. and Mrs. Brightmeadow and then on the card itself and below the wording of the message write in ink "Love to the children, too" or "We all in our house send best Christmas wishes to all of you in your house," or whatever message is suitable.

A CHRISTMAS CARD TO SOMEONE IN MOURNING

A card to someone who is in mourning can be kind if its picture in some way illustrates the promise of peace or the birth of Christ or if its message be of loving friendly thought. But please do not send a picture of a grave or gravestones—nor on the other hand a gay card shouting "Merry Christmas and Happy New Year." Whether or not those who are themselves in mourning send cards depends entirely upon their own feelings. Naturally they would not send cards to mere acquaintances, but certainly there is no impropriety in wishing their friends happiness, if they can forget their own unhappiness enough to do so. On the other hand, no one could possibly want them to do anything that could add to the strain of what must be for them the hardest of days to endure.

Part THREE

AS OTHERS SEE YOU

11

The general rules

"Do not attract attention to yourself in public" is one of the cardinal principles of etiquette, and many of the specific rules and suggestions that appear in this and the following chapters are simply applications of this all-important rule. Just by keeping this one injunction in mind, you can save yourself and others much embarrassment in many situations.

Begin by shunning conspicuous manners and conspicuous clothes. Avoid staring at people or bumping into them or pointing at them. Whether on the street or in a building, don't talk in strident tones. Nothing is in poorer taste than the advertisement of your achievements by loud word of mouth. One should also avoid loudly pronouncing people's names or making personal remarks that may either attract attention or proclaim a person's identity. Do not expose your private affairs, feelings, or innermost thoughts in public. You are knocking down the walls of your house when you do.

A young man walking with a young woman should be careful to draw no attention to her or to himself. Too devoted a manner is always conspicuous. He should never grasp her at the elbow and shove her here and there—except, of course, to save her from being run over!

WALKING ON THE STREET

Older convention rules that a gentleman, whether walking with two ladies or with one, takes the curb side of the pavement. Taking the curb side has not been a necessity since automobiles removed the danger of runaway horses, from which the gentleman was once supposed to protect his fair companion, and today it does seem senseless for him to keep circling behind the lady every time they cross a street, instead of giving her the position of courtesy on his right. In short, modern rules of behavior approve of his walking either on the curb side of the pavement or on the lady's left, as he chooses, but not on any account on her right and away from the curb at the same time.

A gentleman should never sandwich himself between two ladies when walking or sitting with them. From one side, he can look in the direction of both while talking with either one, whereas when he is between them, he must turn away from one when he talks to the other. In addition, if the women happen to be intimate friends, they may have a tendency to talk "across" him, forcing him to turn back and forth as if he were at a tennis match.

THE PROBLEM OF PACKAGES

In Victorian days, it was considered necessary for a man to carry anything and everything for the lady he was with, no matter how feminine in appearance or how light in weight the bundle might be. Nowadays, however, the etiquette of toting is determined by practicality. A lady should certainly carry such feminine articles as her purse, gloves, umbrella, and hat box, and she may also carry any lightweight packages. A gentleman must, of course, carry the heavy items—suitcases, golf bags, or groceries—and he should ask if he can assist her when she has many small packages. Obviously a woman should not ask a man to carry for any distance a heavy or otherwise burdensome load. If, for example, she will be in a situation where there are no porters available, she must plan on sending luggage by other means or restrict her pieces to manageable proportions.

Of course, every man should willingly carry a woman's field glasses or her camera or her polo coat or indeed anything that might seemingly be his own. But only a very inconsiderate woman would ask him to carry a slender, colored umbrella with a long, delicate handle or a coat that is conspicuously feminine. A woman should make sure that any packages she asks a man to carry for her are wrapped neatly and securely. An unthinking young woman who asks an admirer to carry something suggestive of a pillow done up in crinkled paper and odd lengths of joined string is likely to find herself wondering why John Newbeau never calls her any more.

THE PROFFERED ARM OR THE HELPING HAND

To an old lady or to an invalid or to any lady on any occasion when he thinks she may need his support, a gentleman offers his arm. In the daytime, she need not take it unless she wishes. At night, however, when walking for some distance or going down the steps of a house, she is wise to accept his offer, not only because it is a courtesy, but because high-heeled shoes can be somewhat difficult to walk in when it is too dark for a woman to see clearly where she is placing her foot.

When he offers his arm in these situations, he says, "Will you take my arm?" or perhaps "Wouldn't it be easier if you took my arm along here?"

The only other occasions on which a gentleman offers his arm to a lady are when he takes her in at a formal dinner or when he is an usher at a wedding. In crossing a ballroom, couples walk side by side rather than hand on arm.

Etiquette does not permit a gentleman to grab a lady by the arm or the elbow and shove her along. It is only when he is helping her into a car, a taxi, or a bus that he should put his hand under her elbow. When he helps her out of such a vehicle, he should alight first and offer her his hand.

GENTLEMEN BEFORE LADIES

In all ordinary circumstances, indoors or out, the gentleman precedes only if the way is dangerous or uncertain. Over dangerous footing, he goes first and offers his hand, which the woman takes to steady herself. He gets out of a car first and holds the door for her, as well as stepping ahead of her to open the door for her when she enters it.

He also precedes her down a very steep or slippery stairway: "Let me go first; the stairs are bad." The idea of protecting her should she slip is quite out of key with the capable women of today. Even so, etiquette requires that he make the gesture of stepping into a boat first, for example, and being ready to help her. Moreover it is well to remember that charm in a woman still presupposes feminine grace rather than masculine hardihood and in no way denies the fact that a young woman's helplessness is a thing of the past.

A LADY NOT ON THE LEFT

In former days there was a rule of utmost importance: a lady was never seated on a gentleman's left, because according to the etiquette of the day a lady "on the left" was *not* a "lady." But today in America all that remains of this rule is that, when equally practical, it is always more polite that a gentleman seat a lady on his right. (The few surviving rules about sitting on the right include the seating of a guest of honor on the right of the host or hostess or chairman, and the military rule by which the senior officer walks as well as sits on his junior's right.)

In her own car a lady should, if practical, sit on the right-hand side of the rear seat if she is being driven by a chauffeur. This can be awkward, however, because getting into the car on the left side of a one way street, the hostess would have to walk around the car to the middle of the street, or precede her guest, to avoid climbing over her. Therefore, it is really more practical for the lady who enters first to sit in the farthest corner, whether right or left.

SMOKING IN PUBLIC

It is impossible to imagine a true lady walking on a city street either chewing gum or smoking a cigarette. Nor does a gentleman walk with a lady in the city and at the same time smoke. In the country, however, the rules are more relaxed, and there men and women alike smoke more or less whenever they please.

An unfortunate and dangerous habit has arisen in recent years— that of young people smoking on the dance floor. This is inexcusable. Not only does it look unattractive, but there is danger of a spark falling on a synthetic material, which ignites with a flash. Naturally, such behavior would never be permitted at a chaperoned party, but at an impromptu gathering the young people who are the hosts or the organizers of the group should see to it that no one smokes while dancing.

In general, men and women in stores, at sports events, or in restaurants always smoke as much as they wish, provided that smoking is legally permitted. If, however, one is sitting in an audience and notices that his smoke is drifting and annoying people around him, he should make every effort to hold his cigarette in such a position that it is not blowing directly at his neighbors.

» *See also Chapter 64, "For those who smoke."*

THE QUESTION OF PAYING

It is becoming much less customary than it used to be for a gentleman to offer to pay a lady's way, especially if they happen to meet by chance. For example, if a young woman and a man happen to find themselves taking the same train and she stops at the newsstand to buy magazines, the man instinctively starts to pay for them. If she knows him very well and the total is small, she perhaps lets him pay. But if he is someone she knows slightly or if she has bought several of the higher-priced ones, she answers, "Don't bother; I have it!" and puts the money on the counter. It would be awkward for him to protest and bad taste to press the point. In this case, too, she buys her ticket and tips the porter for carrying her bag. On the other hand, if she has gone on his invitation to spend the day in the country, or to lunch, or to dinner, or to a theater, he of course pays for everything.

A man on a train or ferry who finds himself next to a woman whom he knows only slightly need not offer to pay her fare or for anything she may buy from the newsboy or refreshment stand, the reason being that he should on no account put her under obligation to him.

A group of people going on an excursion or dining together in a restaurant should agree beforehand on the handling of the finances. Going "dutch" (each individual or couple paying his own way) is more often done than not. To avoid the confusion of several people trying to divide and pay the bill, it is far better for one man (or woman, but only if it is a women's group) to pay the entire bill, and the others to pay him their share later. Another method is for each to contribute a sum in advance, based on the probable cost, from which fund he may pay and then return in equal amounts any money left over.

LIFE IN CROWDED CITIES

Of great importance is the need for consideration of others among dwellers in city apartments so closely packed that every sound made by one family can be heard by several others. In fact, sound seems sometimes to be intensified by distance. In the same room with the children, their play does not seem overloud, nor does the radio or television set when we are engrossed in the program. But to the family living on the floor below, the patter of little feet sounds like a stable full of Percherons. The toys they drop seem all of iron! The disk jockey crashes through each separate convolution of a neighbor's brain. As for young musicians' practicing—what manager of an apartment house is not at his wits' end to solve this cause of complaint?

There are certain annoyances to others that can't be helped; babies must sometimes cry, children scream, dogs bark, or someone get a hacking cough. The best that considerate people can do is to try to soften such sounds as much as possible by shutting a window temporarily and by trying to train both children and dogs.

Difficult to understand is the fact that in nearly all communal buildings there are always those few who seemingly show no feelings for others because their own sensitivity is, as it were, on another wave length. It is very hard to keep in mind that there can be sounds that greatly annoy some of us—the unceasing sound of a television set, for example, or a record player—but do not disturb others at all, whereas some of the things which we don't mind can quite possibly be unbearable to our neighbors. Difficult as it may be to remember, we must make every effort to do so when we find ourselves in these crowded conditions lest we be classed with the insensitive few. In today's congested cities, behavior that was once strictly private can all too easily become public.

PUBLIC CLEANLINESS

The subject of this section is not a pleasant one; some aspects of it are almost too unpleasant to commit to print. But unless you never go out in public you can hardly be unaware of the increasing messiness (at times actual filthiness) of such places as the lounges and dressing rooms of hotels, theaters, and movie houses. Even the lounges of clubs are not kept in as perfect order as they used to be. As for such really public places as waiting rooms in railroad terminals, rest rooms in overcrowded department stores, or sports stadiums, the problem is becoming overwhelming!

Food-eaters and newspaper-discarders have always been conspicuous offenders, and the gum-scatterers have even ranked with the wall-defacers as doing permanent damage. But in former years their destructive habits were held in check by employees whose present scarcity makes the orderliness of these places the responsibility of the public—and more particularly you and me.

In writing this, there are of course, certain persons to whom I want to make a special appeal. At one extreme are those who are really untidy. We can all name people who throw ashes no matter where, set wet tumblers down on no matter what, drop wet raincoats on the nearest upholstered chair, and burn table edges with forgotten cigarettes. The women of this group wipe indelible lipstick on napkins and towels. They also shake face powder on whatever is near them and leave hairs in the sink when they fix their make-up or arrange their hair-do. Their behavior suggests that in their own homes they would not object if their beds were never made! In other words, those who live in disorder can hardly be keenly aware of the disorder they make others endure.

In the second group are those who are careless because they take it for granted that someone will come along with dust-pan and brush and that it would in fact be wasted effort should there be nothing to brush. These people, if merely made to realize there is no one to brush up after them, would ordinarily be careful to leave no disorder.

The point to be made is that if only each of us who care about the niceties would become sufficiently conscious of our obligation to act as deputy wardens, the situation would be improved. In short, instead of courteously refraining from showing criticism of others, no matter what they do, it is sometimes the obligation of each of us not only to try to become conscious of our own behavior, but to do what we have all been trained NOT to do—frankly correct others. For example, when a woman tosses a used paper towel at a receptacle and leaves it lying on the floor when it misses its mark, we could try to suggest that she make more effort by picking it up ourselves, saying, "Did you notice you missed the basket?"

In the powder rooms of many restaurants and clubs, there are signs that say something like "Please leave this rest room as you found it." But they seem to do little good—in fact I believe that many people don't wish to notice them at all. Having an attendant on duty seems to be the greatest help—people apparently take a little more care if they feel they are being watched. A sad commentary, but in the case of rest rooms—true!

Most familiar and most troublesome to all who have the care of public places is the discarding of chewing gum. I remember being told by a railroad official that the chewing gum ground into the marble floor of a crowded terminal meant patient hand-scraping that cost the building maintenance department hundreds of times the value of a pack of gum!

Details that are too unpleasant to print are those of the washrooms in railroad stations and department stores and other public places which are crowded beyond their capacities and put completely out of order. The greatest offenders of all are people who carelessly throw all manner of waste into toilets not made to serve as trash cans. In washrooms that have no attendants, conditions are sometimes so bad that there is no answer other than a locked door. The owner of a big department store wrote me the other day that he had been forced to hang a large sign on the door leading from the customer's rest room into the washroom reading: "This washroom can remain open for your convenience only for so long as you cooperate in helping to keep it in order."

Every city has the same problem in keeping its streets clean. All the campaigns, the special "Keep our city clean" weeks, the signs, the receptacles put on corners for trash, and the fines imposed for littering, fail to solve the problem completely. As in the public washroom, it is the duty of each and every one of us to take pride in keeping our cities and towns places of cleanliness and beauty and to impress others with the importance of the problem.

As an unbelievable example of the length of carelessness to which a nice person can go, I was myself a witness to the following: Just ahead of me on the street, a prominent citizen bought a Sunday paper, walked along the street ruffling through its pages hunting for an article about himself. Finding it, he stopped and tore it out, then dropped the entire paper on the sidewalk at his feet, stepped over it, and walked on. No credit to him that an apartment-house doorman went into the street and gathered it up. This incident is not necessarily typical, but it did happen!

CONSIDERATION FOR THOSE WHO SERVE YOU

To show lack of consideration for those who in any capacity serve us—whether in restaurants, hotels, stores, or in public places anywhere—is always an evidence of ill breeding as well as inexcusable selfishness. It is only those who are afraid that someone may encroach upon their exceedingly insecure dignity who show neither courtesy nor consideration except to those whom they think it would be to their advantage to please.

In restaurants

Dining out is not only a necessity for the traveler away from home and the man expected to conduct business over the lunch or dinner table; today it is also a pleasant form of relaxation for the family and a popular way of entertaining friends. But whether the meal is taken in a restaurant for social reasons, or of necessity, should make no appreciable difference in the conduct of the diners, and the rules and suggestions that follow are applicable in either situation.

ON ARRIVING

CHECKING HATS AND COATS

On entering a restaurant, a man leaves his hat and coat in the checkroom near the entrance. A woman may leave her coat in the dressing room if there is an attendant on duty to check it, or she may wear it into the dining room, as she chooses. If she keeps it with her, she wears it until she is seated, then throws the shoulders of the wrap back of her, over her chair, with her escort's help if necessary.

In the daytime, she may wear a hat, and she keeps it on. Despite today's trend toward hatlessness, a hat is always correct with a street dress. At night, she wears a hat with daytime clothes, an evening hat or small veil with a cocktail or dinner dress, and no hat, ever, with a formal evening dress.

BEING SEATED

After the coats have been checked, the couple or the group wait just inside the entrance until the headwaiter or hostess comes forward to ask the host about the number in the group and sometimes about his preference as to the location of the table. If there is no host (or hostess), some one member of the group should assume the responsibility for all the duties that are ordinarily assigned to the host. Often one of the older men in the group falls naturally into this role of spokesman. Or if many people are involved, an informal kind of appointment may be made beforehand: "John, won't you please handle things this noon?" This is done only to avoid confusion and the unpleasantness that can arise when, for example, several people are addressing the waiter at once, leaving him in doubt about whom to listen to first and what to do next—a state that never improves the service or adds to the enjoyment of the meal. The person playing the host's role is only a spokesman, however, and cannot be expected to shoulder financial or other burdens that are not properly his.

After the table is reached, the waiter pulls out the choice seat first (meaning the seat that he considers choice because it faces the room or the lake view or whatever is supposed to be of interest). If you are a woman with a man, you naturally take it, unless for some reason you prefer another. In this case, you stand beside the other chair saying, "I'd rather sit here." A lady who has another lady as her guest offers her the best seat, but when the hostess is a much older person, the young guest would naturally refuse, saying, "Oh no, Mrs. Friendly, won't you sit on the banquette?"

When there is no waiter at hand to seat them, the man seats his guests. If he is with two women, he helps first one and then at least makes the gesture of helping the second. He should, of course, help a guest before his wife, who by that time has probably seated herself.

The women always follow the headwaiter and the gentlemen follow them. But if a man is giving a dinner for six or more, the women stand at the table until told by their host where to sit, so in this case it causes less confusion if he goes in ahead of his guests. When a husband and wife are hosts, the wife seats the guests, usually going ahead with the most important lady.

If they are only four and none is married, the ladies seat themselves facing each other. When two married couples dine together, the host and his wife sit opposite each other exactly as they do at a table for six or ten. If, however, neither couple is giving the party, they may sit in any fashion they prefer. At a table of eight or other multiples of four, the most important gentleman sits opposite the host with the hostess on his left.

If there is dancing and an older and more important woman is a guest, the host invites her for the first dance; then he dances with the other ladies and finally with his wife. The other men should invite the women on either side of them to dance before asking others from seats farther away. A woman should never be left alone at a table.

In a restaurant that has continuous sofa-seats or banquettes along its walls, the seating is necessarily somewhat different. Two people dining together are seated side by side against the wall, and the table, which is two places wide, is pushed in front of them. If there are four, the ladies are seated on the banquette and chairs are placed for the gentlemen facing them across the table.

If the restaurant were very crowded, two diners who might otherwise be given wall seats would be seated at a half-width table, at which the lady would be seated against the wall and the gentleman facing her.

In a restaurant with booths, the women go in first and sit against the far wall, facing each other across the table. The men then sit next to them also facing each other. If a woman and two men are lunching or dining, the woman takes her place first against the wall. If one of the men is related to her, he sits across from her, and the one not related sits beside her. If this grouping is reversed, the two ladies sit next to the wall, and the man who is the husband of one sits beside the other, or if no one is related he may sit beside either one.

COCKTAILS AND WINE

When the group is seated, the waiter may ask if any one would like a cocktail. The host asks the others what if anything they would like and then gives the order to the waiter.

No one should be urged to drink cocktails once he has refused, but neither should any guest feel uncomfortable because he would like one. If there are some who say "no" to liquor, the host should ask if they would like to have ginger ale or tomato juice perhaps, while the others are having their cocktails. It is most impolite to prolong the cocktails beyond one or two when others are left with nothing in front of them and only the hope of a meal to sustain them.

If wine is to be served, it should be ordered after the choices for the meal have been made, from the wine steward if there is one, or from the waiter if there is not. The host, or whichever man may be best qualified, should choose a wine that goes well with the greatest number of choices of food. For instance, if more people have ordered chicken or fish, choose a white wine; but if more are having a steak dinner, pick a red. There are also many people who prefer a vin rosé, or pink wine, and it is often a happy compromise, as it goes well with almost any menu.

If you have a definite preference for red or white wine, it is not incorrect to order either with any food. The choices stated above are simply those which usually result in the most pleasing combination of flavors.

You may choose expensive imported wines if you wish, but there are many excellent domestic wines at a fraction of the cost. Some of the imported wines at lower prices are delicious, too, and one should not feel it necessary to spend a great deal to enjoy a fine wine with dinner. If you do not recognize the names on the wine list, by all means ask your headwaiter's advice, giving him an idea of the type you prefer, dry or sweet, domestic or imported.

ORDERING THE MEAL

When a man is taking a woman to dinner, he orders the meal after asking her what she would like. When he knows the restaurant well and sometimes when foreign food is served with which she is not acquainted, he should suggest some choices to her and recommend whatever he thinks she would like. If they are both unfamiliar with the type of food served, he should ask the waiter to recommend one of the specialities of the restaurant. The woman should never give her order to the waiter herself.

Unless she knows that her host is very well off, she should show some consideration for his pocketbook and either ask for a *table d'hôte* dinner, if one is offered, or choose only a soup or appetizer, a main course, and a dessert. The man may always add more, with her permission, but she should give him the opportunity of economizing.

Four people, or even six, may order in the same way, telling their choices to the host, who then gives them to the waiter. If the group is larger, however, it is easier for the waiter to go around the table, taking a complete order from each guest in turn.

THE DIFFERENCE BETWEEN TABLE D'HOTE AND A LA CARTE

Table d'hôte means a set price for a complete meal, irrespective of how many courses are ordered. "Club" breakfasts and lunches, "blue plate" dinners, or any meals at fixed prices are *table d'hôte*.

A *la carte* means that you order from a list of dishes and you pay for each dish ordered, often including the bread and butter.

Usually it is very easy to know which is which, because the price follows each item on an *à la carte* menu, whereas no prices are listed on a *table d'hôte* bill of fare except at the top where the price for the complete dinner is usually printed. Very often a separate card or a box inset on the *à la carte* menu reads, "Special dinner $3.00" or whatever the price may be, and informs you that you can order whatever you choose on this special list for three dollars, but that any item taken from the regular bill of fare will be charged for as an extra.

A very popular type of menu is one that has a price following each entrée. This price includes the choice of an *hors d'oeuvre* or a soup; also a salad and a dessert, and choice of coffee, tea or milk. If any items other than the entrées are followed by a price, this means there is an additional charge for them.

SPECIAL TYPES OF MEALS

The *smorgasbord* is a delightful importation from Sweden. Actually it is simply a buffet, but a buffet of such variety and interest that it has become extremely popular in the United States.

When a man invites a woman to dine in this fashion, he may go to the buffet alone and fill a plate for her, but this eliminates much of the fun of dining in such a restaurant. Aside from the fact that she would be left sitting alone at the table, few women would want to miss the opportunity of seeing the delectable displays of food and choosing a little of everything that appeals to them.

In a restaurant with a smorgasbord table, the individual tables are generally set with the silverware and glasses, so that one takes a plate at the buffet table and serves oneself, although in some cases there may be one or two waiters ready to assist with hot dishes or those that may be difficult to handle.

Japanese and Chinese restaurants often offer interesting variations in service and food. In some of the former, there is a section where the guests may actually remove their shoes, if they choose to, and sit on cushions on the floor at low tables in true Japanese style. Naturally, if you are taking older or crippled people to such a restaurant, you would not sit in that section, but at the regular tables, which are always available for those who prefer them. Chinese restaurants have the seating arrangements in the regular style, but if you wish, you may eat with chopsticks in many of them.

Some distinctive restaurants suggest that each person at the table order a different dish, all of which are placed in the center of the table so that the diners may serve themselves from any or all of them. This is a delightful way to experiment with various dishes—and one that may be helpful in ordering the next time you go to a similar restaurant.

PAYING THE CHECK

When everyone has finished his meal, the host catches the eye of the waiter or headwaiter and says, "The check, please." The check is brought face down on a small plate and presented to the man who ordered the dinner. He looks at it, checks it quickly for mistakes, and returns it to the plate with the necessary money. If he has found an error, he beckons the waiter and points it out quietly; the waiter makes the adjustment, either himself or with the help of the headwaiter or cashier. In no circumstances should a "scene" be made. If the management is unpleasant about making a correction, simply pay the check, leave as quickly as possible, and do not return to that restaurant.

Many restaurants ask their customers to pay a cashier on the way out. This practice is especially common in large city restaurants and in those which are used mostly at the lunch hour. It is a great timesaver, as very often a waiter, when he has finished serving a table, gives his attention to other customers, and those waiting for their checks find it difficult to attract his attention. When it reads at the bottom of your check "Please pay cashier," leave the tip on the table, collect your coats or belongings, and leave, with the host following the group, who wait in the entry while he pays the bill. If by chance he needs change in order to have the right amount for a tip, he pays the check and quickly returns to the table so that the waiter knows he has not been forgotten.

CREDIT CARDS

A popular and practical method of paying for restaurant dinners, entertainments, and even such necessities as gasoline and travel accommodations is that of using a credit card. Numerous credit-card companies exist, and it is a great convenience for those who dine out or entertain frequently but do not wish to carry large amounts of cash. A credit card is sent to you on request with your name, address, and a number. This card may be used as identification at any restaurant or establishment that is a member of the credit organization. All the customer has to do at the time is sign the check and give it and the card to the waiter for processing. The card is returned to its owner, and the restaurant sends the check in to the credit-card company, which in turn bills the customer at the end of the month. The tip may be added to the check, but remember that if you do this, the percentage charged by the credit-card company may be deducted from the amount your waiter receives, and you should therefore adjust your tip accordingly.

TIPPING

It is impossible to give definite rules for tipping, because it depends upon where you go, what you order, and the service that is given you—or that you exact.

That is, if you patronize luxurious restaurants and wear expensive clothes with valuable accessories or if you are critical and difficult to please, greater "compensation" is expected than if your appearance were simpler and your demands less exacting.

WAITER AND HEADWAITER

Fifteen percent is standard in any restaurant, twenty in a night club or if you've been very exacting or if the service has been excellent. Ten percent is too little anywhere, except perhaps at a lunch counter, and never less than ten cents there.

Patrons who make a practice of tipping waitresses less than waiters are being quite unfair, because the service rendered is the same.

If you are having a party of ten, twelve, or more, fifteen percent would be quite adequate for the waiters who serve you and perhaps five dollars for the headwaiter if he has taken pains to give you good service. On the other hand, if he has done nothing beyond seating you and handing you a menu, you give him nothing.

WINE STEWARD AND BARTENDER

If the wine steward has served you, he should receive twelve to fifteen percent of the wine bill. The bartender receives ten percent if you have drinks at the bar.

CHECKROOM AND DRESSING ROOM

The fee to the checkroom boy or girl who takes care of a man's hat and coat in most restaurants is twenty-five cents, in a very expensive one, fifty.

A question often asked by young women is about the fee to the maid in the dressing room. It is never less than twenty-five cents in any restaurant or hotel and sometimes fifty in an expensive one.

In the ladies room there is almost always a small plate with a few coins on it in a conspicuous place. If the attendant hands you a towel or performs some other service for you, you are expected to leave a coin of the same denomination as those on the plate—usually a quarter.

A HOST'S RESPONSIBILITIES

The first thing the host must consider is the choice of restaurant. Do his guests like exotic food or good plain cooking? If they are from out of town, do they have the proper clothes with them for an elaborate restaurant? Do they wish to see a place with a worldwide reputation? Or if a man is taking a girl to dinner, would she like a small, intimate spot, or would she prefer to dance to a good orchestra?

Having made his decision, the host must make every effort to see that the restaurant chosen meets the expectations of his guests. If he has picked a well-known restaurant, he must reserve a table ahead of time, and should his party be on a weekend evening, it is always safer to make a reservation at any restaurant accepting them.

If he has ordered the dinner in advance, he must try to observe the dishes as they are served to make sure that everything is as he requested. If there are any omissions, he quietly calls them to the attention of the waiter and makes sure that the missing items are supplied.

If dinner has not been ordered beforehand, it is the host's duty to take his guests' orders and give them to the waiter or, if the party is too large, to make sure that the waiter gets the order correctly from each person. Again, if there are mistakes, he must see that they are corrected, being sure to be tactful and polite, thereby avoiding embarrassment to his guest.

When paying the check, the host does not display the total, but puts the money (or the signed check if he pays by credit card) quietly on the plate and nods to the waiter that he may remove it. If he has not had the exact amount, including the tip, the waiter will bring his change, but if the sum did include both bill and tip, the host thanks the waiter and indicates that he is ready to leave by rising or by making some such remark as "Well, we should be moving along if we don't want to miss the overture."

If the headwaiter has been especially helpful, given him the best table, or taken special care in serving the meal, the host unobtrusively slips a bill (from one to five dollars, depending on the size of the group) into his hand and thanks him as he is leaving the restaurant.

WOMEN DINING OUT

WHEN A WOMAN INVITES A MAN

When a woman invites a man to dine with her for personal rather than business reasons and it is understood that she is paying the bill, there may be some embarrassment at the time the check is presented. The best solution is for the woman to have a credit card, or possibly a charge account at the restaurant. The act of signing a slip of paper does not somehow seem so objectionable as having the woman check over the bill and count out the money while the man sits helplessly by. In fact, this situation is so awkward that many women without charge privileges prefer to give their guest a sum of cash large enough to cover the bill before they enter the restaurant, thus relieving the man of any embarrassment before the waiter. Incidentally, this solution serves in the case of the husband who has left his wallet behind or has insufficient money with him. Rather than have him embarrassed in front of the staff or his guests, his wife may pass him the necessary sum without calling attention to his situation.

In the case of a woman entertaining a customer for her company, the probabilities are that the company has accounts in the nearby restaurants, and she signs the check as their representative. If they have not made arrangements for her to sign the check, she pays cash, and if her guest protests and tries to pay himself, she explains that he is her company's guest and that the amount of this check is going on her expense account. Or again, if she has a credit card, she may use it and present the bill to her employer.

WHEN WOMEN DINE TOGETHER

When several women are dining out together, the problem of the check is one that can cause concern to and confusion among the waiters, the nearby diners, and the women themselves. Women so seldom are able to separate a check into several parts with grace and speed that the cartoon of feminine heads clustered about the waiter's tab, captioned "Now let's see, Ethel, you had the Tomato Surprise," is familiar to all of us. One way to avoid such a scene is to get separate checks. Or one woman may pay the entire check, and the settling up can be done later. If each one's debt must be figured at the table, make sure at least that the best computer in the group gets the chore so that it is done as quietly and simply as possible.

WOMEN AND MAKE-UP AT TABLE

A well-bred woman always avoids making up in public; cosmetics and food do not go together. At the end of a meal, a woman may quickly powder her nose and put on a little lipstick, but to sit and daub at the face in a little mirror for any length of time cannot fail to impress your host or any onlooker with the blemishes this face must have to need such drastic repair.

The one never-to-be-broken rule is: Don't ever use a comb anywhere outside a dressing room. Don't even slightly rearrange or put your fingers on your hair in any place where food is served.

RESTAURANT COURTESY

When a group about to dine together enters and sees people whom some know and others do not, the members continue on directly to their table, nodding "hello" as they pass. A public restaurant is scarcely the place for group social introductions.

On the other hand, there are occasions when one or two introductions are suitably performed. The man at the table of course rises when a woman is being introduced, as he does whenever a woman stops to talk. But when a woman stopping at a table is introduced to other women seated there, the latter never rise—not even though they be young and the visitor quite old.

Men at the table do not rise when another man stops on his way by. When someone comes across the room to speak to one of the diners, that man only should stand to shake hands. The visitor should then ask him please to be seated while he finishes what he has come to say. But if he intends to say more than a few words of greeting, he might ask a waiter for a chair or as quickly as possible make a later appointment with the one he wishes to talk to.

One act of thoughtlessness is that of an unobserving woman who, when entering a crowded restaurant and passing a table at which her friend Mrs. Evans is dining with Mr. Evans, cannot resist stopping for a greeting that lengthens into a dialogue of many minutes. She overlooks the fact that during her stay the polite husband is obliged to stand and all too often watch the food on his plate grow colder and colder.

True, the visitor does from time to time earnestly urge, "Oh, *do* sit down! Oh, *please* don't stand!" Which Mr. Evans may quite properly do. But usually the poor husband would feel most conspicuous if he were seated while the woman remained standing at the table.

However, the impulse of one husband may quite likely have solved this problem. Gustav Gourmet, just about to eat a perfect soufflé in a noted restaurant, was forced to stand for a friend of his wife who stopped at their table. "Oh, *please* sit down! You must not let your soufflé fall!" said she and, having given this permission, simply thought him stubborn not to sit. Thereupon he solved the problem by lifting the plate and eating—standing.

Let us hope that long-talking standees will take this anecdote to heart and pass the tables of their friends without pausing.

13

The opera, the theater, and other indoor entertainments

The basic principles of public conduct are just as relevant in the formality of an opera house or the free and easy atmosphere of a circus tent: Do not draw attention to yourself by noisy or conspicuous behavior. Do remember that others in the audience (as well as the performers) are entitled to your consideration.

THE OPERA

SEATING IN A BOX AT THE OPERA

Nowhere is greater dignity of manner required than in a box at the opera. As people often dine with their hostess before the opera, they usually arrive together. The gentlemen help the ladies to take off their coats; one of the gentlemen, whichever is nearest, draws back the curtain dividing the anteroom from the box; and the ladies enter, followed by the gentlemen, the last of whom closes the curtain again. If there are two ladies besides the hostess, the latter places her more distinguished or older guest in the corner of the front row nearest the stage. The seat farthest from the stage is always her own. The older guest takes her seat first, then the hostess takes her place, whereupon the third lady goes forward in the center to the front of the box, and stands until one of the gentlemen places a chair for her between the other two. If there are eight, one of the ladies sits in the second row with two gentlemen beside her and the other two in the back row.

One of the duties of the men is to see that the curtains at the back of the box remain tightly closed, so that the light from the anteroom does not shine into the faces of others in the audience across the house.

A common practice today is for three or four couples to subscribe to a box at the opera together, sharing the cost and enjoying each other's company during the season. So that each member of the group may enjoy the better seats and no two men be always relegated to the back row (especially if it is an off center box that does not offer a full view of the stage from all of its seats), these friends may agree to switch their seating arrangements around, even though it violates the old rule of "no gentlemen in the front row."

BETWEEN THE ACTS

Both ladies and gentlemen may visit friends in other boxes between the acts, but the lady must always have an escort. They may go out to enjoy the refreshments that most opera houses provide or simply to enjoy seeing the interesting and beautifully dressed people who are invariably at the opera. No ladies should ever be left alone in the box, however, and no gentleman may stay in a box that he does not belong in after the lowering of the lights. In fact, all who have been out of the box during the intermission must return as soon as the signal is given for the raising of the curtain, for it is very annoying to have people coming in after the performance has resumed, not only to the audience, but to the performers as well.

It should not be necessary to point out that there must be no conversation during the overture or the performance. An enthusiastic audience may applaud at the end of an aria and, of course, after each curtain, but not for the entrances or exits of a performer.

DRESSING FOR MONDAY NIGHT

In New York and some other large cities, there has been a return to very formal dress for Monday night at the opera. In the boxes, many of the men wear white tie and tails, and their companions wear long evening dresses and their most brilliant jewelry. This formality is not required, however, and other men prefer a dinner jacket, and the ladies choose an evening, dinner, or cocktail dress.

In the orchestra, either a dinner jacket or a business suit is correct, and you will feel comfortable in whichever you choose. A lady may wear a long or short dinner dress or, if her escort is in a business suit, a silk dress or a cocktail suit.

In the balconies, daytime clothes are more commonly worn by both men and women.

DRESSING FOR OTHER EVENINGS

On evenings other than Monday, clothing is very much the same as that worn to the theater, but one does see a larger proportion of tuxedos and dinner dresses. One rarely sees tails on a Thursday night, but for men who have the opportunity to change from business clothes, a dinner jacket is still preferred, especially by those in the boxes.

THE THEATER

DINNER AND A PLAY

In any audience there are almost certain to be married couples who are enjoying an evening away from home, devotees of the drama who have come alone, and theater parties of various sizes. One of the more popular and agreeable ways of entertaining people is to ask them to have dinner and go to a play. Unfortunately, however, theater tickets in many cities have become so expensive that a party of four is more typical than one of six or eight.

When an unattached man invites three friends to go to the theater, he usually takes them to dinner in a restaurant; but if the host and hostess have a house or apartment not too far distant from the theater, they are likely to have dinner at home. Among young people especially, this form of entertainment usually involves dining out, and the evening is Dutch treat. If one member of the group wishes to, he (or she) may ask them to meet at his home for cocktails and a chat, but the cost of dinner and the tickets is divided among them.

It is absolutely essential that a host arrange for theater tickets well in advance, and naturally he must get good ones. In New York, for instance, if you buy your tickets at the box office, you must plan weeks ahead in order to get the seats that you wish for the most popular plays. If you plan your party on the spur of the moment, you will have to settle for a less popular play or one that has been running for some time, or else you must buy the tickets from a ticket agency, which charges a certain amount more than the box-office price.

ARRIVING AT THE THEATER

On arriving at the theater, the host (or hostess) holds the tickets in his hand so that the ticket-taker may see them, but he allows his guests to pass in ahead of him. At the head of the aisle, if the usher is there, he gives her the stubs and steps back, and the ladies precede him down the aisle. If, however, the usher is already part way down the aisle, the host may lead the way until he reaches her. If it is a very large party, it is wise for the hostess to tell her guests in what order they are going to sit, so that they may arrive at their row in more or less that order, thereby avoiding a great deal of shuffling about and confusion in the aisle.

The only fixed rule about seating in the theater is that a man should sit on the aisle. Many people feel, and I am inclined to agree with them, that a woman should not go into the row first, as it not only seats her next to a stranger, but leaves her at the end of the line in a more difficult position for joining the conversation before the play starts and between the acts. Therefore, in a group of four, one man should go in first, followed by the two women, and finally the other man. A woman would probably sit next to the man who was not her husband.

When the party is larger, a woman usually does lead the way into the row, and the others alternate, men and women, leaving the host, or one of the men if there is no host, on the aisle.

In the case of a man and a woman alone, she, of course, goes in first, and he follows, sitting on or nearest to the aisle.

Do not, however, judge hastily when this rule is not followed. Arthur Norman, for example, is stone-deaf in his right ear and his wife always sits on his left no matter where that position happens to place her. Others for comparable reasons do the same.

WHEN THE PLAY IS OVER

The man on the aisle, or nearest the aisle, naturally stands in the aisle for a moment so that the lady who follows can walk with him or, if the crowd makes two abreast impossible, precede him. In nearly all situations, a lady goes first. Only when the crowd is really dense does a man go first to make a wedge for her. In a theater party of six, the first man should let the woman who sat next to him go ahead of him, but usually he does not wait to follow the remaining two.

DRESSING FOR THE THEATER

Today it is correct for both men and women to wear day clothes to the theater. During the week, the audience is likely to be made up of a large proportion of couples from the suburbs, and the man who has been at his office all day and has had no opportunity to change his clothes would hardly wish to see his wife arrive to meet him for dinner dressed in an elaborate cocktail or dinner dress. So if Mrs. Franklin has decided to combine her trip to the theater with an afternoon's shopping, she need feel no embarrassment at appearing at the theater in a wool dress, or even a suit, although it should not be a sports suit. Many women carry an extra piece or two of jewelry in their purses with which to dress up their "basic" black dresses for the evening.

On the rare occasion when a hostess plans a large theater party, perhaps to celebrate an anniversary, she may wish to make the evening more gala by requesting that the men wear "black tie." The only other time that more formal dress is required is the opening night of an evening performance, when one sits "down front" in the best seats. Then ladies wear cocktail or dinner dresses, and this, of course, means that the gentlemen wear tuxedos.

COURTESY AT THE THEATER

You must not be late! Nothing is so unfair to others who are keen about whatever it is you are going to see as to make them miss the beginning of a performance because of your selfishness in being late. Other theater-goers, too, dislike being climbed over after the performance has started. If your taxi breaks down or a flat tire causes a truly unavoidable delay, it is far more considerate to wait at the back of the theater until the first scene is over; then the usher can show you quickly to your seat.

Hats off! Even if a woman believes her hat to be so small as not to obstruct the view of anyone, she should be agreeable about removing it if asked to do so. Courteous women whose hats are likely to interfere with the view of the one behind them take them off without having to be asked.

"Excuse me, please" is the natural expression of courtesy when having to disturb anyone in order to get to or leave your seat in a theater or any other place.

If someone is obliged to get up to let you pass, say, "Thank you," or "I'm sorry." Should you by any chance have to pass someone a second time, you say, "I'm sorry to disturb you again," and "Thank you," as they let you go by.

In passing strangers, gentlemen as well as ladies face the stage and always press closely to the backs of the seats they are facing, remembering, however, not to drag anything across the heads of those sitting in the row in front. Some women are very careless about their handbags, which, if swinging from a strap handle, frequently bump into people beside or below them.

When you are seated you must give others enough room to pass. If you can do this by merely turning your knees sideways, so much the better, especially if the play has started. But if there is so little space that the passers-by have to step over your knees, you must of course stand and sit down again—quickly! Remember that during every second you stand, you are cutting off the view of all who are seated behind you.

Young people have much to say about the ill manners of certain middle-aged men as well as women who practically refuse to allow anyone to pass. It is quite true that having to gather up opera glasses, program, and bag and stand while each person on a long aisle leaves and comes back separately after each act can be far from pleasurable. But if you haven't sufficient self-control not only to seem, but to be, amiable about whatever annoyances you encounter, you should at least take enough trouble to avoid the obvious annoyances or else stay at home.

For example, if you do not wish to go out to smoke between the acts, why not take pains to get seats away from an aisle instead of on it? In a theater that has no center aisle, try to get seats in the mid-center and sit undisturbed.

Quiet, please! Most theater audiences are made up of mature people genuinely interested in the performance, but a caution is in order nevertheless. Especially annoying are those who cannot seem to settle down when the curtain first goes up, who must finish that one important story or find a misplaced glove that could perfectly well wait until intermission time. Not much better are the explainers of jokes not understood by their neighbors; rarely is the neighbor enlightened and all too often those in nearby seats miss the next punch line. If you want to discuss the plot or the performance, wait until the act is over.

SMOKING BETWEEN THE ACTS

A woman usually goes out to the lobby with a man who wishes to smoke between the acts. But if a man is with a woman who does not smoke, it is quite proper to leave her briefly during one intermission or, at a play having more than three acts, during two. Of course, it depends somewhat upon whom he is with. He might possibly leave his wife more often than a guest—which does not mean he should leave her at each curtain-fall to sit alone until the house is darkened for the curtain's rise.

THE MOVIES

In general, an evening at the movies is a good deal less formal than one at a play, but other considerations are not too different. Unless you are attending a premier or an especially elaborate benefit performance of some kind, when you would dress as for the opening night of a play, casual clothes are proper—although "casual" must be determined by the location of the theater and the other activities of the evening. For example, slacks might be quite proper in the country, with a stop at your favorite ice-cream stand to follow, but they would be quite out of place in the city, especially should your escort suggest, say, dancing afterward.

FINDING SEATS AT THE MOVIES

How one goes down the aisle in a movie theater—a man and girl, for example—is not a fixed custom. Usually, because they look for their own seats, they go down the aisle together. Either one, seeing seats that are pleasing, says, "There are two—shall we take those?" The other agrees or proposes two farther down.

If you come in after the movie has started, wait at the rear until your eyes have become adjusted to the darkness. By doing this, you may avoid stumbling into the center of a row only to find that there are not the necessary vacant seats, having to back out, and tripping over unsympathetic spectators.

THEATER PESTS

Talking, coughing, jingling bangles—not to speak of rattling cellophane when opening candy boxes—are annoying and disturbing to everyone in the audience. Very young people love to go to the movies in droves and absolutely ruin the evening for others who happen to sit near them. If Julie and Johnny and Susy and Tommy want to talk and giggle, why not let them arrange chairs in rows in a game room, turn on radio or television, and sit there and chatter?

If those behind you insist on talking, it is bad manners to turn around and glare. If you are young, they pay no attention; and if you are older—most young people think an angry older person the funniest sight on earth. The small boy throws a snowball at an elderly gentleman for no other reason! The only thing you can do is to say amiably, "I'm sorry, but I can't hear anything while you talk." If they still persist, you can ask an usher to call the manager.

The sentimental should realize that every word said above a whisper is easily heard by those sitting directly in front, and those who discuss family or other private affairs might also do well to remember this.

But comparatively few people are ever anything but well-behaved. Most people take their seats as quietly and quickly as they possibly can and are quite as much interested and therefore as attentive and quiet as you are, or they would not have come.

CIRCUSES, ICE SHOWS, AND RODEOS

As long as members of the audience obey the basic principles of consideration for others, behavior at such events as circuses, rodeos, or ice shows is unrestricted by rules. Clothing depends entirely on the weather. At a summertime circus held in a hot tent, women would certainly wear the coolest sleeveless dresses imaginable. At a winter ice show, they would appear rather foolish if they did not wear warm boots and heavy coats into a cold arena. There is, however, one rule about clothing that should be followed: unless she is very, very young, a woman should not wear shorts to summer performances of this nature, nor slacks in the winter.

At any show where it is not necessary to hear the performers, the audience may, of course, talk as much as they please. In fact, at such competitive events as rodeos, part of the fun is cheering your favorite on with yells and cheers.

But in spite of all this informality, there are a few things to avoid. As at the theater, don't be late. It still disturbs others who have arrived on time. Don't blow your cigarette smoke into your neighbor's face, and don't let your enthusiasm get so out of hand that your shrill voice may burst his eardrums.

14

Outdoor events

Football, baseball, soccer, ice hockey, and basketball are integral parts of American life. Few parents with young boys have not had to wait their turn for the sports page of the Sunday newspaper. Beginning in earliest grades in school, children learn teamwork and loyalty through participating in team sports. It is natural, therefore, that Americans grow up with an avid interest in one or many sports, an interest that in some cases becomes almost fanatical. In fact, most professional games are so well attended that if you wish to get choice seats, you must get your tickets well in advance.

AT A PROFESSIONAL MATCH

At a sports event you need follow few rules other than those of ordinary courtesy. Arrive on time so that you do not disturb others in reaching your seat. You are expected to shout and cheer for your team or your favorite player, but don't revile the opposing team, as you may very well find yourself in a fight with your neighbor, and you will gain little by being escorted to the nearest exit by an usher or a policeman. Try to refrain from jumping up in moments of crisis; the people behind you are interested in seeing too, and you will be deluged with shouts of "Down in front!" As in other public places, smoke blowing directly into someone's face can be most irritating, so hold your cigarette or cigar in such a way that it does not offend. If it is possible, leave very young children at home. They lose interest very quickly at a long game, and the spectators around you will hardly appreciate repeated requests for candy, ice cream, sodas, or trips to the bathroom. And last but not least, don't shove! If you have an appointment following the game, slip out quietly a minute or two before the end, but if you leave when the game is over, walk slowly *with* the crowd, not *through* it, to the exit.

Clothing is as variable as the weather. At football or soccer games, played in the fall and early winter, warmth is the first consideration. Above all, don't forget boots—a concrete floor is one of the coldest footrests known to man. At indoor arenas, people in the boxes generally dress more formally than those in the balconies, where any costume seems to be acceptable. For the better seats at evening games, a suit or wool dress for women and a sports jacket and tie or even a business suit for men are the usual thing. Baseball, although it is our National Sport, is perhaps the least formal of all, and even in the boxes (unless you are the guest of an official) open sport shirts for men, flat-heeled shoes for women—in short, the most comfortable clothing possible—are the rule.

To sum up, if you do not act or dress in a conspicuous manner, and if you observe the basic rules of consideration for others, you will get the most enjoyment out of any sporting event, as well as adding to the pleasure of neighboring spectators.

AT COLLEGE AND SCHOOL MATCHES

The rules of behavior are the same at any school or college match as they are at professional sport events. There are, however, a few suggestions for girls that may add to their enjoyment and that of their escort. In choosing your clothes, remember to consider where your date may be taking you after the game. If there is a cocktail party or a tea dance before you will have a chance to change, carry a handbag that will hold a pair of suitable shoes to replace your boots, and wear a scarf or hat that will preserve your hair-do for the evening.

If you are unfamiliar with the sport you are going to see, try to get some information about it in advance. The girl who spends the afternoon asking stupid questions—"Why do they do that? What's the score? Which team is ahead?"—is not likely to find herself going to the next game.

And whether you feel any enthusiasm for your date's team or not, let him think you do. Disinterest or lack of loyalty to his school is as bad or worse than lack of knowledge of the sport.

AT A PUBLIC BEACH

At a public beach the first rule is to avoid crowding—at least as much as you possibly can. Those who have children should choose places as near as possible to the spot where the children are going to wade in and out of the water and dig canals and build sand castles. Not only is it dangerous to have little children paddling in the water far away, but it is also natural for a child to fill his pail and run back and forth from his family to the water, kicking sand and spilling water all over those who may be sitting in his path. Even though they may be enchanting children, many people are likely to be irritated by having water poured over them.

It is also important not to let a child thrust his attentions upon strangers. While spontaneous friendliness is one of the most appealing traits that a child can have and most people are inclined to like children, it must be remembered, nevertheless, that there are those who do not. Therefore, before letting Johnny make himself one of a group of strangers sitting nearby, be sure to notice whether the strangers are showing particular interest in Johnny or whether Johnny alone is showing interest in the strangers! If the latter seems to be the case, call him back immediately.

Dogs are forbidden on most crowded beaches, but on more remote ones, they are usually allowed and can be a source of much enjoyment if they are properly controlled. In an area where there are other people, a dog must be kept on his leash so as not to alarm small children or adults who may be distrustful of animals. If your dog is to be free to run and swim, you must find a more deserted part of the beach, being sure to leash him again if a stranger approaches.

Children and dog owners are not the only offenders on the beach. Groups of athletic young men throwing a ball over, around, and between the sunbathers are an all too common annoyance.

An obvious display of affection is out of place, too. Couples who give languid back rubs, lie with heads resting on stomachs, or throw their arms across each other's shoulders, to say nothing of kissing and caressing, show their ignorance of good manners and make their neighbors thoroughly uncomfortable.

And although brief bathing suits and trunks are now accepted wherever there is sun, it is not necessary to throw modesty to the winds and appear among people of all ages and backgrounds in a bikini or any other costume that barely conforms to the legal requirements of decency.

PARKS AND PLAYGROUNDS

Behavior at a public park is virtually the same as at the beach. Again, don't crowd others if you can help it. Don't spread your picnic baskets and personal belongings over two or three tables when your share is one. Although picnic-table manners are less exacting than those at a set table at home, they do not grant to the children the privilege of eating like little savages and offending the sensibilities of those nearby who cannot help but see them.

On the other hand, public parks and picnic grounds are excellent training schools in that they teach a child to take his turn and be satisfied with his own share of time with the slides, swings, seesaws, and any other pleasures offered to all children.

Most important of all, always leave public grounds as clean or cleaner than you find them. Papers, cans, trash, and broken bottles, so frequently strewn over picnic grounds and beaches, completely destroy the beauty of the loveliest landscape.

15

Appearing on television and radio

Except for the special requirements of dressing for a television appearance, the rules are the same for a radio broadcast and for television. Because your radio program is always witnessed by members of the station's staff and sometimes by a studio audience as well, you must dress tastefully but unostentatiously in any case; but because you are not appearing before a camera, the style of your dress, your make-up, and your jewelry is entirely up to you.

DRESSING FOR TELEVISION

You can always decide on appropriate clothing for your television appearance by calling and asking the advice of the producer, but a more satisfactory way is to watch the program two or three times and decide which costumes you think are the most suitable or would be most becoming to you. Pastel or even dark colors televise better than white—men's shirts as well as women's dresses. Almost all networks have make-up artists on hand, and they will see that you are properly made up before you appear. Be sure, however, that they know what your role on the program is to be.

You may wear jewelry if it is necessary to your costume, but remember that brilliant stones will be sprayed with wax to dull the glitter, and the wax may be difficult to remove. Otherwise, choose clothing that is most flattering to your face and figure and appropriate to the time of day and the type of program. A sports suit would seem out of place on an evening variety show, as would a low-necked cocktail dress on a morning "quiz" program.

YOUR VOICE AND MANNER

The most important thing to remember when you are appearing on either radio or television is that you are really a guest in the home of the listener or viewer. Your manners, therefore, should be the same as if you were in their houses in person. You speak in a well-modulated voice, remembering that it is just as if you were in the same room with your audience. Remember, too, that a pocketful of jingling coins and a rattle of notes will sound far louder through the microphone than they ever would across a room, and check before the program begins to make certain you have eliminated all distracting and unnecessary noisemakers.

Once on the air, try not to show off, but rather act naturally. If other people on the program become noisy or the discussion becomes heated, don't compete. Wait until the moderator calms them down or changes the subject, whereby you retain your dignity.

If you are appearing on behalf of a charitable cause or on an intellectual program, be sure that the interviewer knows exactly what your subject is. Otherwise you may have difficulty in bringing out the points you wish to stress. If you are a participant in a discussion group or on a panel show, listen to the views of the other members and don't concentrate on pushing only your own opinions.

Last but not least, don't talk down to or patronize your audience. You are a guest in the homes of people from every walk of life, and you cannot possibly know more than each and every one of them. In other words, don't *under*estimate the intelligence of your listeners. On the other hand, because they have chosen to listen to you, don't *over*estimate their knowledge.

» *For suggestions about preparing your speech, see Chapter 4.*

16

Conducting meetings

Meetings may be held by three or four mothers who want to work out suitable arrangements for transporting their children to school, or they may be the annual gathering of the hundreds of stockholders of the country's largest corporation. Almost all of us are involved in several kinds of meetings each year, and most of us find ourselves from time to time in the position of having to take charge. Situations vary, of course, but some rather generalized suggestions may be useful.

MEETINGS OF LARGE ORGANIZATIONS

The president or chairman of any large organization must run its meetings in strict accordance with the rules of parliamentary procedure. The standard reference book on the subject is *Robert's Rules of Order,* which is available in any library or bookstore. In addition to learning these rules and following them scrupulously, he must control the meeting politely but firmly, so that it does not get out of hand through unnecessary arguments or unpleasant wrangling, and he should prevent discussion from wandering from the business of the day.

Furthermore, he must be neatly dressed in the proper clothes for the time of day and the type of meeting. » *See Chapter 4, "Public speaking."*

BOARD MEETINGS

If you are elected chairman of the board of any organization, you will be called upon to hold meetings, probably once a month and possibly oftener. If the organization is of considerable size or importance (a hospital or a community-fund drive, for example), the meeting must be run with some degree of formality.

Before the members arrive, it is up to you and the secretary to see that the room is in readiness. If it is possible, the meeting should be held in a room furnished for the purpose, with one large table, or several smaller ones, and adequate seating for all. There should be a clean pad and sharp pencil at each place, as well as copies of the minutes of the last meeting and the agenda for that day. If such a room is not available, then pad, pencil, etc. should be placed on the seat of each chair that will be used.

When your board members have arrived (and you should not wait more than ten minutes for latecomers), you say, "Will the meeting please come to order?" If you wish, you may add a word of welcome such as "I'm so glad you could all get here this morning." If your organization requires it, the secretary calls the roll at this point. You then ask him or her to read the minutes of the last meeting. When they have been read, you ask, "Are there any additions or corrections?" If not, you say, "The minutes stand approved as read." If there are corrections, the secretary makes them, and you say "The minutes stand approved as corrected." When the minutes have been distributed to each board member in advance, you may wish to dispense with the reading, but you must ask for a motion and a second from the floor to that effect. Next you call for the treasurer's report and then the reports of the committee chairmen. Even though you know that some chairmen may have no report, you ask each of them in turn, and he or she may simply say, "I have no report to make this month." If there are no questions about the reports, you bring up the business to be discussed, following your prepared agenda.

It is your duty as chairman to see that those who indicate by raising their hands that they wish to speak are recognized one at a time and that no one speaks for too long. Also, if arguments develop, you must, by interrupting if necessary, prevent their getting so heated or involved that the meeting ends in chaos. If possible, wait for a break in his speech but if the speaker is too excited to pause, you may rap your table or stand and break in, saying, "Mrs. Smith, will you please confine yourself to the subject?" or "Mrs. Harris, you have spoken for more than your allotted time, and I will have to ask you to sit down," or even, "Mr. Robertson, it is not necessary to go into personalities, and if you insist on doing so, I must ask you to sit down immediately." By directing the discussion firmly along appropriate lines, limiting speeches, and staying in charge, a good chairman can hasten immeasurably the successful conclusion of the business meeting. Generally, if there is a guest speaker, the business of the meeting is finished as quickly as possible, and the guest's speech concludes the program, with only a brief word of thanks from you before the adjournment.

MEETINGS HELD IN THE HOME

When a group is formed for some special reason, perhaps to raise funds for a charity, or to back a political candidate, or to put on a play, meetings are held in a home, not necessarily the home of the leader or chairman, but of any member of the group who volunteers. Coffee is usually served before or after a morning meeting, and tea or coffee in the afternoon. The member at whose house the meeting is held may provide the refreshments herself, or various others may volunteer to bring a cake, cookies, or sandwiches. Or each member of the group may contribute a small sum, which the hostess uses to buy and prepare the food.

No matter how informal these gatherings are in some ways, certain formalities must be observed if the group is to be successful. First, a chairman should be appointed or elected, because without one person to plan and direct a meeting, it is impossible to coordinate discussions and come to decisions. Second, there must be a secretary to take notes or minutes; a record of each meeting is necessary in order to be able to refer back to earlier ones—to resolve any arguments, to avoid repetition, and also to aid any other group that might continue the work in the future. And last, if there are funds involved in any way, there must be a treasurer to handle them and to keep an exact account of receipts and expenditures.

Beyond the formality of appointing these officers, the group need not follow any particular rules, but may run its meetings as it wishes— semiformally with minutes being read and the roll being called, or as a social meeting with open discussion over a cup of coffee and a piece of cake. The one who has been made chairman must still direct the discussion into the proper channels, however, or no business will be accomplished at all. It is all too easy for friends to become involved in discussion of babies, neighborhood politics, and other subjects close to their hearts and forget entirely the purpose of the meeting. It is her responsibility to get each member to make suggestions or express their views about the current topic. At the same time, each individual who has agreed to participate in the activity should have given it some thought and be willing to discuss and act on suggestions, so that the chairman is not left with all the responsibilities.

Because these groups are made up of good friends, there are no rules about clothing other than the ordinary standards of neatness and cleanliness. Don't come straight from the garden with mud on your shoes and certainly *never* with a curler in your hair! However, if you are dressed in a skirt and sweater, there is no need to change to more formal clothes. In fact, if you live in the country where slacks are accepted as everyday wear, there is no need to change into a dress. And if the group is made up of young mothers, the children are usually brought along to play together in a safe yard or, if they are babies, in a play pen.

Part FOUR

ADVICE FOR TRAVELERS

17

Planning your trip

There are some people who find it so pleasant to make plans for any trip, large or small, that they truly consider the preliminaries "half the fun." But to the joys of poring over maps and collecting suggestions from your friends must be added certain practical preparations without which travel can be a nightmare instead of a restful ramble or an exciting adventure. Dream of castles in Spain if you will, but do not forget that you may well be footsore and weary by the time you have actually toured your first one. A good dinner and a decent bed may make all the difference in your enthusiasm for tomorrow's expedition.

RESERVATIONS

ADVANTAGES OF A TRAVEL BUREAU

The easiest way to plan your trip is to go to a travel bureau. If there isn't one in your own town, write to one that has been recommended to you by a well-traveled friend. Tell the bureau just where you want to go and when and how—in fact, give all the details you can, and let them work out the best possible plan for you. This is their business, and they can do it not only better but much more economically than you can and at no extra cost to you, as they get their commission from the transportation company, the resort, or the hotel.

There is one important point that should be explained to the inexperienced traveler: While a competent travel bureau will engage, if you wish, the best rooms in de luxe hotels, secure automobiles by the week or month, either with or without chauffeurs, and arrange any other elaborate accommodations, they will, with equal interest, provide the same quality service for those traveling on a limited budget.

MAKING YOUR OWN RESERVATIONS

If you cannot, or do not wish to, use a travel agency, start well in advance to make your reservations. If you are refused at the first hotels or resorts you write to, it may take days or even weeks of delay, depending on the remoteness of your destination, before you have word from your alternate choice. It is not unreasonable to make the arrangements for an extensive trip to a popular area six months or more ahead of time. The reservations, in this case, must be reconfirmed a week or two before your departure. It is also well to request a receipt or acknowledgement (and don't forget to carry it with you) to be shown on your arrival, as it is all too easy for a careless innkeeper or hotel manager to fill up the rooms with earlier arrivals and tell you cheerfully when you arrive, hot and exhausted, "But, see, Señor, we have no record of your letter!"

Your travel reservations should be made at the same time as those for hotel rooms—little would be gained by reserving a room that you have no way of getting to. And don't neglect your home-bound ticket. Many people have found themselves in Europe at the end of the tourist season with days of waiting for a plane seat still ahead of them. With a little forethought, your return date can be planned as definitely as that of your departure, and it will prevent a last-minute case of jitters and impatience that could ruin your whole trip.

A tip to parents: When your son or daughter sets off for a summer of traveling, possibly with a knapsack on his back and no planned stopping places other than a list of youth hostels (inexpensive lodgings for bicyclists and motorcyclists found in every European country), be sure that he or she has a return reservation, either with him, or held at the airline or steamship office for him. It is all too easy for a youngster to cable home, "Unable to get reservations until September 15"—three weeks longer than you had expected to finance him!

USING A GUIDEBOOK

If you are young enough so that you don't care where you spend the night—in an inn or in a field—or if you are fortunate enough to be able to travel during the "off" season, when most of the tourists are at home, you may not need reservations. Nothing is more delightful than being able to drive at random, following whatever highway or byway catches your fancy, and stopping for the night wherever you happen to be. And what a joy to have plans so flexible that you can leave a town that has little to offer the day after you arrive or stay for ten in a city that has all the charm you have dreamed of!

To travel in this way is ideal, but there is one requirement—a good guidebook. By looking at the list of available lodgings and eating places in an area, you may avoid, first, hours of searching for a respectable hotel, and second, the danger of falling upon dirty accommodations or dishonest proprietors. The places recommended by all good guidebooks are visited regularly by their staffs, and their information is as accurate and current as it is possible to make it.

» *See also Chapters 18 and 19 for additional suggestions about hotels and transportation.*

LEAVING YOUR HOME IN ORDER

WHEN THE CHILDREN STAY AT HOME

If you wish to enjoy your trip to the full, with a minimum of worries about the people and things you have left behind, there are several precautions that you must take to insure their safety and well being.

The first, and most obvious, is the case of parents who must leave children at home. If you already have a reliable servant (or servants), capable of taking charge while you are away, there is no problem. They simply take over the house with a few extra instructions and a promise of extra pay if all goes well. Otherwise, if you do not have a relative who can come and stay at your house or invite your children to stay at theirs, it is absolutely essential to find a reliable woman to care for them. (Occasionally a couple, or a man if the children are boys, can be found, but generally the position of sitter or temporary mother is filled by a woman.) She should be recommended either by a friend whose judgment is reliable or by a reputable agency. If you do not know her personally, she should arrive two or three days in advance, so that the children may get to know her while you are there to help them over any rough spots and so that she may become acquainted with your house and routine.

There should be definite rules laid down, especially if the children are teen-agers, about what hours they are to keep, what they are allowed or forbidden to do, and with whom they may go out. Otherwise the sitter has no way of knowing what your basic standards are, and the young people will soon find out that they can have many more liberties than they are ordinarily allowed.

Your household should have a complete list of addresses at which you may be reached and also a list of those people, relatives or friends, who may be counted on to help in an emergency. The sitter should also have a list of the stores you ordinarily deal with and the names of dentists and doctors, as well as any appointments that must be kept.

If these matters are conscientiously taken care of before you leave, you will have little reason to be concerned about your family while you are gone.

WHEN NO ONE IS LEFT IN THE HOME

When you are leaving an empty house or apartment, there is a different set of precautions to consider. A house whose owners are obviously away is an open invitation to a burglar. Therefore, in order to make it appear occupied, the following suggestions should be followed. Don't forget:

Cancel milk delivery.

Cancel newspaper delivery.

Request that the post office either hold or forward your mail. Nothing could better advertise your absence than mail and newspapers piling up at your door.

Have all laundry and cleaning delivered before you leave so that it is not left hanging outside for days or weeks.

Leave a light or two burning, or install an automatic light that goes on at dusk.

Check all locks on windows and doors, and be sure that you take a key with you! Not a few people have been horrified to find on arriving home in the middle of the night that they had so thoroughly closed up their house with the key inside that they must either break a window to get in or spend the remainder of the night in a motel.

Leave a spare key with a friendly neighbor and ask him to check the house occasionally.

Either put potted plants outside or make arrangements to have them watered by a friend. A neighbor's child is often happy to take over this chore for, possibly, fifty cents a week.

Take pets to the veterinarian's or wherever they are to be left.

Notify the police of your absence, and ask them to keep watch over your house. Also, if you have a cleaning woman or anyone coming into the house legitimately, give the officer her name so that she will not be accused of unlawful entry.

Never give your travel plans or dates to your local newspaper in advance. There are people who watch the papers every day in order to take advantage of just such information.

There is no way that you can make your home a hundred percent burglarproof, but at the same time all the above suggestions will help to discourage any but the most professional thief. If you travel frequently and wish to go away feeling as confident as possible that all will be in order on your return, make a list of the above suggestions that apply to your home and check it off carefully before every trip.

TRAVEL DOCUMENTS

Several weeks before your departure, you should apply for your passport, visas if they are required, and health certificates. If you already have them, make sure that they are within the required time limit and in good order. These matters have to be attended to in person, although after you have filled out the forms and paid the fee at the passport office, your passport may be sent to you by mail. Your doctor, if he does not have them, will tell you where to get official health forms, and you must go in person to the consulate of the country from which you wish to get a visitor's permit or visa. Everything else can be done for you; and for anyone obliged to go on a suddenly planned trip, a great deal of valuable time can be saved by having an agent who knows the procedures make your reservations anywhere in the world and deliver your tickets to you.

It is advisable to get some foreign money in small bills and change to have in your hand when you land. There are restrictions as to the amount you are permitted to take in or out of some countries, and these should be checked before you leave. It is also very important to take the bulk of your money in American Express or other traveler's checks, which can be replaced if lost and are accepted everywhere as readily as cash. Even though you have a letter of credit, which is advisable if you want to have something to depend on for extra and unexpected expenses, there are many occasions when it is inconvenient or even impossible to go to a bank. » *See also Chapter 20, "Currency and language."*

Motels and hotels

All over America, and recently in foreign countries as well, motels have been springing up like mushrooms. They are becoming more and more luxurious as the competition increases, and many are actually taking the place of resort hotels. The larger ones and those belonging to national chains are equipped with every facility for the traveler's comfort and pleasure, including swimming pools, shuffle board courts, sun bathing areas, television sets (apparently a must in every motel), and individual coffee-makers in each room. At one motel where I have stayed myself, a drive-in movie is directly behind the motel, so that you may sit comfortably in bed and see a movie before going to sleep, with the sound piped into each unit through a private speaker!

Motels can claim many advantages over hotels for the automobile traveler. Because the majority are on the outskirts of towns or between cities, you need not drive into heavy urban traffic to reach them. There is no parking problem, as your car is left directly in front of your room or unit. You may unload only what you need for the night—the rest can be locked up in the car, which is not taken away to a garage as it is at a city hotel. Especially important to women is the fact that, unless she is traveling alone, she need not be seen at all on arrival. Therefore she may travel in shorts, slacks, or whatever costume is most comfortable for driving, even though she would never walk through a hotel lobby in it. Her husband simply goes to the office of the motel, registers, receives the key, and drives to the room allotted to them. There Mrs. Tired Traveler, in her rumpled dress, may slip in with scarcely a chance of being seen by any one at all. Since one pays for the night on arrival, one leaves the next morning with no need to go to the office again, and as there has been no service, neither is there any one to tip.

There are, of course, certain disadvantages to motels. There is rarely (except in the most luxurious resort type, which hopes to attract people to stay longer than overnight) room service. One unloads the luggage alone, gets ice for oneself from an ice machine (always found near each unit), and provides one's own refreshments. Often, there are soft drinks available in vending machines, and cigarettes, magazines, newspapers, etc., are sold in the offices of many motels. Those connected with a chain generally have a restaurant on the premises, but if you are staying at a smaller motel, you may have to go a little distance to find a good eating place. Also, if you are looking for entertainment—dancing, movies, and so on—you may find that you would be better off in a hotel in the heart of the city.

Because of the immense popularity of motels as stopping places, it is wise, especially for a woman alone, to make reservations in advance. If you choose to stay in a chain motel, they will be delighted to call ahead to the member motel in or nearest to your next destination and reserve a room for the following night. The larger chains will also help you plan your trip, providing road maps and lists of restaurants, entertainments, and points of interest, as well as the location of their own or associated motels.

HOTELS

Because of their central locations in most cities and the services that they offer, hotels will never be completely replaced by motels. The business traveler arriving by plane or train naturally chooses a hotel in the center of town, near the offices of the companies he must visit. Tourists, other than those driving their own cars, usually wish to be in a central location where they can easily find transportation to museums, monuments, parks, historical sites, and other points of interest. Finally, many people, and certainly those making their homes in such accommodations, will never forsake the convenience and excellence of the services offered in first-class hotels.

TO ASSURE ACCOMMODATIONS IN HOTELS

It is well to write or telegraph in advance for accommodations in a hotel. A typical telegram reads:

PLEASE RESERVE DOUBLE ROOM WITH BATH FOR WIFE AND SELF AFTERNOON DECEMBER THIRD TO FIFTH. JOHN G. HAWKINS.

A letter is a little more explicit:

Manager of the Lake Hotel,
Chicago, Illinois
Dear Sir:

Please reserve two single rooms with baths or with a bath between for my daughter and me. We are due to arrive in Chicago at five o'clock on the afternoon of December sixth and shall stay a week.

I prefer moderate-priced rooms not higher than the fourth floor.

Very truly yours,
Mrs. George K. Smith

Kindly confirm reservation to
Brightmeadows, Ill.

(Note that this is one of the few occasions when "Mrs." belongs with a woman's signature.)

Both letter and telegram should state clearly the hour of your arrival, number of persons, the accommodations you wish, and the approximate length of your stay.

THE ARRIVAL AT A HOTEL

When you arrive at a first-class hotel, a doorman opens the door of your car or taxi and deposits your luggage on the sidewalk. If the hotel is crowded, he will ask, "Have you a reservation?" If you say, "Yes," all is well; but if you say, "No," the reply may be, "Very sorry, but there is not a room left." This means that you have to go to another or perhaps to several other hotels. So you should not only wire or write, but ask for a confirmation. Usually a day or two is sufficient notice, but at the time of a convention or a big football game, or any other occasion of crowded hotels, you must sometimes write months in advance and not think of going to the hotel unless you have received word that you will be accommodated.

Let us suppose it is an ordinary occasion, however, and that you have your room. A bellboy comes out, takes your bags from the sidewalk, carries them into the lobby, and deposits them not far from the desk. In a typical hotel, there is a counter with one man or two behind it. In city hotels, there are divisions of desks labeled "Rooms," "Accounts," "Inquiry," etc.

In either case you go to the desk, or to the division marked "Room Clerk," and say, "I am Mrs. George K. Smith. I telegraphed you Tuesday and received your confirmation on Thursday." The clerk turns the register around—or more probably he presents a form—for you to fill in and sign.

REGISTERING

A gentleman writes in the hotel register:

> John Smith, New York

He does not use "Mr." if he is alone, but if his wife is with him, the title to their joint names is correct:

> Mr. and Mrs. John Smith, New York

He should not add his street and house number. If instead of a book he has been given a registration card or form, he fills in the blanks, which usually include one for the house address. But his signature is exactly the same whether written in a book or on a card. Neither "John Smith and Wife" nor "John Smith and Family" is good form. If he does not like the "Mr." before his name, he can sign his own without the title on one line and then write "Mrs. Smith" on the one below. The whole family should be registered.

John T. Smith	New York
Mrs. Smith	"
Miss Margaret Smith	"
John T. Smith, Jr.	"
Baby and nurse	"

Or, if the children are very young, he writes:

> Mr. & Mrs. John T. Smith, New York, 3 children and nurse.

"Miss" precedes the names of girls over five, but boys are registered with no title—just "John" or "Henry" or whoever.

One exceptional occasion when a lady signs her name "Miss" or "Mrs." is in a hotel register. "Miss Jean McLean" is correct or "Mrs. George K. Smith"—never "Sarah Smith."

If Mrs. Smith arrives first, she fills in the blank for both herself and her husband. Then when he arrives, he says to the room clerk, "Mrs. Smith has already arrived and registered. What is the number of our room, please?"

As soon as you have registered, the clerk hands the key not to you but to the bellboy, who gathers up your bags and starts in the direction of the elevators. You follow. In your room, the bellboy puts down your bags, turns on the lights, and opens the window or tests the air-conditioning unit. He receives a tip, usually twenty-five cents for each large bag, and extra if there are a number of small parcels.

SERVICE IN A GOOD HOTEL

Any service that you require is requested by telephone. You tell the operator if you wish to be called at a certain time or ask for the desk if you want to inquire about mail or give the name of a visitor you are expecting. You call the porter's desk if you have any inquiries about luggage or trains or reservations. You call the newsstand for magazines, newspapers, or theater tickets, room service when you want food or drinks sent up to you, and valet or maid service if you need a dress or a suit cleaned or pressed.

In the morning, for instance, if you want to breakfast in your room, you say, "Room service, please." Then, when room service answers, you say, "Please send coffee and buttered toast and orange juice for one to Room 117." Many hotels have breakfast menus in each room, and you may choose from that. Presently the waiter brings in a tray with your order. In a first-class hotel, he carries in a long, narrow table that fits between twin beds or stands beside a single one. It is completely set: damask cloth, china, glass, silverware, thermos pitchers, and possibly chafing-dishes to keep the food hot.

It is entirely proper to receive the waiter when you are sitting up in bed or clad in a bathrobe. Waiters are used to carrying breakfast trays into the presence of all varieties of pajamas and negligées, and it is not necessary for even the most old-fashioned lady to be completely dressed to receive him.

In a small hotel, he puts the breakfast tray on a table and then immediately leaves the room. He returns later for the table and check, which can be paid in cash or signed and put on your bill. The room waiter receives a tip, according to the amount of the breakfast check and whether it is for one or two. In addition to this, the hotel makes an extra charge for meals served in your room; room-service charges are usually indicated on the menu.

To have your clothes washed, telephone maid service, unless, as is often the case, there is a bag or receptacle marked for laundry in the bathroom. Pressing is done by the regular valet or maid, but in a small hotel, a woman's dress as well as a man's suit may be sent out to a tailor. It is against the rules in some hotels to use your own iron; therefore, if there is no regular valet service, you ask a chambermaid tactfully, "Where can I have my dress [or suit] pressed?" She answers, "I will do it for you," or tells you who will.

PILFERAGE

An inexplicable urge seems to come over many otherwise decent, honest citizens when they are guests in a hotel. This is the urge to pilfer —to help themselves to articles that can be hidden away in luggage exactly as if such things were put out as gifts to the guests from the management! Bath towels with the hotel's name on them, ash trays, writing paper, soap, dining-room silver, and even bed linen disappear in such quantities as to be a major expense in every large hotel. These pilferers, when accused of stealing, say, "Not at all—the management expects these things to disappear!" How any normal, law-abiding person can thus excuse what is technically petty theft, I cannot understand. All I can do is suggest that the next time you, or any one traveling with you, is tempted to take home such a souvenir, say to yourself or to them, "That ash tray is the property of the hotel, and if I take it home with me, they will have to replace it, and I am no better than a common thief."

HOTEL MANNERS

It is against the rules of every reputable hotel for a guest to receive a visitor of the opposite sex in a bedroom without first speaking to the desk clerk and then leaving the door ajar. If you have a private sitting room, you can have everyone you please take a meal in it with you, or you can receive whomsoever you please, as long as you break none of the ordinary conventions of behavior. Noisy parties, men visitors at unconventionally late hours, or anything that suggests questionable behavior is not permitted in any high-class hotel.

The woman staying alone in a hotel and having no sitting room of her own receives her men visitors in any one of the public rooms that all hotels provide. She is also free to ask whom she will to the restaurant or dining room. There is not the slightest reason why a woman—even though she be very young and very pretty—may not stay in a hotel by herself and have men come to see her and be invited by her to lunch or to dine. It is not so much a question of suitable age as of suitable behavior. A girl who is dignified and whose friends are the sort that pass that sharpest of character readers, the house detective, will never even approach an uncomfortable moment. The woman, on the other hand, who thinks a hotel is a brier-patch where she can hide away all the things she oughtn't to do will find that she might as well have chosen to hide in a show window.

A hotel guest—whether a woman or a man—going down to the dining room alone, usually takes a book or newspaper, because nothing is duller than to sit eating bread and butter and looking at the tablecloth, which is scarcely diverting, or staring at other people, which is impolite, while waiting for one's order.

It is always proper for a woman to wear a hat in a restaurant if she wishes, but she may go into the dining room without one if she is staying at the hotel. In the evening, if she is dressed in evening clothes, she does not wear a hat.

When going to see people stopping at a hotel, you ask for them at the desk and the clerk telephones to their rooms or you go to the house telephone and call yourself. If they are receiving you upstairs, you are told, or your friend tells you, the number of the room you are to go to, and you go up in the elevator alone and find it yourself. You can ask the elevator boy which floor Room 616 is on; in practically every modern hotel this would be the sixth floor.

If the friends you are visiting answer that they are coming down, you sit in the lobby or the lounge, in view of the elevators, until they join you.

WHEN YOU LEAVE THE HOTEL

The courteous guest tells the management when he arrives that he intends to stay overnight only, or several days, or a week or two, as the case may be. When he is ready to leave, he goes to the cashier—or telephones from his room—asking that his bill be made out. When he has finished packing, he telephones for a bellboy to carry down his luggage. Having tipped the boy, he then goes to the desk, or to the window marked "Cashier," pays his bill, leaves his key and a forwarding address if he wishes any mail sent after him, and departs.

TIPS

The following schedule of tips applies to transient visitors staying in the hotel (or the motel with services) for not more than a week. Permanent or long-term residents tip on a monthly or even twice-yearly basis rather than having to produce a perpetual stream of small change for every service. The amount, of course, would vary according to the quality of the service, and the quantity requested. Hotel residents must arrive at their own conclusions, possibly with the help of other permanent guests and even the hotel management.

The usual tip for a dining-room waiter in a first-class restaurant is between fifteen and twenty percent of the bill, but never less than twenty-five cents in a restaurant with tablecloth on table. If you are staying in an American-plan hotel, you give the waiter or waitress at the end of each week about ten percent of the week's board per person, but less if the family is large. When going to the dining room for the first time, you give from two to five dollars to the headwaiter if you would like a table in a particular location. And you tip him, when you leave, in proportion to the service rendered. You give him one or two dollars a week, if he has done little, and five dollars a week for a family that he has been especially attentive to. For a one night stay you need not tip him at all.

The room waiter receives ten to fifteen percent of the bill for each meal. This is in addition to a set sum charged by the hotel for each meal taken to a room.

The chambermaid in a first-class hotel is given about one dollar a week a room, or fifty cents a week in a small inexpensive hotel. If you stay one night only, fifty cents for each person in a room in a large hotel, or twenty-five cents in a small one, is given her if she can be found. If not, it is left on the bureau—in the hope that the chambermaid and not an acquisitive bellboy will get it!

Other tips: Nothing to the doorman for putting a bag on the sidewalk, but twenty-five cents if he helps take the luggage into the hotel or on other occasions if he calls a taxi.

Twenty-five cents for each large bag the bellboy carries to the room.

Twenty-five cents for paging.

Fifty cents to a porter for bringing a trunk to the room, or fifty cents or a dollar if there is much baggage.

Twenty-five cents for ice, drink set-ups, newspapers, packages, telegrams, etc.

Twenty-five cents for checking a man's coat and hat.

Twenty-five cents to the attendant in the woman's dressing room of a high class hotel or restaurant, or twenty-five cents for the coat rack at the entrance to the dining room.

The valet receives a tip only if he brings a large amount of clothing back to your room when you are there. His charge for cleaning or pressing is included in the hotel bill.

Barbers, manicurists, and beauty-parlor specialists are tipped on the basis of fifteen percent of the bill, but not less than twenty-five cents.

Bootblacks are tipped twenty-five cents.

Smart-looking people who frequent expensive hotels and take first-class accommodations on trains, ships, or planes are expected to give larger tips than people traveling economically. The latter may easily be richer, but tips are expected according to appearance.

One piece of advice: You will not get good service unless you tip generously but not lavishly. If you do not care to order elaborate meals, that is nothing to your discredit; but you should not go to an expensive hotel, hold a table that would otherwise be occupied by others who might order a long dinner, and expect your waiter to be contented with a tip of ten cents for your dollar supper!

Tipping is undoubtedly an undesirable and undignified system, but it happens to be in force; and that being the case, travelers who like the way made smooth and comfortable have to pay their share of it.

EUROPEAN HOTELS

Large, first-class hotels in Europe, those most frequented by tourists, are essentially the same as our best hotels in the United States. When you leave the beaten track, however, and venture into less well-traveled areas, it is wise to be prepared for certain differences in facilities and service.

In European hotels all services other than your actual accommodations and meals are provided by a concierge. He corresponds to our porter, but has a much wider range of responsibility and is as important as the hotel management. He presents a separate bill. He and his staff handle luggage and mail, make reservations, rent cars, shop for you, deliver packages, arrange tours, and are altogether indispensible.

Many foreign hotels do not have a telephone in each room. Instead they have a push-button device with charming little pictures of waiters, maids, or valets beside each button to indicate which one you must push. This system certainly overcomes the language barrier!

Most small hotels do not have bathrooms with every room. Many rooms do have wash basins, although in small towns there may just be a pitcher of water and a bowl. In these hotels, you use the public bathrooms on each floor, which are usually marked "W.C."—a universally known abbreviation for "water closet." There may be two, marked for men or women in the language of the country, or there may be just one to be used by all guests. And even the best hotels do not provide soap or wash cloths. Every American tourist should carry a supply of toilet soap, disposable wash cloths, and a roll of soft toilet paper!

Although the hotels in small towns may not be luxurious, the desire to please and the friendliness of the help more than make up for the lack of comfort. The chef who proudly invites you to see his spotless kitchen, the chambermaid who smilingly brings you a cup of coffee when she awakens you in the morning, and the concierge who takes great pains to insure that you miss nothing in this, the most beautiful town in Europe, all leave you feeling that it is the spirit of the place and not the physical comforts that enchant so many Americans who travel abroad.

19

On plane, train, or ship

Plane travel is so much a part of our life and times that it is hardly necessary to point out its advantages over other forms of locomotion. The speed of getting to one's destination by jet, the frequency of flights, the number of airlines and airports, and the safety of flying, all combine to make it the choice of almost all who must, or wish to, travel. In this day of rising costs, air travel is one of the few areas in which prices have actually gone down.

But there are many people who prefer to go by train, and indeed there are some destinations that can be reached in no other convenient way. So too, some prefer the relaxing days of shipboard living to the long flight to Rome or Athens or Beirut. And on a cruise, of course, your ship is your floating hotel as well as your means of transportation.

AIRPLANE TRAVEL

ACCOMMODATIONS

There are now two main classes of air travel—first class and economy. In addition, there are a few overseas airlines that offer extra-cost berths for overnight flights, and a few others advertise special in-between fares. Many small airlines that fly twin-engine equipment or four-motor propeller planes do not offer any choice of accommodations; all seats are the same price and receive the same services. On the large, scheduled airlines, however, you are offered a choice. Both classes fly on the same plane, but the economy-class seats occupy two thirds or more of the space toward the rear of the plane and are divided from first class by a movable partition, the door of which is kept closed except at take-off and landing. These seats are more closely spaced—generally there are three on each side of the aisle. Meals and snacks are included in the fare, but if you wish alcoholic drinks (cocktails are served before meals on overseas flights and on some domestic flights) you must pay for them. Service is somewhat slower than in the first class section, as two or three steward-esses or stewards must take care of approximately ninety people on a full plane. On long flights, most airlines show movies in both economy and first class. The difference in cost between economy and first class on a long flight is quite astronomical, and for this reason, a vast majority of people, even well-to-do people, put up with the discomfort of more crowded conditions on a flight that, with the speed of modern jets, rarely lasts more than a few hours.

For older people who may have difficulty in getting in and out of crowded seats or cannot stand long in line for washroom facilities, for disabled persons, or simply for those who prefer, and can afford, a bit of luxury when they travel, the first-class section has far more appeal. The seats are roomy—two on each side of the aisle, widely spaced so that one may tip far back and stretch one's legs, and large enough tables may be put between them so that passengers may play cards or comfortably spread out their business papers. Cocktails are free, meals are more elaborate, and champagne is sometimes served if you wish it. The steward or stewardess often has only ten or fifteen passengers to attend, and therefore every request is taken care of at once.

LUGGAGE

Airplane luggage should be, above all else, light. There are strict rules about how much weight you are allowed, which vary according to class and whether the flight is domestic or overseas. In general, overseas economy-class passengers are allowed approximately forty-four pounds, and first class, sixty-six. You may carry more, but you pay for the excess at a specified rate per pound.

The ideal luggage is a light-weight, firm metal, such as aluminum, or a composition. The soft bags made of synthetic materials or strong weaves are most attractive, but can be damaged or pierced if handled roughly.

Airlines now weigh almost every piece of baggage, even those you carry with you onto the plane. The only exceptions are handbags, brief-cases (except large, square, or bulging ones), knitting bags, or other light-

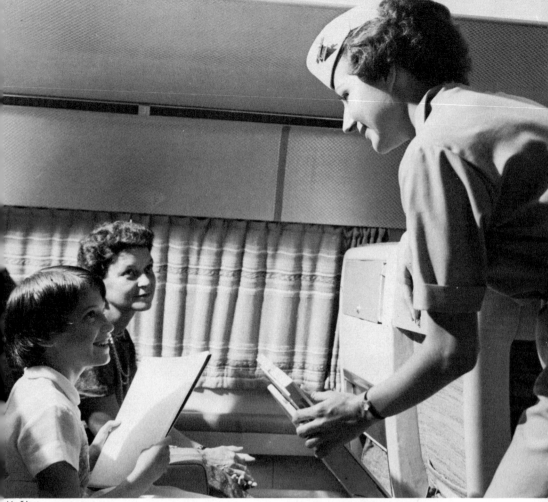

Air Lines

weight articles obviously packed with equipment for use on the flight—
baby's diapers, a book or two, embroidery, etc.

You may not carry any bag or package onto the plane with you unless it can be stowed under your seat. No one is allowed to put any hard
or heavy article on the shelf above the seats.

When you arrive at the airport or terminal, your luggage is taken on
a cart, by a porter, and put in line to be weighed when your turn comes
to check in. If it is overweight, you pay the extra charge at this time.
The porter is tipped twenty-five cents for each bag (not for small hand
pieces) and goes off to help the next arrival. When your ticket is validated, the bags are tagged and the stubs given to you at the same time.
You do not see the luggage again until it is brought into the "baggage
claim" section at your destination. You should make it clear to well-
meaning friends who come to see you off that they should not bring
presents. They will only be added to your weight allowance, or, if you
have been checked in, you may not be allowed to take them onto the
plane.

ARRIVING AT THE AIRPORT

On overseas flights, you are requested to arrive at the airport one hour ahead of departure time, as opposed to the half hour required for domestic flights. This provides the extra time involved in checking travel documents other than tickets.

You go directly to the counter of the airline you are flying on and await your turn to have your ticket validated. Until recently a chart of the plane was hung in plain view, and you could choose your seat from those not marked as taken. Now, however, many airlines are giving up this practice and simply assigning the seats as the passengers arrive. You are given a boarding pass with the seat number on it, to be shown at the departure gate and again to the stewardess when you board the plane.

WHILE IN THE AIR

The seats are clearly numbered, but the stewardesses who greet you with a friendly smile when you board will direct you to your chair and assist you with coats and bundles. Coats are hung on a rack in the rear on some planes or folded and laid on the overhead shelf on others. During the trip, the stewardesses, when not serving meals or drinks, will do their best to assist you in any way they can. You signal them with a light that you find above your head. They will, when they have time, bring magazines, hand out newspapers, bring food or extra pillows or blankets, and even help care for babies by heating bottles, etc. The steward or stewardess is never tipped, nor is any other member of the crew.

Be sure that you wear loose, comfortable clothing that is as wrinkle-proof as possible. Some women like to change into slacks and bedroom slippers during the flight, so that they may curl their legs up and be comfortable with complete modesty. Men are entirely free to remove their jackets, loosen or remove their ties, or change into a sport shirt. Both men and women should carry a loose sweater and wool socks or slippers, if they can—the temperature in an air-conditioned plane can be quite low.

When the sign flashes on to "Fasten Seat Belts," do so promptly. The stewardess has to check on each passenger. Also be prompt in obeying the "No Smoking" sign when it is flashed on. When smoking is permitted, only cigarettes are allowed.

No animals are allowed in the cabin of a plane except a Seeing Eye dog. If you wish to take your pet, he must be in a carrier. His weight is counted as part of the amount of luggage you are permitted, and he rides in the luggage compartment if it is pressurized, or in a special compartment if it is not.

The same rules apply in using the washrooms or lavatories on a plane as do on any public transportation. When there are many passengers, you must wait patiently for your turn, and when it comes, try to take as short a time as possible—unless you are the last. Even so, you should leave the washstand and the dressing table in perfect order. When you have finished washing, wipe out the basin thoroughly with your used towel, which you then throw into the towel basket. Before combing your hair, lay a fresh towel over the wash basin or counter. Leave it there until you have finished your hair-do and put on your make-up. Then gather up that towel and throw it into the towel receptacle. Complete neatness is a first essential of good manners. Never leave any unpleasant trace of untidiness *anywhere!*

The special consideration for the feelings of others that shows itself in a general spirit of friendliness among the passengers is so characteristic of air travel that it has, in fact, brought about new rules of traveling etiquette. The on-the-ground custom of paying no attention to fellow travelers is not observed in the air. Those who are willing to talk—and in a plane nearly everyone is—are entirely free to do so. On the other hand, one who wishes to be left alone can avoid conversation with the explanation, "I'd rather not talk; I'm very tired," which is never resented.

TRAIN TRAVEL

LUGGAGE

The official rate for a porter to take luggage from the entrance of a railroad station to a train is twenty-five cents for each piece, and an additional tip is optional but expected. In many small cities or towns, there are no porters at all, so when traveling to an unknown destination, it is well to restrict your baggage to pieces that can be carried by hand or to send larger bags and trunks ahead by railway express.

If you are spending the night in a single berth, upper or lower, you must carry a very small overnight case with you, as the remainder of your luggage will be stowed at the end of the car. Even in a compartment or drawing room, space is limited, and if you can avoid having to open large bulky suitcases, you will be much more comfortable.

IN THE DINING CAR

On a day-long journey, there is no need to speak to your companions at the table, beyond a possible "May I have the salt, please?" although there is no objection to an impersonal conversation on such subjects as the scenery, the weather, a book the stranger may have with him, etc. On a longer journey, if you happen to sit next to, or near, the same person for a number of meals, it is extremely bad-mannered to sit in wooden silence.

IN THE PULLMAN

During the day in a Pullman section, the seat that faces forward belongs to the occupant of the lower berth; the occupant of the upper berth rides backward. It would be an act of courtesy for you, when you have the right to the seat facing forward, to ask the occupant of the other seat whether he or she minds riding backward—and if he does, to make a place at your side. The window seat naturally belongs to you—unless you prefer the other.

In a bedroom, compartment, or drawing room, all of which have doors that can be tightly closed, there is no reason not to have a friend or two in for a chat. But the partitions between rooms are thin, so voices must be kept low, and the porter should be called to make up the beds by 10:00 or 10:30 at the latest. If you wish to have another drink or continue your talk, you may go to the club or bar car. When you are in a berth in the open section of the car, divided only by curtains from the other passengers, you must cease all conversation as soon as neighbors are in bed, and if you do not feel like sleeping, resort to a good book in the privacy of your berth. Occupants of a section, even though they are strangers, must consult each other as to what time they would like their berths made up for the night.

GOING TO BED IN A PULLMAN

Whether you have a drawing room, compartment, bedroom, roomette, section, or berth, you ring for the porter to make up your berth when you are ready to go to bed. If you have a roomette, drawing room, compartment, or bedroom, you simply shut your door when he is finished, and go to bed. In every variety of room, all bathroom facilities are included so that you do not go to the public dressing room at all. If, however, your berth is in the open car, you wash and prepare for the night in the dressing room while the porter makes up your bed. This is especially necessary if you have an upper berth, so that when you have gone up the stepladder the porter brings for you, you will not have to come down again. You may remove your clothes in the dressing room and return to your berth, dressed for the night and in a bathrobe. But rather than keep others waiting, most people, after washing, return to their berths, close the curtains, and go through the gymnastics of undressing in an impossibly small space! In the morning when you want to get down, you ring the bell inside your berth and ask for the stepladder. You dress, again as much as you can in your berth, because there is no privacy —and less space—in the dressing room. Try to take only a small toilet case or shaving kit to the dressing room.

IF YOU MUST TAKE THE CHILDREN

If you can possibly avoid it, do not travel on a train with very small children. If it is necessary, try to maintain their regular schedule of meals, naps, and bedtime. Those who are sufficiently well-to-do usually take a drawing room or compartment and keep the children in it. Those who are to travel in coaches should take special pains to plan diversions for the children ahead of time; it is unreasonable to expect little children to sit quietly for hours on end and just "be good." But don't let them race up and down the aisles.

TIPS

Dining-car waiters are tipped exactly as waiters are in any restaurant. They are given fifteen percent of the bill, and never less than a quarter.

Waiters or stewards in the bar car or club car are tipped fifteen percent of the bill, and they are given a quarter if they bring "set-ups" (ice, glasses, water, and soda) to you in the Pullman car.

The Pullman porter receives fifty cents to one dollar for each person on an overnight trip—more if he has given additional service other than making up the berths.

TRAVEL ON A SHIP

LUGGAGE

On a ship where you will occupy the same cabin the entire time, particularly if you are to have it alone or with your husband or wife, the amount of luggage you take does not matter. On the other hand, if you are sharing a cabin with strangers, you must limit your luggage to one or two small bags. In other words, you have no right to expect your cabin-

Line

mate to live in a baggage room. Luggage not needed en route is, of course, checked.

On your arrival at a pier, there is a porter to put your luggage on the escalator or elevator to the upper level, for which the tip is twenty-five cents or more a bag. Having seen your luggage all put on the escalator, you then take the elevator or walk up the stairs to the receiving end of the escalator. There, your porter puts the luggage on trucks for delivery to the point from which the luggage goes on board the ship. On some piers, another crew takes over upstairs, and tips are also given to these porters. You then show your passport and ticket at the proper desk, and board the ship.

On the day you sail, be sure to arrive at the ship in plenty of time to be certain your luggage is on board. Any trunks sent to the pier by express or delivered by other means will be covered by numbered checks, the stubs of which will have been given to you. These stubs should be turned in to the baggage master, or whoever is in charge of his desk, on the pier, and the luggage will be stored in the hold, or sent to your stateroom, as requested.

RESERVING DINING-ROOM TABLE AND DECK CHAIR

Immediately after being shown to your cabin, it is well to go to the dining room and reserve a table at the sitting you wish for the voyage. Next, go to the main deck and see the head deck steward about a steamer chair. If you have a preference about the location, this is your chance to get it.

SOCIAL LIFE ON BOARD

You may very well have friends coming to the ship to wish you "Bon Voyage!" This is a fine excuse for a party, and a happy beginning to your trip. There are two ways of giving such a party. If you have a large, comfortable stateroom, your steward will bring soda and soft drinks, hors d'oeuvres, ice, and glasses to your cabin. Often one of the guests will bring a bottle of liquor or champagne as a going-away present. Or, if you are in a small room, possibly shared with strangers, you may have your party in one of the bars or lounges. In either case, you board the vessel as early as possible and make the arrangements with your cabin steward or with the headwaiter in whichever public room you choose.

During the rest of the trip you may entertain your new shipboard acquaintances in the same way. You should tip the stewards who serve such a party fifteen percent of the bill at the time, rather than adding it to your regular tip at the end of the trip.

If you are traveling first class, on a luxury liner, you will find that many people dress in evening clothes—tuxedos for the men and dinner dresses for the women—every night except the first on board. This is not necessary, however, except on the night of the Captain's party (usually

the next to the last night out), and cocktail dresses and business suits are acceptable on other evenings.

Unless your own group is very large or you request a table of your own, you may be seated, in every class, with other people in the dining room. No formal introductions are necessary on board—you introduce yourself to your neighbors, and with luck, you quickly find congenial people with whom you will become fast friends for the length of the voyage. In deck chairs, around the swimming pool, in the lounges, or in the game rooms, this holds true. You may open a conversation with any one who appears to be congenial, but if they do not respond with some enthusiasm, do not force yourself on them; they may honestly wish to be left alone. A short transatlantic crossing may lead to very little friendliness, but a cruise, on the other hand, always has a sociable atmosphere, a holiday spirit, like that of a large house party where the guests speak to each other as a matter of course.

On every cruise there is a "cruise director," who acts as host or hostess and tries to see that the passengers have a pleasant time. Any young girl or man on board who is without friends is expected to go to the director and ask to be introduced to congenial people. If the passenger plays deck games or bridge or likes to dance, the director arranges for games and introduces partners. On the smaller ships, the purser or possibly the chief steward assumes the role of director.

By the time you arrive at your first port, it is probable that you will have made a number of friends. Perhaps you especially like someone who was introduced to you by the director or someone who sits next to you on deck or at table, and you can go ashore with her or him. If this is not the case, then you may always go along in the general group.

Nothing is more mysterious than the way a group of people develops as in a photograph. At first you see a crowd of faces and none of them stands out. Little by little they take on identity, and more often than not, some inconspicuous person whom at first you hardly noticed is the one who becomes your most delightful friend.

On any ship, the Captain usually entertains at cocktails once for first-class and once for tourist-class passengers. He may also give smaller parties for prominent persons, personal friends, or those sitting at his table. These invitations should always be accepted if possible, and a written refusal sent if you cannot attend.

The Captain is always spoken to as "Captain Sawyer" and the other officers are called "Mr."

At mealtime, those seated at the Captain's table or at the tables of the other senior officers must treat them as they would a host in a private home. These passengers should arrive at the same time as the officer, and if he is delayed, wait for him before starting, unless he sends word that they should go on without him. At other tables it is not necessary to arrive all together, as long as each person or group sits down well within the limits of that sitting.

TIPS

There are definite minimum amounts that passengers are expected to give. If you are traveling first class, your cabin steward should receive ten dollars. The dining-room steward receives ten dollars and the headwaiter five. One or two dollars to the bus boy, if there is one, would make him very happy. Lounge and bar stewards are tipped fifteen percent at the time they render their services. The chief deck steward receives five dollars, and his assistant, if he has one, three dollars.

Fifteen percent of the amount of the wine bill is given to the dining-table wine steward.

To the bath steward you give a dollar.

All these suggestions for tipping are per person, on a transatlantic trip.

Tips in the cabin and tourist classes are lower, in proportion to the difference in the passage fare. A good general rule for shipboard travelers is to allow approximately ten percent of their fare for tips. Divide about half of this allowance between the cabin and dining-room stewards, and distribute the rest to others who have served you. Obviously, passengers occupying suites are expected to tip more generously than those in modest accommodations.

To anyone on the ship who has taken pains to please you, show by your manner in thanking him that you appreciate his efforts, as well as by giving him a somewhat more generous tip when you leave the ship.

It should be unnecessary to add that you must on no account attempt to tip a ship's officer! Thank the purser as you would any other acquaintance for courtesy. If you go to see the doctor, or if he is brought to see you, he will probably send you a bill for his services. If he does not and you have had a real illness, it is proper to send him, in an envelope when you leave the ship, the amount that probably would have been charged by your own doctor. If you are ill enough to be hospitalized, an extra charge will be added to your fare.

Currency and language

The two problems that cause the most embarrassment to travelers abroad are language and currency. Lack of understanding of another country's currency can result in most painful situations—you may grossly undertip someone who has done you a real service, or you may overpay highly, thus appearing to be either ostentatious or stupid. But worse than this is the ill-feeling and misunderstanding that can result from having to make yourself understood by someone who knows no more of your language than do you of his.

MONEY MATTERS

The rates of exchanging dollars for each country's currency vary from time to time, but revised and inexpensive wallet-sized guides are printed continually and may be bought at stationery stores or gift shops and are distributed by many travel bureaus, ticket agencies, etc. There are also available adjustable ones that may be changed to give the current exchange. In any case, they are a great help to the tourist who (like myself) has great difficulty in equating seventy-five cents with several hundred (or thousand) lire, francs, pesos, or whatever the local currency may be. Even with the help of these computers, it is wise to learn by heart the corresponding sum for such standard amounts as a quarter, a dollar, and five dollars. The rough equivalent of a quarter is still a standard tip for small services all over the world. And if you know the amount equal to one dollar, it is not difficult to arrive at that corresponding to ten dollars. How much more intelligent one looks in the market place if he says quickly, "Oh, no—that's too much!" than if one has to pull out a card, find the price and its equivalent sum in dollars, and only then start to bargain!

And a word about bargaining. In large city stores all over the world the prices are just as firm as they are at Macy's in New York City. Items are often marked or tagged exactly as are products in the United States, and frequently there are signs saying "Prix fixe" or "Fixed price."

In small towns or rural market places, however, especially in Latin countries, bargaining is part of the fun of making a sale. Not only is the tourist considered an idiot if he pays the "asking price," but he has ruined the day for the vendor, in spite of the exhorbitant amount he has received. In some countries like Mexico, which are overrun by tourists, you may at first be told that the price is firm, but with persistence and a little firmness on your own part (an indication that you are about to walk away and forget the whole thing is usually effective), the price is sure to be lowered.

In most restaurants in Europe, there is a charge on the bill for service. When this is substantial, fifteen percent or more, you need not tip an additional fifteen percent, but you should leave something. The waiter will often bring your change in denominations that make it correct to leave only the coins on the plate, or you may decide that you would like to tip, for example, twenty-five or fifty cents for each person, and leave the equivalent amount. If there is no service charge, or a very small one, you should tip the usual fifteen percent.

THE LANGUAGE BARRIER

We Americans have for years been greatly criticized for our ignorance of the idioms of countries in which we not only travel, but sometimes live. Not even our diplomats have been required to learn to speak the languages of the countries to which they are accredited. The criticism is quite justified.

Although people will tell you time and again that it is not necessary to speak a foreign language because "everyone in Europe speaks English," it simply is not so. Outside the cities and areas frequented by tourists, there are literally millions of foreigners who neither speak nor understand one word of English. I cannot stress enough the importance, first, of knowing a few words of the idiom of whatever countries you are planning to visit and, second, of carrying a small pocket dictionary with you. It is not necessary, of course, to take a course or buy a self-teaching system or even learn all the useless phrases given in so many grammars and phrase books. Who in the world will ever need such a phrase as "Please put the green chair on the other side of the bed," or "My aunt's suitcase was left in the railroad station"? But a few much used words and phrases (the grammar need not be perfect—your inflection can indicate a statement, question, exclamation, etc.) will smooth your path in any strange land:

> "Yes" and "No."
> "Please" and "Thank you."—Most important of all!
> "Hello," "Good-by," "Good morning," "Good evening," "Good night."
> "How much?" "How much does it cost?"
> "The check (or bill) please."
> "Please speak slowly."
> "I don't speak [whatever the language may be]."
> "I don't understand."
> "Where is . . . ?" and "How do you get to . . . ?"
> "Lady's room" and "Men's room."
> "More, please" and "No more, thank you."
> "Beautiful," "Wonderful," "Nice," "Kind," etc.—these single words, said admiringly and sincerely about the place or people you are visiting will warm the heart of the most skeptical native.

All phrase books will give more explicit sentences and questions on many subjects, but the above words should be learned by heart, so that they can be used quickly and easily without having to refer to a book.

For some reason, we all have a natural reluctance to use foreign words if we do not really know the language. This results in a tendency to mumble or else to shout as if your listener were deaf. Obviously, neither of these mannerisms helps him to understand you. The best way to make yourself understood is to say a word or phrase slowly and distinctly, looking at the other person and using gestures if they are meaningful. Waving your arms about may mean nothing, but making a writing motion can certainly help the waiter to understand that you are asking for the check.

Nothing pleases a native of any country, including our own, more than realizing that a visitor has taken the time and made the effort to learn a little of his country's language. If we could all remember this when we travel, we would be far more eager to enter into conversation with foreigners, and thereby a great stride would be made toward furthering friendship among all peoples.

Anyone who has walked through a little alley in a tiny town on a Greek island and seen the beaming smiles and eager response of the old ladies who sit there in the sun and hear "Calimera" instead of "Hello" or "Good morning" will know that this is true.

21

An audience with the Pope

It is possible for American tourists visiting Rome to be granted an audience with the Pope, for, although there are often hundreds of people in a day who wish an audience, no one is denied. Obviously only relatively few can be granted one of the three types of audience that are considered to be personal; group or collective audiences are arranged for the great majority.

Requests by Americans for these group audiences as well as for the personal ones should be cleared by the North American College, and then sent to the Office of the Master of the Chamber known as *Ufficio del Maestro di Camera di Sua Santita*, which is in the Vatican. They should be presented in person, or sent on arrival in Rome, to the Monsignor in charge, whose name, and the address, can be obtained from the concierge of your hotel. All must fill out a form requesting the kind of audience desired and show their credentials, which for a Roman Catholic may be simply a letter of introduction from his parish priest or a prominent layman. The length of their stay in Rome, their addresses and telephone numbers are also included on the form so that they can be notified of the day and hour of their audience. Non-Catholics as well as Catholics are granted audiences, and their requests for audiences must be arranged through prominent Catholic laymen or members of the Catholic clergy.

The reply, and the invitation if the answer is favorable, will be sent to you within a few days. You may receive a general admission ticket, meaning no reserved seat, or, if you are considered sufficiently important, a reserved seat in a special section.

THE GENERAL AUDIENCE

General audiences are usually held at noon, but those without reserved seats should arrive very early if they wish an advantageous location. People often start arriving as early as 10 A.M.

At noon, the audience rises as the Pope appears, seated on a portable throne called the Sedia Gestatoria, carried by eight Swiss Guards. At the end of the aisle, he leaves the portable throne for a fixed one, and when he sits down, the audience may be seated also. He delivers a short address, and then the audience kneels as he gives his benediction to all those present, as well as all articles they have brought with them to be blessed. The group rises and if the Pope has time, he greets each person in the special area. He mounts his portable throne and is carried out, and the audience is over.

For general audiences it is only required that everybody be dressed in a sober and suitable manner. Women must have their hair covered, must wear black or dark dresses with necklines that are not too low and skirts that are not too short, and they may not have bare arms or legs.

OTHER AUDIENCES

The "private" audience is reserved for cardinals, heads of state, ambassadors, or others of first importance. The second type of audience is the "special," which is almost as important as the "private," and is granted only to people of high rank or to those who have an important subject to present to the Pope. The third type of audience is the "baciomano," which is also considered a personal one, as each comes into the personal presence of the Pope, kisses his ring, and exchanges a few words with him, addressing him as "Your Holiness."

In this third type of audience, visitors stand in a single file around the room and when the Pope enters they kneel and do not stand again until the Pope leaves the audience chamber or makes a sign for them to rise. He passes from one visitor to another, extending his hand to each so that all may kiss his ring. He also may ask a question and exchange a few words with each. It is customary, as it is in the general audience, for visitors to take with them one or more rosaries or other small religious objects, which, after the visitor has received the Papal blessing, are also considered to have been blessed.

The rules of dress for visitors to the Pope are not so strict as they once were. But even now for a private or special audience, men traditionally wear evening dress with tails or sack coat and women long-sleeved black dresses and veils over their hair. No one may wear any but the most functional jewelry.

NON-CATHOLICS

At a general audience, every person present must kneel, rise, and sit at the prescribed time. Non-Catholics, if they do not ordinarily do so, need not make the sign of the cross.

In private audiences, they will be told when they arrive the proper manner of kneeling and kissing the Pope's ring. If they object to these requirements on the grounds of their own religion, there may be some slight modification. But the procedures are strictly followed, and rather than making an issue, they would be wiser to forego the private audience.

Representing America abroad

As a result of travel by jet airplane, people at the farthest reaches of the earth have become our neighbors. Every traveler will increase his enjoyment of his trip if he attempts to make friends and exchange ideas with the foreigners he meets. We should try to acquire an understanding of the customs of each country we visit and never presume to set our own behavior up as a pattern to be followed.

To do nothing that can either annoy or offend the sensibilities of others is the principal rule of conduct, abroad as well as at home. In order neither to annoy nor to offend, it is necessary for us to consider the point of view of those with whom we come in contact; when traveling we should know something of the customs that determine the foreign point of view, if we would be thought cultivated and charming instead of boorish and objectionable. The best way to learn about the customs of other lands is also the best way to plan a trip: read books about the people and places you intend to visit.

OUR ATTITUDE

We don't love all the foreigners who come to our shores. We do love those individuals who are appreciative of our country and courteous to us. It is quite plain, then, that corresponding requirements are exacted of us in the countries where we are foreigners.

At first thought, it would seem that there could be no difficulties of understanding between us and those whose language is the same as ours —especially the Australians and New Zealanders, who are said to be so much like ourselves. But slight frictions develop even when there is no language problem, and they suggest that thoughtful observance of other people's reactions to the things we do and say would be helpful. It is said of our soldiers stationed overseas, for example, that not only do they have more money than those of other nations, but the American troops look upon foreign currency as being make-believe money—of no value at all.

To our credit it can be said that we are straightforward; we honor our obligations; we keep our word. But sometimes we make overoptimistic promises, and tact is not one of our virtues. Sensitive perception of the feelings of others is something that few of us possess instinctively. It is necessary, therefore, that we train ourselves to see the point of view of the people of each country we visit, remembering that it is always the stranger who must adapt himself, just as the visitor does to the ways of the house in which he is a guest.

Our travel attitude serves a twofold purpose; it determines, of course, the impression we make on those who meet us, but it also determines the amount of enjoyment we get from our trip. Which one enjoys his travels more—the man who goes with an open mind, eager to see the best in each country and forget the inconveniences, or the man who finds it too hot in Spain, broods all day because he had no hot water for shaving, or can't find a hamburger stand to buy his favorite lunch? This may sound ridiculous, but I have lived abroad, and many a time I shuddered and tried to pretend that I was anything but American when I heard these boorish complaints repeated endlessly in a penetrating voice. The second man was certainly not enjoying his trip, nor was he impressing his neighbors with the charm of Americans.

ENTHUSIASM

You will make yourself thoroughly popular in every part of the world if you show appreciation and enthusiasm for the customs and sights of the country you are in. Of course, there will be annoyances— service in many places is less efficient than that to which we are accustomed, the food may not appeal to you, nor the climate, but it is not necessary to voice your disappointments in public. You need not be falsely ecstatic, but you may be politely noncommittal and attempt to find and dwell on the parts of your stay that you *do* enjoy.

NO COMPARISON

Don't compare everything you see with the United States. We may have taller buildings, bigger automobiles, newer supermarkets, and less poverty, but no one wishes to "suffer by comparison" and it is the surest way of alienating your foreign acquaintances. Every country in the world has something to offer that we do not, so remember that the natives there do not necessarily envy us our material wealth—they may prefer their simpler, less complicated existence.

ADAPTABILITY

Life and culture in northern Europe is more similar to ours than is the case in Latin countries. Therefore, in Germany, the Scandinavian countries, and the British Isles, we have fewer problems in understanding the people, and we find that our ways of life differ little from theirs. This is partly the result of the racial differences between Latins and northern Europeans and partly the climate. Latins, without exception, live in warmer parts of the world. The combination of temperament and the necessity of adapting themselves to hot weather has resulted in a relaxed, unhurried attitude in all things, and "mañana" is the order of the day. This is one of the most difficult adjustments for Americans to make. We are by nature hustlers, and to arrive in a country where no one cares whether everything is ready, where one arrives for appointments hours late or forgets to keep them at all, and where meals are served hours later than one is used to, is quite a shock. Some Americans simply cannot get used to it, and they leave as soon as they can for more northerly climates, but the others, who are more adaptable, soon find that the Latin countries have something to offer that is unique, and it becomes as difficult to return to a clock-watching society as it was to leave it behind in the first place.

MERCENARY AMERICANS

Our greatest fault (so it is said) is that we think the best of everything should be eagerly handed to us—even without our asking. When we're asked "Why?" we believe (even if we are not so rude as to say it) that it is because we can pay for it! If this were true, could anything be more ill-bred?

That we must learn how to pay for it graciously is the true answer. The fact is that some of us have still to learn that the payment we should make is something more and quite apart from dollars—that is; if we are going to be given more than just what dollars can buy! Dollars, pounds, francs, pesos, lire—yes—all these buy objects of ornament or utility, but they don't buy a single gesture of welcome, of admiration, of sympathy.

A little thought, a little preparation, a very great wish to learn and to understand, these alone will reap the beautiful reward—the foreigner's friendship.

OUR CONDUCT

When we are traveling abroad, our conduct as much as our attitude makes the impression we leave either favorable or unfavorable. If, combined with a friendly mien, our manners are impeccable and our actions above reproach, the foreigner cannot help but be left with a good impression of America and its people.

APPEARANCE

The first thing that the native of another country notices is our appearance. Neatness and modesty are the two most important features. Your clothing may be the least expensive you could find, and you may be traveling with only two or three outfits, but if you unpack it when you arrive and keep it clean (always carry a good spot remover and soap powder) and pressed (either by valet service or with your own little traveling iron), you will surely appear well-dressed. Clothing should, of course, be appropriate. Thin clothes for warm climates, dark clothes for large cities, a "dressy" suit or dress for dining out, and the proper clothes for any sports you intend to take part in should be part of your wardrobe. And finally, clothing should be modest. In resorts, on the Riviera or Majorca, for example, you may wear the same things you would wear at any American resort—even less "covered-up" if you wish, but decent foreign women (or men) do not wear shorts or slacks except at resorts, in the privacy of their own yards, or for golf, tennis, boating etc. Tourists only proclaim their ignorance and lack of respect for convention if they appear on the street in such attire. In fact, apart from cities in tropical climates, clothing is more formal than that in our cities. Men are never seen in anything but dark business suits, and well-dressed women wear dark suits or dresses. In the tropics this is not so, however, and sleeveless cottons are often worn. The men in many hot countries do not wear shirts and ties, but a loose cotton or linen shirt-jacket, worn outside the trousers, and sometimes beautifully pleated or embroidered. Women should always have with them some sort of head-covering, if only a scarf, for some churches will refuse them admittance without, and in all, it is only courteous to comply with their requirements.

No matter how you are traveling or for how long, your luggage should be neat and compact. There is no excuse for bags that look as if they'd been with you on a ten-year safari, since durable and light-weight luggage is available at moderate cost. Nothing looks worse or makes a traveler so uncomfortable as broken-down bags and numerous bundles.

GENERAL CONDUCT

The next thing people abroad will notice is your general behavior. Do not attract attention to yourself by talking in a loud voice. Americans have a reputation for being "loud," and it is true that foreigners, Latins especially, are brought up to admire a well-modulated voice. So you will be far more attractive to people abroad if your voice carries only to those with whom you are talking. Your actions should be as inconspicuous as your voice. There is no need to gesture wildly because you may be trying to speak a strange language, and all your actions should be natural but dignified. When you see a friend from home across the square or in a crowded restaurant, it is not necessary to shout and wave violently to attract his attention. Approach him quietly and greet him as you would ordinarily do at home.

Don't push yourself ahead of others in lines or crowds. Europeans are more polite about waiting their turns than we are, and nothing could be ruder than shoving ahead of someone who is too polite to object.

Above all, don't stare! Of course you are interested when you see a Greek gentleman pull out his "worry beads" and toy with them or when a peasant family approaches with mother burdened down with a heavy load while father rides the donkey, but don't stand rooted with your mouth open, obvious surprise or criticism written all over your face. Their customs are natural to them—it is not your place to judge them—and when you are in their country, accept whatever you see as normal, and store it away in your memory as an interesting and different facet of life abroad.

FOOD AND DRINK

Drinking and eating habits are different abroad, but if your table manners are good, you will not be criticized because they are typically American. By this I mean that you will not be considered ill-mannered if you switch your fork to your right hand after cutting your meat with it in your left, but every foreigner in the room will know that you are from the United States.

Cocktails are not a part of life abroad as they are in our country. Because everyone knows, thanks to the movies, that Americans are supposed to drink whiskey and cocktails from morning to night, they are frequently offered to us in private homes, and they are served in bars in all big cities. But beware! They may not taste like any cocktail you have ever had before, and they will more than likely be served lukewarm, possibly with a peanut-sized piece of ice. They may soon cure you of any desire to continue your normal "cocktail habit." Far better to follow the customs of most foreign countries and take, instead, the delicious native wines served with your meals. Of course there are local beverages, alcoholic and nonalcoholic, in each country, and it is interesting to try them at least once. Wines in France, aperitifs in Italy, beer in Germany, and retsina wine in Greece are all examples. While you may not enjoy all (or any) of them, they are a part of the culture and economy of the country and should be sampled by all tourist visitors.

TAKING PICTURES

If you wish to include a native of the country in your pictures, do have the decency to ask his permission. He may appear unusual or picturesque to you, but a poor farmer may be ashamed of the very costume that to you seems charming, and the last thing he wishes is to have his poverty recorded and distributed to strangers from another land.

In countries where the natives still wear a national costume (and these are rare in Europe, except on holidays, but more common in Africa and the Middle and Far East), the people are accustomed to being photographed by tourists, but it is still polite to ask their permission unless you are just taking a picture of a large crowd.

Children may be frightened of the camera, but their fears can usually be overcome by the offer of a small tip or candy. In areas where there are many tourists, they will often crowd around you, offering their services as models.

CHAPERONS

Until very recently in Latin countries, no girl or young woman ever went out alone with a man unless he was her husband. Because many of them, as were their parents, are now being sent away to schools and colleges in more liberal societies, standards are slowly changing, and the chaperon is becoming a thing of the past. In remote areas and in small towns, the daughter's social life is still quite restricted, but in most parts of the world, she may go out with a group of friends without an older chaperon. Brothers are considered excellent guardians, and a man wishing to go out with a girl may often arrange a "double date" through her brother.

Both men and women visitors to Latin countries should remember these customs. Men must not expect to meet a well brought up girl one night and take her out the next. He must be presented to her family, gain their approval, and then arrange, at least on the first few dates, to include mutual friends.

Women do not go out alone after dark. A woman on the street by herself at night is an open invitation to improper advances by any Latin man. In fact, he would consider himself at fault if he did not attempt to approach her. Young girls should stay in groups of three or four, and older women must be accompanied by at least one friend.

EUROPEAN AND SOUTH AMERICAN MANNERS

The manners of Europeans and South Americans are more "flowery" than those of Americans. The men bow more deeply, the women always shake hands when introduced, and hand-kissing is still practiced. If you see that a handsome gentleman is about to lean over and kiss your hand, don't giggle or pull away. Accept the gesture for what it is—a compliment to your femininity—and act as natural as you can. European gentlemen not only tip their hats to ladies; they remove them and bow with a flourish. And ladies are always seated on the gentleman's right, except in a theater when this would place her on the aisle.

FLOWERS AND PRESENTS

Europeans, and especially Latins have a great love of giving presents, not only at Christmas or at someone's birthday, but unendingly. Such gifts are usually foods or flowers, especially those baked in their own ovens or grown in their gardens. Or they may be any trifling or more expensive things.

In accepting these, we on our part must learn how to bow and smile and show our pleasure in accepting the gift—and as soon as possible thereafter we should show our friendliness by a simple appropriate gift to interpret our courteous intentions when grace of speech is lacking.

Flowers are always sent to the hostess when you are invited to dinner. They are also sent as a "thank you" and to greet visitors. In fact, almost any occasion can be called an excuse to send a bouquet.

If it so happens that you can speak not a word of Spanish or Portuguese, or it may be French, or Italian, or Dutch, remember that you can always give a smile and a genuine handshake with confident assurance that your gesture will be received with a cordial welcome. Such gifts are the most heart-warming of all.

Part FIVE

FORMAL ENTERTAINING

Official dinners

To give a perfect dinner is the supreme accomplishment of a hostess, for it means not only perfection of furnishing, service, and culinary skill, but also the ultimate of personal charm and tact. You may never be called upon to entertain with the formality described in this chapter and the next, but the attention to detail, the thoughtful arrangements, and the careful preparation are applicable—indeed necessary—in many other situations.

Although the truly formal dinner is almost a thing of the past (giving way to the informal or "friendly" dinner), its every detail is a definite part of the complete pattern from which all details of even the simplest dinner-giving are chosen. Today this pattern is more commonly used at official functions than in private homes, but nevertheless it cannot be ignored.

This chapter deals only with those aspects of an official dinner which vary from those of any private formal dinner party. Therefore, for all other details as to service, food, and rules of behavior, see Chapter 24, "Formal dinners in private homes."

THE DUTIES OF THE HOSTESS

THE GUEST LIST

When Mrs. Diplomat, wife of the Ambassador to France, gives a dinner, it means little effort on her part beyond deciding upon the date and the guests. For instance, the Senator from Goodlands is to be in Paris for a week, so she picks Wednesday, the tenth of the month, as a suitable date. She then looks through her dinner list and asks her secretary to invite the Oldworlds, the Eminents, the Learneds, the Wellborns, and four other couples, as well as the Senator and his wife. She also picks out three or four additional names to be substituted for those who regret. Then, turning to the "younger" list, she searches for a few amusing or good-looking ones to give life and charm to her dinner, which might otherwise be heavy. But her favorites do not seem appropriate: it will not do to ask the Bob Gildings because Lucy Gilding smokes like a furnace straight through dinner and Mrs. Oldworld disapproves of women smoking at all. So Mrs. Diplomat adds the Kindharts and the Normans, who "go" with everyone, and approves her secretary's suggestions about additional names if those first invited should regret. She tells her to send out invitations for the tenth on the official stationery of the Embassy, sends word to the cook that there will be twenty-four on that date, and later, when the menu is submitted to her, makes whatever changes or suggestions she wishes. She need not think about her table, which the butler will arrange properly, but many times she will give it extra care and a personal touch, perhaps in the arrangement of the flowers or the details of the centerpiece.

THE PLACE CARDS

On the morning of the dinner her secretary brings her the place cards—the name of each person expected is written on a separate card—and she arranges them in the order in which they are to be laid on the table. Starting with her own place at one end and her husband's at the other, she places the lady of honor at his right, the second in importance at his left. Then at either side of herself she places the two most important gentlemen. The others she fits in between, trying to seat side by side those congenial to each other.

When the cards are arranged, the secretary puts the name of the lady who sits at each gentleman's right in an envelope addressed to him. It is placed on a silver tray and passed to him as he enters the drawing room when he first arrives, and he will escort that lady in to dinner. She then picks up the place cards, still stacked in their proper sequence, and gives them to the butler, who will lay them in the order arranged on the table after it is set. » *For details on the use of titles on place cards and the order of precedence at official dinners, see Chapter 58.*

Five minutes before the appointed hour, Mrs. Diplomat is already standing in her drawing room. She has no personal responsibility other than that of being hostess. The whole machinery of equipment and service runs by itself. It does not matter whether she knows what the menu is—her cook is capable of attending to it. The butler will see that the table is perfect. She knows without looking that her chauffeur is outside the door, to assist in parking the cars; that footmen are in the hall; that a maid is in the ladies' dressing room; and that the butler is just outside the door near which she is standing.

So with nothing on her mind she receives her guests with the tranquillity attained only by those whose household, whether large or small, can be counted on to run like a smoothly coordinated machine.

THE DUTIES OF THE HOST

The host who holds an official position may have more to say in the planning of a dinner than the man in private life, whose wife generally makes all the decisions. He may, if he is in the diplomatic corps, for instance, be ordered by his government to entertain important visitors, and he may even be told in what way and to what extent he is to do so. He relays this information to his wife, who takes care of details of food, service, etc. as usual, but follows his suggestions as to the date, what officials must be invited, and other matters important to the specific occasion. When the official list is complete, his wife will, as at any dinner, choose as the other guests those who will be most congenial to the ones who must be invited.

When the guests begin to arrive, the host stands near his wife and shakes hands with them after she has greeted them. If the dinner is in honor of a prominent person, he introduces him to a few people immediately so that he will not be left unattended while others are arriving. Because it is an official dinner, the responsibility for further introductions lies with the host more than it does at a private dinner, although if it is a couple who are being entertained, his wife must see that the lady of honor is not left out.

As at all formal dinners, the host escorts the lady of honor in to the dining room and leads the men to the library for coffee and back to join the ladies before too long a time has elapsed. It is the duty of the host to offer the first toast if the occasion calls for one.

ANNOUNCING GUESTS

A gentlemen falls behind his wife in entering the drawing room. If the butler knows the guests, he merely announces the wife's name first and then the husband's. If he does not know them by sight, he asks whichever is nearest to him, "What name, please?" And whichever one is asked answers, "Mr. and Mrs. Lake."

The butler then precedes the guests a few steps into the room where the hostess is stationed and, standing aside, says in a low tone, but very distinctly, "Mrs. Lake," a pause and then "Mr. Lake." Married people are usually announced separately, but occasionally people have their guests announced "Mr. and Mrs. Gray."

PERSONS OF RANK

All men of high executive rank not only are announced first, but take precedence over their wives in entering the room. The President of the United States is announced simply "The President." His title needs no qualifying appendage, since he, and he solely, is *the* President. He enters first and alone. Then "Mrs. Washington," being announced, follows. The governor of a state is in courtesy announced as "His Excellency," but the correct announcement would be "The Governor of [name of state]" and then "Mrs. Goodland." He enters the room and Mrs. Goodland follows. "His Honor the Mayor and Mrs. Lake" observes the same etiquette; or in a city other than his own he would be announced "The Mayor of Chicago and Mrs. Lake."

Other announcements are "The Honorable the Chief Justice and Mrs. Law," "The Secretary of State and Mrs. Eminent," "Senator and Mrs. Jefferson." The senator, however, allows his wife to enter the room first, because his office is not executive. An ambassador must be announced "His Excellency the British Ambassador," and then "Lady Howard"; he enters the room first. A minister plenipotentiary is announced "His Excellency the Swedish Minister." He enters and a moment later "Mrs. Ogren" follows. But a first secretary and his wife are announced without other title than their own—"Count and Countess European" or "Mr. and Mrs. American."

"Excellency," though strictly a title belonging to none but an ambassador, is always granted by courtesy to a minister plenipotentiary. It may also be used for a chargé d'affaires, although this courtesy is, however, temporary and ceases upon the return of his chief.

The President, the Vice President, the governor of a state, the mayor of a city, the ambassador of a foreign power—in other words, all executives—take precedence over their wives and enter rooms and vehicles first. But senators, representatives, secretaries of legations, and all other officials who are not executives allow their wives to precede them, just as they would if they were private individuals.

Archbishops are always announced as "His Excellency," whether they are Roman Catholic or Anglican.

SPECIAL SITUATIONS

On some occasions, a question may arise about how to announce a foreigner of rank, whether his title is hereditary or political. There is only one general rule, applicable in all situations: whatever the title, it is invariably translated into English. Thus, *M. le Comte* becomes Count, *Marquise* becomes Marchioness, *Duc,* Duke, and so forth. (This, incidentally, eases the difficulty of pronouncing words from a language with which one is not familiar.)

When there is any doubt about the official title or its proper translation, it is always possible to check with the information officer at the embassy or consulate of the country from which the person comes. In almost every case, however, this information would necessarily have been obtained earlier when the invitation was properly addressed and so would be available to whoever is announcing at the official function.

» *See also Chapter 7, "Addressing important persons," and Chapters 58, 59, and 61, on protocol.*

Formal dinners in private homes

The requisites for a perfect formal dinner, whether a great one for two hundred people or a little one for eight, are as follows:

Guests who are congenial to one another (by far the most important requirement).

Food that is good of its kind, and a suitable menu perfectly prepared and served.

Table furnishings in perfect condition and suitable to the occasion and the surroundings, freshly laundered linen, brilliantly polished silver (no matter how little of it), shining glassware.

Service that is competent and expertly suited to *your* requirements.

A *living room* that is invitingly arranged and well aired.

A *cordial and hospitable host.*

A *hostess of charm*, a requirement that means everything—tact, sympathy, poise, and perfect manners—at all times.

For all dinners, these requisites are much the same, but the necessity for perfection increases in proportion to the formality and the importance of the occasion. Still and all, many a perfect or near-perfect dinner has been given that cannot be classed as a *formal dinner*. By definition, it is not possible to give a formal dinner without the help of servants. No matter how elaborate the meal, if the guests have to help themselves from a buffet, or if the hostess has to rise to clear the table, the dinner immediately becomes informal. » *For dinner-giving in the less formal American house without servants, see Chapters 29 and 30, but do read this chapter also.*

EXPERT SERVICE

The fact that few households except such official establishments as embassies have staffs that include butlers, footmen, or kitchen maids need not keep you from entertaining formally. The hostess who wishes her dinner to be formal can hire temporary help. All cities and many smaller communities have catering services that provide not only servants, but excellent meals, either prepared by a cook sent to your home or partially cooked in their kitchens and finished in yours.

If the servants are efficient and well trained, a small (that is, for no more than twelve) formal dinner may be beautifully handled by a cook, a butler, and a footman. The footman may be replaced by a maid, but at a truly formal dinner, those who serve the meal should be men. When the host does not have a chauffeur, a man must be hired to assist the ladies from the cars or taxis, and to direct and help with parking and, later, bringing the cars to the door when the party is over. In the country his job is that of a chauffeur—in the city he acts as a doorman. If there is a permanent cook in the house, she prepares the meal, and only the butler and footman are hired for the evening. They serve and also assist her with the cleaning up.

Let us suppose you have arranged for the temporary servants mentioned above. When such help is used, the hostess naturally must do most of the advance preparation. She sets the table, arranges flowers, and does all else that will relieve her help of any responsibilities other than the preparation and serving of the meal.

The cook arrives early in the day so that the hostess need not concern herself with the preparation of the dinner once she has given explicit directions as to the food and explained the whereabouts and workings of all the utensils and appliances to be used.

The butler and footman and doorman come a little later, but early enough to discuss all details of service with the hostess and to take care of any last-minute polishing or arranging that may be necessary. If cocktails are to be served, the butler mixes them in advance and has them ready to serve as each guest arrives, so that dinner will not be delayed. A few minutes before the hour of the guests' arrival, the butler and footman put on their uniforms, which must be impeccable. The footman takes his place in the hall to direct the guests or help with their wraps. The butler stands near the hostess to announce the guests, or if they are not to be announced, he passes cocktails or simply waits to assist her in any way. It is up to the temporary butler, as it would be if he were permanently employed, to see that all runs smoothly, so that the hostess may devote her attention to her guests.

The butler, footman, and waitress may not leave until the guests have been ushered out, the last glass washed, and the last ash tray emptied. The cook, however, may leave as soon as the cooking utensils and dinner service have been washed and the kitchen made immaculate.

The method of paying temporary help varies in different localities and also depends on the policy of the agency through which they have been hired. Some caterers send a bill for their services and prefer that you do not add a tip. Others send a bill but indicate that you may add a tip if you have been satisfied with the service. If the help has been hired from an employment agency, or by you personally, you may simply pay them before they leave at the rate you have agreed upon. In any case, it is most important to establish the method and amount of payment at the time the servants are hired to avoid embarrassment or unpleasantness that may ruin an otherwise perfect evening.

If your dining-room table seats more than twelve and you wish to entertain a larger group, you will find it desirable and even necessary to hire more than one footman and possibly an assistant to work in the kitchen as well. Otherwise, there will be considerable delay in serving and removing courses, and the last guests served will have a cold dinner.

Temporary help of this sort is the only solution for many housewives today. Nevertheless, this chapter describes in some detail formal entertaining in the establishment with a large staff. Why? Because such a book as this would be incomplete without the inclusion of information about the running of any house, large or small. Some hostesses do have one or more servants; others hire them on occasion; and hostesses and guests alike must be knowledgeable about all possible situations.

SELECTING YOUR GUESTS

The proper selection of guests is the first essential in all entertaining. Some people have a sense for it—others haven't. The first are the great hosts and hostesses; the others, unless they exert considerable effort, are at best mediocre.

Usually it is a mistake to invite great talkers to the same gathering. Brilliant men and women who love to talk want listeners, not rivals. If it seems advisable or necessary to invite two brilliant people, most people think they should be put together. Often they should, but with discretion. If both are voluble or nervous or "temperamental," you may create a situation comparable to putting two operatic sopranos in the same part and expecting them to sing together.

Very silent people should be sandwiched between good conversationalists or at least voluble talkers. Silly people should never be put anywhere near learned ones, nor the dull near the clever, unless the dull one is a young and pretty woman with a talent for listening and the clever one is a man with an admiration for beauty and a love of talking.

The endeavor of a hostess, when seating her table, is to put together those who are likely to be interesting to each other. Professor Bugge might bore *you* to tears, but Mrs. Entomoid would probably delight in him, just as Mr. Stocksan Bonds and Mrs. Rich would probably have interests in common. Making a dinner list is a little like making a Christmas list. You put down what *they* will like (you hope), not what you like. Those who are placed between congenial neighbors remember your dinner as delightful, even though both food and service were mediocre. But ask people out of their own groups and seat them next to their pet aversions and wild horses will not drag them your way again.

One point to remember in making up your guest list is the rigid and unbreakable order of seating at a formal dinner. You may find yourself with a guest of honor who must be placed next to a most unsuitable table companion.

SEATING YOUR GUESTS

WHO IS THE GUEST OF HONOR?

The guest of honor is the oldest lady present, or a stranger whom you wish for some reason to honor. A bride at her first dinner in your house after her return from her honeymoon may be given, if you choose, precedence over older people. The guest of honor is *always* she who is taken in to dinner by the host and placed on his right. The lady of next greatest importance sits on the host's left and is taken in to dinner by the gentleman on whose right she sits. The hostess is always the last to go into the dining room at a formal dinner unless the President of the United States or the governor (but only in his own state) be present. In these exceptional cases the hostess would go in to dinner with the guest of honor, who leads the way, and the wife of the President or governor would follow immediately with the host.

In Washington, even though the dinner be given for a guest of medium rank, the ladies of highest rank have the honor-places on either side of the host. The lady for whom the dinner is actually given is merely "among those present," unless those of higher rank agree to waive precedence. When Mrs. Frances Perkins was Secretary of Labor, she waived her rank and said always to seat her where no one else wanted to sit.

THE ORDER OF TABLE PRECEDENCE

The lady of highest rank is on the host's right. The lady of next highest rank is on his left. The third lady sits on the right of the man of highest rank. The fourth lady on the left of the man of second rank, and so on (see diagram). The lowest in rank is nearest the center. If the dinner is not official and there is no particular distinction in rank or age, the hostess may seat her guests in whatever order she thinks will achieve the most congenial and pleasant conversation. The lady she places on her husband's right is automatically the guest of honor. The "lady of honor" or of first rank must be "taken in" by the host and seated at his right. At ordinary dinners, therefore, the hostess goes in to dinner with the man of the second highest rank. But if the man of honor is of such importance that she must go in with him as well as place him at her right, it is necessary to send the lady who sits on the right of the gentleman of honor and the gentleman who sits on the hostess' left in to dinner together and then to separate them. He sees her to her place, and, discovering his card is not next to her, goes around the table until he finds his own. The diagram (with arrow lines indicating ladies and gentlemen who go in together) makes this seemingly complicated situation clear:

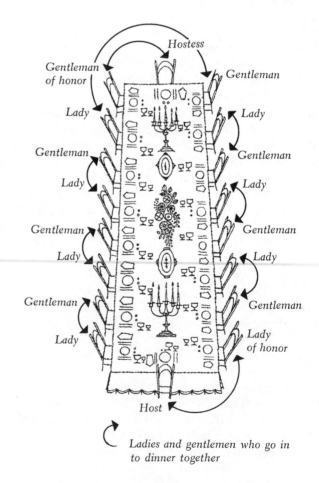

Ladies and gentlemen who go in
to dinner together

SEATING A PARTY OF EIGHT, TWELVE, OR SIXTEEN

At dinners of eight, twelve, sixteen, twenty, and twenty-four, where either two ladies or two men must sit at head and foot of the table, the hostess usually relinquishes her place and the host keeps his. At a dinner of twelve, it is important that she take the place at her left instead of at her right, because otherwise she, instead of the lady at the right of the gentleman of honor, will be served first. An example of this, with the lines showing service:

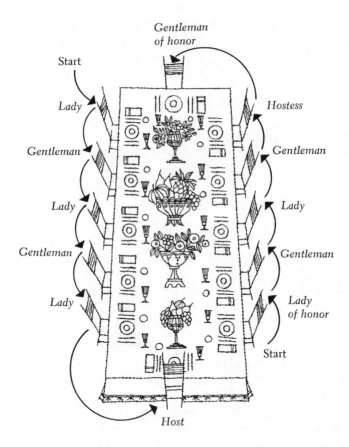

Occasionally, other variations on the usual scheme are necessary for a specific reason. This diagram shows, for example, the correct seating arrangement for a group that has a hostess but no host:

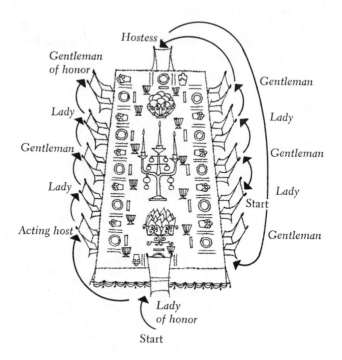

The order of table precedence for such special situations can be worked out suitably by applying common sense to the standard forms and need not be a cause for particular concern.

THE ENVELOPES FOR THE GENTLEMEN

Each gentleman is given an envelope containing a card on which is written the name of the lady he is to take in to dinner. This card just fits in the envelope, which is an inch (or slightly less) high and about two inches long. When the envelopes are addressed and filled, they are arranged in two or three neat rows on a silver tray and put in the front hall. The tray is presented to each gentleman just before he goes into the drawing room, or in the entrance hall on his arrival.

An exceedingly practical method of telling each gentleman where he is to sit at a very large table is to choose a small fold-over card instead of the usual single one. His name is on its front fold and his partner's name inside, and below her name in the lower half of the fold is a small engraved diagram showing the table, the door of entrance, and the location of their seats.

Or if it is so big a dinner that there are many separate tables, the tables are numbered with standing placards (as at a public dinner) and the table number written on each lady's name card. (Do not call it an "escort card.")

THE PLACE CARDS

The place cards are usually plain, about an inch and a half high by two inches long, sometimes slightly larger. Fancy cards, while suitable on such special occasions as Christmas or a birthday, have gone out of fashion on a formal table. The courtesy title and surname—"Dr. Gooding, Mr. Ashley"—are used except when there is more than one guest with the same surname, in which case Mr. Russell Albright and Mr. Lee Albright, for example, should be used to make the distinction. » *See also Chapter 58, if your dinner involves government officials.*

THE IMPORTANCE OF DINNER INVITATIONS

Invitations to formal dinners may be engraved or written by hand, or they may take the form of a card of general invitation. They may even be telephoned. » *See Chapter 52.*

They must be answered immediately—engraved or written ones, by return mail, or those which were telephoned, by telephone and at once! Also, nothing but a serious illness or an unavoidable accident can excuse the breaking of a dinner engagement. To accept a dinner at Mrs. Nobody's and then break the obligation upon being invited to dine with the Importants is inexcusable. But having declined the Nobody invitation in the first place, you are then free to accept Mrs. Important's or to stay at home. The rule is: Don't accept an invitation if you don't care about it.

If, for some unavoidable reason, a guest who has accepted a dinner invitation is forced to drop out at the last moment, the hostess must try to fill in by inviting an intimate friend. She always does this herself, by telephone. The one who receives such an invitation is virtually bound by the rules of good manners to accept if possible.

Tiffan

SETTING YOUR TABLE

Your guest list complete and your seating arrangements worked out, you can turn to the matter of your table and its decoration.

The one unbreakable rule is that everything must be geometrically spaced: the centerpiece in the actual center, the places at equal distances, and all utensils balanced. Beyond this one rule you may vary your arrangement and decorations as you choose.

If the tablecloth is of white damask, which for a formal dinner is always best, a pad must be put under it. (If you do not have a felt pad cut to the dimensions of your table, a folded, white blanket serves very well.) To say that the cloth must be smooth and white—in other words, perfectly laundered—is as unnecessary as to say that faces and hands should be clean. Damask is the old-fashioned but essentially conservative tablecloth, especially suitable in a high-ceilinged room that is either English or French or of no special period in decoration. Lace tablecloths are better suited to an Italian room—especially if the table is a refectory style. Handkerchief linen tablecloths, embroidered or lace-inserted, are suited to all quaint, low-ceilinged, old-fashioned rooms. Either lace or linen goes over the table without felt or other padding.

Whenever a damask or linen cloth is used, the middle crease must be put on so that it is an absolutely straight and unwavering line down the exact center from head to foot. If it is an embroidered cloth be sure the embroidery is "right side up."

Next the centerpiece goes on—usually an arrangement of flowers in either a bowl or a vase, but certainly not too high for guests to see over. It can also be any one of an almost unlimited variety of things: flowers or fruit in any arrangement that taste and ingenuity can devise; or an ornament in silver that needs no flowers, such as a covered bowl; or an ornament of glass or china; or perhaps an arrangement of distinctive conversation-piece objects that blend with the rest of the table setting.

THE INDIVIDUAL PLACES

Next comes the setting of the places. The distance between places at the table must never be so short that guests have no elbow room and the servants cannot pass the dishes properly. When the dining-room chairs are very high-backed and are placed so close as to be almost touching, it is impossible for the most skillful server not to risk spilling something over someone. On the other hand, to place people a yard or more apart so that conversation has to be shouted into the din made by the shouting of all the others is equally trying. About two feet from plate center to plate center is ideal. If the chairs have narrow and low backs, people can sit much closer together. This is especially true of a small round table, the curve of which leaves a spreading wedge of space between the chairs at the back even if the seats touch at the front corners. But on the long, straight sides of a rectangular table in a very large dining room there should be a foot of space between the chairs.

The necessary number of plates, with the pattern properly positioned, are first put around the table at equal distances—spaced with a string if whoever is setting the table does not have an accurate eye. Then on the left of each plate, handle toward the edge of the table and prongs up, is put the salad fork; the meat fork is put next, and then the fish fork. Just to the right of the plate is put the salad knife, next is the meat knife, and on the outside is the fish knife, the cutting edge of each toward the plate. Then the soupspoon and then the oyster fork or grapefruit spoon.

No more than three forks and three knives belong on the table when it is set. Therefore, if there is an additional course (rarely seen these days, but coming between the fish and the main dish when it appears), the

fork for this course is placed between the fish fork and that for the meat, and the salad fork is left out to be brought in later. The salad knife is also omitted, as it is in any case when the salad does not require one.

In short, the silver is arranged so that one uses the utensils farthest from the plate first, taking the next in order for each succeeding course.

Butter knives and plates are never used on a formal dinner table.

Which wineglasses shall be chosen depends of course upon the menu, but their table-setting arrangement will have to be according to size, in that little ones cannot very well be hidden behind large ones. Therefore, the goblet for water is placed directly above the knives at the right of the plate; next to it, at a slight distance to the right, the champagne glass; in front and between these two, the claret or white wine glass, if either is to be served. Then, either in front of this, or somewhat to the right again, the sherry glass. If there is to be a glass for burgundy, it would be back between the goblet and the glass for champagne. Or instead of grouping the glasses on the table, some prefer to have them placed in a straight row slanting downward from the goblet at upper left to the glass for sherry at lower right.

Such an array as this is scarcely ever seen, except at a public dinner, which is more properly classified as a banquet. At the private dinner, two or three glasses, in addition to the goblet, are usual—one for sherry and one for claret and possibly one for a light white wine or a burgundy.

A dinner napkin folded square and flat is laid on each place plate. Very fancy foldings are not in good taste, but if the napkin is very large, the sides are folded in so as to make a flattened roll a third the width of its height. If they have a corner monogram, they also may be folded diagonally in half, and the two long ends folded under.

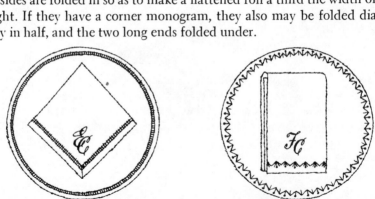

Napkins are put at the side only when it is necessary to put food on the table before seating the guests. To put the napkin at the side of the empty plate in order to display the plate is very much like wearing a ring over a glove—as well as being incorrect for formal table-setting. Bread should not be put in the napkin. The place cards are put on top of and in the center of the napkin, or if unsteady on a folded napkin, they may be placed on the tablecloth above the napkin at the exact center of the place setting.

FINISHING THE TABLE

When the places have been set, two pairs of candlesticks are placed at the four corners about half-way between the center and the edge of the table, or two candelabra at either end half-way between the places of the host and hostess and the centerpiece. The number of candles depends upon whether the dining room is otherwise lighted or not. If the candles alone light the table, there should be a candle a person. You will need two or four candelabra, depending on the length of the table. But if the candles are merely ornaments, four candles will be adequate for a table of eight. Candlesticks or candelabra must be high and the candles as long as the proportion can stand, so that the light does not shine into the eyes of those at table.

Dishes, either bowl- or basket- or paten-shaped, are put at the corners, between the candlesticks or candelabra and the centerpiece, or wherever there are equally spaced vacancies on the table. These dishes, or compotes, hold candy, fruit, fancy cakes, or other edible trimmings, chosen less for flavor than for decorative appearance. Salted nuts do not belong in any dishes that remain on the table after it is crumbed. Properly, nuts may be put on the dinner table either in two big silver dishes or in small individual ones at each of the places, but they are removed with the salt and pepper pots after the salad course. The colloquial description of eating "from soup to nuts" could never apply to a formal dinner. After-dessert "nuts and raisins" belong only on the family dinner table—especially at Thanksgiving and Christmas.

On a very large table, four compotes are filled with candy, and perhaps two larger silver dishes or baskets are filled with fruit and put midway between two of the candy dishes. Flowers are also often put in two or four smaller vases, in addition to a larger and dominating one in the center.

Pepper pots and saltcellars should be put at every other place. For a dinner of twelve there should be six (and never less than four) saltcellars and pepper pots.

Olives and celery are passed during the soup course. When fish, or meat, or salad has its own accompanying condiment, sauce, or relish, it is also passed. Pickles have no place on the correct dinner-party menu, because they are served as an accompaniment or garnishing for cold meats, which belong to lunch, supper, buffets, and picnics.

CIGARETTES AND ASH TRAYS

Whether or not she and her husband smoke, the considerate hostess sees that her guests are supplied with ash trays and cigarettes. A small ash tray is put at each place, and cigarettes are found on the table, either in a tiny holder in front of each diner or in larger holders spaced evenly about the table. The smoker generally does not light his cigarette until he has finished his main or salad course, and he must follow the usual rules of good smoking manners more strictly at the table than at any other time.

There are some hostesses even today who prefer that their guests do not smoke until coffee is served, and no ash trays or cigarettes are placed on the table. Others have them passed at the end of the salad course.

FOOD AND DRINK

COCKTAILS

If cocktails are served, they are prepared in the pantry or kitchen and passed (on a tray) to each guest as he arrives. Two or three varieties should be offered, with the butler indicating what they are: "Would you care for an old fashioned or a martini?" There must also be glasses of tomato juice or some other nonalcoholic beverage on the tray for those who prefer something other than liquor. Unless dinner is delayed by the necessity of waiting for guests who are late, only one cocktail need be served: there will be wine with the meal, and formal dinners should start as nearly as possible at the hour stated on the invitation.

THE MENU

The menu for a modern dinner, no matter how formal, does not consist of more than six courses:

1. soup *or* fresh fruit cup *or* melon *or* shellfish (clams, oysters, or shrimp)
2. fish course (*or* on rare occasions, a dish such as sweetbreads instead of fish)
3. the entrée, or main course (usually roast meat or fowl)
4. salad
5. dessert
6. coffee

One should always try to choose a well-balanced menu; an especially rich dish is balanced by a simple one. Fish timbale with a thick creamed sauce might perhaps be followed by spring lamb, other plain roast meat, or a *filet mignon*; broiled fish by an elaborate meat dish.

Some people love highly flavored Spanish or Indian dishes, but they are not appropriate for a formal dinner. Equally bad is a dinner of white sauces from beginning to end: a cream soup, boiled fish with white sauce or a *vol-au-vent* of creamed sweetbreads, followed by breast of

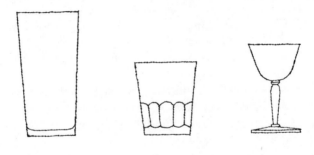

Long drink   Old fashioned   Cocktail

chicken and mashed potatoes and cauliflower, palm-root salad, vanilla ice cream, and lady cake. Or everything sweet: beet soup, fish with apricot sauce, duck basted with currant jelly, a sweet fruit salad with *Bar-le-Duc* jelly, and a sugary dessert. In these examples, each dish is good in itself but unappetizing in the monotony of its combination.

In addition: Although a dinner should not be heavy, neither should it consist of samples, especially if set before men who are hungry. The following menu might seem at first glance a good dinner, but it is one from which the average man would go home and forage ravenously in the icebox: clear soup (no substance); smelts; broiled squab, miniature potato croquette, and string beans; lettuce salad, with one small cheese straw apiece; ice cream.

The only thing that had any sustaining quality, barring the potato which was not more than a mouthful, was the last, and very few men care to make their dinner of ice cream. If the squab had been roast instead of broiled it would have been more adequate because more of the flesh of a roast squab can be eaten. Or if there had been a thick cream soup, or a fish with more substance—such as salmon, or a baked thick fish of which he could have had a generous helping—this would have been adequate. But too many women order trimmings rather than food.

MENU CARDS

Menu cards are most often seen at official dinners or banquets, but they are sometimes used at a formal dinner at home. Usually there is only one, which is placed in front of the host; but sometimes there is one between every two guests.

Menus on fashionable tables never include obvious accessories, such as celery, olives, rolls, peppermints, radishes, currant jelly, chocolates, fruit, any more than they include salt and pepper or iced water.

WINES WITH DINNER

Wines always have their proper place on the menu of a perfect dinner. Let us consider each of them in detail.

Sherry. Customarily this (in a small V-shaped glass) is the first wine served at dinner. It is served with the soup and should always be put into a decanter and served at room temperature. It can stand being decanted indefinitely without spoiling. Sherry is also served at lunch, or at supper, or as a hospitable refreshment at any time. Years ago it was invariably offered with biscuits or cakes to guests arriving from a journey or about to depart on one. Nowadays sherry is often included with cocktails as an alternate.

White Wine. A certain few epicures have always insisted that chilled chablis be served with oysters. Otherwise any dry white wine is served with fish or with an entrée, and a dry or sweet white wine may be the only wine at a women's lunch or at the family dinner table.

Claret. At a simple dinner party, claret is served with meat. Epicures shudder at its appearance before the meat, but at the family dinner table either claret or white wine may be drunk from the beginning of the meal to its close.

Burgundy. Stronger than claret, it is especially suitable with red meats, duck, and all game. Claret and burgundy should both be at room temperature or a degree or so warmer rather than colder if the vintage is very fine. The decanting of vintage wines is a very delicate as well as important operation. Clarets and white wines, if not decanted, should be lifted as gently as possible, without changing the side on which the bottles are lying, into straw baskets of the sort that they are served from in restaurants.

The white wines are carried carefully to a cool—even cold—place. Red wines are carried with equal care to the dining room or pantry, which has a temperature approximating 68 degrees; and all these wines are left in their baskets until as short a time as practical before they are to be served and then, with all the care and gentleness possible, decanted. Some epicures put them through filter papers; others believe that filtering robs them of some of their bouquet. At all events, care is taken not to let any sediment, which has settled at the bottom of the wine, get into the decanter.

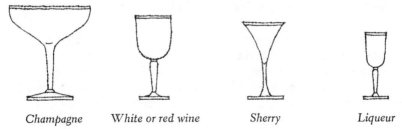

| Champagne | White or red wine | Sherry | Liqueur |

Champagne. Because this is, above all other beverages, that of the formal dinner party, it has, like all other formal details, many exigencies. When other wines are included, it is served with the meat course; but, when it is the only wine, it is served as soon as the first course has begun. Its proper temperature depends upon its quality.

Champagne that is not of especially fine vintage is put in the refrigerator for a day and then chilled further by putting it into a cooler with a very little salt as well as ice and occasionally, holding the bottle by the neck, turning it back and forth a few times. In doing this, take care not to leave the bottle in the salt and ice too long or the champagne may become sherbet! Also, when opening, be sure to wrap the bottle in a towel or napkin as a protection in case it explodes.

An excellent vintage champagne, on the other hand, is packed in ice without salt.

Champagne glasses ought to be as thin as soap bubbles. Thick glasses will raise the temperature at which a really good champagne should be served and spoil its perfection. If they must be used, the epicurean thing to do is to chill them in the refrigerator and put them on the table at the moment the champagne is served.

YOUR GUESTS ARRIVE

THE HOSTESS RECEIVES

On all occasions of formality, at a dinner as well as at a ball, the hostess stands near the door of her drawing room, and as guests enter or are announced, she greets them with a smile and a handshake and says something pleasant to each. What she says is nothing very important; charm of expression and of manner can convey a far more gracious welcome than the most elaborate phrases, which as a matter of fact should be studiously avoided. Mrs. Oldname, for instance, usually welcomes you with some such sentence as "I am very glad to see you," or "I am so glad you could come!" Or if it is raining, she may tell you that you were very unselfish to come out in the storm. But no matter what she says, she takes your hand with a firm pressure and her smile is really a *smile* of welcome, not a mechanical exercise of the facial muscles. She gives you always—even if only for the moment—her complete attention; and you go into her drawing room with a distinct feeling that you are under the roof, not of a mere acquaintance, but of a friend.

Some hostesses are much given to explanations and love to say, "Mrs. Jones, I want you to meet Mrs. Smith. Mrs. Smith is the author of *Dragged from the Depths,* all about psychic insight!" Or to a good-looking woman, "I am putting you next to Mavro Bey—I want him to carry back a flattering impression of American women!" But cultured people do not exploit their distinguished guests with embarrassing hyperbole or make personal remarks. Both are in very poor taste. Do not understand by this that helpful explanations cannot be made; it is only that they must not be embarrassingly made or overdone. Mrs. Oldname might perhaps, in order to assist conversation for an interesting but reticent person, tell a lady just before going in to dinner, "Mr. Traveler, who is sitting next to you at the table, has just come back from two years alone with the cannibals." This is not to exploit her "traveled lion," but to give his neighbor a starting point for conversation at table.

And although personal remarks are never good form, it would be permissible for an older lady in welcoming a younger one, especially a debutante or a bride, to say, "How lovely you look, Adelaide, and what an attractive dress you have on!" Or, to an older lady, "That is a beautiful string of pearls you are wearing." But never anywhere nor at any time may one ask anyone, "How much did it cost?"

THE MANNERS OF A HOSTESS

First of all, a hostess must show each of her guests equal and impartial attention. Also, although engrossed in the person she is talking to, she must be able to notice anything amiss elsewhere. The more competent her servants, the less she need be aware of details herself, but the hostess giving a formal dinner with inexperienced help has a far from smooth path before her. No matter what happens, if all the china in the pantry falls with a crash, she must not appear to have heard it. No matter what goes wrong, she must cover it as best she can and at the same time cover the fact that she is covering it. To give hectic directions merely accentuates the awkwardness. If a dish appears that is unpresentable, she as quietly as possible orders the next one to be brought in. If a guest knocks over a glass and breaks it, even though the glass be utterly irreplaceable, her only concern must seemingly be that her guest has been made uncomfortable. She says, "I am sorry! But the glass doesn't matter!" And she has a fresh glass brought (even though it doesn't match) and dismisses all thought of the matter.

Both the host and hostess must keep the conversation going, if it lags, but this is not so definitely their duty at a formal as at an informal dinner. It is at the small dinner that the skillful hostess has need of what Thackeray calls the "showman" quality. She brings each guest forward in turn to the center of the stage. In a lull in the conversation she says beguilingly to a clever but shy man, "Harold, what was that story you told me—" and then she repeats briefly an introduction to a topic in which Harold particularly shines. Or later on, she begins a narrative and breaks off suddenly, turning to someone else—"*You* tell them!"

THE DUTIES OF THE HOST

Mr. Oldname, who stands near his wife as the guests arrive, always comes forward and, grasping your hand, adds his own greeting to his wife's gracious welcome. And either you join a friend standing near, or he presents you, if you are a man, to a lady; or if you are a lady, he presents a man to you.

At formal dinners introductions are never general, and people do not as a rule speak to strangers, except those next to them at table or in the drawing room after dinner. The host therefore makes a few introductions if necessary. Before dinner, as the hostess is standing (and no gentleman may therefore sit down), and as it is awkward for a lady who is sitting to talk with a gentleman who is standing, the ladies usually stand also until dinner is announced.

A hostess who is either a widow or unmarried asks the man she knows best—a relative if there is one present—to act as host. He gives his arm to the guest of honor and leads the way to the dining table, where he sits opposite the hostess. After dinner he leads the men to the smoking room and later to the drawing room to "join the ladies."

WHEN DINNER IS ANNOUNCED

It is the duty of the butler to "count heads" so that he may know when the company has arrived. As soon as he has announced the last person, he notifies the cook. The cook being ready, the butler, having glanced into the dining room to see that windows have been closed and the candles on the table lighted, enters the drawing room, approaches the hostess, bows, and says quietly, "Dinner is served." Or if she happens to be looking at him, he merely bows.

SEATING YOUR GUESTS

The host offers his right arm to the lady of honor and leads the way to the dining room. All the other gentlemen offer their arms to the ladies appointed to them and follow the host, in an orderly procession, two and two; the only order of precedence is that the host and his partner lead, while the hostess and her partner come last. If by any chance a gentleman does not know the lady whose name is on the card in his envelope, he must find out who she is and be presented to her before he takes her in to dinner. At a very large dinner, if there was no table diagram in the hall, the butler usually stands just within the dining room door with one, and asking each gentleman's name, tells him "Right" or "Left." He has plenty of time to reach the chair of the hostess before her, as she always enters the dining room last.

At a dinner of less than ten, the ladies are not escorted in to dinner, but walk in with whomever they please, in groups of two or three, to avoid crowding at the door.

The guests look for their place cards, assisted by the hostess, who may carry her seating plan with her if she feels that she cannot remember where each guest is to sit. The gentlemen help the ladies on their right into their seats, with the exception of the male guest of honor, who seats the hostess, leaving the man on her left to walk around and seat the lady on the right of the guest of honor.

THE LATE GUEST

Fifteen minutes is the established length of time that a hostess may wait for a belated guest. To wait more than twenty minutes, at the outside, would be showing lack of consideration to many for the sake of one. When the late guest finally enters the dining room, it is she who must go up to the hostess and apologize for being late. The hostess remains seated and the guest merely shakes hands quickly so that all the men at table need not rise. The hostess must never take the guest to task, but should say something polite and conciliatory such as, "I was sure you did not want us to wait dinner." In other days the newcomer was always served with dinner from the beginning unless she was considerate enough to direct the servant who held her chair, "Let me begin with this course." But today so many people arrive late that it has become proper to bring no dish back after it has left the dining room.

CORRECT SERVICE

At a formal dinner in a house with a large staff, the butler always stands behind the hostess' chair, except when giving one of the men under him a direction or when pouring wine. He is not supposed to leave the dining room himself or ever to handle a dish. In a smaller house, where he has no assistant, he naturally does everything himself; when he has a second man or a waitress, he passes the principal dishes and the assistant follows with the accompanying dishes or vegetables.

In any case, whether there are two at table or two hundred, plates are changed and course presented in precisely the same manner. No serving dishes are ever put on the table except ornamental dishes of fruit and sweetmeats. The meat is carved in the kitchen or pantry; vegetables, bread, and condiments are passed and returned to the side table.

From the setting of the table until it is cleared for dessert, a plate must remain at every place. The plate on which oysters or clams are served is put on top of the place plate, and so is a plate holding fruit or cold seafood in a stemmed glass. At the end of the course, the used plate is removed, leaving the place plate. The soup plate is also put on top of this same plate. But when the soup plate is removed, the underneath plate is removed with it, and the plate for the next course immediately exchanged for the two taken away.

If the first course had been a cold dish that was offered in bulk instead of being served on individual plates, it would have been eaten on the place plate, and an exchange plate would then have been necessary before the soup could be served. That is, a clean plate would have been exchanged for the used one, and the soup plate then put on top of that. The reason is that *a plate with food on it must never be exchanged for one that has held food*; a clean one must come between.

Although dishes must be always presented at the left of the person being served, it is better that plates be removed at the right. It is permissible however, if more convenient, to remove them from the left. Glasses are poured and additional knives placed at the right, but forks are put on as needed at the left.

The only plates that are regularly brought into the dining room one in each hand are for soup and dessert. The soup plates are put down on the place plates, which have not been removed, and the dessert plates need merely be put down on the tablecloth. But the plates of every other course have to be exchanged and therefore each individual service requires two hands. Soup plates, two at a time, would better not be attempted by any but the expert and sure-handed, as it is while placing one plate and holding the other aloft that the mishap of "soup poured down someone's back" occurs! If only one plate of soup is brought in at a time, this accident at least cannot happen. In the other way, the spoon and fork on the dessert plate can easily fall off unless it is held level. Two plates at a time, therefore, is not a question of etiquette, but of the servant's skill.

Many years ago it was considered impolite to remove any plates until the last guest at the table had finished eating. Then came one or two decades of speed, during which good service required the removal of each plate the instant the fork was laid upon it, so that by the time the last fork was put down, the entire table was set with clean plates and was ready for the service of the next course.

But the protests of the slow eaters were heard throughout the land and the hostess who a few years ago prided herself on having no used plate left at any place more than a few moments now does not have the plates removed until the slowest eaters have finished.

At every well-ordered dinner there should be a separate service for each six persons; that is, no hot dish should, if avoidable, be presented to more than six, or seven at most. At a dinner of eighteen, for instance, three dishes, each holding six portions, are garnished exactly alike and presented simultaneously: (1) to the lady of honor, (2) to the lady sitting six seats to her right, (3) to the lady six seats on around the end of the table. Study the diagrams on the preceding pages, which explain seating precedence and partner arrangement.

Dishes are passed to the right or passed alternately right and left so that the same gentleman shall not always get the last piece on a dish. Service goes around to the right as usual or reverses for alternate courses, as the hostess chooses, so that there will be two gentlemen who share alternately in being the last served.

While it is thoughtful not to have the same gentleman be the last served all through the dinner, it is not advisable to reverse the direction of service whenever the dinner is large enough to require two services, unless the footmen can be counted on not to become confused by serving first to the right and then to the left, and risk bumping into each other.

THE HOSTESS IS NEVER SERVED FIRST

The hostess who has herself served first when there is another woman at the table is guilty of an act contrary to the highest principles of good manners, or at best of ignorance. Since consideration of others is the first rule of courteous behavior, the hostess who helps herself to the fresh and untouched dish and lets the others take what she leaves, is either unthinking or rude.

In all first-class restaurants, each dish is presented to the host for his approval before it is passed or served to his guests, but he does not help himself. Nor should a hostess in her own house.

FILLING GLASSES

As soon as the guests are seated and the first course is put in front of them, the butler goes from guest to guest, on the right-hand side of each, and fills the water goblet. He then serves the wine, asking each guest, "Sherry, Sir?" (or "Madam?"). All wines are poured at the right of each person and without lifting the glass from the table. Champagne is of course the typical formal dinner-party wine. In fact, it is to many people the evidence of a party, in contrast to the sherry, white wine, and claret of the family table. In France, champagne is often not served until dessert, but elsewhere, sherry is served with the soup (or chablis with oysters), and then champagne is served straight through to the end.

The proper way to serve it is from its own bottle with a napkin around it (put on like a shawl) and wrapped tight. The reason for this is to catch all drops—either of wine or condensed moisture—that might fall, as well as protecting its proper chill from warming hands.

SERVING BREAD

As soon as soup is served, dinner (finger) rolls are passed in a flat dish or a basket. An old-fashioned silver cake basket makes a perfect modern bread basket. Some of the raffia ones from Italy are very attractive. Or, most popular of all, a shallow wicker basket that has a fringed napkin laid in it and several sorts of breads displayed. (Finger rolls, crescent rolls, melba toast, and rye or whole wheat crackers are typical.) A guest helps himself with his fingers and lays the roll or bread on the tablecloth, always. No bread plates are ever on a table where there is no butter, and no butter is ever served at a formal dinner. Whenever there is no bread left at anyone's place at table, more should be passed.

PRESENTING DISHES

Dishes are presented held flat on the palm of the servant's left hand; every hot one must have a napkin placed as a pad under it. An especially heavy meat platter can be steadied if necessary by holding the edge of the platter with the right hand, the fingers protected from being burned by a second folded napkin.

Each dish is supplied with whatever silver is needed for serving it. A serving spoon, somewhat larger than an ordinary tablespoon, and a fork of large size are put on most dishes. Sometimes the spoon alone is used except on the dishes that are hard to help oneself to. String beans, braised celery, spinach *en branche,* etc. need both fork and spoon. Asparagus has various special lifters and tongs, but most people use the ordinary spoon and fork, putting the spoon underneath and the fork prongs down, to hold the stalks on the spoon. Corn on the cob is taken with the fingers, but this dish, delectable though it be, is *never* served at a *formal* dinner party. For this occasion it should be cut off, buttered, seasoned, and served in a vegetable dish. An aspic or mousse should have both fork and spoon, but peas, mashed potatoes, rice, etc. may be offered with a spoon only.

THE SERVING TABLE

The serving table is usually an ordinary table placed in the corner of the dining room nearest the door to the pantry or kitchen and behind a screen, so that it cannot be seen by the guests at table. In a small dining room, where space is limited, a set of shelves like a single bookcase is useful; best of all are shelves made by a carpenter and fitted to the folds of the screen.

The serving table is a half-way station between the dinner table and the pantry. It holds stacks of cold plates, extra forks and knives, and the fingerbowls, and dessert plates. If the serving table is small or too crowded, the latter are sometimes put out on the sideboard.

At informal dinners all dishes of food after being passed are left on the serving table on a warming tray in case they are called upon for a second helping. But at formal dinners, dishes are never passed twice and are therefore taken directly to the pantry after being passed.

CLEARING TABLE FOR DESSERT

At dinner always, whether at a formal one or whether a member of the family is alone, the salad plates, or the plates of whatever course precedes dessert, are removed, leaving the table plateless. The saltcellars, pepper pots, unused flat silver and nut dishes are taken off on the serving tray, and the crumbs are brushed off each place at table with a tightly folded napkin onto a tray held under the table edge.

DESSERT SERVICE

There are two methods of serving dessert. The first, which used to be known as the "hotel method" and has within the last few years become accepted everywhere, is to put the fork and spoon on a china plate. Some people further put a glass plate for ice cream on top of this, but most use only the china plate. After the dessert the fingerbowl is brought in on a plate by itself. In the other service the fingerbowl, as well as the fork and spoon, are brought in on the dessert plate. The diner puts the finger bowl above his plate, and the fork and spoon each to its proper side.

When fruit is to be served, it is passed immediately after the dessert or ice cream; and last are passed decorative sweets. Usually these include chocolates, caramels, peppermints, candied orange, or whatever one chooses for decoration as well as taste.

Before leaving the subject of dessert, it may be well to add that the fingerbowl is less than half filled with cold water; and at dinner parties a few violets, sweet peas, or occasionally a gardenia may (or may not) be floated in it. A slice of lemon is never seen in a well-appointed house in an after-dessert fingerbowl. After broiled lobster, at an informal or family dinner, lemon in *hot* water (or soapy hot water) is excellent.

Coffee is seldom served at a formal dinner table, but is served elsewhere later.

AFTER THE MEAL

LEAVING THE TABLE

At the end of the dinner, when the last dish of sweets has been passed and the hostess sees that no one is any longer eating, she looks across the table and, catching the eye of one of the ladies, slowly stands up. The one who happens to be observing also stands up, and in a moment everyone is standing. The gentlemen offer their arms to their partners and conduct them back to the living room or the library or wherever they are to sit during the rest of the evening.

Each gentleman then leaves his partner and, with the other men, follows the host to the room where after-dinner coffee, liqueurs, and cigars and cigarettes are being passed. It is perfectly correct for a gentleman to talk to any other who happens to be sitting near him, whether he knows him or not. At the end of twenty minutes or so, the host must take the opportunity of the first lull in the conversation to suggest that they "join the ladies" in the living room.

In a house where there is no extra room to smoke in, the gentlemen do not take the ladies to the drawing room, but stay where they are (the ladies leaving alone) and have their coffee, cigars, liqueurs, and conversation sitting around the table.

In the drawing room, meanwhile, the ladies are having coffee, cigarettes, and liqueurs passed to them.

AFTER-DINNER COFFEE

Coffee is served in one of three ways: (1) The footman proffers a tray of cups, saucers, and sugar; the butler follows with coffee pot alone and pours into the cup held in the guest's hand. (2) A tray with filled cups is proffered by the butler to the guests, who help themselves. (3) The tray of cups and sugar is held on the servant's left hand. The guest puts sugar into one of the cups and the servant pours coffee with the right hand.

Liqueurs are offered exactly as coffee in the second or third manner. The guests pour their own, or saying "Cognac" or "Mint, please," their choice is poured for them.

Cigarettes are arranged on a tray with matches or a lighter. There is no modern hostess, even an old-fashioned one, who does not have cigarettes passed after dinner.

At a dinner of ten or twelve, the five or six ladies most often sit in one group, or possibly two sit by themselves, and three or four together; but at a very large dinner they inevitably fall into groups of four or five or so. In any case, the hostess must see that no one is left to sit alone. If one of her guests is a stranger to the others, the hostess draws a chair near one of the groups and, offering it to her single guest, sits beside her. After a while, when this particular guest has at least joined the outskirts of the conversation of the group, the hostess leaves her and joins another group where perhaps she sits beside someone else who has been somewhat left out. Even when there is no one who needs any especial attention, the hostess nevertheless sits for a time with each of the different groups in order to spend at least a part of the evening with all of her guests.

THE GENTLEMEN RETURN

When the gentlemen return to the drawing room, if there is a particular lady to whom one of them wants to talk, he naturally goes directly to where she is and sits down beside her.

Needless to say, gentlemen should not continue to talk together after returning to the drawing room, as it is not courteous to those of the ladies who are thus necessarily left without partners.

At informal dinners, and even at many formal ones, bridge tables are often set up in an adjoining room, if not in the living room. Those who do not play bridge spend an hour or so in conversation and then may go home, unless there is some other special diversion.

TAKING LEAVE

That the guest of honor must be the first to take leave was in former times so fixed a rule that everyone used to sit on and on, no matter how late it became, waiting for her whose duty it was to go. More often than not, the guest of honor was an absent-minded old lady or a celebrity who very likely was vaguely saying to herself, "Oh, my! are these people *never* going home?" until by and by it dawned upon her, or someone reminded her, that the obligation was her own!

But today, although it is still the obligation of the guest who sat on the host's right to make the move to go, it is not considered ill-mannered, if the hour is growing late, for another lady to rise first.

The guest rises, goes to her hostess, and says, "Good night. Thank you so much." The hostess answers, "I am so glad you could come!"

In the dressing room or in the hall, the maid is waiting to help the ladies with their wraps, and the butler is at the door. When Mr. and Mrs. Sewell are ready to leave, for example, the butler goes out on the front steps and says, "Mr. Sewell's car." The host's chauffeur or a man hired for the evening signals to Mr. Sewell's chauffeur and when the car has been brought around reports to the butler, who in turn says to Mr. Sewell, "Your car is at the door, sir," and they go out. If Mr. Sewell is driving his own car, the host's chauffeur or his substitute will bring it to the door and assist Mrs. Sewell into the car.

The bridge players leave as they finish their games, sometimes a table at a time or most likely two together. (Husbands and wives are never, if it can be avoided, put at the same table.) Guests in bidding good night say, "Good night. It was just wonderful!" or "Good night, and thank you *so* much." And the hostess smiles and says, "So glad you could come!" or "Good night!"

SOME ADVICE FOR GUESTS

STARTING A COMPLICATED DISH

When a dinner has been prepared by a chef who prides himself on being a decorative artist, the guest of honor and whoever else may be the first to be served have quite a problem to know what parts of an intricate structure are to be eaten and what parts are scenic effect.

The main portion is generally clear enough; the uncertainty lies elsewhere. Are the flowers edible vegetables, and are the fancy puffs potatoes or trimming? If there is one for each guest, the chances are that they are edible; rings around food are nearly always to be eaten; platforms under food seldom are. Anything that looks like pastry is to be eaten; and anything divided into separate units should be taken on your plate complete. You should not try to cut a section from anything that has already been divided into portions in the kitchen. Aspics and desserts are, it must be said, occasionally Chinese puzzles; but if, in taking what looks like something edible, you do help yourself to part of the decoration, no great harm is done.

REFUSING WINE OR FOOD

If you do not wish wine, it is best—because least conspicuous—to allow a little to be poured into your glass. Unless your host happens to be looking at your glass when the wine is poured, he will not know later on that your almost empty glass was never filled. On the other hand, if he did happen to notice, he could not feel that much wine was wasted. In any case, to turn your wineglass upside down is a needlessly rude way to say "No."

As to this general subject of saying "No" when we want to, many people feel embarrassed when refusing cocktails but have no hesitation whatever in refusing foods—particularly those to which they are allergic! The reason is probably this: The censorious attitude of those who disapprove of alcohol, no matter how temperate its use, has brought about a connotation of disapproval in its refusal. One may refuse to eat bread, or fish, or strawberries, and this may cause regret on the part of the hostess who knows that her biscuits are superlatively good, or the fish caught but a few hours before the meal, or the strawberries picked at just the right hour of the day in her garden, but no disapproval can possibly be implied on the part of the guest who says, "No, thank you."

Not so many years ago, when diet fads had not yet come into fashion and the scientific study of balanced rations, vitamins, allergies, and so on was unknown outside the laboratories, it was considered very discourteous to refuse whatever one's host or hostess proffered. A well-behaved guest took at least a little of everything passed and ate or drank that little. Today, the increasing use of the word "allergic" has been more helpful to the acceptance of the phrase "No, thank you" than anything that ever happened. And after all, if a guest knows that lobster gives him hives, he would be stupid to eat it even though it has just been flown in from Maine.

GLOVES AND NAPKINS

Ladies always wear gloves to formal dinners and take them off at table. Entirely off. It is hideous to leave them on the arm, merely turning back the hands. Both gloves and bag are supposed to be laid across the lap, and one is supposed to lay the napkin, folded once in half across the lap too, on top of the gloves and bag, and all three are supposed to stay in place on a slippery satin skirt on a lap that more often than not slants downward!

It is all very well for etiquette to say, "They stay there," but every woman knows they don't! If you obey etiquette and lay the napkin on top of the bag and gloves loosely across your satin-covered knees, it will depend upon mere chance whether the avalanche starts right, left, or forward onto the floor. There is just *one* way to keep these three articles from disintegrating—cover the gloves and bag with the napkin put cornerwise across your knees, and tuck the two side corners under you like a lap robe, with the gloves and bag tied in place, as it were.

This ought not to be put into a book of etiquette, which should say you must do nothing of the kind. But it is either do that or have the gentleman next to you groping under the table at the end of the meal; and it is impossible to imagine that etiquette should wish to conserve the picture of gentlemen-on-all-fours as a concluding ceremony at dinner.

CIGARETTES AT TABLE

At a truly formal dinner, cigarettes are passed at the end of the salad course, even in the most conservative households. It's true that there are numberless women who light their own cigarettes the moment they are seated at the table—and when young Mrs. Nicotinic lights her cigarette before laying her napkin across her knees and greets the man on her right from beneath an ascending veil of smoke, all others at the table, including the man next to her, feel free to follow her example. To stop this practice, there is really nothing that the conservative hostess can do, except to avoid putting ash trays on the table—a clear indication that she would prefer that her guests wait until the cigarettes are passed. Since no guest can know her hostess's wishes until the table is in sight, one should always put out one's cigarette before going into the dining room.

TALKING TO DINNER PARTNERS

The "turning of the table" is an outmoded custom designed to make people divide their conversation time more or less evenly between their two dinner companions. The hostess, after the first two courses (or at any time she chose), would turn from the man on her right to the one on her left, and each woman at the table was supposed to notice this and switch at the same time. This was a rather forced means of achieving an end that should happen naturally at a convenient break in the conversation rather than at a signal. To be sure, if two diners are engrossed in their conversation, the one sitting by his or her side may be momentarily left with no one to talk to, but a considerate woman will quickly notice this and find a way to end her conversation so that she may talk to her other neighbor, leaving the first man free to turn to the lady on his other side.

One unbreakable rule of etiquette is that you must talk to your neighbors at a dinner table. You must; that is all there is about it!

Even if you are placed next to someone with whom you have had a bitter quarrel, consideration for your hostess, who would be distressed if she knew you had been put in a disagreeable place, and further consideration for the rest of the table, which is otherwise blocked, exacts that you give no outward sign of your repugnance and that you make a pretense, at least for a little while, of talking together.

Luncheons

The formal luncheon, although less formidable than the formal dinner, differs from it only in minor details. Therefore, rather than covering each and every step of preparing for and giving such a luncheon, I shall confine this chapter to the differences. » *For the handling of all other matters, you must read Chapter 24.*

The most significant difference is that luncheons are generally given by and for women. It is not unusual, however, to include an equal number of men on a Saturday, Sunday, or holiday, and their presence or absence may make other differences, as in the heartiness of the menu.

THE INVITATIONS

The word "lunch" is used much more often than "luncheon." Indeed, "luncheon" is rarely if ever spoken, but it is written in books like this one and sometimes in third-person invitations.

Although invitations may be telephoned and occasionally an engraved card is used for an elaborate luncheon, especially for one given in honor of a noted person, formal invitations to lunch are nearly always written in the first person and rarely sent out more than a week in advance. For instance:

Dear Mrs. Kindhart [or *Martha*]:
> *Will you lunch with me on Monday the tenth at half past one?*
> *Hoping so much for the pleasure of seeing you,*
>> *Sincerely* [or *Affectionately*],
>>> *Jane Toplofty*

If Mrs. Toplofty's luncheon were given in honor of somebody—Mrs. Eminent, for instance—the phrase "to meet Mrs. Eminent" would have been added immediately after the hour. If it is a very large luncheon for which the engraved card might be used, "To meet Mrs. Eminent" is written across the top. » *See also Chapter 52.*

ARRIVAL OF THE GUESTS

No matter how large or formal a lunch may be, the hostess, instead of receiving at the door, sits in the living room in some place that has an unobstructed approach from the door. After leaving her wrap, each guest coming into the room is preceded by the butler or the maid to within a short distance of the hostess, where he announces the new arrival's name and then stands aside. Or the guests may greet the hostess unannounced. The hostess rises or, if already standing, takes a step forward, shakes hands, and says, "I'm glad to see you" or "I am delighted to see you." She then waits for a second or two to see whether the guest who has just come in speaks to anyone; if not, she makes the necessary introductions.

When the butler or maid has "counted heads" and knows that all the guests have arrived or when the guests have had time to enjoy a cocktail if it is offered, he or she notifies the kitchen and then enters the room and merely approaches the hostess and bows slightly. But if it is necessary to attract the hostess's attention, he or she says quietly, "Luncheon is served."

If there is a guest of honor, the hostess leads the way to the dining room, walking beside her. Otherwise, the guests go in in twos or threes, or even singly, just as they happen to come, except that the very young make way for their elders, and gentlemen stroll in with those they happen to be talking to or, if alone, fill in the rear. The gentlemen never offer their arms to ladies in going in to a luncheon—unless there should be an elderly guest of honor, who might be taken in by the host, as at a dinner. And even then the others follow informally.

COCKTAILS

Cocktails may or may not be served before lunch, and if they are, they differ a little from those offered before dinner. Although a martini is likely to be on the tray, the preference leans toward sherry, Dubonnet, or a cocktail made with fruit juice, such as a daiquiri. As always, there must be tomato juice or plain fruit juice available for those who wish it.

THE TABLE

Candles have no place on a lunch (or breakfast) table, and the plain white tablecloth that is correct for dinner is not used for luncheon, although colored damask is acceptable. Traditionally the lunch table is "bare," which means set with place mats made in literally unrestricted varieties of linen, needlework, or lace. A runner, matching the mats but two or three times as long, may be used in the center of the table.

The decorations are practically the same as for dinner: flowers or an ornament in the center, and two or four dishes of fruit or candy where they look best. If the table is very large and rather too bare without candles, four slim vases with small sprigs of flowers matching those in the centerpiece—or any other glass or silver ornaments—may be added.

The places are set as for dinner, with a place plate, a fork, a knife, or a spoon for each course. The lunch napkin, which should match the table linen, is much smaller than the dinner napkin and is not folded quite the same: it is folded like a hankerchief, in a square of four thicknesses. The square is laid on the plate diagonally, with the monogrammed (or embroidered) corner pointing down toward the edge of the table. The upper corner is then turned sharply under in a flat crease for about a quarter of its diagonal length; then the two sides are rolled loosely un-

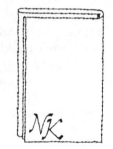
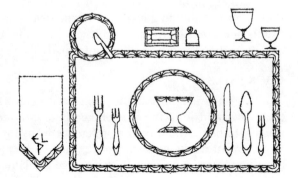

der, with a straight top edge and a pointed lower edge, and the monogram displayed in the center. Or it can be folded in any simple way one prefers.

If it is a large luncheon, place cards are used just as they are at dinner.

THE BREAD-AND-BUTTER PLATE

The bread-and-butter plate is part of the luncheon service always (as well as of breakfast and supper). It is put at the left side of each place just above the forks. The butter knife is placed on the plate diagonally from the upper left to lower right, with knife edge toward the table edge.

Hot breads are an important feature of every luncheon—hot crescents, baking-powder biscuits, bread biscuits, dinner rolls, or corn bread. The several breads are passed as often as necessary. Butter is usually put on the plate beforehand, and it is passed, when necessary, throughout the meal until the table is cleared for dessert. It should be served as butter balls, or curls, rather than in squares.

Bread-and-butter plates are always removed immediately before dessert, with the saltcellars and pepperpots.

SERVING LUNCH

If the luncheon is to be formal, the hostess must have help, whether her own servants or temporary ones. However, the luncheon, as opposed to dinner, may be served by one or two waitresses instead of by men alone.

The formal service is identical with that of dinner. Carving is done in the kitchen and, except for the ornamental dishes of fruit, candy, and nuts, no food is set on the table. The plate service is also the same as at dinner. The places are never left plateless, except after the salad course when the table is cleared and crumbed for dessert. The dessert plates and fingerbowls are arranged as for dinner.

THE MENU

Five courses at most (not counting the ornamental sweets or coffee as a course) and more usually four are sufficient for the longest and the most elaborate luncheon possible. For example: (1) fruit, or soup in cups; (2) eggs or shellfish; (3) fowl or meat (not a roast); (4) salad; (5) dessert.

The menu for lunch eaten in a private house is seldom more than four courses and eliminates either 1, 2, or 5.

A popular first course is melon, grapefruit, or any sort of fruit cut into very small pieces, with sugar and maraschino, rum, or a liqueur. It may be served in special bowl-shaped glasses that fit into long-stemmed and much larger ones, with a space for crushed ice between; or it can just as well be put in champagne glasses, after being kept as cold as possible in the refrigerator until sent to the table.

Soup at luncheon (or at a wedding breakfast or a ball supper) is never served in soup plates, but in two-handled cups. It is eaten with a teaspoon or a bouillon spoon, or after it has cooled sufficiently it is drunk from the cup, which is lifted to the mouth with both hands. It is almost always a clear soup—in the winter a bouillon, turtle soup, or consommé, and in the summer a chilled soup: jellied consommé, madrilene, or vichyssoise.

Lunch-party egg dishes must number a hundred varieties. (See any cook book.) Eggs that are substantial and rich, such as eggs Benedict or eggs stuffed with *paté de foie gras* and a mushroom sauce, should be balanced by a simple meat, such as broiled chicken served with a salad, combining meat and salad courses in one. On the other hand, should you have a light egg course, like eggs in aspic, you could have meat and vegetables, with plain salad, or with an elaborate salad and no dessert. Or with fruit and soup, omit eggs, especially if there is to be an aspic with salad.

The menu of an informal luncheon, if it does not leave out a course, at least chooses simpler dishes: a bouillon or broth, shirred eggs or an omelette, then chicken or a chop with vegetables, a salad of plain greens with crackers and cheese, and a pudding, ice cream, or mousse or any of the light desserts. While cold food is both appropriate and palatable, no meal should ever be chosen without at least one course of hot food. Many people dislike cold food, and it disagrees with others; but if you offer your guests hot soup (or at supper, tea or chocolate), it would then do to have the rest of the meal cold.

All of the menus suggested above are for lunch parties. If you invite women you know are trying to diet, the menu would of course be shorter and simpler. In other words, when lunching with intimate friends, you have the kind of food you know they like.

BEVERAGES

In the winter, a wine is usually served with lunch. Although sherry might be served with soup or a liqueur after dessert, one wine is sufficient, and it should be a light wine such as a dry Rhine wine or a claret.

A chilled white wine may also be served in the summer, but it is not so refreshing as iced tea or iced coffee, and these are the usual choices. Iced tea at lunch is prepared with lemon and sugar and sometimes with cut-up fresh fruit or a little squeezed fruit juice, and it is poured into the glasses (often decorated with springs of fresh mint) already at each place. But coffee should be passed around in a glass pitcher on a tray that also holds a bowl of powdered sugar, a pitcher of cold milk, and another of cream as thick as possible. The guests pour their coffee to suit themselves into tall glasses that are half full of broken ice and furnished with very long-handled spoons.

After lunch, the men, rather than having coffee in the library or at the table, accompany the ladies and have coffee with them in the living room.

Teas and receptions

Afternoon parties range from the very dignified reception, through the more or less formal tea dance or tea, to the quite casual cocktail party. The reception today has become primarily a state affair, a public or semipublic gathering in honor of a prominent personage or an important event. Receptions most frequently take place on the diplomatic or civic levels and are handled, as in the case of official dinners, by a competent staff.

The major difference between a reception and a tea is one of atmosphere, like the difference in furnishing twin houses. A reception always takes itself seriously. A tea, no matter how formal it pretends to be, is friendly and inviting. We do not go to be impressed or instructed, but to enjoy seeing our friends and to be seen by them.

THE INVITATIONS

Afternoon teas are given in honor of visiting celebrities, new neighbors, or a new daughter-in-law, to "warm" a new house, or for a house guest from another city, or, as is most often the case, for no reason other than that the hostess feels hospitably inclined.

The invitation is a visiting card of the hostess with "Jan. 10, Tea at 4 o'clock" in the lower corner, opposite the address, and, if appropriate, "To meet Mrs. Harvey Montgomery" across the top of it. Or it may be telephoned. » *See also Chapter 52.*

THE TEA TABLE

At a gathering of this sort, the tea and the coffee or hot chocolate are sometimes passed on trays, but more often the hostess prefers to have them poured at a table. Many choose their dining-room table as the simplest and most comfortable place from which to serve. However, the tea table may be set up in any room that has adequate space and easy access and exit so that the guests can circulate freely without becoming trapped in a corner after they have been served.

Except on a metal and glass table a cloth must always be used. It may barely cover the table, or it may hang half a yard over the edges. A tea cloth may be colored, but the conventional one is of white linen, with little or much needlework or lace, or both, or appliquéd designs.

A large tray is set at either end of the table, one for the tea, and one for the chocolate or coffee. They may be of silver or of lacquered toleware. Many of these lacquered trays are exquisite in design and color, and some of the old Chinese or English ones are priceless. The Mexican bright tin tray is often used, too.

On one tray should be the most important item of the tea equipment—the practical kettle, in which the water was boiling before being brought in and now with a flame under it. There should also be an empty teapot, a caddy of tea, a tea strainer and slop bowl, cream pitcher and sugar bowl, and, on a glass dish, thin slices of lemon.

The coffee tray is simpler. The coffee is in a large urn or pot with a flame under it, if possible. A pitcher of cream and a bowl of sugar complete the tray. If chocolate is served instead of coffee, there is nothing needed other than the pot of steaming chocolate.

If the trays are carried in by the maid, the flames under the pots are lighted as soon as the trays are set down but never before, as a terrible accident can too easily occur. Her light uniform or organdy apron needs only a stray spark to turn her into a flaming torch.

THE TABLE

The cups and saucers are placed within easy reach of the ladies who are pouring, usually at the left of the tray, because they are held in the left hand while the tea (or coffee) is poured with the right. On either side of the table are stacks of little tea plates, with small napkins matching the tea cloth folded on each one. Arranged behind these, or in any way that is pretty and uncluttered, are the plates of food and whatever silver is necessary. If the table is not large enough to hold all the plates, some may be placed on a sideboard or a small table in a convenient location.

SERVANTS NOT NECESSARY

Because nothing needs to be passed to the guests, it is perfectly possible for a hostess to give a formal tea without the help of servants. If she has no maid, the hostess would of course set out the tray with everything except the boiling water before her guests arrive, leaving the kettle on the stove in the kitchen. She greets the guests at the door, telling them where to leave their coats, and when she is ready for tea, she fills the tea-tray kettle from the kitchen kettle and carries it in to the tea table.

MAKING GOOD TEA

The most important part of the tea service is boiling water and plenty of it. The least amount of water not actually bubbling as it is poured over tea leaves turns the flavor to hay. Nothing is easier than tea-making; nothing is rarer than the hostess who knows how!

To make good tea, first, rinse the pot with a little boiling water to heat the teapot and pour out. Then put in a rounded teaspoonful of tea leaves or one tea-bag for each person or half this amount if the tea is superquality. Then pour on enough *actually boiling* water to cover the tea leaves about half an inch. It should steep at least five minutes (or for those who like it very strong, ten) before additional boiling water is poured on. Now pour half tea, half boiling water for those who like it "weak"; pour it straight for those who like it strong. The cup of *good* tea should be too strong without the addition of a little lively boiling water, which gives it freshness.

When tea has to stand a long time and for many guests, the ideal way to make it is in a big kettle on the kitchen stove, very strong, and let the tea actually boil three to four minutes on the range; then pour it through a sieve or filter into your hot teapot. The tea will not become bitter. Moreover, you do not need a strainer at the table. It does not matter if it gets quite cold. The boiling water poured over no more than the tablespoonful of such tea is hotter than most of us can drink immediately.

DRINKS SERVED AT TEA

At a tea or reception to which men have been invited, the hostess (or maid or butler) often asks a guest who has refused a cup of tea if he or she would like anything else, a whiskey and soda, or a cocktail. If there is a servant, he will serve the drink after it has been made in the pantry. If the hostess has no help, she may ask the guest to mix his own drink from a bar that has been set up in an inconspicuous place in a room separate from the tea table.

THE LADIES WHO POUR

The pouring is usually done by two intimate friends of the hostess. These ladies are always especially invited beforehand and are chosen because they can be counted on for their gracious manners to everyone and in all circumstances. Sometimes after an hour, the first two are relieved by two other intimate friends of the hostess.

It does not matter that a guest going into the dining room does not know the deputy hostesses who are pouring. It is perfectly correct for a stranger to say, "May I have a cup of tea?"

The one pouring should smile and answer, "Certainly! How do you like it? Strong or weak?"

If the visitor says, "Weak," *boiling* water is added and, according to the guest's wishes, sugar, cream, or lemon. (Good tea calls for milk, though it seems always to be called cream!) Or, preferring coffee or chocolate, the guest asks the hostess at the other end of the table for a cup of that. If either hostess is surrounded with people, she smiles as she hands her the cup, and that is all. But if she is unoccupied and her momentary guest-by-courtesy is alone, she makes a few pleasant remarks. She might say when asked for chocolate, "How nice of you! I have been feeling very neglected. Everyone seems to prefer tea." After an observation or two about the beauty of the table or how delicious the little cakes look, the guest moves away with her chocolate and joins a group of friends.

Balls and dances

Balls and dances are very similar, but there are two fundamental differences between them. First, while only those of approximately one age are asked to a dance, ball invitations are sent to *all* the personal friends of the hostess, no matter what their ages. Second, and obviously related, is the fact that fewer people are asked to a dance and so the decorations and refreshments may be but do not have to be simpler.

Although great private balls have become almost unheard of in recent years, this book would be incomplete if a description of them was omitted. Besides, the two types of balls that have replaced private ones all over the country—the charity ball and the debutantes ball—are almost identical with them in terms of customs, rules, and procedures. Thus, although you may never contemplate giving a private ball, you may some time have a daughter among the group of girls to be presented or, even more probably, you may be asked to serve on a charity committee. » *For more details on debutante assemblies, see Chapter 40.*

HOW AND WHERE TO START

The hostess preparing to give a private ball must, of course, assume the final responsibility for every aspect of the evening, but fortunately she may enlist the aid of many and various people. The club or hotel where it is to be held will provide the servants, the food, and the drinks; or, if the ball is in her home, a caterer will provide the same services. A good florist will see to the decorations, and there are social secretaries available who can help her with the lists and invitations. But no matter how much help she is able to amass, the hostess giving a private ball must make the final decisions on all the details that are so important to the success of the party.

A public ball is run by a committee, whose chairman is in some ways comparable to the hostess, but without the full burden of responsibility. Special duties are allotted to each member of the committee: one takes charge of invitations, one of decorations; others are appointed to be responsible for the orchestra, the food, the ticket money, etc. In the following paragraphs, however, wherever the word "hostess" is used, you may substitute "committee member" if the ball is other than a private one.

The first thing the hostess must do is make an appointment to see the manager of the hotel, club, or any other suitable assembly room that she prefers and find out which evenings are free. She then telephones and engages the best orchestra she can for the evening that the ballroom is available. If it can possibly be arranged, there should be two orchestras at all balls, so that the moment one finishes playing, the other begins. Music is of more importance than choice of place. You cannot give a ball or a dance that is anything but a dull promenade if you have dull music. It is also important to try to select an evening not already taken by another hostess or organization in order not to conflict either on lists or, in a small town, on the services of caterers, florists, etc.

Having secured the music and engaged the ballroom and the lounges or other rooms where guests can talk and smoke as well as dance, the hostess next makes out her list and orders and sends out the invitations.

Invitations to balls, private or public, are always formal. There are, however, many variations in good taste. » *For these forms, and also for less formal invitations appropriate to the smaller dance, see Chapter 52.*

ASKING FOR AN INVITATION

It is always permissible for you to ask a hostess if you may bring a man who is a stranger to her; men who dance are always in demand, and the more the better. But it is rather difficult to ask for an invitation for an extra girl, no matter how pretty she is, unless she is to be looked after by the person asking for the invitation. In that case, the hostess is delighted to invite her. Nor are invitations ever asked for persons whom the hostess already knows. This is a definitely established rule of etiquette, which assumes that she would have sent them an invitation had she cared to. It is not at all out of the way, however, for an intimate friend to remind her of someone who, in receiving no invitation, has more than likely been overlooked.

The one who has arranged for the invitation for the stranger should, if possible, accompany him to the ball and introduce him to his hostess. "Mrs. Norman, I would like you to meet John Franklin, my roommate, whom you were kind enough to say I might bring." If the stranger arrives alone he must introduce himself and identify the guest who arranged for his invitation. "Mrs. Norman, I am John Franklin, Bob Whiting's roommate. He was kind enough to ask you if I might come, and he is joining me here later."

A BALL IN A PRIVATE HOUSE

For a ball there is always an awning and a red carpet down the front steps or walk of the house. A chauffeur at the curb opens the car doors. If there is a great crush, there is a detective in the hall to investigate anyone who does not have himself announced to the hostess. In fact, it has become customary in New York and other big cities to have admission cards engraved and sent to all those who have accepted.

All such necessary appurtenances as awning, red carpet, coat racks, and ballroom chairs, as well as crockery, glass, napkins, waiters, and food, can be supplied by hotels or caterers.

Unless a house has a ballroom (which practically none has today), the room selected for dancing should be emptied of furniture. If it is not especially big and if there are adjoining rooms for those not dancing, the floor space can be increased considerably by putting no chairs at all in the dancing room. A more informal grouping of chairs in a large hall or in the library is a far better arrangement than the wainscot row or the wallflower exhibit occasioned by the stiff alignment of straight chairs around the dance floor. The floor itself, it goes without saying, must be smooth and waxed.

DECORATIONS

Decorations for a ball or dance may be as simple or as elaborate as the pocketbook and the taste of the hostess or committee dictate. When the ball is held during a holiday season, for example, Christmas, the decorations generally are in keeping with that time of the year. Christmas tree ornaments, even a beautifully decorated tree in one corner, red, gold, or green ribbons, and so on, might illustrate the central theme of a "Mistletoe Ball." Or the hostess might choose a type of decoration that goes particularly well in her house, perhaps Japanese lanterns and oriental flower arrangements. In any case, whether it be at home or in a public ballroom, some greens behind the orchestra, some flowers on the tables and wherever else they are most effective are all that are necessary for even the most elaborate ball.

THE GUESTS ARRIVE

The hostess must be ready to receive on the stroke of the hour specified in her invitations. If the ballroom opens on a foyer at the head of a stairway, she usually receives there. Otherwise she receives in the ballroom near the entrance.

Guests are announcd as they arrive, and after shaking hands with the hostess, they pass into the ballroom.

THE PERFECT HOST AND HOSTESS

The duty of seeing that guests are looked after, that shy youths are presented to partners, that shyer girls are not left at the wallflower outposts, that the dowagers are taken in to supper, and that elderly gentlemen are provided with good cigars falls to the perfect host. But both host and hostess must try to see that their guests are having a pleasant time.

THE PERFECT GUEST

Guests have responsibilities too. Once they have accepted an invitation, they should be pleasant and act as if they were having a good time, no matter how dull the party may be.

DUTY DANCES

Every young man must dance at least once with the hostess, the girl or girls the dance is given for, the hostess of the dinner he went to before the dance, and both girls he sat beside at dinner. At a dance to which he has brought a girl, he must of course dance the first dance with her. He must also watch during the evening to be sure that she is not stuck too long with any one partner, and he must take her home after the dance.

THE HELPFUL USHERS

The hostess who would insure the success of a dance of any size chooses from among the young men she knows best a number who are tactful and self-possessed to act as ushers. They are identified by white or other distinguishing boutonnières as deputy hosts. They must see that the wallflowers remain chair-bound as little as possible, but they must also relieve any young man who has too long been planted beside the same "rosebud."

The ushers have little chance to follow their own inclinations, and unless the honor of being chosen by a prominent hostess has some measure of compensation, the appointment—which cannot be refused—is a doubtful pleasure. An usher has the right to introduce any man to any girl without knowing either one of them personally and without asking permission. He may also ask a girl (if he has a moment to himself) to dance with him, whether he has ever met her or not. The usher in turn must release every stag he calls upon by substituting another, and the second by a third, and so on. In order to make a ball "go," meaning to keep everyone dancing, the ushers have on occasions spent the entire evening in relief work.

At a ball where there are ushers, a girl standing or sitting alone would at once be rescued by one of them, and a rotation of partners presented to her. If she is hopeless—meaning a very poor dancer—even the ushers are helpless! The answer is, of course, that she must either learn to dance or seek her popularity elsewhere, but the ushers of the evening must still do whatever they can. On the other hand, when none of her friends happens to be present and when there are no ushers, even the greatest belle of the year can spend a miserable evening. Ushers can indeed be useful and their greatest advantage is that their presence gives courage to many a young man because, assured of rescue, he is willing to dance with a girl he would otherwise avoid.

DANCE PROGRAMS

The program or dance card has some undeniable advantages. A girl can give as many dances as she chooses to whomever she chooses; and a man can be sure of having not only many but uninterrupted dances with the one he most wants to be with—if she is willing. But the dance card is unheard of at private balls, probably because the youth of today does not care to take his pleasure on schedule. He likes to dance when the impulse moves him; he also likes to be able to stay or to leave as he pleases. In New York, for example, there are often two or three dances given on the same evening, and he likes to drift from one to the other just as he likes to drift from one partner to another—or not dance at all if he does not want to. A man who writes himself down for the tenth dance must appear on the stroke of the first bar. And if he does not engage his partners at the opening of the evening, he cannot dance at all—he may not want to, but he hates not being able to.

So again we come back to the problem of the average young girl, whose right it is, because of her youth, to be light-heartedly happy, not terrified, wretched, and neglected. The best solution seems to be for her to belong to a group whose members can rely on each other during the evening. Or the problem may be solved for her if her hostess has been thoughtful enough to have efficient ushers at her dance.

THE MANNERS OF THE GUESTS

ASKING FOR A DANCE

When a man is introduced to a girl, he says, "Would you care to dance?" She may reply, "Certainly" or "Yes, I'd like to very much." Usually, however, she says nothing, gets up, or turns to him, and dances. At the end of the dance, whether it has lasted one minute or sixty, the man says, "Thank you!" or "Thanks ever so much!" On occasion he adds, "That was wonderful!" and she might say, "Thank you, I enjoyed it too."

REFUSING TO DANCE

If a girl is sitting in another room or on the stairs with a lone man, a second man should not interrupt or ask her to dance. But if she is sitting in a group, he can go up and ask her, "Would you like to dance?" She either smiles and says, "Yes," or "Not just now—I'm very tired." If she likes him, she may add to her refusal, "Come and sit with us!"

To refuse to dance with one man and then immediately dance with another is an open affront to the first one—excusable only if he was intoxicated or otherwise offensive so that the affront was justified. But in ordinary circumstances, if a girl is dancing, she must dance with everyone who asks her; if she is not dancing, she must not make exceptions.

A girl who is dancing may not refuse to change partners when another cuts in. This is the worst phase of the cutting-in custom; those who particularly want to dance together are often unable to take a dozen steps before being interrupted. Once in a while a girl will shake her head "No" to a stag who darts toward her. But that, in most circumstances, is considered rude. And there are young men who make it a rule never again to ask a girl to dance who has once refused to dance with them.

CUTTING IN

When one of the stags sees a girl whom he wants to dance with dance past, he steps forward and lays his hand on the shoulder of her partner, who relinquishes his place in favor of the newcomer, who then dances with the girl until a third in turn does the same to him.

When cutting in, the following rules must be observed: (1) The partner who was first dancing with a girl must not cut back on the man who took her from him. He can cut in on a third man if he wants to, especially if he is giving her a rush. (2) He must not continue to cut in on the same man when the latter dances with other partners.

SUPPER IS SERVED

A sit-down supper may be served by the caterer at an elaborate ball, but a buffet supper that begins at one o'clock and continues for an hour or more, to which people may go when they feel like it, is pleasanter and easier to manage. If possible, small tables should be set up so that the guests may sit down to eat after they have served themselves at the buffet. They may sit where they please, either a group making up a table or a man and his partner taking any two vacant chairs. A girl is always taken in to supper by the young man who is her escort. If there are unescorted girls at the party, the ushers (or the host, if there are no ushers) should see that one of the stags takes them to supper or that they are included in a group.

Suppers are no longer so elaborate as they used to be. Although hot dishes are still served at some balls, many times the supper consists of a variety of sandwiches, platters of cold meats, and accompanying dishes. There may be such hot drinks as coffee, chocolate or bouillon or bowls of iced fruit punch. And, of course, if it is in accordance with the customs of your community and your own taste, and if the guests are of legal drinking age, nothing is more festive than serving champagne at a ball.

Part SIX

INFORMAL ENTERTAINING

Cocktail parties

Cocktail parties have become, in many parts of the country, the most popular form of entertaining, and they can be the answer to a busy housewife's prayer. The advantages over a dinner party are many in today's society wherein relatively few households have servants and the cost of hiring temporary help or a caterer is beyond the reach of most. Cocktail parties require little preparation, they are less expensive than a dinner party, they are limited as to time, and you can entertain many more people at once in a small house. On the other hand, no one invited to a cocktail party feels as honored as if he had been invited to dinner, and at a large party the host and hostess cannot spend as much time with any one guest as if they were seated at a dinner table.

"PAY-BACK" PARTIES

One of the least attractive customs that has arisen in recent years is that of giving large "pay-back" cocktail parties. A hostess who has been invited to many parties herself and thinks she has not the time or the energy to give a number of small parties invites on one evening all those to whom she is indebted and creates one large horror! The guests are not chosen for compatability, there are not enough places to sit down, the crowd is likely to be such that no one can move freely from group to group, or table, or bar, and the noise level reaches such a pitch that it becomes intolerable. So if you are a popular guest and incur social obligations with any frequency, do make the effort to give small parties from time to time and avoid the necessity of a yearly "pay-back."

COCKTAILS BEFORE A DANCE

A pleasant form of entertaining is having a group of friends for cocktails before a dinner dance or any other function that they would enjoy attending. Invitations are sent out on visiting cards, note paper, or any printed cocktail-party invitation card, but they must state "Cocktails before the dance at the Happy Course Golf Club, 6:00 to 8:00," as well as the place and date. It is also necessary to add "R.s.v.p.," because the hostess usually makes the reservations for those of her guests who wish to go on to the other event.

The invitations may also be extended by telephone, and this is a practical method, because the hostess knows immediately how many will be joining her at the club or dance and so can make the reservations sooner.

When you are the guest, you must pay the cost of admission, dinner, drinks, and anything else at the later party unless your hostess specifically says or writes that she expects you *as her guest*. If you are not a member of the club involved, you must find out in advance whether you may sign as a member of another club or pay in cash. If either is not permitted, then you must ask your host if you may sign his name and add your initials in order to be able to pay him for your share when he receives his bill.

COCKTAIL BUFFETS

A cross between a cocktail party and a buffet dinner party, the cocktail buffet is the choice of many hostesses for entertaining all except the smallest and most informal groups. Because there is usually enough food presented so that the guests need not have dinner afterward and therefore are expected to linger longer, the invitation frequently states only the hour of arrival. In many sections of the country, this is likely to be a little later than a simple cocktail party, often 6:30 or 7:00. It should be made very clear that the gathering is a "cocktail buffet" so that the guests realize that they will be served some substantial food and need not make other plans for dinner.

The menu may vary from simple to very elaborate, but even the simplest must provide more than just hors d'oeuvres. The least that one can expect is a platter of cold meat, ham, chicken, or roast beef, slices of buttered breads, accompanying dishes such as sliced carrots, celery, olives, raw cauliflower, and possibly some sandwiches already made. This mini-

mum type of buffet may be eaten standing near the table without a plate. The meat can be placed on a slice of bread and eaten like a sandwich, and the raw vegetables picked up and dipped in a sauce if one is served. Often a smoked ham or turkey is placed whole on the table, and when the platters of meat are running low, the host, or any of the guests, may carve additional slices as they are required.

The table should be covered with a table cloth, and napkins must be available. If there is room, a centerpiece of flowers or fruit is attractive, but it is better to leave it off and use a prettily decorated cake (or even one of the main dishes) in the center rather than crowd the table.

If you are serving a more elaborate buffet, you will probably include one or more hot dishes, generally casseroles that can be kept warm on an electric hot plate or served in a chafing dish over a flame. In this case, of course, there must be stacks of plates and rows of forks. If the main table becomes too crowded, the hot dishes and plates may be put on the sideboard or on a side table.

If you do not wish to go into the added complication of plates and silver, you may choose a hot dish such as bite-sized meat balls or frank-furters, tiny hot potatoes dipped in salt, and hot bread or rolls with a cheese fondue, all of which may be speared with a toothpick.

JUST COCKTAILS

Many cocktail parties, of course, involve neither a buffet nor a dance afterward, and they may be as large or small, as simple or elaborate as you wish.

The ways of inviting people to such a party are as varied as the parties themselves. If the number of guests is small, the invitation is almost always by telephone. For a larger party, they may be written on your own informal, on note paper, or on a visiting card. (See Chapter 53 for the correct forms.) Or you may buy an attractively printed card with a rooster, cocktail glass, or other eye-catching drawing made just for the purpose.

When there is to be no buffet, the time is usually stated, "Cocktails *from* 5:00 to 7:00" rather than "Cocktails *at* 5:00." While "R.s.v.p." is often omitted, the polite and thoughtful guests let the hostess know whether they are planning to attend the party. If there is an R.s.v.p., the telephone number is usually written beside it, as this type of invitation may always be answered by telephone.

At this kind of cocktail party, you may serve literally every sort of hors d'oeuvre or appetizer that you think tastes good and looks tempting as long as it can be eaten with the fingers. Olives (either chilled or wrapped in bacon and broiled) or very tiny broiled sausages; or thin bread rolled around cheese or bacon, skewered and toasted; or crackers spread with sandwich paste; crabmeat or lobster in mouthful pieces, or shrimps on little wooden picks with which to dip them in mayonnaise or colorful sauces—all are favorites. Don't forget a pile of cocktail napkins— cloth or paper—on the tray. Most hors d'oeuvres are a little greasy, and also, since plates are not used, the napkin may be used to hold an appetizer which is, for the moment, too hot to eat.

WHAT DRINKS TO SERVE?

The most important thing about "what to serve"—whatever you decide on—is to have enough. As a general rule, a host should count on each guest having two to three drinks.

In the winter, martinis, whiskey "on the rocks," and whiskey in a tall glass with water or soda are the most popular drinks. In warm weather a cocktail mixed with fruit juice and gin or rum or tall drinks made from these same ingredients are more often served. But there is an infinite number of other drinks that are offered in different localities, and the host may choose according to his own taste or that of his guests.

Unless you know for certain that your guests all drink alcoholic cocktails, you must have nonalcoholic drinks available. Tomato juice, other fruit juices, Coca Cola, and ginger ale are all popular substitutes, but to avoid remarks that may be embarrassing to a "nondrinker," ginger ale, which looks exactly like a whiskey and soda, is very satisfactory.

Never urge a guest to have a drink—or *another* drink—if he has once refused. Why anyone should find it harder to say "No, thank you" to a cocktail than to shellfish or strawberries makes very little sense, but some people do, to their grief and yours. If someone should answer "Certainly not!" in a disapproving tone of voice, it would be extremely rude, but a polite "No, thank you!" is a courteous way of refusing. If as a guest you are pressed further, say seriously, "No—really, I can't," or as one member of Alcoholics Anonymous says smilingly but firmly, "No can take." In his case, the censure of everyone who knows his situation would rise against anyone so unthinking as to urge him.

BARTENDERS AND WAITERS

If you are planning a cocktail party of more than twelve and if you have no maid in your home, it is wise to consider hiring a bartender for the evening. If it is a really large party, the services of a waiter or waitress will make the evening much pleasanter for the hostess. She may prepare the hors d'oeuvres herself in advance, even days ahead if she has a freezer, or she may hire a waitress or caterer who will both prepare and serve the food.

The bartender attends to the drinks in any one of various ways, or he may combine several means of serving. He may stand behind a large table loaded with every sort of cocktail glass, ice, and bottles of each kind of liquor and soft drink to be served. The guests go to the bar themselves and request the kind of cocktail they wish. A gentlemen usually asks the lady accompanying him what she would like, and she waits at a little distance from the bar while he gives the order to the bartender and brings her the cocktail. If a group of women are talking together, it is perfectly correct for one of them who wishes another drink to go to the bar herself and ask the bartender to mix it for her, rather than interrupting a conversation that her husband or escort might be engaged in.

Another method of serving is for the bartender to pass a tray of drinks, already mixed, to each guest as he arrives. He may continue to do this, but it involves using an enormous number of glasses because a fresh one must be passed each time. After the first serving, therefore, it is more practical for him to watch carefully for empty glasses and, when he sees one, approach the guest and say, "May I bring you another drink?" The guest replies, "Thank you, I am drinking bourbon and soda," and hands him the glass to be refilled.

If your party is large enough to warrant having two men to serve drinks, one, acting as a waiter, may ask each new arrival for his order, go to the bar where the second man (as bartender) mixes the cocktail, and return with it to the guest. This method is rather slow for one man alone, however, especially when a large group of people arrive at the same time.

One important note to remember: Be sure that you instruct the bartender in advance exactly how you like your cocktails mixed, and insist he use a measure. If you are not familiar with the way he mixes drinks and you let him measure "by eye," you may find that your liquor supply is about to run out long before you had planned. Or you may have some unexpectedly boisterous guests on your hands!

HINTS FOR HOSTS AND GUESTS

At a small party, the hostess may introduce a newcomer to all the guests, but at a large one, after introducing a stranger to two or three people, she leaves him on his own. Her roof serves as an introduction, and unless he appears to be completely lost, she may assume that he will talk to whomever he wishes, either asking the people he has already met to introduce him to some one else or introducing himself.

There is no need to shake hands. A girl has trouble enough managing pocketbook, hors d'oeuvres, cigarette, and cocktail—and hands that have been holding a drink are cold and clammy in any case.

SELF-HELP

When there is no extra help for the evening, the host is the bartender and the hostess is the waitress. She passes the trays of hors d'oeuvres once or twice, often with a close friend helping her, and then leaves the food in a conspicuous spot (on a hot plate or in a chafing dish if the hors d'oeuvres are hot), and the guests help themselves. She must watch carefully and remove trays or dishes even before they are empty. There is nothing more unappetizing than one remaining cold, limp shrimp, or a mayonnaise-smeared platter.

The host-bartender asks each guest as he arrives what he would like to drink. If the choice is limited, he may say, "Will you have a martini or bourbon?" rather than "What would you like?" This saves them both from the embarrassment of having the guest request a drink that is not to be had. Also, he may ask the men to refill their own glasses, as well as those of any ladies who wish another. He will have much more time to mix with the group and perform his other duties as host if he does not have to spend the entire evening at the bar.

If there are only a few guests, the host may hang their coats in a hall closet. If there are more wraps than a closet can conveniently hold, the men and women are asked to put them in separate bedrooms, laid neatly on the beds. This scheme is far better than having them piled on chairs or banisters in the entry, and furthermore the ladies have an opportunity to comb their hair and freshen up before they appear in the living room.

Either the host or the hostess should stay within sight of the door to greet arriving guests, and they should try to avoid being out of the room where the party is held at the same time.

OVERSTAYING YOUR WELCOME

Cocktail parties rarely begin—or end—at the hours stated on the invitation. Although the hosts must be ready on time, the guests may—and do—arrive as much as an hour or so after the start of the party. A late arrival, however, should not mean a late departure. Every experienced hostess knows that she must expect some of her guests to linger a half hour or so beyond the indicated time, but that is as much as she should be expected to endure, and she may then take steps to hurry the last survivors out. She and her husband may put on their own coats, saying, "I'm so sorry, but we are expected for dinner in ten minutes," even though it may be the neighborhood restaurant that is "expecting" them. Or they may simply remove the liquor and close the bar. Once the guests finish the drinks in their hands and find no more being served, the party will soon be over.

Informal dinners

Every dinner party that varies even slightly from the rules laid down for "formal dinners" cannot be described as other than informal. But the degree of informality depends entirely on the circumstances and taste of the host or hostess. A hostess who has several servants (or hires several for an evening) may serve a dinner formal in all respects except that she may serve only three courses or choose to have her husband carve the roast or use her linen mats rather than her damask tablecloth, thereby, strictly speaking, making it an informal dinner. For the most part, however, she follows the practices outlined in Chapter 24 on "Formal dinners," changing only a detail or two according to her preferences.

The hostess who belongs to the great majority of women with no help at all, or with only a maid hired for the evening, should consult the chapter on formal dinners, too, for many of the suggestions made there will be equally useful as she plans and prepares for a less formal occasion. For example, the consideration given to her guest list can be no less careful than that bestowed on hers by the hostess whose household regularly includes a butler and two footmen. The rules for the informal dinner are derived from the rules for the formal dinner, and an acquaintance with both will greatly facilitate every step of the proceedings.

SIT-DOWN OR BUFFET?

Having decided to give a dinner party and knowing that, for one reason or another, it cannot be a formal one, you have a further decision to make: Will it be a sit-down dinner or a buffet?

The first consideration is the size of your party. Eight is the maximum number that can be served comfortably at a sit-down dinner without help. If you are planning to invite more than eight, you have a further choice. Should it be possible to seat more than eight at your table, you can chose to have a semibuffet, with the guests serving themselves from a sideboard, but sitting together at the table. Otherwise, you must move on to the next chapter and plan a buffet dinner. Here it is assumed that your guest list, your table, and your preference make it possible for you to give a sit-down dinner.

PREPARATION AND PLANNING

The careful planning and preparation of the meal are of utmost importance to the success of your dinner. If you as hostess wish to enjoy the company of your guests at all, you must choose dishes that can be prepared in advance and served with a minimum of last-minute fuss. You need not worry about fancy hors d'oeuvres—some salted nuts or "niblets" available in packages are preferable to elaborate spreads if you don't wish to ruin your guests' appetites for dinner.

Because the normal routine of your housework must go on along with the added work of preparing for your party, try to spread it out over several days. Cigarette boxes may be filled, flowers arranged (being sure to choose those that will last several days), silver polished, and even your table set in advance. Of course, your husband must agree to eat in the kitchen, and the children must be asked to play in other parts of the house, but any chores that can be attended to ahead make the day of the party so much more enjoyable. If you have a freezer, by all means prepare in advance whatever dishes can be frozen, too.

THE INVITATIONS

Invitations may be written on visiting cards or note paper, but they are usually telephoned. They are extended between ten days and two weeks ahead of time, and the person invited must answer promptly, either by mail or by telephone. » *See also Chapter 53, "Informal invitations," for other details.*

SEATING YOUR GUESTS

Seating arrangements at an informal dinner follow much the same pattern as at a formal one, but they are more flexible. In spite of this flexibility, thought should be given to the seating when the guest list is drawn up, for it is quite possible to make or break a party by the congeniality of dinner partners. In a group of six or ten, the host sits at one end of the table opposite the hostess, who generally chooses the location nearest the kitchen for greater convenience if she must supervise the cook or go back and forth herself. If there are eight or twelve at the table, she must move one seat to the left, putting the male guest of honor on her right opposite her husband. The lady who is guest of honor of course sits on the host's right. Among a group of friends dining together, there may be no particular guest of honor, so the hostess might choose the oldest lady present if there is sufficient difference in ages, or possibly one who has not visited her house for some time. Otherwise, she may seat her guests according to whatever arrangement she thinks they will enjoy the most, alternating the men and women. If there is an uneven number of men and women, she must space them as evenly as possible, and she may keep her place at the end of the table unless doing so puts too many women in a row. She still seats the honored guests at her right and her husband's.

SOME MENU SUGGESTIONS

Menus for an informal dinner are not bounded by rules or conventions, but there are certain practical aspects to consider. Try to avoid dishes that require many extra condiments or sauces. Because you probably wish to eliminate extra plates or silver if you are to clean up alone, restrict your courses to two or three. If you decide on only two, a main course and a dessert, you may serve more substantial hors d'oeuvres beforehand. Some hostesses, to make the serving of dinner less complicated, serve soup or a fish course, such as cold salmon or shrimp, in the living room. If this is done, the host may help his wife by removing the empty plates and ash trays quickly while she is seating the guests in the dining room. Or else the hostess must excuse herself while the guests are finishing their dessert in order to have the living room neat when they return there for coffee. If there is a maid, she should do this tidying up while the guests are eating their main course.

A roast is always delicious, and there is something mouth-watering about watching the meat being carved. If you follow a recipe that calls for it to "repose" (to be removed from the oven after a shorter cooking time than usual and to continue cooking from its own heat), even the gravy may be made before the guests arrive and kept hot in a double boiler. Creamed or curried chicken within a ring of noodles or rice is pretty and saves table space by eliminating an extra dish. Or you may invite your guests for a special dinner—lobsters flown from Maine, or shrimp cooked in beer and shelled and eaten in the fingers. With these delectable and filling dishes, you need only serve a salad, rolls, and dessert.

Whether you serve wine or beer (or milk if there are children present) is entirely up to you, but a glass of iced water should be at every place.

In recent years an increasing number of men have become interested in cooking, especially in cooking meat on a grill or spit. A marvelous sight and a fine conversation piece is a golden, aromatic, roast of beef turning over glowing coals in the fireplace when the guests arrive.

The imagination of the hostess (or host) is really the only limitation on an informal menu. But a word of caution—don't experiment with a new dish at a party. Try it out at least once on the family, so that it will be perfect when you offer it to your guests. And remember, the appearance of a dish is almost as important as its flavor. Choose a menu that has variation in color and texture—never a white sauce on chicken served with rice and cauliflower. Chops should be arranged in a pretty design rather than piled in a heap, just as asparagus neatly laid in the same direction has infinitely more appeal than a helter-skelter pile of broken stems.

CHOOSING AND SERVING WINE

More and more people are serving wine when they entertain and even at family meals. Tradition has always decreed that one particular wine goes with one particular food, but unless the meal is strictly formal, there is no reason why the host may not choose any wine he thinks his guests would prefer. Many fine wines now come from American vineyards, and their lower prices have made wine available to almost every family. Whether you prefer the dry or the sweet varieties is a matter of your own taste, and in many parts of the country, there are regional preferences as well. The most important consideration in choosing a wine is that it compliments the food you are serving it with. » *For details about the traditional choices of wine, see Chapter 24, "Formal dinners."*

SETTING YOUR TABLE

The table may be set as for a formal dinner, with a damask or lace cloth, or it may be set with individual place mats as for a luncheon. Gay,

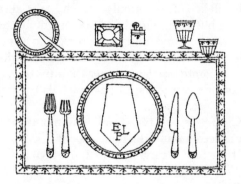

colorful cloths add much to a table set on a terrace or in an informal room, and you can buy special cloths or doilies appropriate to the season, holly-decorated ones for Christmas, or those with designs of autumn leaves or turkeys in the fall. Fruit or a combination of dried plants and flowers makes an attractive variation on the more common floral center-piece.

If a tablecloth is used, you need not set out butter plates, but with place mats, they are necessary to avoid soiling the polished surface with the buttered or crumbly rolls.

All flat silver necessary for the meal is put at each place. As always, the silver to be used last is put nearest the plate, the one to be used first on the outside. The service plate, which is an inseparable item of formal service, is put on the informal table only when it is to be used. Otherwise each place at the table is left plateless.

In many houses, the salad dressing ingredients are arranged in a set of bowls and bottles that, with the salad bowl, are put in front of the hostess, who mixes the dressing herself. In one of the loveliest old houses in the South, salad-mixing is a veritable ritual—and goodness only knows what goes into the mixture. A few drops of this, or shakes of that, or spoonfuls of the other, all stirred with a wooden fork and spoon. It is quite wonderful! And surely its deliciousness is accented by the display of its making.

The same idea exactly has made certain internationally known res-taurants famous—all because the head waiter, or the proprietor himself, cooks and mixes something before your eyes. The ducks of the "Tour d'Argent," the noodles of Alfredo's in Rome, or Japanese sukiyaki seem to acquire an added allure by the visible preparation. In short, preparing a dish at the table (which many hostesses think of as a handicap) may easily become an especially appreciated feature of hospitality.

If a course is to be served before the entrée, it may be on the table when the guests come in to dinner. In the case of fish or shrimp in long stemmed glass bowls, the service plate should be under it, and both are removed to make way for the hot plates of the main course. If your first course is soup, the most practical soup dishes are little pots with lids, which will keep the contents hot while the guests are seating themselves.

The butter should already be on the butter plates, the water glasses filled, and the wine, if it is to be served, in a cooler beside the host or in a decanter on the table. Salad is often served with the main course instead of as a separate one, and rather than putting a crisp cool salad on a hot plate or one swimming in gravy, a salad plate or a bowl may be set at the left of each place.

Cigarettes, ash trays, and condiments must all be in place, conven-iently spaced around the table.

If the host is carving a roast, or serving the meat and vegetables, the stack of warm plates may be in front of him along with the foods to be served and the necessary implements. If there is a course already on the table, however, the hostess or maid must bring the entrée in from the kitchen after the plates have been removed.

GREETING THE GUESTS

The host and hostess stay near the door if possible, or if the living room is out of sight of the door, they go together to greet their guests when the doorbell rings. The host, if he is serving cocktails, brings them what they wish, and the hostess introduces them to those they do not know.

Dinner should be planned for 45 minutes to an hour later than the time on the invitation if cocktails are served, or 20 minutes later if not, to allow late arrivals a moment of relaxation. During this period the hostess may slip out to the kitchen to attend to last minute details, making her absence as brief as possible so the guests will not feel that she is over-burdened.

INFORMAL SERVICE

WITH ONE MAID

One maid cannot possibly do all the preparing and serving of dinner in an elaborate way, but she certainly may do a great deal toward making the dinner go smoothly and allowing the hostess more time to be with

y & Co.
THE ALMOST-FORMAL DINNER TABLE

and enjoy her guests. Before dinner, if she and the hostess have planned well and prepared in advance, she may be on hand to take coats from the guests and serve hors d'oeuvres if cocktails are offered. She should attend to all the last minute details so that the hostess need not leave her guests, and when all is ready she announces dinner, or signals the hostess, who tells the guests that dinner is ready.

If a first course is served, she removes the plates when everyone is finished and either replaces each one with a hot plate or places a stack of hot plates in front of the host, depending on how she is to serve the main course. She may do this in one of two ways. First, if all the food is ready in the kitchen, she may pass the food to the guests, the meat first and then the vegetables. Second, if the host is serving, she takes each plate as he fills it and places it in front of a guest.

When the maid serves directly from the kitchen, she starts on the host's right with the lady who is guest of honor and continues around the table counterclockwise, serving the host last. Some hostesses insist that they be skipped and the maid return to serve them next to last, but this is awkward and delays the rapid serving that is so important to having food remain hot until all are served.

All dishes are served from the left and, if convenient, removed from the right. The condiments, breads, sauces, and salad are usually passed around the table by the guests themselves, but if the group is not large, the maid may pass one or more of them when she has finished with the main dishes. Condiment dishes that hold two or three varieties and divided vegetable dishes are a great help in facilitating serving. There is no reason why a competent maid may not pass two vegetable dishes at the same time, holding one in each hand.

While the guests are eating, the waitress neatens up the living room and prepares the dessert and the coffee tray. When the hostess sees that all her guests are finished, she rings and the maid clears the table. Everything is removed except the glasses and the silver for dessert. She then crumbs the table, using a clean folded napkin to sweep the crumbs onto a small plate held just below the edge of the table.

Dessert may be brought in from the kitchen already on the plates and placed before the guests in the same order as was the main course. Or the plates may be set before the guests and the dessert passed to each one in turn. If she prefers, the hostess may serve it herself at the table, especially if there is a choice, such as two kinds of ice cream.

The second way in which one maid may serve is less formal and more often used for family dinners than when guests are present. The host or hostess has all the dishes to be served arranged about him, and as he fills each plate, the maid lifts it from in front of him and passes it to each person, from the left, starting as before, with the lady on the host's right. When everyone is served, she may remove the serving dishes to be kept warm in the kitchen and pass them herself for a second helping when the hostess signals. Or if they have covers or are of pottery or other heat-retaining material, they may be left where they are. When the host wishes to offer his guests another portion, he may ring for the maid and say, "Mary, would you please bring me Mrs. Harris' plate"; she holds it for him to fill and returns it to Mrs. Harris. Otherwise, the procedure of clearing and crumbing the table is the same as that described above. If dessert is served by the hostess, the waitress passes the plates around in exactly the same manner as she passed the first course.

THE HOSTESS ALONE

When you are giving a dinner party with no help whatsoever, it is best to begin the meal with the main course and provide the equivalent of a first course by serving plenty of substantially satisfying canapés with your cocktails or before you enter the dining room.

You receive your guests and stay with them until all have arrived and "cocktail hour," if you serve cocktails, is over. Then you leave them with your husband and go into the kitchen, take the roast or other meat out of the oven, put it at your husband's place, set the vegetable dishes beside it, and then invite everyone to "Come in to dinner."

Your husband carves the roast or serves the casserole. Perhaps he also serves the vegetables, but the vegetable dishes may be handed around. When the salad is mixed, it is best to pass the bowl, each guest in turn holding it for the one on his right. Dessert may be put on each plate in advance, or you may serve it at the table as your husband did the roast.

In most cases, when the guests see you start to rise to clear the table, they will stand up saying "May I help you?" You *must* refuse, telling them, "No, really, it is easier to do it myself," or "Thank you, but we'll just get in each other's way." The only exception to this occurs when you have a daughter, sister, or very close friend at the table and have asked her in advance if she would mind helping.

In any case, alone or with help, you remove the dishes two at a time, not stacking them, and either put them on a side table or take them to the kitchen. Bread-and-butter plates, salts and peppers, and condiment dishes must be taken off also, but you need not crumb the table. Each time that you take something out to the kitchen, you may bring back dessert plates, salad and salad plates, or whatever is needed for the next course. If you wish, you may put a dessert plate at each place you have cleared as you return to take the next plate. Or as soon as you have removed your husband's plate, you may put a stack of dessert plates and the dessert in front of him and he may serve it while you are finishing the table-clearing. In other words, any system that speeds and smooths the changing of courses is acceptable, so that your guests do not feel that you are going to too much trouble.

There is no need to clear the dessert dishes, as you will say, when every one is finished, "Shall we go and have our coffee in the living room?"

At this point, one of your guests is likely to say, "Let's just wash the dishes quickly. It won't take a minute and we don't mind at all." Even if they are your closest friends or relatives, do your best to dissuade them, and if they are only acquaintances, you must flatly refuse. After all, you have invited them to your home hoping to make a pleasant break in their routine, and allowing them to do the same unpleasant chores they must do every day at home is hardly the way to make their evening the most enjoyable possible. At the same time, the considerate guest will not insist too stubbornly, because the embarrassment it may cause the hostess far outweighs the help that is given.

THE EXTRA SERVING TABLES

The only way that a hostess alone can serve a dinner without leaving the table is by the use of two serving tables, one by her side and one by the side of her husband, and each having at least one lower shelf. Tea carts make ideal tables for this purpose.

As the host fills each plate, it is passed from hand to hand down the table. The first plate goes to the lady guest of honor. The other ladies are served next, then the hostess, and finally the men, starting with the man on the hostess' right and working up the table to end with the host.

At the end of the meat course, your husband puts the meat platter on the lowest shelf of his table and the vegetable dishes beside it. He then removes the plates of the two guests sitting on either side of him, and if you are eight he asks the second beyond, on his left, to pass him his empty plate. You do the same at your end of the table, putting the used plates on the lowest shelf of your table. You both place fresh plates for salad or dessert in front of those next to you; all the silver was put at the places when you set the table, so you are ready to continue at once.

When you are six at table, you would have no trouble with this system, but the one snag at a dinner of eight is that unless you have an uneven number of men and women, you have to sit at the left of your own place at table. Then you must remember to serve only one person on your left and two on your right, because the second on your left is the guest of honor and is served by your husband.

The same plate-changing procedure follows each course, and the dessert or salad is ready beside you on the top of your serving table.

That is perhaps the nicest way of serving an informal dinner, but if you have more than eight guests or have no suitable tables, you must plan to clear the table and serve the courses with as little jumping up and sitting down as possible.

AFTER-DINNER COFFEE

When the guests are seated in the living room, take the cream out of the refrigerator and pour the coffee into whatever pot you are going to serve it from—glass, silver, or, best of all, one that has a flame under it to keep the coffee hot. It may be made and served in an electric coffee-maker, which can be plugged in again in the living room. Arrange the coffee and cream on a big tray, which is already set with sugar, spoons, cups, and saucers. It is a nice gesture to offer either a large cup or a demi-tasse, so many hostesses put some of each size on the tray. When it is all ready, you or your husband carries it in and sets it on a coffee table or on any table that has a chair nearby. You serve the coffee, asking each guest, "How many lumps of sugar?" and "Cream?" Either you or your husband may pass the cups around, or the guests may step up so you can hand it to them directly.

Just as every successful hostess has nonalcoholic drinks available for those who do not drink cocktails, she should be prepared to offer caffeine-free coffee as an alternate to regular after-dinner coffee. Or if she herself prefers caffeine-free coffee, she should offer her guests regular coffee as well.

HINTS FOR GUESTS

While most of the obligations lie with hostess at a party, there are many things that you as a guest can do to make the evening a success.

You should arrive within fifteen minutes of the time for which you were invited. More delay than that indicates that you have not made much effort, and it may ruin the hostess's carefully planned meal.

When dinner is announced, don't ignore the invitation, sitting back and sipping slowly at your full cocktail glass. On the other hand, don't jump up and fly out as if you had been kept waiting to the point of starvation. Watch your hostess and if she seems to be edging toward the door, take one more sip and rise, encouraging your companions to go with you—"Shall we go in to dinner? I think Nancy would like us to." She may say, "Dinner is ready, but don't hurry. It will stay hot for a few minutes." Unless she says, "Please bring your drink with you," don't. She may be serving wine or a meal that she does not feel is complemented by a cocktail.

When you are told which is your place, wait until the hostess starts to seat herself before you sit down, unless she says, "Please sit down. I must bring in another dish." Men, as at any meal, should help the women on their right to be seated. Don't start to eat until your hostess picks up her silver for the course. She may very well say, as the plates are passed, "Please start. I don't want your dinner to get cold," but unless she does or starts herself, you should wait for everyone to be served.

When your hostess rises to clear the table, don't jump up to help unless she has asked you to beforehand. You'll probably only get in her way. However, it can only be a help if you wish to offer to pass the cups around when she serves coffee after dinner.

And most important—remember to talk to the guests on either side of you or to enter with enthusiasm into a general conversation if the table is small.

If games are suggested after dinner, no matter how you feel about them, try to look as though you think it's a fine idea and help your hostess to organize the group. Very often, especially if the guests do not have a great deal in common, entertainment that you would ordinarily avoid can be the means of pulling a party together and making a riotous evening out of what started out as a very dull one.

30

Buffet dinners

There are three great advantages to a buffet dinner that appeal to all of us. First, you can accommodate many more guests than your dining-room table will seat—but it is important not to have so many that there will not be places for all to sit down somewhere.

Second, lack of service is no handicap. Because a buffet is truly a "do-it-yourself" party, even the hostess without a maid may spend almost the entire evening with her guests.

And third, it has the informality that most of us so much enjoy. There is something about sitting in one place before dinner, then going into the dining room and foraging for yourself, then coming back to the same place or finding a new place, that makes buffet parties the informal and popular gatherings that they are. If people are not sitting beside those they find particularly congenial, women as well as men are free to move elsewhere. A woman can even escape the most persistent of bores by going back to the buffet table and then joining whomever she chooses. So if you have never given a buffet lunch or dinner, you can't begin too soon to discover the charm and ease of this delightful form of entertaining.

WITH OR WITHOUT HELP

The duties of a hostess serving a buffet dinner alone are far lighter than those at a sit-down dinner, assuming that she has planned carefully and prepared the food well in advance. Just before she announces dinner, she must, of course, attend to such details as lighting candles, putting out iced water, and arranging the platters, casseroles, or serving dishes on the table. But the food can be all ready—in double boilers or chafing dishes or, if it is to be cold, in the refrigerator—and her last-minute chores will take her away from her guests for only a little while. After eating, the guests take their empty plates back to the dining room themselves, putting them on a side table—not on the buffet—and serving their own dessert. She and her husband may remove the dessert plates, or the guests may do it themselves. If the dining room has a door, it can be closed; or a screen can be pulled across the entrance, once all the plates have been taken there. If, however, the dining area opens onto or is a part of the living room, the hostess should remove the soiled plates to the kitchen while the guests are drinking their coffee.

If she has a maid or has hired a waitress for the evening, she has very little to do at all. When cocktails are served, she must advise the waitress when to put the food on the buffet table, watching to see that her guests are ready. The maid, in turn, signals to her when all is prepared in the dining room. The waitress should remove cocktail glasses and clean the ash trays while the guests are serving themselves, and she should take out empty plates as they set them down. She may or may not, as the hostess wishes, pass the dishes around for second helpings. Because everyone will not finish simultaneously, she should have adequate time to remove the food from the buffet table and replace it with dessert plates and dessert, or salad and cheese, or whatever is to finish the meal.

After the waitress has removed the last of the plates, she may bring in the coffee tray and the hostess pours. From then on the host takes over the serving of liqueurs and after-dinner drinks, and the maid is free to clean up the kitchen and dining room.

THE INVITATIONS

The invitation is usually written on an informal, on your note paper or across the top of the face of your "Mr. and Mrs." visiting card. » *See Chapter 53, "Informal invitations," for additional details.*

The invitation must be answered promptly for otherwise the hostess will have no idea how many to provide for. The answer can be telephoned or sent on a visiting card, merely saying "Sat. Oct. 2 with pleasure." » *See also Chapter 55, "Acceptances and regrets."*

SEATING ARRANGEMENTS

There are two ways of seating guests at a buffet dinner. First, they may simply return to the living room (where enough chairs have been placed to accommodate all), hold their plates on their laps, and set their glasses on the nearest table. Your guests will be much more comfortable and there will be much less chance of an accident, either to your rug or to your guests' clothes, if you set a small table (the folding kind that fit in a rack are ideal and easy to store) by each chair, or at least by each chair not within easy reach of a coffee or side table.

The second way of seating guests is to set out small tables—sturdy card tables, perhaps—in your living room, dining room, or library. This arrangement is, of course, dependent on your having large enough rooms so that the tables will not be in the way before dinner or while the guests are serving themselves. If you do have the space, most men and many women prefer to be seated in this way. The tables are covered with cloths that can be purchased in all colors and styles, in bridge-table size. The places are set exactly as for an informal dinner, so that the guests need not carry silver, napkins, or glasses with them, and a great deal of space is saved on the buffet table. The guests serve themselves as at any other buffet, going themselves for second helpings and removing their used plates. If the living room is used, however, the hostess must take the tables out after the meal to make room for conversational groups or whatever activity she may have planned. At a bridge party, of course, she simply takes out whatever is left on the tables and removes the cloth, leaving the tables ready to be used.

SEMIBUFFET

A pleasant way of serving a small group of friends or a family party is to arrange the food on the sideboard or a side table and set the dining room table as for a sit-down dinner. Two variations are possible. First, after the guests are seated, the host serves each plate, asking the guests, "Do you like your meat rare or well done?" or "Do you take cranberry sauce and stuffing?" The hostess passes the plate, seating herself with her own plate next to last, and the host helping himself last. She may say as she hands the plates around, "Please start, so that your dinner won't get cold." Or second, the guests may serve themselves as at a regular buffet and carry their plates to the table while the hostess watches to see whether she may help or whether they miss any of the sauces or side dishes. Again the hostess serves herself after the guests, and the host is the last.

THE INVALUABLE ELECTRIC HOT PLATE

Whichever type of buffet you are serving, the most valuable piece of equipment you can have is one that keeps things hot. I recommend an electric hot plate or tray, because on them, plates can be heated and your meal kept warm for an almost indefinite period of time. As long as your finished dish is covered so that it will not dry out, it may be placed on a hot plate an hour or more before dinner and be as delectable when it is served as it was the moment it was taken from the stove. The only exception, of course, is a soufflé, which must be served at once, and for this reason is not recommended for any large serve-yourself party. Furthermore, with an electric appliance on the buffet table, there is no need to take the dishes to the kitchen to be kept warm for second helpings. And, finally, it is unnecessary to watch and replace fuel for flame-heated chafing dishes.

SETTING THE TABLE

The difference in the principle of buffet and ordinary table setting is that objects of utility are of first importance, and unless there be ample space for both, objects that are solely for ornament are omitted. Flowers in the center of the table are lovely, of course, but if it is a question of choosing between decorative flowers and edible fruit, a centerpiece of dessert fruit is preferable.

In the same way, if the table is crowded and candles are not needed to see by, they are better left off. If candles are needed, candelabra are better than candlesticks because, first, they give better light and, second, they are less likely to be knocked over by a guest reaching for a plate of food.

If the party is large, it is better to leave the table in the center of the room, so that two lines of guests may serve themselves at once. Then the most important dish is divided into two parts, and one plate or casserole placed at each end of the table. The plates are in two stacks beside them, and the napkins and silver neatly arranged next to the plates. Dishes of vegetables, salads, bread and butter, and sauces and condiments are on each side of the table so that the guests need to pass down only one side—greatly speeding the service and keeping them from turning back and bumping into each other.

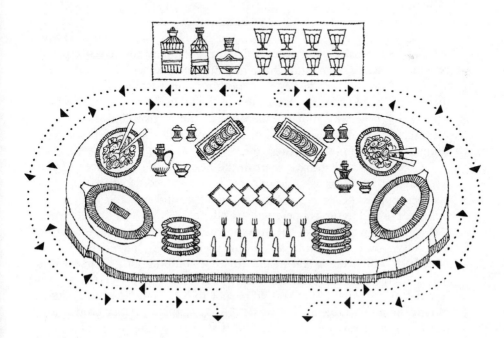

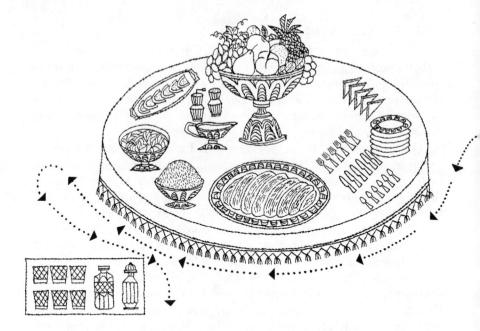

If the table is set against the wall, place your plates and main dish at the end that makes for the best flow of traffic, usually the one farthest away from the door so that the guests may leave the dining room without pushing through the line waiting to be served.

The table may be set as formally or informally as you wish. If you use a white damask cloth, silver candelabra, and an elaborate centerpiece, your buffet will appear quite formal. But you may go to the other extreme and use pottery dishes with nothing but a hot-plate pad under them and a bowl of fruit in the center of the table. The thing that makes your table attractive is not the elegance of the utensils and decorations you use, but the combination of dishes, linen, and silver and the way in which they are arranged on the table.

Color plays an enormous part in the beauty of a buffet table. If you have copper bowls or a kettle or a copper-bound beer keg, red-cheeked peaches, apples, pears, purple grapes, bananas, and oranges, even a few tomatoes to add to the coppery red, are effective.

With copper, keep all the autumn tints in mind: green, red, russet, and yellow on a bare table. Or if you prefer, a red or green or yellow tablecloth will make a warm and inviting combination. Coarse white damask tablecloth and napkins dyed a fairly strong color make an ideal foundation for a table that you prefer not to have bare. Especially suitable for the buffet table are strong colors like eggplant, russet brown, lobster red, leaf green, and dark blue; or if you are setting your table with stainless steel, additional colors of tablecloths to choose from include turquoise blue, emerald green, and charcoal gray.

Generally red and white wine, possibly a punch or other cold drink, iced water, and beer left in its cans or bottles, together with glasses, are on the sideboard as well as a large urn of coffee, which should be available during the meal as well as afterwards.

Because the coffee is already on the sideboard, the guests may serve themselves, but the hostess, if she wishes, may take an additional tray, set with cups, a coffee pot, cream, and sugar in to the living room to serve those guests who may not have noticed it or wanted it with their dinner.

When there are no little individual stands or tables and guests must put their glasses beside them on the floor, it is wise to use iced-tea glasses or highball glasses as they are steadier than goblets. If the beverage is served with ice in the glass, it should not be put down on a table unless coasters are provided.

THE MENU

It does not matter what foods you happen to choose so long as they are good of their kind and easy to eat with fork alone (although this is not important if you are seating your guests at tables). Otherwise, merely

use a reasonable amount of common sense in selecting dishes that will be satisfying to the people invited. Don't feed hungry men bouillon, dabs of hors d'oeuvre, samples of fruit salad, and meringues. For women alone, food might be trifling; but for normal men with good appetites, you should provide three or four dishes that are substantial, and at least one of these should be hot.

Substantial dishes include, for example, most meats, fish in a sauce such as Newburg, potatoes, and the heavier desserts. Nearly everything made in a baking dish or casserole is ideal for a buffet meal, not only because it is hearty, but because it is easily kept hot.

There are countless delicious menus to be tried; the only limit is your imagination. If you wish to be very elaborate, or if you have a great many guests, you may wish to serve two main dishes, possibly a lobster Newburg at one end of the table and beef stroganoff at the other. But choose two dishes that will be complemented by the same vegetables and condiments, or you will have more preparation than you can easily handle and not enough space on your table for all the dishes.

Here are some menu suggestions, ranging from an elaborate buffet to a very simple family-type menu. You may, of course, use any combination that appeals to you, omitting or adding to each menu as you wish.

Veal Scaloppine   Roast Turkey
Mashed Potatoes
String Beans with Mushrooms
Cranberry Sauce, Stuffing, Gravy
Buttered Rolls
Fresh Fruit Compote
Cookies
Coffee

Italian Spaghetti and Meatballs or Lasagne
Mixed Green Salad
Choice of Roquefort, French, Italian Dressing
French or Italian Bread, Butter
Lemon Ice
Coffee

Hungarian Goulash or Beef and Kidney Pie
Noodles
Glazed Carrots
Green Salad with Mandarin Oranges
Buttered Rolls
Coffee

Curried Lamb or Chicken
Rice Ring
Chutney, Raisins, Ground Nuts
French Bread, Butter
Raw Spinach Salad
Ice Cream and Cake or Cookies
Coffee

For a summer evening:

Three or four varieties of cold sliced meats such as
Ham, Turkey, Roast Beef, Lamb, or Cold Cuts
Scalloped Potatoes
Vegetable Salad
Buttered Rolls
Vanilla Ice Cream with Green Mint Sauce
Cookies
Coffee

A good suggestion for a Friday evening when some of your guests may not wish to eat meat:

Lobster or Shrimp Newburg   Beef Stroganoff
Rice
Green Peas and Onions
Croissants
Caesar Salad
Cheese and Crackers
Fresh Fruit (apples, pears, seedless grapes)
Coffee

THE PARTY ITSELF

So let us say that the table is set with all the cold foods and the dining-room lights are lighted and the hot foods are ready to be brought in from the kitchen or are already on their hot plates or in their chafing dishes, and let us go with the host and hostess into the living room and wait for the guests to arrive.

As people enter the room, the host and hostess go forward to greet them and perhaps introduce any who may for the moment find themselves alone. It must always be remembered, of course, that at every small and particular party (as distinguished from a huge and general one) the roof of a friend's house serves as an introduction, and one talks with those whom one finds nearby, whether he knows them or not.

When the guests have arrived and the cocktails, if served, are finished, the door into the dining room is opened and people in more or less of a queue file around the dining table. The women as well as the men help themselves, because they like to see what there is to eat and to take just what they want. Sometimes, however, and quite correctly, a man may ask a woman what she would like, fill a plate, and take it to her.

A man seeing a woman sitting without a plate or with an empty one naturally asks her (whether he knows her or not), "Can't I get you something to eat?" If she says, "Yes, please," he brings her whatever it is she would like. But most likely she says, "Thank you, but I'm going into the dining room in a moment."

If people continue to sit and wait to be served, the hostess has to direct them as she would direct children at a party, saying, "Please go into the dining room and help yourself to what you like." Then, if they stand blockading the table, carrying on a long conversation, she has to say, "Won't you please take your plate and go into the other room again and sit down?"

Important item: plenty of ash trays. For a buffet supper recently, a New York hostess went to a ten-cent store and bought fifty ash trays. She put two of them on each step of her staircase—one next to the wall and one on the outer edge and the others in every space that could possibly serve as a cigarette parking place.

The only serving detail of importance in a buffet meal is the clearing away of used dishes and the unceasing emptying of ash trays. In a house with servants, every plate is removed as soon as it is put down and filled ash trays are constantly replaced. Also, if there are servants, the glasses of those seated are refilled from time to time, and the main dishes may be passed for second helpings. But the only thing the servantless hostess can do is to ask one or two members of her family—or her most intimate friends—to help her put used dishes in several spaces provided, from which she can stack them and take them away as easily and unobtrusively as possible.

31

Informal luncheons

Just as the informal dinner is a less elaborate version of the formal dinner, so the informal luncheon resembles the informal dinner. Because of the hour, the guests are usually all women, although on weekends or holidays it is not uncommon to have a mixed group. If men are included in the guest list, the meal is likely to have a stronger resemblance to the informal dinner, for the menu, though shorter than the dinner menu, must be fairly substantial lest half the guests go away hungry.

Again, the type of luncheon you give depends upon the resources of your dining room, the number that can be seated at your table, and the help that you will have with the serving. If you are one of those who have a very small dining room, or perhaps no dining room at all, but have a living room or a patio large enough to permit two or three small tables to be set up, a luncheon of eight or twelve, perhaps followed by bridge, is one of the nicest parties imaginable.

Each card table should be set with a cloth, either white or colored, a yard and a half square, which is much the best covering for lunch as well as dinner on small tables. Any style of small tablecloth will do, of course, but they should, if possible, be exactly alike. Better to have simple, matched ones than assorted, elaborate ones. A small flower arrangement makes the prettiest centerpiece.

SERVING THE LUNCHEON

THE HOSTESS ALONE

If you are serving without the help of a maid, you will be wise to make your party a buffet luncheon. The food is set out as for a buffet dinner, on the dining-room table or any table with sufficient space, but for a ladies' luncheon, the fare is much simpler than for a dinner. Among a group of eight or twelve women, there are almost always some who are watching their calories, so a delicious but light meal is far more appreciated than one dressed with rich sauces and ending with "gooey" sweets.

As soon as you announce that luncheon is served, your guests file past the table and serve themselves, taking their plates to the card tables and seating themselves with whomever they wish. If you are having a course before the entrée, it should already be on the tables when your guests arrive, and they sit down and finish it before going to the table for the main course. If there is no maid to help, the guests should take their empty plates and leave them on a side table as they go to get their next course. While they are helping themselves, you may remove the soiled dishes to the kitchen.

The same procedure is followed when the guests are ready for the salad or dessert. You then ask them to go to another room, or at least to leave the tables and sit on more comfortable chairs to have their coffee, giving yourself a chance to clear away the remaining glasses and silver and the cloths from the table and, if bridge is to follow, set out the cards. There should always be two decks of *clean* cards, and at least two score pads and two pencils on each table. » *For further details about card parties, see Chapter 35, "Other informal gatherings," and Chapter 68, "In games and sports."*

WITH THE HELP OF A MAID

When you have a maid to help you, she can serve eight or twelve guests quite easily if the first course is already on the table. She may clear the plates by standing at the table corner, taking two at a time, one in each hand. The menu should be limited to a single dish and salad, or it will take a rather long time to serve, as she must pass the food in the usual way, from each person's left. The salad may be all ready in small bowls or plates, which she may bring in two at a time to place on the guests' left. Rolls, butter, and iced water and any other beverage should be put on the table beforehand.

When dessert is finished, the waitress carries the coffee tray to another room and, if part of the plan, readies the tables for bridge, while the hostess pours the coffee.

ON FOOD AND DRINK

If you wish to serve cocktails before lunch, you may, but the time should be limited, especially if everyone is looking forward to playing cards. And the drinks should be of a milder type than those served before dinner. Sherry, Dubonnet, and vermouth, either "on the rocks" or in a wine glass, are ideal luncheon cocktails, but you may, if you know your friends prefer them, serve martinis or daiquiris, too. A "Bloody Mary" is very popular nowadays, made with seasoned tomato juice and vodka, and you may serve a "Bloodless Mary" to those who prefer their tomato juice without the vodka.

Two or three courses are sufficient at any informal luncheon. If you serve many more than that and then move to the bridge table, you will find some of your players falling asleep over their hands!

Four of the following menus have been planned with the idea that you can have all the preparation finished in advance. But the main dishes in the first and last should be cooked and served at an exact moment, and I would save those menus until a day when you have some help in the kitchen.

Fresh Fruit Cup
Filet of Sole Amandine
Spinach Salad with Chopped, Hard-boiled Egg, Tart Dressing
Buttered Rolls
Orange Chiffon Cake
Coffee

Clam or Oyster Chowder with Oyster Crackers
Fruit Salad and Cottage Cheese
Melba Toast
Chocolate Mousse
Coffee

Cold Salmon with Green Mayonnaise Sauce
Sliced Cucumber and Tomato
Protein and White Toast
Lemon Chiffon Pie
Coffee

Curried Chicken with Rice Ring
Mixed Green Salad
Baking Powder Biscuits
Jello made with Fresh Fruit
Coffee

Little Neck Clams, or Oysters
Cold Sliced Roast Beef, Horseradish Sauce
Potatoes au Gratin
Watercress and Tomato Salad
Fresh Strawberries and Sour Cream
Coffee

Cheese Soufflé (if your guests can be trusted to arrive on time)
Asparagus Vinaigrette
Croissants
Crackers and Cheese
Coffee

BEVERAGES

Iced tea and iced coffee are delicious with luncheon, especially in the summer. It is nice to give your guests a choice by passing a tray with a pitcher of each or by having both available close to the buffet table. A bowl of fruit punch may take the place of iced tea or coffee and appears cool and refreshing if it is prepared with floating slices of orange and lemon and is surrounded by glasses or cups adorned with fresh sprigs of mint.

In the winter, many hostesses like to have hot coffee or tea or chocolate in a convenient spot where the guests may help themselves.

A light wine may be served, although it is not necessary, especially if you have offered cocktails.

A pitcher of iced water, from which the guests may help themselves, should always be in evidence, or glasses of water may already be on the table if it is not a buffet luncheon.

LATER IN THE AFTERNOON

On a hot summer day when people have been playing cards for an hour or a little over, a tray should be brought in with a large pitcher of ice water and perhaps another pitcher of iced tea and put it down on a convenient table. The one thing that hostesses tend to forget is that five people out of six long for a cold drink in the afternoon more than anything else. Occasionally sandwiches and cookies are brought in, as well as the iced tea, but these are not necessary when bridge follows a luncheon. (If you were inviting people to come at two and play for the afternoon, light refreshments would be considered necessary between half past four and five o'clock.)

32

Informal dances

Dances that are less sumptuous and less formal than balls may be given for any number of reasons, from the very specific—introducing a new neighbor, perhaps—to the very general—your friends like to dance and no other excuse is necessary. But whatever the occasion and the degree of informality, certain points should be kept in mind if your dance is to be a success.

EVENING DANCES

If the dance is for adults, the invitations are usually written on a visiting card or an informal. For a dance for young people, they may be written in the same way, but unless it is quite a formal affair, invitations are more often sent out on commercial "party" invitations, which have attractive drawings on the outside and spaces for writing time, address, and type of party on the inside. Remember to include at the bottom a hint about clothes. Nowadays, young peoples' parties, even dances, are so informal that clothing may be anything from suits for the boys and "party" dresses for the girls to Bermuda shorts for both. An R.s.v.p. with a telephone number beside it is the surest way of having some idea of how many will be at the party.

For a young person's party or for an adult's, the invitation may always be by telephone. » *For additional details, see Chapter 53.*

DECORATING THE ROOMS

When the dance is held in your own home rather than a public room of any sort, the most important thing is a large enough clear space and a floor properly prepared for dancing. If it is possible, all the furniture should be removed from the room, but if it is not, take out whatever you can and move the rest close to the wall. The rugs must be rolled and put away and the floor freshly waxed.

Decorations are not too important. A few flowers placed where they are not in the way—on a mantle, for instance—are sufficient. If the party is held during a holiday season, such appropriate decorations as Christmas ornaments or Valentines on the walls add a festive note.

TEA DANCES

An afternoon tea dance often takes the place of the old-fashioned debutante ball. » *See Chapter 27, "Balls and dances."* It may equally well be given to introduce a new daughter-in-law. On occasion, it may be your responsibility to see that someone who has moved to your community is properly introduced, and a tea dance serves this purpose very well.

Invitations, especially to a dance given to introduce the bride of a son, are usually written on the visiting card of the hostess with "To meet Mrs. Grantham Jones, Jr." across the top. It is equally correct, however, to use the inside of a fold-over card or an informal. They may also be telephoned.

Nowadays houses large enough for dancing are comparatively few, and growing fewer. As a result, the tea dance is usually given at a club or in a small ballroom of a hotel. Remember, however, that it is a mistake to choose too large a room, for too much space for too few people gives an effect of emptiness that is always indirectly suggestive of failure. Also one must not forget that an undecorated public room needs more people than a room in a private home to make it look filled. Although a crush may be unpleasant, it does always give the effect of success. Nothing is more dismal than a half-empty room with bored looking guests.

The arrangements for a tea with dancing are much the same as for an evening dance. A screen of greens in front of which the musicians sit, perhaps a few green vines here and there, and flowers on the tables form the typical decorations.

Whether in a hotel, club ballroom, or a private drawing room, the curtains are drawn, and the lights lighted as though for a dance in the evening.

Usually only tea, chocolate, breads, and cakes are served. In some localities coffee is offered instead of chocolate. There may be all sorts of sandwiches, made with rolls or bread, and there may be layer cake, sliced cake, and all imaginable kinds of little cakes. Nothing more elaborate is necessary. At the end of the table or on a separate table nearby are bowls or pitchers of orangeade or lemonade or punch for the dancers, exactly as at an evening dance.

Guests go to the table and ask whoever is serving for chocolate, coffee, or tea and help themselves to the sandwiches or cakes, which they eat standing at the table, with cup and saucer held in the left hand.

OUTDOOR DANCES

If you are fortunate enough to have a smooth terrace, a stone patio, perhaps beside a swimming pool, or even a built-in dance floor in the lawn, an outdoor dance on a summer evening is one of the most romantic and gay ways of entertaining. Small tables should be set up near the dance floor, with enough chairs for all who are not dancing. The bar, if you are serving liquor, and the table with refreshments should be nearby.

Plenty of light is important. If the music is provided by an orchestra, there must be light for them to see their music, and also for the bartender and waiters if you have them. Your guests may be delighted to dance on a moonlit floor, but when they are ready to sit down, uneven ground or steps may be a hazard if not well lighted.

Before planning an outdoor dance, arrangements should be made to insure the guests' comfort in case of rain. Either you must have a large enough tent or marquee available to cover chairs, tables, and dance floor, or you must be prepared to move the entire party into your house.

THE IMPORTANCE OF GOOD MUSIC

Probably the most important thing in assuring the success of a dance is good music. Therefore, although you may save as much as you can on decorations and refreshments, spend as much as your pocketbook can afford on the music. If it is within your means, hire the best orchestra you can obtain, even though you may only be able to get three pieces. Rhythm, gaiety, and a knowledge of the taste of the age group at the party are the essential qualities that the orchestra must have. If the guests are people in their fifties, they will probably not want to dance the latest fad of the teen-age set all night. By the same token, teen-agers would think a party a miserable failure if the orchestra played nothing but fox-trots and waltzes.

If you simply cannot hire an orchestra and are planning to use a phonograph, choose records that were specifically intended for dancing and ones that will appeal to your guests. If you borrow records from your friends—and many people do in such a situation—be sure the owner's name is clearly printed on the label in indelible ink or put on with marking tape.

DANCE MANNERS

Good manners at a dance are the same for young and old alike. Whatever the local customs about cutting in, double cutting (that is, switching partners on the dance floor), and so on, a man must dance with his hostess, and he must dance the first and last dances with the lady he brought to the party, be it friend or wife.

At a dance where the guests are married couples, there may be few or no extra men, and the only time to change partners may be during the intermission or when the music starts again. At this type of party, there are almost always tables to which the couples return between dances, and the men must ask their wives, as well as the women next to them and their hostess, to dance. If the hostess is at another table, a man should not ask her to dance until he is sure that all the women at his table have partners or at least that there are several men and women remaining at the table so no one woman is left alone. Under no circumstances should the men hold a "stag party" in the bar, leaving the women at the table without partners.

When the dance is over, every guest must, of course, find his host and hostess, thank them, and say "good night."

33

Picnics

From earliest spring until latest autumn the very proposal, "Let's give a party," is almost certain to suggest a picnic to those who enjoy them. In its essential outline, going on a picnic means the packing of a lunch basket—possibly several baskets—with things to eat and drink, and then either walking or sailing, bicycling or driving to some pleasant outdoor spot, and eating this lunch or supper.

Although picnics can be utterly delightful when well managed, they can be altogether awful when bungled! Therefore here are a few general directions for the benefit of those who want to have a successful picnic.

WHAT KIND OF PICNIC?

DUTCH TREAT OR HOST'S TREAT?

There are several ways of organizing a picnic.

The first is to give the entire picnic yourself, inviting the guests by telephone and saying "John and I are giving a picnic on the South Beach on Friday evening. I hope you and Harry can come." If they accept, tell them the hour and where to meet and possibly ask them to bring a blanket or back rest if the party is large and you do not have enough for everyone.

Or you may call and say, "Mike and I are trying to get a group to-gether for a picnic Saturday night. We'll bring the steaks, and we're ask-ing each couple to contribute one dish. Would you rather bring dessert or salad?" Others might be asked to bring the condiments, chowder, corn, or the drinks.

Lastly, a group of friends may simply arrange to picnic together, each family bringing their own food and cooking it over a community fire. It is rather fun to see what the others have prepared, and often there is considerable trading and sharing. "I'll trade you a chicken leg for a lobster claw" or "Do try some of this special steak sauce that Susie taught me to make." This sort of picnic is especially good if children are in-cluded, as each mother knows best what her young ones will eat most happily.

TAIL-GATE PICNICS

Tail-gate picnics have come into being with the universal popularity of the station wagon. They are particularly suitable on two occasions. First, if you are making a long trip and do not wish to take too lengthy a break for lunch, you may pull over to the side of the road (preferably in a "rest area" if you are on a big highway, because of the receptacles provided for garbage, etc.), let down the tail-gate, spread out your picnic on it, and eat, in no time at all.

The other occasion that has gained tremendous popularity is the lunch before a college football or baseball game. Call your classmate who lives in another town—"How about meeting us at the No. 2 parking lot at the stadium, before the State vs. Hometown game in October? We'll bring the food and you bring the drinks, and we'll have a reunion!" Hav-ing arranged the meeting place specifically, you load your whole family into the station wagon and enjoy the game after a sumptuous meal cooked on your folding grill and a chance to catch up on all the news of old friends. In fact, many of those friends may turn up in the same parking lot.

The tail-gate takes the place of a folding table, and the only extra piece of equipment that is necessary is a piece of oilcloth or plastic to lay on it, as the floor of the car and the inside of the tail-gate are likely to be dusty or sandy.

CLAMBAKES

The preparations for a clambake are quite specialized; but if you know how a seaweed oven is made (practically, as well as theoretically), and you have a loyal friend who is willing to help or if someone on your beach has had long experience in preparing and timing the baking of corn on the cob and potatoes and the clams and lobsters, nothing is more in keeping with a holiday at the seaside than a clambake. In recent years, it has become necessary to suggest that you make sure there is enough seaweed on your beach as well as rocks to line your pit, before you think of a clambake—and I repeat, do not attempt one at all if you are not an expert, or if you are not willing to devote the entire day to the preparation. The fire must be lit in the morning and from then on must be tended constantly or your pit will not be hot enough to cook the "bake."

YOU'RE THE HOSTESS

If you wish to entertain friends by taking them on a picnic, your first task is to consider your guest list very carefully. Nothing is so dampening to the enjoyment of a picnic as the presence of one or more fault-finders who never lift a finger, but sit and complain of the heat, of the sun, or the chill of the wind, or a possible shower, or the danger of sitting on the ground, or of their personal sufferings caused by mosquitoes or black flies, as though their tender skins alone were sensitive to these trials. On the other hand, if you select your company from among those who have a genuine passion for picnics (these are really the only ones to invite for an enjoyable time), not only will they make everyone forget blowing sand and inquisitive ants or hungry mosquitoes, but most likely they will work like beavers.

Knowing that you have a congenial group and considering the ages and preferences of your guests—whether adults and children or just adults—you may now decide whether you are going to give what is merely an outdoor lunch or supper, meaning that you will take only things that are ready to serve—a basket of sandwiches, or cold chicken and salad, and a thermos of liquids—or whether you are going to build a fire and cook.

Then you must choose the location. If you live near the mountains, you may decide to climb or drive to a site that has a beautiful view, but if there are children in the party, be sure there is a field nearby for games or races, or a stream in which they may swim. Advice scarcely necessary to offer is that for your picnic you select a site that you know something about—because you have picnicked there before and know that the ground is not swampy, or that it is not more mosquito or ant-infested than anywhere else, or that it is not covered with poison ivy.

If it is to be on a beach, it is well to remember to make some preparation to shield both your guests and the food they are to eat from blowing sand. For this nothing is better than a few ordinary five-foot garden stakes and a few yards of burlap with a hem at each end of each length, through which stakes are inserted and then thrust into the sand to form a windbreak. If you are going to be on the beach all day, an umbrella is a must for those who are not well tanned or accustomed to so much sun.

By the way, if you are giving a large picnic and including a number of people of average variety—by this I mean not picnic addicts—it is important to select a site that is easy to get to or away from. You may have a jeep or "beach buggy" and can arrive at a remote part of the beach with no effort at all, but don't expect your guests to tramp through miles of soft sand, carrying blankets, beach towels, and back rests.

Having made up your mind as to what to cook and where to cook or eat it, it is important to make as careful preparations as you would were you inviting people to dine or to lunch with you at home. You wouldn't ask people to lunch at one o'clock and then think it quite all right to serve at three; nor would you be blissfully content to give them fish, or steak, or chicken, one side of which is raw and one side charred to a cinder, and there is no more reason to do this at an outdoor meal than an indoor one.

HOT OR COLD?

The very simplest type of picnic is a "continental" picnic, straight from the farmers of Europe. It consists of a loaf of bread, a piece of cheese, and a bottle of wine. If the cheese and wine are good and the bread fresh, this menu has all the advantages of being delicious, nourishing, requiring no preparation, and costing next to nothing. But in spite of the ease of getting together and carrying the ingredients of a "continental" picnic, most Americans prefer to expand the menu in varying degrees. Using the three items above as a base, you may add whatever you wish—fruit for dessert, little tomatoes as a vegetable, tins of sardines or meats, and so on.

If there are children included in the picnic, sandwiches are the most popular food of all. Peanut butter and jelly outstrip any other variety in popularity contests among the very young. Adults and children alike enjoy meat sandwiches, well seasoned and with a little butter or mayonnaise to moisten the bread. Don't, however, make the mistake of using too much mayonnaise or using tomatoes and other "runny" ingredients, as the sandwiches will turn to mush on the way to the picnic grounds. Don't attempt to take bread and fillings separately and let people make their own. The messiest picnic that can be imagined is one at which knives and plates and bread and butter and a half dozen jars of jams and meat pastes are all spread around and flavored with sand or ants.

It is wise to offer a choice of two or three kinds of sandwiches, and by all means label each variety, especially if they are wrapped in foil. Wrapping and unwrapping and pulling apart to view the insides can make a hash of the most beautifully prepared sandwich.

To accompany the sandwich menu, there should be a selection of potato chips, pickles, tomatoes, carrot and celery sticks, or jars of potato or macaroni salad. Cake or cookies or any other dessert that may be eaten with the fingers (seedless grapes are among the most popular with all ages) makes a perfect ending. Thermos jugs of milk or soft drinks for the children and beer, iced tea, or coffee for the adults complete the meal.

Cold menus may be much more elaborate than sandwiches. In fact, if you have the necessary equipment, you may have an entire buffet spread on a folding table. But most people prefer a simpler picnic, and the main requirement is that the food is the best of its kind. Cold fried chicken, or cold boiled lobster, accompanied by coleslaw or lettuce brought in a damp cloth and mixed with dressing when the group is ready to eat, bread and butter, and fresh fruit for dessert make a meal that is truly "fit for a king."

When the nights are cool, or simply because you prefer it, you may wish to serve a hot dish on your picnic. Again you have a choice to make. Do you wish to bring a main dish already made, in an insulated container, or do you wish to build a fire and cook your meal at the picnic site? Stews complete with potatoes and other vegetables, creamed chicken with noodles, roast-beef hash made with potatoes, or filling chowders are all excellent choices. All keep indefinitely in big thermos jugs or any other well-insulated container.

Many men enjoy cooking meat over an open fire, and they generally have more assistance and suggestions than they need from their male guests. If your husband likes to do it, or if you do yourself, there is nothing more delicious than meat or fish cooked over coals. Steak, lamb chops, chicken, swordfish, or lobster are all superb when done in this fashion, and hot dogs and hamburgers change from an uninspired meal to a delectable treat. Whole potatoes or corn, wrapped in foil and roasted in the coals, and a mixed green salad make the best accompaniments, along with as many condiments such as mustard or ketchup as you can fit into your baskets. Cold, sliced watermelon or perhaps an angel food cake and fresh strawberries, already sugared, might finish the meal.

Your plates for a "hot" picnic must be of something more substantial than uncoated paper, and plastic ones are really most satisfactory, even though they must be taken home to be washed. Plastic bowls or cups for chowder are far more leak-proof and easier to hold than paper cups. As long as you are bringing the utensils for this type of meal, there is no reason not to accompany your main dish with a salad already mixed in a big bowl and breads kept warm by several layers of foil wrapping.

Good strong coffee in a thermos, and plenty of beer and soft drinks kept cold in a tub of ice should be on hand for the singing around a roaring fire that should be a part of every evening picnic.

EQUIPMENT

Several items of equipment available at hardware stores, chain stores, or specialty shops are a delight to any picnic enthusiast. Styrofoam containers, which will keep food either hot or cold and weigh almost nothing, are a must. Another excellent item is an insulated wide-mouthed jug or thermos to carry anything from cold vichysoisse to hot lamb stew.

Portable grills with folding legs are a great help if you are planning to cook, although on the beach you may simply scoop a hole in the sand, put in the charcoal, and lay a grill from your oven across it, resting it on a sturdy board pressed into the sand on either side of the hole.

Charcoal briquettes in a cardboard container save the trouble of taking newspaper or lighting fluid, and they are easier to carry than a large bag of charcoal. All one has to do is to touch a match to the cardboard and your fire is started. And one warning—don't try to cook until the flame has died down and the coals have turned white, with a faint red glow here and there.

A two-sided grill, hinged on one end, and with a long handle, is wonderful for holding and turning hamburgers, hot dogs, and steaks. It eliminates the danger of the hot dogs rolling between the rungs of a larger grill into the fire, or the hamburgers sticking and crumbling when they are turned.

A pair of long tongs is useful for arranging coals and for moving anything that is hot. They are ideal for turning potatoes or corn as they cook in the coals and better for turning a steak than a fork, which pierces the meat and allows the juices to escape.

There are many other items that add greatly to the ease of preparing a picnic, and each picnic fan must decide which please him most. In general, it is best to choose those articles that are the most compact and lightweight and those that may be used for several purposes so that they are not limited to a sandwich-and-cold-drink picnic or to a cooking picnic, but can be useful in transporting or preparing either.

A CHECK LIST

The perfect picnic manager, like the perfect traveler, has made simplification an exact science. She knows very well that the one thing to do is to take the fewest things possible and to consider the utility of those few.

Fitted hampers, tents and umbrellas, folding chairs and tables are all very well in a shop—and all right if you have a trailer or a station wagon for hauling them. But the usual flaw in picnics is that there are too many things to carry and look after and too much to clean and pack up and take home again.

Therefore, for those who organize picnics frequently, it is a good idea to make up a list of all items that may be needed and check it each time before leaving. All the equipment may not be necessary for every picnic, but a list will prevent the salt or the bottle opener from being omitted!

LEAVING THE PICNIC SITE

No matter where your picnic has taken place, make sure not only to tidy up before you leave, so that no trace will be left, but to be careful, while you are eating and opening papers, that you don't carelessly throw them aside where they will blow out onto the road. Many of our highways have pleasant wayside parks for picnickers, equipped with rustic tables, safe drinking water, and incinerators. On the property of a private owner, the least payment you can make is to be sure that you do nothing that might despoil any of his property.

Most important of all, *never* leave a fire without being absolutely certain that it cannot spread or ignite any dry material nearby, causing a major blaze. In the woods, water may be poured on the logs until there is no sign of steam, or if you have a shovel or other means of lifting them, the embers may be carried to a nearby pond or stream and thrown in. On the beach, the fire may also be put out with water. Do *not* cover the coals with sand, however, as they will retain the heat for hours, and someone walking by with bare feet, unable to see the remains of the fire, may step on the hot sand and receive a terrible burn.

Barbecues

A barbecue is essentially a cooking picnic in your own yard, but because of the proximity to your house, your menu and equipment may be more elaborate because you are not limited by how much can be transported in your car.

ARRANGING YOUR DINING AREA

If you have a built-in grill in your yard or patio, you are fortunate indeed, but it is not at all necessary. A portable grill, either one on wheels or the folding variety, serves just as well. There should be a table, or tables, near the fire to hold the food and the plates, cooking utensils, and any other necessary equipment. There must be seating facilities for every guest. If your garden has a wall or if the patio has steps leading to it, these may be used as seats, but it is thoughtful to provide cushions, if you have them, to cover hard stone or cement. If you do not have enough small chairs that can easily be carried to the yard, it is possible to rent them for very little money from a caterer.

SETTING THE BARBECUE TABLE

In setting the table for a barbecue, you may give your flair for color and decoration a free rein. Checked or striped tablecloths, ones with splashy designs of fruits or flowers, or those with bright red lobsters or colorful chefs' hats are eye-catching and set the tone for a gay party. They may be of cotton or linen if you wish, but more practical are plastic ones that can be wiped clean in a jiffy. Paper napkins in every imaginable color and design are available, but if your cloth is patterned, a solid colored napkin is best.

Disposable plates and cups of paper or plastic lighten the hostess' duties, and they too can be bought in many colors and varieties. Be sure, however, that they are of a sturdy material—plastic or plastic-coated paper rather than the somewhat flimsy carboard-paper type. If you are serving a hot drink, the cups must have handles or your guests will have difficulty holding them, and the package should be labeled "for hot drinks" or they will leak.

Some hostesses do not like to use disposable plates, and for them there are many alternatives. The new hard plastic sets of "china" now come in lovely patterns and, although unbreakable, feel much like real china. Drink containers, too, come in many break-proof materials that are ideal for use outdoors, where uneven ground or stone patios add to the ordinary number of broken glasses.

Also of great use to the barbecue cook are the colorful enamelled flame-proof pots and pans. What a joy to be able to cook or heat a casserole over your fire and serve it in the same handsome container! This enamelware also can be purchased for individual servings—little casseroles with covers, perfect for hot chowder, stew, meat pies, etc.

Styles of centerpieces and decorations are unlimited, but you will receive more compliments if they are appropriate to the meal or the season. For example, Chinese lanterns strung above the table and a centerpiece of gay paper parasols might accompany a Chinese dinner. Or a fish-net tablecloth with colorful felt cut-outs of fish sewed on is decorative on the table set for a lobster dinner. Half a watermelon, filled with fresh melon balls and other fruits and decorated with sprigs of mint, makes a cool and appealing centerpiece for a hot summer evening. And fresh flowers arranged in a container that fits into the barbecue theme are always attractive—yellow daisies, for instance, arranged in a copper kettle.

THE HOST AS COOK

At most barbecues, the host is the cook, but this is not a hard and fast rule. If he dislikes cooking and the hostess wants to entertain their friends in this way, there is no reason why she should not act as chef— and she is almost sure to be deluged with suggestions and assistance from her male guests. But the party will run more smoothly if she is relieved of the duties at the grill and is free to bring the other dishes from the kitchen, to help the guests serve themselves, and to see that every one is having a good time.

MENU SUGGESTIONS

Rather than discuss menu possibilities generally, I am going to give you some sample menus, all of which may be enlarged upon or changed to fit the taste of the guests and the hosts. These suggestions are intended as a guide, to show the infinite variety that may be presented at this type of party; they are not in any way meant to be a complete list. In each case, the main dish—meat, fish, or fowl—is prepared on the grill, and unless specified, the others are prepared in advance and kept on the stove indoors or brought out to sit on a corner of the grill where the temperature must be neither too hot nor too cold.

The least expensive, but always popular, especially with young people:

Hamburgers and/or Hot Dogs
Buttered Rolls
Casserole of Baked Beans
Potato Chips
Celery and Carrot Sticks
Watermelon Slices

An exotic menu that calls for more preparation beforehand (pieces of meat or shrimp, mushrooms, tomatoes, onions and bacon are marinated and threaded alternately on long skewers, ready to be laid on the grill):

Beef, Lamb, or Shrimp "Kabobs"
Rice
Watercress and Tomato Salad
Hot Rolls
Chocolate Eclairs

Especially good for the seashore:

Grilled Swordfish
Casserole of Scalloped Potatoes
Spinach Salad
Croissants
Fresh Fruit Compote and Cookies or Cake

Messy to eat, but delicious. Be sure your guests are informally dressed for this one:

Spare Ribs with Barbecue Sauce
Baked Potatoes
Coleslaw
Hard Rolls
Apple Pie with Vanilla Ice Cream

The classic barbecue menu:

Sirloin Steak
Potato Chips
French Fried Onions
Mixed Green Salad
French or Garlic Bread
Assorted Pastries

Beer, any soft drink, and pitchers of milk all go well with the informality of a barbecue. In hot weather, iced tea and iced coffee are delicious. Pots of coffee should be kept hot on the grill for serving either during or after the meal.

Cocktails may be served, but since the food is hearty, elaborate hors d'oeuvres are not necessary. A few dishes of nuts or potato chips scattered about are sufficient.

A side table loaded with a variety of condiments is a nice touch. As each guest fills his plate (the host usually cuts and serves the meat), he passes by this table and helps himself to ketchup, mustard, relish, sauce, or whatever may be offered.

SOME GENERAL HINTS

Remember to have plenty of light; it is very difficult for the chef to tell whether the meat is done if he cannot see it. Floodlights directed up into the trees give a beautiful effect. Japanese lanterns are gay and colorful and can be purchased strung on electric wires like Christmas-tree bulbs. Candles give a soft light, but they must be in hurricane lamps to protect them from the breeze. Some candles contain an insect repellent, an excellent idea for a summer night.

Entertainment after the meal depends on your facilities and the preferences of your guests. A lunch-time barbecue may be followed by a swim if you have a pool or are near the beach. If not, you may want to organize a game of softball or badminton. Many adults enjoy a game of catch or touch football on a brisk day. When there are children present, suitable games and races are almost a necessity to keep them from getting into mischief.

In the evening, a phonograph may be plugged in for dancing, if the patio or terrace has a suitable surface, or, if you have a stone fireplace, the fire may be built up to a blaze and the guests gathered round it to sing or chat. If you notice your guests shivering or putting on sweaters or coats, you must be prepared to move the party into the house—one of the advantages of having a barbecue in your own yard. No matter how good the food or how pleasant the company, your guests will disappear soon after dinner if they are allowed to freeze as the sun goes down.

Other informal gatherings

There are many ways of entertaining informally that have special descriptive names or specific purposes but do not otherwise differ very much from the informal gatherings discussed in earlier chapters. A housewarming, for example, may be a cocktail buffet with tours of the new house added, or a surprise party might be, in effect, an informal dance given in someone else's home. Therefore, it is perfectly proper for a hostess to combine the suggestions made here with those from another appropriate chapter.

HOURS FOR PARTY-GIVING

The hour chosen for a meal, or a party, or a game, or a visit should always be that of neighborhood custom. To invite friends to dine two hours later than their habitual meal is far more likely to distress than impress them with what may be intended as a fashionable innovation. People dine in London at nine and in Spain or Mexico at ten or even later, but this is no reason for upsetting the digestions of those who prefer to dine at seven. If weddings in the evening are customary in your neighborhood, then have your wedding in the evening too. If, on the other hand, a nine o'clock dinner hour and a noon wedding are customary, then even though you forage in the refrigerator an hour or more before dinner, at nine you dine and at noon you marry.

If neighbors pay visits in the evening—or if morning is the hour preferred—you take your protesting husband with you in the evening—or go by yourself in the morning—no matter how inconvenient either hour may be to you.

The same is true of a dessert-bridge party or the meeting of your sewing circle. If you cannot manage to have the group at the time decreed by custom, you should find another way to entertain your friends that can be conveniently fitted into your schedule and theirs.

HOUSEWARMINGS

When you have put a great deal of time and effort into making a lovely home, you are naturally as eager to show it off as your friends are to see it. The nicest way to do so is to call your friends and ask them to a housewarming. Or you may invite them informally whenever you see them. Invitations on visiting cards are quite suitable, too. Because the object of the party is to show them the house, it is far better to have two or three small parties at which you will only have to make the tour a few times. If you have too many people at once, you may spend the entire time leading groups from one room to another.

A housewarming is generally a cocktail party or a cocktail buffet. It may be as simple or as elaborate as you wish, but it is fun to keep the style of your house in mind when you plan your decorations. For instance, if it is 'an Early American type, a brown table cloth set with copper or pewter may be more appealing than lace with crystal or silver. » *For additional suggestions, see Chapter 28, "Cocktail parties."*

The guest generally takes a small gift to a housewarming. It need not be expensive, but it is more thoughtful to find something that will be of permanent use rather than flowers, which will only last a short time, or paper napkins, which would soon be used up. An ash tray, a few pretty dishtowels or place mats, a cigarette box, or a brush for the fireplace are a few possibilities.

OPEN HOUSE

An open house is literally what the name implies. The door is open to all those invited at any time between the hours stated on the invitation. Most open houses nowadays are held to celebrate a holiday—New Year's Day, perhaps, or Christmas Eve. They also may take the place of a housewarming.

Invitations are generally sent out on informals or commercial cards bought for the occasion. Because an answer is never expected, refreshments are generally simple and of a sort that may be expanded or not set out all at once. Dips, bowls of nuts, or other "nibbles," and a punch rather than individual drinks are good choices. People drop in to greet their hosts, and friends wish each other a "Happy New Year" or "Good luck to you in your new home." They generally stay no more than a half hour to an hour.

If the open house is to celebrate a holiday, the decorations are generally appropriate to the season. At Christmas time, the tree would be trimmed, and whatever other decorations you might wish to use would be arranged as beautifully as possible. For a Fourth of July party, red, white, and blue streamers, balloons, or bouquets might add a note of gaiety. But if the open house is not held to celebrate any particular holiday, no decorations are necessary other than some vases of pretty flowers or greens.

The food and beverages may be set out on the dining-room table if you have enough plates of cookies or sandwiches so that it will not look bare. If your refreshments are restricted to one or two plates of food and a punch bowl, they may be set out on any conveniently placed table in the hall or living room, or on a side table in the dining room. You may wish to surround a bowl of eggnog with holly twigs or a fruit punch with flowers, but otherwise, only the attractive arrangement of glasses, little napkins (cloth or paper), and food is necessary to assure the charm of your refreshment table.

BRUNCHES

Brunch—a combination of breakfast and lunch that relies heavily on breakfast for its menus but is taken closer to the usual hour for lunch—is a pleasant sort of informal, even casual, entertaining. It is not unusual to find brunches being given on the day after a large party, especially if there are many out-of-town guests who have come for the "big" occasion. But no such excuse is necessary if you find the late morning hours convenient for you and your friends.

In any event, informality is the rule. In the country, slacks or simple dresses may be worn by the women, or if the host is having the party beside his swimming pool, people may come in shorts and bring their bathing suits. In the city, any daytime dress or a suit is correct for a woman, and a man usually wears a sports jacket rather than a business suit.

Invitations may be telephoned ahead of time, but so casual is this kind of gathering that the host may simply say to his friends as they are leaving someone else's party, "Would you come over around 11:30 tomorrow for a late breakfast?" or "Would you all come for a late breakfast after church tomorrow?"

Sometimes a "Bloody Mary" or a mixture of chilled consommé and vodka is served, but tomato juice or consommé must also be offered without the liquor for those who prefer it that way.

The food is arranged on a buffet table less elaborately set than for lunch or dinner, but attractively and conveniently laid out. Breakfast and lunch dishes are combined. For example, a platter of scrambled eggs surrounded with bacon or little sausages, accompanied by hot rolls or toast, and sautéed potatoes and broiled tomatoes. Or platters of waffles to be covered with maple syrup by some or with creamed chicken by those who prefer a heartier meal. Pitchers of fruit juice and pots of coffee should be on a table beside the buffet.

CARD PARTIES

ON PLANNING YOUR TABLES

In giving a card party, whether of two tables or of ten, the first thing to do is to make a list of those to be invited. Then divide those who accept into groups of four, and try to seat at each table only those who like to play together. The tables may all be different—one with good players, another with beginners, one where the stakes are high, another where they play for nothing—but you must do your best to put those who play approximately the same kind of game at the same table. In addition to playing, it is important to remember temperament. Don't put people who take their game seriously (and "play for blood") with others who unceasingly chatter and keep asking, "What's trump?" Don't put one who plays rapidly at a table with hesitators and dawdlers who take a whole minute to decide which card they'll play—and who even then take half a minute more in daring to lay an intended finesse face up on the table!

We all know hostesses who apparently seat players by drawing names out of a hat without the slightest regard for who plays well and who plays badly or for what stakes they like to play. At an evening party, the unthinking hostess will put two men who are the best players in town at a table with one woman who, imagining herself a wit, thinks of nothing but the next bright remark she can make, and a second woman who is beautiful to look at but who knows scarcely more than a child of eight about bidding. A man will be delighted to find a pretty woman next to him at the dinner table, but at the card table he hopes for an expert partner. If she is pretty or charming, or both, so much the better, of course, but these attributes are secondary. The real point is that one poor player spoils the whole evening—or afternoon—for the three who play well.

And now your preparations. It seems scarcely necessary to say that the packs of cards on each table must be fresh and that the pencils laid beside the score pads must be sharp. On each table you leave a slip of paper on which you have written distinctly the names of the four players who are to play there together. They, of course, cut for their seats and partners. It is also of importance to see that each table is comfortably lighted, because poorly placed light that is reflected from the shiny surface of the cards is just as bad as darkness so deep that red cards are indistinguishable from black ones. If you have any doubt about light, sit in each place, hold cards in your hands, lay a few on the table, and see.

REFRESHMENTS

The kind of refreshments you offer your card-playing guests depends, of course, on the time of day. While small sandwiches and tiny cakes, accompanied by tea or coffee, might be suitable when served at four o'clock to a group of women, they would hardly please the men at an evening gathering. Then a selection of cold meats and cheeses and a variety of breads for do-it-yourself sandwiches, served with coffee and beer, would be more appropriate. In either case, however, the food may be attractively arranged on the dining-room table, and, having served themselves, the guests may be asked either to return to the cleared card tables or to take their plates to the comfortable chairs in the living room (each having a small table nearby).

A note of warning: If you have invited avid card players, you will be well advised not to interrupt their game to serve some lavish concoction of whipped cream, cake, frosting, and cherries, no matter how long it took you to prepare. Men in particular will be most unlikely to accept your next invitation if they feel that in your home card playing is secondary to such culinary productions. Give another kind of party if you wish to indulge yourself in the kitchen!

PRIZES

If it is customary in your community to play for prizes, then you must select a first prize for the highest score to be made by a woman and a first prize for the highest score to be made by a man; but at a party to which no men are invited, a second prize is usually given. In any case, all prizes are attractively wrapped before being presented. Those who receive the prizes must, of course, open the packages at once and show some evidence of appreciation when thanking the hostess. Needless to say, a well-behaved person does not show disappointment upon receiving a prize that happens not to please her, nor does she "forget" to take it home.

DESSERT CARD PARTY

A dessert card party is a happy compromise for the hostess who may feel that she cannot provide a full luncheon for her guests, yet wishes to do more than simply invite them to play cards. When there are four present, or even eight if her dining-room table is large enough to seat them, dessert may be served in the following way: The dining table is set for the dessert course only. Individual place mats are set with a china dessert plate, a lunch napkin on the plate, a fork at the left and a spoon at the right, and a glass of water. The table should, furthermore, be set with a

org Jensen, Inc.

coffee tray in front of the hostess; while her friends are having their dessert, she pours the coffee, and it is handed around the table. After coffee, they begin playing on tables already set up in the living room.

If there are more than eight, the dining table may be set as a buffet, using a pretty table cloth or place mats or round lace doilies (paper ones will do if you have no lace mats) under the stack of plates and the dishes on which the dessert is served.

The guests serve themselves and take their plates to the living room to eat, but unless the hostess asks them to, they do not sit at the card tables, which have already been set up and readied for bridge. They help themselves to coffee, and if they wish to start playing immediately, they may take their cups with them to the bridge tables.

STAG DINNERS

A man's dinner is sometimes called a stag or bachelor dinner and, as its name implies, is a dinner given by a man for men only. It usually celebrates some special event or person, as a welcome or farewell, or, most frequently, as the groom's last party with his good friends before his wedding. Occasionally a man may have a quantity of game that he has shot, or fish that he has caught, and want to share them with his friends.

Nearly always a man's dinner is given at the host's club or in a private room in a hotel or restaurant. But if he chooses to give a stag dinner in his own house, his wife (or mother or sister) should *not* appear.

For his wife to come downstairs and receive the guests with him is most definitely out of place. No matter how much you may want to say "How do you do" to your husband's or son's friends—*don't*.

So if a man does decide he would like to entertain his friends at home, he must discuss his plans and the menu with his wife, who will then prepare it ahead of time and unobtrusively set out the dishes on a buffet table at the time agreed upon with her husband. After the men have eaten, she may remove the plates and clean up if they have gone to a living room or library separated from the dining room, but if they are still in close proximity, she would do better to leave the cleaning up until the next day. If there are servants in the house, they may prepare and serve the meal as at any dinner party.

THE SURPRISE PARTY

Popular now as it ever was is a surprise party, given sometimes for new householders but equally suitable for any special occasion. The general plan of a surprise party is, as everyone knows, the arriving by surprise at a friend's house in the eager hope that it will really be a surprise!

AN ELABORATE BIRTHDAY-SURPRISE PARTY

Tiffany

The preparation may be made in different ways. For an evening party, you might make your plans for a date on which John and Mary White are having dinner alone at home. The company who are to surprise them meet nearby and then troop in a procession to storm the house. Or you may arrange to have the Greens invite John and Mary for dinner. While dinner is progressing, the others who are giving the surpise take possession of John's and Mary's house. On some pretext, the Whites and Greens return to the White's house, where the party is in full swing. On a weekend, it may be even easier to get them out of the house—by inviting them to inspect the new puppies, perhaps, or enjoy a special exhibit of sculpture at the nearby gallery. In any case, provisions for refreshments are always brought by the unexpected guests, and they never leave a mess for Mary to clean up when they have left.

Such parties, needless to say, always consist of a group of intimate friends and usually take place on John's or Mary's birthday or some other suitable anniversary, particularly the wedding anniversaries that are celebrated in paper, wood, tin, or crystal.

A word of warning for those who might be inclined to celebrate a golden wedding anniversary with a surprise party. If the bride and groom are young for their ages, it is possible that they would enjoy this type of party. But if they were not married in their earliest youth, the disturbance of too great a surprise might very well have the opposite of happy results.

SINGING, READING, OR DISCUSSION GROUPS

In a rather special category of entertaining is your turn to entertain the neighborhood singing or reading or discussion group to which you belong. Especially if they include both men and women, they usually meet in the evening at a time agreed upon as convenient for all when the group is first established; therefore, the hostess has little to say about the hour. But a group of women interested, for example, in reading French plays together, may find that an afternoon or even a morning meeting is the only solution to the problem of family schedules. The convenience of the members carries more weight in such circumstances than any prescribed hour, and even neighborhood custom should not discourage a determined group from picking their own time or changing it by mutual consent.

Refreshments are usually served after the activity of the meeting, and of course the kind depends on the hour, the preferences of the group, and the inclination of the hostess-of-the-day. Coffee and sandwiches, Welsh rarebit and beer, cider and doughnuts would all be appropriate after an evening gathering. Earlier in the day, coffee and rolls or tea and cookies might very well be adequate.

Very often, musicians give a concert at the end of the year or the theatrically inclined present a reading of the play that they have labored over. In these cases, the refreshments and service may be somewhat more lavish and resemble a buffet supper.

Otherwise, there are no rules for such groups—except to be firm with those who can't keep in tune or with the gossipers who wander from the topic under discussion.

SEWING GROUPS

The hostess at whose house a sewing group meets should have a supply of different-sized thimbles, extra needles, and several pairs of scissors and spools of thread. What is sewed depends upon the purpose of the group, which may be to make garments for a nursery, hospital, or other organization; or, having no object other than meeting socially, the members sew for themselves—which perhaps means doing needlepoint, or darning socks, or sometimes even knitting. Sometimes a sewing circle is also a lunch club that meets weekly or fortnightly at the houses of the various members. They sew from eleven until about one and then have a sit-down or buffet luncheon. More often coffee and light refreshments, such as coffee cake, cookies, or doughnuts, are served approximately half-way through a session that may run from ten to twelve or from two to half past four.

36

Showers

Showers are friendly gatherings held in honor of a bride-to-be or in welcome of a new clergyman or in expectation of the arrival of the stork—for almost anything, in fact, that imagination can invent. So, too, the setting for a shower can be almost anything—a luncheon, a dinner, an afternoon tea, an evening party, or even a morning coffee. The only distinguishing characteristic of the shower is the giving of presents to the guest of honor.

Bridal showers are never given by members of the bride's immediate family, because a gift is obligatory (as it is not even for those who are invited only to the wedding ceremony). Whether a wedding present is sent in addition to a shower gift depends upon the custom of one's own community; it also depends on how well one knows and how much one cares for Mary Jones. And most of all it depends upon the depth of one's purse. It is perfectly permissible to give a shower for someone who is being married for the second time, whether she be widow or divorcée. But the hostess, as she plans her party, would do well to keep in mind the elaborateness of the wedding plans and make hers accordingly. In other words, the bride-to-be who for one reason or another is having a very quiet, simple wedding might easily be embarrassed by an extremely elaborate shower, however kindly her friend's intention.

THE INVITATIONS

Invitations to showers are often telephoned: "I'm having a kitchen shower for Betsy Jones on Tuesday at three o'clock." Or they may be written on a visiting card—"Larder shower for Dr. Smythe" or "Stork shower for Helen"—with the day and the hour. Or one of the shower cards found at stationers' shops is just as appropriate. Make certain, however, that it is perfectly clear to the guests exactly what kind of shower it is to be, including all details you have that may be helpful. For example, if you know that Betsy Jones's kitchen is to have red trim, do let the guests know, too, so they can choose appropriately colored items.

THE HOUR

A shower for a bride may be given at any hour of the day or evening. Evening is chosen when the shower presents take the place of wedding presents, and when men as well as women are invited. Originally shower presents were the kind of things, most often to wear, that girls can give to girls but that would be embarrassing to display if any men were present, and therefore showers were for girls only.

The shower for a clergyman is usually given in the early evening. A stork shower is always given in the early afternoon and only intimate girl or women friends of the mother invited—that is, when the shower is an anticipation shower. Sometimes a combination of stork shower and surprise party is given at the house of the mother when the baby is five or six weeks old. Although a surprise party, this is one occasion when it would be excusable for someone to give her a hint at least half an hour in advance, so that both she and the baby will be found ready for company. Also, the guests usually bring light refreshments with them as at all typical surprise parties, and surely they would do so in the case of a surprise shower for an unmarried clergyman.

THE GIFTS

Many times the type of shower being given allows wide leeway in the choice of presents. At a stork shower, they may include anything for a new baby. A larder shower, which is often given for a new clergyman, includes everything eatable. On the other hand, the shower for a bride is sometimes specified as a linen shower or a kitchen shower or a stocking shower or a general shower. Only in the last case does one have the option of bringing anything at all that seems appropriate.

At a "round-the-clock" shower, each guest is given an hour of the day on her invitation and brings a present appropriate for the hour. For example, at a bridal shower, if her hour is 10:00 A.M., she might take a

dustpan and brush, or if it is 6:00 P.M., she might take a set of four or six cocktail glasses.

Sometimes the shower presents are given in place of wedding gifts. Usually, however, they are an extra expression of generosity and of much less importance than the wedding gifts. Sometimes they are the donation of the bride's bridge club or a small group of her most intimate friends who have been busy throughout a number of weeks hemming or embroidering a set of friendship table linen or kitchen towels, each piece of which is embellished and signed by the sewer. For those who in this busy age have time for such expressions of affection, such gifts have a charming and personal sentiment that the bride or anyone else is certain to appreciate.

PRESENTING THE GIFTS

When everyone—or almost everyone—expected has arrived, Mary opens the packages one by one and thanks each giver. "Thank you, Susie—how lovely!" The cards of donors should be enclosed, because otherwise each giver must say more or less self-consciously as her present is unwrapped, "That's from me."

After that, if the party is at tea time, the guests are offered light refreshments of tea or coffee and cakes. If it is in the evening, coffee or punch and sandwiches are suitable, as are cider and doughnuts, or liqueurs or highballs, especially if men are included.

Although wedding presents are sent from the shop where they are bought, gifts for a shower are brought by hand and given personally— usually upon each donor's arrival, although sometimes the packages are taken at the door and put unopened with the others on a table in another room.

In some localities all the presents are sent to the hostess several days before hand. She leaves the packages as they are, but puts each in a uniform outer gift wrapping so that the whole stack of packages are attractively alike. For this purpose, the assortments to be found at all stationery counters are enchanting. When all are wrapped, the presents are piled on a table, perhaps in another room or behind a screen, or perhaps in full view against one wall of the living room.

37

House parties and overnight guests

Although the day of the great house staffed by a horde of servants is almost gone, there is no reason why the simple house with a relaxed hostess and enthusiastic guests cannot be the setting for a house party that is just as much a success as the elaborate affair of other years.

The size of the house party in the smaller houses of today is limited mainly by the number of available beds. Furthermore, for a hostess who has no help, it is certainly easier to cook, serve, and keep the house in order with two guests than it is with eight, as she should remember even after she has counted the beds.

THE INVITATIONS

Invitations are generally telephoned, but, if your guests live in another town, they are written on your note paper.

June 15th

Dear Ellie,

John and I are hoping that you and Bob and the children can spend the weekend of the fourth with us in Edgartown. If Bob could leave the office a little early on Friday, the second, there is a 4:00 P.M. ferry that would get you here in time for dinner, and there are ferries leaving at 5:00 and at 8:00 on Sunday. The fishing should be great, and our children are counting on Sally and Jimmy for the annual picnic. Please come—we have wanted to show you our island for so long.

Affectionately,

Ann

With the rising popularity of winter sports, more and more people are acquiring lodges in the mountains, and ski weekends are becoming almost an institution in all sections of the country with nearby slopes.

January 4

Dear Joan,

The forecast is for snow and more snow, and Dick and I are hoping that you and Bill will spend the weekend after next skiing with us at Stowe. Come as early as you can on Friday the eighth, and stay until Sunday night, so as not to miss a minute of it. The Hortons are coming, too, and perhaps you could drive up together. To find us, you turn off Route 7 on Skyline Drive, exactly three tenths of a mile beyond the traffic light in Hampton, and we are the second house on the right.

No formal clothes, only your ski outfits, and slacks or a skirt for the evening. Plenty of woolies and flannels—it's cold!

We're counting on you, so do say "yes."

Love to you both,

Barbara

In your letter or on the telephone, you must give the details of transportation or, if your guests are coming by car, the route. If they will be arriving by public transportation, you must tell them to be sure to let you know at what hour they will arrive, so that you can meet them at the station or airport.

To make it easier for a woman to know what to bring, it is wise to indicate what the main activities will be. "We're planning a deep-sea fishing expedition on Saturday," "The Jones have asked us to a beach picnic on Sunday," or "There is to be a dance at the club on Saturday night."

ROOM FOR YOUR GUESTS

TEMPORARY ARRANGEMENTS

Most families today do not have a room in their house that is intended solely for the use of guests. When they wish to have friends spend a night or a weekend (or more), the children are moved around to vacate a room, or the library or den, which is furnished with convertible sofas, is put in readiness. The toys are hidden from sight, the clothes are removed from the closet, sufficient drawer space is cleared so that the guest may unpack his suitcase, and the room is made sparkling clean. If he is to share a bath with other members of the household, his towels should be hung on a rack in his bedroom, so that children do not inadvertently use them. Although it may seem that not much more can be done to make a guest room out of one that is used every day, many of the suggestions made in the following section describing the permanent guest room can be adapted—to the comfort and convenience of your visitors.

THE GUEST ROOM

It is by no means idle talk to suggest that every hostess be obliged to try her guest room by spending at least one night in it herself. If she does not do this, she should at least check the facilities thoroughly. She should go into the guest bathroom and draw the water in every fixture to see that there is no stoppage and that the hot water faucets are not seemingly jokes of the plumber. If a man is to utilize the bathroom, she must see that there is an outlet for an electric razor and a receptacle for used razor blades and, furthermore, that there is a mirror by which he can see to shave both at night and by daylight. Even though she can see to powder her nose, it would be safer to ask her husband to bathe and shave both in the morning and in the evening in the bathroom and then listen to what he says about it.

She may have a perfect maid, yet it is not unwise occasionally to make sure herself that every detail has been attended to, that in every bathroom there are plenty of bath towels, face towels, a washcloth, bath mat, a new cake of bath soap in the bathtub soap rack, and a new cake of soap on the washstand.

It is not expected, but it is often very nice to find eau de cologne, bath salts or bath oil, mouthwash, bath powder, hand and sunburn lotion in decorated bottles on the washstand shelf. But to cover the dressing table in the bedroom with brushes and an array of toilet articles is more of a nuisance than a comfort. A good clothesbrush or whiskbroom is a good idea, because guests almost invariably forget these.

Good beds are most important. The mattresses should be firm— many people develop serious backaches from sleeping on a sagging bed. The most desirable arrangement is to have twin beds placed together, possibly with a single headboard. This satisfies both the couple who cannot sleep in the same bed and the couple who are used to the closeness of a double bed. It also serves perfectly well for two girls (or two boys), and if there is space, the beds may even be pushed apart and a table put between them if the girls are not intimate friends.

It is nice but not necessary to provide two pillows for each guest, one medium hard and one soft, so that one may make one's choice. There must always be plenty of covers, of course, and in the winter there should be, in addition to the blankets, a quilt laid across the foot of the bed.

If there are servants in the house, the bell should be checked to see that it is in working order.

There must, of course, be a light at the head of the bed. Not just a decorative glowworm effect, but a 75- or 100-watt bulb with an adjustable shade that is really good to read by while lying in bed. Moreover, if there are twin beds, there should be a light for each bed, so shaded from the other that the occupant of one can read while the other sleeps. And always there should be books—chosen more to divert than to strain the reader's attention. The sort of selection appropriate for a guest room might best comprise one or two nonfiction books of the moment, a light novel or a mystery novel, a book of modern short stories, and a few of the latest magazines. It is very important that this selection be revised for each guest, for even though one may not guess accurately the taste of another, one can at least avoid making the guest room either a wastebasket or a catch-all for books selected because their bindings look pretty.

There should also be cigarettes, matches, and ash trays on the tables, and a wastebasket beside the bureau. In hot weather, every guest room should have an electric fan, if the house does not have some type of air-conditioning; and in August, even though there are screens, a fly swatter!

The hostess should do her own hair at the dressing table to learn whether there is a good light over it, both by electric light and by daylight.

And a pincushion! Complete with pins that are usable and not rusted. As well as straight pins, there should be black and gold safety pins in several sizes. Three or four needles threaded with white, black, gray, and beige thread are an addition that has many times proved welcome.

Facial tissues in pretty containers should be on the dressing table, beside the beds, and in the bathroom.

If there is a desk in the room, one must be sure that the ink is not a mere patch of black dust, that the pens are in working order, and that the writing paper textures and sizes are not at odds with the envelopes. There should be a fresh blotter and a few stamps. Again, thoughtful hostesses put in some convenient place a card giving the post office schedule and saying where the letters may be mailed. And a calendar. And a clock that runs and shows the right time. Is there anything more typical of the average spare room than the clock that is at a standstill or, worse, a half-hour slow?

In the closets must be plenty of clothes hangers made of wood or plastic and not the thin wire ones from the cleaners that may even be rusty. For women a few hat stands, and for men trouser hangers or coat hangers that have a bar for the trousers. In hunting country, there should be bootjack and boot-hooks in the closet as well.

It should be unnecessary to add that every bureau drawer and closet should be looked into to see that nothing belonging to the family is filling the space that should belong to the guest and that the paper lining the bottom of the bureau drawers is fresh.

People who like strong perfumes often mistakenly think they are giving pleasure in filling all the bedroom drawers with pads heavily scented. Instead of feeling pleasure, some people are made almost sick, but a very lightly scented sachet is delightful. Everyone—hay fever patients excepted—loves flowers, and vases of them beautify rooms as nothing else can. Even a shabby little room embellished with a few wild flowers or a potted plant loses all effect of shabbiness and is inviting instead.

A shortcoming in many houses is the lack of a newspaper. The thoughtful hostess who has servants and has a morning paper sent up with each breakfast tray deserves a halo, and it takes no effort to see that one is placed on or near the breakfast table.

Guest rooms should have dark shades for those who like to keep the morning sun out. The rooms should also, if possible, be away from the kitchen end of the house and the nursery.

At night, a glass and a thermos jug of water should be placed by the bed. If you have no thermos jugs, be sure that there are glasses in the bathroom, or suggest that your guest take a glass of iced water with him when he goes to bed.

THE HOUSE WITH SERVANTS

When house guests arrive at a house run by a staff of servants, the personal maid of the hostess (if she has one—otherwise, the housemaid) unpacks the lady's luggage, lays toilet articles on the dressing-table and in the bathroom, puts folded things in the drawers, and hangs dresses in the closet. If as she unpacks, the maid sees that something of importance has been forgotten, she tells the hostess; or, in case she has been long in the house and knows where to find a substitute for the missing article, she supplies the guest with such articles as comb and brush or clothes-brush or toothbrush without asking. (This last article afterward is packed in the guest's luggage.)

Whoever looks after the host's clothes performs the same service for the men. If there is no lady's maid or valet, the housemaid is asked to press ladies' dresses, and send gentlemen's clothes to be pressed. There are some maids who can do this last themselves.

In a house with a large staff, breakfast trays for the ladies are usually carried to the bedroom floor by the butler and are handed to the lady's maid or to the housemaid, who takes the tray into the room. In small houses they are carried up by the waitress.

Trays for men visitors are less common, but when ordered they are carried up and into the room by the butler or, if there are no menservants, by the waitress.

Unless breakfast is at a set time and everyone comes down promptly, the advantage of having one's guests breakfast upstairs is that no delayed breakfast prevents the dining room's being put in order or the lunch table set. Trays, on the other hand, can stand all morning "all set" in the pantry and interfere much less with the dining-room work. Many hostesses therefore much prefer guests to have trays.

Every china store carries breakfast sets, of course, but only in open stock patterns can one buy extra dishes or replace broken ones—a fact it is well to remember. The set always has a coffee- or tea-pot, a hot-milk pitcher, a cream pitcher and sugar bowl, a cup and saucer, two plates, an egg cup, and a cover. A hot cereal is usually put in the covered dish, toast in a napkin on a plate, and eggs and bacon on a plate with a cover. This with fruit or fruit juice and coffee completes the tray.

When a guest rings for breakfast, the maid goes into the room, opens the blinds, and in cold weather closes the windows, lights the fire, if there is fireplace in the room, and turns on heat. Asking whether a hot or cool bath is preferred, she goes into the bathroom, spreads a bath mat on the floor and a big bath towel over a chair and draws the bath. (As few people care for more than one bath a day and many people prefer to bathe before dinner instead of before breakfast, this office is often performed at dinner time.) If the hostess has not asked her guests the night before, the maid asks what they would like for breakfast at this time.

Anyone breakfasting in the dining room is expected to dress before going down to the table. On some rare and informal occasions, the hostess may suggest the night before that dressing gowns are in order, but this is not usually the case.

TIPS

In the United States, when you dine in a friend's house, you do not tip anyone—ever. But when you go to stay overnight or longer as a house guest, you do give a gratuity. A fixed schedule of the amount to tip is really impossible to prepare, inasmuch as each occasion is different.

To an average servant in an average house, two dollars is about right for a weekend. Mrs. Lavender, staying with the Littlehouses and not making more work than the least possible, might quite acceptably give no more than five dollars for a week. Intimate friends in a house with two or three servants tip perhaps only a dollar or two apiece, but no one is forgotten. In a very big house, this is never done; you tip only those who have served you.

A gentleman (very unfairly) scarcely ever remembers any of the women (except a waitress) and tips only the butler and the valet and

Tiffany & Co.

AN ELABORATE HOUSE-PARTY BREAKFAST

sometimes the chauffeur. The least he can offer any of the menservants is two dollars and the most is usually five.

In a few houses, especially official establishments, the tipping system is abolished, and in every guest room, in a conspicuous place either on the dressing-table or on the bathroom mirror where you are sure to read it, is a sign saying:

PLEASE DO NOT OFFER TIPS TO MY EMPLOYEES. THEIR CONTRACT IS WITH THIS SPECIAL UNDERSTANDING, AND PROPER ARRANGEMENTS HAVE BEEN MADE TO MEET IT. YOU WILL NOT ONLY CREATE A SITUATION, BUT CAUSE THE IMMEDIATE DISMISSAL OF ANYONE WHO MAY BE PERSUADED BY YOU TO BREAK THIS RULE OF THE HOUSE.

The notice is signed by the host. The arrangement referred to is one whereby every guest means a bonus of so much per day added to the wages of all employees. This system is much to be preferred for two reasons. First, self-respecting servants dislike the demeaning effect of tips—an occasional few won't take them. Secondly, they can count on the fact that so many visitors will bring them a precise amount.

Just before the time for saying good-by to your hostess, when the maid has finished packing your bag and the chambermaid is probably doing up your room, you give each her tip. And you give the butler his or the waitress hers in the front hall. You may always give the butler a tip for any other menservants.

In a small house, if the waitress is not in the hall, you go to the pantry and put the money into her hand. If you are a frequent visitor and know her name, you say, "Good-by, Anna, and thank you." Then you go into the kitchen and do and say the same thing. Or you may, after giving Anna her own tip, hand her a second sum of money saying, "Please give this to the cook for me." If Anna has pressed your dress, let us say, or sewed something that had ripped or done any other special service, you give her a dollar or two extra; and when you say good-by, you add "Thank you" for whatever the service was.

PLANNING THE MEALS FOR YOUR GUESTS

If you are fortunate enough to have servants, meals for your guests present few, if any, problems. Prepare the menus, discuss them with your cook, and think no more about them until you sit down at the table.

When you must entertain without help, the more planning and preparation that can be done ahead, the more effortless and pleasant the result. House parties do not generally last for more than two days and nights, or possibly three. With the help of a freezer, or even the freezing compartment of your refrigerator, your meals can be largely prepared in advance. A casserole, warming in the oven, can be ready at whatever hour your guests arrive, early or late. A steak cooked on the beach in summer or over the coals of the fireplace in winter, served with potato chips and salad, takes little effort. And you may wish to treat your guests to a dinner in a local restaurant that specializes, perhaps, in foods native to the region. At most summer resorts, yacht clubs or night clubs provide dinner and dancing on Saturday night.

For lunches, you may prepare the ingredients for a chef's salad, lobster rolls, chowder, and sandwiches in advance, ready to be mixed or spread at the last moment.

The one meal that the hostess cannot organize in advance is breakfast. Because one of the joys of a weekend away from home is being able to sleep as late as they want, the guests should not be awakened unless there is an activity planned in which they truly wish to participate.

The hostess should get up at an early enough hour to precede all her guests to the kitchen. She makes coffee, prepares fruit or juice, and cooks sausage or bacon enough for all, keeping them warm on a hot plate or in a very low oven. She may then put butter, eggs, and frying pan—or pancake batter and griddle—by the stove, bread by the toaster, and an assortment of cereals and milk and cream on the table, which she sets with places for every one. She may wait for her guests, or she may eat her own breakfast and be ready to help the late comers as they arrive. If some of the group want to make an early start, to the beach or to ski, for instance, plans should be made the day before. The host and hostess may accompany the ones who are leaving, as long as everything is left in readiness for those who wish to sleep or relax and arrangements have been made for their joining the group later on if they wish.

A very friendly custom is gaining popularity in many localities—when two or three couples go to visit good friends, they may offer to bring a roast or a casserole to provide one evening's meal. There is no reason why the hostess should not accept such an offer. On this type of intimate party, all feel more comfortable if they can contribute, and it certainly adds to the pleasure of the hostess.

THE PERFECT HOSTESS

The abilities of a perfect hostess are called upon long before the actual start of the house party. They begin with choosing guests who have the same interests and will enjoy each other's company. There is little pleasure in having one couple who enjoys staying up all night to play

A SIMPLE HOUSE-PARTY TABLE SETTING

bridge, while the others wish to go to bed early in order to be up at sunrise to go on a fishing expedition.

Arrangements for whatever activities you know your visitors will enjoy must be made ahead of time. If they like tennis, be sure that you sign up or reserve a court at a convenient hour, or if you are sure that they would love to go to the dance at your club, don't forget to make a reservation for a table or you may be disappointed when you arrive at the door. Don't try to fill every minute with strenuous projects, however; it is probable that your guests would like some time to relax and visit with you and the other guests, and they may very well have some suggestions of their own about a special landmark they would like to see, perhaps, or a shopping trip to stores carrying merchandise made in the area.

A perfect hostess in a household with servants gives the impression that she has nothing whatever to do with household arrangements, which apparently run themselves. In a servantless household, she has the cleaning, marketing, and as much cooking as possible done in advance, so that an absolute minimum of her time is spent on these chores while her guests are with her.

Certain rules are easy to observe once they are brought to attention. A host or hostess should never speak of annoyance of any kind—no matter what happens. Unless actually unable to stand up, they should not mention physical ills any more than mental ones.

If anything goes wrong with the household they must work a miracle and keep it from their guests. If, for instance, the cook leaves, then a picnic must be made of the situation as though a picnic had been planned from the beginning. Should a guest be taken ill, the hostess must assure him that he is not giving the slightest trouble; at the same time, nothing that can be done for his comfort must be overlooked.

And above all, they must not be "overanxious." The overanxious host or hostess is one who fusses and plans continually, who thinks the guests are not having a good time unless they are being rushed, tourist fashion, from this engagement to that, and crowded with activity and diversion—never mind what so long as it is something to see or do—every moment of their stay.

A variation of this type of hostess (or host) is she who does not insist on your ceaseless activity, but is no less persistent in filling your time. She is always asking you what you would like to do next. If you say you are quite content as you are, she nevertheless continues to shower suggestions that leave no time for peace and quiet.

DO'S AND DON'TS FOR HOUSE GUESTS

Having accepted an invitation, guests may shorten their visit, but they must not stay beyond the time they were asked for unless very especially urged to do so. Even then they would be much wiser to go early and be missed rather than to run the risk of outstaying their welcome.

The laws governing the behavior of the ideal guest are by no means easy to follow. Whether it is easy or not, you as a guest must conform to the habits of the family with whom you are staying. You take your meals at their hour, you eat what is put before you, and you get up and go out and come in and go to bed according to the schedule arranged by your hostess. And no matter how much the hours or the food or the arrangements may upset you, you must appear blissfully content. When the visit is over, you need never enter that house again; but while you are there, you must at least act as if you were enjoying it.

If you know anyone who is always in demand, not only for dinners, but for trips on yachts and visits in country houses, you may be very sure of one thing—that popular person is first of all unselfish or else extremely gifted, and very often both.

The ideal guest not only tries to wear becoming clothes, but tries to get into an equally becoming frame of mind. No one is ever invited very often if he or she is in the habit of telling people all the misfortunes and ailments he has experienced or witnessed, though the perfect guest listens to other's grievances with apparent sympathy.

Another attribute of the perfect visitor is never to keep people waiting. You are always ready for anything—or nothing. If a plan is made to picnic, you like picnics above everything and prove that liking by enthusiastically making the sandwiches or the salad dressing or whatever you think you make best. If, on the other hand, no one seems to want to do anything, the perfect guest always has a book to be absorbed in, or a piece of sewing or knitting, or else beyond everything would love to sit in an easy chair and do nothing.

When you have accepted the invitation and assuming that you want to be an ideal guest, there are four details that demand your attention: selection of clothes to be taken, selection of luggage to put them in, selection of gifts, and selection of the ideal guest's state of mind.

It is not necessary, but it is always courteous to take your hostess a gift—or better, if she has children, to take presents to them. The conventional list of flowers, fruit, candy, or a book is perfectly acceptable, but be sure you know of a book she wants, or that she eats candy, has no flowers in her garden or fruit on her trees. Some people prefer to send a present after their visit, having made note of something that their hostess would find useful or that would go perfectly in one of the rooms. As to the children, if they are young, a collection of small amusing articles from the ten-cent store often gives them more pleasure than a single present of value.

Your next concern when going on a visit is to condense your luggage in both quantity and size. If you are going in your own car, this is not so important; but if you are being taken in someone else's car or going by train to a place where there are no porters to carry heavy bags, too much luggage can be a near tragedy.

It is sometimes impossible to go for a weekend without a good deal of luggage. An athletic man who is likely to ride and play golf and tennis might easily be taken for a vaudeville star carrying his properties with him. Beside the necessary sport clothes, a dinner coat (you should ask your host if it is necessary to bring one) and one or at most two sports jackets with the necessary shirts, shoes, ties, etc. will suffice.

If you are going where you are to swim or ride or play games, be sure you take your own bathing suit (it is safer to take two in case of damp weather and slow drying; better still, of course, are the quick-drying synthetics to solve this problem), riding habit, tennis racket, or golf clubs. Not only will your hostess be glad not to have her own good things used and perhaps ruined, but you will avoid having to use borrowed clothes or equipment that may not fit or may be totally unlike that to which you are accustomed.

It too often follows that the borrower is likewise an abuser of the lender's property. The guest no one invites a second time is the one who runs a car to destruction and a horse to a lather, who dog-ears books, who burns cigarette trenches on table edges, who uses towels for cleaning shoes, who stands wet glasses on polished wood, who tracks into the house in muddy shoes and then puts them up on the sofa or bed, and who leaves his room looking as though it had been visited by a cyclone. Nor are men the only offenders. Women have been known to commit every one of these offenses and more besides. Think of what they can do to fine linen with the lipstick! Or to a dressing table surface with nail polish!

Perhaps the greatest damage that any of us is ever asked to bear is that caused by a lap dog that is taken everywhere and allowed to run free because of its owner's bland unawareness that, although it may be house-trained in its own home, all strange places are "outdoor places" to a dog. » *See also Chapter 72, "For pets and people."*

Besides these actually destructive shortcomings, there are those guests whose lack of consideration is scarcely less annoying. They may be late for every meal; or they help themselves to a car and go off and fail to come back for meals on time. Then there are those who write no letters afterward, nor even take the trouble to go up and speak to a former hostess when they see her again. This abuse of hospitality is, of course, more often met with by hostesses of large estates who have frequent weekend parties than by the hostess of a little house who seldom has anyone staying with her except a really intimate friend.

Aside from the more or less general rule of behavior, there are a few more specific rules that are worthy of mention.

A guest in someone's home should never suggest taking his hosts to a meal in a restaurant. While you are their guest, you eat the food they provide. If, however, your host suggests dining at a restaurant, you might well say, "That sounds wonderful, and we would love to be *your* hosts for dinner—you are giving us such a wonderful time!" Otherwise, you show your gratitude by inviting them to a restaurant sometime when they are in town or by sending a suitable present.

If you have friends in the neighborhood and they invite you and your hosts over for a swim or to play tennis, you should never accept the invitation and then relay it to your hostess. It is better to leave the "door ajar" and make a noncommittal reply such as, "May I call you back, as I'm not sure about Joan's plans?"

If you are not needed to make up a foursome at bridge and you are tired and want to go to bed before your hosts and the other guests do, it is perfectly all right to say to your hostess that you've had a "rugged" week at the office and would like to go to bed.

When you are visiting in a large household, do not use the staff as your own servants, and unless you have been told to ring for breakfast, do not do so. The thoughtful hostess, however, will suggest to an aged guest that if he or she would like any help in dressing, John, the house-man, or Marie, the maid, will be glad to do anything possible.

When you are visiting a house run with one maid or none, it is in-considerate to make your visit a burden through the extra picking up that your careless disorder entails. Even should you be staying in a house where there are many servants, it should be remembered that each has a share of work to do. If the housemaid offers to press a dress that has be-come mussed in packing, you of course accept her offer and later give her a gratuity—but you should not ask this service unless the pressing is really necessary.

If the hostess does her own housework, you may certainly, and in-deed you must, make your bed, tidy up your room, and offer to help in clearing the table and cleaning up in the kitchen.

One of the most trying things to people of very set habits is an un-usual breakfast hour. When you are one who wakes with the dawn and the household you are visiting has the custom of sleeping on a Sunday morning, the long wait for your coffee can quite truly upset your whole day. On the other hand, to be aroused at seven on the only day when you do not have to hurry to your own affairs, in order to yawn through an early breakfast and then sit around and kill time with the Sunday paper, is just as trying. The farsighted guest with the early habit can in a measure prevent discomfort. He can carry in a small case his own little electric water-heating outfit and a package of instant coffee or tea, sugar, pow-dered milk or cream, and a few crackers. He can then start his day all by himself in the barnyard hours without disturbing anyone. Or, in an in-formal household, he may slip quietly into the kitchen and make him-self a cup of coffee and a piece of toast to sustain him until the others are ready for a full breakfast. Few people care enough to fuss, but if they do, these suggestions for a visitor with incurably early waking hours can make a great difference to his enjoyment of the entire day.

Perhaps the entire guest situation may be put in one sentence. If you are an inflexible person, very set in your ways, don't visit! At least don't visit without carefully looking the situation over from every angle to be sure that the habits of the house you are going to are in accord with your own. If you have confidence in your adaptability, go and enjoy yourself!

THE GUEST ON A YACHT

The sole difference between being a guest at a country house and a guest on a yacht is that you put to a very severe test your adaptability as a traveler. You live in very close quarters with your host and hostess and your fellow guests and must therefore be particularly on your guard against being selfish or out of humor. If you are on shore and don't feel well, you can stay at home; but off on a cruise, if you are ill, you have to make the best of it, and a seasick person's "best" is very bad indeed! Therefore, let it be hoped you are a good sailor. If not, do not accept that yachting invitation!

If you are involved in a racing cruise of any sort, remember that it may be vitally important to your host to win—or at least to make a good showing. In these circumstances you will almost certainly be expected to assist, or act as crew, and presumably your host knows the extent of your sailing ability. You may never have sailed with him before, however, and you must be prepared to accept orders quickly, adjust yourself to his routine, respect his regulations, and forgive and forget any impatience or ill temper that he may show in moments of stress. » *See also Chapter 68, "In games and sports."*

THE OVERNIGHT GUEST IN A CITY APARTMENT

Today an increasing number of people live in apartments where a guest room is a rarity. Sometimes a couch in the living room can be converted into a comfortable bed at night for an overnight guest, or if a child is away at camp or boarding school, his room may be available. No matter how hospitable your host or hostess may be, a guest should remember that an extra person in small quarters is, inevitably, something of an imposition—no matter how charming the guest may be. Household regulations should be meticulously observed, and the visitor should stay no longer than necessary. He should take up as little room with his possessions as possible and keep his belongings neat. Above all, he should be prepared to fit in with the household schedule and not inconvenience his host or hostess.

Part SEVEN

SPECIAL OCCASIONS

The new baby

The first announcement of the birth of a baby is usually made to the nearest and dearest friends and relatives as soon as the proud father or delighted grandparents can get to the telephone. Some time before the blessed event actually takes place, or immediately thereafter, the prospective parents usually visit a stationer's and select an announcement card to be sent to their own friends and those friends of the grandparents who are close to the family. After the birth and as soon as the name is determined, the father notifies the stationer, and in a few days the cards are ready.

The nicest type of birth announcement, and one that is happily coming back into general use, consists simply of a very small card with the baby's name and birth date on it, tied with a white or pastel ribbon to the upper margin of the "Mr. and Mrs." card of the parents.

A large variety of commercially designed announcement cards, with space for the baby's name, date of birth, and parents' names to be written in by hand, are also available, and as they are much less expensive, they are very popular. The least desirable of these include such data as the baby's weight and length and some foolish phrasing or coy design. One of those in poorest taste shows a baby's head peering out of a white pack-

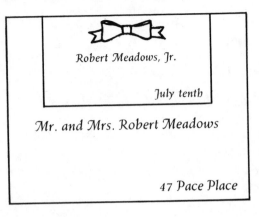

Robert Meadows, Jr.

July tenth

Mr. and Mrs. Robert Meadows

47 Pace Place

age carried by a stork and says: "My mommy and daddy want me to tell you I landed." Good taste rules that the simplest card is the best, *always!*

ANNOUNCEMENT OF ADOPTION

It is a nice gesture to send a card announcing this happy event to your friends and relatives. A card such as this will also bring reassuring comfort to the child later on, should she ever doubt her place in the hearts of those who chose her to be their own.

Mr. and Mrs. Nuhome
have the happiness to announce
the adoption of
Mary
aged thirteen months

Or, if announcements are sent during the legal proceedings, the wording may be changed:

Mr. and Mrs. Nuhome
have the happiness to announce
the arrival
and prospective adoption of
Mary
aged thirteen months

NEWSPAPER ANNOUNCEMENT OF BIRTH

In the week following the birth, the father may send a release to the local newspapers announcing the event: "Mr. and Mrs. Robert Meadows of 202 Park Avenue, New York City, announce the birth of a son, Robert, Jr. on July 10, 1959, at Doctors Hospital. They have one daughter, Jane, 4. Mrs. Meadows is the former Miss Mary Gilding." Or "A daughter, Mary Jane, was born to Mr. and Mrs. John Phillips of 19 Maple Avenue on

February 9th at St. Joseph's Hospital. Mrs. Phillips is the former Miss Mary Star of New Haven, Connecticut." The same announcement may be sent to the editor of the church newsletter or bulletin.

CHOOSING A NAME

Parents should be careful to avoid giving the baby a name that will be a handicap because it is too long or difficult to pronounce clearly or forms an unpleasant combination with the last name. Simple or biblical names will go well with most family names. It is nice for a name to have some significance, perhaps because of its original meaning or because it is traditionally carried by some member of the family. A child may also be named for a highly respected national figure or a beloved friend.

Many Christian first sons are given the same name as their fathers; when a child is named for a parent he may be given a middle name different from that of the parent, and in adult life he may decide to be known as "R. William Meadows," instead of "Robert Meadows, Jr." Roman Catholic babies, by canon law, are named after a saint. Although they may be called by any diminutive, their baptismal certificates must record a saint's name as the baby's first or middle name. Most Jewish babies are traditionally named for a deceased relative, and thus the name of a loved one is perpetuated.

PRESENTS FOR BABY AND MOTHER

Everyone who receives a birth-announcement card should write a note of congratulations to the new parents. Or a note may be enclosed if a gift is sent. It is not necessary to send a present, however, even if you receive an announcement.

Gifts may be sent for the baby, addressed to the parents at home, or you may bring your present with you when you visit the hospital. It is thoughtful to bring something for the new mother, too—cologne (if she uses it) or handkerchiefs, or perhaps a plant or flower arrangement.

CHRISTENINGS AND OTHER RELIGIOUS CEREMONIES

TIME OF CHRISTENING

In other days of stricter observances, a baby was baptized in the Roman or High Episcopal church on the first, or possibly the second, Sunday after its birth. In the Catholic church, the baptism still takes place when the baby is very young—usually not over a month old—and always in the church or baptistry (unless its baptism is *in extremis*). In Latin countries, babies are often baptized in the hospital, within a day or two of their birth. In Protestant churches, the average age for christening is from two to six months, although in some denominations or under special conditions, children may not be christened until they are several years old. In all churches, it is customary for the mother to be present if she is able.

THE GODPARENTS

If your faith requires godparents, before setting the day of the christening, the godparents should be asked and their consent obtained. They may be asked to serve when the baby's arrival is announced to them and occasionally before; or perhaps when they visit the hospital. In Protestant practice, there are usually two godfathers and one godmother for a boy, two godmothers and one godfather for a girl. A Catholic baby has one godparent of each sex, who must be Catholics, too. (Catholics are not allowed to serve as godparents for children of other faiths.)

It is perfectly correct to send a note if the godparent lives at a distance, or he may be asked by telegraph: "IT'S A BOY. WILL YOU BE GODFATHER?" But in any case do not write anything so formal as "My husband and I sincerely hope that you will consent to be our son's godmother." It would be the height of presumption to ask anyone so slightly known as this wording implies to fill so intimate a position.

If a godparent whom the parents particularly want is unable to be present, a proxy acts for him or her at the ceremony, the consent of the real godparent having first been given. It is considerate for the real godparent to send a note to the clergyman authorizing the proxy.

One must never ask any but a most intimate friend to be a godmother or godfather, for it is a responsibility not lightly to be undertaken and also one difficult to refuse. Godparents are usually chosen from among friends rather than relatives, because one advantage of godparents is that they add to the child's stock of relatives. Should the child be left alone in the world, its godparents become its protectors. But when a child is born with plenty of relatives who can be called upon for assistance, godparents are sometimes chosen from among them.

The obligation of being a godparent is essentially a spiritual one; therefore, the godparent should be of the same faith as the parents. The godparent is supposed to see that the child is given religious training and is confirmed at the proper time. Beyond these obligations, he is expected to take a special interest in the child, much as a very near relative would do.

At the christening, he gives the baby as nice a present as he can afford. The typical gift is a silver mug or porringer, inscribed: "*Robert Meadows, Jr./December 5th, 1965/From his godfather/John Strong.*" Other typical presents are a silver fork and spoon, a silver comb and brush set, a government bond, or a trust fund to which the donor may add each year until the child is grown.

CHRISTENING INVITATIONS

Usually, christening invitations are given over the telephone or in a personal note to "Dear Linda and Jeff" or "Dear Mr. and Mrs. Kindhart," and signed "Mary" or "Mary Meadows."

Dear Jane,

    We are having Karen christened on Sunday at 3:00 in Christ's Church. Would you and Bob come to the ceremony at the church, and join us afterward at our house?

Affectionately,

Sally

Or a message may be written on the "Mr. and Mrs." card of the parents, saying simply: "*Baby's christening, St. Mary's Church, Jan. 10, 3 o'clock. Caudle at our house afterward.*" All invitations to a christening should be very friendly and informal.

THE CHILD'S CLOTHES

The baby's christening dress is often one that was worn by the baby's mother, father, or even one of its grand- or great-grandparents. Everything the baby wears on this occasion should be white, although this is merely a custom and not a church requirement. The traditional christening dress is long, made of sheer, soft material with lace and hand embroidery trim, and worn with delicate, long petticoats. It is not necessary to go to the expense of buying a traditional christening dress if there is no family heirloom; any long, or even short, plain white dress will do. However, some very pretty christening dresses are available in the new miracle fabrics, and they are quite inexpensive.

In Protestant churches, when the children are no longer babies, little girls wear white dresses, even though they may be well past the baby stage. Little boys, however, do not have to wear white suits. An Eton jacket, dark blue with matching shorts, is appropriate for very little ones, and older boys may wear a dark blue or dark gray suit.

WHAT THE GUESTS WEAR

The guests at a christening wear what they would wear to church. The mother wears a light-colored dress; she should not wear black on this occasion, and she should wear a hat or a veil. If she is not sure of the custom of the church, every woman should wear a hat—it is *never* incorrect.

THE CHURCH CEREMONY

The clergyman, of course, is consulted about the place and hour for the christening before the guests are invited. The ceremony may take place at the close of the regular Sunday service, the guests remaining after the rest of the congregation leaves. Roman Catholic parishes generally schedule baptisms for a specified time on Sunday afternoons, and the parents make an appointment at the rectory in advance. If a large party is planned to follow a Protestant christening, it is best to choose a weekday and an hour when the church is not being otherwise used. Guests seat themselves in the pews nearest the front.

As soon as the clergyman appears, the baby's coat and cap are taken off and the godmother, holding the baby in her arms, stands directly in front of the clergyman. The other godparents stand beside her, and relatives and friends nearby.

The godmother holding the baby must be sure to pronounce his name distinctly; in fact, if the name is long or unusual, it is wise to print it on a slip of paper and give it to the clergyman beforehand, because whatever name the clergyman pronounces is fixed for life. More than one baby has been given a name not intended for him. The godmother states the given name or names only, and not the surname.

In the Presbyterian church and others that do not require godparents, the father holds the baby and gives its name. There is no separate service—it is done during or immediately after the regular Sunday service.

As soon as the ceremony is over, the baby and all the relatives and friends go to the house of the parents or grandparents, where a reception —the traditional caudle usually replaced by punch or champagne—has been arranged.

Baptism is a sacrament of the church, for which no fee is ever required. A donation, however, is presented in an envelope to the clergyman after the ceremony, commensurate with the elaborateness of the christening.

A HOUSE CHRISTENING

If permitted by the church to which the baby's parents belong, the house christening is a safer and prettier ceremony—safer, because the baby is not likely to catch cold by being taken out and brought in, and prettier, because the baby's dress has not been crushed by having a coat put over it and also because a baby whose routine has not been upset is generally "good."

The arrangements for a house christening are quite simple, the only necessary decoration being the font. This is always a bowl—usually of silver (often borrowed)—put on a small, high table.

A white napkin on the table suggests a restaurant rather than a ritual and is therefore an unfortunate choice; most people prefer to cover the table in a dark fabric, such as old brocade or velvet. Flowers may be arranged around the bowl in a flat circle, the blossoms outside, the stems toward the center and covered by the base of the bowl.

At the hour set for the ceremony, the clergyman enters the room and takes his place at the font. The guests naturally make way, forming an open aisle. The godmother, or the father if there are no godparents, carries the baby and follows the clergyman; the other participants walk behind and all stand near the font. At the proper moment, the clergyman takes the baby, baptizes it, and hands it back to the godmother or father, who holds it until the ceremony is over.

After performing the ceremony, the clergyman, if he wears vestments, goes to a room that has been set apart for him, changes into his street clothes, and then returns to the living room as one of the guests.

THE CHRISTENING PARTY

The only difference between an ordinary informal reception and a christening party is that the latter features christening cake and caudle. The christening cake is generally a white "lady" cake elaborately iced. A real caudle is a hot eggnog, drunk out of little punch cups. But today champagne or punch is usually substituted for the caudle, and those who have an aversion to a punch are often offered a highball.

Guests eat the cake as a sign that they partake of the baby's hospitality and are therefore his friends, and they drink the punch to his health and prosperity. But by this time the young host or hostess is peacefully asleep in the nursery.

JEWISH CEREMONIES FOR THE NEWBORN

On the eighth day after birth, in the ceremony known as *Brith Milah*, a boy is initiated into the Jewish covenant between man and God. The circumcision is accompanied by a religious ceremony during which the boy is named. After the ceremony, which may take place in a special room in the hospital, there is a light collation. The guests drink to the baby's future and toast the parents, grandparents, and godparents (there is always a godfather and usually a godmother). Relatives and close friends are invited to the *Brith* by telephone or informal note. They dress as they would for any service in a synagogue, and both men and women customarily wear hats.

Girls are named in the synagogue on the first Sabbath after birth, when the father is called up to the Torah. Sometimes the naming is postponed until the mother is able to be present. In some Reform congregations, boys are also named in the synagogue (in addition to being named at the *Brith*) when both parents are present, and a special blessing is pronounced by the rabbi. The mother may be hostess at the collation following the service. Friends and relatives may be invited to attend the religious service during which the baby will be named.

The ceremony of redemption of the first-born, the *Pidyon Ha-Ben*, which takes place only if the first-born is a boy, is performed when the baby is thirty-one days old. According to ancient custom described in the Bible, the first-born son was dedicated to the service of God. It became customary for a *Cohen* (a descendant of the priestly tribe) to redeem the child from his obligation, entrusting him to the care of his father for bringing up in the Jewish faith. The *Pidyon Ha-Ben*, consisting of a brief ceremony and a celebration, is held in the home, informal notes of invitation having been sent about ten days previously to close friends and relatives.

Graduation

Because the activities differ widely in each of our thousands of schools and colleges, no definite schedule for commencement week can be given. Graduation or commencement programs at the high school level are much the same as at the colleges, but on a modified scale. The senior class dance is more likely to be attended by the graduates and their dates only, with a few parents included as chaperones, although at some preparatory schools all families are invited, too. There may be a class play or a varsity game attended by parents and dates, or there may be nothing other than the graduation ceremony itself.

Although "commencement week" festivities may start for the students a week or more in advance of the actual graduation day, the events to which families and dates are invited take place only on the last day or two before commencement. These events usually consist of any or all of the following: A senior class ball, attended at some colleges by dates only, and at others by parents and brothers and sisters of the graduates as well. A senior class play, generally a comedy or review, sometimes involving the class history, and attended by everyone. Fraternity parties, tea dances, or cocktail parties, to which all the graduates' dates are invited. A varsity baseball game or possibly a Seniors vs. Alumni game. Special events peculiar to a particular college, such as torch light parades or barn dances. And finally, winding up all commencement week festivities and attended by every guest, the baccalaureate service, usually held in the chapel on a Sunday morning, and the commencement exercises themselves, held that afternoon or the following morning.

MAKING RESERVATIONS

It is essential in this day of large college classes for the families of the graduates to make reservations well in advance of graduation day. Many hotels and inns have no rooms left to reserve by the time Christmas vacation arrives, so it is well to think of this during the fall term, especially if the college is in a small town that does not have too many accommodations. The parents may find out from the college how many guests each student may have and then consult with their son or daughter as to whom he or she wishes to invite. If the graduate has a fiancé or a serious boy or girl friend, the family makes a reservation for him, too.

INVITATIONS

Colleges and universities provide each graduating student with the number of invitations he is allowed to send. Some also distribute announcements to those students who wish to send them out after graduation day. Considerable thought should be given to sending announcements, and the list should be limited to those really interested, because the recipients are inclined to feel that they must send a gift.

REQUIREMENTS FOR THE SENIOR'S DATE

The senior's date, whether a fiancé or a very good friend, a boy or a girl, stays with the family of the student. He or she naturally attends all those events which are for dates only, but at parties or games to which all guests are invited, the date goes with the parents and does not try to monopolize the attention of the graduate.

If a young man's family cannot attend the commencement or if he has no family, he or his date must try to find another graduate's family (preferably the parents of a close friend) willing to adopt her for the occasion. If this proves impossible, the young man may ask one of his favorite professors if it would be possible for her to stay in his house. In no circumstance may she stay alone in a motel or an inn.

CLOTHING

Clothing varies with the activities planned, of course, but it is much the same as for similar social events elsewhere. Guests are usually sent a program well in advance, either by their son or daughter or by the college, and can determine then what may be needed.

The senior dance is always formal, so the date must bring an evening dress or a tuxedo. Girls generally wear shorts or simple cotton dresses for daytime sporting events or picnics, and the boys wear shorts or slacks and a sport shirt. Since June is graduation month and the weather is usually hot, the guests may be told to bring a bathing suit.

For the baccalaureate and commencement services, mothers and girl friends will look prettiest and most comfortable in cool, short-sleeved dresses, in a print or a pastel color, and perhaps of silk or an easily packed synthetic. Grandmother may be happiest in a silk suit. Hats or veils are worn at a chapel service, but are not necessary if the commencement ceremony is held out of doors.

Men and boys wear light-weight suits of any color for the formal services.

PRESENTS

Graduation presents are unlimited in variety, but the closer to the graduate the giver, the more elaborate the gift. Parents may give a fine watch, a set of evening jewelry, an automobile, or even a trip to Europe. If these gifts are beyond their means, anything that is lasting and of the best quality that they can afford is always appreciated. A nicely bound book on a favorite subject, for instance, or a set of cuff links or other simple jewelry can be a source of much pleasure.

A fiancé or a "steady" boy friend might choose a charm or a locket, and a girl friend might consider a handsome wallet or a gold or silver tie clip.

The gifts of other relatives and friends may depend on the future plans of the graduate. If he is taking a trip, a passport case or a suitcase would be a good choice. If he is about to be married, something for his home—a cigarette box with the college seal, perhaps, or a silver tray with the graduation date on it—would be appreciated.

THANK-YOU NOTES

A note of thanks, written by hand and on note paper, must go to every one who has sent a present whenever the giver has not been at the commencement to be thanked in person. This note need not be long, but it should express appreciation and be written as promptly as possible.

> *Dear Aunt Mary,*
>
> *I can't thank you enough for the check you sent me, which will be such a help toward my summer in Europe. I'm looking forward to seeing you in the fall to tell you all about the trip.*
>
> *With much love,*
>
> *Jane*

Or:

Dear Uncle Jim,

Thank you so very much for the cuff links you sent me. How did you know they were the things I needed most of all? I was disappointed that you couldn't make the graduation, but I'll drive down to see you and thank you in person as soon as possible.

Thanks again,

Bill

Debuts

"Presenting a debutante to society" has a quaint flavor and, in this age of female equality, may seem to echo social customs long past. Yet, when her daughter is eighteen—never before and rarely long after—a mother may want to present the young lady to the adult world with a certain degree of formality. For this "coming-out," she has a choice of several forms.

The most elaborate, possible only for parents of considerable means, is a private ball. Less elaborate and more common is a small dance that presents the debutante to her own and her parents' friends. Third is a tea dance. Fourth, and by far the most popular today, is the big dance for all or several of the debutantes in the area. In a very large city, it may be given cooperatively by a group of parents who get together and share the expense of a single coming-out party for their daughters. In other cases, it may be given by an organization that invites a group of girls to participate. Many balls or cotillions of this kind are benefit affairs, handled by a committee of the sponsoring charity and thus serving a double purpose, as the parents of the girls invited to participate are expected to give a substantial donation to the charity involved. » *The correct forms for the invitations and their answers to all these functions may be found in Chapters 52 and 55.*

DEBUTANTE BALLS

THE RECEIVING LINE AT A PRIVATE DEBUT

The ball for a debutante is typical of all balls. The debutante "receives" standing beside her mother or whoever else may be hostess, and farthest from the entrance, whether that happens to be on the latter's right or left. As they enter, the guests approach the hostess first, who, as she shakes hands with each, turns to the debutante and, repeating the name that has been announced to her, says, "My daughter" or "You remember Cynthia, don't you?" or merely "Cynthia."

Each arriving guest shakes hands with the debutante as well as with the hostess. If there is a queue of people coming at the same time, there is no need of saying anything beyond "How do you do?" and passing on as quickly as possible. If there are no others entering at the moment, each guest makes a few pleasant remarks—for instance, "How beautiful your bouquets are!" A friend of her mother probably says, "Cynthia dear, how lovely you are tonight!" or "Your dress is enchanting!" A young man exclaims, "My, you look wonderful tonight!" The girls assure her, "Your dress is simply divine!"

At a ball, where the guests begin coming at eleven o'clock, the debutante receives until about twelve o'clock—or later if guests continue to arrive. Then she is free to join the dancing. She usually dances the first dance with her father and the next with the young man (or men) she has asked to be her escort for the evening.

SENDING FLOWERS

It is still customary in most cities to send a debutante flowers at her coming-out party. They may be bouquets, or baskets, or any other decorative flowers, and they are sent by relatives, friends of the family, and her father's business associates, as well as by the younger men who are her friends. These flowers are usually banked as a background for her when she stands to receive. The debutante always holds one of the bouquets while receiving, sometimes the same one, sometimes several in succession so as not to show partiality to any special giver.

AT SUPPER

The debutante goes to supper with a partner whom she herself chooses, her escort, if she has invited one. She always makes up her own table, which includes her most intimate friends. If she is very popular and does not wish to center her attention on one man, an easy way out is to ask a brother or other relative. Her table is usually in the center of the dining room, is somewhat larger than the tables surrounding it, and has a card on it saying "Reserved."

DINNER DANCES

Since the times of the year when young people are at home in large numbers are restricted to school vacations, there are often more girls who wish to come out at private parties than there are evenings available. In many communities, two girls whose guest lists overlap arrange for one of them to be presented at a dinner dance and the other at a late dance on the same evening. This is a very convenient arrangement for both families. The one who goes to the expense of serving the dinner knows that she needs to provide drinks and refreshments for only a limited time after dinner, and the other girl only needs to worry about a light supper served around one o'clock, and the champagne, punch, or whatever she chooses to serve for the rest of the night.

The two debutantes attend each others' parties, and the one giving the second party leaves, with her escorts, immediately after dinner to help her mother with last minute arrangements. Guests are usually invited to a dinner dance at 7:30 or 8:00, and the debutante and her hostess receive until dinner is served at 8:30 or 9:00. The late dance begins at approximately 11:00.

TEA DANCES

The afternoon tea dance to introduce a debutante is described in Chapters 26 and 32, and the very small dance needs little comment, because, except for size and decoration, its pattern is precisely the same. As at every coming-out party, the debutante and her mother or hostess stand in line and receive the guests as they arrive.

ASSEMBLIES, COTILLIONS, AND COMMUNITY DEBUTS

Eliminating the expense and rigors of a private ball and coming out instead as a member of a group, large or small, is becoming more and more common. If she wishes, a girl's mother may give a small debut party or tea at home and still accept an invitation to participate in one of the assemblies or cotillions.

Customs vary widely in different areas, and because debutante balls are generally planned by the more knowledgeable people in a community, it is safe to assume that whatever local practices have become traditional and are accepted by the participants are, in that city or town, quite correct.

Some committees invite both boys and girls (other than those "coming out") to the dance; others invite only the girls and request that they bring two escorts. When this is done, the girls are expected to send in the names of the escorts as soon as they have accepted, and the committee then sends the boys a formal invitation. The girls are expected to pay for their escort's ticket if it is a charity-sponsored ball. At most multiple de-

buts, the committee does not invite guests, but each debutante's family is allowed a certain number of invitations, and they are responsible for paying for those they invite.

There may be entertainment in the form of a dance performed by the debutantes and their fathers or escorts, or nothing more than the formal presentation, by their fathers, of the girls to the committee members who are acting as hostesses. There may or may not be professional entertainment—a singer or dancer, perhaps.

The party may be a dinner dance, but it is more likely to be a late ball. If it is private, friends will frequently give dinner parties preceding it; and if it is run by a committee, the members often have dinners for debutantes and their escorts. This may also be done by the families of the girls themselves.

Whatever the local traditions, these "mass debuts" are a great success. By sharing the costs, many families can afford far more elaborate decorations, prettier dresses, and better music than they could otherwise hope to obtain. The girls, if they are at all shy, are spared the nightmare of being alone in the spotlight. And any mishaps that may occur seem smaller when the responsibility is divided, whereas sharing a success with friends makes it doubly sweet.

THE FATHER'S PART

The role of the father at a private debut is simply that of the good host at any party. He does not stand in the receiving line, but he stays nearby, greets friends and acquaintances, and sees that everything is running smoothly. He dances the first dance with his daughter, and then he dances with his wife, with the grandmothers if they are present and wish to dance, and then with the other guests, young and old alike.

At many cotillions and community debuts, the fathers participate in a parade and a simple cotillion dance with their daughters. They cross the ballroom, one couple at a time, and each father presents his debutante daughter to the hostess or to the committee giving the dance. Although the young men guests nowadays may wear tuxedos to debut parties, the escorts of the debutantes who are coming out and the fathers must wear white tie and tails.

THE DEBUTANTE'S DRESS

At a ball, the debutante wears the very prettiest evening dress she can buy. Old-fashioned sentiment prefers that it be white and that it suggest something light, airy, gay, and, above all, young. For the girl who prefers to wear colors, a pastel—faint rose, pale blue, or light yellow—is perfectly suitable. But not scarlet or a bright blue, and on no account black, no matter how sophisticatedly chic she thinks she would look in it. At a multiple debut, the girls wear the same color, almost invariably white, but they choose their own style. The mothers of the debutantes wear evening dresses in any color except black.

At an afternoon tea the debutante wears a cocktail dress. Her mother wears an afternoon dress, not an evening one. Both mother and daughter wear gloves, and neither wears a hat.

SOME HINTS FOR THE "BELLE OF THE BALL"

Let us suppose that you are a young girl on the evening of your coming-out ball. You are excited! Of course you are! It is your evening! But don't let your excitement overwhelm your sense of courtesy.

It takes scarcely five seconds to listen to a name that is said to you, to look at the one to whom the name belongs, to put out your hand willingly and not as though doing something hateful to you, and with a smile say, "How do you do, Mrs. Holmes?" who then passes on. It takes no longer to be cordial and attentive than to be distrait and casual and rude, yet the impression made in a few seconds of time may easily gain or lose a friend. When no other guests are arriving, you can chatter to your own friends as much as you like; but as you turn to greet another, you must show pleasure, not annoyance, in giving her or him your attention.

As friends who have sent you flowers approach, you must thank them; you must also write later an additional note of thanks to older people. But to your relatives or your own intimate friends, your oral thanks, if appreciatively made, are sufficient.

41

Engagements

The courtship period is a time of excitement and fun, but as it progresses and as the young people find themselves more and more attracted to each other, it becomes as well a time of serious consideration. At some point, the girl begins to think, "This is the man I want to marry—I wonder if he feels the same way about me?" And Jim is saying to himself, "Sally is the only girl in the world for me—I wonder if she'll say 'Yes' if I ask her." So their conversation becomes more personal and more serious and they start to "sound each other out." Very often nowadays the man never actually says "Will you marry me?" They agree to marry through a sort of understanding and acceptance of each other that has grown with their deepening acquaintance.

It is very important, during this pre-engagement time, that these young people do not avoid the company of others. While the evenings when they are alone are surely their favorite ones, it is essential for them to get to know each other's friends. A marriage in which either partner is incompatible with those who have always been part of the other's life has one strike against it to begin with. This is even more true of the couple's families. Each should be entertained in the home of the other so that they can see the surroundings and the family to which they will be expected to adjust. Although it may not be possible if either or both of the families live in another area, an overnight or weekend visit can be helpful in making the decision as to whether to propose and whether to accept if the proposal comes. The family that is to entertain the young people should be advised beforehand what the situation is by their son or daughter, in order to avoid embarrassing their guest.

> *"Mother, may I bring Sally Foster up for the night next Saturday? We have been seeing a lot of each other, and I'm eager to have her see Waterbury, and to introduce her to you."*
>
> Love,
>
> Jim

Or:

> *Dear Mom,*
>
> *I recently met a most attractive man, Jerry Boyd, from Syracuse, and I'm very eager for you to meet each other. So I wondered if it would be convenient for us to spend next weekend with you and Dad. Please let me know as soon as you can.*
>
> Love to you both,
>
> Sue

The parents receiving such a note or a telephone call are prepared to meet their possible son or daughter-in-law, but should realize that unless they are told otherwise when the couple arrives, the engagement is still in the future.

THE FUTURE GROOM AND HIS FIANCÉE'S FATHER

The very first thing the couple does after he proposes and she says "Yes" is to see her father or whoever is head of her family, and the prospective groom asks for his or possibly her consent. If her father refuses, the girl then is faced with the problem of changing her "Yes" to "No" or else marrying in opposition to her parents. The honorable young woman who has made up her mind to marry in spite of her parents' disapproval tells them that on such and such a day her wedding will take place and refuses to give her word that she will not marry. The height of dishonor is to give her word while intending to break it.

In most instances, however, when John goes to see Mary's father, the latter has a perfectly good idea of what he has come to say and has for some time been planning how he will word his answer to his prospective son-in-law.

It may be that John's finances seem to the father not to be quite up to supporting his daughter, and he may decide to give her some sort of allowance, which will make the life of the young couple less of a struggle. But if her father is not able to make up for the shortcomings of John's finances himself, he may have to advise that they wait before marrying or even possibly before he can approve the engagement. On the other hand, if everything is satisfactory, he makes no objection to an immediate announcement.

THE ENGAGEMENT RING

It is doubtful that the man who produced a ring from his pocket upon the instant that she said "Yes" ever existed outside romantic novels. In real life, it is both correct and wise for *him* to consult *her* taste. The fiancé first goes alone to the jeweler, explains how much he can afford, and has a selection of rings set aside. He then brings his fiancée into the store and lets her choose from among them the one she likes best.

It might be a charming one of platinum and diamond design. Or it may be a lovely ring of more important size in her own birthstone. If there are family heirlooms to be chosen from, he may show them to his fiancée and have her selection set to her taste.

One quite popular trend today is the widespread fashion of using semiprecious stones, beside which the tiny diamond has lost its appeal.

An aquamarine is today's first choice as a solitaire diamond's substitute. An amethyst, or topaz, or transparent tourmaline are all lovely as selections for an engagement ring. But if a birthstone seems appropriate:

JANUARY—*Garnet* (Its rather dark glow makes a pleasing engagement ring). The *zircon*, a white crystal-clear stone, makes a very attractive ring and closely resembles a diamond particularly when square cut and kept brilliantly clean. Because it does resemble a diamond, many a bride will, I am afraid, fear that people will feel she is trying to fool them into thinking it really is a diamond. There is also a beautiful steely-blue variety.

FEBRUARY—*Amethyst* (Big one; square cut effective).

MARCH—*Aquamarine*, first; then *bloodstone* or *jasper*. Aquamarine, square cut—very popular and a really beautiful substitute for a diamond.

APRIL—*Diamond* (The stone of stones, but high-priced when of first quality).

MAY—*Emerald* (Also very costly if perfect in color and without noticeable flaw).

JUNE—*Pearl* (Nothing more becoming to a very beautiful smooth white hand).

JULY—*Ruby* (Of very high value when of the desirable pigeon-blood color).

August—*Sardonyx, peridot* (a rare and beautiful stone), or *carnelian*.
September—*Sapphire* (A favorite engagement ring of yesterday and always beautiful).
October—*Opal* (The opal is believed to be the stone of good fortune for those born in October, but unlucky for those not born in this month).
November—*Topaz*.
December—*Turquoise* or *lapis lazuli*.

The engagement ring is worn for the first time in public on the day of the announcement. But *the engagement ring is not essential to the validity of the betrothal*. Many confuse the engagement ring with the wedding ring and believe the former is as indispensable as the latter—which is not the case. The wedding ring is a requirement of the marriage service. The engagement ring is simply evidence that he has proposed marriage and that she has answered "Yes!"

Countless wives have never had an engagement ring at all. Many another receives her ring long after marriage, when her husband is able to buy the ring he has always wanted her to have. Some brides prefer to forego an engagement ring, and put the money it would have cost toward furnishing their future home.

IF SHE GIVES HIM AN ENGAGEMENT PRESENT

It is not obligatory, or even customary, for the girl to give the man an engagement present; but there is no impropriety in her doing so. In fact, if she wants to call it that, she can even give him an engagement ring.

The more usual presents include such articles as a set of studs and a matching pair of cuff links, or a watch band or a key chain, or a cigarette case. Probably because the giving of an engagement ring is his particular province, she very rarely gives him a ring or, in fact, any present at all.

HIS PARENTS' CALL ON HERS

Following the acceptance of the engagement, the parents of the man should go to call on the parents of the girl. At least his mother goes at once to see hers. If they do not live in the same city, letters of welcome to the girl should be written, and letters to her parents, expressing their pleasure. After the engagement is announced, all the near relatives of the bridegroom-to-be—sisters, brothers, aunts, and even cousins, if they are close to him—should as soon as possible call upon or write to the bride and her family. The telephone, of course, can help two families who live at a distance to know each other. When they live some distance apart it may be more practical for the bride's parents to visit those of the groom first, and this is perfectly correct. In this case the invitation to visit corresponds to the groom's parents paying the first "call," and it is arranged by mutual consent. If for any reason the man's family does not call on the parents of the girl, her father and mother should be very careful not to permit an oversight to develop into a situation that may cause great distress. The point to be made is that this time should be a happy one for the young couple and that both sets of parents should act with spontaneity and in a spirit of friendship.

It is also of great importance that the girl try to understand and accept the attitude of her future family (whatever it may be) and that she must *not* stand inflexibly upon what she unwittingly might consider to be her own rights. After all, the objective that she should keep in mind is the happiness of the relationship between herself and her future in-laws.

ANNOUNCING THE ENGAGEMENT

PERSONAL ANNOUNCEMENT

Usually a few days—perhaps a week—before the formal announcement the girl and man each write to or call aunts, uncles, and cousins, and their most intimate friends, telling of their engagement and asking them not to tell anyone else until the determined date. This is so those closest to them will not read of it first in the newspapers. It is expected, however, that these relatives telephone or write the bride as soon as they receive the news, and call, when it is convenient. She must, of course, answer the letters as soon as possible.

If his people are in the habit of entertaining, they should promptly ask her with her fiancé to lunch or to dinner, and after the engagement is publicly announced, give a more general party in her honor. If, on the other hand, they are very quiet people, they should merely call upon her to show their welcome.

In case of a recent death in either immediate family, the engagement should be quietly announced by telling families and intimate friends. (The wedding announcement in the newspaper serves to inform other acquaintances.)

THE FORMAL ANNOUNCEMENT

The formal or public announcement is made by the parents of the bride-to-be. This is done either by notes, or at the engagement party, and after that publicly through the newspapers. Engraved announcements are not correct.

NEWSPAPER ANNOUNCEMENTS

The newspaper announcement of the engagment is sent by the "bride's" parents, with all the information to be included (and, if you wish, a picture of the bride) to the society editor of all the papers in which it is to be printed. If you live in the suburbs of a large city or in a small town, a copy should be sent to the local paper (which may be a weekly). Others go to the paper of your choice in the nearby city and to the paper suggested by the groom's family in their locality.

The announcement should be sent to the papers a week or more in advance of the date on which you wish it to appear, and that date should be clearly stated, so that the announcement comes out simultaneously in all the papers. Many people think it important to have it appear in the Sunday paper, probably because the party announcing the engagement may have been held on the Saturday before. There is a far better chance of having all the information printed, and the photograph used, on a weekday when the demand for space is not so pressing. If your local paper is a weekly, the date given the other papers should coincide with the day on which it is published.

The usual form is as follows:

Mr. and Mrs. Herbert Coles Johnson of Lake Forest, Illinois, announce the engagement of their daughter, Miss Susan Bailey Johnson, to Dr. William Arthur Currier, son of Mr. and Mrs. Arthur Jamison Currier of Atlanta, Georgia. A June wedding is planned.

Miss Johnson was graduated from Bentley Junior College. She made her debut in 1960 at the Mistletoe Ball in Chicago, and in May will complete her nurse's training at Atlanta General Hospital. Dr. Currier was graduated from the Hill School, Yale University, and the Yale Medical School. He completed his residency at the Atlanta General Hospital and is now in practice in that city.

In unusual situations, the information as to schools and employment remains the same, although the identification of the bride and groom and their parents may vary.

When one parent is deceased: The announcement is worded the same whether made by the mother or father of the bride.

Mrs. Herbert Coles Johnson announces the engagement of her daughter, Miss Susan Bailey Johnson, to Dr. William Arthur Currier . . . etc. Miss Johnson is also the daughter of the late Herbert Coles Johnson. . . .

If her parent has remarried:

Mr. and Mrs. John Franklin announce the engagement of Mr. Franklin's daughter, Miss Helen Susan Franklin, to . . . etc. Miss Franklin is also the daughter of the late Mrs. Sarah Ellis Franklin. . . .

If a parent of the groom is deceased:

Mr. and Mrs. Harry Brown announce the engagement of their daughter, Miss Mary Francis Brown, to Mr. Robert Lewis, son of Mrs. Allen Carter Lewis, and the late Mr. Lewis. . . .

When the bride is an orphan: The engagement of an orphan is announced by the girl's nearest relative, a godparent, or a very dear friend. If she has no one close to her, she sends the announcement herself:

> The engagement of Miss Jessica Towne, daughter of the late Mr. and Mrs. Samuel Towne, is announced, to Mr. Richard Frost. . . .

This form may also be used if the parents live very far away or if she has, for some reason, separated herself completely from her family.

If the parents are divorced: The mother of the bride usually makes the announcement, but, as in the case of a deceased parent, the name of the other parent must be included.

> Mrs. Jones Farnham announces the engagement of her daughter, Miss Cynthia Farnham . . . . Miss Farnham is also the daughter of Mr. Henry Farnham of Worcester, Mass. . . .

If the parent with whom the bride lives is remarried:

> Mr. and Mrs. Samuel Harvey announce the engagement of Mrs. [*or* Mr.] Harvey's daughter, Miss Jane Barber Cutler [Harvey] to . . . . Miss Cutler [Harvey] is also the daughter of Mr. David Soames Cutler [*or* Mrs. James Little] of Menlo Park, California. . . .

If divorced parents are friendly: On occasion, divorced parents may remain good friends and their daughter's time may be divided equally between them. If this is true, they may both wish to announce the engagement.

> Mr. Gordon Smythe of Philadelphia, and Mrs. Howard Zabriskie of 12 East 72nd Street, New York City, announce the engagement of their daughter, Miss Carla Farr Smythe. . . .

If the bride is adopted: If the bride has been brought up with the family since babyhood and has the same name as her foster parents, there is no reason to mention the fact that she is adopted. If she joined the family later in life, however, and has retained her own name, it is proper to say:

> Mr. and Mrs. Warren La Tour announce the engagement of their adopted daughter, Miss Claudia Romney, daughter of the late Mr. and Mrs. Carlton Romney. . . .

Older women, widows, and divorcées: A woman of forty or more, even though her parents are living, generally does not announce her engagement in the newspaper, but instead calls or writes her relatives and friends shortly before the wedding. A widow or divorcée announces her second engagement in the same way.

THE ENGAGEMENT PARTY

Invitations to engagement parties are generally written on informals or visiting cards, and do not necessarily mention the reason for the party. They are generally sent in the name of the bride's parents or of the relative or friend who is announcing the engagement. Occasionally the parents wish to include their daughter's name with theirs, and add "To meet Mr. John Watkins." Or, they may prefer, "In honor of Sally Jones and Robert Coolidge," clearly indicating the nature of the occasion. The invitations also may be issued by telephone.

Cocktails Dec. 10, 7-9
in honor of
Sally Jones and Robert Watkins

Mr. and Mrs. William Jones

R. s. v. p.

10 Lake Rd
Rye N Y

Presents are never taken to an engagement party even though it is not a surprise, because only intimate friends or relatives give gifts, and it might be embarrassing to other guests.

Cocktails
Dec 10, 7-9

Mr. and Mrs. William Jones

Sally Jones
to meet Robert Watkins

10 Lake Rd.
R. s. v. p.
Rye, N. Y.

The engagement party may be of any type that the mother of the bride prefers, but it is generally a cocktail party or a dinner. The guests are relatives and close friends of the bride and groom, and probably a few close friends of the parents. The news may be told by the girl herself, or by her mother, as the guests arrive and find the fiancé standing with their hostess. Or perhaps, if the party is a dinner, it is announced by the father, who proposes a toast to the couple. Little announcing is necessary, however, when the young woman is wearing a shining ring on the fourth finger of her left hand.

To those who ask about using a novel way to announce an engagement, it can be said that there is really no logical objection to whatever may be pleasing to you. Whether you let a cat out of a bag with your names written on a ribbon around its neck, float balloons with your names printed on them, or distribute bouquets tagged with both names, or whether guests receive the glad tidings in telegrams used as place cards, there is not a rule in the world to hamper your own imagination.

THE TOAST

This is the conventional announcement made by the father of the bride at a dinner: After seeing that all glasses at the table are filled, the host rises, lifts his own glass, and says: "I propose we drink to the health of Mary and the young man she has decided to add permanently to our family, James Smartlington."

Or: "A standing toast: To my Mary and to her—Jim!"

Or: "I want you to drink to the happiness of a young pair whose future welfare is close to the hearts of all of us: Mary [holding up his glass and looking at her] and Jim [looking at him]!"

Everyone except Mary and Jim rises and drinks a little of whatever the beverage may be. They then congratulate the young couple, and Jim is called upon for a speech.

Generally rather fussed, Jim rises, the color of black-raspberry sherbet, and says something like this: "I—er—we—thank you all very much indeed for all your good wishes," and sits down. Or if he is an earnest rather than a shy youth, perhaps he continues, "I don't have to tell you how lucky I am; the thing for me to do is to prove, if I can, that Mary has not made the mistake of her life in choosing me, and I hope that it won't be very long before we see you all at our own table with Mary at the head of it and I, where I belong, at the foot." Or: "I can't make a speech and you know it. But I surely am lucky and I know it."

The custom in some areas is for the party to be given on the afternoon or evening of the day of the newspaper announcement. In this case, the engagement is never proclaimed to the guests as an assembled audience. The news is "out," and everyone is supposed to have heard it. Those who have not cannot long remain ignorant, as the groom-elect is either receiving with his fiancée or is brought forward by her father and presented to everyone he does not know. Everybody congratulates him and offers the bride-to-be wishes for her happiness.

BEHAVIOR OF THE ENGAGED COUPLE

There is said to be still preserved somewhere in Massachusetts a whispering reed and through its long hollow length, lovers were wont to whisper messages of tenderness to each other while separated by a room's length and the inevitable chaperonage of the fiancée's entire family. At the opposite extreme is the engaged couple of today who persist in embarrassing all about them with constant displays of their emotion. It is not necessary to demonstrate one's feelings with caresses and kisses in front of others, but how attractive to indicate their affection by frank approval of whatever the other may do or say and by their radiant look! Even more proper is their obvious friendliness toward all people, their air of wishing the whole world to be beautiful for everybody because it is so beautiful for them. That is love—as it should be! And its evidence is a very sure signpost to their future happiness.

NO OTHER SINGLE DATES

It is unnecessary to say that an engaged man shows no marked interest in other women. Often it so happens that engaged people are together very little because he is away at work, lives in another city, or for other reasons. Rather than sit home alone, he or she may, of course, go out with their friends, but they must avoid going out with any one man or woman alone.

CHAPERONING THE ENGAGED COUPLE

The question of a chaperon differs with locality. Southern girls used to be more carefully chaperoned than their Northern sisters, and Western girls have long been the most independant of all. But there are few places left today where an engaged pair may not spend as many hours alone together as they wish, so long as it is not overnight. In order to reach a destination where they will be chaperoned, they may travel overnight by a public conveyance, but their accommodations must not be adjoining and their behavior must be irreproachable. They should never take an automobile trip that requires them to pass the night en route in a hotel or motel.

Unmarried friends are not suitable chaperons, but married couples, even though of the same age, are acceptable. Otherwise, for any overnight stay, the engaged pair must be in the company of an older man, woman, or couple, either relatives or friends.

It is perhaps sufficient to say that if a man is thought worthy to be accepted by a father as his daughter's future husband, he should be considered worthy of trust no matter how far any situation they might find themselves in may be lacking in propriety.

PRESENTS THAT MAY AND MAY NOT BE ACCEPTED BY THE BRIDE-TO-BE

The fiancée of a young man who is "saving in order to marry" would be lacking in good taste as well as good sense were she to encourage or allow him to send her many flowers and other charming but extravagant presents. On the other hand, if the bridegroom-elect has ample means, she may accept anything he chooses to select, except wearing apparel or anything that can be classified as maintenance.

They may, if they wish, open a joint bank account shortly before the wedding, in order to deposit the checks they receive as gifts. They may draw on this account to help in furnishing their future home.

It is perfectly proper for her to drive his car, and she may select furniture for their house, which he may buy or have built. But if she would keep her self-respect, she must not live in the house or use its furniture until she is given his name. He may give her all the jewels he can afford; he may give her a fur scarf, but not a fur coat. The scarf is an ornament; the coat is wearing apparel.

If she cannot afford to buy a new dress, she may have to be married in the prettiest dress she already has, but her wedding dress and the clothes she wears away on her wedding day must not be supplied by the groom or, in most circumstances, by his family. There are, of course, exceptions. If his mother has long known the girl and loves her dearly, there is no reason why she should not give her everything she chooses. But it would be starting life on a false basis and putting herself in a compromising position were the bride-to-be to be lodged and clothed by any man, whether he is soon to be her husband or not.

THE LENGTH OF THE ENGAGEMENT

A long engagement is likely to be a strain on all involved. The ideal duration is from three to five months, which allows time for the wedding arrangements to be made and for the couple to come to know each other very well. If one or both are finishing school, but want to be engaged during the last year so that they do not have to become involved in more social life than they wish, or if a man is serving his military term and his fiancée wishes everyone to know that she will not be going out with other men, then of course it is right and proper to announce the engagement long before the wedding. Nonetheless, it may be a somewhat trying period. The young people, trying to see as much of each other as possible and at the same time continue studying or working, are often exhausted. The bride has the added time-consuming responsibilities of planning the wedding, and her mother, who may be left to make the arrangements almost alone, is also in a difficult position. Therefore, unless there are good and sufficient reasons for a long one, a short engagement period ensures that the bride, the groom, and their families will arrive at the wedding in good health and a happy frame of mind.

THE BROKEN ENGAGEMENT

In the unfortunate event of a broken engagement, the ring and all other gifts of value must be returned to the former fiancé. Gifts received from relatives or friends should also be returned with a short note of explanation:

Dear Sue,

I am sorry to have to tell you that Jack and I have broken our engagement. Therefore I am returning the towels that you were so sweet to send to me.

Love,

Jane

A notice reading "The engagement of Miss Sara Black and Mr. John Doe has been broken by mutual consent" should be sent to the newspapers that announced the engagement.

If the man should die before the wedding, his fiancée may keep her engagement ring. If it happens to be an old family heirloom and she knows that his parents would like to have it remain in the family, she would be quite correct and considerate to offer to return it. She may keep any gifts that were given her by friends.

BUYING THE WEDDING RING—OR RINGS

Shortly before the wedding, it is not only customary but important that the bride go with the groom when he buys the wedding ring. One reason is that since she may not intend to take it off, it stays for life on her finger, and she should be allowed to choose the style she prefers. No ring could be in better taste than the plain band of yellow or white gold, or platinum. A diamond band, no matter how fashionable, is more suitable as a guard than as a wedding ring, especially as any ring with stones must be taken off to be properly cleaned or to have a stone tightened or replaced.

If the bridegroom wishes to have a ring, the bride buys a plain gold band to match hers but a little wider—or it may be any type of ring he prefers and she is able to buy. Preferably, a man's ring is worn on the fourth finger of his left hand, but the fourth or fifth finger of either hand is correct.

The wedding ring may be engraved with whatever sentiment the bridegroom chooses. On the broad rings of many years ago, it was not unusual to have a quotation of twenty-five letters or more, as well as the initials "A.Y.X. and L.M.N., September 2, 1900." On the rings of today, however, only the initials and date are usually engraved.

The bridegroom's ring is also marked with initials or a sentiment, as the bride chooses.

ENGAGEMENT PRESENTS

It is not unusual for a bride-to-be to receive a few engagement presents sent either by her relatives, her very intimate friends, and her godparents, or by members of her fiancé's family as special messages of welcome to her. It is not necessary to give engagement as well as wedding presents. But if one wishes to do so, the gifts are usually table linen, towels, bed linen such as a set of embroidered sheets, or possibly an inexpensive novelty gift—a "his and hers" cocktail shaker with two glasses, or an artificial flower arrangement. They are presents directed particularly toward the bride's pleasure, and if they are monogrammed, her initials alone are used.

Shortly after the engagement is announced, it is wise for the bride to go to the local stores and indicate her preferences in colors and styles so that engagement presents will fit in with her choice of trousseau.

THE HOUSEHOLD TROUSSEAU

A trousseau, according to the derivation of the word, was the "little trusse or bundle" that the bride carried with her to the house of her husband. At present, the extravagant trousseaux of yesterday's daughters of the very wealthy are dwindling to items of actual requirement. Household linens enough to run an enormous house—and for a lifetime—are a thing of the past. Few modern linen closets would hold them. The well-appointed house of today's bride will be adequately equipped to start married life with the following items, but she will wish to add to them as her family and household expand:

BED LINEN (amounts are for *each* bed)
   6 sheets (for master bed)
   4 sheets (for guest bed)
   4 pillow cases (for each single bed; 8 for double bed)
   1 blanket cover (washable silk or drip-dry cotton)
   2 quilted mattress pads
   1 light-weight wool blanket for summer
   1 electric blanket (dual control for double bed) or 2 heavy-weight wool or wool-blend blankets
   1 comforter for winter (preferably eiderdown)
   1 bedspread

Bath Linen (quantities are for each bathroom)
- 6 large bath towels
- 6 small towels to match
- 6 washcloths to match
- 6 guest towels
- 1 shower curtain
- 2 bath mats

Kitchen
- 8 sturdy dish towels (I prefer terry cloth to linen)
- 6 dishcloths or 2 sponges
- 4 potholders

Small bath towels and washcloths are needed for a maid who comes in by the day.

Remember that terry-cloth towels are very practical because they show only soil. Huck towels rumple the moment they are used.

Table Linen
- 1 damask tablecloth, white or pastel color, 3½ yards long (if you ever plan to give a dinner for as many as twelve seated at one table) or 2½ to 3 yards long (to fit a smaller table)
- 12 napkins to match, 24″ x 24″
- 2 or 3 yard-and-a-half-square linen tablecloths for bridge tables; matching napkins optional.
- 1 or 2 sets of linen place mats with matching napkins
- 12 linen or cotton napkins in a neutral color that will go with any odd place mats that you may be given
- 1 set (4 to 6) plastic mats with smooth, hard surface, or treated paper mats for everyday use
- 1 set (6 or 8) plastic, straw, or any attractive mats of a more elaborate design, for use at informal parties

Optional, but very useful—large monogrammed paper napkins
Cocktail napkins, paper or cloth

Remember that a damask cloth is very useful for any buffet setting because, with a felt pad under it, every inch of space is available—which is not the case with the bare table spaces if mats are used. An embroidered handkerchief-linen cloth or one of lace is also practical with the addition of a heat-protecting mat under any exceptionally hot platter or dish.

Small place mats of linen with or without a runner to match are most practical. A dozen mats with one runner can be used for some time as your one and only tablecloth. No matter how pretty your plastic mats may be, linen or lace ones always make your table a little dressier.

You should try your best to have cloth napkins to use with your tablecloths or linen mats. They need not be of the same fabric if they are appropriate to your equipment. Paper napkins are so attractively made today that they do solve one household problem very practically, but they *are* informal and should be used only with other casual table appointments.

If your dining room is likely to be very small, or if you have none at all, it may be practical to set three sturdy, and they must be sturdy, bridge tables with matching tablecloths and napkins. They will be more pleasing in appearance if they are all of a color that is becoming to your room. Odd tablecloths grouped together are not pleasing and give the impression of a haphazard household.

MARKING LINEN

It is, of course, very decorative for the linen to be embroidered with monogram or initials. An initial designed with additional embellishment to give the appearance of a monogram is more effective than two initials —and usually the cost is less.

Towels are marked so that, when they are folded and hung on the rack, the marking is centered.

The monogram should be in proportion to the size of the piece. If it is too small, it will look skimpy; if too large, it is overly conspicuous.

Years ago, when Muriel Barbara Jones married Henry Ross, not a piece of linen or silver in their house was marked otherwise than "MBJ." But because this proved a confusing and senseless custom, it is now recognized as more practical, when initials are used, to mark everything with the bride's future initials: "MJR". Her monogram could also be simply "R".

Long tablecloths are marked on either side of center, midway between table center and edge of table. Small yard-and-a-half square tablecloths are marked at one corner midway between table center and the edge. Square monograms look well set in line with the table edge; irregular ones look best at corner.

Very large damask napkins are marked in the center of one side, smaller ones in one corner—cross-cornered usually, but sometimes straight. To decide about the place for marking the napkins, always fold the napkin exactly as it is to be folded for use and then make a light pencil outline in the center of the folded napkin.

Sheets are always marked with base of letters toward hem—when on the bed, the monogram is right-side up and can be read by a person standing at foot of bed—and it is put at half the depth at which the sheet is turned back. Pillow cases are marked half-way between edge of case and beginning of the pillow. On square French pillow cases the monogram is put cross-cornered with top of initials to corner.

CHOOSING CHINA, GLASS, AND SILVER

Before her wedding invitations are sent out, every bride should go to each gift shop or department store in her neighborhood, or anywhere that she knows her friends will be shopping, and select those patterns of glass, china, and other items that she would like to receive as wedding presents. All stores of this type are prepared to cooperate with the bride in keeping a record of her choices, and it is of an immeasurable help to those selecting the gifts.

CHINA

Today the stores are filled with such entrancing sets of pottery, plasticware, and china in every variety imaginable, thick, thin, plain, or decorated, that the problem is not to find sufficiently attractive table decorations in china, but to decide from among the many to choose from. There is, however, one item of important advice. Keep in mind the subject of replacements. And remember that any pattern not easily replaced means that breakage will leave you helplessly handicapped. It is always wise to ask if a pattern is in open stock. Remember, too, that soap-bubble thin glass, or glass that is very finely chased or cut, is naturally most becoming to porcelains, whereas the heavier glassware is best suited to pottery.

But let us consider a few general principles that apply to a table set entirely with china. Its one exaction is that it be in harmony, meaning that it have some matching detail—such as texture or at least a repeated note of color. In other words, service plates of one variety, bread and butter plates of another variety, centerpiece of another, dishes for sweets of another, candlesticks of still another, would look like an odd-lot table selected at random unless these pieces were closely allied.

Whether you decide on decorated china or plain is your own choice. All white china of the same color and texture need not match in pattern or shape, but it would be unpleasing, for example, to use translucent milk glass with opaque white earthenware. The tastefulness of china in any other plain color necessarily depends upon the color of the cloth or table upon which it is to be set.

The following lists are really what the bride should *basically* have to start out with. If her funds are limited and if she is not given enough dinner and dessert plates, for instance, to complete eight or twelve place settings, she may add a piece or two as often as she can, completing one place setting at a time rather than buying two or three more dinner plates and still having an incomplete setting.

FOR EVERYDAY USE:

1 complete set of 4 or 6 place settings of inexpensive china, pottery, or unbreakable plasticware, which now comes in most attractive patterns. This set should include:

dinner plates
dessert plates (may also be used for salad)
cereal dishes (used also for soup, puddings, canned fruit, etc.)
cups
saucers
cream pitcher and sugar bowl
2 platters
2 vegetable dishes

FOR ENTERTAINING:

The bride may choose between:

(1) A complete service of fine matching china for 8 or 12 place settings. Each place setting should include:

soup cup (two handled, for both clear and cream soups)
saucer
dinner plate
salad plate
butter plate
dessert plate

Optional:

cups and saucers
cream soup plates
cream pitcher and sugar bowl
platters and vegetable dishes
demitasse cups
gravy boats
sauce bowls for hollandaise, mayonnaise, etc.

(2) Odd sets of 8 or 12 dinner plates and dessert plates in any pattern she chooses.

If the bride prefers variety to a single set of china, she must choose her accompanying items carefully. Glass, silver, pewter, and the beautiful new easy-to-care-for stainless steel may be combined with any china to make a charming dinner table. To go with the odd dinner and dessert plates, the bride will need:

8 or 12 glass or silver butter plates
8 or 12 glass salad plates (the crescent shaped ones are pretty and take
    up less space on the table)
12 cups and saucers in any pattern
8 or 12 demitasse cups and saucers in any pattern

2 platters and 3 vegetable dishes of silver or stainless steel
1 cream pitcher and sugar bowl, silver, glass, or stainless steel

Other essential items that may be of any material or style that the bride prefers are:

4 salts and peppers—silver, glass, stainless steel, wood, china, or a combination of silver and wood *or* salt and pepper dishes
1 salad bowl and servers—wood or glass
1 bread dish—silver or wicker
1 gravy or sauce boat—silver or china
3 condiment dishes—glass, china, or pottery
1 water pitcher—any material
8 or 12 fingerbowls
silver tea service or china tea pot
1 silver coffee pot, or a presentable coffee maker (stainless steel, glass, etc., whether an electric one or not) that may be brought from the kitchen for serving after-dinner coffee
8 deep dishes for serving ice cream with sauce or a "runny" dessert—glass dishes are best—they look very pretty on a plate with a colorful pattern showing through
6 or 8 tiny dinner table ash trays—china, glass, or silver
enamelware pots and casseroles, which come in innumerable sizes, shapes, and patterns—invaluable to a busy bride, as dishes may be cooked and served in the same utensil
1 electric warming tray—the most valuable thing in my kitchen!
4 trays—wood, tin or plastic—necessary in this age of frequent meals out of doors or in front of the living-room fireplace.

GLASSES

Glasses are so easily broken and good glass so expensive to replace that a bride who wishes to have a matching set for any length of time should have far more than she actually needs to start out with.

In order to save her good glass for entertaining, she should have for the everyday use of herself and her husband and for casual drop-in visitors:

8 "kitchen glasses" or tumblers
4 juice glasses
4 old-fashioned glasses
4 stem cocktail glasses (may also be used for wine)
8 ice tea or highball glasses

Beyond this, she should have, depending on the number of place settings she has decided upon:

goblets
wine glasses
liqueur glasses
sherbet glasses
8 highball glasses
8 stem cocktail glasses
8 old-fashioned glasses

Since the chances are that not all her guests at a large party will request the same type of drink, this should be adequate for a party of twelve. Also, she may bring out her plainer cocktail and highball glasses if necessary.

SILVER

A large amount of silver is neither so desirable nor as fashionable as it used to be. In fact, many brides request that they be given pewter or stainless steel platters, serving dishes, or any other such item, rather than silver, as they require little care and are more durable. However, although the bride may ask for a set of stainless steel eating utensils for daily use, nothing can replace a set of beautiful sterling flat silver on the dinner party table. There are innumerable patterns; the bride whose home is "traditional" may choose one of the older, more ornate patterns and she who lives in a modern house or apartment will probably prefer a very plain design. Each has its advantages. The modern, undecorated piece is easier to clean, but it also shows wear and tear more quickly and is sometimes dulled by scratches. Whichever the bride chooses, she should remember that it is probably the silver she will use all her life, and possibly her children after her, so it is safer to select a pattern that is not extreme in any way—neither too severely modern, nor so ornate that it easily appears out-dated.

As with china, it is wiser to complete one place setting at a time rather than have twelve forks and no knives with which to cut the meat. If she is getting her china and silver place setting by place setting, the bride will simply start out with smaller parties, which will grow as her implements permit. This is not a disadvantage, however. A girl who has had little practice in party-giving will do far better to start out with two or four guests and enlarge her group as her experience increases.

The necessary silver for one place setting is:

1 large fork
1 large knife
1 small fork
1 small knife
1 dessert spoon

1 teaspoon
1 butter knife

In addition—and these items need not be in the same pattern as the above list:

12 oyster forks
3 serving spoons (tablespoons in the chosen pattern may be used)
2 serving forks
12 after-dinner coffee spoons
2 gravy or sauce ladles
4 extra teaspoons (for sugar, condiments, etc.)

Optional—and often received as wedding presents:

salad or fish forks (broad tines)
sugar tongs
butter server
ornamented spoons for jellies or jams
cake knife
pie server

If the flat silver is monogrammed, a triangle of block letters, last-name initial above and the first-name initials of bride and groom below, goes well on a modern pattern. When Jane Ann Ross marries Henry Cranmore:

C
J H

Or the initials of her name after she is married:

C
J A

If a single initial is used, it is, of course, the last-name initial of the groom.

Any initialing should be simple in style. Elongated Roman goes well on modern silver, and Old English on the more ornamented styles.

A wedding gift of silver may be marked if the giver is absolutely sure that it is something the bride truly wants and that no duplicate will arrive, but generally it is safer to leave it unmarked so that it can be exchanged if desired.

42

Funerals

As a person reaches the age when he makes a will, he should also consider how and where he would like to be buried. These wishes may be put into his will; and while they are not irrevocable, the family will naturally give them every consideration. If he does not include them in his will, he should at some point discuss the question with those closest to him so they will be able to arrange for the type of burial that he would have chosen himself.

If his parents have a plot in a cemetery, he should know whether there is space for him (and his wife, if she wishes) to be buried there, or he should think about purchasing a plot for himself and his own family. If, as so many people do, he wishes to be cremated, the law requires that his nearest relatives give permission. Therefore, he should make it very clear to his wife (or husband, if we are speaking of a woman), his children, and his brothers or sisters what his desires are.

Although few people like to think of death in personal terms, it is wise for the head of the family, at least, to have a space set aside in which he keeps a copy of his will and the name of the attorney who drew it up, a deed to a burial plot if he has one, a list of the location of safe deposit boxes, mortgages, bank accounts, etc., and any personal instructions he may wish to leave in case of his death. The other members of the family should know the location of these papers and something about their contents. The small amount of effort necessary to put such a sensible precaution into effect is nothing compared to the help it can be to a stunned and confused family at the time of death.

IMMEDIATE STEPS

At the time of actual bereavement, when we stand baffled and alone, etiquette performs its most real service by smoothing the necessary personal contacts and making sure that the last rites of our beloved shall be performed with beauty and gravity.

When you hear of the death of a friend, you should go at once to the house, write "With sympathy" on your card, and leave it at the door. Or, if such a call is not practical for some such reason as distance, you must write a letter to the family at once. Telephoning is not improper, but it may cause inconvenience by tying up the line, which is always needed at these times for notifying members of the family and making necessary arrangements.

Intimate friends are expected to go to the house of mourning and ask whether they can be of service. There are countless ways in which they can be helpful, from assisting with such material needs of the family as food and child care to sending telegrams and answering the door. » *See also Chapter 57, "Calls and callers."*

At this time it is of immeasurable help if a very good friend is willing to take charge of the funeral arrangements. Those closest to the deceased may be in such an emotional state that it is impossible for them to make rational decisions, and they may rush, or be pushed, into situations that they later regret. If no such friend is at hand, then decisions must be made by a relative, possibly one who is not of the immediate family, a nephew or a cousin, perhaps. This lot often falls to a son of the deceased, however, and he must exercise strict self-control.

NOTIFYING FAMILY AND CLOSE FRIENDS

If members of the immediate family are not already present, the first act of someone at the bedside of the deceased is to notify them and one or two intimate friends whose capability as well as sympathy can be counted on. If the deceased had suffered a long illness, and the family has become attached to the trained nurse, no one is better fitted than she to turn her ministrations from the one whom she can no longer help to those who now have a very real need for her care. She, a friend, or a member of the family must look after many details.

Members of the family and very close friends should be called on the telephone. Close relatives, even though they live at some distance, should also be called, but if expense is a factor, friends and more distant relatives may be notified by telegram.

THE DEATH CERTIFICATE

The death certificate is filled out and signed by the physician in attendance at the time of death. If the death was very sudden or caused by an accident, or if there was no doctor in attendance for whatever reason, the county medical examiner or coroner must be called in to ascertain the cause of death and sign the certificate. This must be done immediately, because no other steps can be taken until the death certificate is properly signed.

NOTIFYING AN ATTORNEY

The next step is to notify an attorney, preferably the one who has drawn up the will of the deceased. If he, or his firm, are unavailable, then any other attorney who is reputable, perhaps one who has been retained by another member of the family or one who is a personal friend, may be called.

THE FUNERAL DIRECTOR AND THE CLERGYMAN

The next most immediate matter is that of selecting a funeral home. If the family belongs to a church or synagogue, they may call the church office, which will give them all the information about the funeral directors in the area and probably recommend one who will suit their needs. The family doctor can also provide this information.

The funeral director will come to the home as soon as possible after he is called and remove the body to the funeral home. Whoever is in charge for the family will discuss all the arrangements with him at that time, telling him how elaborate a funeral the relatives wish or can afford and how they wish the details to be handled. If the service is to be held at the funeral home or in the home of the deceased, the day and hour may also be settled. If it is to be held in a church, the clergyman must be consulted immediately to fix the time. If the family is not affiliated with a church, the funeral director or a friend can recommend a clergyman of any faith the family chooses.

NEWSPAPER NOTICES

Notices of the death should go to morning and evening papers in a large city and to the local paper (daily or weekly) in towns or suburbs. They usually contain the date of death, names of immediate family, place and time of funeral, and, frequently, a request that a contribution be given to a charity instead of flowers sent to the deceased. The notice may be telephoned by the person making the funeral arrangements, but often the funeral director handles it as part of his services.

CONSTANTINE—Mary Phillips, on March 19th, 1964. Beloved wife of Henry S. Constantine, devoted mother of Henry S. Constantine, Jr., and Barbara Constantine Franklin, sister of Dorothy P. Hill. Reposing at the Frederick Carter Funeral Home, Farmingdale, Mass., Monday and Tuesday, 2:00 P.M.-9:00 P.M. Funeral Wednesday, 11:00 A.M., at Christ Church, Farmingdale. In lieu of flowers, please send donations to the New York Cancer Fund.

HASKELL—John Woods, suddenly, on February 12th, 1964. Beloved brother of Robert C. Haskell, George F. Haskell, and Sally Haskell Simpson. Funeral service Friday, February 14th at 11:30 A.M. at the Riverside Funeral Home, 10 Lawton Street, Clinton, Mass.

When the notice reads "Funeral private" and neither time nor place is given, only very intimate friends are given this information, either by telephone or on the personal card of the relative or friend in charge: "Mr. Brown's funeral will be at Christ Church, Monday at eleven o'clock." Others are not expected to attend.

When the notice reads "Please omit flowers," this wish should be strictly followed.

If the person who has died was prominent in any way, it is probable that the newspapers have a file on him and, in the case of an older person, an obituary already written. They should be notified immediately, and the information that they have should be checked by someone who is acquainted with the facts, so that no errors will be made in the published articles. The paid notice of death is inserted as with less well known people, when the details of resting place, funeral, flowers, etc. have been decided.

THE CLOTHING FOR BURIAL

The person who has been put in charge of arrangements, with the help of someone very close to the deceased who may know of some special preference or a favorite piece of suitable clothing, delivers the clothes to the funeral director. Members of some faiths, the Orthodox Jewish among them, still prefer to bury their dead in shrouds, but most religions have no restrictions on clothing for burial. Dresses should be in solid, subdued colors, of a style that might be worn to church. Young girls are usually buried in white and children in their Sunday school clothes. Men are also dressed as for church; a cutaway is sometimes worn, but generally the family chooses a dark suit. Wedding rings are usually left on, but other jewelry is removed.

EMBLEM OF MOURNING ON THE DOOR

To indicate that there has been a death in the house, the funeral director may hang streamers on the front door: white ones for a child, black and white for a young person, or black for an older person. Flowers are, of course, most beautiful and the choice of those who can afford them. Usually they are ordered by the family directly from their own florist, but quite possibly the funeral director orders them. White flowers are used for a young person, purple for one who was older.

Any emblem is removed by a member of the funeral establishment before the family returns from the services.

HONORARY PALLBEARERS

The member of the family who is in charge will ask (either when they come to the house or by telephone or telegraph if they are at a distance) six or eight men who were close friends of the deceased to be the pallbearers. When a man has been prominent in public life, there may be eight or ten of his political or business associates as well as his six or eight lifelong friends. Members of the immediate family are never chosen, as their place is with the women of the family.

One cannot refuse an invitation to be a pallbearer except because of illness or necessary absence from the city. The pallbearers meet in the vestibule of the church, a few minutes before the time set for the service.

Honorary pallbearers serve only at church funerals. They do not carry the coffin. (This service is performed by the assistants of the funeral director, who are expertly trained.) They sit in the first pews on the left and, after the service, leave the church two by two, walking immediately in front of the coffin.

SENDING AND RECEIVING FLOWERS

If there is a notice in the papers requesting that no flowers be sent, you send none. Otherwise, they are addressed "To the funeral of [name of the deceased]," either at the funeral home or the church. When you did not know the deceased, but only his close relatives, flowers may be sent to them at their home, with a card addressed to one of the family, on which you might write "With sympathy," "With deepest sympathy," "With heartfelt sympathy," or, if appropriate, "With love and sympathy."

It is also especially kind to send flowers to any bereaved person who is particularly in your thoughts. A few flowers sent from time to time—possibly long afterward—are very comforting in their assurance of continued sympathy.

To avoid confusion, whoever is in charge of arrangements for the family should appoint one person to take charge of flowers and he or she must carefully collect all the accompanying cards. On the outside of each envelope is written a description of the flowers that came with the card. Sometimes this is done by the florist and the cards are delivered to the bereaved family after the funeral. For example:

Large spray Easter lilies tied with white ribbon
Laurel wreath with gardenias
Long sheaf of white roses—broad silver ribbon

Without such notations, the family has no way of knowing anything about the flowers that people have sent. Moreover, these descriptions are necessary when writing notes of thanks.

If some friends have sent potted plants or cut flowers to the house, their cards are removed and noted for later acknowledgment.

If the family is Protestant, an hour before the time set for the service one or two women friends go to the church to help the florist or someone on the church staff arrange the flowers, which have been placed in the chancel. Their duty is not to arrange the flowers but to see that those sent by relatives are given a prominent position, because effective grouping and fastening of the heavy wreaths and sprays is difficult for novices, no matter how perfect their taste may be, and the florist is capable of doing a more effective job.

The sexton or one of his assistants will have collected the cards, noting the variety of flowers as above, and will give them to these friends who will in turn deliver them to the one who is responsible for all the cards.

Friends of any faith may send a "spiritual bouquet" (a Mass said for the deceased) to a Catholic family. Any priest will make arrangements for the mass and accept the donation. A card is sent to the family, stating the time and place of the mass and the name of the donor.

CALLING AT THE FUNERAL HOME

More often than not, nowadays, the body of the deceased remains at the funeral home until the day of the funeral. Very often the family receives close friends there, rather than at home. If they choose to do so, the hours when they will be there to accept expressions of sympathy are usually included in the death notice in the newspaper. At other times, people who wish to pay their respects but do not feel that they are close enough to intrude on the privacy of the bereaved may stop in and sign the register that is always provided by the funeral parlor. Their signatures should be formal, including their titles—"Dr. and Mrs. Harvey Cross" or "Miss Deborah Page" and not "Bill and Joan Cross" or "Debbie Page"— in order to simplify the task of any one who may be helping the family acknowledge these visits. The family need not thank each and every caller by letter, but if some one has made a special effort or if no one of the family was there to speak to him, they may wish to do so.

WHO ATTENDS THE FUNERAL

All members of the family find out when the funeral is to take place and go to it without waiting to be notified, of course. But if the notice reads "Funeral private," a friend does not go unless he has received a message from the family that they wish him to come. If the hour and location of the service is printed in the paper, that is considered an invitation to attend. It is entirely up to you to decide whether you knew the deceased or his family well enough to wish to be at his funeral. But it is heartlessly delinquent not to go to the public funeral of one with whom you have been closely associated in business or other interests, or to whose house you have been often invited, or when you are an intimate friend of the immediate members of the family.

It is no longer considered necessary to wear black when you go to a friend's funeral unless you sit with the family or have been asked to be one of the honorary pallbearers, but you should choose clothes that are dark and inconspicuous.

Enter the church as quietly as possible, and as there are no ushers at a funeral, seat yourself where you think you belong. Only a very intimate friend should take a position far up on the center aisle. If you are merely an acquaintance, you should sit toward the rear of the church.

FUNERAL SERVICES

AT THE CHURCH

The church funeral is the most trying for some people in that the family has to leave the seclusion of the house and be in the presence of a congregation. On the other hand, others find the solemnity of a church service with the added beauty of choir and organ helpfully soothing.

As the time appointed for the funeral draws near, the congregation gradually fills the church. The first few pews on the right side of the center aisle are always left empty for the family and those on the left for the pallbearers.

The trend today is to have the casket closed. Protestants may follow their own wishes. At a Catholic or Jewish service it is obligatory that the casket be closed.

At most funerals, the processional is omitted. The coffin may have one or several floral pieces on it, it may in some churches be covered with a pall of needlework, or, for a member of the armed forces or a veteran, it may be draped with the flag. It is placed on a stand at the foot of the chancel a half-hour before the service. The family usually enter through the door nearest the front pews.

Should the family prefer that there be a processional, it forms in the vestibule. If there is to be a choral service, the minister and choir enter the church fom the rear and precede the funeral cortege. Directly after the choir and clergy come the honorary pallbearers, two by two; then the coffin covered with flowers; and then the family—the chief mourner being first, walking with whoever is most sympathetic to him or her.

Usually each woman takes the arm of a man. But two women or two men may walk together, according to the division of the family. For example, if the deceased is one of four sons and there is no daughter, the mother and father walk together immediately after the body of their child, and they are followed by the two elder sons and then the younger, and then the nearest woman relative. Although the arrangement of the procession is thus fixed, it is of greater importance that those in deepest affliction should each be placed next to the one whose nearness may be of most comfort. A younger child who is calm and soothing would be better next to his mother than an older one who is of more nervous temperament.

At the chancel, the choir takes its accustomed place, the clergyman stands at the foot of the chancel steps, the honorary pallbearers take their places in the front pews on the left, and the casket is set upon a stand previously placed there for the purpose. The actual bearers of the casket, who are always professionals furnished by the funeral director, walk quietly to inconspicuous stations on the side aisles. The family occupy the front pews on the right side; the honorary pallbearers on the left; the rest of the procession fills vacant places on either side. The service is then read. Upon its conclusion, the procession moves out in the same order as it came in, except that the choir remains in its place.

If the family so wishes, one of the male relatives may stop at the back of the church to thank those who have attended the services. He needs to say nothing more than "Thank you," with perhaps a special word for close friends, but the gesture will certainly be warmly received.

Outside the church, the casket is put into the hearse, the family enter automobiles waiting immediately behind the hearse, and the flowers are put into a covered vehicle (for it is very vulgar to fill open landaulets with floral offerings and make a parade through the streets). Or they are taken in the closed car by a different route and placed beside the grave before the hearse and those attending the burial service arrive.

AT THE HOUSE

Many prefer a house funeral. It is simpler and more private, and it obviates the necessity for those in sorrow to face people. The nearest relatives may stay apart in an adjoining room where they can hear the service yet remain in seclusion.

A few decades ago, there seldom was music at house funerals because at that time nothing could substitute for the deep, rich tones of the organ. At the present time, however, phonographic recordings of organ and choir music are excellent and readily available and may be used most helpfully as a beautiful addition to a house funeral.

Arrangements are usually made to hold the service in the living room. The coffin is placed in front of the mantel, perhaps, or between two windows, but always at a distance from the door. It is usually set on stands brought by the funeral director, who also supplies enough folding chairs to fill the room without crowding.

At a house funeral, the relatives either take their places near the casket or stay apart in seclusion. If the women of the family come into the living room, they wear hats, as in a church.

All other women keep their wraps on. The men, if they are wearing overcoats, keep them on or carry them on their arms and hold their hats in their hands.

It is unusual for any but a small group of relatives and intimate friends to go to the cemetery from the house.

AT THE FUNERAL HOME OR CHAPEL

In recent years, the establishments of funeral directors have assumed a new prominence. There is always a chapel in the building, actually a small and often very beautiful nonsectarian church. There are also many retiring rooms and reception rooms where the families may remain undisturbed or receive the condolences of their friends.

Services are conducted in the chapel quite as they would be in a church, although sometimes there is a private alcove to one side so that the family need not sit in the front pews.

THE BURIAL

If the burial is in the churchyard or otherwise within walking distance, the congregation naturally follows the family to the graveside. Otherwise, those attending the funeral, wherever the services are held, do not expect or wish to go to the interment. Except at a funeral of public importance, it is witnessed only by the immediate family and the most intimate friends. The long line of vehicles that used to stand at the church, ready to be filled with mere acquaintances, is proper only for a public personage.

CREMATION

Many people whose religion does not forbid it prefer the idea of cremation to burial. The preceding service is exactly the same as that preceding a burial. The family may or not, as they wish, accompany the body to the crematorium. If they do, a very short service is held there also.

The ashes may later be delivered to the family, to be disposed of in any way that the deceased would wish (as long as it is not contrary to any law). Often, however, the urn is deposited in a building or section set aside in the cemetery or churchyard, and sometimes it is buried in the family plot.

A MEMORIAL SERVICE

In some circumstances, as when the deceased has died in a far country, a memorial service is held instead of a funeral.

Notice of this service is put into the obituary column of the paper, or, in a small town, people are telephoned and each given a short list of his own nearest neighbors whom he is asked to notify.

These services are very brief. In general outline, two verses of a hymn are sung. Then follow short prayers and a very brief address about the work and personality of the one for whom the service is held. It is closed with a prayer and two verses of another hymn.

Usually, no flowers are sent except a few for the altar. On those occasions when flowers are sent, they are arranged as bouquets (not sheaves) so that they may be put into the wards of a hospital without having to be taken apart and rearranged.

Since this is more like a church service than a funeral, some of the men in the family may, before joining the women, escort guests to their seats as at a Sunday service.

CHURCH FEES

No fee is ever asked by the clergyman, but the family are expected to make a contribution in appreciation of his services and should do so. The fee may be anything from $10.00 for a very small funeral service to $100.00 for a very elaborate one.

A bill rendered by the church office includes all necessary charges for the church.

ACKNOWLEDGMENT OF SYMPATHY

When messages of condolence, many of them impersonal, mount into the hundreds, as may well be the case when a public figure or perhaps a prominent business executive or even a member of his family is involved, the sending of engraved or well-printed cards to strangers is proper:

The Governor and Mrs. State
wish gratefully to acknowledge
your kind expression of sympathy

The family of
Harrison L. Winthrop
wish to thank you for
your kind expression of sympathy

If such cards are used, a hand-written word or two and a signature *must* be added below the printed message when there is any personal acquaintance with the sender. And in no circumstances should such cards be sent to those who have sent flowers or to intimate friends who have written personal letters.

Perhaps as the result of the use of cards in these rare but permissible cases, a most unfortunate custom has recently sprung up. The funeral director supplies printed cards, and the recipient merely signs his or her name to it. A poor return, indeed, for a beautiful spray of flowers or even a bouquet of garden flowers.

A personal message on a fold-over card is preferable to any printed card. It takes but a moment to write "Thank you for your beautiful flowers," "Thank you for your kind sympathy," or "Thank you for all your kindness." Nor is it much more of an effort to write: "Thank you, dear Mrs. Smith, for your beautiful flowers and your kind sympathy," or "Your flowers were so beautiful! Thank you for them and for your loving message," or "Thank you for your sweet letter. I know you meant it!" or "I cannot half tell you how much all your loving kindness has meant to me."

If the list is very long, or if the person who has received the flowers and messages is in reality unable to perform the task of writing, some member of the family or possibly a near friend may write for her or him: "Mother [or whoever it is] asks me to thank you for your beautiful flowers and kind message of sympathy." No one expects more than a short message of acknowledgement, but that message should be *seemingly personal* and written by hand!

» *For suggestions on writing letters of condolence, see Chapter 9, "Personal letters."*

MOURNING CLOTHES

During the past twenty-five years, no other changes in etiquette have been so great as those in the conventions of mourning. Until then, the regulations about dress were definitely prescribed according to the precise degree of relationship of the mourner. One's real feelings, whether of grief or comparative indifference, had nothing to do with the outward manifestation one was expected to show as a sign of respect.

A greater and ever greater number of persons today do not believe in going into mourning at all. There are some who believe, as do the races of the East, that great love should be expressed in rejoicing in the rebirth of a beloved spirit instead of selfishly mourning one's own earthly loss. It is certain, however, that the number who can actually attain this spirit are few indeed. Most of us merely do the best we can to continue to keep occupied, to make the necessary adjustments, and to avoid casting the shadow of our own sadness upon others. The sooner that we can over-come our grief and turn our thoughts to the future, the better. Because mourning is a continual reminder of the past, it can only delay the wearer's return to a normal life.

A WIDOW'S MOURNING

A widow of mature years may still, if she chooses (and in some Latin countries they do), wear mourning for life. On the other hand, deep mourning for a year is now considered extreme, and more than six months is very rare.

The young widow, if she wishes to wear mourning, should wear all-black for six months. Black clothes are never appropriate in the country, however; any sports clothes may be worn, provided they are of an incon-spicuous nature.

She should, of course, *never* remain in mourning for her first husband after she has decided she can be consoled by a second. There is no reason why a woman—or a man—should not, in time, find such consolation. But to welcome the attentions of a new suitor while still in mourning is likely to be thought heartless—especially if the marriage had been a happy one.

MOURNING FOR OTHERS

A mother who has lost a grown son or daughter may wear all-black for six months or a year, depending on her inclination.

A daughter or sister, if she wishes, wears mourning for one season. Counting by season is very practical because of the expense of buying ex-tra clothes. When going into mourning in the spring or summer, for ex-ample, wear deep mourning until winter clothes are appropriate; then go back to regular clothes.

MOURNING FOR BUSINESS WOMEN

Since mourning is the outward evidence of a personal frame of mind that has no place in the impersonal world of business, mourning that at-tracts attention is as unsuitable in an office as a black uniform would be on a soldier.

Inconspicuous mourning, on the other hand, is entirely proper. The fact that a woman invariably wears a black dress or a gray mixture suit at-tracts no attention if she has a little white at the throat. Too-solid black, including a black-bordered handkerchief, would be out of place in the office.

If a woman arrives at her office a day or so after the death of a close relative in the clothes she ordinarily wears, no one looks askance. She also must consider the effect her wearing mourning would have on any cus-tomers she comes into contact with.

MOURNING FOR MEN

It is entirely correct for a man to go into mourning for a few months by the simple expedient of putting a black band on his hat and on the left sleeve of his clothes. Also, he wears black shoes, gloves, socks, and ties, and white instead of colored linen. In the country a young man continues to wear his ordinary sport clothes and shoes and sweater—no matter how gay—and without any sleeve band.

The sleeve band is from three and a half to four and a half inches in width and is of dull cloth on overcoats or winter clothing and of serge on summer clothes. The sleeve band of mourning is sensible for many reasons, the first being economy.

There is an objection to even a sleeve band on business clothes—the implied bid for sympathy, which most men want to avoid. Many men, therefore, go to the office with no evidence of mourning other than a black tie and black socks.

THE BEHAVIOR OF THE FAMILY AFTER THE FUNERAL

As soon as possible after the funeral, the life of the family should return to its normal routine. There are many things that must be attended to at once, and while these may seem like insurmountable chores to a grieving husband or wife, the necessity of having to perform them and, above all, in so doing, to think of others rather than oneself is in reality a great help in returning to an active life.

Letters must be written to the clergyman, thanking him for his services and his help. The pallbearers must also be thanked, and there are always others who have performed some service for the family who will appreciate a note of thanks. The gifts of flowers must be acknowledged, and each letter of condolence answered. As stated above, when thousands of letters have been received, it is correct to use printed cards of acknowledgment, but in the ordinary family, a hand-written note, be it only two lines long, should be sent.

The return of the close relatives of the deceased to an active social life is, nowadays, up to the individual. If he or she is not wearing mourning, he may start, as soon as he feels up to it, to go to a friend's house, to a movie, play, or sports event, or to classes or meetings. He may wish to avoid large gatherings for a time, but little by little he increases the scope of his activities until his life has returned to normal. A man or woman may start to have dates when he or she feels like it, but for a few months they should be restricted to evenings at the home of a friend, a movie, or some other inconspicuous activity.

Those who are wearing mourning do not go to dances or other especially formal parties, nor do they take a leading part in purely social functions. But anyone who is in public life or business or who has a professional career must, of course, continue to fulfill his duties. The fact that many women have gone into business or are following careers is another cause of the lightening of mourning and the shortening of its duration. In sum, each year the number increases of those who show the mourning in their hearts only by the quiet dignity of their lives.

CHILDREN

On no account should a child be put into black at any time. They wear their best church clothes to a funeral, and afterward, whatever they ordinarily wear.

Many people are uncertain about whether children who have lost a parent should participate in their usual school activities and after-school entertainments. The answer is "yes." They of course take part in sports and school concerts or plays. However, older children may not wish to go to a purely social party, within two or three weeks, or even longer, after the death of a parent. The normal routine of a small child should not be upset—more than ever they need to romp and play.

Part EIGHT

WEDDINGS

Planning the wedding

A wedding, be it large and elaborate or small and simple, is always an important occasion—beautiful, impressive, and the bride's day of days. But it must be remembered that the groom has a place in it too and that his wishes should be consulted from first to last. Furthermore, the details involved in even the simplest wedding are so many that careful planning and preparation are necessary if everyone is to enjoy the day itself. And, of course, for a large wedding, expert help should be arranged for well in advance to avoid last-minute confusion. Without adequate preparation, Father may be irritated, Mother jittery, the bride in tears, the groom cross—and who could look forward to a situation like that with any sort of equanimity, much less pleasure. It is to the avoidance of such discomfort that this chapter and those that follow are dedicated.

Let it be said at the outset that our discussion of wedding plans will include a complete description of the most elaborate wedding possible. Not because more than a very few will want or be able to carry out every detail, but because only then can the pattern be complete. In other words, it is important to explain all possible details of perfection so that you can follow as many as you find pleasing and practical for you.

THE RESPONSIBILITIES, FINANCIAL AND OTHERWISE

The first fact to remember is that all the expenses of a wedding belong to the bride's parents. The cost of a wedding varies as much as the cost of anything else that one has or does. A big fashionable wedding can total several thousand dollars, and even a simple one entails considerable outlay. This cost can be modified, however, by those who are capable of doing many things themselves instead of employing professional service at every point.

THE BRIDE'S PARENTS PROVIDE:

The engraved invitations to ceremony and reception, and the announcements. While true engraving is most beautiful and a required expense for a wedding of superfection and extreme formality, there are methods of simulating engraving that are very pleasing and entirely suitable when cost must be counted.

The service of a professional secretary who compiles a single guest list from the various ones provided her; addresses the envelopes, both inner and outer; encloses the proper number of cards; seals, stamps, and mails all the invitations or announcements. She may also handle such details as making arrangements with florists, orchestra, etc. This item of cost may be omitted if the work is done by members or friends of the family.

The service of a bridal consultant, if desired.

The trousseau of the bride, consisting not only of her clothing but of her household linen as well.

Floral decorations for church and reception. Bouquets for the bride and bridesmaids, corsages for the bride's mother and grandmother, and a boutonnière for the father of the bride. In some American communities, it is customary for the groom to provide the bouquet carried by the bride. In others, it is the custom for the bride to send boutonnières to the ushers and for the groom to order the bouquets of the bridesmaids, but in most areas the bride's as well as the bridesmaids' bouquets are looked upon as part of the decorative arrangements, all of which are provided by the bride's parents.

Choir, soloists, and organist at chuch, and the fee to the sexton. Some churches send a bill covering all these services; if not, they must be paid for separately.

Orchestra at reception. This may mean twenty pieces with two leaders; or it may mean one violinist or a phonograph.

Automobiles for the bridal party from the house to the church and to the reception and for the bride and groom to drive away in, unless they are going on their journey in a car of their own.

The refreshments, which may be the most elaborate sit-down meal or the simplest afternoon tea.

The wedding cake and, if desired, boxes of cake (usually fruitcake) to be given to the guests.

Champagne and/or other beverages.

The bride's presents to her bridesmaids. They may be jewels of value or carefully selected trinkets of trifling cost.

Hotel accommodations for bride's attendants if they cannot stay with friends and neighbors.

A wedding present to the bride, often her flat silver or "good" china.

Photographs taken of the bride in her wedding dress, and candid pictures taken the day of the wedding. If a bridesmaid or usher wishes to have a wedding photograph, she or he may properly order and pay for a print from the photographer.

Awnings, tent for outdoor reception, and carpet for church aisle if desired.

The bride herself gives a wedding present or a wedding ring, or both, to the groom, if she wants to.

THE BRIDEGROOM'S EXPENSES

The engagement ring—as handsome as he can afford.

A wedding present to the bride—jewels if he is able, always something for her to keep forever.

His bachelor dinner if he gives one.

The bride's bouquet, where local custom requires it, and in any case, a corsage for her to wear when they go away.

The marriage license.

A personal gift to his best man and to each of his ushers; and their hotel expenses, unless they are invited to stay with neighbors or friends.

Unless the entire outfit is rented (and this is rarely the case), he gives his best man and each usher his wedding tie and gloves.

He provides each of the above with a boutonnière, as well as his own and that of his father.

The wedding ring.

The clergyman's fee. Clergymen do not charge a regular fee, but a donation is expected, and it should be in accordance with the circumstances of the family.

From the moment the bride and groom start off on their wedding trip, all the expenditure becomes his.

EXCEPTIONS

No matter whether a wedding is to be large or tiny, there is a supposedly fixed rule that the reception must be either at the house of the bride's parents or grandparents or other relatives or close friends, or else in rooms rented by her family. Etiquette has always decreed that the groom's family may give entertainments of whatever description they choose for the young couple after they have returned from the honeymoon; but the wedding breakfast as well as the trousseau of the bride, however simple these may need to be, must be furnished by her own side of the house!

There might be circumstances, however, when it would be caviling not to break this rule. If, for instance, the bride were without family, she might perfectly well be married in the church or the rectory and go afterward to the house of the bridegroom's parents for the reception. After all, there are few rules that permit no exceptions under extenuating circumstances. But in the average case, she would put herself in a false position and bring criticism upon her own family's inability to assume the wedding obligations which properly belong to them.

WHEN, WHERE, AND HOW BIG?

Before deciding the date of the wedding, the bride must find out definitely on which day her church or synagogue and the clergyman who is to perform the ceremony will be available. If it is to be a large wedding, she must also coordinate the time available for the church with the time that is possible for the caterer or the hotel or the club.

The next step is to decide the time of day that will be best for the ceremony. Religion, climate, local custom, and transportation schedules may be important factors, as well as the bride and groom's own plans for their wedding trip. Also, due consideration should be given to the probable convenience of a majority of the relatives and friends who will want to come.

Having settled upon a day and hour, the bride next decides on the number of guests who can be provided for; this is determined by the type of reception intended, as well as by the size of the bride's house or the club, and the amount that her family can afford for the reception.

Remember, too, that if the reception comes at a customary meal hour, a substantial wedding breakfast or collation is usually provided. In this case, expense may restrict the number of guests invited to the reception.

Only a very small church or chapel or the cost of the invitations would limit the number of guests invited to the ceremony.

THE INVITATIONS

The bride-elect and her mother then go to the stationer and decide details, such as size and texture of paper and style of engraving, for the invitations. The order is given two months or more in advance for the estimated number of invitations or announcements. Once the plates are engraved, it is not difficult to increase the order if necessary. » *For all details of the forms, see Chapters 49, 50, and 51.*

Invitations are sent out three weeks before a formal wedding, and as little as two weeks or ten days before a small, informal wedding.

THE WEDDING LIST

Four lists are combined in sending out wedding invitations; the bride and the groom make one each of their own friends, to which are added the list of the bride's family, made out by her mother or other near relative, and the list of the groom's family, made out by his mother or a relative.

The bride's mother consults with the groom or, if possible, with his mother, about how the list is to be divided between them. If the families have long been friends and live in the same community, the invitations should be divided more or less equally between them. If it is decided that one hundred may be included at the reception, this would suggest that some seventy names would probably be the same and would mean then that each would be able to add fifteen of their own to the seventy already on their shared list. But if they have never known each other well and their friends are unknown to each other, each would have to limit her list to fifty.

On the other hand, if the groom's people live in another place and this may mean that not more than twenty will be able to come, the bride's mother will be able to invite as many as will result in eighty acceptances. Both mothers may risk being a little overliberal because there are always a few who, having accepted, are then prevented for one reason or another from coming.

It is most important to harmony among the future in-laws that the family of the out-of-town groom estimate *realistically* the number of guests who will make the trip to the wedding. When the bride's mother tells them the total number that can be invited and how many of this total she expects to accept on her side, they should make every effort to restrict their list to stay within the total. It is up to the out-of-town family to respect the requests of the bride's family in this matter, as they may not be aware of the limitations of space or expense that are a factor in the number of invitations.

Nor should a great number of invitations to the reception be sent to distant acquaintances who could never be expected to attend, as they only appear to be invitations to send a gift. These far-away friends should be sent announcements or invitations to the church alone, neither of which carries any obligation.

LODGING FOR OUT-OF-TOWN GUESTS

If the groom lives far enough away from the bride so that his family and attendants cannot return home after prewedding parties and the wedding itself, the bride (or more generally her mother) makes arrangements for their lodging. The groom's mother must, as soon as possible, tell the bride's family exactly how many of their relatives will definitely attend the wedding. Friends and neighbors of the bride, if they possibly can, usually offer accommodations for bridesmaids and ushers and occasionally (especially if they happen to be acquainted with them) for the immediate family of the groom. Because they would certainly feel that they were imposing on strangers to visit in the usual servantless house of today, aunts, uncles, cousin, and friend stay at nearby hotels, inns, or motels. If the bride's family or some of their close friends are members of a club that has guest accommodations, it is an ideal solution for grandparents or older relatives, as they will be provided with all services and meals when they are not attending wedding festivities.

Some weeks before the wedding, the bride's mother reserves the necessary number of rooms in the best inn or hotel nearby, or, if there is a choice, she may send pamphlets or brochures (adding her own recommendation) to the groom's family. They select the one that appeals to them and make their own reservations. In either case, unless the bride's family is very wealthy and that of the groom can barely pay for its transportation to the marriage, the cost of the accommodations is paid for by those using them.

CHURCH INVITATIONS UNLIMITED

Invitations to a big church wedding may be sent to the entire list of personal acquaintances, and often to business acquaintances of both families, no matter how large the combined number may be or whether they will by any chance be present or not. People in mourning are included, as well as those who live miles away, for the invitations not merely proffer hospitality but are messengers carrying the news of the marriage.

At a typical wedding, friends are asked to the reception as well as to the church, and acquaintances to the church only. If the wedding is to be in the house or is otherwise very small, so that none but families and intimate friends are invited, announcements may be sent to all uninvited acquaintances.

When, as often happens, one family is several times the size of the other family, and has also a list of intimate friends that is twice the length of that of the other, a certain number of pews that would customarily be occupied by the smaller family are made available for members of the larger family.

CHOOSING THE BRIDE'S ATTENDANTS

The bride's closest sister is always maid (or matron) of honor. If she has no sister of suitable age, she chooses her most intimate friend.

In addition to a maid or matron of honor, a bride may have a veritable procession; eight or ten bridesmaids, flower girls, pages, and a ring bearer.

At the average wedding, however, there are from two to six bridesmaids. Sometimes, when a bride's best friends have married before her, the "maids" may be "matrons," but they are always called "bridesmaids" and not "bridesmatrons."

Although a bride need have no attendants, it is best that she have at least one. The picture of her father or the best man holding her bouquet and stooping to adjust her train would be difficult to witness with gravity.

As ushers and bridesmaids are chosen from the most intimate friends of the bride and groom, it is scarcely necessary to suggest how to word the asking. Usually they are told at the time the engagement is announced that they are invited to serve; or they are told whenever one happens to meet them. If school or college friends who live at a distance are among the number, they are invited by telephone, telegram, or letter.

CHILDREN AS ATTENDANTS

Junior bridesmaids are young girls, usually between seven and twelve, who are too big to be flower girls and too young to be regular bridesmaids. They attend the rehearsal, of course, and usually the rehearsal dinner (for a little while, at least), but are not necessarily included in other festivities. *Flower girls* are present only at the rehearsal and at the reception, where they do not stand in line.

If the bride would like to have her little brother or nephew be the *ring bearer*, he is dressed in white, carries the ring on a small firm white cushion, and walks ahead of her. The ring is either lightly sewed to the cushion or fastened by having an ordinary pearl-headed flower pin thrust into the center of the cushion and the ring encircling this. The best man should be shown beforehand whether he is to pull or lift it off.

Train bearers, as the name implies, hold the bride's train. They, too, must be very little boys and dressed in white. The train trailing smoothly by itself is really more assuring than a train in the hands of very little children whose manner of bearing it is apt to be uncertain, to say the least.

THE COST OF ATTENDING THE BRIDE

With the exception of the flowers they carry, which are presented by the bride, every article worn by the bridesmaids, flower girls, and pages, although chosen by the bride, must be paid for by the wearers (or their parents).

It is perhaps condemnation of the modern wedding display that many a young girl has had to refuse the joy of being in the wedding party because a complete bridesmaid's outfit costs a sum that neither she nor her parents can provide. And it is seldom that the bride herself is in a position to give six or eight complete costumes, much as she may want all her most particular friends with her on her day of days. Therefore, unless her bridesmaids have unusually deep purses, the bride who has a conscience tries to choose clothes that will not be too expensive. Department stores as well as specialty shops are prepared to submit enchanting ready-to-wear models that can be ordered in different colors, or even different materials, and within almost any budget.

The other expenses are shared this way: All attendants of the bride and bridegroom pay for their own transportation from wherever they are to wherever the wedding is to take place. "Conveyance of the bridesmaids" means merely to and from the church and the bride's house, etc. The girls are always the guests of the bride and the men the guests of the bridegroom, from the moment they arrive in the bride's town until they leave.

CHOOSING THE BEST MAN AND USHERS

No matter how small the wedding, the bridegroom always has a best man. It is not an unbreakable rule, but it hints of a family quarrel if the brother of the bridegroom is not best man, or the sister of the bride is not maid of honor, unless, of course, brother or sister is many years senior or junior. When the bridegroom has no brother, his next selection is his most intimate friend; or, if deciding upon this best one is difficult he perhaps chooses a cousin, or the brother of the bride. Frequently an only son who is very devoted to his father will ask him to serve as best man.

The number of ushers is in proportion to the size of the church and the number of guests invited. At a house wedding, ushers are often merely honorary, and the bridegroom may have many or none, as he chooses.

It is unheard of for a man to refuse the honor unless a bridegroom, for snobbish reasons, asks someone who is not really a friend at all. Of course, the groom is careful not to ask someone whom he knows will have problems of time and distance that will be difficult to overcome.

THE HEAD USHER

In certain localities, courtesy designates the usher who is selected to take the bride's mother up the aisle as the head or first usher. Very occasionally, too, the groom appoints an especially reliable friend head usher so as to be sure that all details will be carried out, including the prompt and proper appearance at the church of the other ushers. The ushers divide the responsibilities among themselves. The groom decides who goes on which aisle. One volunteers or is asked to look out for the bride's coming and to notify the groom. Others are detailed to take the two mothers up the aisle. But very often this arrangement is arbitrarily decided by height. If one mother is very tall and the other very short, each goes up with a different usher, but if a brother of the bride or groom is among the ushers, he always escorts his own mother to her place.

JUNIOR USHERS

For a boy who is too big to be a ring bearer and too young to be an usher, a very useful position (especially if there are two) is that of running the ribbons in front of the pews. When there are two, one takes the right side of the aisle, the other one the left, and then they stand at the front holding the ribbon.

When there is only one boy, he can quite well run the ribbon up the left side of the aisle and stand beside the first pew holding the ribbon until the bride's father takes his place. Then he can put the ribbon across the end of the pew and stand in front of it. In this case, an usher has placed the ribbon on the right side.

ANOTHER WORD ABOUT ATTENDANTS

RELATIVES OF BRIDE AND GROOM AS ATTENDANTS

Unless attendants are limited to her sister and his brother, a brother of the bride or, if she has no brother, then her favorite cousin is usually asked by the groom to be usher out of compliment to her. The bride returns the compliment by asking the sister of the groom who is nearest her own age to be bridesmaid, or if he has no sister, she asks a cousin. If she is to have a number of bridesmaids—especially if the groom has no sister—she very often shows her courtesy by asking the groom to name a close family friend or a cousin. The bride in asking the groom's relative does not say, "Will you be one of my bridesmaids because Jim wants me to ask you?" If the bridesmaid is not a particular friend of the bride, she knows perfectly that it is on Jim's account that she has been asked. It is the same with the bride's usher. If the groom is choosing from six to ten ushers, he often includes one who is an especial friend of the bride and asks him exactly as he asks the others.

When the homes of the bride and bridegroom are a great distance apart, so that none but the bridegroom's immediate family can make the journey to the wedding, it is not unusual—if he has no brother—that he choose his father or even stepfather as his best man. The ushers, in such situations, are chosen from among the friends of the bride.

MARRIED ATTENDANTS

It is entirely correct for a married man to act as usher, or for a married woman to be matron of honor or a bridesmaid. Neither the wife of the first nor the husband of the second need be asked to take part. The one not officiating is of course invited to the wedding, and sits at the bridal table.

PLANNING THE CHURCH SERVICE

Some time before the day of the wedding, the bride and groom go together to visit the clergyman who will perform the ceremony. They discuss the service they would like to have, whether they wish the choir or a vocalist to sing, possible pieces (often consulting the organist also), and any customs or rules peculiar to that church. The clergyman, in turn, may very well have, because of his experience with other marriages, suggestions as to decorations and other details. For example, if there are to be many elderly people in the audience or simply because it will be easier for the congregation to see the ceremony sitting down, the couple may ask the clergyman to announce that the guests may be seated, if he approves. Or they may wish to discuss with him the suitability of a nuptial kiss at the end of the ceremony.

If the marriage is to be performed by a minister or rabbi from another parish, the couple should visit both him and clergyman of the church or synagogue where the wedding is to take place.

PLANNING THE "WEDDING BREAKFAST"

The "wedding breakfast" is a term applied to the meal served at the reception, whether it be morning, noon, or night. It may be an elaborate sit-down meal, it may be a buffet to which the guests help themselves, or it may simply be sandwiches and hors d'oeuvres passed on trays.

If the reception is held at a club or hotel, the food and drinks will be prepared and served by the staff of the organization. They may also provide some decorations, which most keep on hand for such occasions. The bride and her mother should discuss the menu and all other arrangements with the manager, or whoever is in charge of social activities, as soon as the wedding date is set.

THE SIT-DOWN BREAKFAST

The sit-down breakfast is the most elaborate wedding reception possible and, when not held at a club or hotel, is always supplied by a caterer, who brings all the food, tables, chairs, napery, china, and glass, as well as the necessary waiters. If there are servants in the house, they may assist or oversee or be detailed to other duties.

In the country, a canopied platform is erected on the lawn. The platform is filled with little tables, but in the center is a large one reserved for the bridal party. At a large breakfast a second table is reserved for the parents of the bride and groom and a few especially invited friends.

Place cards at the bride's table and at the parents' table are of white bristol board embossed in silver to match the monograms on the wedding-cake boxes if they are to be distributed. Or plain white cards may have a strap cut (like a double buttonhole) and small white flowers thrust under the strap.

Place cards are not put on any of the small tables. All the guests, except the few placed at the two reserved tables, sit with whom they like. Sometimes they do so by prearrangement, but usually they sit where they happen to find friends—and room!

Small menu cards printed in silver are usually put on all the tables. Sometimes these cards have the crest of the bride's father embossed at the top, but usually the initials of the surnames of bride and groom are stamped in silver to match the wedding-cake boxes.

Lobster Newburg
Suprême of Chicken
Peas
Aspic of Foie Gras
Celery Salad
Ices
Coffee

There may be bouillon or vichyssoise, lobster Newburg or some other seafood. The main dish might be beef stroganoff with wild rice, sweetbreads and mushrooms, or chicken pâté.

Any variety of aspic or salad may be served.

Individual ices are accompanied by little cakes of assorted variety.

At a wedding breakfast of this extreme elaborateness, the accepted beverage has always been champagne. For those who do not serve alcohol, orange juice and ginger ale, or white grape juice and ginger ale, with mint leaves perhaps, are two attempts at a satisfying substitute.

THE STAND-UP BREAKFAST OR SUPPER

For the stand-up breakfast, a single long table is set in the dining room of home or club. It is covered with a plain white damask cloth. In the center is a centerpiece of white flowers. On it are piles of plates (preferably white, or white and gold), stacks of napkins, and rows of spoons and forks at intervals. This table should be so situated that the guests pass on directly to the buffet table to help themselves to the food.

If there is a bridal table, it is usually set elsewhere. If not, the wedding cake is the feature of the buffet, put at the center of this table with a centerpiece of white flowers behind it or two floral pieces flanking it. In evenly spaced places are such cold dishes as chicken and celery salad or ham mousse with chopped hearts of lettuce and such hot dishes as creamed crabmeat, chicken à la king, or chicken croquettes. Whatever the choice is, there are two or three cold dishes and at least two hot dishes. Of first importance is to select food that can be easily eaten with a fork while the plate is held in the other hand. There should also be finger rolls and sandwiches, substantial yet small enough to eat easily.

There are dishes filled with fancy cakes, chosen for looks as much as taste. Usually there are also peppermints, caramels, and chocolates. Ice cream is the typical dessert.

After-dinner coffee is put on a side table, as is champagne or its substitute, punch.

THE SIMPLEST RECEPTION REQUIREMENTS

A morning wedding followed by a high-noon breakfast would mean substantial food; and in the evening one rather expects an elaborate wedding—evening clothes, dinner, etc. An afternoon reception can, however, be very simple. All that is required is champagne or a fruit punch in which to drink the bride's and groom's health, and the wedding cake. A slightly more elaborate reception would include either tea or coffee and thin sandwiches.

The table decorations and the wedding cake should of course be white. Although a number of small tables may be set up in the downstairs rooms of the house, typically the collation (whether simple or lavish) is set out on the dining table and the guests eat standing. The bridal table, if there is one at all, is necessarily placed in another room, or in summer possibly on the porch or in the garden. If the bride has no attendants, she chooses a few of her best friends to sit at her table.

IF THERE IS TO BE NO RECEPTION

When the marriage takes place in a church and there is to be no reception afterward, the bride and groom often follow the friendly and charming custom of waiting after the recessional in the vestibule of the church, with the bridal party and their parents, in order to receive the good wishes of their guests as they leave.

THE WEDDING CAKE

Wedding cake is an essential of every wedding reception. Black fruitcake is traditional—and most expensive. Therefore, nowadays, a white cake or pound cake is the more frequent choice.

The wedding cake is almost always ordered from a caterer who delivers it shortly before the hour of the reception. It is usually in several tiers, beautifully decorated with white icing and topped by small figures of bride and groom, flowers made of frosting, or real flowers. It is large enough to serve the wedding party, the families, and often the close friends. If the reception is not too large, every guest may receive a piece.

A nice custom that is becoming less prevalent because of the expense, but still seen at some large weddings, is that of having cake (usually fruitcake) put into individual white boxes tied with white satin ribbon and ornamented with the combined initials of the bride and groom. These boxes are stacked on a table close beside the front door. Each departing guest is expected to take one. On occasions when another member of a family has been expected but prevented from coming, a second box may be taken home to him or her. Otherwise, it is very bad manners to take more than one's own box.

Although the cost of ordering such a cake may be prohibitive, the charm remains, and it might be a suggestion for an unusual and thoughtful wedding gift (after a consultation with the bride) from a family friend who is skilled in the art of baking—or very rich. Then the individual pieces of cake need not be put into expensive boxes, but may be wrapped in white paper and tied with white or silver ribbon, possibly with a little flower or greenery put through the knot.

THE FLOWERS

As soon as the date and general plans for the wedding are decided upon, the bride and her mother should go to see their florist and ask him for an estimate for the decoration of the church and house and for the bridesmaids' bouquets. Whether they or the bridegroom are to order the bride's own bouquet depends upon the custom of the community, but in most places it is the custom for the bride's parents to order the bride's bouquet as well as those of the bridesmaids when they order the flowers for the church and house.

The bridegroom sends the bride a corsage to wear when she leaves the reception with him. He always buys the boutonnières for his ushers, his best man, and himself—but not for the bride's father, who, unless he is a widower, receives his boutonnière from his own "bride," the bride's mother. In certain communities it is customary for him to send flowers for the mothers and grandmothers to wear at the wedding. When the bride's bouquet is the responsibility of the bridegroom, the corsage is often inserted in the center of the larger bouquet and removed when the time comes to throw the bouquet to the bridesmaids or later when the bride dresses for going away. Of course, the flowers appear to be one bouquet.

At a very elaborate wedding, whether in the city or the country, the church is decorated with masses of flowers arranged as standards or sprays tied to the pew ends, as well as the floral embellishment of the chancel. Later, at the reception, not only is there a floral background against which the bridal couple receives, but every room has been adorned with greens and flowers. An orchestra—sometimes two, so that the playing may be without intermission—is hidden behind smilax or other greenery in the hall or wherever most convenient.

But at a more typical wedding, the floral arrangements are merely a modification of the one outlined above. The chancel of the church is decorated, but less lavishly—perhaps two bowls on the altar and a spray at the end of the choir stalls, or an arrangement on either side of the chancel steps. Sometimes there are flowers at the ends of the ten to twenty reserved pews, or possibly only at the ends of the two pews that mark the beginning of the ribboned section.

There is very little floral decoration at the reception. There are usually flowers on the bridal table and the buffet table, but the decorations at all receptions in all seasons consist in greatest degree—and most often wholly—of smilax and plants of green. It is in fact true that a confusion of flowers detracts from the dresses and bouquets of the bride and the bridesmaids.

Flowers for the church, incidentally, need not be white, but may blend with the color scheme of the bridesmaids's dresses and bouquets.

MAKING A BIG CHURCH SEEM SMALLER

If the wedding is to be in a large church instead of a chapel and only a comparatively few pews are to be occupied, the effect of emptiness may be overcome entirely by making a hedge of branches or potted shrubbery behind the pews that form the boundary. Altar, chancel, and necessary pews would be lighted brilliantly and the pews behind the screen of greens left dark, thus making the church seem as small as need be.

If there is no side door, a narrow opening would have to be left in the aisle to admit the guests, but the bridal party would enter from the vestry or waiting-room, instead of going up the long aisle. Or at less expense, if there are choir stalls, they may be used as pews and the church so lighted as to include only the chancel. This arrangement gives to the smallest possible wedding all the solemn beauty of church surroundings, including the music of the organ.

OTHER DECORATIONS AND ACCESSORIES

As well as flowers, there are other decorations and accessories that must be ordered in advance. If a canopy is to be used at the church entrance, the sexton must know so that he can arrange for it to be put

up the morning of the wedding day. A carpet is often laid down the aisle of the church after the bride's mother is seated, to protect the bride's train, and this must be ordered, either from the church or the florist. If the reception is to be held under a tent or a marquee, it is provided by the caterer for a home garden, or by the club where the reception is to be held, and usually put up a day or two in advance.

Many brides, especially when boxes of wedding cake are not to be distributed, provide mementos of the wedding in the form of white match books with the bride's and groom's names and the date printed on them in silver. These are placed about in bowls, as well as in or beside ash trays in sufficient quantities so that the guests feel free to take them home. Another attractive custom is that of having the couple's names printed on paper cocktail napkins. These are passed with sandwiches or hors d'oeuvres and also with glasses of cold drinks, which tend to drip on a warm day. These printed accessories should be ordered six weeks or two months ahead of the wedding date if the bride wishes to be sure of their delivery.

MUSIC FOR CHURCH AND RECEPTION

The questions of the kind of music that may be played in the church and whether the couple would like to have the choir or a soloist sing are in the province of the choirmaster or the organist. At a majority of weddings, the march from Wagner's *Lohengrin* is the choice for the wedding procession. The recessional is usually Mendelssohn's. If the bride and groom have their hearts set on music that they are advised is too worldly to be played in their church, they can, of course, have many of these selections played at the reception.

On occasion, a notable singer, or even possibly an organist, who is a member of the bride's or bridegroom's family (or perhaps merely a special friend) may quite properly be included in the musical arrangements. But it would be very discourteous to invite an outsider without consulting and receiving the consent of the church organist.

The size and the formality of the wedding determine the type of music to be provided at the reception. If it is a formal wedding with an elaborate reception held in a large tent or ballroom, the bride's family usually hires a full orchestra, and the guests dance themselves as well as watching the bride as she enjoys the most wonderful party of her life. For romantic effect, the orchestra leader generally features his string section rather than bringing a large percussion or brass section. The bride and groom may give him a list of the pieces they would like to have played.

But it is by no means necessary to go to this extent, and for smaller, less formal weddings a trio or a piano and violin, or even a phonograph, can easily provide music for a small dance floor—possibly one room of the house, cleared for the occasion.

If there is to be no dancing, a wandering violinist or accordionist, playing the music chosen by the couple, makes a gay and happy background for toasts and conversation.

THE WEDDING PICTURES

THE FORMAL PHOTOGRAPH

At some time before the wedding, often at the final fitting of the bridal gown, the photographer takes the formal wedding pictures of the bride. If pictures are to be sent to the newspapers, it must be done well in advance to allow time for choosing those to be used, the final printing, and mailing to the papers two to three weeks before the wedding day.

A small print of this formal picture in a silver frame, with or without the date and the initials of the couple engraved on it, makes a charming present from bride to bridesmaid.

CANDID PHOTOGRAPHS

If the candid shots on the wedding day are to be taken by a professional, he must be engaged far ahead of time, especially if the wedding is to be in June. However, amateur photographers are often almost as well equipped and as skillful as the professional, and if you are fortunate enough to number one of these among your friends, he will surely be delighted to record the events of the day. If he covers the entire day and uses quantities of film, the bride's family must certainly pay for the supplies and the printing, which, especially if color film is used, can be exorbitant. But if he uses a roll or two at the reception of his own volition and not at the specific request of the bride, this is not necessary, and often camera enthusiasts present these pictures as a wedding present to the bride.

A candid album may start with the bride leaving the house before the wedding and continue through the day—the arrival at the church with her father (or whoever is giving her away), leaving the church after the ceremony, the bridal party and receiving line at the reception, many shots of the bride dancing, the guests, the toasts, the cutting of the cake, and finally, the departure of the happy pair on their honeymoon.

Pictures of the actual ceremony are in poor taste when flash bulbs detract from the solemnity of the service, but one time exposure, if made with the clergyman's permission, would not be out of order. Once the service is over and the bridal procession is coming down the aisle, however, the camera may start to work, and pictures of the radiant bride and groom who suddenly realize that they are "Mr. and Mrs." are often among the best souvenirs of all.

WEDDING PRESENTS AND OTHER GIFTS

If the presents, which begin to arrive as soon as the invitations are out, are likely to be many, each one should be entered at once in a gift book. There are many kinds published for the purpose, but any book with ruled pages about eight to ten inches square will answer the purpose. The usual model spreads across the double page as follows:

Present Received	Article	Sent by	Sender's Address	Where Bought	Thanks Written
May 20	Silver Dish	Mr. and Mrs. White	1 Park Place	Criterion's	May 20
May 21	12 Plates	Mr. and Mrs. Hardy	2 South Street	Crystal's	May 21

All gifts as they arrive should be numbered with a paste-on sticker, and the corresponding number should be listed in the gift book. There might be many silver dishes and also dozens of plates—meaning that a sticker goes on one of each design or pattern.

THE BRIDE'S THANKS

In return for the many presents showered upon a happy bride, there is a correspondence task that may not be evaded. On a sheet of note paper—not a folded visiting card—and in her own handwriting, she must send a separate letter for each present she receives—and, if humanly possible, she writes each letter of thanks on the day the present arrives. If she does not, they soon get ahead of her and her whole honeymoon is taken up with note-writing. » *For the wording of bride's notes, see Chapter 9.*

It would not be possible to overemphasize the inexcusable rudeness of the bride who sends a printed or even an engraved card of thanks for wedding presents sent her. Whoever devised this flagrant affront to the traditions of common decency was, obviously, more concerned with making sales to stationers than with the ordinary precepts of polite behavior.

In a few most unusual cases, such as the hurried marriage of a bridegroom who is unexpectedly being sent overseas, or the marriage of a person of such prominence that the gifts arrive in overwhelming numbers, a printed acknowledgment, *always* to be followed later by a note of thanks, is permissible, but seems a waste of effort. A minute or two more would complete a note of thanks to enclose in each stamped and addressed envelope instead of addressing and stamping every acknowledgment twice. Also, it seems pretentious because it implies that so many presents were expected that special preparations were made in advance to take care of the avalanche. Moreover, this engraved notice, which attracts formal attention to the promised letter, exacts that the letter be longer and better than an unheralded note in which a few brief sentences could say all that is necessary.

If circumstances demand it, however, the engraved note reads

Miss Joanne Carter
[or *Mrs. John Franklin,*
if the notes are sent after the wedding]
gratefully acknowledges the receipt of
your wedding gift
and will write you a personal note at
the earliest possible date.

WHEN THE PRESENTS ARE SHOWN

There is absolutely no impropriety in showing the presents at the wedding reception. The only reason for not showing them is lack of space in a small house or, of course, an apartment. If there is an extra sitting room, such as a library, they are shown there. Otherwise a bedroom from which all the furniture has been removed is suitable. Tables covered with plain white damask tablecloths or sheets are put like counters around the sides of the room. They may be decorated with white ribbon or artificial flowers, and the sides may be draped with tulle net or pleated cheesecloth.

If the reception is not held at home, relatives and friends are often invited to the house shortly before the wedding day to see the display of presents.

ARRANGING THE PRESENTS

Not so much in an effort to parade her possssions as to do justice to the kindness of the many people who have sent them, a bride should show her appreciation of their gifts by placing each one in the position of greatest advantage. Naturally, all people's tastes are not equally pleasing to the taste of the bride—nor are all pocketbooks equally filled. Very valuable presents are better put in close contrast with others of like quality—or others entirely different in character. Colors should be carefully grouped. Two presents, both lovely in themselves, can be completely destructive of each other if the colors are allowed to clash.

Sometimes china is put on one table, silver on another, glass on another, but I think a more attractive arrangement can be made by combining textures and shapes. Pieces that "jar" when appearing together must be placed as far apart as possible and perhaps even moved to other surroundings. A badly designed piece of silverware should not be left among beautiful examples, but be put among china ornaments or other articles that do not reveal its lack of fineness by too direct comparison. To group duplicates is another unfortunate arrangement. Eighteen pairs of pepper pots or fourteen sauce boats in a row might as well be labeled: "Look at this stupidity! What can she do with all of us?" They are sure to make the givers feel at least a little chagrined at their choice.

Porto

WHETHER CARDS ARE LEFT ON

There is no definite rule as to whether or not the cards that are sent with the gifts are removed. There is no impropriety in leaving them on, which certainly saves members of the family from repeating many times who sent this and who sent that, especially the family of a bride whose father is a governor, or a mayor, or a much-loved clergyman, or a notable person in the business community and who therefore receives an unusual number of presents. On the other hand, many people feel that it is a private matter between the bride and the giver and do not wish the world to know how elaborate a gift they were able to send.

DISPLAYING CHECKS

Ordinarily, it would be in very bad taste to display gifts of money. But because it would not be fair to a generous check-giving relative or very intimate friend of the family to have it supposed that he or she sent no gift at all, it is quite proper to display checks with amounts concealed. This is done by laying them out on a flat surface one above the other so that the signatures alone are disclosed. The amount of the one at the top is covered with a strip of opaque paper and then a sheet of glass laid over them all. The glass should be sufficiently large to lay other presents around the margin to keep a curious someone from lifting it.

EXCHANGING WEDDING PRESENTS

Some people think it discourteous if a bride changes the present chosen for her. But it has been a time-honored custom to permit a bride to exchange all duplicate presents, and no friends should allow their feelings to be hurt unless they have chosen the present with a particular sentiment. A bride never changes the presents chosen for her by her own family or by the bridegroom's family, unless especially told that she may do so. But to keep twenty-two saltcellars and sixteen silver card trays when she has no pepper pots or coffee spoons or vegetable dishes would be putting sentiment above sense.

GIFTS FOR THE BRIDE'S ATTENDANTS

If the bridesmaids give a party for the bride shortly before the wedding or, if not, when they arrive to help the bride dress for the wedding, she gives each of them her present, which is usually something to wear. The typical bridesmaid's present is a bracelet, earrings, a pin, a clip, or other trinket, and this, according to the means of the bride, may have great or scarcely any intrinsic value. The gift to her maid or matron of honor may well match those given the bridesmaids or be quite different. If it is something that can be engraved, such as a small silver picture frame, the date and the initials of the bride and groom commemorate the occasion.

GIFTS FOR THE USHERS

The bridegroom's gifts to his ushers are usually put at their places at the bachelor dinner if one is held. If not, they may be presented at the rehearsal dinner or just before leaving for the church. Cuff links are the most popular gift. Silver or gold pencils, belt buckles, key rings, cigarette cases, billfolds, and other small and personal articles are suitable. The present to the best man is approximately the same as, or slightly handsomer than, the gifts to the ushers.

THE BRIDE AND GROOM EXCHANGE PRESENTS

He is a very exceptional and enviable groom who is financially able to take his fiancée to the jeweler and let her choose what she fancies. Customarily, and better, the bridegroom goes shopping alone and buys the handsomest ornament he can afford. If he has great wealth, a diamond pendant, brooch, or bracelet, or if he hasn't, the simplest bangle or charm. But whether his gift is of great or little value, it must be something for her personal adornment.

The bride need not give a present to the groom, but she usually does if she can. Her favorite gift is something permanent and for his personal use—ranging from cuff links to a watch or ring.

44

The clothes for the wedding party

Although the bride's gown is usually the center of attention at any wedding, the fact remains that all other members of the wedding party, as well as the parents of bride and groom, must appear in special and appropriate apparel on the day itself. As with other preparations, nothing can be left to chance or a last-minute flurry, and as soon as the kind of wedding—formal, or informal, morning, afternoon, or evening, large or small—has been determined, the bride must turn her attention not only to her own dress and the dresses of her attendants but also see to it that the groom has the necessary information to inform his best man, the ushers, and, of course, his parents about the arrangements.

THE BRIDE'S COSTUME

Before choosing her costume, the bride and groom together (always consulting the bride's family) must come to a decision on several things. First, they must decide on the degree of formality and the size of the wedding. When the date is set they must consider the probable temperature, which will affect the material and style to be chosen. And they must also think of the setting and local customs. Will the reception be held indoors in a small house or a large club room, or will it be outdoors in a shady garden? Will the ceremony be held in a large cathedral, or a tiny chapel, or possibly in the living room of the bride's home? All these questions and many more must be answered before the bride can choose a dress that will be not only beautiful, but comfortable and appropriate.

THE DRESS

At her first wedding a bride suitably wears a dress of white and a bridal veil whether she be sixteen or forty! Beyond that age, she will probably feel more comfortable in a pretty cocktail dress in a pastel shade. Naturally a veil of tulle would be too youthful for the bride of forty, just as a veil of yellowed lace would be unsuitable at eighteen.

The traditional bridal material is satin for all seasons of the year. But few brides wish to wear such a warm material on a summer day. Therefore, although satin is the favorite choice for fall and winter, other materials have become more popular for the rest of the year.

In addition to satin, those suitable for autumn and midwinter weddings are faille, velvet, and moiré. In the spring, lace and taffeta are lovely and in midsummer, chiffon, organdy, mousseline-de-soie, cottons, piqués, and linens. An infinite variety of synthetic materials have added to the bride's choice for every season.

A very young bride in a veritable cloud of tulle is at her loveliest. Lace of course adds dignity and is most becoming to a mature bride. It is very important that a bride in her thirties or over choose both veil and dress in a creamed white, particularly if the dress be of satin. There is really a very marked difference in the becomingness to the skin of an almost imperceptible accent of blue or pink or ivory. For a bride beyond her twenties, the right one of these off-white tints is as flattering as the wrong one is cruel.

The length of the train of the bride's dress depends somewhat upon the size of the church. In a large church the train can be very long; in a small chapel, short. A moderately short train extends one yard on the ground. The length of the train also depends to some extent on the height of the bride. The dress should be on the conservative side of fashion.

In the case of an informal marriage ceremony, such as a civil ceremony before a justice of the peace, or a second marriage when the bride or groom does not wish a large celebration, the bride chooses the prettiest dress she has, or can afford to buy, which will be appropriate to whatever the couple plan after the wedding ceremony. If a few friends are gathering to wish them happiness, she wears an afternoon or cocktail dress or suit. If they are leaving on a wedding trip directly following the ceremony, she may be married in the suit or traveling dress that she will wear away.

THE BRIDE'S VEIL

The face veil is rather old-fashioned and is appropriate only for a very young bride of a demure type. Traditionally, she is a maiden too shy to face a congregation unveiled and reveals her face only when she is a married woman.

If she chooses to wear a veil over her face up the aisle and during the ceremony, the front veil is always a short, separate piece about a yard square, gathered on an invisible band of some kind. It is taken off by the maid of honor when she gives the bride's bouquet back to the bride at the conclusion of the ceremony. It may be pinned with a hairpin at either side, after the long veil is arranged, but more often is mounted by a milliner on a foundation, so that it need merely be put on.

Every girl has her individual idea of what she wishes her wedding veil to be, and she may choose to put it together herself, have it done by some particular friend whose taste and skill she especially admires, or rely on one of the many attractive styles available in all bridal shops.

SHOES AND GLOVES

Her slippers are of white satin or moiré. In either case, she should be sure that they are comfortable because she not only has to walk up the aisle in them, but she has to stand at the reception.

If short, loose gloves happen to be in fashion, she merely pulls one glove off at the altar so that her ring can be put on. But if she wears elbow-length or longer evening gloves, the under-seam of the wedding finger of the glove is usually ripped for about two inches, and she only needs to pull the tip off to have the ring put on. Or she may wear no gloves at all.

JEWELRY SUITABLE FOR THE BRIDE

If the gift of the bridegroom is jewelry the bride always wears it even though it may be composed of colored stones. Otherwise she wears colorless jewelry such as a pearl necklace or possibly a pin of pearls or diamonds.

MAKE-UP

If the bride customarily wears make-up, naturally she will wear it for her wedding, but skillfully applied in moderation. Nothing could be more inappropriate than the bride and her attendants coming down the aisle of the church made up as though they were in a chorus line in a musical comedy.

THE BRIDEGROOM'S WEDDING CLOTHES

Having decided on the degree of formality of the wedding, the season, and the *type* of dress the bride will wear, the groom plans his outfit accordingly (and therefore that of the ushers, whose suits are the same style as the groom's). The following are correct for every occasion:

(1) *Formal Wedding, Daytime*

Cutaway coat or, slightly less formal, black sack coat

Waistcoat to match or gray (or white or fawn in summer if the bridegroom prefers)

Gray-striped trousers or black with white pin stripes

Stiff white shirt for cutaway; soft white collarless shirt for sack coat

Wing or fold-down collar for cutaway; stiff fold-down collar for sack coat

Black-and-white tie or gray or white ascot, if preferred

Plain black shoes and socks. Shoes should be freshly polished and have new soles and heels. Bridegrooms should blacken the soles of their shoes with waterproof shoe dye so that when they kneel at the altar, their shoes look dark and neat

White boutonnière

White buckskin gloves preferred, but when gray is chosen, they should be as light as possible

Silk hat with cutaway; black homburg with sack coat. More often, no hats at all

(2) *Most Formal Wedding, Evening*

Full dress (tail coat, stiff white shirt, wing collar, white lawn tie, white waistcoat)

White evening gloves

White boutonnière

Patent leather pumps or oxford ties

Black socks

Silk hat, if worn at all

(3) *Informal Wedding, Daytime* (when the bride does not wear a wedding dress and veil, but suit or daytime dress)

Dark blue, black, or very dark gray suit

White shirt

Starched turn-down or soft fold collar

Bow or four-in-hand tie in conservative stripe or dark solid color

Black socks and calfskin oxford shoes

White boutonnière

No gloves

Gray or black homburg hat

(4) *Informal Evening Wedding* (the bride wearing wedding gown or cocktail dress—if she is in a daytime dress, the groom wears outfit 3)

Dinner coat (tuxedo)
White shirt with pique or pleated bosom
Black waistcoat or cummerbund
Black silk bow tie
White boutonnière
No gloves
Patent-leather oxford shoes

(5) *Summer Daytime Wedding in Country*
Either dark blue or gray flannel coat and waistcoat (or if coat double-breasted, no waistcoat)
White or gray flannel or white linen trousers
With blue coat, blue and white tie; with gray coat, black and white tie or plain gray
White buckskin shoes and white wool or lisle socks, or plain dark blue or gray socks (matching coat)
No hat
No gloves

(6) *Informal Daytime Wedding in Torrid Weather*
All white Palm Beach or linen suit
Plain dark blue tie, bow or four-in-hand
White socks
White buckskin shoes
White handkerchief

(7) *Evening Wedding in a Hot Climate*
White dinner coat, double-breasted so as to avoid waistcoat
Black tie, and other details same as 4

» *See Chapter 74 for more information about the correct accessories for evening and daytime formal wear.*

THE BRIDESMAIDS' COSTUMES

The costumes of the bridesmaids—slippers, stockings, dresses, bouquets, gloves, and hats—are selected by the bride, without consulting them as to their taste or preferences. The dresses may be long or short, straight or full, light or dark, but the bride will do well to consider the coloring and build of her bridesmaids when making her choice. On occasion, a bride will try to consult her attendants and get all to agree, but long experience has proved that six girls almost certainly will have six opposing opinions to one idea. Bridesmaids, therefore, customarily wear and pay for what the bride chooses. That is the rule. They are always dressed exactly alike as to texture of materials and style, but sometimes their dresses differ in color. The two who follow the ushers might wear green, the next two chartreuse, and the next two lemon yellow, and the maid of honor pale yellow; and all carry the same kind of flowers.

Sometimes the bridesmaids wear the same color, but in graduated value. The first two would wear American Beauty rose, the next two a lighter tint, and the next two a still lighter color, while the maid of honor would be in palest flesh pink. Although a bride seldom cares to run the risk of having the white of her attendants detract from the effect of the single whiteness of her dress, a sash or other detail of color may solve the problem, and an all-white wedding can be entrancing, especially in a garden with a background of dense greens.

The other important item is the selection of a material for the bridesmaids' dresses that will complement the material of the dress of the bride.

The dress of the maid or matron of honor, by the way, never precisely matches that of the bridesmaids, though it is usually similar in style but different or reversed in color. For example, for an autumn wedding, the bridesmaids might wear deep yellow and carry rust and orange chrysanthemums and the maid of honor might wear rust and carry yellow chrysanthemums.

WHAT THE BRIDESMAIDS CARRY

The bridesmaids almost always carry flowers—bouquets sometimes, or baskets, but usually sheaves which they hold on their outside arms. Those walking on the right side hold them on the right arm with the stems pointing downward to the left; and those on the left hold their flowers on the left arm, with stems toward the right. Bouquets or baskets are, however, held in front.

Occasionally, bridesmaids carry muffs in winter, or in summer fans or parasols, more often flower-filled baskets or hats made into baskets by tying their wide brims together with ribbons. Flowers matching those in the basket might be worn in the hair, in which case the bridesmaids need not buy either hats or hair ornaments.

BRIDESMAID IN MOURNING

A bridesmaid who is in mourning may wear colors on this one day, as bridesmaids' dresses are looked upon as uniforms, not individual costumes.

CHILDREN ATTENDING THE BRIDE

Young girl attendants, aged from about seven to fourteen, who are too big to be flower girls and too young to be regular bridesmaids, are junior bridesmaids. The clothes of junior bridesmaids are modified copies of those worn by the bridesmaids.

Flower girls and pages may be dressed in quaint old-fashioned dresses and suits of white silk or satin of whatever period the bride fancies as being especially picturesque. Or perhaps they are dressed in their ordinary white clothes, with wreaths and bouquets for the girls and white boutonnières for the boys.

Ring bearers and train bearers are most often dressed in white suits, preferably with short pants.

At large weddings little girls often wear picture bonnets. At simpler weddings they wear narrow wreaths on their heads. These should be carefully measured for size and must be neat in outline. Small artificial flowers are far better for this purpose than real flowers, which are likely to be ragged as well as too heavy.

Tiny boys and girls wear slippers with a strap and white socks. If they are dressed in white, their slippers are white, but if they wear color, their slippers are colored, either to match their clothes or of a contrasting color—more often the latter. Children's strap slippers usually come in several colors, but white ones are easily dyed. Kid is in better taste than satin.

Junior ushers may be dressed exactly like the other ushers. If not, they wear blue suits, as most suitable to their age group.

WHAT THE BEST MAN AND USHERS WEAR

At the formal daytime wedding, the best man wears precisely what the bridegroom wears. The groom and best man often wear ties that are different from those worn by the ushers and occasionally, if cutaways are being worn, white waistcoats. Otherwise the two principal men are dressed like the ushers.

To make sure that his ushers will be alike (in the event that the outfits are not being rented from one agency), a fastidious bridegroom sends each one instructions covering every detail of the equipment required. For example:

Please wear for the wedding:
Black calfskin low shoes
Plain black socks
Gray striped trousers—the darkest available
Morning coat (cutaway) and single-breasted black waistcoat
White dress shirt; cuffs to show three-quarters of an inch below coat sleeves
Stand-up wing collar
Tie and gloves are enclosed [Groom had already found out size of gloves and size of collars, since bow ties had been selected]
Boutonnière will be at the church

When sending this list, the groom should include information as to when the usher should arrive in town, where he will be staying, what festivities are planned, etc.

It is of greatest importance that in dress each usher be *almost* a counterpart of his fellows, if the picture is to be perfect. Everyone knows what a ragged-edged appearance is produced by a company of recruits whose uniforms are from odd lots. The clothes of the bride's father need not match those of the ushers, but must look well with theirs.

That one word "almost" in the above paragraph is important: The clothes of the men of the bridal party including bridegroom and best man and ushers need not and indeed should not match too precisely.

Their ties, boutonnières, and gloves are exactly alike of course, because they are gifts from the bridegroom and not bought individually. But otherwise, unless they have been rented in one group, there may be differences in stripes of trousers, shape of waistcoats, and slight but quite apparent differences in materials and measures of coats.

RENTING THE USHERS' CLOTHING

If the ushers are members of the diplomatic corps or in high government positions, they may very well own the cutaways or tail coats necessary for a formal wedding. Otherwise, since few young men nowadays possess such suits, the ushers' clothing is usually supplied by a rental agency.

Each may rent his own suit in accordance with the groom's instructions, or, for the sake of uniformity, the groom may prefer to rent them all from one agency in the area of the bride's home. In this case, he is responsible for obtaining the measurements of each out-of-town usher who cannot be measured by the store ahead of time, and he also arranges a time for a final fitting as soon as the ushers arrive, probably a day or two ahead of the wedding date.

One of the ushers who lives in the area is appointed to return the clothes on the first weekday after the wedding, or if they all must leave town immediately, a member of the bride's family should volunteer to take charge of this duty.

CLOTHES OF THE PARENTS

THE BRIDE'S MOTHER

At a wedding held at any hour between 8 A.M. and 6 P.M., the mother of the bride wears a daytime dress, preferably light in color or bright—never black unless relieved with color. Her dress varies in degree of elaborateness according to the other wedding preparations. For example, at a formal wedding her dress follows an equally formal pattern—even, if she wishes, to a long skirt. Always she should wear hat and gloves and usually flowers, although these last are not a requirement. Flowers or other hair ornaments or perhaps veiling or a lace mantilla would fill the requirements for head-covering in church when it is not in current fashion to wear evening hats.

In the evening, dinner dresses are in best taste. A low-cut dress is unsuitable in a church, but a fur piece or some other shoulder covering may be worn over it. As a rule, the mother of the bride leaves her wrap in the vestibule with those of the bridesmaids. If she knows that the church is likely to be cool and if she has an attractive fur piece, she carries or wears this. Otherwise, someone can put a light wrap in the pew for her just before she herself comes up the aisle. In other words, the bride's mother should not wear or carry anything that might spoil the effect of her dress.

THE BRIDE'S FATHER

There is no hard and fast rule governing the clothes of the bride's father. In other words, he may wear whatever is becoming to him, or he may wear whatever the bridegroom is going to wear.

Ordinarily a young father wears a cutaway like that of the bridegroom and his ushers. If they wear black sack coats with their striped trousers and her father is both young and slim-waisted, he may very properly wear the same. But it would not be quite suitable for him to wear the less formal as well as more youthful sack coat when the younger men are wearing cutaways.

THE BRIDEGROOM'S MOTHER AND FATHER

Since the two mothers stand together to receive at the reception, the bridegroom's mother should if possible choose a dress similar in type to that chosen by the bride's mother. Obviously, one should not wear a tailored street dress if the other is wearing a long formal dress, but the bride's mother should choose and the groom's mother do her best to dress in similar style.

At a formal wedding, the bridegroom's father may wear the same type of clothes as those worn by the bride's father. In other words, cutaway in the daytime, tail coat in the evening. He has, however, no part in the ceremony and therefore what he wears is not so important.

ON WEARING BLACK

Nearest relatives should not choose black unless they wear nothing else ever, and, in this case, its somberness should be relieved with some trimming of color. This even applies to one who is wearing mourning; the color in this case would be violet or white.

» *Clothes worn by wedding guests are discussed in Chapter 48.*

Parties, dinners, and the rehearsal

Engaged couples are entertained in a multitude of ways, but there are a few traditional occasions that bear special mention because they differ somewhat from the usual luncheon or dinner, not in the food or service, but in details that pertain to the bride and groom as distinct from other guests.

THE PARTIES BEFORE THE WEDDING

THE BRIDESMAIDS' LUNCHEON

In many American communities, the bridesmaids give the bride a farewell luncheon (or it may be a tea) in addition to the regular showers.

There is no special difference between a bridesmaids' luncheon and any other lunch party, except that the table is more elaborately decorated, often in pink, with bridesmaids' roses or the bride's chosen colors for the wedding. The bride may give her bridesmaids their presents at this time, and if they are giving her a single present from all of them, this would be the occasion for the presentation.

THE BACHELOR DINNER

Bachelor dinners are not held as often as they used to be, especially if the ushers are scattered far and wide or if they, as well as the groom, are working until the day before the wedding. If they are held, it is generally in the private dining room of a restaurant, or in a club.

Popularly supposed to be a frightful orgy, the bachelor dinner was in truth, more often than not, a sheep in wolf's clothing. As a matter of fact, an orgy was never looked upon with favor by any but silly and misguided youths, whose idea of a howling good time was to make a tremendous noise, chiefly by singing at the top of their voices and breaking glasses. A boisterous picture, but scarcely a vicious one! Especially as a lot of the cheapest glassware was always there for the purpose.

The breaking habit originated with drinking the bride's health and breaking the stem of the wine glass, so that it "might never serve a less honorable purpose." And this same time-honored custom is followed to this day. Toward the end of the dinner, the bridegroom rises and holding a filled champagne glass aloft says, "To the bride!" Every man rises, drinks the toast standing, and then breaks the delicate stem of the glass. The impulse to break more glass is natural to youth, and probably still occurs and it is not hard to understand. The same impulse is seen at every county fair where enthusiastic youths delight in shooting or throwing balls at clay pipes and ducks and crockery.

Aside from toasting the bride and its glass-smashing result, the bridegroom's farewell dinner is exactly like any other stag dinner.

SHOWERS

For a full description of bridal showers, see Chapter 36.

PARTIES FOR OUT-OF-TOWN GUESTS

In order to take care of out-of-town family and guests who may arrive two or three days before the wedding, and also to relieve the bride's parents of extra meals and housework, friends of the family frequently give luncheons and dinners for the early arrivals as well as members of the wedding party who live nearby. These parties are likely to be much less formal than the actual wedding festivities and may be given at home, in a club, or in a restaurant. If it is summertime, they may be in the form of an outdoor barbecue or a swimming party; in the winter a sleigh ride or skating party could be organized for the young people, and a cozier fireside buffet for their elders. Whatever the party, the attendants, the families of the couple, their own close friends, and friends of their parents who might also be entertaining for them may be included.

THE REHEARSAL DINNER

The night before the wedding a dinner is generally given for the bridal party and the immediate families of the bride and groom. It may be followed by the rehearsal, but more often the rehearsal is in the late afternoon, followed at 6:00 or 7:00 o'clock by the dinner.

It has now become an accepted custom all over the country, although it is not obligatory, that the parents of the groom give this party. This seems to me an extremely nice gesture—a slight repayment to the family of the bride for all the courtesies extended throughout the wedding activities to the family of the groom. If they come from another city, they may ask the mother of the bride to reserve a room in a club or restaurant for the dinner and consult with her on the number of her family who should be included, so that they can make the reservations in advance. When they arrive for the wedding, they go at once to see the facilities and make the final arrangements. If the groom's family does not, or cannot, give the rehearsal dinner, it is arranged by some member of the bride's family or by a close friend.

The party is usually a gala affair with many toasts to the bride and groom, the families, and every other possible subject. The bride and groom and her parents leave shortly after dinner, so that they will get a good night's sleep, but the rest of the group may stay on, especially if there is music and dancing. This, in many cases, is a reunion for the ushers and takes the place of a bachelor dinner.

LUNCHEON BEFORE THE WEDDING

A small luncheon for the bridal party may be held on the day of the wedding, again to relieve the bride's mother of extra responsibility. It is usually given by a relative or a friend of the bride's family and may be as simple or elaborate as the host and hostess wish. The bride and groom may not even attend. There is an old superstition that the groom should not see his bride before the ceremony on the day of the wedding—but this is an outmoded idea, and they usually come for a short time, probably not together, but each with his own family.

THE REHEARSAL

The bride always directs her wedding rehearsal with the help of her parents and her clergyman, but rarely takes part in it herself, as that is supposed to be bad luck. Someone else, anyone who happens to be present, is appointed her stand-in. Some clergymen, however, feel that superstition has no part in religion and, unless she feels strongly, insist that the bride play her own part.

Most of us are familiar with the wedding service, and its form seems simple enough. But unless one has by experience learned to take care of details, the effect can be hitchy and disjointed. It is not that awkward happenings are serious offenses; but any detail that destroys the smoothness of the general impression is disastrous to dignity, which is the qualification necessary above all in every ceremonial observance.

THE PROCESSION

At a Protestant wedding with choral service, the choir may enter in advance of the hour set for the ceremony and so take no part of the wedding procession. But at an important Catholic wedding and also at Protestant weddings, if the bride and groom wish it that way and the minister and organist agree, the choristers lead the wedding procession, singing as they go. The ushers immediately follow them.

In any event, whether the wedding be Catholic or Protestant, the most elaborate possible or the smallest and simplest, the organist must always be at the rehearsal, as one of the most important details is marking the time of the wedding march.

A wedding rehearsal should proceed as follows:

First of all, it is necessary to determine the exact speed at which the march is to be played. The ushers are asked to try it out. They line up at the door, walk forward two and two. The audience, consisting of the bride and members of the families, decides whether the pace looks well. It must not be fast enough to seem brisk, nor slow enough to be funereal. At one wedding the ushers were told to count two beats as one and the pace was so slow that they all wobbled in trying to keep their balance. On the other hand, it is unsuitable to trot briskly up the aisle of a church.

The audience having decided the speed and the organist having noted the tempo, the entire procession, including the bridesmaids and the stand-in for the bride on her father's arm, goes out into the vestibule and makes its entry. Remember, the father is an important factor in the ceremony, and he must take part in the rehearsal.

The procession is arranged according to height, the two shorter ushers leading—unless others of nearly the same height are found to be more accurate pacemakers. Junior bridesmaids come next, if there are any. If not, the bridesmaids come directly after the ushers, two and two, also according to height, and again the shorter in the lead. After the bridesmaids, the maid or matron of honor walks alone; flower girls, ring bearer, and last of all, the understudy bride on the arm of the father, with pages, if she has any, holding up her train. Each pair in the procession follows the two directly in front by four paces or beats of time. In the vestibule, everyone in the procession must pay attention to the feet directly in front; the pacemakers can follow the army sergeant's example and say very softly, "Left, left!" At the end the bride counts eight beats before she and the father put the left foot forward. The whole trick is starting; after that they just walk naturally to the beat of the music, but keeping the ones in front as nearly as possible at the same distance.

AT THE CHANCEL

At the foot of the chancel, the ushers divide. In a small church, the first two go up the chancel steps and stand at the top, one on the right, the other on the left. The second two go a step or two below the first. If there are more, they stand below again. Chalk marks can be made on the chancel floor if necessary, but it ought not to be difficult, except for very little children, to learn the positions.

In a big church they go up farther, some of them lining the steps or all of them in front of the choir stalls with the line sloping outward so that the congregation may see them better. The bridesmaids also divide, half on either side, and always stand in front of the ushers. The maid of honor's place is on the left at the foot of the steps, exactly opposite the best man. Flower girls are put above or below the bridesmaids, wherever it is thought "the picture" is best.

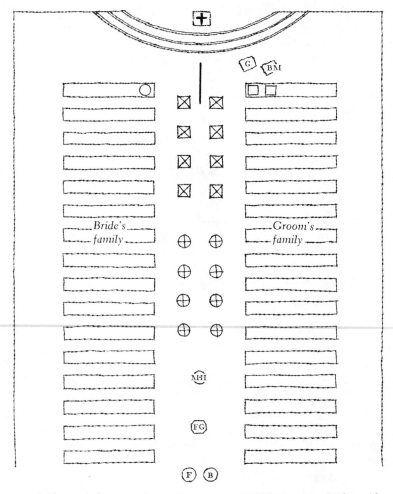

B, *bride*; F, *father*; FG, *flower girl*; MH, *maid of honor*; ⊕, *bridesmaid*; ⊠, *usher*; G, *groom*; BM, *best man*; ⊞, *clergyman*

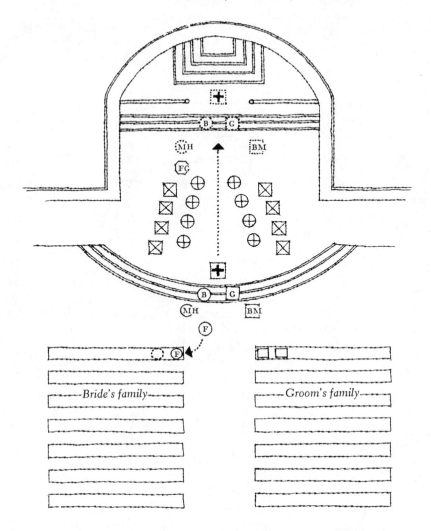

The grouping of the ushers and bridesmaids in the chancel or lining the steps also depends upon their number and the size of the church. In any event, the bridesmaids stand in front of the ushers, half of them on the right and half on the left. They never stand all on the bride's side, with the ushers on the groom's.

In a Roman Catholic ceremony, the father of the bride joins her mother as the groom joins the bride. He does not give his daughter away.

In a church with two main aisles, the guests are seated according to aisles and not according to the church as a whole. All the seats on the right aisle belong to the bride's family and guests. The left aisle belongs to the bridegroom.

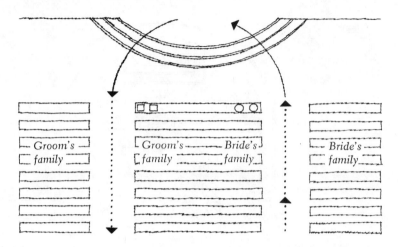

The bride's mother is seated in the front pew at the left (as always) of the bride's aisle—exactly as she would be in a center-aisle church. On the other side of the church the bridegroom's mother occupies the front pew on the right of the groom's aisle (also as always).

For the processional, the bride's (right) aisle is chosen because people naturally turn to the right rather than to the left. After the ceremony, the bride and groom come down the groom's (left) aisle. These directions make it quite clear why the aisles are necessarily chosen so as to place the immediate families in center pews. The left pew must be entered from the aisle at the right. If the bride's mother were to choose the left aisle, this would seat her in a side pew instead of a center one.

However, if the church is very large and the wedding small, so that only the right aisle is used, then the bride's family sits on the left of this aisle and the groom's family on the right, while the marriage takes place at the head of this aisle.

ENTRANCE OF THE BRIDEGROOM

The clergyman who is to perform the marriage comes into the chancel from the vestry. At a few paces behind him follows the groom, who in turn is followed by the best man. The groom stops at the foot of the chancel steps and takes his place at the right, as indicated in the diagram, and his best man stands behind him. The ushers and bridesmaids always pass in front of him and take their place as noted above. When the bride approaches, the groom takes only a step to meet her.

REHEARSING THE MARRIAGE SERVICE

At the rehearsal, the bride, if she does not take part, watches carefully how the substitute bride takes her left hand from the real father's arm, shifts her bouquet from her right hand to her left, and gives her right hand to the real bridegroom. In the performance proper, the groom takes the right hand in his own right hand and draws it through his left arm, at the same time turning toward the chancel. If the service is undivided and all of it is to be at the altar, this is necessary, as the bride always goes up to the altar leaning on the arm of the groom. If, however, the marriage ceremony is to be read at the foot of the chancel, as is done at many weddings, he may merely take her hand in his left one and stand as they are.

No words of the service are ever rehearsed, although all the places to be taken by the several participants in the marriage ceremony are rehearsed. The minister does explain the order of the service and the responses.

The substitute for the bride takes the bridegroom's left arm and goes slowly up the steps to the altar. The best man follows behind and to the right of the groom, and the maid of honor, or first bridesmaid, leaves her companions and moves forward at the left of the bride. The bride, in pantomime, gives her bouquet to the maid of honor; the best man, in the same way, hands the ring to the groom, this merely to see that they are at a convenient distance for the services they are to perform.

THE RECESSIONAL

The recessional is played, and the procession goes out in one of two ways. In reversed order, the bride and groom go first, she on his right arm, then the maid or matron of honor, then bridesmaids, then ushers,

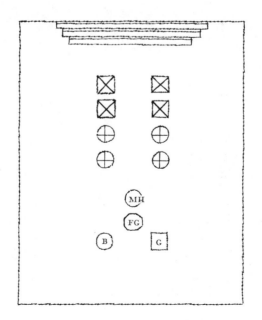

again all taking pains to fall into step with the leaders. In this form of recessional, the best man goes out through the vestry, picking up the groom's coat if he has one, and rejoins him at the front door.

In the other form of recessional, the maid or matron of honor and the best man walk out together behind the bride and groom. Then the bridesmaids and ushers pair off and follow two by two. One of the ushers or the best man will have put the groom's coat in the vestibule before the ceremony so that he need not go back to the vestry or waiting room for it.

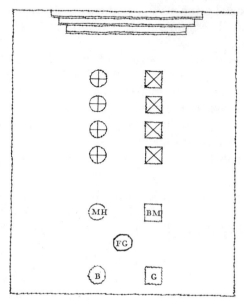

46

The wedding day

On the day of the wedding, the busiest person is the best man! Quite literally, he finds himself thrust into a position that is a combination of secretary, valet, and general manager of the entire wedding procedure as well as the bridegroom's best friend, whose understanding and patience are unfailing.

Bright and early in the morning (especially if it's to be a daytime wedding), he goes to the house of the bridegroom, generally before the latter is up. Very likely they breakfast together. In any event, he takes charge of the groom precisely as might a guardian. He takes note of his ward's general condition; if he is normal and fit, so much the better. If he is up in the air with nerves, the best man must bring him to earth and calm him down as best he can.

BEST MAN'S DUTIES

BEST MAN AS BAGGAGE MASTER

His first duty is to see that everything necessary for the honeymoon is packed and that the groom does not absent-mindedly put the furnishings of his room in his luggage and leave all his clothing behind in the closet. If the groom is to dress in formal clothes for the wedding, those which he is to wear away are put in a bag to be taken to wherever the reception is to be, where he, as well as the bride, must change from wedding clothes into traveling ones. The best man becomes expressman if the first stage of the wedding journey is to be to a hotel in town. He puts all the groom's luggage into a car, drives to the bride's house, or the site of the reception, and carries the bag with the groom's traveling suit in it to the room set aside for his use. He then collects—according to prearrangement—the luggage of the bride, drives with that of both bride and groom to the hotel where accommodations have already been engaged, and sees that their bags are placed in their room and that everything is as it should be. If he is thoughtful, he may himself have flowers put about as a decorative welcome. He also registers for the newly-weds, secures the hotel key, returns to the house of the groom, gives him the key, and assures him that everything at the hotel is in readiness. This maneuver allows the young couple, when they arrive, to go quietly to their own room without attracting the notice of every curious soul in the lobby.

Or if they are leaving directly after the reception by boat, plane, or train, the best man takes the luggage to the point of departure and either checks it (remembering to give the tickets to the groom) or sees that it goes to the proper stateroom. If they are leaving by car, he personally loads the luggage into the car which he has previously hidden in a spot safe from the pranks of the possible practical jokers among the ushers or the groom's other friends. He himself may well drive the couple from the reception to their hidden car.

BEST MAN AS VALET

His next duty is that of valet. He must see that the groom is dressed in plenty of time, even to standing ready with a styptic pencil if he cuts himself shaving. He may need to find the cuff links or even to point out the "missing" clothes that are lying in full view. The marriage license must be safely stowed in the groom's wallet or pocket. He must also be sure to ask for the wedding ring and the clergyman's fee and put them in his own pocket.

BEST MAN AS COMPANION-IN-ORDINARY

With the bride's and groom's luggage properly stowed, the ring and fee in his pocket, the groom's traveling clothes at the bride's house (or wherever he will be changing into them), the groom in complete wedding attire, and himself also ready, the best man has nothing further to do but be gentleman-in-waiting to the bridegroom until it is time to escort him to the church, where he becomes chief-of-staff.

AT THE END OF THE CEREMONY

If the best man is not to walk out with the maid of honor, he disappears through a side door. While the procession goes down the aisle he dashes out of the side entrance and around to the front to give the groom his hat and coat.

Sometimes the sexton takes charge of the groom's hat and coat and hands them to him at the church door as he goes out. But in either case the best man always hurries around to see the bride and groom into their car, which has been standing at the entrance to the awning since she and her father alighted from it.

He returns to the vestry, where he gives the fee to the clergyman befor going to the bride's house or wherever the reception is to be held.

AT THE RECEPTION

After seeing that there is nothing he can do for the groom while he is in the receiving line, the best man may mingle with the guests until the bridal party sit down at the bridal table. It is then his responsibility to give the first toast to the bride and groom.

When the couple leave to change out of their wedding clothes, he again becomes valet to the groom. He helps him dress, takes care of the discarded clothing, and finally sees that the groom has with him everything necessary for the wedding trip. Money or traveler's checks, car keys, baggage-check stubs, plane, train, or boat tickets, and if the best man has registered in advance, hotel or motel keys, are all too easy for the groom to overlook in his excitement.

The best man leads the couple through the waiting guests to the door, and when they have pulled away in a shower of rose petals, he may finally breathe a sigh of relief and join the rest of the wedding party in a final celebration.

HEAD USHER

Unless there are special reasons to the contrary, it is well for the groom to pick the man who has had the most experience to be head usher. The latter then assigns, according to their height, the order in which the ushers are to walk in the processional and where each is to stand during the ceremony.

He tells each usher which lady he is to escort to the vestibule after the recessional.

It is the head usher's duty to see that the ushers arrive at the church at the appointed hour and to decide which ushers are assigned to the center and which to the side aisles. If the groom has not already told them, he may suggest which of them will escort various members of the families to their seats. He himself takes the mother of the bride, unless one of her close relatives—a son or a nephew—is among the other ushers.

THE HOUR APPROACHES

AT THE BRIDE'S HOME

The first bridesmaid arrives dressed and ready. She at least is on time. All activity stops while she is looked at and admired. Then panic seizes someone! Confusion reigns! The time is too short—nothing will be ready! Someone else, realizing that the bridesmaid is far too early, says so —there is no end of time.

Upstairs everyone is still dressing. The father of the bride—one would suppose him to be the bridegroom himself—is trying on his third shirt and desperately searching for his cuff links. The mother of the bride is hurrying into her wedding array so that she will be ready for any emergency, as well as ready to superintend the finishing touches to her daughter's dress and veil.

As the hour approaches, everyone seemingly is in the bride's room— her mother, her grandmother, three aunts, two cousins, three bridesmaids, four small children, and possibly a bridal consultant. Every little while a maid brings a message or a package. Her father comes in and goes out at regular intervals, in sheer nervousness. The rest of the bridesmaids gradually appear and distract the attention of the audience so that the bride has moments of being allowed to dress undisturbed. At last, even her veil is adjusted and all present gasp their approval: "How beautiful!" "Darling, how wonderful you look!"

"Oh, Mary," shouts someone, "how about

Something old, something new,
Something borrowed, something blue,
And a lucky sixpence in your shoe."

"Let me see," says the bride. " 'Old,' " I have old lace; 'new,' I have lots of new! 'Borrowed,' and 'blue'?" A chorus of voices: "Wear my ring," "Wear my pin," "Wear mine! It's blue!" and someone's pin, which has a blue stone in it, is fastened under the trimming of her dress and serves both needs. If the lucky sixpence—a dime in her shoe will do—is produced, she must at least pay in discomfort for her "luck."

PROCESSION TO THE CHURCH

The bridesmaids always meet at the house of the bride, where they also receive their bouquets. When it is time to go to church, several cars are waiting. The bride's mother drives away in the first, usually alone, or she may, if she chooses, take others of her children or one or two bridesmaids with her; but she must reserve room for her husband who will return from church with her. Maid of honor, bridesmaids, and flower girls follow in as many cars as may be necessary.

Last of all comes the bride's car, which is usually a rented limousine.

The bride drives to the church accompanied only by her father. Her car arrives last of the procession and stands without moving in front of the awning until she and her husband—in the place of her father—return from the ceremony and drive back to the breakfast or reception.

AT THE CHURCH

Meanwhile, about an hour before the time for the ceremony, the ushers arrive at the church and the sexton turns his guardianship over to them. They leave their hats in the vestry or in the coat room. Their boutonnières, sent by the groom, should be waiting in the vestibule unless the best man has distributed them beforehand. Each man puts one in his buttonhole and puts on his gloves.

Those of the ushers who are the most likely to recognize the various friends and members of each family should be detailed to the center aisle. A brother of the bride, for instance, is always chosen for this aisle because he should be best able to recognize and look out for the family's best friends. A second usher should be either a brother of the groom or a near relative who is able to recognize the family and intimate friends of the groom. The parents of the bride always sit in the first pew on the left, facing the chancel; the groom's parents in the first pew on the right. If the church has two aisles, her parents sit on the left of the right aisle, and his on the right of the left aisle.

RESERVED PEWS

A few pews on either side of the center aisle are reserved for the immediate families of the couple, and the people to sit there may have been given or sent pew cards (see Chapter 49) to show the ushers, who otherwise might not recognize them or know where to seat them. Sometimes pew cards are not sent, but the ushers are given a list of guests to be seated in the first few pews. These pews are called "in front of the ribbon." Formerly a ribbon was actually put across the aisle behind them and raised at one end by the usher to allow the guest to pass into the reserved section. Nowadays, however, these pews are generally designated by a bouquet or white bow on the end, and the aisle is not closed. The ribbon that is laid over the ends of the pews the length of the aisle just before the procession starts generally ends at the reserved pew farthest from the chancel, so that the family may be escorted out and leave for the reception quickly, while the other guests must wait until it is removed.

A few pews may be taken from one family to give to the other when the one family is very small and the other large. Let us say the bride needs seven pews and the groom three (as often occurs when the groom is from a distant part of the country and few members of his family and almost none of his friends can be present). Then the families may agree to instruct the ushers that behind the first three pews, those with pew cards may be seated evenly on both sides.

THE GUESTS ARRIVE AT THE CHURCH

It is the duty of the ushers to show all guests to their places. An usher offers his right arm to each lady as she arrives, whether he knows her personally or not. If the vestibule is very crowded and several ladies are together, he sometimes gives his arm to the oldest and asks the others to follow, but only when the crowd is great and the time short. Customarily, he asks them to wait until he can come back or another usher is available.

The usher does not offer his arm to a man unless he is quite old and it is obvious that he may need assistance. If the older man is accompanied by a younger, the latter is asked to follow so that he can seat them together.

If the usher thinks a guest belongs in front of the ribbons, though she fails to present her card, he always asks, "Have you a pew card?" If she has, he then shows her to her place. If she has none, he asks whether she prefers to sit on the bride's side or the groom's and gives her the best seat vacant in the unreserved part of the church. Unless he is acquainted with the guests, he always asks whether they wish to be seated on the side of the groom or the bride.

Ushers are not supposed to escort guests in total silence, even when they are strangers. A few casual remarks are made—perhaps about the weather or the decorations—in a low voice, but not whispered or solemn. The deportment of the ushers should be natural, but dignified and quiet, for they are in church. They must not trot up and down the aisles in a bustling manner; yet they must be fairly swift and efficient, as everyone must be seated as expeditiously as possible.

The guests without reserved cards should arrive early in order to find good places. Members of the families and the few guests who have places in front of the ribbon may come later.

SEATING DIVORCED PARENTS

THE BRIDE'S PARENTS DIVORCED BUT FRIENDLY

Because it is obviously happier for the childern when friendliness rather than hatred exists between their divorced parents, yesterday's ban against contact between them no longer exists. If a friendly relationship has been possible, not only Mary's parents but also both of her stepparents are present at the church and possibly at the house. The one unbreakable ban is the sending of a joint wedding invitation by the divorced parents.

Her mother and stepfather sit in the front pew, her mother's immediate family behind them. Her father (after giving her away in a

Protestant ceremony) sits with her stepmother and their family, in the next pew.

WHEN THEY ARE NOT FRIENDLY

In the entire subject of etiquette, there is perhaps no situation that brings such unavoidable distress as the wedding of a daughter whose parents are divorced, with both families bitterly estranged. This is especially unhappy for the bride who loves her father and all of his family quite as much as—sometimes even more than—she loves her mother and her family. Yet according to the exactions of convention, the wedding of their daughter must be given by her mother.

It is true that she does drive with her father to the church, walks with him up the aisle, and even has him share in the marriage ceremony. After giving his daughter away, he sits in the pew behind the immediate family of her mother. His second wife may sit with him if the bride wishes, or, if there is great bitterness involved, she does not attend at all. He does not have so much as a glimpse of his daughter after the ceremony, since he does not go to the reception given by his ex-wife and, quite possibly, her present husband.

It is also probable that no member of his family—neither the grandparents nor the aunts or uncles of his daughter—has so much as a glimpse of their granddaughter or their niece on her wedding day, since it is quite possible that they may not be invited even to the church.

THE WEDDING GIVEN BY THE BRIDE'S FATHER

In the few instances when the wedding is given by the bride's father and stepmother while her own mother is also living, it is evidence that the daughter has made her home with her father instead of her mother.

The bride's own mother sits in the front pew with members of her family, but her second husband usually sits farther back. (She is not usually invited to the reception, although she may be if the bride requests it.) The father gives the bride away and then takes his place in the second pew with his present wife and their family.

SEATING DIVORCED PARENTS OF THE BRIDEGROOM

Even if they have remained on friendly terms, it would be in very bad taste to seat any divorced parents together. The groom's mother and whomever she would like to have with her should be given the first pew on the bridegroom's side of the church, and his father and others of his family seated in the third pew behind. At a large reception their presence need not be conspicuous nor make anyone uncomfortable.

THE LAST FEW MINUTES

THE BRIDEGROOM WAITS

Meanwhile, about fifteen minutes before the wedding hour, the groom and his best man arrive at the church and enter the side door.

They sit in the vestry or in the clergyman's study until the sexton or an usher comes to say that the bride has arrived. They then wait for and follow the clergyman to their places. » *See diagrams for procession provided in Chapter 45.*

THE LAST FIVE MINUTES

The groom's mother and father are waiting in the vestibule. As the bride's mother drives up, an usher hurries off to tell the groom of her arrival as the bride and her father will be close behind. Any brothers or sisters of the bride or groom who are not to take part in the wedding procession and have arrived in their mother's car are now taken by ushers to their places in the front pews. The moment the entire wedding party is in the church, the doors between the vestibule and the church are closed. No one is seated after this except the parents of the young couple.

The groom's mother goes up the aisle on the arm of the head usher and takes her place in the first pew on the right; the groom's father follows alone and takes his place beside her. The same usher or a brother or cousin of the bride escorts the bride's mother to the first pew on the left. (When the bride has a stepfather and especially when they are very close but he is not to give her away, the stepfather may follow her mother and the usher, in the same manner as the groom's father.)

If a carpet is to be laid, it is already arranged in folds so that two ushers may now pull it quickly down the aisle. At the last moment, a white ribbon is draped over the ends of the pews from the back of the church to the nearest reserved pew on each side of the center aisle. Having done this, the ushers return to the vestibule and take their places in the procession. The beginning of the wedding march should sound just as they return to the foot of the aisle.

To repeat: No person should be seated after the entrance of the mother of the bride. Nor must anyone be admitted to the side aisles while the mother of the bride is being ushered down the center one. Her entrance should not be detracted from by late arrivals scuttling into their seats behind her. Guests who arrive late must stand in the vestibule or go into the gallery.

THE BRIDE ARRIVES

At a perfectly planned wedding, the bride arrives exactly one minute after the hour in order to give the last comer time to find a place. A maid or other volunteer is waiting in the vestibule to help the bride and bridesmaids off with their wraps and to help again after the ceremony.

THE WEDDING CEREMONY

The sound of the music is the cue for the clergyman to enter the chancel, followed by the groom and the best man.

The groom stands on the right-hand side at the head of the aisle; but if the door opens onto the chancel, he sometimes stands at the top of the steps. In order to make it easier for him to put the ring on his bride's finger he is not wearing his gloves. The best man remains always directly back and to the right of the groom and does not remove his gloves.

HERE COMES THE BRIDE

And finally the processional advances. First come the ushers two by two, four paces apart; then the bridesmaids—at the same distance exactly; then the maid of honor alone; then the flower girls (if any); then the ring bearer (if any); then, at a double distance (eight paces), the bride on her father's right arm.

As the bride approaches, the groom waits at the foot of the steps, unless he comes down the steps to meet her. If there are no steps, he waits at the head of the aisle. The bride relinquishes her father's arm, changes her bouquet from her right to her left arm, and gives her right hand to the groom. The groom, taking her hand in his right, puts it through his left arm—just her finger tips should rest near the bend of his elbow—and turns to face the chancel as he does so. It does not matter whether she keeps his arm, or whether they stand hand in hand or merely side by side at the foot of the chancel in front of the clergyman.

In a Protestant ceremony, her father has remained where she left him, on her left and a step or two behind her. The clergyman stands a step or two above them and reads the betrothal. When he says, "Who giveth this woman to be married?" the father goes forward, still on her left, half-way between her and the clergyman, but not in front of either. The bride turns slightly toward her father and gives him her right hand. The father puts her hand into the hand of the clergyman and says distinctly "I do." A recent innovation, which has caused many very favorable comments, is that of the bride's father replying "Her mother and I do." He then takes his place next to his wife at the end of the first pew on the left. The clergyman, holding the bride's hand in his own right, takes the bridegroom's hand in his left and very deliberately places the bride's hand in that of the bridegroom.

If it should happen that the bride has neither father nor any very near male relative or guardian, she may walk up the aisle alone. At the point in the ceremony where the clergyman asks, "Who giveth this woman to be married?" her mother stays where she is standing in her proper place at the end of the first pew on the left and bows her head very distinctly to indicate "I do." There is no rule against her going forward as the bride's father would have done, but this would be unusual.

The organist or the choir then plays softly and sings while the clergyman slowly moves to the altar before which the marriage is performed. The bride and groom follow slowly, the fingers of her right hand on his left arm.

The maid or matron of honor then moves out of line and follows on the left-hand side until she stands immediately behind the bride. The best man takes the same position exactly on the right behind the groom. At the termination of the anthem, the bride hands her bouquet to the maid of honor—or her prayer book to the clergyman. If the bride wishes her own prayer book to be used for her marriage, she carries it instead of a bouquet. And the bride and groom plight their troth.

When it is time for the ring, the best man produces it from his pocket, the minister blesses it, and the groom slips it on his bride's finger.

The wedding ring must not be put above the engagement ring. On her wedding day a bride either leaves her engagement ring at home when she goes to church or wears it on her right hand. Afterward she wears it above her wedding ring.

When it is to be a double-ring ceremony, the maid of honor hands the groom's ring to the bride at the moment that the best man gives her ring to the groom, and the bride puts it on his finger immediately after she has received her ring from him. The ceremony then proceeds.

AFTER THE CEREMONY

At the conclusion of the ceremony, the minister congratulates the new couple, and if they have decided to do so, the couple kiss. The organ begins the recessional. The bride takes her bouquet from her maid of honor, who then lifts the face veil, if one is worn. The bride turns toward her husband—her bouquet in her right hand—and puts her left hand through his right arm, and they descend the steps.

The maid of honor hands her own bouquet to a second bridesmaid while she arranges and straightens out the train and veil. The bride and groom go on down the aisle and are followed by their attendants in the way that has been rehearsed. » *See Chapter 45.*

The conveyances are drawn up in the reverse order from that in which they arrived. The bride's car leaves first; next come those of the bridesmaids; next that of the bride's mother and father; next that of the groom's mother and father. Then follow the nearest members of both families, and finally all the other guests in an order determined only by their being able to find their conveyances.

To return to the church for a moment: As soon as the recessional is over, the ushers hurry back and escort to the door all the ladies who were in the first pews, according to the order of precedence; the bride's mother first, then the groom's mother, then the other occupants of the first pew on either side, then the second and third pews, until all members of the immediate families have left the church. Meanwhile it is a breach of etiquette for other guests to leave their places. As soon as the occupants of the first pews have left, the ribbons along the ends of the pews are removed and all the other guests go out by themselves. The ushers are by that time hurrying to the bride's house to make themselves useful at the reception.

The best man goes back into the church, gives the fee to the clergyman, collects his coat, and leaves for the reception.

THE CLERGYMAN'S FEE

The fee of the clergyman may range anywhere from ten dollars to one or two hundred dollars, according to the means of the groom and the importance of the wedding. Whatever the amount, it is enclosed in an envelope and taken in charge by the best man, who hands it to the clergyman in his vestry room or office immediately after the ceremony.

When the clergyman comes from a distance, either because he is a relative or a special friend of the bridegroom's family, his traveling and hotel accommodations are, of course, paid by the groom or his family.

ORTHODOX AND REFORM JEWISH WEDDINGS

The Orthodox wedding ceremony differs somewhat from the Reform Jewish ceremony. In the Orthodox ceremony, the bride is veiled and is escorted by her father and mother under a cloth canopy supported by four poles, usually held by hand. The groom is escorted by his parents. Hats are worn by all men attending the ceremony. Within recent years, the canopy, called "chupah," has been made stationary, that is, the posts rest upon a platform, and the bride's parents simply escort her up the aisle. Sometimes the canopy is of flowers instead of cloth—but the underlying idea is that there must be a covering over the heads of the couple to be married. The principals stand under the chupah before the Ark of the Covenant.

The service is read in Hebrew. The groom places a ring upon the finger of the bride, repeating the following formula: "Thou art consecrated unto me with this ring, according to the law of Moses and Israel." The officiating rabbi then makes the benediction over the wine, giving the groom and bride the goblet, from which they drink. A document is read in Aramaic, giving in detail the pledge of fidelity and protection on the part of the groom toward the bride, and also indicating the bride's contribution to the new household. At the conclusion of the ceremony, a glass is broken, symbolizing the fact that one must never overlook, even at the height of happiness, the possibility of misfortune.

In the Reform service, English (or the native language) is used in addition to Hebrew, and the canopy may be dispensed with. The young couple may decide to include many elements traditionally associated with the Christian wedding ceremony; they should consult with their rabbi about this a few weeks beforehand. The groom is usually ushered in by his best man, and the bride is escorted on the arm of her father. The attendants function as in a Christian ceremony. The groom repeats either the Hebrew formula or its English equivalent. The bride and groom also drink wine out of the same cup, symbolizing the cup of joy. Usually the clergyman delivers a brief address on the significance of marriage.

ROMAN CATHOLIC WEDDINGS

The wedding of the Roman Catholic Church is customarily centered around the Nuptial Mass celebrated between eight A.M. and noon. Inasmuch as the Nuptial Mass follows the schedule of masses in most parishes, it is often necessary for the engaged couple to make arrangements at the rectory several months in advance. The banns, an announcement of intention to marry, are usually proclaimed from the pulpit three times or are published in the church calendar prior to the wedding. The couple should therefore complete church arrangements before making reception plans. It is also recommended, though not obligatory, that the Catholic members of the bridal party receive Holy Communion at the Nuptial Mass.

Whether the bride and groom and best man and maid of honor, or the whole bridal party are permitted within the altar rail is determined by individual church practice. The bride's father does not give her away, so, after escorting her down the aisle, he steps into the front pew to join his wife. Since some churches have strict rules about procedure, it is incumbent on the couple to ascertain the restrictions in advance and be guided by them.

Although afternoon weddings usually take place between four and five o'clock, they may be held any time from one to six. A Catholic wedding may take place any time during the year; but during the closed seasons of Lent and Advent, the Nuptial Blessing is not given, unless, under extraordinary circumstances, permission is granted by the bishop.

THE RECEPTION

On arriving at the house or club where the reception is to be held, the bridal party may pose for pictures before the other guests arrive. This finished, they form the receiving line, and the reception is under way.

THE RECEIVING LINE

The actual receiving line is made up of the bride and groom and the bride's attendants. The ushers and best man have no place in it.

The bride's mother greets the guests at the beginning of the line nearest the entrance to the room. Sometimes she, with the bridegroom's mother and possibly his father, comprise a receiving line of three because they may stand apart from the bridal party to greet the guests as they arrive. Or possibly the bride's father makes a fourth, but more often the two fathers walk about together, leaving the two mothers to receive alone.

The bridegroom's mother almost always receives with the bride's mother if she is from another town. But if she is as well known to the guests as the bride's mother, she is likely to receive in another part of the room where her own friends can talk with her at greater length. The bride's mother of course decides upon whatever arrangements she thinks will be most pleasant for all concerned.

In any case, the bride's mother always stands nearest the door of entrance to the principal room. At a very elaborate reception there may be an announcer, either her own butler or one furnished by the caterer. He asks each guest his or her name and then repeats it aloud. The guests shake hands with the hostess and, making some polite remark about the "beautiful wedding" or "lovely bride," continue in line to the bridal

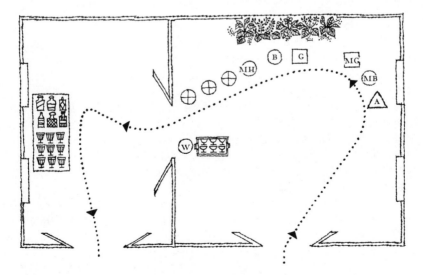

A, *announcer*; MB, *mother of bride*; MG, *mother of groom*; G, *groom*; B, *bride*; MH, *maid of honor*; W, *waiter*

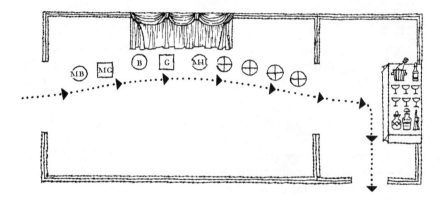

pair. If there is no one announcing, guests unknown to the hostess announce their own names.

The bride always stands on the bridegroom's right. The direction of
the queue depends upon the plan of the room. If, in the room shown in
the diagram, the door to the dining room were at the right, the mothers
would stand at left and the queue would naturally swing away from that
door and approach the line from the opposite direction, and guests
would greet the bride first, instead of the bridegroom.

Usually the bride and groom receive against the wall opposite the
door of entrance; but this is not a fixed rule, and they choose whichever
side of the room will make the most convenient background. This is usually decorated with leaves and flowers, but may equally well be the closed
curtains of a window or a fireplace with flowers on the mantel.

The bride stands on the bridegroom's right, the maid of honor next
in line. The bridesmaids stand beyond the maid of honor, according to
height.

RECEIVING THEIR GUESTS

To a relative or friend of the bride, but a stranger to the groom, the
bride always introduces her husband, saying "Aunt Kate, I want you to
meet Jim," or "Mrs. Neighbor, this is Jim!" or, formally, "Mrs. Faraway,
may I present my husband?"

The groom, on the approach of an old friend of his, says, "Mary,
this is Cousin Carrie" or "Mrs. Denver, Mary" or "Hello, Steve. Mary,
this is Steve Michigan." If Steve is an older man or old-fashioned, he says,
"How do you do, Mrs. Smartlington!" And Mary says, "How do you do.
Jim often speaks of you!" If he is young or modern, he says, "I'm glad to
meet you, Mary." And she replies, "I'm glad to see you, Steve."

The bride with a good memory thanks each arriving person for the
gift sent her: "Thank you so much for the lovely candlesticks" or "The
platter is just what we wanted." The person who is thanked says, "I am so
glad you like it," or "I hoped you might find it useful," or "I didn't have

it marked, so that in case you have a duplicate, you can change it." But these verbal thanks do not lessen her obligation to write her thank-you note. If she has received a large number of presents and if she doesn't trust her memory, she had better not run the risk of thanking Mr. and Mrs. Worthington for a glass ash tray when they sent a piece of sterling silver.

To all expressions of best wishes and congratulations, the bride and groom need only answer "Thank you."

It is wise to have the refreshments ready for guests as soon as they have passed down the receiving line—particularly if the reception is a large one. Some are sure to want to leave or to have other engagements.

THE BRIDE'S TABLE

Very frequently the bride and groom prefer not to have a bridal table, but to mingle with the guests. When they do this, one of the regular tables should be reserved for them, however, so that they may sit down when they feel like it. When there is a bridal table, it may be at the side or end of a large room, or in a room apart, decorated with white flowers. In front of the bride, as its chief ornament, is the wedding cake—always elaborately iced and often surmounted by little figures depicting the bride and groom.

When the queue of arriving guests has dwindled and melted away, the bride and groom decide that it is time they go to their table or join their guests. Arm in arm they lead the way, followed by the ushers and bridesmaids.

The bride and groom always sit next to each other, she at his right, the maid or matron of honor at his left. The best man is at the right of the bride. Around the rest of the table are bridesmaids and ushers alternately. Sometimes one or two others—intimate friends who were not included in the wedding party and husbands or wives of the attendants—are asked to the table. When there are no bridesmaids, the table is always made up of such intimate friends. The bridal table is always served by waiters even when the rest of the guests eat buffet style.

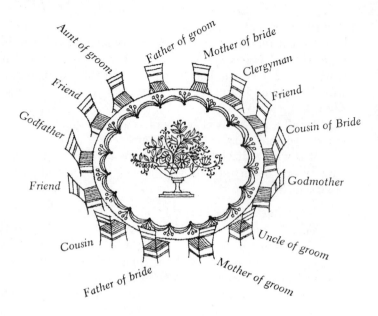

Aunt of groom · Father of groom · Mother of bride · Clergyman · Friend · Friend · Godfather · Cousin of Bride · Friend · Godmother · Cousin · Uncle of groom · Father of bride · Mother of groom

THE TABLE OF THE BRIDE'S PARENTS

The table of the bride's parents differs from other tables in nothing except its larger size and the place cards for those who have been invited to sit there. The groom's mother always sits on the right of the bride's father, and opposite them the groom's father is on the right of the mother of the bride. The other places at the table are occupied by especially intimate friends of the bride's parents or distinguished guests, who may or may not include the clergyman who performed the ceremony. If a high church dignitary has performed the ceremony, he is always included at this table and is placed at the left of the hostess, and his wife, if present, sits at the bride's father's left.

When the wedding guests are to be served standing up, the only sit-down table is the one for the bridal party.

THE TOAST TO THE BRIDE AND GROOM

At a sit-down bridal table, champagne is poured as soon as the party is seated. The glass of the bride is filled first, then that of the bridegroom, and then on around the table, starting with the maid of honor at the groom's left and ending with the best man seated at the right of the bride. Then someone—it is really the duty of the best man—proposes a toast to the bride and bridegroom. All (except the bride and groom) rise, raise their glasses, and drink the toast. Then the groom rises and replies with thanks from them both. Other toasts may be drunk should anyone care to propose them; for instance, the groom might wish to propose a toast to the bride's mother. At a large reception these are necessarily confined to individual groups, but at a small one, all the guests may join in drinking together to the couple's health and happiness.

DANCING AT THE RECEPTION

If a regular two- or three-course meal, or wedding breakfast, is to be served, the first course is passed shortly after the bridal party sits down, and the dancing does not start until after dessert has been eaten and the cake cut. But at a reception where no full meal is served, but sandwiches and snacks are passed or eaten from a buffet table, the bride and groom may start the dancing as soon as they have had a chance to rest a bit from standing in the receiving line.

All the guests watch and applaud while the bride and groom dance the first dance. Her father-in-law usually asks for the second dance and then her father. The groom follows the same pattern and dances with his mother-in-law and with his mother.

After the bride and groom have danced alone for a few moments, the bride's father asks the groom's mother for the first dance and his father asks the bride's mother. As the groom dances with each bridesmaid and the ushers with the bride, the guests may start cutting in, and dancing becomes general for the whole group.

CUTTING THE CAKE

At a sit-down bridal table dinner, the cake is cut just before the dessert is served, and slices are passed with the ices or ice cream. If there is no bridal table, the cake may be cut later, often just shortly before the couple leave the reception.

The bride, with the help of the groom, cuts the first slice from the bottom tier (if it has more than one) with a silver cake knife. Sometimes she cuts two slices, one for her groom and one for herself. After this, a waiter cuts slices until the bottom tier has been cut away. The cake then is removed from the table, and the tiers are separated and cut into slices. The baker has supported each tier on a heavy cardboard disk. When possible, the small top layer surmounted by figurines is set aside for the bride and groom to keep. At any rate, a large piece should be saved for them.

THE DIVORCED FATHER SHARES IN THE WEDDING

When the devoted but divorced father of the bride wishes to have a share in his daughter's wedding, there is a practical solution. The bride who, although she lives with her mother, is equally fond of her father and his family, knows very well that because bitterness exists between her parents, few if any of her nearest relatives on her father's side will be at the church. She also knows that her father will leave the church as promptly as possible and that neither he nor his immediate family, nor his special friends—many of them hers, too—will be at the reception.

So at the same time that the wedding invitations are sent out by her mother, the following invitations to a small second gathering are sent out by her father:

Mr. John Pater
requests the pleasure of your company
at the wedding supper of his daughter
Mary
and her bridegroom
James Martin
Saturday, the tenth of April
at seven o'clock
4 Monroe Place

If he has remarried, the invitation may read:

Mr. and Mrs. John Pater
request the pleasure of your company
at the wedding supper of his daughter
etc.

One change in the mother's invitations is an earlier-than-usual hour for the reception. Another deviation from the established wedding procedure: instead of leaving the reception at the bride's mother's in their traveling clothes, the bride and groom remain in their wedding clothes. In these clothes they leave the house, accompanied by her bridesmaids and his ushers (also, of course, in their wedding clothes) and drive to the home of her father.

After greeting his family and special friends, a buffet supper or a supper served at small tables is ready. At the end of this, the bride and groom change into traveling clothes, which have been brought to her father's house earlier in the day, and depart under the customary shower of rose petals and confetti.

For the children who care equally for their parents, a family divorce brings unavoidable unhappiness, and to the bride whose love for her father and his family is quite as great as her love for her mother and her family, this plan can be a very important contribution to the thoughtful kindness that is always the test of perfect behavior!

THEY'RE OFF!

Sometimes the bride and groom continue dancing or chatting for so long that those who had intended to stay for the "going away" grow weary and leave—which is often exactly what the young couple wants! And unless they have to catch a train, they usually stay until the crowd thins before going to dress for their journey. At last the bride signals to her bridesmaids and leaves the room. They all gather at the foot of the stairs. About half-way to the upper landing as she goes up, she throws her bouquet, and they all try to catch it. The one who succeeds is supposed to be the next married. If the bride has no bridesmaids, she collects a group of other girls and throws her bouquet to them.

Sometimes if a very close relative is too ill to attend the wedding, the bouquet is sent to her.

As soon as the bride has gone upstairs, followed by her mother, sisters, and bridesmaids, who stay with her while she changes into her traveling clothes, the groom goes to the room reserved for him and changes into the traveling clothes that the best man has already taken there for him. He waits upstairs until the bride appears in her going-away clothes. All the ushers shake hands with them both. His immediate family, as well as hers, has gradually collected. Any that are missing are sent for. The bride's mother gives her a last kiss. Her bridesmaids hurry downstairs to have plenty of paper rose petals ready and to tell everyone below as they descend, "Here they come!" A passage from the stairway and out the front door, all the way to their automobile, is left free between two rows of eager guests, their hands full of confetti and petals.

Down the stairs, out through the hall, into the car, slam the door, and they are off!

The wedding guests stand out on the street or lawn looking after them for as long as a vestige can be seen—and then gradually they disperse.

Many young couples spend a good deal of thought and planning on making their going away unusual and dramatic. Every sort of departure has been tried—on skis, in sleighs, on horseback or in horse-drawn carriage, and even in a helicopter! But the loveliest and most memorable I have ever seen took place when the reception was held at a yacht club on a beautiful June evening. The bride and groom raced down the dock and hopped onto a handsome yacht, polished and shining, with all flags flying. They pulled away from the pier with horns of other boats tooting, the cannon firing a salute, and a carpet of rose petals floating on the blue water. It was truly an ending never to be forgotten by the bride and groom or by any who were there to see them go!

A THOUGHT FOR BRIDEGROOM'S PARENTS

At the end of the reception and as soon as she is in her traveling dress, a thoughtful bride will send a bridesmaid or someone out into the hall and ask her husband's parents to come and say good-by to her.

It is very easy for a bride to forget this act of thoughtfulness and for a groom to overlook the fact that he cannot stop to bid his parents good-by on his way out of the house. Many a mother and father, seeing their son and new daughter rush past without even a glance, have returned home with a let-down feeling and an ache in their hearts. One may exclaim, "How stupid of them! Why didn't they go upstairs?" But often the groom's parents are strangers; they may have met their new daughter only a few days before the wedding; and if by temperament they are shy or retiring people, they hesitate to go upstairs in an unknown house until they have been invited to do so. So they wait, feeling sure that in good time they will be sent for. Meanwhile the bride forgets; and it does not occur to the groom that, unless he makes an effort while upstairs, there will be no opportunity in the dash down to the car to recognize them any more than anyone else.

THE NEWLY MARRIED COUPLE

A completely beautiful wedding is not merely a combination of wonderful flowers, beautiful clothes, smoothness of detail, and delicious food. These, no matter how pleasing, are external attributes. The spirit, the soul of it, must have something besides; and that something is seen in the behavior and in the expression of the bride and groom.

The most beautiful wedding ever imagined could be turned from sacrament to circus by the indecorous behavior of the groom and the flippancy of the bride. She must not reach up and wigwag signals while she is receiving, just as she must not wave to people as she goes up and then down the aisle, although she may relax and smile her joy on the way out of the church. She must not cling to her husband as though unable to stand or lean against him or the wall or any person or thing. She must not swing her arms as though they were dangling ropes; she must not switch herself this way and that; she must not shout; and she must not, while wearing her bridal veil, smoke a cigarette. No matter how young or natural and thoughtless she may be, she must, during the ceremony and the short time that she stands beside her husband at the reception, act with dignity.

The happiness of both the bride and groom must dominate a perfect wedding. An unhappy-looking bride, an uncomfortable-looking groom, turns the greatest wedding splendor into sham. Without love it is a sacrament profaned, and the sight of a tragic-faced bride strikes chill to the heart.

The radiance of a truly happy bride is so enhancing that even a plain girl is made beautiful. A happy bridegroom quite plainly may have the quality of radiance, but it is different—more directly glad. They both look as though there were sunlight behind their eyes, as though their mouths irresistibly turned to smiles in visible proof of perfect happiness that endears them to all beholders and gives beauty even to the simplest of weddings.

Weddings in special situations

Not always do the bride-to-be and her fiancé choose to be married in church—and for a number of perfectly acceptable reasons. These occasions require our attention, for they should be as perfect of their kind as are the most elaborate of church ceremonies. Then, too, there are variations on the usual form, as when two sisters wish to be married at the same time or when the bride has been married before. Anniversaries, especially Golden Anniversaries, should be a re-choing of the wedding day and so have been included here as very special "situations."

THE HOUSE WEDDING

A house wedding involves somewhat less expenditure but a good deal more work for the bride's family than does the church wedding. It also has the disadvantage of limiting the number of guests. The ceremony is exactly the same as it is in a church, except that the procession advances through an aisle of white satin ribbons from the stairs or hallway down which the bridal party comes to the improvised altar. Chairs for the immediate families may be placed within a marked-off enclosure, but if the room is small, space is merely kept free for them to stand in.

In the country, a house wedding may be performed in the garden, with the wedding procession under the trees, and tables out on the lawn —a perfect plan for California or other rainless-season states, but often difficult to arrange along the Atlantic seaboard where the weather is all too likely to spoil everything.

In some forms of the wedding ceremonies, a cushioned bench is provided for the bride and groom to kneel on during the prayers. It is placed directly in front of the space reserved for the clergyman and is often backed by an altar rail. In this case the bench is usually six or eight inches high, and between three and four feet long; at the back of it an upright on either end supports a crosspiece or altar rail. It can be made in the roughest fashion by any carpenter or amateur, as it is entirely hidden under leaves and flowers. The top of each upright is usually decorated with a spray of white flowers.

At a house wedding, the bride's mother stands at the door of the room in which the ceremony is to be and receives people as they arrive. But the groom's mother takes her place near the altar with the rest of the immediate family. The ushers are purely ornamental, as no one is escorted to seats. The guests simply stand wherever they can find places behind the aisle ribbons. Just before the bride's entrance, her mother goes forward and stands in the reserved part of the room.

In a house, the procession usually starts from the top of the stairs. In an apartment, it starts in the foyer or bedroom hall. The wedding march begins, and the ushers come in two and two, followed by the bridesmaids, exactly as in a church, the bride coming last on her father's arm. There are seldom many bridal attendants at a house wedding—two to four ushers, and one to four bridesmaids—unless the house is an immense one. The clergyman and the groom and best man have, if possible, reached the altar by another door. If the room has only one door, they go up the aisle a few moments before the bridal procession starts.

A HOUSE WEDDING WITH LEAST EXPENSE

At the smallest wedding possible, the clergyman enters, followed by the bridegroom; the bride then enters with her father, or alone; and the wedding service is read.

When there are no garden flowers to be had, a suitable background can be made by drawing heavy curtains or hanging curtains of damask, velvet, or any other plain fabric, from the picture molding across a flat wall space. Against this, the colorful clothes of the bride's attendants (if she has any) and her own white dress and veil are entirely effective. For music, nothing could be more beautiful than the phonograph recordings of organ and choir purposely made for such weddings. The collation may consist of nothing but ginger ale or fruit juice, wedding cake, and a few varieties of sandwiches, with the refreshments placed on a small table covered with a tea cloth. But the spirit of the day remains, and the young couple should leave as joyously as if they had been wed in a cathedral.

THE DIFFERENCES

The chief difference between a church wedding and a house wedding is that the bride and groom do not take a single step together. The groom meets her at the point where the service is read. After the ceremony, there is no recessional. The clergyman withdraws, an usher removes the prayer bench, if there is one, and the bride and groom merely turn where they stand and receive the congratulations of their guests, unless, of course, the house is so big that they receive in another room.

When there is no recessional and if bride and groom have decided in favor of the wedding kiss, it is always given before they turn to receive their guests. In any event, it is against all tradition for anyone to kiss the bride before her husband does.

AFTER THE CEREMONY

Usually, but not always, there is a bride's table, decorated exactly as that described for a larger reception and placed perhaps in the library; but there is no special table for the bride's mother and her guests—or for anyone else.

At a very simple stand-up breakfast, the food would be the same, except that in place of the elaborate dishes there would be one hot dish and one salad. If chicken salad is served, there should be a hot dish of some thing like eggs or creamed fish. Moreover, if the hot dish is chicken croquettes or chicken à la king, there is usually a salad of mixed vegetables. Bouillon and ice cream are served as at a large wedding.

SEATING AT A VERY SMALL WEDDING BREAKFAST

At the smallest wedding possible, where only the immediate families and a few friends are present, they very often all sit together at one lunch or dinner table. (See illustration on the next page.)

THE BRIDE'S DRESS

At a home wedding, the bride has her choice of a formal wedding gown, long or short (without long train, however) or a daytime dress or suit worn with a hat. The other items of her costume correspond to those suitable for a similar church wedding.

THE EVENING WEDDING

All through the South and generally throughout the West, many weddings are celebrated at eight or nine o'clock in the evening. There is a reason for the evening wedding in the South. The heat of the day has passed and the coolness of the evening, which lends itself better to festivities and to dancing (always a wedding-supper feature), prevails.

The details are precisely the same as those for the morning or afternoon. In large Southern cities, the bride and bridesmaids may wear dresses that are perhaps more elaborate and more "evening" in type, and the bridegroom and ushers wear full evening clothes. Guests, both men

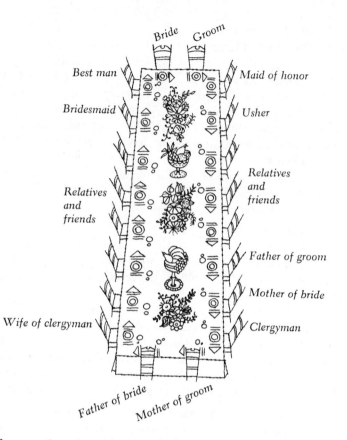

and women, dress as though going to a ball. For the church ceremony, the women should wear light scarfs of some sort around their shoulders and over their hair, in compliance with the regulations forbidding the uncovering of women's heads and shoulders in consecrated places of worship.

At simpler ceremonies, especially in smaller communities, the guests wear exactly what they would wear to evening service in church—a good dress and hat for a woman, and a dark daytime suit for a man.

THE EARLY MORNING WEDDING

Among Roman Catholics, an eight o'clock morning wedding is not unusual, and its details may be precisely the same as for later hours. But for others, who are perhaps boarding an early morning train or ship and would especially like the informality to which such an hour lends itself, a wedding may be carried out as follows:

The bride may wear any simple dress. She would probably wear a veil, but of tulle instead of lace, either falling to the hem of her dress or of finger length. She carries a bouquet of moderate size, unless she carries a prayer book, and wears no gloves. Her attendants might wear the simplest sort of morning dresses and hats; the groom and his best man, business suits or flannels. And the breakfast menu—really breakfast—might be fruit, coffee, and hot biscuits.

In fact, a small, early morning wedding—where everyone is dressed in morning clothes and where the breakfast truly suggests the first meal of the day—can be perfectly enchanting.

MARRIAGE AT THE RECTORY

Marriages are often performed in the clergyman's study or in another room at the rectory or parish house. Although the words "marriage" and "wedding" are the same in meaning, the latter to most people connotes the picturesque ceremonial of long-established custom, so "marriage" is here used advisedly.

When the bride and groom decide on a ceremony in the rectory, the clergyman must be consulted ahead of time as to the date and hour. The bride and bridegroom go together and are met at the parsonage by the members of their families and the two or three friends invited. When all are assembled, the bridegroom tells the clergyman that they are ready. The clergyman takes his place. The bride and bridegroom stand before him, and the service is read. Afterward those present congratulate them, and that may be all. But they may all go to the house of the bride or of a witness or to a restaurant and have lunch, tea, or dinner together. At such a marriage, the bride rarely wears a white wedding dress and veil, but it is entirely proper for her to do so if she chooses—especially if there is to be a wedding dinner at someone's home afterward.

MARRIAGE BY A JUSTICE OF THE PEACE

The general procedure is exactly the same as that for a marriage at the rectory. However simple and informal the plans, there are always two guests, preferably relatives but often friends, who act as witnesses as well.

The traditional wedding dress and veil are not suitable in the circumstances, but the bride will certainly wish to wear a pretty daytime dress or suit. And again, the radiant happiness of the couple best reflects the spirit of the occasion.

THE RUNAWAY MARRIAGE

To elope, according to the dictionary, is to run away from home with a lover, but to most of us an elopement means that a young couple has run off and been married without the consent of the young girl's parents. I am sure, however, that many such marriages have had their quiet blessing; for some reason, financial or otherwise, the family felt that a big wedding would be impossible.

When the parents had approved before the marriage or when they have decided after it to make the best of what has happened, they send out the announcements in their name. Should the parents be unalterably opposed, however, and wish the world to know that they are withholding their blessing, they do not send out the announcements. The married pair may, if they wish, send them out themselves. » *See Chapter 51.*

If the bride's mother and father wish to give a belated reception after the marriage, it is generally an informal affair, attended by close friends and relatives. This is often done to introduce an out-of-town groom. The invitations are telephoned or sent on informals, and, if written, should include the bride's married name—"In honor of Mr. and Mrs. Harvey Kirk, Jr."

THE DOUBLE WEDDING

At a double wedding, the two bridegrooms follow the clergyman and stand side by side, each with his best man behind him, the groom of the older sister nearer the aisle. The ushers—half friends of the first, and the others friends of the second bridegroom—go up the aisle together. Then come the bridesmaids of the older sister followed by her maid of honor, who walks alone. The older sister follows, holding her father's arm. Then come the bridesmaids of the younger sister, her maid of honor, and last, the younger bride on the arm of a brother, uncle, or nearest male relative.

The first couple ascends the chancel steps and takes their place at the left side of the altar rail, leaving room at the right side for the younger bride and her bridegroom. The father stands just below his older daughter. The brother takes his place in the first pew.

The ceremony is a double one, read to both couples, with the particular responses made twice. The father gives both brides away—first his older daughter and then his younger. Then he takes the place saved for him beside his wife in the first pew.

At the end of the ceremony, the older sister and her husband turn and go down the aisle first. The younger couple follows. The bridesmaids of the older are followed by those of the younger, and the ushers follow last. Or bridesmaids and ushers pair off and go out together.

"ATTENDING" EACH OTHER

It is not usual, but it is quite possible, for each bride at a double wedding to serve as maid of honor for her sister. Each in turn holds the other's bouquet during her sister's ceremony.

But the wise bridegroom, if he dispenses with a best man and uses the services of his brother groom, keeps his own bride's ring in his own waistcoat pocket.

One difficulty of a double wedding is the seating of the parents of the two bridegrooms, who must either share the first pew or draw lots for the occupation of first or second. This question they must decide for themselves.

Occasionally the brides are cousins, in which case the front pew on the bride's side must be shared by both mothers, the older being given the aisle seat.

REMARRIAGE

THE GROOM'S SECOND MARRIAGE

The fact that a bridegroom has been married previously has no bearing on the wedding preparations made by his maiden bride. She may wear a white gown and veil, and the wedding and reception may be as elaborate as she chooses.

THE MARRIAGE OF A WIDOW

The marriage of a widow differs from that of a maid in that she cannot wear a bridal veil, orange blossoms, or a myrtle wreath, which are emblems of virginity. Nor does she have bridesmaids, though she may have a maid or matron of honor.

If she has not done so long before, she should either remove her first wedding and engagement rings or else transfer them to the fourth finger of her right hand as soon as she becomes engaged. When her second engagement ring is given her, she of course puts aside the first, and if her second marriage is to take place soon, she removes her wedding ring as well. She may keep the engagement ring for her daughter by her first marriage, or by and by it may be that she will again wear it on her right hand. If the stone is valuable, she might have it reset into a clip or pin, either for herself or for her daughter. This, however, depends upon the feelings of her second husband. If she knows that he objects, her future happiness may quite possibly depend upon its permanent discard.

Usually a widow writes personal notes of invitation to a quiet wedding, but this is no reason why she cannot have a lovely ceremony. Sometimes—especially if she is young and her family and the groom's are very large—it becomes necessary to send out engraved invitations. » *For the correct form, see Chapter 49.*

Although she almost always chooses a dress and hat of color, she may wear white, but never a bridal veil or orange blossoms.

A wedding in very best taste for a widow is held in a small church or chapel or in her home, with a few flowers or some branched greens in the chancel or at the altar rail. There would be few ushers or quite possibly only honorary ones, out of consideration for the groom. There are no ribboned-off seats, as only very intimate friends are invited. Usually the bride wears an afternoon dress and hat or possibly a cocktail dress and tiny veil. There may be a fairly large reception afterward or the simplest afternoon tea. In any case, the breakfast, tea, or dinner is, if possible, at the bride's own house, and the bridal pair may stay where they are and have their guests take leave of them and then drive away afterward.

A DIVORCÉE REMARRIES

Whether or not a divorcée may be married in her church depends upon the circumstances of her divorce and the approval of her clergyman. Usually the remarriage takes place in her own house, performed either by a clergyman or a justice of the peace. A small reception follows.

She may not wear a typical white bridal dress, veil, or orange blossoms, and she should not wear white. The dress should be a simple street-length gown worn with a hat, in any style she prefers.

Engraved invitations are not in good taste. Handwritten notes or possibly messages on visiting cards are best.

Children of divorced parents do not attend the marriage ceremony unless they are totally reconciled to the situation and fond of their future stepparent. In any case, they may, if they wish, attend the reception.

WEDDING ANNIVERSARIES

The eight anniversaries known to us all are:

> 1 year, Paper
> 5 years, Wood
> 10 years, Tin
> 15 years, Crystal
> 20 years, China
> 25 years, Silver
> 50 years, Gold
> 60 years, Diamond

Because the first wedding anniversary is of great importance and the selection of paper gifts is comparatively limited, the trend toward making plastics also an accepted first-year gift is too appealing to disallow.

Until comparatively modern times, the eight anniversaries were all that were acknowledged. About fifty years ago, anniversaries were added until there was one for each year up to fifteen, and one for every five years after that.

1, paper or plastics. 2, calico or cotton (calico is the more amusing word and suggests, perhaps, a more amusing party). 3, leather. 4, silk. 5, wood. 6, iron. 7, copper or woolen. 8, electric appliances (showing that innovation has supplemented tradition). 9, pottery. 10, to the tin of this year is now added aluminum. 11, steel. 12, linen. 13, lace. 14, ivory. 15, crystal (as it has ever been, and of course it includes everything made of glass).

After this there are four giftless anniversaries and then:

> 20, china. 25, the Silver Wedding Anniversary, which has surely been celebrated more often than all the others put together. 30, pearls. 35, coral and jade. 40, ruby. 45, sapphire. 50, the Golden Wedding Anniversary. 60, diamond.

Suitable parties to celebrate any of the earliest wedding anniversaries are a housewarming or perhaps a stork shower, a calico fancy-dress party, a barn dance, a treasure hunt, or any informal party that appeals to the imagination. For that matter, it can also be a surprise party arranged for the bride and groom by their friends. The first years suggest much more informal gatherings than the Silver Wedding, for example, which is perhaps celebrated by a big dinner or a dance to which everyone who was a guest at the wedding is invited. The clergyman who performed the ceremony is there, and if many of the bridal party can attend, a table is often set up exactly as it was. The most important anniversary, the Golden Wedding, is usually celebrated by a somewhat formal afternoon or evening at home, or by a family dinner either in the evening or at midday, after which other relatives, friends, and neighbors come in to offer their congratulations.

Some couples like the custom of reaffirming their marriage vows on an important anniversary such as the twenty-fifth or even the fiftieth. As many of the original wedding party as possible gather, and a party follows the ceremony.

GIFTS NOT OBLIGATORY

No one must feel that a present is obligatory, especially when the anniversary year is one that suggests an item of value. Sometimes the invitation carries a line reading "Please omit gifts." Intimate friends, however, usually take or send something if possible. Flowers, of course, are always an appropriate remembrance of such an occasion or any anniversary.

The wedding guest

The mere fact of receiving a wedding announcement or even an engraved invitation to the church obligates you to much or to nothing, according to your own personal situation or your impulse of the moment. In other words, an announcement informing you that a marriage has taken place between Mary Anthony and John Ballard may require no more attention than it takes to change the name of the bride in your address book. On the other hand, the wedding of a dear friend or a godchild necessarily entails certain responsibilities.

"THE HONOUR OF YOUR PRESENCE . . ."

As soon as you receive an invitation, whether to the ceremony, the reception, or both, and see that it includes R.s.v.p., you must reply at once. It is most inconsiderate as well as impolite not to do so. Remember that the family will have to make definite preparation for every guest who has not refused just as they have for those who do attend. Failure to reply causes extra trouble and expense. » *For the correct form of acceptances and regrets, see Chapter 55.*

"AND FAMILY"

An invitation reading "and Family" does include each and every member of the family living under the same roof—and this means every child from walking and talking age (at about two) up to great-grandparents. Married daughters or sons who live in their own houses are not included because, if invited, they are sent separate invitations.

In general, however, guests should not take small children unless they have been specifically invited, and even then not unless they themselves will look after them. Well-behaved children are very sweet at a wedding, but children out of hand can be most annoying to everyone and detract from the solemnity of the occasion.

THE WEDDING PRESENT

Having sent your acceptance—or your regrets—you should next turn your thoughts to whether or not you will send a gift to the bride, for wedding presents should, if at all possible, arrive before the ceremony.

If you are not an intimate friend of the bride or groom or of their families and if you are not invited to the wedding reception, you are not expected to send a present (unless, of course, you know that there is to be no reception). Obviously the more personal the invitation the greater the obligation to send a gift. An invitation by written note definitely indicates that you are considered an especially dear friend, and you will therefore certainly want to send a present. And you must always send a present to one who is marrying into your immediate family. While it is not an absolute obligation, most people who refuse an invitation to a wedding reception do feel like sending a present.

PRESENTS FOR A SECOND MARRIAGE

An occasional few special friends and perhaps close relatives send presents to someone being married for a second time. When one of the couple has never been married before, his or her friends will most probably wish to send gifts.

PRESENTS FOR ELOPERS

One receiving an announcement of an elopement, either in the name of the parents or without their names, is in no way obligated, nor even expected, to send a present. If, of course, anyone out of love or affection for either the bride or the groom or their families wishes to give them something, it will be an especially appreciated gesture.

DELAYED PRESENTS

If, because of illness or absence, your present is not sent until after the wedding, a note should accompany it, giving the reason for the delay. Delayed presents are sent to Mr. and Mrs. Newlywed at their own new address. If you do not know their address, they may be sent in care of the bride's family.

WHAT KIND OF GIFT

Typical wedding presents include almost anything ornamental as well as useful for the furnishing of a house or the setting of a dining table, from a piece of silver to a glass ash tray, a picture frame to a clock, a paper cutter to a lamp, a cigarette box to an occasional table or chair. Naturally, the less you know about the future living plans of the bride and groom, the more necessary it is to choose a gift that can be used by anyone living anywhere.

Many gifts are beautified by marking; a certain few require it. Objects of plain silver or untooled leather are enhanced by engraved or tooled initials. Linen, unless heavily embroidered or lace-inserted, may seem rather impersonal without an embroidered monogram or initials. But unless you know for certain that your gift is something that the bride wants and that it will not be duplicated, it is safer to send presents unmarked.

The most important thing is that your gift be lovely and useful. To fulfill these two requirements, it need not be expensive. No bride or groom would want you to spend more than you can afford. And one type of gift to avoid is the dust-catching ornament.

PRESENTS FROM BRIDEGROOM'S FRIENDS

You seldom send a present to the bridegroom. Even if you are an old friend of his and have never met the bride, your present is sent to her —unless you send two presents, one in courtesy to her and one in affection to him. Rather often friends of the bridegroom do pick out things suitable for him, such as a decanter or a rather masculine-looking desk set, which are sent to her but are obviously intended for his use.

CHECK-GIVING

Nearest relatives may properly give their gifts in the form of money. Since checks given as wedding presents are usually of important size and frequently intended for a definite purpose, they are not necessarily drawn to the bride. Often they are drawn to the couple jointly; on occasion they are drawn to him. The check to be cashed after the wedding is drawn to John and Mary Smith. Godparents also sometimes send checks so that the bride can make her own choice—perhaps a coffee table or an occasional chair or whatever she wants. » *For display of checks with the other wedding presents, see Chapter 43.*

CARDS WITH PRESENTS

A visiting card is practically always enclosed with a wedding present; sometimes nothing is added, but usually you write "Best wishes" or "All best wishes for your happiness." If you have no visiting card at hand, write the same message on a blank card and sign it. If you are a contemporary or very little older than she, you sign it "John and Mary Friendly." If you are a friend of her parents or John's, you would write "With best wishes from" and place it so that "Mr. and Mrs. Your Name" engraved on your card forms the signature. And unless you are certain that the bride knows it, be sure your address is included.

WHAT TO WEAR TO A WEDDING

Always, the choice of clothes depends upon the size and time of the wedding as well as the customary practices of the community. Wedding guests today are wearing simpler clothes than they used to.

At very big daytime weddings, correct clothes for men used to be gray striped trousers with a cutaway coat or the less formal black sack suit. However, today very few men wear anything more formal than plain business suits, whether dark blue or dark gray. During hot weather, especially at simple seashore and country weddings, light suits or white or light gray flannel trousers with plain flannel coats are suitable. The sport coat is as out of place for a guest as it should be for a groom!

In certain cities, especially in the South where evening weddings are customary, tail coats are still seen. In those of less formality, the tuxedo coat is the only one ever worn in the evening. In simpler communities, men wear plain navy-blue suits on all dress occasions in the evening as well as during the day.

As a general rule, at a formal evening wedding the women wear low-neck-and-no-sleeves evening dresses, with flowers or clips or hair ornaments or perhaps a lace scarf over their hair and shoulders in church. At a very simple wedding in the evening or during the day, they wear afternoon dresses, with small becoming hats or else a flower.

When not going to the reception, whatever clothes are worn habitually to church are correct.

Children always wear their best party clothes.

AT THE CHURCH

When you enter the church, you go as far as the back of the center aisle, and wait until one of the ushers comes up to you. If you get there early there will be plenty of seats. If you are a member of either family or a very intimate friend of the bride or the groom, you will tell him your name. If it is a wedding at which those to sit in the pews in front of the ribbons have been sent cards with a pew number, he will ask you for your card. At a wedding without pew cards he would ask your name and look on his "in front of the ribbons" list in order to seat you. If you say nothing to indicate that you should be seated in front, he will ask you whether you are a friend of the bride or of the groom, in order to seat you on her or his side of the aisle. In any case, a lady puts her hand on the inside of his proffered arm, and he escorts her to a seat. A gentleman alone walks beside the usher or if he comes with a lady he follows the usher and the lady, unless there is room for the three of them to walk abreast.

AISLE SEAT NOT RELINQUISHED

If you have arrived early enough to be given an aisle seat, there is one rule of etiquette that is a seeming contradiction to politeness and therefore important to know: It is entirely proper for you to keep your aisle seat, no matter who or how many enter the pew later. Now and then an inconsiderate latecomer, seeing someone much younger or a stranger sitting on the aisle, unfairly demands, "Move up, please." Nine out of ten well-bred people do so instinctively and find themselves pushed along to the sixth seat in. To stand up where you are and to make room for the latecomers to pass you and take their places farther in is all that is required by etiquette, even though the one on the aisle be a young man and the newcomer an elderly woman. In other words, aisle seats at a wedding are held exactly as reserved seats are held in a theater.

GREETING OTHER GUESTS

At a wedding it is proper to smile and bow slightly to people you know—even to talk briefly in a very low voice to a friend sitting next to you. But when you find yourself among strangers, you just sit quietly until the processional starts.

A STRANGER TO THE RITUAL

In most Protestant churches, the congregation rises and stands throughout the service. But whatever the sect, you may, whenever you are in a church of a religion other than your own, observe those in front of you: stand if they stand, kneel if they kneel, and sit if they sit.

When the service is over and the recessional has passed by, those in the pews farther back must wait in their places until the immediate families in the front pews have left. If you wait until those around you start to leave, you will be sure of not making any mistake.

FROM CHURCH TO RECEPTION

When invited to the reception, you are expected to go directly from the church to wherever the reception is to be held. But do give the bridal party a little while to arrange for wedding pictures and form the receiving line. No provision is ever made for taking any of the guests from the church to the house. You go in your own car, or you call a taxi, or, if the distance is short, you walk.

AT THE RECEPTION

Whether in a house, club, or hotel, you will be met at the entrance by someone who tells you, "Ladies' dressing-room to the right, men's through the hall on the left." If you are a woman, you leave your wrap, if you choose to, but you do not take off your hat or your gloves. Men always remove coats and hats. Then you go to the door of the room in which the reception is held. You will see people going in, and if there is an announcer he will be announcing their names. As you approach, he asks you, "What name, please?" You give your name with title. If he says nothing, you say to him, "Miss Pauline Panic" or "Mrs. John Jones" or "Dr. Henry Roberts." He then repeats in a clear rather than loud voice, though it may sound loud to you, "Miss Pauline Panic," and you start down the line.

The bride's mother will be standing closest to you. She offers you her hand, smiles, and if you are unknown to her, she says, "How do you do." If she knows you, she says whatever is suitable. In the first place, you also say, "How do you do"; in the second, you reply to what she says to you. If she says, "I am very glad to see you," you answer, "Thank you" or "It was very kind of you to invite me," and add something pleasant about the bride, the day, or the wedding in general. If the groom's mother is standing next to her, you must shake hands with her too, whether you are introduced to her or not. Even if you know both of the mothers very well, there is no time to say more than perhaps something such as "What a lovely day Mary and John have for the wedding!" or "How beautiful Mary looks!" There is, however, one real rule: Do not launch into a conversation about yourself, how you feel or look, or what happened to you, or what you wore when you were married! Your subject should be confined to the young couple themselves, their wedding, their future.

Above all, be brief in order not to keep those behind waiting longer than necessary. If you have anything particular to tell them, you can return later when there is no longer a line. But even then, any long conversation is out of place.

You then move along with the queue of guests who are waiting to greet the bride and groom. You congratulate the groom, but you wish the bride happiness, because it is a breach of good manners to congratulate a bride on having secured a husband.

If you are in doubt about being known to either of them, you give your name, shake hands with the bride, and add, "I wish you every happiness!" Then you shake hands with the groom and say, "Congratulations, and all good wishes." If the bride does not introduce you because she is being greeted by someone following you, and the groom seems to be trying to remember your name, you tell him who you are. Otherwise, you don't.

In the excitement of the day, the bride and groom may easily forget the names even of their best friends, and they are quite likely not to remember Aunt Mary, who last visited ten years ago. It is thoughtful for a guest to mention her name even though she thinks she is known to the couple. Never choose this moment to play "Guess who I am," as some unbelievably inconsiderate people do.

If you have been invited to bring a friend who is unknown to the bride and groom, you should introduce the friend to them both.

You greet any of the bridesmaids with whom you are acquainted. Otherwise you walk on—or smile perhaps if you happen to be looking directly at one of them who also looks at you. But there is no chance to stop and really talk to anyone unless you arrived early.

The bride's father sometimes stands beside his wife, but he usually circulates among his guests just as he would at a ball or any other party where he is host. Therefore, you speak to him either on your arrival or, as at other important occasions, whenever you encounter him acting as host.

The groom's father is a guest, and it is not the obligation of strangers to speak to him unless he stands beside his wife and receives. But it is certainly courteous, especially if he is a stranger, to introduce yourself and tell him how well you like his son or his new daughter-in-law or, best of all, both.

After greeting the bride and groom, you look around for friends of your own. If you see no one whom you know well enough to join, the best thing to do is to make your way slowly and nonchalantly to wherever refreshments are being served.

You take your time to look at the table and then either ask one of the waiters to serve you or help yourself to what you want. You can linger and nibble as long as you like or just sit down and watch people. And you may speak to anyone who is alone and looks willing to be spoken to.

A SIT-DOWN BREAKFAST

If you are a stranger at a sit-down breakfast, you cannot very well join a group of people whom you do not know. Therefore, it is best to sit down at an unoccupied table and let others join you. If you wait until every table has several people sitting at it, you have no alternative but to run the risk of making yourself an unwelcome intruder.

WHEN YOU MAY LEAVE THE RECEPTION

When you want to leave you just do so. It is not necessary or even polite to attract attention to your going if it is soon after your arrival. You do smile at anyone you happen to be talking with and say something about being sorry you have to leave early—and go.

Part NINE

ON THE SUBJECT OF
INVITATIONS

Wedding invitations

The engraved forms of invitations and announcements that we use are almost as unchangeably fixed as are the letters of the alphabet. The third-person wording of an invitation and its acceptance or regret has remained unchanged throughout countless years. It is true we no longer "present our compliments" and invite our neighbors to come in "for a dish of tea." On the other hand, third-person invitations to a dinner of ceremony or a dance are worded and engraved exactly as they have always been.

All formal invitations are recognized as such because they are worded in the third person, and their acceptances and regrets are invariably answered in this same form, and by hand. The words must be placed on specified lines and centered as evenly as possible. Names of hosts belong on the first line, the "request the pleasure of" on the second, the name of the guest on the third, and so on.

Invitations to the largest and most elaborate of weddings consist of an invitation to the church ceremony, a card of admission or "pew card," and, for relatives and close friends, an invitation to the reception. But many variations are possible and perfectly correct, as we shall see.

When a guest is expected to attend the church service only, no invitation to the reception is enclosed.

If the wedding is to be in a very small church or chapel and the reception in a very big house, then many will receive invitations to the reception and very few to the ceremony.

If it happens that not only the church but also the reception is limited to a very few who are sent hand-written invitations or are given oral invitations, then engraved announcements in place of invitations of any kind may be sent to the friends who could not be included as well as to acquaintances.

The invitations to a large wedding are sent three weeks beforehand; those to a simpler wedding can be mailed as late as ten days before the wedding day.

» *See Chapters 51 and 50, for wedding announcements and reception invitations.*

CORRECT STYLE

Correct invitations to any wedding, whatever its size, are engraved on the first page of a double sheet of heavy paper, ivory or white, either plain or with a raised margin called a plate-mark or panel. It may be about 5 1/2 inches wide by 7 3/8 inches deep or slightly smaller and thus fold once for insertion into its envelope. Or it may be about 4 3/8 by 5 3/4 inches and go into the envelope without folding. The fashion varies from time to time and other sizes may be used, according to the current custom.

The engraving may be in whichever lettering style the bride prefers among the several offered her by the stationer.

This is one time when, should the family of the bride's father have one, it is proper to have the coat of arms, or a crest only, embossed without color at top center of the sheet. When the invitations are sent out by the bride's mother (or any woman alone), a coat of arms is not used. If the family has no coat of arms, the invitation bears no device of any kind. But if it does, plain script is the best taste for the engraving.

TWO ENVELOPES

Two envelopes are definitely associated with wedding invitations. The inner envelope has no mucilage on the flap and is addressed to Mr. and Mrs. Brown with neither first name nor address. Then it is put into an outer "mailing envelope" that has mucilage on its flap, addressed side toward the flap. This envelope is then addressed by hand.

ADDRESSING THE ENVELOPES

In all formal correspondence it is in bad taste to abbreviate the state name.

Mr. and Mrs. George Brown
26 Parkway
Hometown, Illinois

Envelopes should *not* be addressed:

Mr. and Mrs. James Greatlake
and Family

The phrase "and Family" has never been correct for invitations because it is considered too indefinite as to how many of the family are involved. Correctly, Miss Mary Greatlake, or the Misses Greatlake, may be written beneath the names of their parents, but a separate invitation should be sent to "The Messrs." All members of the family not living at the family's home address certainly have to be sent separate invitations.

The names of children under twelve or thirteen are written on the inner envelope this way:

Priscilla, Penelope, Harold, and Jim

and enclosed in an outer envelope addressed to "The Misses and Messrs. Greatlake."

On the inside envelopes of the invitations to relatives who are very dear to the bride or to the groom, "Aunt Kate and Uncle Tom" or "Grandmother" may be written in the handwriting of the bride or the groom. This, however, is a personal exception and quite apart from etiquette, which is more particularly concerned with the wording of the engraving and with the addressing of the outer envelope.

FOLDING AND INSERTING

When preparing to send out the invitations, all the envelopes are addressed first. An envelope-size invitation is inserted in the inner envelope, folded edge down, with the engraved side toward the flap. An invitation designed to fit an envelope half its size will require a second fold, which should be made with the engraving inside, and inserted, folded edge down, into the envelope. With the unsealed flap of this filled inner envelope away from you, insert it in the mailing envelope. If the invitation is folded, all insertions (such as the reception card or pew card) are placed inside the second fold with the type facing the flap of the envelope. If the invitation is not folded a second time, they are inserted in front of it (nearest you), with the reception card next to the invitation and any smaller cards in front of that.

Engravers generally use tissue sheets to protect the pages from the fresh ink. These tissues may be removed, but many stationers recommend that they be kept to prevent the ink from smearing.

CORRECT WORDING

The wording of the wedding invitation varies as little as the conventions governing its size and mailing. For example, the invitation to the ceremony itself should always request "the honour"—spelled with a "u"

—of your "presence" and never the "pleasure" of your "company." It is the invitation to the reception that requests the pleasure of your company. But, on the other hand, it is perfectly proper for those communicants of the Roman Catholic Church who so wish to use a form in which the phrase "at the marriage of" is replaced by "*at the Marriage in Christ of*"; and where appropriate there is added beneath the name of the groom the lines "*and your participation in the offering of the Nuptial Mass.*"

In the examples of correct wording, spacing, and styles of engraving that follow, it is important to note the omission of punctuation, except after abbreviations and initials and when phrases requiring separation by punctuation occur in the same line.

GENERAL FORMS

The following illustrations show proper forms for wedding invitations.

The wording of an invitation to a house wedding gives a house address in place of the name of a church, and R.s.v.p. is added at bottom left.

Mr. and Mrs. Charles Robert Oldname

request the honour of your presence

at the marriage of their daughter

Pauline Marie

to

Mr. John Frederick Hamilton

Saturday, the twenty-ninth of April

at four o'clock

Church of the Heavenly Rest

New York

Doctor and Mrs. John Huntington Smith

request the honour of

Miss Pauline Town's

presence at the marriage of their daughter

Mary Katherine

to

Mr. James Smartlington

Tuesday, the first of November

at twelve o'clock

St. John's Church

WEDDING AND RECEPTION INVITATION IN ONE

Occasionally, especially for a country wedding or when the reception is taking place in the assembly room or parish house of the church and everyone is invited to remain, the invitation to the reception or to the breakfast is included in the invitation to the ceremony.

Mrs. Alexander Oldname

requests the honour of your presence

at the marriage of her daughter

Barbara

to

Mr. James Town, junior

Tuesday, the twenty-first of October

at three o'clock

Church of the Resurrection

Ridgemont, New York

and afterwards at the reception

Bright Meadows

R.s.v.p.

INVITATION TO A WEDDING IN THE HOUSE OF A FRIEND

Invitations are issued by the parents of the bride even though the wedding takes place at a house other than their own. The names of the parents at the head of the invitation means that *they* are giving the wedding (and probably assuming all expenses) though not in their own house.

Mr. and Mrs. Richard Littlehouse

request the honour of your presence

at the marriage of their daughter

Betty

to

Doctor Frederic Robinson

Saturday, the fifth of November

at four o'clock

at the residence of Mr. and Mrs. James Sterlington

Tuxedo Park, New York

R.s.v.p.

When the reception follows a house wedding, it is not mentioned in the wedding invitation as it is assumed that everyone invited will stay on.

WHEN THE BRIDE HAS A STEPFATHER

When the bride's own father is not living and she has a stepparent, or her mother has divorced and remarried, the invitations are worded:

Mr. and Mrs. John Huntington Smith
request the honour of your presence
at the marriage of her daughter
Mary Alice Towne
etc.

WHEN THE BRIDE'S MOTHER IS WIDOWED OR DIVORCED

If the bride's mother is giving the wedding alone:

Mrs. Bertram Jones
requests the honour of your presence
at the marriage of her daughter
Helen Jeffrey Jones
etc.

WHEN THE BRIDE IS AN ORPHAN

It is important to remember that good taste does not permit "Miss" or "Mrs." as titles before the bride's name but the three cases that follow are exceptions.

If the bride has no relatives and the wedding is given by friends, the wording is:

Mr. and Mrs. John Neighbor
request the honour of your presence
at the marriage of
Miss Elizabeth Orphan
to
Mr. John Henry Bridegroom
etc.

If she has brothers, the oldest one customarily sends out her wedding invitations and announcements in his name. Or if another relative has taken the place of a parent, his or her name is used. The bride whose several sisters or brothers are younger than she may prefer to send her invitations in her own name. The following form might be used:

The honour of your presence
is requested
at the marriage of
Miss Elizabeth Orphan
to
etc.

WHEN THE BRIDE IS A WIDOW OR DIVORCÉE

Invitations to the marriage of a widow—if she is very young—are sent in the name of her parents exactly as were the invitations for her first wedding, except that her name, instead of being simply "Priscilla," is now written "Priscilla Banks Loring," thus:

Doctor and Mrs. Maynard Banks
request the honour of your presence
at the marriage of their daughter
Priscilla Banks Loring
to
etc.

Sending out engraved invitations to the remarriage of a divorcée is not good taste.

On the other hand, the fact that the groom has been divorced does not interfere with the invitation to, or announcement of, his new bride's marriage.

WHEN THE BRIDE HAS A PROFESSIONAL NAME

When the bride has a career, uses a professional name, and therefore has many professional friends to whom she would like to send invitations, but who are unlikely to recognize "Pauline Marie Oldname," the invitations may have her professional name engraved in very small letters and in parentheses under her Christian name:

Pauline Marie
(Pat Bond)

to

Mr. John Frederick Hamilton

This is most practically done by having the name (Pat Bond) added to the plate after the order for regular invitations has been completed. As many invitations as are to go to her professional friends are then struck off with this addition.

WHEN PRINCIPALS ARE IN THE SERVICES

On the wedding invitations, the name of a bridegroom whose rank is below Commander or Lt. Colonel is given this way:

John Strong
2nd Lieutenant, United States Army
or
Ensign, United States Navy

The title of higher ranking officers precedes their name, and the service may or may not be included on the line below.

Colonel John Spring
United States Air Force

The name of a noncommissioned or an enlisted man in the Armed Forces is engraved John Strong, and Signal Corps, U.S.N.R., or Coast Artillery, U.S.A., or whatever designation is his, in smaller type directly beneath the name on the wedding invitations. Or if the bride chooses to include Pvt. 1st Class, U.S.A., or Apprentice Seaman, U.S.N.R., she may do so.

The name of the bride who is in the Armed Forces is engraved:

marriage of their daughter
Alice Mary
Lieutenant, Women's Army Corps

When the bride's father is in the Armed Forces and absent on duty, his name appears as follows:

Major (overseas) and Mrs. John Jones
request the honour of your presence, etc.

An officer in the Reserves does not use his title unless he is on active duty.

High-ranking officers continue to use their title and include their service on the line below with "retired" following the service.

General George Harmon
United States Army, retired

THE DOUBLE-WEDDING INVITATION

Mr. and Mrs. Henry Smartlington

request the honour of your presence

at the marriage of their daughters

Marian Helen

to

Mr. Judson Jones

and

Amy Caroline

to

Mr. Herbert Scott Adams

Saturday, the tenth of November

at four o'clock

Trinity Church

The elder sister's name is given first.

It is unusual but not unheard of for two brides who have been lifelong friends—or possibly cousins, but with different names—to have a double wedding.

The wording of such invitations must necessarily include the surnames of both parents and brides:

Mr. and Mrs. Henry Smartlington
and
Mr. and Mrs. Arthur Lane
request the honour of your presence
at the marriage of their daughters
Marian Helen Smartlington

to
Mr. Judson Jones
and
Mary Alice Lane
to
Mr. John Gray
etc.

WHEN THE BRIDEGROOM'S FAMILY GIVES THE WEDDING

In the unusual situation when the young bride comes as a stranger from abroad, or from any distance, without her family, it is entirely proper that the groom's family give the wedding and send the invitations in their name. This is the only other case where the title "Miss" is used.

Mr. and Mrs. John Henry Pater
request the honour of your presence
at the marriage of
Miss Marie Mersailles
to
their son
John Henry Pater, junior
etc.

Announcements, but not invitations, may be sent from abroad by her own family.

PERSONAL INVITATIONS

The most flattering wedding invitation possible to receive is a note of invitation personally written by the bride:

Dear Mrs. Kindhart,

Dick and I are to be married at Christ Church Chantry at noon on Thursday the tenth. We both want you and Mr. Kindhart to come to the church and afterward to the reception at the home of my aunt, Mrs. Salde, at Two South Beach Street.

With much love from us both,

Affectionately,
Helen

The bride may, of course, write similar notes to the groom's relatives and special friends.

CARDS FOR RESERVED PEWS

To the family and those intimate friends who are to be seated in specially designated pews, a card (approximately 2 by 3 inches) may be enclosed, with "Pew No. " engraved and the number filled in by hand. The style matches that of the invitation.

But the more usual and less expensive custom is for the mother of the bride and the mother of the bridegroom each to write on her personal visiting card the number of the pew that each member of the family and each intimate friend is to occupy.

Pew No. 7

Mrs. John Huntington Smith

600 East Fifty-Seventh Street

A similar card for a reserved enclosure consisting of a certain number of front pews, although for no special pew, and inscribed "Within the ribbon" may be enclosed with the invitations, or "Within the ribbon" may be written on a visiting card and included with the invitation.

Pew cards are often sent, or given in person, after acceptances have been received, when the families of the bride and groom know how many reserved seats will be needed.

ADMISSION CARDS

Except in the case of a wedding held in a cathedral or other church which attracts sightseers, admission cards are no longer used. If it is necessary, a card of approximately 2 by 3 inches is engraved in the same style as the invitations:

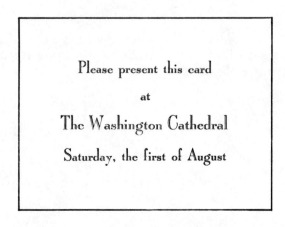

Please present this card

at

The Washington Cathedral

Saturday, the first of August

Only the holders of these cards will be admitted to the church at the time of the wedding.

AT HOME CARDS

The bride- and groom-to-be cannot call themselves Mr. and Mrs. before they are married, so if they want their friends to know what their address is to be, an At Home card is included with the invitation. Today this card is most often as follows:

At home

after the fifteenth of November

3842 Olympia Drive

Houston 19, Texas

Or:

Will be at home

after October sixteenth

1730 Taylor Street

Del Monte, California

The size of the cards is about 4 by 2 3/4 inches, slightly smaller than the reception card. » *For At Home cards to accompany wedding announcements, see Chapter 51.*

50

Invitations to wedding receptions

The correct form for the invitation to a wedding reception depends upon the combined plans for wedding and reception. That is, the invitation sent to guests who are also invited to the church differs from that used when the ceremony is private and invitations are sent out only for the reception.

INVITATIONS TO A RECEPTION FOLLOWING THE CEREMONY

The invitation to the breakfast or reception following the church ceremony is usually engraved on a card to match the paper and engraving of the church invitation. If the latter is folded for the envelope, then the card is a little smaller than half the full size of the invitation. If it is to go with the smaller invitation that does not fold, it may be from 2½ to 3 inches high by 3½ to 4 inches wide. The most commonly used form is this:

Reception
immediately following the ceremony
Essex County Country Club
West Orange

The favour of a reply is requested
Llewellyn Park, West Orange

Although it is perhaps better suited to the unfolded church invitation because of its larger size, it is also perfectly correct to use this longer form:

Mr. and Mrs. John Huntington Smith
request the pleasure of

Miss Pauline Town's

company at the reception
following the ceremony
43 Park Avenue

R.s.v.p.

The forms R.s.v.p. and R.S.V.P. are both correct. It is to be noted that in France and in diplomatic circles the capital letters are the correct form.

RECEPTION AT THE CLUB OF A FRIEND

When the wedding reception (or any other entertainment, for that matter), is given at a club through the courtesy of a friend of the hostess, the following announcement is always engraved in the lower right corner: "Through the courtesy of Mrs. John Smith Jones." This is put in the right corner because the left corner is reserved for the R.s.v.p.

INVITATION TO THE RECEPTION ONLY

On occasion, the ceremony is private and a big reception follows. In these circumstances, the invitations to the ceremony are given orally, and general invitations to the reception sent out for a somewhat later hour. The size and style of these invitations are exactly the same as those to the wedding itself. The wording for this is:

Mr. and Mrs. John Huntington Smith
request the pleasure of
[name or names written in] *company*
at the wedding breakfast [or *reception*]
of [or *for*] *their daughter*
Millicent Jane
and
Mr. Sidney Strothers
Tuesday, the first of November
at half after twelve o'clock
555 Park Avenue
R.s.v.p.

A RECEPTION FOLLOWING A HOUSE WEDDING

When the reception follows a house wedding, it is not necessary to send any sort of separate invitation as it is assumed that those attending the wedding will stay on.

Wedding announcements

When the number of guests who can be accommodated at the marriage service or the reception is limited, announcements are sent to those friends of both families who would otherwise have been invited to be present. They require no gift or acknowledgment except what your own interest and impulse suggest. Announcements are never sent to anyone who has been invited to the wedding or the reception. And they should always be sent as soon after the wedding as possible.

CORRECT STYLE AND WORDING

The form of the wedding announcement resembles the form of the wedding invitation in almost everything except wording. The note paper, the styles of engraving, the use of a crest, the two envelopes, the manner of addressing the envelopes are all the same. » *See Chapter 49.*

The standard wording is this:

Mr. and Mrs. John Fairplay
have the honour of
announcing the marriage of their daughter

Madeleine Anne

to

Mr. George Followes Highseas
Ensign United States Navy

Tuesday, the twenty-seventh of March
One thousand nine hundred and sixty-five

Washington, D. C.

Three forms of phrasing are equally correct: "have the honour to announce," or "have the honour of announcing," or merely the one word "announce." Although "Tuesday, April 24, 1965" is not incorrect, the use of "Tuesday, the twenty-fourth of April" on one line and "One thousand nine hundred sixty-five" on the next is most formal.

The variations in wording necessitated by special circumstances (when the bride has a stepfather, or professional name, etc.) correspond to the variations in wedding invitations (see Chapter 49) with these few exceptions:

Whenever possible, announcements go out in the name of the bride's nearest kin, whether they have been present at the wedding or not. For example, invitations to a wedding given by the groom's parents carry their names, whereas announcements of the same marriage carry the names of the bride's parents.

Announcements for a young widow's marriage are the same as for a first wedding:

Mr. and Mrs. Maynard Banks
announce the marriage of their daughter
Priscilla Banks Loring
etc.

The announcement of the marriage of a widow of maturer years reads differently:

Mrs. William Phillip Hoyt
and
Mr. Worthington Adams
announce their marriage

on Monday, the second of November
One thousand nine hundred and sixty-five
at Saratoga Springs
New York

The parents of a young divorcée may announce her second marriage in the same form as if she were a widow.

Mr. and Mrs. Harvey Strong
announce the marriage of their daughter
Mary Strong Brooks
etc.

Or a divorcée may, with her husband, announce her own marriage.

Mrs. Strong Brooks
and
Mr. Robert Hanson
announce their marriage
on Saturday, the tenth of May
etc.

The bride who is an orphan and the bridegroom may announce their own marriage this way:

Miss Elizabeth Orphan
and
Mr. John Henry Bridegroom
announce their marriage
etc.

Or if the wedding was given by a relative or friend, the announcement may be made in this way:

Mr. and Mrs. John Neighbor
announce the marriage of
Miss Elizabeth Orphan
etc.

AT HOME CARDS

When announcements are sent, the At Home notice may be engraved in the lower left hand corner.

After the first of December
25 Elm Street, Greattown

Or cards in the same form as those used with wedding invitations may be enclosed (see Chapter 49). Either form is perfectly correct. There is a third possibility, also. Because the marriage has already taken place, the card may read:

Mr. and Mrs. John Newlywed
will be at home
after November twelfth
25 Elm Street
Greattown

Other formal invitations

All formal invitations are engraved (never printed) on white cards, either plain or plate-marked like those for wedding receptions, or written by hand on personal note paper.

Formal third-person invitations are sometimes written on paper headed by a very small monogram, but are never engraved on paper headed by an address. If the family has a coat of arms, it or the crest may be embossed without color on engraved invitations.

The size of the card of invitation varies with personal preference. The most graceful proportion is three units in height to four in width, or four high by three wide.

The lettering is a matter of personal choice, but the plainer the design the safer. Punctuation is used only when words requiring separation occur on the same line, and in certain abbreviations, such as R.s.v.p. The time should never be given as "nine-thirty" but as "half past nine o'clock" or, the more conservative form, "half after nine o'clock."

If the dance or dinner or whatever the entertainment is to be is given at one address and the hostess lives at another, both addresses are always given.

BALLS AND DANCES

TO A PRIVATE DANCE

The form most often used by fashionable hostesses is this:

Mr. and Mrs. Harold Gilding

request the pleasure of

Miss Sally Waring's

company at a small dance

Monday, the first of January

at ten o'clock

400 Lake Shore Drive

R.s.v.p.

The expression "small dance" is often used no matter what the size of the ball, but it is not absolutely necessary.

Mr. and Mrs. Sidney Oldname

request the pleasure of your company

at a dance

Monday evening, January the third

at ten o'clock

The Fitz - Cherry

Kindly send response to
Brookmeadows,
Long Island

Even when the ball is given for a debutante daughter, her name does not necessarily appear, and the above forms may be used.

Other proper invitations in such cases are these:

THE MOST FORMAL INVITATION

The most formal invitations to a private ball, no matter whether the ball is to be given in a private house or the hostess has engaged an entire

Mr. and Mrs. Alexander de Puyster

request the pleasure of

Miss Rosalie Grey's

company at a dance in honour of their daughter

Miss Alice de Puyster

Monday, the tenth of January

at ten o'clock

One East Fiftieth Street

R.s.v.p.

Mr. and Mrs. James Town

Miss Pauline Town

request the pleasure of

Mr. and Mrs. Greatlake's

company on Monday, the third of January

at ten o'clock

400 Lake Shore Drive

Dancing

R.s.v.p.

floor of the largest hotel in the world, announce merely that Mr. and Mrs. Somebody will be "At Home"—both words written with capital letters—and the word "Dancing" is added, almost as though it were an afterthought, in the lower left or right corner. This is the most punctilious and formal invitation that it is possible to send. It is engraved, usually in script, on a card of white bristol board about 5½ inches wide and 3¾ inches high. Like the wedding invitation, it is plain or it has an embossed crest without color. The precise form is this:

Mr. and Mrs. Davis Jefferson

At Home

Monday, the third of January

at ten o'clock

Town and Country Club

Kindly send reply to
Three Vernon Square   *Dancing*

But it may of course be engraved in whatever style of lettering the family prefers.

THE INVITATION TO A PUBLIC BALL

The word "ball" is rarely used except in an invitation to a public one, or at least a semipublic one, such as may be given by a committee for a charity or by a club or association of some sort. For example:

> *The Entertainment Committee of the Greenwood Club*
> *requests the pleasure of your company*
> *at a Ball*
> *to be held at the club house*
> *on the evening of Thursday, the seventh of November*
> *at ten o'clock*
> *for the benefit of*
> *The Neighborhood Hospital*
> *Tickets five dollars*

INVITATIONS TO A DEBUTANTE ASSEMBLY

An invitation to present the debutante at an assembly reads thus:

The Committee of the Westchester Cotillion

invites

Mr. and Mrs. David L. Williams

to present

Miss Penelope Williams

at the Cotillion

on Friday, the ninth of September

at ten o'clock

Shenorock Shore Club

Rye, New York

An invitation to debutantes *not* being presented at the ball reads thus:

The Committee of the Mayfair Assembly

has the honor to extend to

Mrs. David L. Williams

an invitation for her daughter

Miss Penelope Williams

to attend

The Mayfair Assembly Dinner Dance

on

New Year's Eve

Saturday, December 31, 1964

Hotel Pierre Roof

nine o'clock

R.s.v.p.

An invitation to other guests invited to the ball:

The Governors of the Tuxedo Club
invite you to subscribe to
The Autumn Ball
to be held at
The Tuxedo Club
on Saturday, the twenty-second of October
Nineteen hundred and sixty-six
at eleven o'clock
Tuxedo Park, New York

R.s.v.p.

These invitations are accompanied by a card stating the amount of the subscription, where it should be sent, etc. A list of the debutantes being presented, the committee, and sometimes the patrons is printed inside the invitation.

INVITATION TO BE A PATRON

If the list of those invited to become patrons is very long, the correct wording is as follows:

The Committee of the Midwinter Ball
has the honour to invite

to be a Patron of the Ball
for the benefit of
The Children's Hospital
at the Hotel Grand
Friday evening, the thirtieth of October
at nine o'clock

Usually a card with return envelope is enclosed with the invitation for the convenience of the patron's answer.

INVITATIONS TO RECEPTIONS AND TEAS

Invitations to receptions and teas differ from invitations to balls in that the cards on which they are engraved are usually somewhat smaller. The words "At Home" with capital letters may be changed to "will be at home" with small letters or "at Home" with a small "a." The time is not set at a certain hour, but extends over a definite period indicated by a beginning and a terminating hour. Also, except for very unusual occasions a man's name does not appear. If the tea is given for a debutante, her name is put under that of her mother, and sometimes under that of her sister or the bride of her brother.

To a tea dance:

Mrs. Grantham Jones
Miss Muriel Jones
at Home
on Tuesday, the third of December
from four until seven o'clock
The Hilton Hotel
3751 Wildwood Boulevard   *Dancing*

Or to a tea for a debutante:

Mrs. James Town
Mrs. James Town, junior
Miss Pauline Town
will be at home
Tuesday, the eighth of December
from five until seven o'clock
850 Fifth Avenue

Because afternoon teas are supposedly given by women, Mr. Town's name is omitted from this invitation. Mr. Town shares his wife's responsibility if the party is given in the evening, and he, of course, assumes the responsibility of host in the afternoon as well.

Probably Mr. Town's name would appear with that of his wife if he were an artist and the reception were given in his studio to view his pictures; or if a reception were given to meet a distinguished guest, such as a bishop or a governor, in which case "In honour of the Right Reverend William Ritual" or "To meet His Excellency the Governor of California" would be engraved at the top of the invitation.

Suitable wording for an evening reception:

To meet the Honorable George Stevens
Mr. and Mrs. James Town
at Home
Tuesday, the eighth of December
from nine until eleven o'clock

This use of the small a and capital H as in the example above is pleasing, because it emphasizes the hospitable thought of Home and denotes neither the ceremoniousness of At Home nor the impersonal attitude that "will be at home" announces.

THE CARD OF GENERAL INVITATION

Invitations to important entertainments are nearly always especially engraved, so that nothing is written except the name of the person invited. But for the hospitable hostess, a card that is engraved in blank, so

Mr. and Mrs. Harold Foster Stevens

request the pleasure of

company at

on

at   o'clock

Two Knob Hill

that it may serve for dinner, luncheon, dance, lecture, musicale, or whatever she may care to give, is a great help.

Another card of general invitation may be useful for those who do not wish to go to the expense of having the full form engraved, for they need not be specially ordered.

Mr. and Mrs. Charles Watson James

request the pleasure of the company of

Mr. and Mrs. Maxwell

at *Cocktails*

on *Tuesday, December 4th*

at *6* o'clock

R. s. v. p.   *785 Meadow Rd.*

INVITATION BY MORE THAN ONE HOSTESS

There is no rule about the order in which the names of two or more hostesses should appear, but the one at whose house the party will be is usually put first. Or if one is a great deal older, her name may head the list. The invitation should make very clear where the event is to take place and where the acceptances and regrets are to be sent. For example, if the luncheon is to be at Mrs. White's house, the correct form would be this:

Mrs. Walter David White
Mrs. Henry Edward Black
Mrs. Theodore Jamison Gray
request the pleasure of your company
at luncheon
Tuesday, the tenth of November
at half after one o'clock
123 Sutton Place

R.s.v.p.
Mrs. Walter David White

If, on the other hand, the luncheon is to be at a club or hotel, the form is this:

Mrs. Walter David White
Mrs. Henry Edward Black
Mrs. Theodore Jamison Gray
request the pleasure of your company
at luncheon
Tuesday, the tenth of November
at half after one o'clock
Hotel Pierre

R.s.v.p.
Mrs. Walter David White
123 Sutton Place

INVITATION SENT BY AN ORGANIZATION

An example of this type of invitation:

The Alpha Chapter
of
Beta Chi Delta
requests the pleasure of your company
on Monday, the twenty-third of February
at four o'clock
at the Beta Chi Delta House
2 Campus Row

INVITATION TO COMMENCEMENT

Each school, college, and university follows its own established customs for Commencement Week. » *See Chapter 39.*

Of the varying forms of invitation to commencement exercises sent, the following is the most usual:

The President and Faculty
of Hotchkiss College
request the pleasure of your company
at the Commencement Exercises
on Wednesday morning
the twentieth of June
at eleven o'clock
in the Sterling Gymnasium

HANDWRITTEN INVITATIONS

When the formal invitation to dinner or luncheon is written instead of engraved, note paper stamped with house address or personal device is used. The wording and spacing must follow the engraved models exactly.

Mr. and Mrs. John Kindhost
request the pleasure of
Mr. and Mrs. Robert Gilding Jr.'s
company at dinner
on Tuesday, the sixth of December,
at eight o'clock.

If the device stamped on the paper does not contain the address, it is correct to write this below the hour. It is never proper for a telephone number to appear on a formal invitation. Note that "Jr." is used when appropriate.

An invitation should not be written like this:

Mr. & Mrs. J. Kindhost request
the pleasure of Mr. & Mrs. James
Town's company at dinner on Tuesday
etc

This incorrect example has three faults: (1) Invitations in the third person must follow the prescribed form, and this does not. (2) The writing is crowded against the margins of the note paper. (3) The full name "John" should be used instead of the initial "J."

THE FORMAL INVITATION BY TELEPHONE

It is proper to telephone formal invitations as well as informal ones. Such calls, if placed and received by members of the household staff, should follow a prescribed form:

"Is this Lenox 2-0100? Will you please ask Mr. and Mrs. Smith if they will dine with Mrs. Grantham Jones next Tuesday, the tenth, at eight o'clock? Mrs. Jones's telephone number is Regent 4-0011."

The person receiving the call should repeat the invitation and, of course, write it down.

The answer:

"Mr. and Mrs. Huntington Smith regret very much that they will be unable to dine with Mrs. Jones on Tuesday, the tenth, as they are engaged for that evening. Please thank Mrs. Jones for asking them."

Or:

"Please tell Mrs. Jones that Mr. and Mrs. Smith will dine with her on Tuesday, the tenth, at eight o'clock, with pleasure."

If the one being called is home at the time:

"Will Mrs. Smith play bridge with Mrs. Grantham Jones this afternoon at the Country Club, at four o'clock?"

"Just a moment, please . . . Mrs. Smith will be delighted to play bridge at four o'clock."

53

Informal invitations

With the exception of invitations to house parties, those sent to out-of-town guests, and those requiring a certain amount of formality, the invitation by note is almost a thing of the past. On informal occasions, the telephone is used almost exclusively, and nothing needs to be said about the correct form beyond a reminder that you should be perfectly clear about dates and hour and leave your guests in no doubt about what is intended. If you feel that a written invitation is needed, you have a choice of several possibilities.

VISITING-CARD INVITATIONS

For an informal dance, for a tea to meet a guest, or for bridge, a lady may use her ordinary visiting card. (See Chapter 56 for their style and form.) Because the Post Office will not accept very small envelopes, a practical size should be ordered for visiting cards or other small-sized cards. These larger envelopes, being thinner but of the color and texture of the cards, do not need to look unmatched.

The following examples are absolutely correct in every detail—including the abbreviations. They should be written, if possible, in black ink.

To meet
Miss Millicent Gordon

Mrs. John Kindhart

Tues. Jan. 7
Dancing at 9 o'ck.

1350 Madison Avenue

Wed. Jan. 8.
Bridge at 2. o'ck.

Mrs. John Kindhart

R. s. v. p.   1350 Madison Avenue

INFORMALS

The use of informals (small folding cards, described in Chapter 56) for invitations is correct and practical. If the card is engraved with your name, the invitation is written in this way:

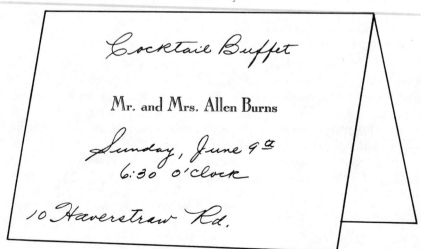

Cocktail Buffet

Mr. and Mrs. Allen Burns

Sunday, June 9th
6:30 o'clock

10 Haverstraw Rd.

If the card is monogrammed or if it is unmarked, the informal invitation must include your name or the recipient may not know by whom it was sent. If the card is going to a close friend, the signature need only be the first name, but if there should be any question whether the receiver knows from which "Lucy" the invitation comes, it is safer to include the last name.

THE "SINGLE NOTE" CARD

A useful variation of the informal is an unfolded card, about 4½ by 3½ inches, with the address engraved in the upper right corner and the name slightly above the center, leaving room beneath for the message.

HANDWRITTEN NOTES AND ANSWERS

Informal invitations are those which are written in the second person, and, though called informal because they have greater latitude than the utterly prescribed pattern of the third-person invitation and reply, they too follow a fairly definite formula. The colon is not used after the form of address in a social note. Either no punctuation or a comma, as you prefer.

The informal dinner and luncheon invitation is not spaced according to set words on each line, but is just written in two paragraphs. From younger to older couple:

Jan. 2, 1964

Dear Mrs. Steele

Will you and Mr. Steele dine with us on Thursday, the seventh of January, at eight o'clock?

Hoping so much to see you then, I am

Very sincerely
Caroline Robinson Town

Or to a woman engaged to a man unknown to the writer of this invitation:

Jan. 2, 1964

Dear Phyllis

Will you and your fiancé lunch with us this coming Saturday, at one o'clock?

Looking forward to meeting him,

Affectionately
Caroline Town

Acceptance:

Dear Mrs. Town

We would be delighted to dine with you on Thursday the seventh at eight o'clock.

Thanking you for your kind thought of us,

Sincerely yours
Phyllis Steele

Regret:

Dear Mrs. Town

We are so sorry that we cannot accept your kind invitation for Saturday because of another engagement.

With many thanks for thinking of us, and I will bring John over to meet you soon.

Sincerely
Phyllis Steele

» *For invitations to a house party, see Chapter 37; to an engagement party, see Chapter 41.*

REMINDER CARDS AND NOTES

When invitations have been telephoned, cards reminding guests of their acceptance are in good usage and very sensible. Those who entertain a great deal have cards engraved with blank spaces to fill in with the word lunching, dining, playing bridge, or whatever.

Otherwise you write on your visiting card: "To remind you— Wednesday 10th, 7:30."

To expected house guests, one perhaps writes a note.

Dear Helen

Just to remind you that we are expecting you and Dick on the sixth.

Love
Muriel

A BACHELOR'S INVITATIONS

The bachelor's invitations are the same as those sent out by a hostess. There is absolutely no difference. He himself telephones or, if he has one, his houseboy or maid telephones: "Will Mr. and Mrs. Norman dine with Mr. Bachelor on Wednesday?" Or he writes a note or (for formal occasions) uses the engraved dinner card.

In giving a party of any size, it is correct for him to write on his visiting card.

Saturday, April 7.
at 4. o'ck.

Mr. Anthony Dauber

To hear Tonini play.

Park Studio

This card is an artist's and somewhat larger than a man's ordinary visiting card. But it would be proper for any host to send for any informal party he cares to give.

Recalling and requesting invitations

If because of illness or for some other reason, invitations have to be recalled, the following forms are correct. They are always printed instead of engraved, there being no time for engraving.

Owing to the sudden illness of their daughter
Mr. and Mrs. John Huntington Smith
are obliged to recall their invitations
for Tuesday, the tenth of June

When an engagement is broken off after the wedding invitations have been issued:

Mr. and Mrs. Benjamin Nottingham
announce that the marriage of their daughter
Mary Katharine
to
Mr. Jerrold Atherton
will not take place

ASKING FOR AN INVITATION

One may never ask for an invitation for oneself anywhere! Nor ordinarily does one ask to bring a house guest to a meal, unless one knows it is a buffet at which one or two unexpected persons could make no difference.

When regretting an invitation, it is quite proper to explain that you are expecting to have weekend guests. Ordinarily the hostess-to-be says, "I'm sorry!" But if it happens that she is having a big buffet lunch or a tea or cocktail party, she may say, "Do bring them. We will be delighted to have them!"

An invitation for any general entertainment may be asked for a stranger—especially for a house guest—still more especially for a man.

> *Dear Mrs. Eminent,*
>   *My nephew, David Park, is staying with us. May he come to your dance on Friday?*
>
> > *Very sincerely yours,*
> > *Caroline Robinson Town*

If the nephew had been a niece instead, Mrs. Town would have added, "If it will be inconvenient for you to include her, please do not hesitate to say so." This would give Mrs. Eminent a chance to answer, if necessary, that her list of men was rather short and that she would be glad to have Mary at the dance if Mrs. Town can find a man to escort her. Most probably Mrs. Town would call Mrs. Eminent on the telephone, which would enable them to discuss the problem, if there were one, and arrive at a solution at once.

A young girl may of course ask her hostess if she may bring a man to her dance; and in fact several men would almost certainly be welcomed!

Acceptances and regrets

The form of acceptance or regret depends upon the form of the invitation received, for the degree of formality or informality must be the same. On the telephone, of course, this presents no problems, but for the handwritten answer, there are formulas that are invariably used.

THE FORMAL ACCEPTANCE OR REGRET

Whether the invitation is to a dance, a dinner, or whatever, the answer is identical, with the exception of the pertinent word—that is, the following form may be used with the substitution of "a dance," etc. for "dinner."

Mr. and Mrs. Donald Lovejoy
accept with pleasure
the kind invitation of
Mr. and Mrs. William Jones Johnson, Jr.
for dinner
on Monday, the tenth of December
at eight o'clock

Also used but not quite so formal is this form:

> *Mr. and Mrs. Donald Lovejoy*
> *accept with pleasure*
> *Mr. and Mrs. Johnson's*
> *kind invitation for dinner*
> *on Monday, the tenth of December*
> *at eight o'clock*

Note that in the first form the full name, including "Jr." when appropriate, must be used, whereas in the second, "Mr. and Mrs. Johnson's" is sufficient.

The formulas for regret:

> *Mr. and Mrs. Timothy Kerry*
> *regret that they are unable to accept*
> *the kind invitation of*
> *Mr. and Mrs. Harvey Brent Smith*
> *for Monday, the tenth of December*

> *Mr. Sidney Hartford*
> *regrets that he is unable to accept*
> *Mr. and Mrs. Worldly's*
> *kind invitation for dinner*
> *on Monday, the tenth of December*

"Monday, December the tenth" is sometimes used, but the wording above is better.

In accepting an invitation, the day and hour must be repeated so that, in case of mistake, it may be rectified and prevent one from arriving on a day and hour when one is not expected. But in declining an invitation, it is not necessary to repeat the hour.

TO MORE THAN ONE HOSTESS

If the names of two or more hostesses appear on an invitation, the envelope is addressed to the one at whose house the party is to take place; or if it is to be at a club or hotel, to the name and address indicated below the R.s.v.p. (Without such indication, you must address it to all of them at the hotel or club.)

But when you write your answer, you repeat the same order of names that appeared on the invitation, no matter how the envelope is to be addressed:

> Mrs. Donald Lovejoy
> *accepts with pleasure*
> *the kind invitation of*
> Mrs. White and
> Mrs. Black and
> Mrs. Grey
> *for Tuesday, the tenth of November*
> *at half after one o'clock*

TO A WEDDING

An invitation only to the church requires no answer whatever (except when the wedding is so small that the invitation is a personally written note). An invitation to the reception or breakfast is answered on the first page of a sheet of full-sized letter paper or on a fold-over note paper; and although it is written by hand, the spacing of the words must be followed as though they were engraved.

Acceptance:

> Mr. and Mrs. Robert Gilding, Jr.
> *accept with pleasure*
> Mr. and Mrs. Smith's
> *kind invitation for*
> *Tuesday, the first of June*

Regret:

> Mr. and Mrs. Richard Brown
> *regret that they are unable to accept*
> Mr. and Mrs. Smith's
> *kind invitation for*
> *Tuesday, the first of June*

The alternative form is equally acceptable:

> *the kind invitation of*
> Mr. and Mrs. Roger James Smith
> *for Tuesday, the first of June*

COMBINATION ACCEPTANCE AND REGRET

It is entirely proper for a wife or husband to take it for granted that either one alone will be welcome at a general wedding reception and to send an acceptance worded as follows:

> Mrs. John Brown
> *accepts with pleasure*
> Mr. and Mrs. Smith's
> *kind invitation for*

Saturday, the tenth of June
but regrets that
Mr. Brown
will be absent at that time
or
will be unable to attend

If it were the wife who could not attend, the wording would merely transpose Mr. and Mrs.

FORMULAS FOR OTHER OCCASIONS

TO AN ORGANIZATION

Miss Mary Jones
accepts with pleasure
the kind invitation of
The Alpha Chapter
of
Beta Chi Delta
for Monday afternoon, February 23rd

TO A COMMITTEE

If the name of the committee or its organization is very long or complicated, you may write your reply in the following form:

Mr. and Mrs. Geoffrey Johnson
accept with pleasure
your kind invitation
for a Ball
on Saturday, the first of January

TO A MULTIPLE DEBUT

Doctor and Mrs. Ronald Graham
Miss Joan Graham
accept with pleasure
your kind invitation
for a dinner dance
Saturday, February tenth
at nine o'clock

INFORMAL REPLIES

When an invitation is sent on a visiting card or an informal, the reply may be telephoned or written briefly on your own card.

VISITING-CARD REPLIES

The reply is no more than this:

Accepts with pleasure!
Wednesday at 4.

Mrs. Robert Gilding, junior

14 Water Street

Sincere regrets
Wed. Jan. 8

Mr. and Mrs. Henry Osborn

INFORMALS

In replying on an informal, you use the same degree of formality as was used in the invitation.

June 4

Dear Sue

We'd love to come to dinner on June 10th at 8:00.

Thanks so much
Betsy

Brook Street   Holyoke   Mass.

So sorry we can't make it on the sixth. We'll be at the Cape.

Gloria

If your informal is engraved as a visiting card, you may write:

Accept with pleasure Sat. at 7:00

Mr. and Mrs. Carl Keeley

On a plain informal you might write:

Accept with pleasure Saturday at 7:00

Fran and Carl Kelley

ANSWER CARDS

It is regrettable that it is necessary to write this section at all, but the custom of sending "answer cards" with invitations to debut parties and subscription dances is so widespread that it must be discussed.

This custom has risen out of sheer necessity. Years ago, even teenagers would not have thought of appearing at a party without having answered the invitation. Also years ago, when parties were given in houses with large staffs it was not as important to the hostess to know the exact number of guests she might expect. Both costs and service were more flexible than they are today, when parties are served and food prepared by catering services, who must know the exact quantity of food to be sent and waiters to be hired.

Therefore, while we deplore the lack of good manners which makes the sending of these cards necessary, we recognize the problem of the hostess who sends them, and it must be admitted that it seems the only way to obtain the answers.

An answer card is usually small and engraved in the same style as the invitation with a box to check, indicating whether the invited guest will attend or not.

Mr. Allen Lordyee

☐ accepts

☐ regrets

Friday, January second
Columbus Country Club

Many invitations to private parties also include a self-addressed stamped envelope with the card. Subscription dance committees may send the envelope, but generally do not stamp it as they are more concerned with costs. Another arrangement is to enclose a self-addressed stamped postcard.

Etiquette has been made so simple for the receivers of these invitations that they can hardly fail to answer them. And having returned the card, they should not also send a formal reply, as the hostess or committee undoubtedly is keeping a filing box, and does not wish to receive the answers in a variety of shapes and sizes.

Part TEN

CARDS AND CALLS

Visiting cards, informals, and business cards

Today, one seldom leaves his card at the house of another as evidence of his presence there, but "visiting card" or "calling card" is still the proper name for these small but useful objects. Business or professional cards differ somewhat in format, but should be considered in conjunction with their social counterparts. To these two long familiar forms has been added a third—the informal. Although it cannot substitute for a business card or perform all the functions of a visiting card, it has in recent years earned a well-deserved place of its own.

VISITING CARDS

Cards used to be left in great quantities at the homes of acquaintances, but in these hectic days, people are simply too busy to make formal calls in the old-fashioned way. Only in military and diplomatic circles are they still an expected custom. » *See Chapter* 57.

Nowadays, the visiting card (in its matching envelope) has taken the place of the written note of invitation to informal parties of every description. Messages of condolence or congratulation are often written on visiting cards. And they are usually enclosed when one sends a present, although the small white card and envelope provided by many shops may be substituted if you do not have your own with you.

SIZE AND ENGRAVING

Of necessity, the size of visiting cards varies, according to length of name, but a married woman's card is usually from 3 to 3½ inches wide and from 2¼ to 2½ inches high. (Very young girls customarily use a smaller card.) A man's card is narrower, from 3 to 3¼ inches long and from 1¼ to 1 5/8 inches high. The cards are made of white or cream-white glazed or unglazed bristol board of medium thickness, and they are not plate-marked. Those made of thin parchment paper are convenient if, for some reason, a greater quantity must be carried.

The engraving much in use is shaded Roman, and script is always good form. Various other letterings, brought out by engravers from time to time, have a temporary vogue, but all overly large or ornate lettering should be avoided.

ADDRESSES

People who live in cities often have the address in the lower right corner, engraved in very small letters. In the country, addresses are less important, as everyone knows where everyone else lives. People who have both town and country houses occasionally have separate cards for each.

In America, it is not customary for a married man to have a club address on his card. Unmarried men may use the address of a club, but if they do not regularly receive their mail there, they of course use their home address.

ENVELOPES

Because visiting cards are so often mailed these days, it is wise to order a supply of matching envelopes for them. Postal regulations make it necessary for the envelopes to be somewhat larger than the cards themselves, but color and quality of paper prevent any seeming mismatch and the larger size ensures their safe delivery.

CORRECT NAMES AND INITIALS

To be impeccably correct, one should not use initials on a visiting card. A gentleman's card should read "Mr. John Hunter Titherington Smith"; but because names are sometimes awkwardly long, he may have his cards engraved "Mr. John H. T. Smith" or "Mr. J. H. Titherington Smith," as suits his fancy. His wife's card must, of course, be the exact duplicate of his, and not read "Mrs. J. Hunter Smith" when his reads "Mr. John H. Smith." She uses "Jr." if he does, and drops it, if he does, when his father dies.

CARDS OF A MARRIED COUPLE

A married woman's card: A married woman uses her husband's name in exactly the same form that he does, and her card is approximately 3¼″ by 2¼″.

Mrs. John Foster Hughes

"*Mr. and Mrs.*" *cards:* "Mr. and Mrs." cards are just as useful as individual cards. They are used for invitations, as enclosures with presents, or for any communication that comes from both husband and wife. They are approximately 3½″ by 2½″.

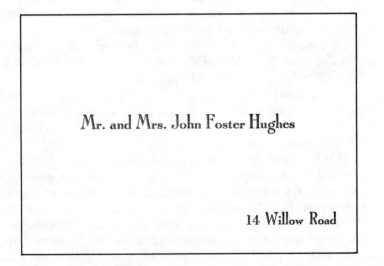

Mr. and Mrs. John Foster Hughes

14 Willow Road

A married man's card: A man's card is engraved with his title, Doctor or Mr., even though he may have "junior" after his name. Although Mr. is *never* written "Mister," Doctor rather than Dr. is preferred. The size is 3¼″ by 1½″.

Mr. John Foster Hughes, Jr.

CARDS FOR OTHERS

A widow's name: A man gives his name to his wife for life—or until she herself through remarriage relinquishes it. A widow, therefore, should always continue to use her husband's Christian names. She is Mrs. John Hunter Titherington Smith (or Mrs. J. H. Titherington Smith), but never Mrs. Sarah Smith, if she cares at all about good taste.

If a widow's son has the name of his father, the widow may have "Sr." added to her name when her son marries. This use of Sr. is necessary if they live at the same address—or in a village where no street address is used. If they live in different cities, both mother and daughter-in-law can be Mrs. John Hunter Titherington Smith.

If the widow lives in the same city but at a different address from her son and his wife, she can have her address engraved in small letters at the lower right-hand corner and so identify herself.

John Smith, Jr., John Smith, 2nd, and their wives: The fact that a man's name has "Jr." added at the end in no way takes the place of "Mr." His card should be engraved "Mr. John Hunter Smith, Jr." and his wife's "Mrs. John Hunter Smith, Jr." "Junior" may be engraved in full; when it is, it is not spelled with a capital *j*. John, second, or John, third, may have 2nd or 3rd after their names, but II or III in Roman numerals gives a very handsome appearance.

It is improper, unless he has a good reason, for a man to continue adding "Jr." to his name after the death of his father or grandfather. But on occasion, the reason may be sufficient. For example, he may well wish to retain the *Jr.* if he lives in the same locality as his mother and his wife might be confused with the older Mrs. Smith. Or when the widow, who is perhaps the young stepmother of the son, does not wish to be known as *Sr.*, it may be the only practical solution. Or when a father has been so celebrated that the son cannot possibly take his place (and sometimes for other professional reasons), it is practical or very important for the son to keep his identity as junior.

The same considerations apply in continuing to call a boy "John Smith, 3rd" if John Smith, Jr. (or 2nd) has died. *Junior* always means the son—or possibly the grandson—of a man of the same name; *2nd* means the nephew or cousin of a man of the same name. The following diagram will perhaps make this much misunderstood order clear:

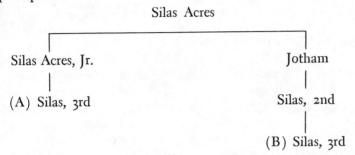

Silas Acres

Silas Acres, Jr.   Jotham

(A) Silas, 3rd   Silas, 2nd

                        (B) Silas, 3rd

Because there is no way to distinguish between (A) and (B), the latter is usually given a different middle name and is christened Silas John Acres. Since this changes the name, he has no suffix, and his son could be called Silas John Acres, Jr.

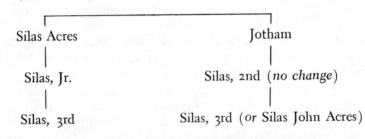

Silas Acres   Jotham

Silas, Jr.   Silas, 2nd (*no change*)

Silas, 3rd   Silas, 3rd (*or* Silas John Acres)

A *divorcée's card:* Some women, if they have no children and if their divorce has been a bitter one, prefer to give up their married name entirely and return to being "Miss Agnes Fulbright." This is understandable and permissible. The proper name for a divorcée, however, is her maiden name combined with her husband's surname. Miss Susan Coleman, who is divorced from Franklin Butler, becomes Mrs. Coleman Butler, and her cards should be engraved in this form. Because some surnames are overly long and awkward, there is a tendency for a woman to let herself become Mrs. Susan Butler, but this is not correct and should not be condoned.

A *professional woman's card:* A woman who has earned a professional title uses her title or professional name in public, while in private life she uses the name of her husband. A spinster who is a practicing physician uses the title of Doctor socially as well as professionally. But if she is, for instance, a Doctor of Philosophy, a woman should not call herself "Doctor" except in a classroom or when she is introduced as a speaker.

The best solution for a woman who is a medical doctor is to have two cards—one for business purposes engraved "Helen Corbin, M.D." or "Doctor Helen Corbin," and one for social use engraved "Mrs. Richard Ford Corbin." On a "Mr. and Mrs." card, she would remain "Mrs.," not "Dr.," as it would be most awkward to have "Mr. and Dr. Richard Ford Corbin" on one card. If her husband is also a doctor, the card reads "Dr. and Mrs. Richard Ford Corbin."

A boy's card: A boy never puts "Mr." on his cards until he leaves school or becomes eighteen, and many use cards without "Mr." until they have finished college.

Cards of a young girl: A young girl's cards, after she is fourteen, have "Miss" before her name, which should be her real and never a nickname: "Miss Sarah Smith," not "Miss Sally Smith."

Cards for children: That very little children should have visiting cards is not so "silly" as might at first thought be supposed. To acquire perfect manners, training cannot begin early enough, since it is through lifelong familiarity with good behavior that much of the distinction of a well-mannered person is acquired. Many mothers think it good training for children to have their own cards, even though they are used only to send with gifts and on a very few other occasions. Children's cards are always smaller than regulation size, and the younger the child, the smaller the card. They may seem a bit extravagant, but as a present from a doting grandmother or aunt, they need not be.

Titles on cards: A doctor, a clergyman, or a military officer in active service, and holders of title-bestowing offices all have their cards engraved with their titles: Doctor Henry Gordon (an M.D.); The Reverend William Goode; Colonel Thomas Doyle; Judge Horace Rush; Senator James Widelands. But a person holding high degrees does not add their letters to his name, and his cards are not engraved "Professor." The double card reads Doctor and Mrs. Henry Gordon, Judge and Mrs. Horace Rush, etc.

It is always best to engrave titles in full.

The correct card for a governor is

The Governor of Nevada

on a card that is slightly larger or more nearly square than an ordinary man's card. Less correct, but not inadmissible, is his ordinary card with Governor of Nevada added in small letters under his name. Occasionally an overmodest incumbent objects to the correct form because he thinks it looks too self-important. But he must remember that the card is representative of the highest office of his state and not the card of a private citizen.

The card of a mayor may read

The Mayor of Chicago

or, if he prefers,

Mr. John Lake
Mayor of Chicago

is also correct.

A diplomat uses his title and United States of America rather than America or American.

It is unnecessary to continue this list, as each official certainly knows his own name! But it may be as well to add that titles of courtesy have no place either in a signature or on a visiting card: The American title of courtesy, "The Honorable," unlike this title given to sons of British earls, viscounts, and barons, is never correct on a card.

The professional card of a doctor or surgeon is James Smith, M.D. His social card is Doctor or Dr. James Smith, as he prefers. (Dr. is not incorrect; but Doctor is somewhat better form.)

THE P.P.C. CARD

This is merely a visiting card, whether of a lady or a gentleman, on which the initials P.P.C. (*pour prendre congé*—to take leave) are written in ink in the lower left corner. This is usually sent by mail to acquaintances when one is leaving and means nothing except "I've gone away—good-by." It is in no sense a message of thanks for especial kindness, for which a visit should be paid or a note of farewell and thanks written.

MESSAGES WRITTEN ON CARDS

"With sympathy" or "With deepest sympathy" is written on your visiting card with flowers sent to a funeral. This same message is written on a card and left at the door of a house of mourning, if you do not know the family well enough to ask to be received.

"To inquire" is often written on a card left at the house of a sick person, but not if you are received.

At the house of a lady whom you know well and whom you are sorry not to find at home, it is friendly to write "Sorry not to see you!" or "So sorry to miss you!"

» *For the use of visiting cards as invitations, see Chapter 53.*

INFORMALS

The small fold-over cards known as informals are convenient when you want, for example, to write a very brief note, but one that requires more space than is afforded by a visiting card.

Plain white informals of good quality are available at all stationers and are perfectly acceptable. If you wish, however, you may have them engraved. This should be done exactly as you would have your visiting cards engraved. Or you may simply have your monogram in the upper left corner.

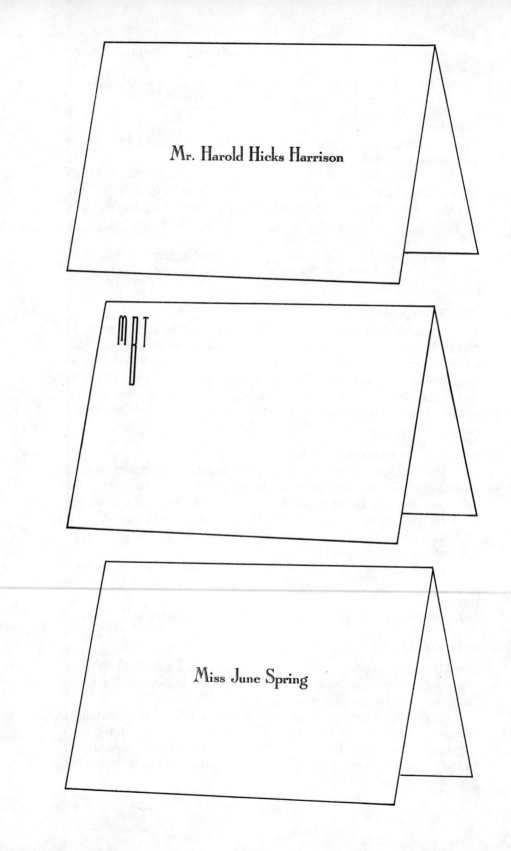

Mr. Harold Hicks Harrison

Miss June Spring

Because informals are usually somewhat larger than visiting cards, the envelopes present fewer problems when it comes to the size acceptable for mailing.

Informals are correct and practical for invitations (see Chapter 53), but they cannot substitute for visiting cards when you make a formal call. They may be enclosed with a gift only if you wish to write a personal message on the inner page.

BUSINESS AND PROFESSIONAL CARDS

Although business cards are never used for social purposes and must not be confused with visiting cards, their principal use is very like the original and now uncommon function of the visiting card: When an employee or an executive of a company makes a business call on another company or on a client or a prospective client, he sends in his card or leaves it as a record of his visit.

The card of an employee usually has the name and address of the company in the center of the card with the employee's name in the lower left corner and the telephone number in the lower right corner.

An executive has his or her name in the center with his or her position in the company in smaller letters under the name. The name and address of the company are then put in the lower left corner. Although the telephone number is often omitted, it is so convenient not to have to look up the number that it is usually put in the lower right corner.

Business cards are approximately 3½ inches by 2 inches in most cases. They do not require the use of full names to the extent that is usual with visiting cards. That is, a man's business card may read "Mr. John Smith" (whereas his social card reads "Mr. John Hunter Titherington Smith") if he is known simply as "John Smith" in his business life and, for example, signs his letters in that form.

Professional cards may differ from business cards in that no company name appears.

HAROLD HICKS HARRISON

500 WALL STREET
NEW YORK, N. Y.   MARKET 6-7272

Calls and callers

The custom of making formal calls, in this day of high pressure and lack of leisure time, is no longer a part of our lives. But there are circumstances in which even those most indifferent to social obligations must call and leave their cards: In Washington, members of diplomatic or military circles exchange calls. Members of the military or the diplomatic service arriving at a new post call on their superiors. Calls are exchanged between officers on military posts.

In addition to these official calls, there are certain visits that all of us must make.

VISITS THAT EVERYONE MUST PAY

Paying visits differs from leaving cards in that you must ask to be received. A visit of condolence should be paid at once to a friend when a death occurs in the immediate family, but in this case you ask if Mrs. Jackson feels like seeing you. And further, the would-be-visitor asks if there is anything he or she can do. A lady does not call on a man, but writes him a note of sympathy.

When going to inquire about a friend who has been very ill, the question of whether or not you ask to see her depends upon how well you know her. It is always proper as well as thoughtful to take a gift of a book or fruit or flowers or perhaps, if you know of something she likes that you or your cook makes and that she is allowed to eat, something from your kitchen.

When the engagement of a man in your family—or family-in-law—is announced, you should go to see his fiancée. Should she be out, you do not ask to see her mother. You do, however, leave a card upon both ladies, and after this you show your future relative whatever hospitality you can.

A visit of congratulation is paid a new mother, and, of course, it is always very pleasing if you can take a present to the baby.

HOW TO MAKE A FIRST VISIT

In large cities, neighbors seldom call on each other. But when strangers move into a neighborhood in a small town or more especially in the country, it is very unfriendly of the residents nearby not to call on them. The newcomers always must wait for the old residents to call on them—or at least invite only those much younger to come to see them. Or if two ladies meet and they are both newcomers, either one may say, "I wish you would come to see me." To which the other replies, "I'd love to."

Everyone invited to a wedding may call upon the bride on her return from the honeymoon. And when a man marries a girl from a distant place, courtesy absolutely demands that his friends and neighbors go to see her as soon as she is at home.

WHAT TO DO

Let us say you go to see a stranger who has come to live in your neighborhood, and when you ring the bell the lady herself opens the door—or let us say you find her sitting on her porch. In either case, you say, "How do you do—I'm Mrs. Jones. I live in the brick house across the street."

The new neighbor says, "How do you do. I'm very glad to see you," or "How kind of you to come to see me!" She then invites you into her living room or asks whether you think it pleasanter on the porch. In any case you sit and talk.

From ten to fifteen minutes is the time allotted for a formal visit. This is not a strict rule, but it is well to keep within this time unless you have much to talk about, and unless your hostess says, "Oh, do stay a little longer" or "Oh, don't go so soon," in which case you stay for a few minutes longer or say, "I'm sorry! I've love to, but I can't today. Do come and see me soon!" The new neighbor says, "I'll be glad to." You both say, "Good-by," and that's all.

RETURNING A FIRST VISIT

People who are old friends pay no attention to how often or how seldom one goes to see the other, unless there is an illness, a death, a birth, or a marriage. Nor do they ever consider whose turn it is to invite whom. But first visits should be returned with considerable punctuality—especially the visit that should be paid after a *first* invitation to lunch or dine.

If hospitality has been shown you by two or more hostesses together, you are indebted to both or all equally, if you know them equally. But if you know only one of the hostesses, it is not necessary that you return the hospitality of the other (or others) unless opportunity offers. In any event, when returning the hospitality of these several hostesses, it is never necessary that you invite them together.

CALLS OF CONDOLENCE

Calls of condolence should be made as soon as possible after hearing of the death of a friend, or a member of a friend's family. If they are very close friends, you will probably be admitted to speak to them and in this case, you should offer your services to help in any way that you can. If they do not need anything, you offer your sympathy and leave without delay.

When you are not so well acquainted with the family, and do not wish to intrude on their privacy, you may leave your card, with "With deepest sympathy" written across the top. Visits of condolence need not be returned.

SOME SPECIAL SITUATIONS

THE BUSY NEWCOMER

If a new neighbor, struggling to get her house in order, opens her door to an unexpected visitor, it is obviously only human for her to exclaim frankly, "Oh dear, I would so much like to ask you to come in but, as you can *see*, my house and I are in just too much of a mess to have you. Won't you please come back when I am straightened out?" Because this is so likely to happen when someone has just moved, it is a good idea to telephone first, introduce yourself, and ask when it might be convenient to call.

IF THERE ARE SERVANTS

In a household with servants, the door is opened by a waitress or a butler, and, if the hostess is at home, the guest is led into the living room. In a very formal household, the butler presents a tray for the card, reads it himself, and, going to the door of the living room, he announces, "Mrs. Henry Stowe." If the lady of the house is at home but upstairs, the visitor is asked to take a seat in the living room, and the servant takes the card to the hostess.

On an exceptional occasion, such as paying a visit of condolence or inquiring for a convalescent, when the question as to whether he will be received is necessarily doubtful, a gentleman does not take off his coat or gloves, but waits in the hall with his hat in his hand. When the servant returning says either, "Will you come this way, please?" or "Mrs. Town is not well enough to see anyone, but Miss Lillian will be down in a moment," the butler then takes the gentleman's hat, helps him off with his coat, and shows the way to the living room.

The butler or maid must stand with the front door open until a visitor re-enters her car, or if she is walking, until she has reached the sidewalk. It is bad manners ever to close the door in a visitor's face or while she is still going down the front steps.

"NOT AT HOME"—NO DISCOURTESY

When a servant at a door says, "Mrs. Jones is not at home," this phrase means that the lady of the house is "not at home to visitors." This answer neither signifies nor implies—nor is it intended to imply—that Mrs. Jones is out of the house. But it is more polite than "Not receiving," a phrase that actually means the same thing and is used by many people.

To be told "Mrs. Jones is at home but doesn't want to see you" would certainly be unpleasant. And to "beg to be excused"—except in a case of illness or bereavement—is very chilling. But the message "not at home," given at her door, means merely that she is not sitting in her living room ready to receive visitors. Actually she may be resting, she may be ill or extremely busy, or she may simply be unpresentable.

If it should happen that, catching a glimpse of you or recognizing your voice, she should call, "Oh, do come in. I am at home to *you!*" this certainly is no discourtesy. Nor are you "catching her in a lie." She is merely showing great friendliness to you personally, and you should certainly be pleased and not consider her an untruthful person.

While "not at home" is merely a phrase of politeness, for Mrs. Jones to say "I am out" after a card has been brought to her is both an untruth and an inexcusable rudeness. Or to have an inquiry answered, "I don't know, but I'll see," and then to have the servant, after taking a card, come back with the message "Mrs. Jones is out" cannot fail to make the visitor feel rebuffed. Once a card has been admitted, the visitor *must* be admitted also, no matter how inconvenient receiving her may be. Mrs. Jones may send a message that she is dressing but will be very glad to see her if she can wait ten minutes. The visitor can either wait or say she is pressed for time. But if she does not wait, then it is she who is rather discourteous.

MANNERS DURING A CALL

A gentleman visitor always leaves his hat and coat in the hall and also removes and leaves his gloves—and overshoes, should he be wearing them. But a lady keeps on her coat, hat, and gloves, unless it is very warm and her hostess asks her to remove them. A gentleman entering a room in which there are several people shakes hands with his hostess and slightly bows to all the others, whether he knows them personally or not. He, of course, shakes hands with any who are friends, and with all men to whom he is introduced, but with a lady only if she offers him her hand.

Before entering a room full of people, it is best to pause on the threshold and see where the hostess is and the most unencumbered approach to her. The way *not* to enter a room is to dart forward and then stand awkwardly bewildered and looking about in every direction. After greeting the hostess, talk with her for a few moments, and then either join friends of your own or those to whom the hostess introduces you.

The duration of a formal visit should be in the neighborhood of fifteen minutes. But if another visitor is announced, the first one—on a very formal occasion—may cut her visit shorter. Or if conversation becomes especially interesting, the visit may be prolonged by five or ten minutes.

CORRECT NUMBER OF CARDS TO LEAVE

When the visitor herself rings the doorbell and the message is "not at home," the butler or maid proffers the card tray on which the visitor lays a card of her own and one of her daughter's for each lady in the house and a card of her husband's and son's for each lady and gentleman. The number of cards to leave is very simple. You leave your own cards for ladies only, because you do not call upon a gentleman. But your husband's card is left upon every gentleman as well as every lady.

That is all there is to it. But three is the greatest number ever left of any one card. In calling on Mrs. Town, who has three grown daughters and her mother living in the house and a Mrs. Stranger staying with her whom the visitor was invited to a luncheon to meet, a card on each would mean a packet of six. Instead, the visitor should leave three—one for Mrs. Town, one for all the other ladies of the house (not one for each), and one for Mrs. Stranger. In asking to be received, her query at the door should be, "Are any of the ladies at home?" Or in merely leaving her cards she should say, "For all of the ladies."

CALLING WITHOUT A CARD

The fact that you may not have any visiting cards is no reason for you not to make any calls that you may wish to. If the person on whom you are calling is home and greets you herself, she obviously knows that you have made the effort to see her. If no one is home, you may leave a note in her mailbox, "So sorry to have missed you, Sally." If she does not know you well, you sign it "Sally Brown."

When the door is opened by a maid, you say, "Would you tell Mrs. Carter that Mrs. Brown is calling?" If Mrs. Carter is not home or cannot see you, you may ask for a pencil and paper and leave her a note or ask the maid to tell her that you have called.

POSTSCRIPTS ON VISITS

If a servant has met you at the door, do not hand him your card. If he has not offered you a tray to place it on, step inside the door and place the card (or cards) on the nearest table.

A lady never pays a call on a gentleman. But if the gentleman who has given a dinner has his mother or sister staying with him, you may, of course, pay a call on them both.

While one should not perch stiffly on the edge of a chair, neither should one sit on the middle of one's spine as if stretched on a sofa. One foot should always be flat on the floor.

Don't outstay other visitors who arrive after you. And do not linger because someone who may have come before you, but who is plainly an intimate friend with special news, has not yet left. In such a situation, the rule of safety is to leave after ten minutes.

Never make such remarks as "I'm afraid I have overstayed my welcome" or "I must apologize for hurrying off" or "I am afraid I have bored you to death talking so much." All such expressions are self-conscious and stupid. If you really think you are staying too long or talking too much—don't!

VISITING THE SICK

"Making calls" brings to mind one subject that certainly is at one time or another in the thoughts of all of us. This is the occasional visit we must make to a hospital when members of our families or our close friends are ill. The same general rules apply to visiting a sick person at home, although if he is well on the way to recovery, they may be slightly relaxed.

The whole routine of a hospital is highly organized and kept in smooth running order by the doctors and nurses and staff. Whether we go as a patient or visitor, we must behave so that our presence there, when we are visitors, fits into an orderly pattern and so that, as a patient, the hospital's staff can do its best for us.

Far too often visitors are thoughtless and careless. One should think of the problems that a visitor makes under the busy, crowded hospital conditions of today. Courtesy to nurses and the other hospital personnel, quietness of manner and approach in the hospital buildings, avoidance of asking for special attention from busy people, these we can show—and above all we must not act in any way that will be tiring or harmful to the patient we are visiting. We must make our visits short and friendly, leaving our small gifts without fuss or any expectancy of more than a simple thank you for them. We must not engage the patient in long discussions, nor ask questions about his or her illness that properly are in the sphere of the doctor and the nurse. We must time our visits so that the patient becomes neither tired nor anxious and, of course, we must alway follow the rules as they are given to us by the staff. A surgeon that I know claims that visitors kill more patients than do operations, certainly an overstatement, but be sure that you are not one of those visitors. Here are a few do's and don'ts that may be helpful for visitor and patient.

Don't bring as your gift foods such as chocolates or cakes that the patient may not be permitted to have.

Whenever it is possible, bring your flowers with their own container and let them be of a size that can easily be handled. Hospitals are invariably short of containers, and it is an additional chore for the nurses to have to hunt for a suitable vase. Most florists realize this, and if you mention that your purchase is to go to a hospital, they will arrange the flowers in inexpensive (sometimes even disposable) containers at no additional charge.

Patients often prefer potted plants to cut flowers. They are easy to care for, last longer, and can be taken home by a member of the family if more space is needed for those which arrive at a later date. There they continue to give the patient many further moments of pleasure.

It should be clear that heavily scented flowers have no place in the sickroom.

Don't think that the hospital routine has been devised to bedevil you as a visitor or the patient himself. It is only a part of a long-range plan carefully worked out to serve everyone in the best way possible. Limited visiting hours, early meals, and rules governing smoking may seem unreasonable to you, but you must remember that they have not been made just for the benefit of your sister Susie, who may have nothing more than a broken finger, but rather for the sicker patients, who, without a carefully planned routine and the best possible conditions for rest and quiet, might not recover at all.

Don't talk about his illness in front of the patient. Ask the necessary questions quietly, from those who are competent to answer them for you, out of his hearing and sight. Also, remember that floor nurses are not allowed to give out certain information. If one of them says to you, "You will have to ask Dr. Smith about that," you need not feel that she is hiding information from you or that she is being deliberately unfeeling; it is a hospital rule, and she has no choice.

Don't worry a patient about anything that you feel might upset or

disturb him. The fact that Bobby is failing algebra, or the dog had a disastrous fight with the neighbor's cat, is not news calculated to improve
the mental outlook of the patient, and in any case, he or she can do
nothing about it. The best thing you can do, if you wish his speedy return home, is to bring him cheerful, encouraging news, which will make
him want to get there quickly.

Remember that the average patient is not his normal self and the
burden of good behavior is on your side, not his. He may show little enthusiasm for the things that usually interest him, or he may react over-
excitedly to a minor incident. If he does either, simply tell yourself that
this reaction is only temporary, and change the subject to a safer one. But
it is up to you to lead the way.

Don't overstay your welcome. Visit briefly, cheerfully, and leave the
patient rested and encouraged. Make up your mind before you arrive
that you will stay no more than fifteen or twenty minutes, and stick to it,
no matter how much your friend may beg you to stay. If other visitors
arrive while you are there, leave sooner, so that they may have their share
of the patient's time without overtiring him. Nothing is more exhausting
to a person in bed than to have to try to follow a conversation among
several people who may be seated on all sides of the room. If it is possible,
when two or three people are present, stand or put your chairs on the
same side of the bed.

If, possibly because of the shortage of nurses in many hospitals, the
doctor or a member of the family asks you, as a close friend, to stay with
the patient, do not let him feel that he must entertain you or even talk.
Take a book along, attend to any simple things he may wish you to do,
and settle yourself where he may know that you are there, but at the
same time, indicate that you are quite happy to have an hour or two in
which to enjoy your book quietly.

SEMIPRIVATE ROOMS AND WARDS

The number of private rooms in every hospital has been greatly de-
creased, partly because of the shortage of nurses, partly because they are
too costly for most people, and partly because there always seems to be a
need for more hospital beds than exist. The vast majority of hospital patients nowadays find themselves in semiprivate rooms or larger wards.

The rules governing visitors to these rooms must be stricter than
those for visitors to patients in private rooms. Your friend may not object
to cigarette smoke, but it may cause the man in the next bed to have a
coughing attack which could be the worst thing for him. Therefore, if it
is allowed at all, it is essential to ask the others nearby if it will bother
them if you smoke. And please, cigarettes only! Cigar and pipe smoke
can actually cause nausea in many people.

Voices must naturally be kept lower, not only for privacy's sake, but in order not to disturb the other sick people who may badly need their rest.

If you are going to the snack bar or restaurant to bring a dish of ice cream or a candy bar to your friend, it is only thoughtful to ask the other person in a semiprivate room if you can bring him anything at the same time. This would not be necessary in a larger ward, unless one of the patients actually requested you to do an errand for him.

If there is a television set in the room—and this rule applies between patients as well as visitor and patient—do not turn it on without asking the other's permission and consulting him as to his choice of program. Unless he shows real enthusiasm, keep the volume very low.

If another patient in a room wishes to rest, draw the curtains between the beds, to give him as much privacy and quiet as possible. On the other hand, if he and your friend have become friendly, include him in the conversation, and your visit will be doubly appreciated.

TIPPING

The question of tipping the nurses may arise, but its answer is simple—don't. It is perfectly proper, however, to bring a box of candy or the like that can be shared by all the staff caring for the patient. The package should be left with the nurse on duty at the desk nearest his room, with a word or two to the effect that "this is for everyone who has been so nice."

FLOWERS FOR YOUR FRIENDS

There are certain occasions when sending flowers, if we can possibly afford them, is really obligatory. We try to send flowers to an intimate friend who is or has been seriously ill, to a new mother, to a debutante on her coming out, to a guest speaker when we are hostess, and on anniversaries—either joyous or tragic—of our nearest friends. We must send flowers to the funeral of a friend, or a member of an intimate friend's family. Certain thoughtful people are constantly sending flowers; others seldom do. Certainly the majority of us send them much less often than we might, sometimes because we think those we can afford to buy or those growing in our garden are not good enough.

At all events, there is scarcely any situation in which flowers are not a suitable as well as probably the most beautiful messengers of friendship or sympathy or love that can be chosen. They may be sent by almost everyone to almost anyone. It is always proper, for example, for a woman to send flowers to any man she knows when he is seriously ill or convalescing—cut flowers, a plant, or perhaps best of all, a terrarium or cactus garden, which requires very little care.

Whatever the occasion, remember that the true measure of your thoughtfulness is not the cost but your feelings when you decide to send flowers to a friend.

Part ELEVEN

PROTOCOL IN OFFICIAL CIRCLES

Precedence and titles

Although most people are kind and those who have been long in government service instinctively try to help the inexperienced, it is imperative that each new arrival in Washington, whether an official or a private citizen who expects to take part in the social life of the capitol, learn first of all the proper title by which each diplomat, government official, and military officer is addressed and the order of his rank. When a man has been promoted to high position, the respect due his office should not be overlooked. And placing a foreign representative below his proper seat at a dinner table, showing less than proper concern for his rank, may actually endanger diplomatic feeling between nations.

Precedence is the bane of the Washington hostess. It is easy enough to know that a general outranks a lieutenant, a duke a count, or a member of the President's cabinet a state assemblyman. The difficulty begins in determining, for instance, whether a general of the army should rank the governor of a state, or whether a rear admiral, or a mayor or a justice of a state court should go in to dinner first, or where to seat the Archbishop of X and the Duke of Y.

The hostess who plans to entertain several government officials, military officers, or foreign diplomats must try to arrange her seating without slighting any of her guests. But she should also realize that her dinner is a private occasion and that her charm and hospitality are of more importance than any minor and unintentional errors in precedence.

In an American house, the ranking foreigner should insofar as possible be given precedence. He could never be a rival of the President of the United States, for he would be either a presidential guest of honor or the host at his own country's embassy and thus never outrank him.

In a foreign embassy in Washington, the ranking American (or any other stranger) is given precedence. The President of the United States takes precedence over the representative of the country that is receiving him. In the President's absence, the Vice President, the Chief Justice, or the Secretary of State—whoever represents the United States—outranks all foreign ambassadors. In the diplomatic service, the highest ranking ambassador is the one who has been longest in residence in Washington —not longest in service of his country.

As the Protocol Staff of the Department of State has explained, "The White House and the Department of State prescribe the protocol to be used only for ceremonies of state. The protocol differs somewhat for each ceremony, and the rules used are not considered as binding at private functions. For this reason it is the policy of The White House not to make the rules public or to give out the order of precedence of Government officials." Therefore, the following list must be understood to be an unofficial order of rank among those in government service.

> The President of the United States
> The Vice President of the United States
> The Speaker of the House of Representatives
> The Chief Justice of the United States
> Former Presidents of the United States
> The Secretary of State
> Ambassadors of Foreign Powers
> Widows of former Presidents of the United States
> The Secretary General of the United Nations
> United States Representative to the United Nations
> Ministers of Foreign Powers (Chiefs of Diplomatic Missions)
> Associate Justices of the Supreme Court of the United States and Retired Associate Justices
> The Cabinet
> > The Secretary of the Treasury
> > The Secretary of Defense
> > The Attorney General
> > The Postmaster General
> > The Secretary of the Interior
> > The Secretary of Agriculture

The Secretary of Commerce
The Secretary of Labor
The Secretary of Health, Education and Welfare
The Senate
Governors of States
Acting Heads of Executive Departments (in the absence of the Cabinet member)
Former Vice Presidents of the United States
The House of Representatives
Under Secretaries of State
Administrator, Agency for International Development
Director, United States Arms Control and Disarmament Agency
Chargé d'Affaires of Foreign Powers
Secretaries of the Army, the Navy, and the Air Force (ranked according to date of appointment)
Director, Bureau of the Budget
Chairman, Council of Economic Advisers
Chairman, Board of Governors, Federal Reserve
Under Secretaries of the Executive Department and Deputy Secretaries
Chairman, Joint Chiefs of Staff
Chiefs of Staff of the Army, the Navy, and the Air Force (ranked according to date of appointment)
Commandant of the Marine Corps
Five Star Generals of the Army and Fleet Admirals
The Secretary General, Organization of American States
Representatives to the Organization of American States
Director, Central Intelligence Agency
Administrator, General Services Administration
Director, United States Information Agency
Administrator, National Aeronautics and Space Administration
Chairman, The Atomic Energy Commission
Director, Defense Research and Engineering
Director, Office of Emergency Planning
Administrator, Federal Aviation Agency
Chairman, Civil Service Commission
Director, The Peace Corps
Special Assistants to the President
Deputy Under Secretaries of the Executive Departments
Assistant Secretaries of the Executive Departments
United States Chief of Protocol
Members of the Council of Economic Advisers
Active or Designate United States Ambassadors and Ministers (career rank, when in the United States)
Under Secretaries of the Army, the Navy, and the Air Force (ranked

according to date of appointment)
Four Star Generals and Admirals
Assistant Secretaries of the Army, the Navy, and the Air Force (ranked
    according to date of appointment)
Lieutenant Generals and Vice Admirals (3 Star)
Ministers of Foreign Powers (serving in Embassies, not accredited)
Deputy Assistant Secretaries of the Executive Departments
Counselors of Embassies or Legations of Foreign Powers
Major Generals and Rear Admirals (2 Star)
Brigadier Generals and Commodores (1 Star)
Assistant Chiefs of Protocol
The Secretary of the Senate

OFFICIAL TITLES

Just as there is a certain order of precedence within official circles, so there are forms of address that differ somewhat from those to which we are accustomed in unofficial life. For example, the following sentences indicate the way persons in the diplomatic world are introduced, announced, and spoken of and spoken to.

"Mr. Ambassador, may I present Mr. Worldly?" (Mr. Worldly finds out for himself, if he does not already know, *which* ambassador.)

But in the case of Mrs. Worldly the order is reversed.

"Mrs. Worldly, may I present The Speaker?"

"Mrs. Worldly, may I present Mr. Justice Lawson?"

"Mrs. Worldly, may I present the British Ambassador?"—or more formally—"his Excellency the British Ambassador?"

A man of lesser rank is always introduced to one of greater.

Members of the Cabinet are usually "Mr. Secretary," but if several are present, one is designated "Mr. Secretary of State," the other "Mr. Secretary of Commerce." And you say, of course, "Mr. Chief Justice" or "Mr. Justice Lawson"—even after he has retired. You also say "General Pershing," and "Admiral Sim," and "Senator Lake," and not merely "General," "Admiral," or "Senator" without a surname.

The Chief Executive and the Vice President are *always* spoken to without a surname:

"I appreciate the honor, Mr. President."

"Thank you, Mr. Vice President."

It is utterly improper to call a governor "Mr." no matter how informal and simple his own inclinations may be. And only those who know him well say "Governor" without adding his surname. In public, he is "Governor Jones" or "The Governor."

Captains and commanders and those of higher rank are generally addressed by title and surname: Captain Brown, Commander Gray, Colonel Steel, but to call them by title alone is not objectionable, as it would be in the case of a governor.

Military and naval titles are used only by officers in active service or retired "regulars." It is not in good taste for reserve officers or those who held temporary commissions during the war to continue having their cards engraved Captain, Major, or Colonel. Often a man is affectionately called "Colonel" by his friends, but he should not have the title engraved on his visiting cards; neither should he use it as a part of his signature. A civilian staff officer (such as a colonel on a governor's staff) shows very poor taste in using his title, or rank, when his political chief is out of office.

In contrast to the abbreviation of "Mr." or "Mrs.," which is *never* written in full, it is both correct and courteous to write out all military and naval titles—especially when addressing a social note. Impersonal communications may be sent to 2nd Lieut. John Smith, Lieut. Johnson, or Lt. Col. Graham, but other ranks are more properly written in full.

When introducing or addressing a letter to one who has both a military and an inherited title, military rank is put first: Colonel, Lord London.

TITLES ON PLACE CARDS

Place cards present another problem, for at official functions some carry only the title whereas others have title and surname. The following appear without names on all formal occasions:

> The President
> The Vice President
> The Archbishop of ———
> The Ambassador of ———
> The Minister of ———
> The Chief Justice
> The Speaker
> The Secretary of ——— *or* The Attorney General *or* The Postmaster
> General

So, too, at public dinners place cards are inscribed "His Excellency, the Archbishop of New York." "His Honor, the Mayor of Chicago," etc. "The Assistant Secretary of the Navy," for example, is never used alone, however, because there is more than one assistant secretary in all executive departments. The same is true in the case of the following and similar titles:

> Mr. Justice Fox
> Senator Essex
> Governor Lansing
> Rev. Father Stole
> Dr. Saintly

At a private dinner, when the title alone sounds overly stiff and formal, the hostess may modify the official form (except in the cases of the President and Vice President) by adding the surname: "Ambassador Santorino," "Chief Justice Howard," "Secretary Knowles." For other notables, she uses the name by which she would address them in speaking: "Governor Street, will you sit here?" "Father Gaines, I'd like you to meet . . ." Everyone else appears as Mr., Mrs., or Miss at dinners given by a host and hostess in their own house. Remember that the object of a place card is twofold: to show the owner of the name (or title) where he is to sit and to give his neighbors at the table a clue about how to address him.

An invitation to The White House

An invitation to lunch or dine at The White House is a command and automatically cancels any other engagement that is not of the utmost importance. The reply must be written by hand. It must be mailed the day the invitation is received if it is not delivered by hand to The White House. There are very few acceptable excuses for refusing such an invitation, and the reason must be stated in the note of regret—unavoidable absence from Washington, the recent death of a close relative, or actual illness.

The correct forms for replies are:

Mr. and Mrs. Richard Worldly
have the honour to accept
the kind invitation of
The President and Mrs. Washington
for dinner on Thursday, the eighth of May
at eight o'clock

Mr. and Mrs. Robert Franklin
regret extremely
that owing to Mr. Franklin's illness
they will be unable to accept

the kind invitation of
The President and Mrs. Johnson
for dinner on Friday, the first of May

The note to a disappointed hostess:

Mr. and Mrs. Richard Worldly
regret extremely
that an invitation to The White House
prevents their keeping
their previous engagement for
Tuesday, the first of December

INFORMAL INVITATIONS

Informal invitations to dinner or luncheon at The White House are now used more frequently than formerly. They may be sent by letters, telegrams, or telephone messages from the President's secretary or his wife's secretary. The replies should be sent in the same form to whoever issued the invitations. Acceptances (or regrets, when the reasons are valid) should be written on personal stationery, either engraved or plain.

A typical invitation might be worded something like this:

Dear Mrs. Heathcote,

Mrs. Harrison has asked me to invite you to have lunch with her at The White House on Thursday, the sixteenth of May. Luncheon will be at one o'clock.

Yours truly,
Eleanor Smithers
Secretary to Mrs. Harrison

The reply might read:

Dear Miss Smithers,

Will you please tell Mrs. Harrison that I shall be delighted to lunch with her at The White House on Thursday, the sixteenth of May. Thank you very much.

Sincerely,
Frances Heathcote

To the luncheon Mrs. Heathcote wears a dress that she might wear to any similar gathering, but in this instance she should wear hat and gloves as well.

DINNER AT THE WHITE HOUSE

An engraved invitation to The White House means black tie unless white tie is specified on the invitation. For black tie the men wear stiff shirts and collars and a dinner jacket. Women wear evening clothes, and if it is a white-tie dinner, they wear long gloves.

All the names of guests expected at The White House are posted with the guards at the gate. You announce your name and wait a few seconds until you are recognized.

After the guests arrive, the President and his wife enter and speak to each guest and shake hands. Guests, of course, remain standing.

At a formal dinner, the President goes into the dining room first with the highest ranking woman guest. His wife follows with the highest ranking man guest.

DETAILS OF WHITE HOUSE ETIQUETTE

Although customs vary somewhat during different administrations, the following details represent the conventional pattern from which each administration necessarily adapts its own procedure.

When you are invited to The White House, you must arrive several minutes, at least, before the hour specified. No more unforgivable breach of etiquette can be made than not to be standing in the drawing room when the President makes his entry.

The President, followed by his wife, enters at the hour set and makes a tour of the room, shaking hands with each guest. When your turn comes, you bow. If he talks to you, you address him as "Mr. President." In a long conversation it is proper to vary "Mr. President" with "Sir" occasionally. You call the wife of the President "Mrs. Washington" and treat her as you would any formal hostess. You do not sit down as long as either the President or his wife remains standing. No guest, of course, ever leaves until after the President has withdrawn from the room, but they then bid each other good night and leave promptly.

Requests to see the President on a business matter should be made through one of the Presidential aides—the one closest to the subject you wish to discuss—or through your congressman. Your reason should be a valid one, you should be sure that no one else can solve your problem, and your letter should be stated in such a way that, if possible, the matter can be settled without a personal interview.

If you have a business appointment with the President, it is most important that you arrive a few minutes ahead of the appointed time. No doubt you will be told how much time you are allowed. Make your call brief and, if possible, take less time than that allotted.

If a buzzer should ring when you are in a corridor, an attendant will ask you to step behind a closed door. The buzzer means that the President or members of the family are leaving or entering. This precaution is for their safety and their privacy.

Don't smoke unless you are invited to.

Gentlemen always remove their hats as they reach the portico.

Do not take a present unless you have cleared it with an aide; a small package taken from a briefcase or a handbag will alarm the Secret Service men who are always present.

GIFTS TO THE PRESIDENT

Not only should you not take a present to the President unless it has been cleared with an aide, but you should not *send* anything to The White House without receiving permission from his secretary or one of his aides. You may have had a successful hunting trip and wish to send the President a brace of pheasants. The gift must be cleared with the proper authority; otherwise he will never see or taste it.

The flag of the United States

There are certain rules and customs that all of us who love this symbol of the United States should know and always follow because it shows our true respect for our country.

Every day in the year between sunrise and sunset is a proper time to fly the flag, though customarily it is not flown in inclement weather unless there is a particular occasion that requires its display. It may also be displayed at night as part of a patriotic display.

On Memorial or Decoration Day, May 30th, the flag is displayed at half-staff until noon and at full staff thereafter till sunset. Flag Day is June 14th—the day when we especially celebrate this emblem. It is a widespread custom also for most of us to display the flag on other national holidays.

There are certain clear-cut situations in which the flag should never be used, for example, as decoration on a portion of a costume or athletic uniform, as embroidery on cushions, scarves, or handkerchiefs, or on paper napkins or boxes. Of course, it should never be used as a covering for articles on a speaker's table or so placed that objects may be placed on it or over it. When the flag is used in the unveiling of a statue or monument, it should not be used as a covering of the object to be unveiled. It

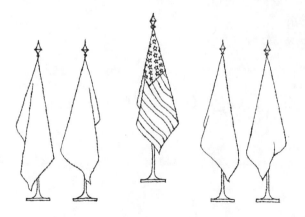

is unlawful to use the flag in a registered trade mark which comprises "the flag, coat of arms, or other insignia of the United States or any simulation thereof." It goes without saying that the national emblem is never displayed in connection with advertising of any kind. When festoons, rosettes, or other draperies are desired, bunting of blue (uppermost), white, and red should be used, but never the flag itself.

DISPLAYING THE FLAG

When displayed over the middle of a street, the flag should be suspended vertically with the union (the blue field) to the north in an east-west street, or to the east in a north-south street.

When displayed with another flag from crossed staffs, the flag of the United States should be on the right (the flag's own right) and its staff should be in front of the staff of the other flag.

The flag should be raised briskly and lowered slowly and solemnly.

When it is flown at half-mast, the flag should be hoisted to the peak for a moment and then lowered to the half-mast position. Before lowering the flag for the day, it should again be raised to the peak.

When flags of states or cities or pennants of societies are flown on the same halyard with the flag of the United States, the latter should always be at the peak. When flown from adjacent staffs, the national flag should be hoisted first and lowered last.

When the flag is suspended over a sidewalk from a rope, extending from house to pole at the edge of the sidewalk, the flag should be hoisted out from the building, toward the pole, union first.

When the flag is displayed from a staff projecting horizontally or at an angle from a window sill, balcony, or the front of a building, the union of the flag should go clear to the peak of the staff (except when at half-mast).

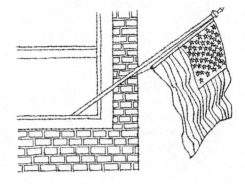

When the flag is used to cover a casket, it should be so placed that the union is at the head and over the left shoulder. The flag should not be lowered into the grave or allowed to touch the ground.

When the flag is displayed in a manner other than flown from a staff, it should be flat, not tucked or draped, whether indoors or out. When displayed vertically against a wall, the union should be uppermost and to the observer's left. When displayed in a window it should be displayed in the same way, with the union to the left of the observer in the street.

When carried in a procession with another flag or flags, the American flag should be either on the marching right or, when there is a line of other flags, it may be in front of the center of that line.

When a number of flags of states or cities are grouped and displayed

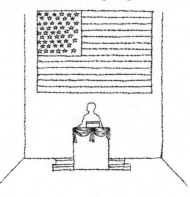

from staffs, our national flag should be at the center or at the highest point of the group. If the flags of two or more nations are displayed, they should be flown from separate staffs of the same height and the flags should be of approximately equal size. International usage forbids the display of the flag of one nation above that of another nation in time of peace.

When the flag is used in a church, on the chancel or on a platform, it should be placed on a staff on the clergyman's right, other flags on his left. When displayed in the body of the church, the flag should be on the congregation's right as it faces the chancel.

When used as an identifying symbol on an automobile, it is flown on a small staff affixed on the end of the front bumper, on the right looking forward and within the line of the fender. When used this way, the staff should be tall enough so that the flag clears the car hood. Alternately, a small flag may be flown from the radiator cap. If the flag has become soiled or wind-torn, it should be promptly removed and replaced.

The flag should *never* be hung upside down except as a signal of distress.

CARE OF THE FLAG

The flag of our country should be carefully protected in storage and in use so that it will not be damaged. Every precaution should be taken to prevent it from becoming soiled or torn. It should not be permitted to touch the ground, or water, or a floor, and in handling it should not brush against other objects.

If it should get wet, it should be hung smoothly until dry, never rolled or folded while still damp.

Flags should be dry-cleaned, not washed.

61

The United Nations

Because of the diversified membership of the United Nations, precedence and protocol have always evidenced a kind of fluidity quite in keeping with its multinational character. Therefore, when guests of almost equal rank are being entertained, the host and hostess may consult the Chief of Protocol (Protocol and Liaison, United Nations, New York).

It is quite understandable that members of an organization comprised of persons from countries of widely varied systems of diplomatic protocol and social custom will largely follow the customs of their home countries in such matters. On the other hand, since the United Nations Headquarters is located within the United States, it is often, but by no means always, the case that they follow American custom.

There are three broad principles that in general are followed. First, the order of diplomatic precedence—prime minister or chief of state, cabinet minister, ambassador extraordinary and plenipotentiary, envoy extraordinary and minister plenipotentiary, counselor of embassy, and attaché. Second, no seniority in terms of rank or service is recognized; the various member countries are listed alphabetically as they are spelled in the English language. Third, delegates and personnel are selected to serve in an international capacity by the nations solely on personal merit, and regardless of nationality or diplomatic status.

As there is a system of rotation employed in many of its component organizations that reflects the international aspect of the United Nations, the determination of precedence is often qualified by a date, as in the Security Council, for instance, where the presidency is rotated monthly. The Secretariat itself characteristically differs from that of the embassies of one nation to another, for they serve as international civil servants and not as representatives of a single country.

Remembering that those serving at the United Nations are in a sense the guests of our country, and some are very distinguished guests indeed, the thoughtful host or hostess will get from the Chief of Protocol the necessary information about his or her guests-to-be.

Part TWELVE

GOOD MANNERS FOR EVERY DAY

On the telephone

When you are talking on the telephone, whether in your home or in an office, the quality of your voice and your ability to express yourself clearly and concisely are of utmost importance. The person at the other end of the line cannot, after all, see your facial expressions or your gestures, and the impression he receives must depend entirely on what he hears.

The telephone is designed to carry your voice at its natural pitch. It is not necessary to shout. In fact, raising your voice, especially during a long-distance call, will only distort it. The telephone transmitter should be held about one inch from your lips and the earpiece close to your ear. Speak clearly and distinctly, with the same inflections that you would use in a face-to-face conversation. If you must put the telephone down during the conversation, do it gently, and when you hang up, do not slam the receiver down—the person at the other end may still have the phone close to his ear and the sudden sharp bang can be quite deafening.

THE BUSINESS TELEPHONE

ANSWERING THE OFFICE PHONE

When telephone calls go through a switchboard, the operator often answers the ring by giving the name of the company. Some firms, however, feel that a more friendly impression is made on the caller by the greeting "ABC Company, good morning" or "Good afternoon, ABC Company."

When the call goes directly through to an office or has been transferred by the switchboard operator, it should be answered promptly, before the second ring if possible. The person answering should identify himself and his department: "Mr. Hugo, accounting department." If answering for some one else, as a secretary does, she should give her employer's name as well as her own: "Mr. Carlson's office, Miss Norton speaking." If her employer is not in, or if she wishes to protect him from unnecessary calls, she should then offer to help the caller if she can or, if not, take a message: "He's not available at the moment. May I take a message?" or "He's out of the office just now. May I have him call you?" or "He's attending a meeting this morning. Could I help you?" If he is in his office, she asks "May I tell him who is calling?" Any of these phrases should elicit the necessary information without the abruptness of "Who's calling?" But if the caller is evasive, you may have to ask for his name more directly. "Who is calling, please?" is sometimes necessary.

A pad and pencil must be kept next to the phone to avoid the irritating "Just a minute. I have to find a pencil," when you are asked to take a message.

PLACING A CALL

When placing a call, be sure that you have the correct number. Next to all business phones there should be a list of the numbers frequently called.

As soon as your call is answered, you must identify yourself, and unless the person you are calling knows you well, you must also name your organization. "This is Robert Kramer, of the Hobbs Company. May I speak to Mr. Hughes?"

It is in very poor taste for a salesman to announce himself as Sam Sales to a woman. Correctly he says, "This is Mr. Sales of the Blank Company." But to a gentleman he may omit the "Mr."

A young woman in business says, "This is Miss Caesar of the Wheel Tyre Co." or "Transcontinental Railroad—Mr. Train's secretary speaking."

All names must be given as briefly but as explicitly and as clearly as is humanly possible.

The most discourteous telephone habit is that of the businessman who tells his secretary to call Mr. Jones and then is not waiting to take the call. The secretary, for example, dials the number; a voice announces, "A. B. Jones Company"; the secretary says, "Mr. Brown is calling Mr. Jones." Promptly Mr. Jones says, "Hello, Brown!" but instead of hearing Brown's voice, he hears a secretary explain, "Mr. Brown is busy on another wire. He'll be with you in a moment." Mr. Jones listens good-temperedly—a few seconds, and more seconds. Mr. Brown is evidently unaware that seconds seem minutes to a busy person listening to a dead receiver.

The point is that the person who has been called has the "right of way"—even though he has not yet come to the telephone. It is picking up the second telephone after putting in a call on the first that results in rudeness to the one who, having been called to the telephone, is then asked to wait!

THE TELEPHONE IN THE HOME

"HELLO" CORRECT AT HOME

The correct way to answer a house telephone is still "Hello." It is like looking out through shutters, as it were, to see who is there. "Yes" is abrupt and a bit rude, but "This is Mrs. Jones's house" leaves the door standing open wide, and "Mrs. Jones speaking" leaves her without chance of retreat.

This is not nonsense. It is a really important aspect of modern telephone etiquette. In all great cities, telephones are rung so persistently by every type of stranger who wants to sell something to Mrs. Householder, or to ask a favor of Mrs. Prominent, or to get in touch with Mr. Official (having failed to reach him at his office) that many persons of prominence are obliged to keep their personal telephone numbers unlisted. The last thing that they want to do, therefore, is to announce "Miss Star speaking." It is far more practical to say "Hello" and let the one calling ask "Is this Miss Star's house? Mr. Director would like to speak to her." Or if she herself answers, a friend recognizing her voice says, "Hello, Mary. This is Kate."

WHO IS CALLING, PLEASE?

When the telephone in the home is answered by someone other than the head of the household, the response to "May I speak to Mrs. Brown, please?" is usually "Just a moment, please." If, however, Mrs. Brown has told the maid, or a child, that she is very busy and can only take the most important calls, the one who answers is correct in saying, "Mrs. Brown can't come to the phone just now; may I have your name and she will call you as soon as she can."

If the caller should say, "I want to speak to Mrs. Brown personally—never mind my name!" whoever has answered replies, "I'm sorry, but I can't interrupt Mrs. Brown. May I give her a message later?" If he then refuses to leave a message or give his name, he can hardly expect Mrs. Brown to speak to him, nor is there any reason why she should.

GIVING ONE'S NAME

Whether to give one's name with or without title is a question often raised. When talking with strangers, titles are always used, but in other situations, usage may vary.

The following rules hold good: An older person announcing herself or himself to one who is much younger says, "This is Mrs. Elder" or "Miss Spinster" or "Mr. Elder."

A younger lady, whether married or single, says, "This is Marie Manners," or to one whom she knows socially, but who is not on a first-name-calling basis, "Hello, Mrs. Knox? This is Mary Bailey." Mrs. Knox answers, "Good morning, Mrs. Bailey!"

A gentleman calling a lady of his acquaintance never under any circumstances announces himself as "Mr. Smartling." Instead, if the call is social, he says, "This is George Smartling."

If you are a young man calling a friend and the answering voice is that of a friend or a member of the friend's family, you say, "This is Jim Brown" or probably "This is Jim." If the voice is that of a maid or a butler, you say, "This is Mr. James Brown. May I speak to Mr. Allen Gray?" or if the friend is the only man in the house, "to Mr. Gray."

INVITATIONS BY TELEPHONE

When Mrs. Jones issues an invitation by telephone, there is no long conversation, but merely:

Mrs. Jones: "Is that you, Mrs. Smith [or Sarah]? This is Mrs. Jones" [*if she is elderly, but* Alice Jones *if she is fairly young, or* Alice *if an intimate friend*]. "Will you and your husband [*or* John] dine with us next Tuesday?"

Mrs. Smith: "I'm so sorry we can't. We are busy that night." Or "We'd love to," or "Yes—with pleasure." And probably she repeats "Next Tuesday at eight" to be sure there is no misunderstanding of date or time.

Invitations for a weekend visit are as often as not telephoned:

"Hello, Ethel. This is Alice. Will you and Arthur come for the weekend on the sixteenth?"

"The sixteenth? That's two weeks from tomorrow. We'd love to!"

» *If Mrs. Jones is not telephoning herself and the message is given by or received by a butler or a maid, see the discussion of the formal invitation by telephone, Chapter 52.*

A bad habit is the prefacing of any invitation with, "Hello, John. What are you doing Saturday night?" Or "Are you going to be busy Monday afternoon?" This maneuver puts John in the position of finding it embarrassing to refuse after having answered, "Nothing," and then being told that he is expected to dine with the Borings or to play bridge with the Revokes. On the other hand, if he answers, "I have an engagement," and is then told that he would have been invited to something he likes very much, it is disappointing not to be able to go—without seeming rude to the person he has at first refused. A young woman who says she has an engagement and is then told, "Too bad you can't come, because John Brilliant was looking forward to meeting you," cannot change her mind and say, "Oh, then I'll get out of my dinner somehow and come." To do so would be the height of rudeness to all concerned, and there is no need for her to be put in this position.

THREE IMPORTANT DON'TS

When the number you get is evidently wrong, don't ask, "What number is this?" Ask instead, "Is this Main 2–3456?"

Don't answer and then say, "Wait a minute," and keep whoever called you waiting while you vanish on an errand of your own. If the doorbell is ringing and you can't listen at that moment, say "I'll call you back in a few minutes!" And do so.

Don't let too young a child answer the telephone. A lot of the caller's time is wasted trying to make the child understand a message and relay it to the right person. If there is a long silence, there is no way of knowing whether the child is hunting for Mother or playing with his dog, quite forgetful of the caller and the telephone.

LONG-DISTANCE CALLS

When making a long-distance call, it is most important not to shout —amplifiers on the circuits will step up your voice all the way. On overseas calls, it is also important to wait for the other person to finish speaking before you start. It is a one-way-at-a-time circuit, and if both speak at once, both are shut off until one or the other stops talking.

Keep on the tip of your tongue what you have to say, and say it promptly. If you have several things to say, write them down and read them off.

If you call long distance often, a telephone timer is a must. It is a small second-counting gadget that rings a bell before each three minutes. If you are making a personal call and the person on the other end of the line likes to talk on and on, you may ask the operator, when you put in your call, to interrupt when the three minutes are up. But in these days of direct dialing, you will do well to have a timer at hand, for you may never have a chance to speak to the operator.

INFORMATION, PLEASE

It is quite true that the telephone operator who answers when we dial Information is prepared to answer our perplexities, but it is not at all true that she can be expected to overcome our lazy carelessness.

Strangely enough, it is not our oldest generation who find it difficult to read the small print in the telephone book (a small magnifying glass near the telephone will help the far-sighted, or a great effort will get you out of the big easy chair to lift the heavy book) that gives Information an unnecessary amount of work. On the contrary, investigation by the telephone company has found that the overcrowding calls that are at times literally crippling to the service, especially in our greatest cities, are made by the lazy young who have seemingly neither the strength of muscle nor the sense of fairness to lift themselves off their spines long enough to look up a number, rather than ask Information to do it for them. If for some reason you have to ask for a number, and if it is one you think you will call again, write it down.

ON A PARTY LINE

When it is realized that the usual number of families sharing a party line is four (and the maximum ten) and that as long as one person is talking, no outside call can reach any other person on that line, the consideration required of each sharer is obvious. For this reason the telephone company has taken pains to make—and expects the subscribers to keep—the following rules:

Ordinarily, when you find the line in use, you hang up for three minutes before signaling again. In an emergency, it is permissible to break in on a conversation and call out clearly "EMERGENCY!" and then "Our barn is on fire," or "Johnny's had an accident," or whatever it is. But unless all on the line hang up, your telephone is cut off.

A personal memory: During the last war, a soldier tried to say a few last words to his wife before sailing. For fifty minutes the long-distance operator repeatedly received a "busy wire" signal. He had to go without a word to her. What he could have done (and we can all do) is remember that while the operator is not permitted to cut in on a busy wire, her supervisor can. In this case, the husband could have asked for the supervisor of the station called and briefly explained. At her discretion, she could then have cut in, announced a long-distance call for Mrs. Soldier, and asked those talking to hang up, please, and permit her to take it.

PAYING FOR YOUR CALLS

ON A NEIGHBOR'S TELEPHONE

Today, almost everyone has his own telephone, but sometimes, especially in resort areas, there are those who become embarrassing and expensive nuisances by using a neighbor's telephone over and over again, not only for local calls, but for long-distance ones, too.

To those who live in a town where local calls are not charged for individually or whose allotted number of calls is seldom used up and no long-distance ones are made, frequent use of your telephone may very well be annoying, but it does not add to your bill. In a city where even a local call is charged for, it is just as correct to present an itemized bill for the charges on your telephone bill as it would be to present a bill for eggs or chickens, a thing you would never hesitate to do.

For an occasional local call, you might let it go, but for those who make many long-distance calls, it is simplest as well as most accurate to show your telephone users the toll list and let each check his calls and pay his total.

It is not too finicky to ask those who live where local calls are charged for to leave ten cents (or whatever the charge may be) for each city call, when they make a large number.

Try to avoid making calls from a busy doctor's office, but if you have to, pay the nurse for the call.

BY VISITORS AND HOUSE GUESTS

Many guests mistakenly hesitate to proffer payment for their calls. The definite rule is this: Should one be obliged to make a single local call, one would not ordinarily offer payment for it, but it is absolutely required that one pay for every long-distance call. Moreover, it is the only way a house guest can feel free to telephone as often as he or she may want to. One should always call the operator as one has finished speaking and ask for "the toll charge on XY-2368 Great Town" and then leave this amount with a slip, giving date and number called. Or if one has made many during a long stay, the complete list of telephone calls and telegrams sent, with the amounts of each and their total, should be handed to the hostess and paid for when one says good-by. This is not humiliating, and no matter how rich the host may be, it is the correct way to pay this debt.

THE TELEPHONE COURTESY TEST

If it interests you to know how good or otherwise your telephone manners may be, the number of times you can answer "Yes" to the following questions will give you your rating. If every one is "Yes," you deserve not merely a crown, but a halo!

1. Do you make sure of the correct number so as not to risk disturbing strangers by "calling from memory"?

2. Do you make sure conversations with busy people are as brief as possible?

3. When calling intimate friends who do not recognize your voice, do you resist playing a game of "Guess who?" and announce yourself promptly?

4. Do you try to time your calls so as not to interfere with the occupations of those you call most often?

5. Do you make business calls well before the close of office hours, especially if calling a person you know is a commuter?

6. In a business office, do you explain to personal friends inclined to talk at length that you will call them after hours?

7. Do you treat wrong-number calls as a mutual inconvenience and

answer, "Sorry, wrong number," in a tone of polite sympathy instead of showing ill-tempered annoyance?

8. On a dial telephone, do you always wait for the dial tone?

9. When the number you are calling is not answered quickly, do you wait long enough for someone to lay aside what she may be doing so that when she reaches the telephone she will not have been disturbed just to answer a dead telephone when you have already hung up?

10. Do you, when making a number of calls on a party line, space them so that others on the line may have a chance to use their telephones?

63

Motoring

If every driver would follow the rule "Do unto others as you would have others do unto you," there would be very few accidents on our highways. No one who has a license to drive can fail to appreciate the good manners of the driver who signals his turns, makes his stops smoothly, and gradually pulls into the proper lane well before making a turn. This type of consideration not only shows "good manners," but may actually save the lives of others—as well as your own.

Really fine drivers do exist, and very good ones are not uncommon; and, moreover, both these groups are aware of their own expertness. This chapter is certainly not for either of these, but for tens of thousands who in ever-increasing numbers swarm out upon the highways to have their lives saved time and again (though they don't know it) by the experts who step in between the Grim Reaper and the bad driver. And if we think seriously of the power in all of these machines running freely upon our streets and roads and realize that no examination in driving courtesy is required of one applying for a license, the wonder is not that there are accidents, but that there are not more.

SOME BAD ROAD MANNERS THAT CAUSE ACCIDENTS

One of the worst offenders (and he ought to be sent to jail to think it over) is the driver who, when the road is crowded, pulls out of a solid line of cars to steal his way forward. Finding himself in sudden danger of a head-on collision, he makes a frantic effort to push his way back into the line he has left—possibly forcing someone off the road or at the least crumpling fenders. The bad manners of any driver who shoves to get ahead, tries to beat the lights, crowds another off the road, and never considers anybody's rights but his own can easily cause a fatal motor crash.

Reprinted from "How to Drive," published by the American Automobile Association

It is hard to understand, but nevertheless quite true, that these same people in other circumstances are perfectly well behaved. The man who tried to force his way ahead of the line of cars would not think of trying to force his way ahead of others in a box-office queue; nor would he shove a fellow pedestrian off the sidewalk. Should he by unhappy accident do such a thing, he would be abject in his apology, mortified by his own rudeness. But in his car, with a palm pressed firmly on the horn, he is quite likely to swear roundly at his victim for getting in his way.

Equally dangerous is the annoying snail—long known by other unflattering sobriquets because of his insistence upon crawling along in the center of the road, or on the left, or in the passing lane of a superhighway. Behind him horns can blow, but he does not budge an inch. Or if he does, beware of his pet trick: he starts for his proper lane, but instead of staying there, goes right back, so that the passing car is forced to brake suddenly and risk being rammed by a third car—and perhaps even a fourth. And yet this same snail, when he is walking on the street, does not refuse to let another pass him by. Needless to say, courtesy demands of one who likes to crawl that he stay far over on the right side to let faster cars go by and if he won't, there ought to be a special truck of largest size detailed to push him—and keep him pushed.

Timid Caspar Milquetoast also drives at ten miles below the speed limit on a narrow, twisting road through hilly country and accumulates a long line of impatient drivers behind him. These in their exasperation end by taking desperate chances on passing too close to a curve or the top of a hill, and the net result is that Caspar is much more likely to be involved in a serious crash than if he were to drive a little faster and not exasperate the drivers behind him.

At night, an annoying and dangerous driver to meet is one who will not dim his headlights, although knowing perfectly well that other drivers facing him are helplessly blinded by the glare of his lights.

All cars now have electric directional signals that permit one to indicate the direction in which he is going to turn. It is up to the drivers to use those turn indicators—and use them invariably. A point worth emphasis is that hand signals differ in various localities, but your turn indicators are universally understood, so the driver behind you cannot possibly misinterpret your intentions.

Also, in order not to confuse the driver following you, don't put your arm down outside the car and shake ashes off your cigarette. Don't put your hand out when you throw away your cigar. Don't put your hand out and point at the scenery, and don't let anyone else in your car wave his hand out of a window.

DRINKING AND DRIVING

It is unnecessary to emphasize the menace of the drunken driver; certainly there is nothing to be said in his defense, nor can anyone want him to escape the full penalty of the law. And furthermore, not half enough emphasis is laid on the exhilarated driver who has had one or two cocktails and certainly cannot be called drunk by any standard, but who with overjoyful recklessness takes chances that he would not think of taking when he has had nothing to drink. Alcohol and gasoline do not mix!

DISCOURTEOUS HORN BLOWERS

Trumpet horns—those raucous, penetrating signals designed for use on the open road—are as out of place in city driving as hobnailed shoes in a ballroom. Another impoliteness is the unnecessary blowing of any horn in a traffic line when it can do no good and is merely annoying to others.

The sounding of a horn at pedestrians caught midstreet by a changing light is not only unkind, but may even cause the pedestrian to jump into the path of another car.

If more people realized that the horn, as the voice of the car, is in reality the voice of the driver, there would be less raucous thoughtlessness in its use. People who would never dream of bawling a vocal protest will at a moment's delay blast away on their motor horns at every hesitancy of the car ahead. No polite young man would announce his arrival to a lovely lady by standing at the curb outside her door and yoohooing. Yet this is the identical offense that so many commit who, arriving by car, sit at the wheel and blast away at the horn. A well-mannered visitor will, of course, alight and ring the door bell.

CITY DRIVING MANNERS

When driving in a city, remember that discourtesy to pedestrians can turn out to be manslaughter. Don't rush traffic lights; that is, don't start suddenly in the yellow light interval before your light has changed to green and possibly frighten pedestrians or find yourself in a collision with a crossing car whose driver has been slow in stopping. A gentleman will no more cheat the lights than cheat at cards. Don't fail, at a crossing where the lights have turned against you, to stop far enough back to be sure that you are not blocking the proper path of pedestrians crossing the street. Don't, if you can possibly help it, run through puddles and splash pedestrians or other cars; if you cannot avoid a puddle, at least slow down as much as possible. Don't almost run down someone who is trying to signal a bus or a taxi when a little consideration requires only a few seconds. Courteous drivers should, before starting on the green light, give pedestrians who are caught in the middle of the roadway a chance to get across. Be sure to avoid starting with a jerk to pass an elderly woman. Instead of hastening her, fright is likely to root her to the spot. Be sure to slow down to a crawl when you see the sign "School Crossing." You simply cannot tell when a moppet might appear out of the blue.

DRIVERS WE LIKE—AND DISLIKE

The best test of a perfect driver is that when riding with him you never find yourself driving the car. When you see a passenger involuntarily tensing his muscles and pressing his own feet on an imaginary control, this evidence subtracts by just so much from the driver's rating. Certainly the outstanding characteristic of an abominable driver is complete lack of courtesy to his passengers, almost jerking their heads off every time he stops and scaring them half to death with his carelessness.

We are all made nervous by the driver who keeps looking out all the time, expatiating on the view and paying no apparent attention to what is happening on the road. Or the one who turns around to talk to those on the back seat (who can't hear what he says because they are so busy praying that the car will stay on the road). Or the one who carelessly lets go of the wheel while he lights a cigarette or tries to get a new station on the radio, meanwhile letting his car meander toward the ditch or over toward the wrong side of the road.

Another bad-mannered driver is the one in a hurry. Among the thousands of car accidents listed on the police blotters, at least half are said to be made by people who have not learned to discipline themselves to be on time. The driver, suddenly becoming conscious that he should have left home earlier, flings his good driving manners to the wind, starts weaving in and out of lines, clipping red lights, pushing his way, and taking chances which he would never take if he were not in a hurry!

DRIVING SPORTSMANSHIP

The good sportsmanship of all well-bred drivers is indicated in the following exactions:

It is just as unfair and unsporting to lag when the traffic light turns green (holding up the cars behind you) as to beat the light by starting while it is still red.

The fair-minded driver, if driving slowly, keeps well over to the right so that another, who may be anxious to get somewhere, may overtake him safely. When making turns, it is not much to ask of a driver to turn the steering wheel enough to enable him to stay on the right when he turns right and on the left when he turns left. The boorish driver who swings to the left before a right turn, and vice versa, is plainly a person so selfish or so lazy that he would rather risk his own and the following driver's life than turn the steering wheel the little extra required to make the sharper turn from the proper lane.

Reprinted from "How to Drive," published by the American Automobile Association

Well-bred people neither monopolize space for two parked cars nor park so close to others as to prevent them from pulling out. In marked parking places, thoughtful people stay within the marks.

It shows thoughtfulness to slow up a little at a side road and let a car whose driver has been trying to join your unbroken procession come into the line ahead of you.

AS FOR THE MANNERS OF PEDESTRIANS . . .

When anyone is run over by an automobile, the driver's guilt is *invariably* taken for granted. Often the blame belongs to him, but often again it does not. In other words, motor manners are every bit as important to those who want to escape being injured as to those who want to avoid injuring them. First rules for pedestrians include:

Don't cross before the light turns green or the signal reads "Walk." Don't cross streets in the middle of a block. Don't dart forward after hiding behind a parked car and imagine that an oncoming driver, whom you yourself could not see, could know by means of clairvoyance that you were there! Don't, when the lights change while you are in the middle of the street, turn and run back to the side you started from. If you keep on going exactly as you were, drivers will automatically wait and give you time to pass in front of their cars. But not one of those you have already passed can possibly be prepared to have you about-face and suddenly dash back again in front of his wheels.

One of the serious causes of pedestrian accidents is the practically universal (and a very natural) habit of walking on the right side of a road that has no sidewalk. This habit, obviously acquired from the correctness of this position on a sidewalk, is a not infrequent cause of accidents as well as annoying delays to car drivers. A pedestrian on the right side cannot see a car overtaking him. If another car is coming from the other direction, the pedestrian unfortunately stays on his right-hand half of the road, directly in the path of the unseen or unheard overtaking car. Pedestrians should walk on the left-hand side of the road—always.

SOME TIPS FOR MOTOR TRIPS

YOUR CAR AND EQUIPMENT

When starting out on a motor trip that will take you away from your normal garage or repair shop, make certain that your equipment is in the best possible condition. Tires are the most important item—never start on a trip on which you will undoubtedly be driving at higher speeds than you normally would around your home, with worn tires or, if you are likely to find winter driving conditions, without snow tires or chains. Your fuel, oil, brakes, and automatic transmission should be checked before starting, and frequently during the trip. In strange territory you have no way of knowing when you will find the next gas station. Windshield-wiper blades should be replaced if rough or worn, and headlights, turn indicators, and brake lights checked. And of course, your car registration must be in order and easily available, as well as your driver's license.

AVOID FATIGUE

On long trips it is essential to make frequent stops to stretch your legs, take some refreshment, and allow your engine and tires to cool off.

If you are accompanied by a licensed and capable driver, you should, of course, take turns at the wheel. A good rule is to stop and change drivers every hundred miles or every two hours, whichever comes first.

If you are stopping at motels along the way, it is wise to make a reservation for the following evening before you set off in the morning. The many chains of excellent motels all over the United States are delighted to help you estimate the distance you will cover and call ahead, free of charge, to one of their member motels, to reserve a room for that night. You will find yourself much less tired if you plan to arrive at your destination by four in the afternoon to allow time for a rest, a little sightseeing if there are attractions in the neighborhood, and a leisurely dinner.

TRAVELING WITH CHILDREN

Traveling with children who are old enough to read, write, or play games need not be a problem. By taking along a supply of papers, crayons, or one of the excellent game books that are sold just for the purpose, the time can be made to fly. Verbal games, too, such as "Twenty Questions," help to pass the hours. You may find that more frequent stops are necessary—young stomachs seem to demand a steady flow of nibbles when motoring—but the stops will help to avoid restless wiggling while in the car.

For little children, a mattress laid in the back of the station wagon, or a little play pen with a well-padded mat on the back seat is a boon to the parents. The baby is free to move about safely, rather than endure the restraint of a car seat or his mother's lap. Even the older child will enjoy the luxury of being able to stretch out on such a mattress if you can afford to use the space in this way, and many children will sleep away many hours if they can lie down comfortably.

FOR COMFORT AND SAFETY

Many states require that all new cars be equipped with safety belts. If you do not have them, I can only recommend most strongly that you have them installed. Figures on accident deaths prove that while they do not prevent accidents, fatalities are far less frequent among drivers and passengers wearing properly installed belts or shoulder harnesses. They should be snugly fastened, so that you are not thrown hard *against* the belt by a sudden stop.

It is an excellent idea to keep a pair of sun glasses in the glove compartment of your car. If they are always there, you will never be caught unprepared by an unexpected change in the weather, and many people find that prolonged glare can cause severe headaches.

Your clothing should be loose and comfortable. A girl who is comfortable in slacks or shorts will find that they are excellent for traveling. They allow maximum mobility, and now that so many travelers stop at motels, she need not be seen in public until after she has had a chance to wash and change. A man, even though he may be dressed in a business suit, will probably be more comfortable if he removes his tie and replaces his jacket with a loose sweater or, if it is warm, drives in his shirt with the collar loosened.

IN AN EMERGENCY

If you do, in spite of all your precautions, have an emergency such as a flat tire or a broken fan belt, *pull off the road*, raise the hood, and tie a white handkerchief or cloth to your door handle. This is the universal signal of distress on the road, and any policeman, and often a kind-hearted motorist, will stop to offer assistance. On a superhighway, stay near your car, or in it. On a smaller road, if there is a house or shop nearby where you can go to call for help, walk well off the road and return to the car immediately after making your call.

CAR POOLS

Many thousands of Americans go to work in a "car pool." It is a practical and economical arrangement and means that other members of their families may have the car except on those days when it is their turn to provide the transportation.

For those who are about to join a car pool there are several basic rules of courtesy to be observed.

1. Be on time! If you keep the others waiting, you may be causing three or four or five others to be penalized for their late arrival at work.

2. Don't carry quantities of articles, and if you must take a package or two, don't pile them where they will obstruct the driver's view, either directly or in the rear-view mirror.

3. Don't open or close windows without asking permission of the other passengers.

4. Don't bring an extra passenger without asking the driver if there is room. Some drivers do not object to three in the front seat, for example, but to others this might be a considerable annoyance.

5. Ask the permission of the other riders before smoking. When you do smoke, make sure that a window is opened, if only a little, to allow the smoke to escape.

6. If you are a woman, don't use the rear-view mirror to fix your make-up. Carry a compact with a mirror or a small mirror in your purse.

7. If you must carry an umbrella when it rains, shake it well (and your raincoat, too) before getting in the car instead of soaking your neighbor.

8. If you are not planning to use the car pool, let the driver know in advance so that he does not go out of his way to pick you up or wait for you unnecessarily before continuing his trip.

64

For those who smoke

The universal custom of smoking in nearly all places at nearly all hours and by all sorts of people makes it seem advisable to gather in this special chapter rules that will permit the enjoyment of smoking by those who smoke with the least unhappiness to those who don't, as well as to each other.

TIMES WHEN NO ONE MAY SMOKE

One may not smoke in a church, or during any religious service or ceremonial proceedings. One may not smoke in a sickroom unless the patient himself is smoking. Good taste still forbids smoking by a woman on a city street. It should be unnecessary to say that no one should think of smoking or carrying a lighted cigarette when dancing.

Smoking is forbidden on local buses and on some coaches on the railroad. These cars are clearly marked "No Smoking."

Smoking is permitted in the mezzanine seats in most movie houses —and of course in all eating places, but it is true that the theaters devoted to plays are still smoke-free.

Smoking is forbidden in most museums, although some have designated areas where it is allowed.

To these restrictions should be added those in business (regulated by the rules of each firm) and those of consideration for the customs of the community which you may be visiting or for the prejudices of the people with whom you personally come in contact.

Most important of all, and so frequently disobeyed, never, never light a cigarette, pipe, or cigar when a "No Smoking" sign is displayed.

WHEN GUESTS SMOKE

The answer to the hostesses who ask how they can protect their possessions from careless guests is that hospitality need never be helpless. It is true that after a guest has burned a hole in the upholstery or a groove on a table edge, nothing can be done about it, although the guest should insist on paying for whatever repairs are necessary. But when a hostess sees a smoker pick up an ornament of value to use in place of an ash tray, she can certainly take it away and put an ash tray in its place. Perhaps she says nothing or perhaps she smiles and says, "'Let me give you this," as though she were thinking of the smoker's convenience.

The sensible solution for the wise hostess is to see to it that there is an ash tray within easy reach of every seat in her house that may be occupied by a smoking guest. A thoughtful hostess, even one who does not smoke herself, will see that there are cigarette boxes, with fresh cigarettes in them, and a lighter that is filled and that works, or plenty of match boxes, for the comfort of her smoking guests. Ash trays should be reasonably large and have a wide lip or groove to hold a cigarette.

Cigars need be passed only after dinner and when the ladies have left the dining room.

SMOKING DON'TS

First of all, it is unforgivable to lay a cigarette (or cigar) on the edge of a table or other piece of furniture—ever! Forgetting it and letting it burn a charred groove on a table edge or a brown scar on a marble mantel is merely the result of putting it down on the wrong place to begin with. Find an ash tray to lay it on—or ask for one.

Striking a match directly toward someone is dangerous—the head may fly off and cause a painful burn.

Never press a cigarette out without being sure that the object pressed on is intended for that purpose. Cigarettes put out against lamp bases, ornaments, and the like may mar or destroy objects of value. And potted plants do not thrive on ashes or unburned tobacco!

Lighted cigarettes should not be thrown into fireplaces. If the fire is laid, a roaring blaze started on a hot July day may be the reward of such carelessness, and if it is not, remains of cigarettes or unburned filter tips look dreadfully messy in a freshly-swept fireplace. Never toss a cigarette out the window—it may land on an awning or the top of someone's new convertible parked outside.

Other don'ts include such untidiness as spilling ashes on the floor or upholstery, or throwing filter-tipped cigarettes on a lawn or terrace where the fire-proof, rain-proof tip will remain until some one rakes or sweeps it away. And worst of all is the smoker who leaves his lighted end in the ash tray to burn itself out, making even the other smokers present ill from the smell.

CIGARETTES AT THE TABLE

Whether it is proper to smoke at table depends upon the setting of the places. If each place is set with cigarettes, a lighter, and an ash tray, naturally people may smoke as soon as they choose. But in the houses of those who do not put them on the table or who have them passed only after dessert, it is still bad manners to light one's own cigarette and smoke throughout the meal.

It is also extremely bad manners and thoughtless to pay no attention to whether smoke from the cigarette you are holding is blowing into the face of someone who may not be smoking.

A FEW HINTS ON SMOKING MANNERS

Smokers should carry their own cigarettes. Even though the thoughtful hostess has filled her cigarette boxes (to put filter-tips in some boxes and "regulars" in others is thoughtful), she will appreciate the guest who does not depend entirely on her supply.

When a man is about to smoke, it is polite to offer a cigarette to those next to him, or in his immediate group, but he need not pass them further afield. And a warning to the ladies—the feminine cigarette "sponge" is no more popular than the male.

A man should light a woman's cigarette if he is close to her, but not if he is on the other side of a table or if it would be awkward in any way.

A woman smoker should carry her own matches or lighter and *use* them. She only looks ridiculous sitting with a dangling cigarette, waiting for a group of men to break up their conversation in order to provide her with a light.

Pipe smokers must exert extra caution when emptying a pipe since it sometimes takes a sharp rap to loosen the burned tobacco in the bowl. They should select a large sturdy ash tray, for they may shatter a delicate glass or fine china receptacle or, if it is too small, find their ashes spraying all over the table top.

And two final words to the cigar smoker. First, don't leave cigar butts in ash trays. They *do* smell, and they *are* unattractive in appearance. Unless you see that some one is prepared to remove the ash tray when you are finished smoking, try to find another means of disposing of the finished cigar—into a lighted fire, down the toilet, anywhere, as long as it is out of sight.

Second, you *must* ask permission to smoke a cigar in mixed company. Naturally, when cigars are passed to the men after dinner or offered (traditionally) in an office to celebrate the birth of a baby or at any male gathering, you are expected to smoke them, but many women find cigar smoke unpleasant, if not actually nauseating, and your popularity with the opposite sex will quickly wane if you do not determine the feeling of your companion before lighting a cigar.

65

In clubs

A society is an organization composed of persons who band together for a common purpose and are not infrequently obligated to one another by bonds of brotherhood. A club is an organization composed of persons who have joined it for their individual convenience or pleasure. Its membership, whether composed of men or women or both, may be limited to a dozen or may include several thousands, and the procedure of joining may be easy or difficult, according to the type of club and the standing of the would-be-member.

Membership in many athletic associations may be had by walking in and paying dues, and many country golf clubs are as free to the public as country inns. But joining an exclusive club is a very different matter. To be eligible for membership in such a club, a man must have among the members friends who like him enough to be willing to propose him and second him and write letters for him; furthermore he must be disliked by no one—at least not so much that a member might raise a serious objection to his company.

There are two ways of joining a club: by invitation and by having application made for you. To join by invitation means that you are invited when the club is started to be one of the founders or charter members, or if you are a distinguished citizen, you may at the invitation of the governors become an honorary member; or in a small or informal club you may become an ordinary member by invitation or at the suggestion of the governors that you would be welcome. A charter member pays dues, but not always an initiation fee. An honorary member pays neither dues nor initiation fee; he is really a permanent guest of the club, or a temporary one, as in the case of a mayor, for example, who may be an honorary member just for the duration of his term in office. A life member is one who pays his dues for twenty years or so in a lump sum and is thereafter exempted from dues even though the annual dues should be greatly increased in later years or he should live to be a hundred.

Different clubs offer different types of membership. At a country club, you might be a "golfing member," using only the golfing facilities, or a "house member" using only the restaurant and facilities of the club house. Or it may depend on where you live—the ordinary members of a club might be resident, meaning that they live or have their office within fifty miles of the club, or nonresident—living beyond that distance and paying smaller dues but having the same privileges.

BECOMING A MEMBER

"PUTTING UP" A NAME

Since no sensible man is likely to want to join a club in which the members are not his friends, he says to a member of his family or an intimate friend, "Do you mind putting me up for the Nearby Club? I think that Dick would second me." The friend answers, "Delighted to do it!" and Dick says the same.

More likely the suggestion to join comes from a friend, who remarks one day, "Why don't you join the Nearby Club? It would be very convenient for you." The other replies, "I should like to," and the friend says, "Let me put you up, and I'll ask Dick to second you." And he arranges with Dick to do so.

It must be remembered that a man has no right to ask anyone who is not really one of his best friends to propose or second him. It is an awkward thing to refuse in the first place; in the second, it involves considerable effort and on occasion a great deal of annoyance, to say nothing of responsibility.

For example, let us suppose that Jim Struthers asks Donald Cameron to propose him and Henry Bancroft to second him. Jim's name is written in the book kept for the purpose and signed by both proposer and seconder:

Struthers, James
  Proposer: Donald Cameron
  Seconder: Henry Bancroft

Nothing more is done until the name is posted—meaning that it appears among a list of names put up on the bulletin board in the clubhouse. In many clubs, a list of proposed names is also sent to each member. It is then the duty of Cameron and Bancroft each to write a letter of endorsement to the governors of the club, to be read by that body when they hold the meeting at which Struther's name comes up for election.

Board of Governors,
The Nearby Club
Dear Sirs:

It affords me much pleasure to propose for membership in The Nearby Club Mr. James Struthers. I have known Mr. Struthers for many years and consider him qualified in every way for membership.

He is a graduate of Northsouthern University, class of 1941, and was a member of the Center Club. He is now with the firm of Jones, Fairbanks, & Co.

Yours very truly,
Donald Cameron

In most clubs, the number of members is limited by the bylaws. Therefore, there may be a waiting list, necessitating a considerable delay before your name comes up for consideration. Before making a decision as to which clubs you wish to join, it is wise to find out about the length of waiting time, and discuss the possibilities with your sponsor.

MEETING THE GOVERNORS

Cameron must also at once select with Struthers six or more of his friends who are members of the club (but not governors) and ask them to write letters endorsing him. Furthermore, the candidate cannot come up for election unless he knows several of the governors personally so that they can vouch for him at the meeting. Therefore, Cameron and Bancroft must take Struthers to several governors and personally present him.

At many clubs the governors appoint an hour on several weekend afternoons before elections when they are in the visitors' rooms at the clubhouse in order to meet the candidates whom their proposers must present. Or a large reception may be held, attended by the governors, the candidates, and their sponsors.

IMPORTANCE OF GOOD LETTERS OF ENDORSEMENT

Jim Struthers, having popular and well-known sponsors and also being very well liked himself, is elected with no difficulty.

But take the case of young Breezy. He was put up by two not very well-known members who wrote half-hearted endorsements themselves and did nothing about getting letters from others. They knew none of the governors, and trusted in the fact that two members who knew

Breezy slightly would do. His casual proposers forgot that enemies write letters as well as friends—and that, moreover, enmity is sometimes active whereas friendship is often passive. Two men who disliked his "manner" wrote that they considered him "unsuitable." As he had no friends strong enough to stand up for him, he was turned down. A man is rarely blackballed, as such an action could not fail to injure him in the eyes of the world. (The expression "blackball" comes from the custom of voting for a member by putting a white ball in a ballot box, or against him by putting in a black one.) If a candidate is likely to receive a blackball— two disqualify him; in some clubs, one—the governors do not vote on him at all, but inform the proposer that the name of his candidate had better be withdrawn, which is almost invariably done, rather than run any risk of the stigma of a blackball. Later on, if the objection to him is disproved or overcome, his name may again be put up.

QUALIFICATIONS FOR ELECTION

The more popular the candidate, the less work for his proposer and seconder. A stranger, if he is not a member of the representative club in his own city, would need strong friends to elect him to an exclusive club in another community and an unpopular man should never be proposed.

However, in all but very rare instances, events run smoothly; the candidate is voted on at a meeting of the board of governors and is elected. A notice is mailed to him next morning, telling him that he has been elected and that his initiation fee and his dues make a total of so much. The candidate at once draws his check for the amount and mails it. As soon as the club secretary has had ample time to receive the check, the new member is free to use the club as much or as little as he likes.

THE NEW MEMBER

The new member usually, though not necessarily, goes to a club for the first time with his proposer or his seconder or at least with an old member, who briefs him on unwritten information: "That chair in the window is where old Snodgrass always sits. Don't occupy it when you see him coming in or he will be disagreeable to everybody for a week." Or "They always play double stakes at this table, so don't sit at it unless you mean to." Or "There's an unwritten rule that we never walk on the grass in the circle." "The roasts are always good, and that waiter is the best in the room." And so on.

A new member is given or should ask for a copy of the Club Book, which contains, besides the list of the members, the constitution and the bylaws or "house rules," which he must study carefully and be sure to obey.

COUNTRY CLUBS

Country clubs vary greatly in both characteristics and expense. A few are more expensive to belong to than any clubs in New York and are precisely the same in matters of membership and management. It is also quite as difficult to be elected to them as to any of the exclusive clubs in the cities—more so, if anything—inasmuch as they are open to the family and friends of every member. Whereas in a man's city club his membership gives the privilege of the club to no one but himself personally, in a country club his family and possible guests must be as agreeable to the governors as he is.

Nearly all country clubs have, however, one open door unknown to city clubs. People taking houses in the neighborhood or vacation visitors in a resort are often granted "season privileges"; that is, on being proposed by a member and upon paying a season's subscription, new householders are accepted as transient guests. In some clubs, this subscription may be indefinitely renewed; in others, a man must come up for regular election at the end of three or six months' or a year's time.

Apart from the few that may be called very exclusive country clubs, there are hundreds—more likely thousands—that have very simple requirements for membership. Merely having one or two members vouch for a candidate's integrity and good behavior is sufficient.

In almost all country clubs, the atmosphere is less formal than in a city club. Members speak to each other without introductions, form tennis games and golf foursomes with comparative strangers, and otherwise behave in a more casual and informal manner.

WOMEN'S CLUBS

Except that the luxurious women's club has an atmosphere that a man rarely knows how to give to the interior of a house, no matter how architecturally perfect it may be, there is no difference between women's and men's clubs.

In every state of the Union, there are women's clubs of every kind and grade: social, political, sports, professional. Some are housed in enormous and elegant buildings designed especially for them and others in only a room or two, usually in a hotel.

When the pioneer women's club of New York was started—a club that aspired to be in the same class as the most important men's club— various governors of the latter were unflatteringly outspoken. Women could not possibly run a club as it should be run—it was unthinkable that they should be foolish enough to attempt it! And the husbands and fathers of the founders expected to have to dig down into their pockets to make up the deficit, forgetting entirely that the running of a club is merely the running of a house on a large scale and that women, not men, are the housekeepers. Today, no clubs are more nearly perfect in appointment or more smoothly run than the best women's clubs.

IN THE CITY CLUB

Good manners in clubs are the same as good manners elsewhere—only a little more so. A club is for the pleasure and convenience of many; it is never intended as a stage setting for a star or clown or monologist. There is no place where a person has greater need of restraint and consideration for the reserves of others than in a club. In every well-appointed one there is a reading room or library where conversation is discouraged. There are books and easy chairs and good light for reading by day and night, and it is one of the unspoken rules not to speak to anybody who is reading or writing.

It is courteous of a governor or habitual member, on noticing a new member or a visitor—especially one who seems to be rather at a loss—to go up and speak to him; but the latter should not be the one to speak first. In the dining rooms of many clubs, there is a large table, sometimes known as the social table, where members who are lunching alone may sit and where the conversation is general, and all are expected to talk whether they are friends or total strangers. Through no intent to be disagreeable, but just because it is not customary, members of certain clubs in New York do not speak to those they do not know. It does not occur to them that strangers feel slighted, until they themselves are given the same medicine.

The fundamental rule for behavior in a club is the same as in the living room of a private house. In other words, heels have no place on furniture; ashes belong in ash trays; books should not be abused; and all evidence of exercising should be confined to the courts or gymnasium, and the locker or dressing room.

VISITORS IN A CLUB

When a men's club moves into a new clubhouse, it is quite usual for the members to give an opening reception to which ladies are invited to see the house. After this, in most clubs, women are barred except perhaps for one day a year on which they are invited to a cocktail party or dinner.

A well-known and most distinguished men's club in New England has an annex with dining rooms to which ladies as well as gentlemen who are not members are admitted; and this annex plan has been followed by other clubs elsewhere.

All men's clubs have private dining rooms where members can give dinners that include nonmembers, either men who are local residents but do not belong to the club or men who are merely visiting the city.

When a woman gives a lunch or any party in a club, either a women's club, or in the "open" dining room of a men's club, she waits for her guests in the lobby, entrance hall, or, if there is one, the reception room. As her guests arrive, they join her and stand or sit near her.

If the room is filled with others, she herds her own group, as it were, a little apart. When all have arrived, they go to the dining room and sit at the table, which should always have been prepared in advance for them. And if they are more than four, the food should have been ordered in advance and the meal be ready to serve as soon as they sit down.

In every club in the United States, a member is allowed to introduce a stranger—one who lives at least fifty miles away—for a varying length of time determined by the bylaws of the club. In some clubs, guests may be put up for a day only; in others, the privilege extends for two weeks or more. Many clubs allow each member a certain number of visitors a year; in others, visitors are unlimited. In many city clubs, the same guest cannot be introduced twice within the year. In country clubs, members usually may have an unlimited number of visitors. When these are golf or tennis players, the host is responsible for greens' fees or court charges.

As a rule, when a member introduces a stranger, he takes him to the club personally, writes his name in the visitors' book, and introduces him to those who may be in the room at the time—very possibly asking another member whom he knows particularly well to look out for his guest. If for some reason it is not possible for the stranger's host to take him to the club, he writes to the secretary of the club for a card of introduction.

> Secretary
> The Town Club
> Dear Sir [*or* Dear Mr. Jones]:
>> Kindly send Mr. A. M. Strangleigh, of Wilkes Barre, Pa., a card extending the privileges of the Club for one week.
>> Mr. Strangleigh is staying at the Carlton House.
>>> Yours very truly,
>>> *Henry Bancroft*

Note the degree of formality. One does not write "Dear Jim," because this is not a personal letter, but a formal request to be put on file.

The secretary then sends a card to Mr. Strangleigh.

> The Town Club
> Extends its privileges to
> *Mr. Strangleigh*
> from *Jan.* 7 to *Jan.* 14
> Through the courtesy of
> *Mr. Henry Bancroft*

Mr. Strangleigh goes to the club by himself. A visitor who has been given a card to a club has, during the time of his visit, all the privileges of a member except that he is not allowed to introduce others to the club and he cannot give a dinner in a private dining room. The guest must arrange at the club's office to have his charges rendered to himself—he must be scrupulous about asking for his bill upon leaving and pay it immediately and without question. Otherwise his bill must be paid by the member who issued the invitation, and such an invitation never means automatically that the member is his host.

The visitor's status throughout his stay is founded on the courtesy of the member who introduced him, and he should try to show an equal courtesy to everyone about him. He should remember not to intrude on the privacy of the members he does not know. He has no right to criticize the management, the rules, or the organization of the club. In short, he behaves exactly as a guest would behave in the private home of his host.

UNBREAKABLE RULES

Failure to pay one's debts or behavior unbefitting a gentleman is cause for expulsion from every club, a disgrace that is looked upon in much the same light as a dishonorable discharge from the Armed Forces. In certain cases, expulsion for debt may seem unfair, because one may find himself in unexpectedly straitened circumstances, and the greatest fault or crime could scarcely bring down upon a man a more severe penalty than being expelled from his club.

If a man cannot afford to belong to a club, he must resign while he is still in good standing. If later on he is able to rejoin, his name is put at the head of the waiting list; if he was considered a desirable member, he is re-elected at the next meeting of the governors. But a man who has been expelled—unless he can show that his expulsion was unjust—can never again belong to that club, nor probably can he be elected to any other club, because the fact he has been expelled from one will almost certainly come up should another ever consider him for election. And this would cancel his chances for membership.

RESIGNING FROM A CLUB

When one wishes to resign from a club, it is necessary to write a letter of resignation to the secretary well before the date on which the next yearly dues will be due. The letter would read something like this:

Mrs. James Town
Secretary, Colonial Club, New York
My dear Mrs. Town,

It is with great regret that I find it necessary to resign from the club and to ask you therefore to present my resignation at the next meeting of the governors.

Very sincerely,
Mary Smartlington

At the table

All the rules of table manners have been made for a very few basic reasons, and keeping them in mind can solve many problems automatically. There are, in addition, a number of trifling decrees of etiquette, some of them unreasonable and silly, others merely finicky. No one will disapprove if you follow the latter quietly and without ostentation, but before you concern yourself with them, you should be sure that you have thoroughly mastered the basic ones and act accordingly.

THE "WHYS" OF GOOD TABLE MANNERS

Most rules for the table were made to avoid ugliness. To let anyone see what you have in your mouth is offensive. To make a noise is to suggest one of the lower animals. To make a mess is disgusting. But if you consider, before doing something, what impression it will make on the others at the table, few problems will arise that cannot be solved by common sense alone.

The second "why"—and it should not even need mention—involves the safety of the eater and those around him. To saw away at one's meat with elbows high is to risk hitting one's neighbor. To wave one's arms about is to endanger one's own back if just then a waitress is about to serve a plate of scalding soup.

The third is the general principle that we have met before: Do not attract attention to yourself in public. Chairs scraped on the floor, knives and forks rattled against the plate, and other unnecessary noises can only cause disapproval among those near by.

A certain easy gentleness will prevent many an unfortunate experience at table. It will avoid the cramming, jabbing, clashing, and other harsh uglinesses that offend one's table companions. It will do much to keep accidents from happening, and it will be noticed, if at all, with pleasure and appreciation.

ARRIVING AT THE TABLE

Going into the dining room at a formal dinner presents a special and, for most of us, not too common situation (which is discussed in Chapter 24). At the informal gatherings and family meals that all of us have each day, a man holds the chair for the woman on his right. But if the men or boys do not arrive simultaneously with the women, as may happen when Mother calls, "Dinner's ready" to her home-working children, the women (and girls) seat themselves without delay.

GRACE BEFORE MEALS

The custom of giving a family blessing or thanks before meals is a very gracious one though it is not observed as widely as it used to be. Some families are seated with bowed heads and touch nothing until the grace has been said; others remain standing—both forms are correct.

Usually the mother or the father offers the prayer, but it is sweet to allow the younger members of the family to take turns in asking grace. There are a number of shorter and longer variations, but the following three are typical examples.

Bless us, O Lord, and these Thy gifts, which we are about to receive from Thy bounty. Through Christ our Lord. Amen.

Lift up your hands toward the Sanctuary and bless the Lord. Blessed art Thou, O Lord our God, King of the universe, who bringest forth bread from the earth. Amen.

Bless, O Lord, this food to our use, and us to Thy service, and make us ever mindful of the needs of others, in Jesus' Name. Amen.

POSTURE AT THE TABLE

The distance from the table at which it is best to sit is a matter of personal comfort. One should not sit so close that his elbows are bent like a cricket's, nor so far back that food is likely to be dropped in transit from plate to mouth.

Elbows are *never* put on the table while one is actually eating. To sit with the left elbow propped on the table while eating with the right hand or to prop the right one on the table while lifting fork or glass to the mouth must be avoided.

Elbows are seen on the table in some situations when they are not only permitted but are actually necessary—especially in restaurants when people are lunching or dining at a small table of two or four, and it is impossible to make oneself heard above music or conversation and at the same time not be heard at other tables nearby, without leaning far forward. And in leaning forward, a woman's figure makes a more graceful outline supported on her elbows than doubled forward over her hands in her lap as though she were in pain! *At home*, when there is no reason for leaning across the table, there is no reason for elbows. And *at a dinner of ceremony*, elbows on the table are rarely if ever seen, except perhaps at the ends of the table, where again one has to lean forward in order to talk to a companion at a distance across the table corner. And even in these special situations, *never* when one is eating.

Slouching or slumping at the table is most unattractive, too, and tipping one's chair—a most unfortunate habit among young people—is unforgivable. It not only looks dreadfully sloppy, but it is fatal to the back legs of the chair.

Ideal posture at the table is to sit straight but not stiffly, leaning slightly against the back of the chair. Your hands, while not actually eating, are best off in your lap; this position will automatically prevent you from fussing with implements, playing with breadcrumbs, drawing on the tablecloth, and so forth. Hands should also be kept away from the face, from nervous scratching, and from twisting or touching the hair.

It is correct to reach for anything on the table that does not necessitate stretching across your neighbor or leaning far across the table yourself. When something is out of reach, simply ask the person nearest to it, "Would you please pass the jelly, Mrs. Betts?"

THE NAPKIN

As soon as you are seated, you put your napkin in your lap. It does not matter how you do it, so long as you do not give it a violent shake to open it up. You take it from the table, put it on your lap (if it is large enough, you may tuck a corner under you to keep it from sliding off, or if it is not, you arrange it as safely as you can), and unfold it as much as necessary with both hands.

When using the napkin, avoid wiping your mouth as with a washcloth. Blotting or patting the lips is much more delicate.

When the meal is finished, or if you leave the table during the meal, put the napkin on the right side of your place, or if the plates have been removed, in the center. It should not be refolded, nor should it be crumpled up; rather it is laid on the table in loose folds so that it does not spread itself out. At a dinner party, the hostess lays her napkin on the table as a signal that the meal is over, and the guests then lay their napkins on the table—not before.

SERVING ONESELF AND BEING SERVED

When helping yourself, the first rule is to pay attention to what you are doing and not handle a serving fork or spoon in such a way as to scatter food particles over either the floor, the table, your neighbor or yourself.

Anything served on a piece of toast is lifted off on the toast, unless you don't want the toast, in which case you may take the quail or help yourself to asparagus and leave the toast in the dish. For sweetbreads, mushrooms on toast—foods that seem to be an arrangement—take the toast and all on the spoon and hold it in place with the fork. If there is only a serving spoon and no fork in the dish, you must balance the food with great care.

When helping yourself, you say nothing; but when declining a dish offered by a waiter, you say, "No, thank you." Your voice is barely audible and in fact a negative shake of the head and "No thanks" more nearly describes the usual refusal.

Gravy should be put *on* the meat, and the condiment, pickles, and jelly *at the side* of whatever they accompany. Olives, radishes, or celery are put on the bread and butter plate if there is one, otherwise on the edge of the plate from which one is eating. Salted nuts are put on the tablecloth or place mat.

When passing your plate to the head of the table for a second helping, always leave knife and fork on the plate and be sure the handles are far enough on not to topple off.

It is good manners to take at least a little of every dish that is offered to you, but if it is a food you especially dislike and if you are among friends, you may refuse with a polite "No, thank you." In fact, because it is definitely impolite not to finish the food on your plate, it is better to refuse it; that which remains on the platter can be used again, while that which remains on your plate must be thrown away. You need not give your reason for refusing a dish, but if it is because of an allergy, diet, or other physical cause, you may avoid hurting your hostess' feelings if you quietly tell her your problem, always without drawing the attention of the entire table.

WHEN TO START EATING

At a small table of two, four, or even six people, when the delay will not be sufficient to cause the food to become cold or the soufflé to fall, it is certainly polite to wait to start eating until all have been served. In this case, the hostess should pick up her implement first, and the others follow suit.

If the group is larger, however, it is *not* necessary to wait until all have been served. The hostess, if she is at all aware of her guest's comfort, will say, as soon as the first two or three guests have their food, "Please start—your dinner will only get cold if you wait," and the guests take her at her word and start immediately. If the hostess says nothing and you realize that her attention has been devoted to serving or supervising, or that she has simply forgotten to say anything, it is not incorrect to pick up your spoon or fork after five or six people have been served, and the others will soon follow your lead. At family meals, as Mother or Father fills and passes the plates, the children should say "May I please begin?" if they are not old enough to be expected to wait.

There should never be any question of which silver to use: *You always start with the implement farthest from the plate.* This question arises again and again, and the answer is always the same, with one exception. If the table is incorrectly set, possibly by a maid who is not trained or experienced, and the error is such that you cannot use the implement for the course that its position indicates, you must, of course, choose the next one that is appropriate. For example, if the small shellfish fork has been put next to the plate, you would not use the dinner fork for the shrimp cocktail, leaving the little fork for the main course, even though they were placed in that order. Otherwise, you assume that the table is correctly set, and starting at the outside, you work your way with each course toward the center.

USING THE KNIFE AND FORK

The proper way to use the knife and fork can best be explained by the accompanying illustrations. Study them carefully and you will see that they depict easy and graceful ways of cutting food and bringing it to your mouth.

The American custom of "zig-zag" eating (changing the fork

from left to right hand after cutting meat) is not incorrect, but it is unnecessarily complicated. Therefore, it does not have as pleasing an appearance as the simpler method of leaving the fork in your left hand, that is, raising the meat to your mouth, after cutting it, with the fork still in the same hand rather than turning the fork over and switching it to your right.

Dessert may be eaten with spoon or fork or both. Stewed fruit is held in place with the fork and cut and eaten with the spoon. Peaches or other very juicy fruits are peeled and then eaten with knife and fork, but dry fruits, such as apples, may be cut and then eaten with the fingers. Incidentally, *never* wipe hands that have fruit juice on them on a cloth napkin without first using a fingerbowl, because fruit juices leave injurious stains.

FINGERS OR FORKS

All juicy or soft fruit and all cake is best eaten with a fork; in most cases it is a matter of dexterity rather than rule. If you are able to eat a peach or ripe pear in your fingers and not smear your face, let juice run down, or make a sucking noise, you are the one in a thousand who *may*, and with utmost propriety, continue the feat. If you can eat a Napoleon or a cream puff and not let the cream ooze out on the far side, you need not use a fork. But if you cannot eat something—no matter what it is—without getting it all over your fingers, you must use a fork, and when necessary, a spoon or a knife also.

PUSHERS

There is no better pusher than a piece of dry crust. Lacking this, the knife is also correct—if properly used. Held in the left hand in the same position as it is when held in the right hand, with the tip of the blade helping to guide and hold each mouthful for the fork to lift, it is a natural motion in no way incorrect.

A more conspicuous way of using the knife as a barricade is often dexterously and unobjectionably done by well-mannered men (though rarely practiced by women) by holding the whole length of the knife blade, sharp edge down, as a barrier and pushing the fork against it.

OTHER THAN THE MAIN COURSE

SOUPS

Either clear soup or thick soup may be served in a cup with one handle or with handles on both sides. After taking a spoonful or two, if the soup is cool enough, you may pick up the cup, using both hands if it has two handles, or you may continue to use your spoon.

Clear soups are often served in a soup plate rather than a cup. When the level of the soup is so low that you must tip the plate to avoid scraping the bottom nosily, lift the near edge in your left hand and tip the plate away from you. Then the soup may be spooned away from you or toward you, whichever is less awkward.

BREAD AND BUTTER

Bread should always be broken into moderate-sized pieces—but not necessarily single mouthful bits—with the fingers before being eaten. If it is to be buttered, a piece is held on the edge of the bread-and-butter plate, or the place plate, and enough butter spread on it for a mouthful or two at a time, with a butter knife. If there is no butter knife, use any other knife you find available.

This buttering of bread is not an important rule. There are always common-sense exceptions. For instance, hot biscuits can of course be buttered immediately, since they please most palates only when the butter is quickly and thoroughly melted. Bread must never, however, be held flat on the palm and buttered with the hand held in the air. If a table knife is used, care must be taken not to smear food particles from the knife onto the butter. Jellies and jams as well as butter are spread on bread with a knife, never with a fork, though you do put butter on vegetables and jelly on meat with a fork.

BREAD AND GRAVY

Certainly you may sop bread into gravy, but it must be done properly—by putting a small piece down on the gravy and then eating it with knife and fork as though it were any other helping on your plate. A very good sauce may also be finished in this way—in fact, to do so is a compliment to the cook.

SALAD

Why one should not cut one's salad in small pieces—if one wants to —makes little sense unless, that is, one cuts up a whole plateful and makes the plate messy. Until a stainless steel was invented, a steel knife blade was not usable for salad or fruit, because it turned black; but silver-bladed knives have always been used for salads as well as for fruits, and today stainless steel has joined its older brother silver.

Anything more difficult than managing leafy salad with a fork alone —especially the fresh, crisp, springing variety—is difficult to imagine. At all events, beware of rolling the fork and wrapping springy leaves around the tines in a spiral. Remember what a spring that lets go can do! At present, and happily ever since stainless steel was introduced, there has been no possible reason why anyone should be denied the efficiency of a salad knife.

SALT

If there is no spoon in the saltcellar, use the tip of a clean knife. If the saltcellar is for you alone, use your knife or take a pinch of salt with your fingers.

Putting salt on the tablecloth and then pinching it between the fingers to put on food is a very old custom and therefore not incorrect if it so happens that a saltcellar is not on one side or the other of one's plate. But dipping celery or radishes into this salt on the tablecloth is never permitted. Salt that is to be dipped into should be put on the bread-and-butter plate or on the rim of whatever plate is before you.

FRUIT AT TABLE

The equipment for eating fruit at table consists of a sharp-bladed fruit knife and fork, a fingerbowl, and a napkin that fruit juice will not permanently stain. In a restaurant, when no knife is given you, it is proper to ask for one.

Raw apples and *pears* are quartered, usually with a knife. The core is then cut away from each quarter, and the fruit is eaten in the fingers. Those who do not like the skin pare each quarter separately.

Bananas. Although it is not bad manners to peel the skin half-way down and eat the fruit bite by bite at table, it is better to peel the skin all the way off, lay the fruit on your plate, cut it in slices, and eat with a fork.

Berries. Strawberries as well as all other berries are usually hulled or stemmed ahead of time, served with cream and sugar, and eaten with a spoon. When especially fine and so freshly picked that they are still warm from the garden's sun, they are often served with their hulls on and sugar placed at one side of each person's plate. The hull of each berry is held in the fingers, and the fruit is dipped in the sugar and so eaten.

Cantaloupes and *muskmelons* are served in halves, or sometimes quarters, and eaten with a spoon.

A honeydew melon is cut into new-moon-shaped quarters or eighths, depending on size, and eaten with either spoon, or knife and fork—whichever you prefer. Similarly with Persian or Casaba melons.

Watermelon is cut into large-size pieces or slices and usually eaten in the fingers. If eaten with fork, remove seeds with tines and then cut piece with side of fork.

Raw cherries and *plums* are eaten in the fingers of course. The pit of the cherry should be made as dry as possible in your mouth and dropped into your almost-closed cupped hand and thence to your plate. The plum is held in your fingers and eaten as close to the pit as possible. On occasion when you do remove a pit in your fingers, be sure that you do it with your thumb underneath and your first two fingers across your mouth, and not with your fingertips pointing into your mouth.

Hothouse grapes are eaten two ways: One, lay a grape on its side, hold it with fingers of left hand, cut into center with point of knife, and remove seeds. Then put grape in mouth with left hand. The other way is to put a whole grape in your mouth, chew it, swallow the pulp and juice, and drop the bare seeds into your almost-closed fist. In this way, the seeds are conveyed unseen from lips to plate.

With *garden or Concord grapes*, you press the stem end of a grape between your lips and against your almost-closed teeth and the juice and pulp will be drawn into your mouth and the skin left to be discarded.

Little *seedless grapes* are no problem since they are eaten whole.

Oranges. A favorite table orange is the rather rough-skinned firm fruit, usually seedless. An enjoyable way to eat it is to slice the two ends of the rind off first, then standing it on one end and holding it on the plate with fingers of left hand, cut the peel off in vertical strips with the knife. You then cut the peeled orange in half at its equator. After this, each half is easily cut and eaten mouthful by mouthful with knife and fork together. They can also be halved, the sections loosened with a curved grapefruit knife, and then eaten with an orange spoon or teaspoon.

A thin-skinned orange, filled with seeds, is extremely difficult to eat. About the only way is to cut it into eighths, take out the seeds from the center with the tip of the knife, and eat the new-moon-shaped pieces as daintily as you can in the fingers.

Tangerines seemingly present no problem because the skin is removed easily and the segments separate readily. But the pulp, seeds, and fibers must be taken neatly from between the lips with the thumb and first two fingers (fingers above and thumb underneath).

A *freestone peach* or *a nectarine* is cut into the pit, then broken in half and eaten. A clingstone you can't break apart; therefore only if you don't mind the fuzz, as most of us do, you eat it whole. If you do this you take very small bites to prevent the juice from running down your wrist. It is better to peel the peach whole and then eat it with knife and fork.

THE FOODS THAT ARE SOMETIMES DIFFICULT

ARTICHOKES

Artichokes are always eaten with the fingers; a leaf at a time is pulled off, and the edible portion dipped in the sauce, and then bitten off. When the center is reached, the thistlelike part is scraped away with a knife, and the heart eaten with a knife and fork.

ASPARAGUS

By reputation this is a finger food, but the ungraceful appearance of a bent stalk of asparagus falling limply into someone's mouth and the fact that moisture is also likely to drip from the end have been the reasons that most fastidious people invariably eat it—at least in part—with the fork. That is, cut the stalks with the fork to where they become harder, and then pick up the ends in the fingers if you choose. But don't squeeze the stalks, or hold your hand beneath the end and let juice run down your arm.

Hothouse asparagus, or any other that has no hard end, is eaten entirely with a fork. All hard ends should be cut off asparagus before serving it at a dinner party, since picking up stalks in the fingers is scarcely compatible with formal table manners.

BAKED POTATO

Baked potato, whether white or sweet and not otherwise prepared before serving, is usually eaten by breaking it in half with the fingers (cutting a slit with a knife first, if necessary), scooping all the inside of the potato onto the plate with a fork and then mixing butter, salt, and pepper in it with a fork.

Another way to eat baked potato is to break it in half with the fingers and lay both halves, skin down, on the plate. Mix a little butter in a small part of one half with a fork and eat that. Then mix a little more, and so on, eating it out of the skin without turning it out on the plate.

A third way—for those who like to eat the skin as well as the inside—is to cut the baked potato into two halves with the knife and fork. Then cut them again into pieces, a few at a time, of eatable size. Butter the pieces with the fork alone and eat, of course, with the fork held in right hand, tines up. If you wish to eat the skins separately they may be placed on the side of the plate, or on the butter plate, and eaten a small piece at a time, exactly as you would bread and butter.

BACON

Breakfast bacon should, when possible, be eaten with a fork. But when it is so very dry and crisp that it scatters into fragments when broken by the fork, fingers are permitted.

BOUILLON

Drink any thin soup that is served in a cup or sip it from a spoon as you prefer (sipping must, of course, be silent). Usually you sip a few spoonfuls and then, when it is cool enough, drink from the cup, holding both handles if the cup has two. Remember not to hold your fingers curled in exaggerated cockscombs. Imagine the double-curl effect!

BUTTER

Every sort of bread, biscuit, toast, and also hot griddle cakes and corn on the cob are buttered with a knife. But corn that has been cut off the cob, or rice, or potato—or anything else on your plate—has seasoning or butter mixed in it with a fork.

CHEESE

Cheese is one thing that may be spread with either a knife or a fork. If eaten with a salad, with which one is using no knife, one may break off a piece of cheese and put it on lettuce or a cracker with one's fork. Runny or soft cheeses, such as Brie, Camembert, or Liederkranz, should always be spread with a salad knife or butter knife if there is one. A hostess should remember that ever since the coming of stainless steel, salad knives are a useful addition to table-setting.

CONDIMENTS

The thought of smearing condiments with a knife on food already impaled on a fork is quite unpleasant if more than a small amount is taken. The proper way to manage a quantity of cranberry sauce, dressing, jelly, pickle, etc., is to lift it onto the fork and either eat it as a separate mouthful or take some of it with a small piece of meat on the tips of the tines.

CORN ON THE COB

To attack corn on the cob with as little ferocity as possible is perhaps the only direction to be given, and the only maxim to bear in mind when eating this pleasant-to-taste but not-very-easy-to-manage vegetable is to eat it as neatly as possible. It doesn't matter whether you break the ear in half, or whether you hold it by its own ends or by special little handles. The real thing to avoid is too much buttering all at once and too greedy eating. If you like much butter, then spread it across only half the length about two rows at a time. If you take a moderate amount of butter, you can spread it across the whole length of two rows, add salt and pepper, hold the ends in both hands, and eat those two rows, and repeat the buttering and eating until all is finished.

Cutting corn off the cob is chiefly a question of the sharpness of the knife. Considerate housekeepers should supply small sharp vegetable knives (steak knives would do nicely) to those who like to cut the corn off. When corn is served for a dinner party, it should be cut off the cobs in the kitchen and creamed or buttered.

CHICKEN (ROAST OR BROILED), SQUAB, GAME HEN, AND OTHER SMALL BIRDS

At a formal dinner, no part of a bird is picked up in the fingers. Among family and friends, however, it is permissible to eat as follows:

The main body of the bird is not eaten with the fingers. You cut off as much meat as you can and leave the rest on your plate. If you know how to manage very small bones, such as joint or wing, or the second joint of a squab, you put the piece of bone with meat on it in your mouth, eat it clean, and remove the bare bones between forefinger and thumb. Larger joints, such as the drumstick of a roast chicken, may be picked up after the first few easily-cut-off pieces have been eaten.

CLAM CHOWDER—THICK SOUPS

Clam chowder is one of the soups that should be served in a soup plate or bowl, but not in a cup. You should be able to drink cup soups easily. Thick soups are eaten by taking about one third of the spoon into the mouth and doing what really amounts to pouring the soup into the mouth from the end of the spoon.

CRACKERS OR CROUSTARDS WITH SOUP

Croustards, which are very small forcemeat pastries, are scattered on the soup after it has been ladled into the plate to be served. Croutons (tiny French-fried cubes of bread) are either put on the soup or else passed separately in a dish with a small serving spoon and each person puts a spoonful in his soup. Oyster crackers, as well as any others, are put on the bread-and-butter plate, or on the tablecloth—and dropped two or three pieces at a time into the soup.

FRENCH-FRIED POTATOES

When French-fried potatoes accompany a hamburger, hot dog, or other sandwich, they may be eaten in the fingers. At all other times, they must be cut into reasonable lengths and eaten with a fork.

LAMB CHOPS

At a dinner party or in a restaurant, lamb chops must be eaten with knife and fork. At the family table or among an informal group of friends, the center may be cut out and eaten with the fork, and the bone picked up and eaten clean with the teeth. This is permissible, too, with veal or pork chops, but only if they are broiled or otherwise cooked without gravy or sauce.

LOBSTER, BROILED

This is called a finger food because unless the claws have been broken in two, their meat cannot be eaten at all. So you must pick up the claw in its shell to pry out the meat with a lobster fork, but you put the meat (and that from the main body) on your plate, cut it with a knife, and eat it with the fork.

Properly, a big paper napkin (or bib) and a fingerbowl with hot water and lemon slices, should be put at the side of each place at table as soon as people are served and carried away, of course, as soon as the plates are removed.

OLIVES

Eat with your fingers. Bite off the meat, but don't nibble too avidly around the stone. Bite a stuffed one in half. Put only a very small stuffed olive in your mouth whole.

OLIVES, ONIONS, AND CHERRIES IN COCKTAILS

When the glass is drained, it is easy enough to tip the glass and drop the cherry, onion, or small olive into your mouth. Since a large olive is too much of a mouthful, lift it out with the fingers and eat it in two or three bites.

SANDWICHES

All ordinary sandwiches, not only at picnics but everywhere, are eaten from the fingers. Club sandwiches and other inch-thick and whole-meal sandwiches are best cut in smaller portions before being picked up and held tightly in the fingers of both hands, or if literally dripping with mayonnaise they should be served on a plate with a knife and fork. If you are not sitting at table and you have no knife, you bite into an over-large and hugely thick piece as nicely as you can or, quoting previous advice in the matter of eating corn on the cob, attack it with as little ferocity as possible.

SHRIMP

Shrimp as a first course present one of the most difficult problems encountered by the diner. If not too impossibly large, each shrimp should be eaten in one bite. But when they are of jumbo size, the diner has no alternative but to grasp the cup firmly with his left hand and cut the shrimp as neatly as possible with the edge of his fork. It is impractical to use a knife because the stemmed shrimp cup will tip over unless held with one hand. At home, the problem can be avoided by arranging the shrimp attractively on a small plate, where they can be cut easily with knife or fork, and I can see no reason why restaurants should not do the same.

SPAGHETTI

The method of eating spaghetti by winding it on a fork held against a spoon is correct neither here nor in Italy, its former home. A few pieces are held against the plate with the end of the fork, which is then twisted to wrap the spaghetti around the tines and then conveyed to the mouth. If necessary this can be done against the curve of the plate, which will substitute for the spoon in keeping the slippery pieces on the fork while they are being wound around it. An extra amount of grated Parmesan cheese will help a novice because it makes the strands less slippery.

EMBARRASSING DIFFICULTIES

If food is too hot, quickly take a swallow of water. Never, NEVER spit it out! If food has been taken into your mouth, no matter how you hate it, you must swallow it. It is offensive to take anything out of your mouth that has been put in it, except dry fish bones and equally dry fruit pits or seeds. If you choke on a fish bone, cover your mouth with your napkin and leave the table quickly. To spit anything whatever into the corner of your napkin is too nauseating to comment on. It is horrid to see anyone spit wet skins or pits on a fork or onto the plate, and it is excusable only if you get a bad clam or something similar into your mouth.

Even then the best—because least noticeable—method is to take it from your mouth in your fingers—thumb underneath and four other fingers forming a screen over whatever it is from lips to plate. And then gently wipe off on your napkin any moisture still on your fingertips.

THE TECHNIQUE FOR BONES, PITS, AND SEEDS

Fish bones or other incidental bones are taken between finger and thumb and removed between compressed lips. Pits and seeds must be eaten quite bare and clean in the mouth and dropped into the cupped fist and then into the plate. The pits of stewed prunes or cherries that are eaten with a spoon are made as clean and dry as possible in the mouth with the tongue and teeth, and then dropped into the spoon with which you are eating, and conveyed to the edge of the plate.

SPILLS

If you should spill jelly or a bit of vegetable or other solid food on the table, pick up as much as you can neatly with a clean spoon or the blade of your knife. If it has caused a stain, apologize to your hostess, who, in turn, should not add to your embarrassment by calling attention to the accident, but quietly assure you that "No harm was done—the cloth will be washed tomorrow in any case."

If you spill wine or water at a formal dinner, try quietly to attract the attention of the butler or footman, who will bring a cloth to cover the spot. At the family table or informal dinner without servants, offer to get a cloth or sponge to mop up the liquid, and help the hostess clean up in any way you can.

SOME TABLE DON'TS

Don't encircle a plate with the left arm while eating with the right hand.

Don't push back your plate when finished. It remains exactly where it is until whoever is waiting on you removes it. If you wait on yourself, get up and carry it to the kitchen.

Don't lean back and announce, "I'm through." The fact that you have put your fork or spoon down shows that you have finished.

Don't *ever* put liquid into your mouth if it is already filled with food —this really means filled. You might have a little bread in your mouth when you drink your coffee, if it be so little as to be undetectable to others. But a good habit is *never*.

Don't dunk, although it is an approved practice in lunch wagons according to the movies. If you must soften your doughnut or slice of toast, at least break it in half and dip an end, or cut the toast into one-inch strips and dip them lightly, or better, break a small piece at a time into your coffee, milk, or soup, and eat it with a spoon.

Don't apologize and thus call unnecessary attention to anything so unpleasant as having to blow your nose at the table. The only thing to do is to end it as quickly as possible.

Don't wait until all the plates are served; after a few guests have been served, it is perfectly all right to start eating.

Don't wipe off the tableware in a restaurant. If you do happen to find a dirty piece of silver at your place, call a waiter or waitress, show him the soiled article, and ask for a clean one.

Don't, if you are a woman, wear an excessive amount of lipstick to the table, out of consideration for your hostess's napkin, and also because it is very unattractive on the rim of a glass or on the silver.

Don't spread jelly or jam directly onto a piece of bread from the dish in which it is served. Put a small portion on your butter plate, or the rim of your dinner plate if there is no butter plate, using the spoon provided to serve the condiment. If there is no spoon with the jelly, you may use a clean knife to put a little on your plate.

Don't crook your finger when picking up your cup. It's an affected mannerism.

Don't—ever—leave your spoon in your cup. Not only does it look unattractive; it is almost certain to result in an accident.

Don't leave half the food on your spoon or fork to be waved about during conversation. One often sees this done with ice cream, but the coldness is no excuse—one should put less on the spoon and need only one bite.

Don't cut up your entire meal before you start to eat; it only makes a mess on your plate.

Don't bend your head so low over the plate that you seem to be bobbing up and down for each bite like a robin for a worm. Of course, you must lean forward slightly to avoid carrying the food too far and risking a spill on your lap, but there is a happy medium.

WHEN CHILDREN COME TO THE TABLE

No child under five can be expected to use a napkin instead of a bib, although, if he wishes, he may be given a napkin in addition to the bib to become accustomed to using it to wipe his mouth. No matter how nicely behaved he may be, there is always the present danger of his spilling something, sometime. Soft-boiled egg is hideously difficult to eat without ever getting a drop of it down the front, and it is much easier to supply him with a clean bib for the next meal than to change his clothes for the next moment. By quietly experimenting with the individual child, it can easily be ascertained just when he is ready for the next step in the training program. But until he is ready to accept the new way, do not force the issue unduly.

Very little children usually have warming plates—made as a double plate with hot water space in between—on which the food is cut up and the vegetables "fixed" in the kitchen. It is brought to them before other people at the table are served, not only because it is hard for them to wait when their attention is too easily attracted by food not for them, but because they naturally eat slowly and deliberately. As soon as they are old enough to eat everything on the table, they are served, not last, but in the regular rotation in which they come at table.

When children are learning to help themselves, they must especially try to handle the serving spoon evenly and to guard against "flinging" it quickly and so spattering the table. In fact, this principal cause for a spotted tablecloth is something to which even grown people should pay attention.

THE LEFT-HANDED CHILD

To the many who ask whether it is best to set the place at table in reverse of usual order for a left-handed child who has to "cross over" for every implement, the answer is definitely "No!"

Nothing could turn out to be a greater handicap than letting him become accustomed to reversed place-setting. It is only by being obliged to make this maneuver at every meal at home that he becomes adept at it. If his place is set especially for him at home, he will be conspicuously as well as helplessly awkward at every meal he ever eats away from home where his place will not be so set.

TABLE TRICKS THAT MUST BE CORRECTED

To pile mashed potato and other vegetables on top of meat on the convex side of the fork for two inches or more of its length is an ungainly habit dear to the hearts of schoolboys and sometimes of their fathers—a habit that is more easily prevented in the beginning than corrected later. In fact, taking a big mouthful (next to smearing the face and chewing with mouth open) is perhaps the worst offense at the table.

To sit up straight and keep their hands in their laps when not occupied with eating is very hard indeed for children, but it should be insisted upon in order to forestall a careless habit that all too readily degenerates into flopping this way and that and fingering whatever is in reach. The child must not be allowed to warm his hands on his plate, or drum on the table, or screw his napkin into a rope, or make marks on the tablecloth. If he shows talent as an artist, give him pencils or modeling wax in his playroom, but do not let him bite his slice of bread into the silhouette of an animal or model figures in butter at the table. And do not allow him to construct a tent out of two forks, or an automobile chassis out of tumblers and knives, or tie the corners of his napkin into bunny-rabbit ears. Food and table implements are not playthings, nor is the dining-room table a playground.

Children should be taught from the time they are little not to talk at table about what foods they like and don't like. A child who is not allowed to say anything but "No, thank you," when offered something he doesn't want at home, will not mortify his mother in public by screaming, "I *hate* spinach. I *won't* eat potato. I want ice cream and cookies!"

Older children should not be allowed to jerk out their chairs, to flop down sideways, to flick their napkins by one corner, to reach out for something, or to begin by eating candy, fruit, or other table decorations. A child as well as a grown person should sit down in the center of his chair and draw it up to the table (if there is no one to push it in for him) by holding the seat in either hand while momentarily lifting himself on his feet. It makes no difference whether he approaches the chair from the left or the right. The only rule is to take his place quietly, and not jump or rock his chair into place at the table. In getting up from the table, again he must push his chair back quietly, using his hands on either side of the chair seat, and *not* by holding onto the table edge and giving himself, chair and all, a sudden shove!

In business

Every executive knows how important etiquette is, both in managing his office and in dealing with other businessmen. No man can ever tell when a knowledge of it may be to his advantage, or when the lack of it may suddenly turn the scale against him. The man who remains "planted" in his chair when a lady speaks to him, who receives customers in his shirt sleeves, who does not take off his hat when talking with a lady or take his cigar out of his mouth when addressing her, impresses others, not only by his lack of good manners, but by the business incompetence that his attitude suggests.

THE WELL-MANNERED BUSINESSMAN

In the well-run business office, the more important the executive, the greater courtesy does he show to those who come to see him. A president of a large industry, for example, employs several assistants chosen partially because of their tact and good manners. If an unknown person asks to see Mr. Prominent, one of these aides goes out to find out what the visitor's business is; and instead of telling him bluntly that the executive can't see him and to write a letter, he not only says, "Mr. Prominent is in conference just now," but adds, "I know he wouldn't like you to be kept waiting. Can I be of service to you? I am his assistant." If it is important that he see the president, he is admitted to the executive's office, since it should be the latter's policy to see everyone that he possibly can.

The president has a courteous manner that makes every visitor feel there is nothing in the day's work half so important as what he, the client, has come to see him about. Nor is this manner insincere, for he has made it a practice to give anyone he talks with his undivided attention. Should his time be short and the moment approach when he is due at an appointment, his secretary has been taught to come in a few minutes before the hour and remind him, "I'm sorry, Mr. Prominent, but your appointment with the traffic committee is due." Mr. Prominent, with seeming unconcern, uses up most of these few minutes in an unhurried close of the previous conversation, giving his visitor the impression that he may, indeed, be late at his appointment and just because of his interest in the subject that his visitor brought before him.

This is neither sincerity nor insincerity, but merely bringing social knowledge into business dealing. To make a pleasant and friendly impression is not alone good manners, but equally good business. That this is understood by modern businessmen is shown by the importance they give to public relations. The less experienced man might show his eagerness to be rid of his visitor and, after offending the latter's pride by the discourtesy of inattention, possibly even be late for his own appointment! The man of skill saw his visitor for fewer actual minutes, but gave the impression that circumstances over which he had no control forced him unwillingly to close the interview. He not only gained the good will of his visitor, but had plenty of time for his own appointment.

THE SELF-MADE MAN

It is not in order to shine in society that good manners are an asset; comparatively few people in a community care a rap about society anyway. A man of affairs whose life is spent in doing a man's work in a man's way is not likely to be thrilled at the thought of getting dressed up and going out with his wife to a tea or a ball. But what many men do not realize is that a fundamental knowledge of etiquette is no less an asset in business or public life, or in any everyday contact with people, than it is in society.

Just as any expert, whether at a machine bench, an accountant's desk, or at golf, gives an impression of such ease as to make his accomplishment seem to require no skill, a bungler makes himself and everyone watching him uneasy. And as inexpertness is quite as irritating in personal as in mechanical bungling, so there is scarcely anyone who sooner or later does not feel the need of social expertness. Some day he will envy the accomplished manners of men he thought of as being "soft" when he felt himself strong and manly in his crudeness! Does anyone think of

Theodore Roosevelt as soft or effeminate because he was a great master of etiquette? Washington was completely a gentleman—and so was Abraham Lincoln. Though Lincoln's etiquette was self-taught, it was no less mastered for that!

WOMEN IN BUSINESS

Women have come to stay in not only every branch of business but every profession as well. Women are the successful heads of their own offices, and very few are the businesses that do not have women secretaries, bookkeepers, receptionists, switchboard operators, clerks, and typists.

The ideal business woman is accurate, orderly, quick, and impersonal, whether she is a typist or the top executive of a great concern. By "impersonal" is meant exactly that! Her point of view must be focused on the work in hand, not on her own reactions to it or on anyone's reactions to her. If she is an executive, she avoids being dictatorial and still maintains her dignity.

At the very top of the list of women's business shortcomings is the inability of many of them to achieve this impersonality. Mood, temper, jealousy, especially when induced by a "crush on" her employer or a fellow worker—these are the chief flaws of the woman in business and a constant source of annoyance in every office where she works. The greatest handicap to woman's advancement in business is her inability to leave her personal feelings and affairs at home.

An anonymous expert on business gave as the recipe for success: "The ability to work efficiently and pleasantly with other people." The recipe is perfect—there is nothing to add except to acknowledge that it takes no small amount of will and self-control to get on with any constant companion under the daily friction of an enforced relationship that is unrelieved day after day, week after week. It is wonderful that human nature stands the strain as well as it does, especially in situations where one's own work is dependent upon the cooperation of others for its complete efficiency.

Women who work must learn not to waste their employers' time. And employers should know that the effect on morale of a ten-minute make-up repair or coffee break more than makes up in increased efficiency for the actual loss in time. No employer, however, will stand for a coffee-break atmosphere throughout the working day. Women should avoid wasting time in idle conversation during working hours, since this only interrupts the office routine and is a very unbusinesslike habit.

SEX BANNED IN BUSINESS

A woman who goes into an office because she thinks herself pretty and hopes to meet romance in the form of her employer, or at least to rise quickly because of her physical charm, has clerkship and chorus work mixed up. Sex is one thing that has no place in business. Much as a man may admire a pretty or magnetic or amusing woman in his leisure hours, in his hours of work he wants someone to help him with that work. The more help she can give him, the more he values her and the more salary he is willing to pay.

Naturally he likes one who is attractive, but business personality and leisure personality are two different things. They are sometimes combined in one person, and sometimes romance is an outcome of business, but that is the exception that proves the rule. And every time the prospect of romance intrudes into a business situation, think not just twice but a dozen times before allowing an office relationship to become a personal one. The woman who happens to work in an office with her husband should remember to be as impersonal and efficient during working hours as any other woman would be.

Every businessman likes a woman who is neat, impersonal, and efficient, just as he likes an automobile that is ready to go any distance without any danger of breaking down. A successful business personality has as its first attribute *efficiency*, not sex appeal.

THE PERFECT SECRETARY

The function of the perfect secretary is to complement her employer's endeavor and not make any intrusions which would be more likely to impede than help.

Needless to say, a secretary must not betray the secrets of her employer. His business dealings must be regarded as professional secrets that it would be dishonorable to divulge—no matter how inconsequential they may seem to her.

THE CORRESPONDENCE OF HER EMPLOYER

Business training surely teaches every secretary to know everything she can that will be of service to her employer, but to know as little as possible about the things that are not her concern. When sorting his mail, she leaves unopened the obviously private letters—envelopes written by hand on stationery not suggestive of business—and having opened his other letters and clipped them in whatever order he likes to have them, she should then clip a sheet of blank paper on the top of each pile, or put the mail in a manila folder, so that visitors or others who have access to his office will not have the contents of letters displayed before them.

TAKING DICTATION

When a secretary enters a man's office in response to his summons or because it is the hour set for her appearance, she should take a chair and place it near enough to hear him easily. Where she sits depends very much on the office—where the light comes from and where she can best hear his voice. It is not expected that he get up and offer her a chair or show her the sort of personal attention that a man in social life shows to a woman.

IN UNCONVENTIONAL SITUATIONS

The young woman who is a confidential secretary to an executive may very well on occasion be required to stay late into the evening working with him alone; or if the nature of his business or profession requires that he go on long tours of investigation or conference with firms in distant cities, she may accompany him on these purely business trips. Theoretically and according to the normal conventions, nothing could be more improper than a young woman—an attractive and personable one, no doubt—traveling about the country with a man alone. But practically, and according to the exactions of the modern business world, it is necessary that every professional or business woman shall write her own code of propriety. She must! In the case of Miss Secretary, no one in the world can advise her as well as she can advise herself. She knows exactly how necessary she is or is not to the work her employer must do; she knows his attitude toward her, and certainly she knows her own attitude toward him. Therefore, she knows beyond the shadow of a doubt whether she must or whether she need not go with him.

It is true the business woman is free from criticism—unless she herself gives cause for it. It isn't the bald fact of taking trains and staying in hotels and being off in a distant state alone with Mr. Employer that will hurt Miss Secretary's good name. Nothing will hurt her good name except her own or Mr. Employer's unprofessional and therefore improper attitude of mind. And now having said that Miss Secretary may defy convention, it is necessary to add a fairly formidable array of qualifying exactions that the critical world expects her to follow.

In preparation for the journey, she orders whatever accommodations he always expects. On trains, she engages a drawing room or a section for him, and a section or lower berth for herself in the same car; but in hotels she engages a suite for him, and a room and bath on another floor for herself. To put herself in another car or in another hotel would be a mistake, because she will make her employer conscious of the fact that she is conscious of him.

If she should by chance find herself shown into a room adjoining that of her employer, the question of what to do depends somewhat upon the type of man he is. Perhaps she says as a matter of fact, "This is not what I ordered. I'm sorry!" Or maybe she says, "This is a mistake. I'll go and change it." She then goes down to the desk and tells the clerk that her room is not the one that was ordered and tries to get another.

To those who may think it stupid as well as prudish to do anything about this at all, since everyone must know as well as she does that the relationship between Mr. Employer and herself is one of professional necessity, the answer is that much more is at stake than a question of social gossip. The greater his prominence, the more seriously could carelessness of propriety endanger his career, and this not at the moment but years later when exaggeration of the fact of their adjoining rooms can distort the truth.

HER BEHAVIOR OUTSIDE BUSINESS HOURS

Questions concerned with whether the secretary traveling with her employer may have lunch or dinner or go to the theater with him are in the area where professional propriety crosses into dangerous territory. It is almost certain that she will lunch with him or have dinner with him—especially on trains or boats or in hotels or restaurants. On rushed days, she may have to eat in his rooms where they are working. In other words, she takes eating alone or eating with him as incidental to convenience. The danger point appears when the pleasure of dining becomes social.

WHEN SHOULD A SECRETARY RISE?

A question often raised is whether a secretary should rise when visitors enter the office. Many a young woman thinks it very rude not to meet the friendliness of such persons as she would do were she at home.

The answer to this is that unless the visitors are persons of importance to her employer—so important that the time she takes from her work is spent in her employer's interest—it would not be expected of her, or even proper, to greet them in such a way as to encourage their talking to her at length. On the other hand, if she is the private secretary of an executive and part of her job is to make a pleasant impression, she would naturally leave her desk to greet a stranger or an important customer but not (if she is otherwise busy) to greet one who comes into the office constantly. A secretary's duties do not include helping a visitor off and on with his coat, unless he actually needs help. This same approach to these problems applies to all similar office personnel.

THE RECEPTIONIST

A tactful person at the reception desk in an office is of great importance. Neither a condescending nor gushing attitude is suitable—anywhere! A pleasant, quiet, but cordial attitude can do much to further the good will of the firm for which you work.

When a recumbent, gum-chewing office boy flings at you from behind a locked gate "Who d'ja wanna see?" and then shuffles off and returns with "Mr. Brown's busy. Can't see ya t'day! Y' c'n try t'morrer if ya like!"—the customer will *not*, unless he really must see Mr. Brown and cannot take his business to anyone else. Many offices—especially those which have many personal contacts—are putting middle-aged women and men at the reception desk because it has been found that people do not resent being refused admittance by a tactful older person as they resent being barred by one who is young and callous. Good public relations have become an important part of good business management.

THE WELL-RUN OFFICE

OFFICE DISCIPLINE

A business organization is, in one sense, like a military one. You should take as much pride in helping to keep up the tone of the office you work in as you take pride in your own efficiency.

An employee ought to have that same feeling for the spirit of the organization or the office he works in that is characteristic of the "school spirit" of young people. He and his associates, his superiors, his inferiors are fellow members who can all add to or detract from the firm's importance.

The possession of tact whereby you know how to please people and make them pleased in turn with your firm is one of the surest ways of getting an increase of salary. Putting on airs and thinking yourself too good for your job is pretty close to asking for a job not half so good as the one you hold.

Do not bring your personal problems to the office. You may rest assured no one is interested. Leave them at home, or, if you must, discuss them with a friend during lunch.

In the office of a large company, the executives should call their employees "Miss [or Mrs.] Jones" rather than "Mary," and they, in turn, always call him "Mr. Smith." There are, however, varying degrees of formality in business organizations. Offices today tend to be more casual than formerly. Many employers feel that in a more relaxed atmosphere employees will be more efficient, more reliable, and more loyal. These employers try to hire personnel who will be congenial and who will work well together to the benefit of the company. The employer or ranking executive determines the degree of formality in his office. He may, for instance, prefer to be on a first-name basis with his staff and the informality does not itself imply a too-familiar relationship. This is invariably true in the office of a small company, where the total staff may not exceed ten or twelve people.

A young woman in a subordinate position does not go out to lunch with her superior or employer. But if she holds a responsible position and has matters of business to discuss, there is no reason—unless her own—why she should not on occasion lunch with him. It would, however, be courting criticism should their going out together become a habit.

A man does not rise when a woman employee comes into his office. But he must stand to receive a woman visitor and remain standing until she is seated. He stands again when she prepares to leave and usually goes with her to the door, opens it for her, and "bows her out."

Personal messages over the telephone are at times unavoidable, but long chatty conversations are not only out of place, but wasteful of time that does not belong to the employee. Social "chatter" annoys other people in the office who can't help but overhear your discussion of the movie you saw last night. Personal calls that interfere with the routine of office procedure, either incoming or outgoing, are inexcusable except in genuine emergencies.

Discourage visits from your family and friends at the office. Your baby brother may be a most enchanting child, but his place is not in the office in which you work.

BUSINESS GIFTS

Gifts from a firm to its employees are usually in the form of a bonus or a proportion of one's salary. At Christmas a man may give his personal secretary a present. Candy is conventional, although when she has been with him for some time, he might choose something he thinks she would rather have. It is hardly necessary to add that wearing apparel is NOT suitable. A private secretary known well to a man's wife is sometimes, but not usually, remembered by the wife at Christmas. Occasionally employees give presents to their employers, but it is not common. There are exceptions: If there is a wedding in the employer's family, or if a baby is born, then the employees may all contribute and send a gift. They also as a group may send flowers to a funeral. A committee usually collects contributions and makes an appropriate selection.

Gift-giving to one's fellow workers who are also personal friends should always be arranged for out of office hours.

STORE ETIQUETTE

The technical aspects of salesmanship are much too specialized to be discussed by anyone who has not learned the subject at first hand and practiced it with success—success, moreover, that is measured by tangible proof of satisfactory sales slips, and best of all, an increasing number of customers who ask for Mrs. Keen or Miss Personable when they come again to buy. A saleswoman can be very helpful, and she can also be a nuisance.

But the aspects of salesmanship that depend for their success upon tactful and pleasing manners belong very decidedly in a book such as this. Also very decidedly belong good manners that are to be expected of all customers who make any pretense to being well-bred.

First let us consider the point of view of a customer, since this is something that we all know from personal experience. We surely do not all agree as to the type of saleswoman we like or dislike. A clever saleswoman must have different methods with different customers. After all, if customers were identical, perfect salesmanship would not be the difficult accomplishment it is. It is quite possible for methods that are unendurable to some of us to be acceptable to others.

THE SUCCESSFUL SALESWOMAN

Really great saleswomen have cultivated not only an expert knowledge of the commodities they sell, but an equally expert ability to appraise each of the customers to whom they sell. It is essential to know, therefore, whether a customer likes to be "dearied" or "madamed" or chatted to about every topic under the sun, whether she is one who likes to have her mind made up for her, or whether she is one who, knowing exactly what she wants, prefers to have her own questions answered intelligently without any unasked-for advice.

But the saleswoman whom an intelligent customer is certain to like best—and return to—is one who listens to what she says and tries to give her what she wants, instead of trying to sell her what the store seems eager to be rid of.

For example, when you ask for something she can't supply, the ideal saleswoman would listen attentively to what you say and answer, "I am very sorry we have nothing at all like that in the color you want; but I could give you something in a small pattern of yellow," and then with certain eagerness she would ask, "Have you time to let me show it to you?"

You are pleased, because the saleswoman showed eagerness to help you find what you want, and you as a customer would be very lacking in courtesy not at least to let her show you what she so much hopes may please you. When she brings it, you are inclined to be pleased because, though you know it is not just what you want, you are sure it is not going to be thrust upon you. And the possibilities are that if you can make it do, you will take it. And even if you do not, you will certainly come back to that saleswoman another time when you are looking for something else.

Of all the varieties of poor saleswomen, the worst is she who simply brushes aside what you say you want and blandly spreads before you something that is exactly what you have explained to her you do NOT want, at the same time trying to force you to like it by extolling its beauties or its bargain values and capping the climax by telling you that Mrs. Uppity thinks this is exquisite! That kind of saleswoman would have difficulty in selling a steak to a starving man.

I do not think that any of us like high-pressure salesmanship or that it ever pays in the long run. One wonders how many customers who have been high-pressured into buying what they did not really want or into spending more than they could afford have thereafter avoided not only that particular salesperson, but that particular store as well.

THE INCONSIDERATE CUSTOMER

The behavior of the customer is as important as that of the saleswoman. Indeed, a saleswoman is, so to speak, at the mercy of any customer who is ill-bred or unreasonable for as long as that customer chooses to keep her in attendance. Moreover, an unjustifiably irate customer can cause, by her complaints, a mark against a saleswoman, and whether deserved or not, many such marks may mean loss of a job.

As a guess, one might say that an inconsiderate customer can be at her worst and cause the greatest strain upon a saleswoman's sportsmanship and good temper in the ready-to-wear clothing department. And what a careless customer often does to the merchandise is scarcely believable. Perhaps she smears the dresses with lipstick as she pulls them on or off. Perhaps she tears them in her haste or sheer carelessness; perhaps she scorches one with her cigarette although smoking is not permitted in stores. Rarely does she think *she* did the damage. And in the end she orders none, or perhaps she buys several and then returns everything looking still more shopworn the next day.

It is true that we all at some time buy something which for one reason or another we are obliged to send back. But neither this practice nor that of being inconsiderate of salespeople or the merchandise belonging to the store is typical of any considerate person.

Another lack of consideration is shown by those who go shopping ten minutes before closing time. The salespeople have had a long day and have routine chores to do before they can leave.

Another fault—but probably only belonging to housewives who have had no business experience—is to think it fair or honest to expect favors from their friends who are no longer women of leisure and who are not in a position to give below-cost prices, or to put all other customers aside and spend their time in gossiping with a former friend. And finally it is hard to believe but there are women who, with no thought of buying anything, will go into a dress department solely to pass an hour or so before a lunch date, and waste the time of a saleswoman who is paid at least in part by commissions on the dresses she sells—and not on the ones she shows.

Is the customer always right? It would not seem likely. Unfailing patience and good temper are qualities expected of every saleswoman, whereas there is nothing to restrain the ill-humor or unreasonableness of a customer—except her own good manners.

68

In games and sports

The basic requisite for good manners at any game table or sports area is that age-old quality *sportsmanship*. The training schools for sportsmanship are three: first, easiest and best, the nursery; secondly, school and college; thirdly, the adult school of competitive tournaments.

The quality that perhaps more than any other distinguishes true sportsmanship is absence of any show of temper, not temper brought along and held in check, but temper securely locked and left at home. After all, if you can't take sports with grace and good temper, don't go in for them. Cursing out your faults or your luck, excusing, complaining, and protesting against unfairness won't get you anywhere—except in trouble. You win or you lose; that is all there is to it! To throw down your clubs or racket in a temper is to throw down your chances of ever holding them again without penalty. Never to display ill-humor is the first rule of sportsmanship. This does not mean that never by expression or gesture may you show either satisfaction or chagrin. Stoicism is often a means, not an end. The imperfect sportsman, whether he has traits of character that he cannot otherwise control, or whether he is a child or novice at the sport and still uncertain of his own reactions, learns that stoicism is the rule of safety.

The perfect sportsman meets every situation with easy grace. He shows chagrin, he shows elation, but only for the briefest moment and never without a smile. The onlookers always make him their favorite because he is "human." Every now and then his expression lights with a quick smile, a distinctly happy grin, or it creases into a grimace at a bit of bad luck or a bungled play. There is no reason whatever why a player may not on occasions smile, unless the smile broadens into triumphant affront or verges on the smugness of conceit. When he wins, he takes his satisfaction lightly or perhaps the better word is transiently. If he loses, he takes it good-naturedly—and still more transiently. Furthermore, when the game is ever, the subject is finished. Why he won or lost or how he felt or played is not to be talked about.

It is entirely proper, even advisable, for the tournament player to win popularity if he can. One often notices that a player does almost better than he knows how to when the public is cheering him—no champagne is equal to it. On the other hand, silence for himself and cheering for his adversary are quite as real a handicap as extra pounds strapped upon his back—a weight that every player must at least sometimes steel himself to bear.

The second rule is always to give your opponent the benefit of the doubt. Nothing is more important to your standing as a sportsman, though the loss of the particular point in question may seem very important at that moment. Never argue with the umpire. If he rules a line ball on the tennis court is out, it is out. You do not turn toward the spectators with an expression that says, "See how unfairly I am being treated!"

Among the lesser shortcomings of an unsportsmanlike player is his practice of understating his ability before a match. It is not necessary to point out the lack of fair play in this procedure before the handicaps are given out; but it is a commonplace occurrence to hear from a man who is perfectly satisfied with his skill, "I am not much of a player," or "I know I'll make a poor showing; I've got a 'bad' arm!" The motive is not necessarily dishonest—though on many occasions it is difficult to see it as anything else—but is often a show-off impulse to create admiring surprise should he play brilliantly on the one hand and on the other to save face should his game be off. The only time a player may declare himself unskilled is when he really is, and would otherwise be a source of annoyance in a game beyond his class.

One last and earnestly urged "don't" is the loser's practice of complaining of illness after having lost a match. This is one real flaw in many a woman's sportsmanship. "I had such a pain in my side [or knee, or back] that I don't know how I ever got through the match!" is heard so frequently that one consciously resists the temptation to taunt every woman loser, "I'm *sure,* poor dear, you were in such pain you could not see the ball!"

For the benefit of those who seem to believe that a man is rated a good sport because he spends money freely, it should be stated clearly that they have confused the term "sportsman"—one who competes fairly in any contest—with "sporting man," a man of far from admirable habits. A player's reputation as a good sportsman is the one thing that money can *not* buy. Neither by giving away boxes of tennis and golf balls, nor by offering colossal silver cups, nor even by a million-dollar endowment, can the richest man that ever was increase by the thickness of a leaf of beaten gold his rating in sportsmanship.

Sportsmanship can be very well acquired by following a few simple rules. Keep your mind on the game, but not on your feelings. If you win, don't at once begin to fancy yourself a star in the firmament. A gloating winner is detested even more than a bad loser. But when you lose, don't sulk, or protest, or long-windedly explain. If you are hurt, whether in mind or body, don't nurse your bruises. Get up and light-heartedly, courageously, good-temperedly get ready for the next encounter. This is playing the game—and the only successful way to take life.

CARD PLAYERS, PLEASANT AND UNPLEASANT

Bridge is probably the most popular "mixed-company" card game, but the same rules of etiquette apply to players of gin rummy, hearts, poker—mixed or stag—and any other game.

That no one likes a poor partner—or even a poor opponent—goes without saying. In a "team" game, the ideal partner is one who never criticizes or seems even to be aware of your mistakes, even though you trump his ace unnecessarily; on the contrary, he recognizes a good maneuver on your part, is pleased over a clever play, and gives you credit for it whether you win the hand or lose. The inferior player is likely to judge you merely by what you win and blame you if you lose, though your play may have been exceptionally good and the loss occasioned by a wrong move on his part. To be continually found fault with makes you play your worst, whereas appreciation of your good judgment acts as a tonic, and you seem to play better than you know how to.

Nothing more quickly reveals the man whose gentlemanly appearance is only a veneer than the card table, for that veneer melts equally with success or failure. Being carried away by the game, he forgets to keep on his company polish. If he wins, he becomes grasping or overbearing because of his skill; if he loses, he complains constantly about the cards he has been holding and sneers at the luck of others.

ANNOYING MANNERISMS

Mannerisms must always be avoided like the plague. If there is one thing worse than the horrible post-mortem, it is the incessant repetition of some jarring habit by one particular player. A common offensive one is that of snapping down a card as played, or picking it up and trotting it up and down on the table.

Other pet offenses are drumming on the table with one's fingers, making various clicking, whistling, or humming sounds, massaging one's face, scratching one's chin with the cards, or holding the card one is going to play aloft in the air in smart aleck fashion as though shouting, "I know what you are going to play! And my card is ready!" All mannerisms that attract attention are unpleasant—and in the long run even unendurable—to one's companions.

Many people whose game is otherwise admirable are rarely asked to play because they have some such silly and annoying habit. Don't hold a post-mortem on anybody's delinquencies, unless you are actually teaching.

THE GOOD LOSER

The good loser makes it an invariable rule never to play for stakes that it will be inconvenient to lose. The neglect of this rule has been responsible for more bad losers than anything else, and needless to say a bad loser is about as welcome at a game table as rain at a championship tennis match. Of course, there *are* people who can take losses beyond their means with perfect cheerfulness and composure. Some few are so imbued with the gambler's instinct that a heavy turn of luck, in either direction, is the salt of life. But the average person is equally embarrassed in winning or losing a stake that matters and the only answer is always to play only for what one can easily afford.

THE THOUGHTFUL HOSTESS

There is one point of consideration which every hostess owes her guests: protection from being forced into playing for stakes which can embarrass them. Giving a guest a chance to decline her invitation beforehand is really much more important in the case of a man than in the case of a woman. A woman usually feels free to say, "I'm sorry, but I never play for more than so much." But a man sometimes feels that his refusal is an embarrassing confession of financial failure—a position into which no good hostess would ever put him. If people coming to her house, for instance, are known to play together, nothing need be said; but if strangers are invited to play with others who play for certain stakes, the hostess should say when she invites them, "The Smiths and Browns and Robinsons are coming. They all play for a cent. Is that all right?" The one invited can either say, "I'm sorry. I don't play for money," or

"My limit is a tenth of a cent," or "They must be way out of my class! Do ask me again when you are having people who play for less."

CONTRACT BRIDGE

A trick that is annoying to moderately skilled players is to have an overconfident opponent (who usually is a better player than they are) throw down his hand, saying, "The rest of the tricks are mine!" Often it is quite possible that they might not have been his if the hand had been played out. Knowing themselves to be poorer players, the others are not likely to challenge the move, even though they feel that their rights have been taken away.

A rather trying partner is the nervous player who has no confidence in his own judgment and will invariably pass a good hand in favor of his partner's bid. If, for instance, he has six perfectly good diamonds, he doesn't mention them because, his partner having declared a heart, he thinks to himself, "Her hearts must be better than my diamonds, and if I have to play the hand, I'll probably butcher it."

An equally serious failing—and one that is far more common—is the habit of overbidding. In poker, you play alone and can therefore play as carefully or as recklessly as you please; but in contract bridge, your partner has to suffer with you, and you therefore are in honor bound to play a sound game—the best you know how—and the best you know how will surely keep you from overbidding more than very occasionally indeed.

If luck is against you, it will avail you nothing to sulk or complain about the awful cards you have been holding. Your partner is suffering just as much in finding you a "poison vine" as you are, in being one— and you can scarcely expect your opponents to be sympathetic. You must learn to look perfectly tranquil and cheerful even though you hold nothing but poor cards for days on end, and you must on no account try to defend your own bad play. When you have made a play of poor judgment, the best thing you can say is, "I'm very sorry, partner," and let it go at that.

Always pay close attention to the game. When you are dummy, you have certain duties to your partner, so do not wander around the room or look into your opponents' hands. If you don't know what your duties are, read the rules until you know them by heart and then—read them all over again! It is impossible to play any game without a thorough knowledge of the rules that govern it.

Don't be offended if your partner takes you out of a bid, and don't take him out for the glory of playing the hand. He is quite as anxious to win the rubber as you are. It is unbelievable how many people really seem to regard their partners as third opponents.

VARIOUS SPORTS

There are fixed rules for playing every game—and for proper conduct in every sport. The details of these rules must be studied in the books of the game, learned from instructors, or acquired by experience. A small boy perhaps learns to fish by himself, but he is probably taught by his father how to hunt with a gun or ride a horse. But apart from the technique of each sport, or the rules of each game, the basic principles of good sportsmanship are always the same. In no sport or game can any evasion of rules be allowed. Sport is based upon an impersonal and indiscriminating enforcement of all rules on everyone alike.

It would be impossible to discuss good manners in every game played by sports-loving Americans. Nor is it necessary, as most are governed by a combination of adherence to the rules of the game and common courtesy.

I have chosen four sports, however, in which good manners beyond the rule book are most important. They are yachting, tennis, golf, and skiing. The latter two I will dwell on at some length for three reasons. First, because of the enormous number of people who enjoy them. Second, because their popularity has increased so tremendously in very recent years that there are more people who do not know the rules—in fact, the rules are still being formed. And third, in both cases, adherence to the rules of etiquette is essential to the safety of the sport.

YACHTING

If you are the proud owner of a new yacht, be it a sail boat or power boat, and especially if it is your first venture in ownership, you must learn thoroughly and completely the rules of safety on the water. These rules and regulations can easily be obtained from the United States Coast Guard. After complying with the rules affecting other boats, the captain may establish the routine for his own boat in as rigid or as relaxed a way as he wishes. But there are certain procedures that have come to be regarded as most correct and most practical, and every guest should be acquainted with these conventions before accepting an invitation to go cruising.

On all but the most elaborate yachts or houseboats, space is very limited. Therefore, one takes as few clothes as possible. If you are going on an extended cruise, you must find out where and in what circumstances you will be going ashore. You may attend receptions, cocktail parties, or dances in five different ports, but remember that the people ashore will not have seen you in the other ports, and the people on other boats understand the space problem, so the same dress or two will serve for several trips to shore. Most captains keep foul weather gear on their boats, but before you sail be sure that he has sufficient, and if not, bring your own.

Some cruises, for example the New York Yacht Club cruise, do not allow laundry to be hung on deck. All participants should find out the regulations and plan their wardrobes to last the number of days between ports where a laundromat can be found.

Although many boat owners do not object to hard shoes on board, it is only polite to find out how your captain feels. If he does object, carry your party shoes in your hand until you reach shore, where you may change into them. Remember that regular rubber soles are slippery. If you are to be on board a boat that will be "heeling" (tipping with the wind) or one small enough so that it will pitch about in a rough sea, you should have grooved, nonskid sneakers, especially made for sailors.

All clothing must be packed in canvas bags or duffel bags, never in a hard suitcase. The latter is impossible to stow away, whereas the canvas ones can be squashed into a minimum of space.

If you are cruising on a luxurious yacht with a large crew, you treat them exactly as you would the servants in a house on land. There is no fraternization, but they are treated with friendliness and respect, and if a steward has taken care of you and your clothing, you may leave him a tip, just as you would a chambermaid, before going ashore.

There are no other rules that are not simply those of good manners anywhere. Remember that, even more than a host on shore, the skipper is boss, and, as much for safety as for politeness, his word is law. He, after all, is the one who knows the limits of his boat and also the capabilities of his guests or crew, and he has planned for the greatest enjoyment (and in racing, the greatest chance of success) that he possibly can.

Because of the close community living on board a boat, consideration for the other people with you is of utmost importance. Before you make any move, ask yourself if you will disturb one of the others, and try to be constantly aware of the special habits and likes and dislikes of your fellow cruisers.

TENNIS

Good manners on the tennis court are generally the rule, but one does see enough violations of etiquette to make them worth mentioning. More often than not, tennis is a partnership game, and one cannot, as he can in golf or skiing, play alone. Therefore, the most important rules of etiquette are those which deal with considerate manners between players.

First of all, never question the ruling of the linesmen or referee. You may think your ball landed "in" by a foot, but he is in a better place to see each line, and his decision must be final.

If your ball bounces out of your court and into the occupied court next to you, wait until those players have finished the point. Don't call "Ball, please" or dash over to retrieve it while their ball is still in play.

Change sides on every odd game if the sun or wind give an advantage to one court. This is a requirement in tournament play, and even in a friendly game, the offer should be made.

Children and beginners should not sign up for courts (at many clubs they are not allowed to) on weekends or other days that are the only ones on which the businessmen can play. If those happen to be the only times available to the novice as well, he should arrange to play very early in the morning or late in the afternoon.

When you arrive at the hour for which you have signed up and find the players on the court are playing what are probably the last points, wait patiently without pacing, bouncing balls, or glaring at them. In fact, it is polite to say, "Go ahead and finish. We don't mind waiting a few minutes." At the same time, when you are the one on the court, don't try to finish if you are not near the end of a set. Never finish out more than the game you are playing, and if that does not end the set, leave the court anyway.

At the end of a match, it is not necessary to hop over the net as the players do in the movies, but to do go up to the net and, shaking hands with your opponents, congratulate them for the good game if they won, or thank them for the excellent match if they lost.

Clothing for the tennis court is fully described in Chapter 75. Suffice it to say here that white is the tennis color, if it is not actually required, as it often is, and that clean, neat, modest shorts or dresses are correct on every court in every locality.

GOLF

Golf was originally considered (and with reason) a rich man's game. Today, however, with the appearance of the thousands of public courses that eliminate the necessity of joining an expensive club, millions of people are enjoying the game. For those who have recently started to play, there are—above and beyond learning to hit the ball correctly—many rules of etiquette to be learned.

Golf is a particularly severe strain upon the amiability of the average person, and in no other game, except probably bridge, is serenity of disposition so essential. No one who is easily ruffled can keep a clear eye on the ball, and exasperation at lost balls seemingly bewitches successive ones into disappearing like puffs of smoke. In a race or other test of endurance, a flare of anger might even help; but in golf, it is safe to say that he who loses his temper is almost certain to muff his shot and lose the match.

Golf players, of course, know the rules and observe them; but it quite often happens that idlers, having nothing better to do, walk out over a course and watch the players. If they know the players well, that is one thing; but they have no right to follow strangers. A diffident player is easily put off his game, especially if those watching him are so ill-bred as to make audible remarks. Those playing matches of course expect an audience; and erratic and nervous players ought not to go into tournaments—and certainly not into two-ball foursomes where they will handicap a partner.

Let us first consider those rules which help to eliminate the danger on a crowded golf course.

Never, in any circumstances, hit your shot until the group ahead of you is out of range. On weekends, there is generally a starter on the first tee who will tell you when to drive, but if not, you *must* wait until those who teed off before you have hit their second shots. And this rule is followed on every one of the eighteen holes. The only exception occurs when the group ahead feels that they are holding you up and signals to you to "go through." In this case, at least wait until they have moved to the edge of the fairway, and also be sure that they are all watching your ball in case it should go astray.

If you hit a wild shot that heads toward a player on another fairway, or if someone appears unexpectedly from behind a bush where he was searching for a ball, yell "Fore!" at the top of your lungs. Although he will not have time to locate your ball in flight and dodge, your shout will generally cause him to throw his arms over his head and possibly avoid serious injury.

On a blind hole (a hole where the green is not visible from where you are hitting), send a caddy or another player to the point at which he can see the area where your ball may be expected to land. If there are still other golfers in range, he holds up his hand to signal you to wait and then, when it is safe for you to hit, waves and steps to the edge of the fairway.

While waiting on a tee for your turn to drive, look around before taking a practice swing. Not only may you hit someone with your club, but if you are swinging toward them, you may blast them painfully with bits of stone or turf from the ground. This is true while playing other shots as well—your caddy or companions may be closer behind you than you think, and it is always safer to look before you swing.

In addition to these rules affecting safety on the golf course, there are many that add to the pleasure of the player and the orderly progression of the game.

Never speak, rattle your clubs, or move when another player is making his shot. This is especially true on the green, where intense concentration is required, but it can be disturbing on any part of the course. Even though you may think you are far enough away from the player whose turn it is to hit, the wind may carry a sound right to him, or he may catch your movement from the corner of his eye in the middle of his backswing.

It is a matter of convention rather than etiquette, but should be mentioned because it is important to the smooth functioning of the twosome or foursome, that the person whose ball is farthest from the pin, or hole, plays first. Around the putting green, there are certain set golf rules that apply to special situations, but in an informal match the ball farthest from the hole is played, even though it is not on the green, or putting surface. Usually, however, it is agreed that if a player's ball stops close to the hole, he will "putt out," or tap it in, to save the time involved in marking the spot, moving his ball, waiting for the others to play, replacing the ball, and then sinking the putt.

A foursome is obligated to allow a twosome to "go through," or pass them, if there is an empty hole ahead of them. This "if" is important, because when there are players directly in front, the twosome will be prevented from moving on, there will be a pile up of six or more players on the same hole, and those behind will have an even more lengthy wait. In the case of a foursome following a foursome, or a twosome following a twosome, the first one obviously holding up the second, it is very rude of the slower one not to allow the others to go through.

It is customary for the player who has had the lowest score on the previous hole to "tee off," or drive, first on the next hole. If two or more are tied for the "honor," as this privilege is called, the one who had the lowest score on the last hole on which there was a difference plays first. In the case of teams, all members of the team that won the last hole go first and usually keep the same order no matter which one of them had the low score.

The final three rules relate to the proper care of the course. It should hardly be necessary to say that divots (pieces of turf dug up by the club head) should be replaced, but if one walks over a course after a busy weekend, it is apparent from the number of brown pits all over the fairways that golfers' education has been sadly neglected in this area. Equally important is the need for repairing the little pits made in the green by a high approach shot.

After playing a shot out of a trap (or bunker), the player must see that his caddy rakes the sand to eliminate his footprints, and the hole made by his club. If he has no caddy, he must do it himself. In the event that there is no rake by the trap, he may do his best to smooth the sand with the head of his club.

Beyond these rules, all golfers will continue to enjoy the sport more and more if tempers are restrained and everyday rules of courtesy are observed.

SKIING

The number of people who have recently become enthusiasts makes skiing in winter comparable to golf in the summer, and as in golf, many of the rules of etiquette for skiers have developed from a need for safety regulations. In fact, on the ski slopes, except for the ordinary rules of good behavior and consideration for others, almost all the etiquette is derived from an effort to eliminate dangerous situations.

Never ski alone. Even the most expert skier in the world can have an accident—in fact the best skiers may have the most serious falls, as a result of their speed—and cold and emptiness are no respectors of skill if one falls on a lonely trail when no one knows his whereabouts. There has been more than one case reported of a skier's foolishly going off by himself and never being found until the melting snow uncovers his body in the spring.

Never ski on a closed trail. The commonest reason for blocking it off is that it is considered too dangerous for skiing at the time. Some young daredevils, thinking that nothing is too difficult for them, are occasionally tempted to ski a trail that has been marked "Closed." First and foremost, this is foolish, as the ski patrols have no obligation to patrol that slope and in case of accident the skiers are far from help. Secondarily, the trail may be closed in order to keep the snow in condition for a time later in the season or for a special competition. In the latter case, it is thoughtless to the management of the area, and also to the skiers who were to enjoy it when it opened.

Never ski on a trail or slope that is too difficult for you. All ski areas mark their trails "Novice," "Intermediate," or "Expert," or possibly a combination of two—"Novice-Intermediate." If you have only been skiing a few times, don't assume that because in other sports you are as good as your friend Sally, who has been on the slopes since she was three, you are capable of accompanying her to the top of the mountain to try the new "expert" trail. Not only are you likely to break a leg, but you will infuriate the true experts who are entitled to use the trail and who will hardly appreciate rounding a curve at high speed only to find a novice "snow-plowing" down the middle of the trail in front of them.

The other side of the coin must be cited, too. If you are an expert, high-speed-loving skier, stay off the novice and intermediate slopes as much as possible. There is no need to make them more crowded than they ordinarily are, and nothing is more terrifying to a beginner than a hurtling skier rushing past him or even, as I have seen so often, running over the tips of her skis or actually knocking her down.

Skiers cannot be put on little tracks labeled 10 mph, 20 mph, 40 mph, and so forth, however, and there are certain to be occasions when a faster skier must pass a slower skier on a narrow trail. In order to warn him (or her) that he is about to pass, he calls "Track, right" or "Track, left" indicating that he will pass on that side, thereby warning the slower skier to pull to the other side—or at least not to make a sudden turn toward him as he passes.

If, because of a miscalculation, or for any reason whatever, you do knock another skier down, STOP! Apologize, and make absolutely sure that he is not injured before you continue on down the hill.

If he appears to be having difficulty in regaining his feet, it is only common courtesy to go back and assist him. If he really is unable to move or get up or is in pain, do not fly off hysterically looking for help, but stay with him, doing whatever you can, such as undoing his harnesses, to make him more comfortable, until another skier comes near. Then, and only then, having asked the new arrival to stay with the injured person, you may go as fast as you possibly can to the nearest ski patrol. Never try to move the fallen skier. If he is suffering from a broken bone you may cause a much more serious injury if you move him incorrectly. The ski patrol is trained to do this and will have the proper equipment with them when they arrive.

Remember that the mountain may be very large, and it is very difficult to find another person at any given time. When you are a member of a group, family or friends, it is wise to set a specific place and time at which to meet for meals, to go home, or just to "check in."

Otherwise, good manners for skiers are simply a matter of employing consideration for others at all times. Don't ridicule the novice even jokingly, and don't boast of your own skill. When the line waiting for the lift is long, don't shove your way in ahead of those already waiting, but take your place patiently and cheerfully. If you are with a group, don't hold the better skiers up by insisting that they wait for you, and if you are one of the more expert, don't insist that the beginners accompany you where they are not capable of staying in control and enjoying it.

Skiing is a wonderful sport, both for physical thrills, and for the social life that is a part of it. But more than in almost any other sport, consideration of others and good manners are essential to the enjoyment and safety of everyone.

69

For the newcomer

Moving to a new community presents problems to all but the most seasoned of transient households. Mrs. Engineer, whose husband stays in one spot only long enough to complete a bridge and then transports his family to another river half way across the continent, may after a few years develop her own packing and moving system to a high degree of perfection and find it not too difficult to adjust to a new neighborhood. But Mrs. Newlywed, leaving her life-long home for the first time, can find the change very difficult, and it is primarily, but not solely, to her that these remarks are directed.

THE NEW BRIDE

The young woman who is a stranger, but whose husband and his family are well known in the community, has no problem other than to make herself liked in her new surroundings. The best way to do this is to be ready to like others, to be interested in what interests them, and to try to adapt herself to their points of view. This does not mean that she is to be double-faced, but merely that she is not to ride roughshod over their pet prejudices before she has even discovered what they are. The bride, for example, who comes from Chicago or San Francisco to

Bright Meadows and rudely criticizes the smaller town's ways, who insists on comparing Bright Meadows' new six-story office building with fifty-story skyscrapers, is being not merely discourteous but stupid.

The best ingredients for likableness are a happy expression of countenance, an unaffected manner, and a sympathetic attitude. A young woman with an affected pose and bad or conceited manners will never make friends anywhere. The best rule to follow, as always: Be your own natural self.

The newcomer, whether a new bride or not, should particularly avoid forcing herself on her neighbors. It is fatal to be pushing or presumptuous. She should remain natural when anyone approaches her, but she should not herself approach anyone more than half-way. A smile to the passing acquaintance, the friendlier the better, is never out of place, but after smiling she should continue on. Enthusiasm should, of course, be shown to friends, in contrast to the more impersonal courtesy displayed to strangers.

WHEN BOTH ARE STRANGERS

Let us say the young Lakes from Chicago are about to move to Strangetown, where John Lake will be employed in the new branch office his firm has just opened. Business is the usual reason for moving to a new community. John will, of course, meet a few people through business. If the town is small and characteristically friendly, Mary will probably get to know her neighbors quickly. The Lakes will become members of the church and, by participating in a variety of church and community activities, gradually enlarge their acquaintance.

A LETTER OF INTRODUCTION

Before the Lakes left Chicago, they told Mrs. Oldname about John's new location, and Mrs. Oldname offered to send a letter introducing the young couple to a friend of hers in Strangetown.

A letter of introduction is better sent than taken in person by the newcomers. If the Lakes themselves were to take a letter to Mrs. Welcome, this lady would be obligated, whether she felt like it or not, to show them immediate and particular hospitality, or risk affronting both the newcomers and the writer of the letter. A letter of introduction sent by Mrs. Oldname and telling her friends about Mary and John Lake gives Mrs. Welcome time to consider when and how best she may introduce the young couple to other and congenial young people. It does not force the Lakes upon the intimate hospitality of Mrs. Welcome as a letter taken by them to her would do. » *For further details, see Chapter 9.*

NEWCOMERS TO A BIG CITY

Because so many young people have the notion that life in a great city is glamorous, those who come from a small, neighborly community into a huge city of titanic size and crushing indifference are likely to be greatly disappointed and unhappy. The young bride will find herself bereft of a position such as she had at home or would have had in almost any other small community. This is not because the great city refuses to accept her; it simply doesn't know of her existence. In a small town she would not remain for long an unrecognized stranger. If she walked down Main Street a dozen times, dozens of people would have seen her every time.

If you plan to move to one of our large cities, try not to go into a neighborhood where you will know no one at all. If you have any friends or relatives in the city, try to find an apartment within easy traveling distance of them. Or perhaps a man's business associates in a new city can recommend a neighborhood with which they are familiar. If you know no one at all in the city, you may be more at home in a suburb where the casual informality will provide new friends more easily.

But even if you do take an apartment in, let's say, the heart of New York, you will, in time, find a circle of friends. Even in the largest city in the world, people can be friendly. Just give a few of them a chance to get to know you. You'll meet your next-door neighbors in the laundry room or the elevator, or in the park a block away. If you as well as your husband have a career, you will meet people of similar interests through business. Become an *active* member of the nearest church of your denomination; perhaps it has a Young Couples' Club, a Bible Study class, or some other activities you both can participate in. The YMCA and similar organizations sponsor a variety of clubs and classes. And every large city has several universities offering evening extension courses. Study French literature or interior decorating and make friends with the others taking the same courses. Above all, be sure to keep busy; never stay at home moping about the town you came from. The bigger the city you move to, the more there is for you to do and discover in it.

YOUR FIRST VISITORS

Very probably some of your new neighbors will come to call before your home is ready to receive visitors. If they find you at the top of a stepladder or in a paint-spattered smock, you are really in luck. If you think about it, you will realize that this is a far more friendly setting than a formal hostess-visitor scene could be. Before you know it, you will be showing your neighbors the objects you have painted and the curtain material you are going to sew; and before they know it, they are giving you their best advice which perhaps you take or perhaps you don't. By the time they go they seem like friends, and probably they soon become just that. But for the more formal first call, see Chapter 57.

BEWARE OF IMMEDIATE INTIMACY

If you wish never to seem to be a snob, beware of rushing into intimacy with every welcoming but not necessarily congenial neighbor, and then later having to break with your earlier acquaintances when you meet people you really like. After you have been in your new home for a while, you will come to know people whose interests are the same as your own. You can avoid suddenly having to neglect those with whom you were too intimate at first, if you are selective and somewhat reserved from the beginning. If, however, you *are* a snob, and transfer yourself from the Nextdoor circle to the Highhills, who are richer or more important, you will deserve the opinion that others will most certainly have of you.

Between being a snob and being selective is the entire distance between being contemptible and admirable—between worst and best.

70

With regard to artists, entertainers, and other celebrities

When we meet a performing artist or a distinguished lecturer or a celebrity of any kind, ordinary good manners and common courtesy should cover almost every situation, but only too often problems arise. Indeed, the forms of impoliteness may cover a very wide range—from the debutante's mother who thinks nothing of being rude to the musicians hired to play for the tea dance to the lion-hunting hostess who invites a theatrical star to dinner not because of any genuine feeling of friendship for him, but merely because of a misguided wish to impress her other guests—which she certainly will not do in any desirable way.

THE ARTIST IS EMPLOYED

Apart from the courtesies that every hostess instinctively shows to friends, acquaintances, or strangers alike when they are admitted to her house, particular rules that apply in reference to professional artists hired to entertain depend upon circumstances. Unless their presence is to be a surprise, all entertainers should be admitted at the front door, of course.

Musicians who play at a dance or at a wedding reception necessarily arrive long before the guests, and they are shown at once to a dressing room and then to the place where they are to play. They should be greeted briefly by whoever is in charge of arrangements. Refreshments should be taken to them at the times that fit in best with their program.

Soloists or actors who are to make their entrance from behind scenery as on a stage should be shown to the dressing rooms and then to a sitting room or other convenient spot, to await the hour of their performance. They should be greeted as soon after their arrival as possible by the host or hostess or both, who naturally ask whether there is anything that would add to their comfort. Whether after their performance they meet many of the guests or none depends upon their own standing no less than upon their personality and their wishes. When musicians or actresses or actors are especially charming or talented, or both, guests will almost surely ask to meet them.

COURTESY TO A CELEBRITY

A real celebrity, whether a star in the musical world or a notable person who is to lecture, is usually the guest of honor and treated as such in every particular. Since the hostess may be busy with the guests, the host or another member of the family is delegated to greet the celebrity upon his arrival and to conduct him to whichever is the most suitable room in which to wait until it is time for his entrance. The host or delegate-host remains with the artist or speaker until the hostess herself appears. She greets the celebrity and conducts him to the music room or to the platform and introduces him to the audience. At the end of the program, the hostess stands beside him and introduces those of her guests who come up to be introduced.

But no matter in which category an artist belongs, there is a certain purely business matter-of-factness to the situation of a professional fulfilling an engagement. He goes prepared to do to the best of his ability what he has agreed to do, and at the close of his performance he receives the sum that has been agreed upon. Whether in addition to this he has a delightful evening or a trying one is, as far as his business contract goes, beside the mark.

THE ARTIST IS A FRIEND

For obvious reasons, a most indefensible creature is the hostess who considers the talents of professional friends—and even mere acquaintances—as assets to which she has proprietary rights. Don't we all know Mrs. Hi Wayman, who invites Mr. Barrytone Tops or Mr. Hitshow to dine on Sunday evening? After dinner she coyly announces that she just knows that Mr. Tops will be delighted to sing, or that Mr. Hitshow will *of course* do that delicious scene that is the only reason why the theater is packed to bursting every night in the week except this—his one evening of rest!

It is often true that at a party of considerable size a star-ranking professional can, or possibly must, decline on the plea that contracts prohibit his performance. But at an informal dinner at which one or two others of lesser talent have contributed their part, it is often embarrassing to refuse because it seems ungenerous to all those present who so eagerly look toward him. But actually it is distinctly unfair to expect someone to return the courtesy of a little food and a place at table between no matter how pleasant companions with an entertainment commercially valued at something approaching, or possibly surpassing, four figures! And even if he is not at or near the top of his profession, remember that your guest is not a trained poodle to be put through a bag of tricks for the entertainment of your other guests.

FAVORS TOO MUCH TAKEN FOR GRANTED

Much might be said about the unthinking casualness with which numberless people ask favors of their professional friends. Put bluntly, one would not go to a bank and ask for money, nor to the shop of a milliner and ask to be given a hat, and yet the friends of a professional artist will think nothing of asking for a sketch or a recital. And the work of every professional is his livelihood. If he gives to one person, how can he refuse to give to another—and who will want to buy what is given so freely?

Of much less importance, but merely illustrating the point: The barest acquaintances of an author think nothing of asking him for his books. Apparently most people imagine that books grow like daisies in the field and that an author need merely pick them at random. Doctors and lawyers are constantly asked for professional advice by people they meet casually in the houses of their friends. As for people of the theater, no others in all the professions in the world are so persistently asked to give their time, their vitality, and their talent. And in nearly all cases they are delighted to give generously to someone they care for or to a cause in which they are interested; but when they are asked to give, a conventional "I'm so sorry" should be respected without forcing them into a position that seems to make them appear ungracious.

If musicians are amateurs, however, their friends can perfectly well ask them to play at a musicale. But they should not be asked to provide a background accompaniment to chatter. No one with any sensibility would invite first-class artists to play or sing and then make no effort to preserve a courteous silence during their performance. On the other hand, professional dance orchestras and other party musicians who play at dances and at weddings do not expect, or even want, to face a room full of completely silent people.

AUTOGRAPHS

The number of people who recognize the celebrity on the street and the number who wait outside the stage door to get his autograph are among the principal measures of his success. If he is rude or impatient with these fans, it can only have an adverse affect on his popularity, and therefore most entertainers or professionals whose success depends on their public image are willing to be watched, followed, and hounded for their signatures. The greater the degree of friendliness and tact with which they submit to these annoyances, the greater their success with the public.

By respecting the fact that their idol cannot defend himself against invasions of his privacy without alienating people, his fans should confine their efforts to the times when he expects to sign their books and otherwise fulfill his obligations as a public figure. When a prominent person is in his home or dining out, even though he may be in a public restaurant, or shopping, or seeking a little relaxation in a sport or a hobby, or otherwise attempting to lead a normal life, he should be allowed his privacy.

71

With the handicapped

It is probably true that a majority of the people in the world have little contact with the unfortunate ones who are handicapped or disabled. If we have a cripple of any sort in our homes, or in the home of a relative or friend, we quickly become accustomed to the situation and learn how to act so as to be of the most help to him and to those around him. Should the disabled one be a member of our own family, we make every effort to learn all that we can about his problem, to seek professional advice, and to make his life, as well as our own, as normal as possible. This chapter, therefore, is devoted to those who meet the handicapped only from time to time and who, in making an effort to be helpful, may go about it, through lack of knowledge, in the wrong way. Their intentions may be the very best, but an act of kindness, tendered in the wrong way, may be a cause of much embarrassment and even actual harm to the very person they are trying to help.

There are certain rules that apply to your behavior in regard to all handicapped people, and the most important by far is this: NEVER stare, or indicate that you are conscious that the person is different from others in any way. People who are getting themselves about in wheelchairs, have mastered the use of crutch or brace, or can manipulate a mechanical hand dexterously take great pride in their independence and approach to normalcy. The last thing they wish is to be reminded by curious or overly solicitous persons that they have not achieved their goal. An offer of help to a man in a wheelchair who must navigate a steep curb in order to cross the street or an arm proffered to a lady with a cane and a leg brace who is trying to get down a rail-less set of steps is, of course, in order. But before grabbing the wheelchair or seizing her arm, ask politely if, and in what way, you can be of assistance.

Another important rule is never to make personal remarks, or ask personal questions of one with an obvious disability. If he wishes to talk about the accident that caused it or discuss his condition, let him introduce the subject, but never, never pry into his feelings or his clinical symptoms—subjects that he may be doing his best to forget.

Of all forms of disabilities, deafness and blindness are the two with which the greatest number of people come into frequent contact. Therefore, I am making some suggestions, not only for those meeting deaf or blind people, but for those so handicapped themselves.

DEAFNESS

There are, of course, all degrees of deafness, from partial loss of hearing in one ear, to the more unusual extreme of complete deafness, which cannot be helped even by a hearing aid. It may only be necessary to speak a little more distinctly to one who is partially deaf or to repeat a remark that he may have missed. If you know that the hearing loss is in one ear, it is considerate to sit on the side of his good ear in movies, restaurants, or any place where you may not face him. In the case of total hearing loss, the only means of contact is visual—through lip reading—so the rules are quite different from those applying to someone with partial hearing.

You must speak distinctly and reasonably slowly.

Don't use exaggerated mouth movements. Distorted lip motions may confuse him, as he has been taught to read normal lip movement.

To attract his attention, it is useless to shout. If he is not facing you, tap him gently on the arm or shoulder.

Be patient in talking to him and willing to repeat or make your statement in words that are easier for him to understand.

Encourage him to participate in family and social activities. Persons with severe handicaps tend to withdraw into themselves, but it is not to their own good, and it only upsets their family and friends. A little extra urging and enthusiasm over their presence can make the handicapped feel much more like leading a normal life.

Between the slightly deaf and the totally deaf fall the many thousands with intermediate degrees of the disability. The first thing to be recommended for them is that they wear a hearing aid. There is no more stigma or embarrassment in this than in wearing glasses, and the family and friends of those who are reluctant should do their best to persuade them to overcome their hesitation. Once persuaded, they will find that their life will attain a normalness they had never thought possible. Here are some rules that should be observed for conversation with the partially deaf:

Don't raise your voice or shout—his hearing aid is probably adjusted for a normal voice.

Call him by name to attract his attention.

As with the more severely handicapped, be patient—willing to repeat if necessary. And if you must repeat, don't shout or appear annoyed. This will only embarrass him and make it harder for him to understand.

Don't exclude him from conversation, but try to place him so that he may see you or the group. Even normal people read lips unconsciously, and it is a great help to one handicapped by partial deafness.

If you are one of those handicapped by deafness yourself, a few of the following suggestions may add to your comfort and that of your friends.

DO wear a hearing aid—they are now made in such a way as to be almost invisible, and even if they weren't, loss of hearing is no more "shameful" than loss of sight, and few people refuse to wear glasses.

Having gotten a hearing aid, wear it! A strained expression of concentration, a constant, "What did you say?" and answers that make no sense make you appear inattentive, or stupid, when there is no need to. Keep your aid turned on, and gain the admiration of your friends for so capably overcoming your handicap.

With or without your aid, do listen attentively and concentrate on what people are saying. Even people with normal hearing miss many remarks through inattention.

Look at the people talking to you—their expression and their lips will help you to "hear" them.

Don't take advantage of your impairment by trying to arouse sympathy. There is no justifiable reason for sympathy—a deaf person can, with a little extra effort, lead a perfectly normal life.

BLINDNESS

The most important thing to remember when coming in contact with some one handicapped by blindness is that in every other respect he is exactly like you. His other facilities are in no way impaired; his interests and his way of life may be much the same as yours. He certainly has a problem to overcome that does not face a person with normal sight, but it is a problem with which one can learn to live, and most blind people have done so with considerable success.

Therefore the cardinal rule is this: Treat the blind man as you would any other person. Talk to him, in a normal voice, about the same subjects that would interest your other friends, including blindness, if it should come up. Don't avoid the use of the word "see." Blind people use it as much as any one else. There is no reason to show surprise that he can dial telephone numbers, light a cigarette, dress himself, or perform any of the daily chores that we all do. He has simply made a little more effort to learn to do them by touch or sound.

Aside from your attitude, there are several specific suggestions that will make your contacts with a blind person more pleasurable to you both.

When you are with, or pass by, a blind person on a street corner, you are perfectly correct in asking if you can help him to cross, but never grasp his arm or try to give assistance without first asking whether he wishes it or not. If he does, let *him* take *your* arm, which will give him far more confidence than being propelled forward by you. If he should ask you for directions, be sure to use left and right from his viewpoint—the direction he is facing.

If you go to a restaurant with a blind person, do not hesitate to read him the menu, including the prices if the occasion demands. You certainly may tell him quietly where the salt and pepper are and help him to the sugar and cream if he wishes. You may tell him how the items on his plate are arranged and help him cut his meat if necessary. But much of this he will prefer to do himself if you simply locate the food for him.

When he visits your home, lead him to a chair and then just place his hand on the arm or back. If he is staying with you for any length of time, remember to tell him where the furniture is, mention it if anything is rearranged, and keep doors open or closed—never half way.

When taking him to a strange place, tell him quietly where the furniture is located and who is present. And before you leave him alone, be sure that he has someone to talk to—one thing he cannot do (unless he is among good friends whose voices he recognizes) is single out a person who would, from his appearance, be congenial.

When there is a blind person in a room you have just entered, make your presence known, and tell him, if he does not recognize your voice, who you are. Tell him also when you leave, so that he will not be left talking—to himself.

Last of all, if the blind person has a Seeing Eye dog, do not attempt to play with or distract the dog in any way. His attention must remain fully on his master, whose safety and well being may depend entirely on his strict adherence to his training.

72

For pets and people

A dog may be man's best friend and a cat by the hearth a very cozy sight, but all who own pets are responsible for seeing that they behave in such a way as to make them the real friends of everyone with whom they come in contact. Pets other than dogs and cats may be fewer in number, but their good manners are just as important. And, if your children's rabbit cannot be trained not to make a nuisance of himself, *your* good manners must take over and insist that he be kept in his pen when visitors are in the house.

DOGS

For years people have complained to me, about the unnecessary problems created by neighbor's pets. Is there anything that the Joneses can do to protect themselves from the ill-mannered dogs of neighbors or visitors or even house guests? I could quote instances by the dozen of pleasant neighborhood friendships that have become strained and even broken by the Smith dog that barks all night, or the Pope dog that runs through flower beds and possibly rolls or digs in them, too. Then there are other dogs brought by their owners into friends' houses and allowed to jump up on the furniture, in spite of muddy paws or sharp claws that dig into the sofa cushions. We have all known owners who complacently believe that their pet is perfectly trained to stay wherever they tell him to stay. It never occurs to them, engrossed in conversation, to notice that in less than a minute after he was told to stay there, he has quietly slipped away on an exploring expeditioh. If he is a dog of mature intelligence, he may, it is quite true, make an entirely impersonal and dignified survey of the premises. But if he is young and eager to test the taste, texture, and toughness of every new thing he sees, his investigation may all too well become a foray of destruction. » *For suggestions about the note of apology to be written after such an unfortunate episode, see Chapter 9.*

The behavior of a dog—like that of the rest of us—is seldom better out in company than it is at home. If Kiltie (bright little Scottie though he is) is allowed to run around the dinner table and beg, he will do the same in every other house. Moreover, he is naturally more restless out where new surroundings tantalize his curiosity than he is at home where everything is familiar to him and he can be allowed the freedom of the house.

On the subject of that seemingly unaccountable lapse from trustworthy behavior that *can* overtake a dog who is allowed to wander at liberty in a strange house—particularly a new house—owners sometimes fail to realize that it is the thoroughly impregnated scent of "human habitation" that tells him he is indoors. To his sense of smell, new upholstery or a newly laid carpet, which has had almost no human handling, is easily mistaken for outdoors. He can't tell the difference between indoor decoration and outdoor view just by sight! It is always safest in a strange house to keep him on a short leash unless his obedience to command is so complete that wherever he may be, he pays attention to nothing but his position at his master's side. On the street, he does not even glance in the direction of another dog unless his master releases him by saying in a changed tone, "Go run," and he is free to go where he pleases. At the command "Heel!" he takes his place at his master's side with the precision of a soldier obeying the command of his sergeant. In fact, you might test your own dog's training by noticing when you take him out, whether he is welcomed by your neighbor, "Hello, Topsie," "Good morning, Blackie!" or by a frown that clearly says, "Oh dear, there's that dreadful dog again!"

It is true, some people do not like dogs at all. Plainly then, if you are invited to stay with those who do not welcome four-footed visitors, this is one of the occasions when ownership of a dog exacts its payment, and you must stay home unless you have someone with whom you can leave him or a good kennel at which you can board him. On the other hand, no absolutely obedient dog has ever—so far as I know personally—been objected to by anyone, even as a house guest. But the dog who is told "Come here" only to have him run in the other direction, the puppy who nips people on the ankle, the one who chews on everything he can get his teeth into, the big, loose-lipped dog who on hot days drools like a teething baby over the suits and dresses of visitors instead of being made to lie down in the coolest unspoilable floor space—and stay there—are not social assets even in the opinion of dog-lovers.

But to train a dog to such a degree that he obeys on the second every word spoken, or every wordless gesture made to him, requires consistent as well as persistent patience directed by practical common sense. That perfect training is entirely possible has been proved not only by the miracle dogs who are Seeing Eyes for the blind and by the dogs trained as assistants to the police, but by all other breeds of dogs who perform in the theater, by those which herd sheep, and by those who work flawlessly in the hunting field. Surely then, it is not too much to ask that adequate education be given to the four-footed members of the family. One thing is certainly true: the rewards of beautiful manners are very great. Not only does the behavior of a canine gentleman (or lady) quite actually enhance the social prestige of his master, but the dog himself acquires stature as a companion, a guardian, and a friend—in short, a recognized personality.

CATS

In some ways, cats present different problems, for they are taken visiting far less often. When your cat has the run of the neighborhood, however, you may have to take steps to see that he does not become an inadvertent but regular visitor to the house of someone who once innocently set out a saucer of milk in the kitchen, only to find the cat perched between the Dresden figurines on the mantel. It is perfectly proper, before the accident has a chance to occur, to ask your neighbors not to feed your pet, as the bad habit is hard to break and can easily become a neighborhood problem.

In your own house, you may be quite accustomed to having your cat jump into your lap without warning, but remember that your guest probably isn't. Not only will there be a suit or dress covered with hairs and possibly snagged; there may be a broken teacup or a burned carpet as a result of the natural and involuntary start of surprise. Until you know your visitor well, it is far safer to put Fluffy securely in another room and in no way unkind to your pet, for very likely you are saving him from the discipline his overenthusiasm deserves.

Some people, of course, have real aversions to all cats, even the best behaved, and you should no more force Fluffy's presence on them than you would force crabmeat on a guest who is allergic to it.

OTHER PEOPLE

If you are one of those who have an allergy or an aversion to dogs, cats, hamsters, white mice, or any of the other pets you are likely to encounter, it is only polite of you to tell your host or hostess quietly and unobtrusively, just as you would mention a food allergy to avoid embarrassment at the dinner table. No one will wish you to suffer as a guest in his house, and a few words can usually prevent much discomfort and possibly an unpleasant misunderstanding.

On the other hand, if you are fond of household animals, you should take every care to respect their training and encourage their good habits. Don't, for example, thump the sofa beside you and invite Kiltie to jump up until you have asked whether he is allowed to sit on the furniture. Don't feed an animal without his owner's permission, any more than you give a child candy without asking his mother first. If you wish your pet-owning friends and neighbors to respect your rights, do remember that your thoughtless actions may undo months of careful training.

73

Women's clothes and fashions

Clothes do more than add to our appearance; in one sense, they are our appearance. The first impression that we make upon others depends almost entirely upon what we wear and how we wear it. Manners and speech are noted afterward, and character is discerned last of all.

Character is, of course, the true essential; but for the transient impression that we make everywhere in public, two superficial attributes are indispensable—good manners and a pleasing appearance. And such an appearance is impossible without an average degree of smartness.

THE CLOTHES THAT SUIT

The woman who knows how to wear clothes is like a stage director who skillfully presents—herself. This skill in presentation is something for which it is difficult to give directions, because it is a talent rather than a formula. Naturally, one who is young, whose skin is clear, and whose figure is size ten or twelve can wear almost any dress she fancies and have it become her to perfection. And yet a woman lacking the knack of personal adjustment will find the buying of a becoming hat such a trial that she finally buys, not one she likes, but the one she dislikes least.

The sense of what is becoming and the knack of wearing clothes well are the two greatest assets of smartness. And both are attainable by anyone willing to look at herself as she really is.

SHORT WOMEN

There are certain basic principles that all women should consider when they are buying their clothes. Very short women should choose clothes with long vertical lines rather than those broken at the waist by a belt or band of contrasting color. High heels add height, but better to choose a moderate heel than a "spike" if one is unable to walk gracefully on the latter. Hair-dos that are high on top of the head and tall hats add inches to the short woman.

TALL WOMEN

Tall girls should feature outfits with a break in the middle—a wide belt, a suit with a long jacket, or costumes with contrasting colors in skirt and top. Pretty shoes are sold for the tall girl, with slim graceful heels of low or moderate height. When a hat is worn, it should not add inches to the head, nor should the hair-do.

FAT WOMEN

The plump woman must avoid large prints, wide plaids, and bulky materials. Black and navy blue are the most slimming colors, but any solid color or small print also looks well if it is becoming to her complexion. Clothes should not be tight enough to reveal a bulge, but neither should they be "baggy" or gathered at the waist. A flared skirt (often called the A-shape) is much more flattering than either a "dirndl" or a straight style. Upswept hair-dos, if becoming to the face, and long earrings help to lengthen a short neck. Evening dresses should be as simple as possible, and, if practical, a style that covers the upper arm (having a matching stole, for example) is desirable. Bathing suits with a skirt of a reasonable length help to hide chubby thighs, and please, no "stretch" suits "to hold in the tummy"! The fat girl, alas, must give up wearing shorts and slacks in public.

THIN WOMEN

The thin girl has relatively few problems, as most clothes look well on a slim figure. If the neck bones are prominent, however, a low neck line should be avoided, and because a long neck often goes with a thin figure, turtle neck blouses, high collars, and scarves are usually most becoming. The interesting "nubbly" materials, which so many women cannot wear, go well on the thin girl, as do more extreme styles, such as short straight skirts. This type is also fortunate in being able to wear shorts or slacks with style.

THE AVERAGE FIGURE

If you have a more or less average figure, choose clothes that exaggerate your good points, either in color or style. Minimize your poorer features, heavy hips, perhaps, or a thick waist, by choosing clothes that disguise those faults. And consider your age. The older woman may feel she is still a "sport," but she might better carry on her athletics in a smartly tailored skirt rather than brief shorts. Nor does graying hair look well in a long loose hair-do; the shorter, fuller, or upswept styles are more becoming to a mature face.

FAD FOLLOWERS

Fashion has the power to appear temporarily in the guise of beauty, though as often as not it is the antithesis of beauty. If you doubt it, look at old fashion plates. Even the woman of beautiful taste succumbs occasionally to the epidemics of fashion, but she is more immune than most. All women who have any clothes sense whatever know more or less the type of things that are their style—unless they have such a temporary attack of "fashionitis" that they are irresponsibly delirious.

There is one unchanging principle which must be followed by everyone who would be well dressed—*suitability*. A great number of American women do dress with this in mind, but less numerous, although far more conspicuous, are the dressed-to-the-minute women who, like sheep exactly, follow every turn of latest fashion blindly and without the slightest sense of whether it is a good one or absurd, or even if it is in the least becoming to her. As each new season's fashion is defined, all the sheep run and dress themselves each in a replica of the other; their own types and personalities have nothing to do with the case. Fashion says, "Wear a three-cornered handkerchief instead of a bodice," and daughter, mother, grandmother, and all the neighbors wear the same. If emerald green is fashionable, all the yellowest skins will be framed in it. Utility, becomingness, suitability, and beauty are of no importance. Fashion is followed to the letter—therefore they fancy, poor sheep, that they are the last word in smartness. Those whom the fashion suits are "smart" but they are seldom, if ever, distinguished because—they are all precisely alike.

VULGAR CLOTHES

To define differences between clothes that are notable because of their smartness and clothes that are merely conspicuous is to define something very elusive. Vulgar clothes are those which, no matter what the fashion of the moment may be, are always too elaborate for the occasion, are too exaggerated in style, or have accessories out of harmony with the dress and the wearer.

Beau Brummell's remark—when someone attracted too much notice, he could be sure of being, not well dressed, but overdressed—has for over a hundred years been the comfort of the dowdy. It is, of course, very often true, but not invariably so. A person may be stared at for any one of many reasons. A woman may be stared at because she is ill-behaved, or because she looks like a freak of the circus, or because she is enchanting to behold.

THE WOMAN WHO IS CHIC

The woman who is chic is always a little different. Not different in being behind fashion, but always slightly apart from it. Chic (pronounced *sheek*) is a borrowed adjective, but unfortunately no word in our language expresses its meaning. Its nearest description today is the combination of sophistication and fastidious taste. By way of comment, the word chi-chi (pronounced *she-she*) is not a synonym for chic, but a flashy imitation of it.

The woman who is chic adapts fashion to her own personality. This is in contrast to the woman who will merely buy the latest hat or dress and adapt herself to it, whether the fashion is suited to her or not. When it is conspicuously *not*, it is likely to be chi-chi.

ACCESSORIES

Accessories are as important to the budget-conscious woman as the basic dress. They provide the accents that can vary the costume, giving it versatility, as well as adding to its beauty. In planning your wardrobe, it is well to stick to a narrow range of colors, so that the same accessories may be used with a number of outfits. That is not to say, however, that accessories should limit your wardrobe; instead they should broaden it. A simple black dress may be perfect for lunch at a restaurant or an afternoon of shopping when it is worn with a gold circle pin, single-pearl earrings, and a daytime watch or wide gold bracelet and accompanied by black kid pumps and a plain leather pocketbook. But change these accessories to a diamond or zircon clip (or instead add a single or double strand of pearls), diamond (or pearl drop) earrings, a bracelet, perhaps, or a ring of glittering stones, suede pumps, and a small suede purse, and you may appear at any but the most formal party that night.

JEWELRY

It has always been the rule of the well dressed not to wear too many jewels in public places because such a display is considered ostentatious and in poor taste. But with the improvement in quality, and the consequent rise in popularity, of costume jewelry, smart women all over have increased the amount of jewelry they wear in public as well as at home. Certain gems, such as sapphires, can actually be manufactured now, and others are beautifully imitated. Cultured pearls rival "real" pearls in beauty, and such semiprecious stones as zircons, garnets, or jade come in an infinite variety of colors. With the lower cost of these substitutes for expensive gems, many more women than ever before are able to wear beautiful jewelry.

As with clothing, jewelry should be chosen and worn with an eye to suitability rather than to fad. A woman with stubby unattractive hands, for example, should not draw attention to them with a large flashing ring, no matter how popular the style. Furthermore, the type of jewelry worn changes with the time of day and the activity. When engaging in an active sport, jewelry of any kind is out of place. In the daytime, a gold or silver bracelet, a string of pearls, and earrings unadorned by large stones are more suitable than the brilliant gems that go well with evening clothes. A pretty pin or clip to set off a dress or suit is lovely at any hour. In short, the choice of jewelry is limited only by the good taste and the budget of the wearer.

GLOVES

Gloves are worn on city streets, to luncheons, dinner parties, and other social gatherings, to churches, and to restaurants, theaters, and all other public places of entertainment. At a restaurant, theater, or the like, they may be removed on arrival, but they are generally left on in church except during communion or when it is very warm.

A lady never takes off her gloves to shake hands, no matter when or where, and *never* apologizes for not doing so. But she *always* removes them for dining. On formal occasions, the hostess should wear gloves to shake hands with her guests—and keep them on until food is served. Gloves are *always* worn when standing in a receiving line. When long gloves are an intrinsic part of your costume at a ball, they may be left on for dancing—otherwise they are taken off. A bracelet may be worn outside a long glove, but never a ring.

HATS

If you look well in hats—wear them! If well chosen, a hat may add a dash and distinction to your outfit that a bare head can't possibly achieve. If you are one of the many women who feel that there is no hat in the world becoming to you, you must settle for a little veil on those occasions when it is necessary to cover your head. You *must* wear a hat to all Roman Catholic church ceremonies, and it is always correct at churches of every faith. At official luncheons and receptions, they are almost a requirement, and beyond that, hats may be, and are, worn at any time and on any occasion that you wish to during the day. A small hat or veil is appropriate, but not necessary, with a cocktail dress. Except for the necessary head covering at an evening wedding, a hat, even the smallest veil, is never worn with an evening dress. The only exception, and it is not truly an exception, is the practical one of wearing a plastic or net scarf tied over your beautiful new hair-do to protect it from wind and rain on the way to a formal party.

SHOES

The first thing to consider in buying shoes—and this cannot be stressed too strongly—is the importance of comfort. The most beautiful pair of shoes in the world will destroy the appearance of the wearer if the height of the heel causes her to teeter or hobble, or the tightness of the toes causes her to stand painfully, first on one foot and then the other or, worse yet, to sink thankfully onto the nearest chair, saying, "My feet are killing me—do you mind?" and kick off the offenders! When you find a last (the form on which the shoe is made) that really fits your foot, you will do well to continue to choose shoes produced by the maker of that last.

When picking out shoes, try to find colors and styles that will go with more than one dress. Red, for instance, is an excellent choice for spring and summer as it goes well with black, navy, white, and many of the light summer shades.

If you are more comfortable in "flats" or low heels, stick to them for daytime wear—there are attractive styles available even for city wearing. Dressier shoes are now made with low, medium, or high heels to fit every requirement. Loafers, sneakers, sandals, and gaily colored flat-soled shoes in every conceivable material and to fit any budget are cool and comfortable in summer.

In winter, a pair of handsome wool-lined boots is invaluable for daytime use in the country, and even city dwellers are finding them more practical than arctics or rubber boots, which must go on and off a dozen times a day.

The working girl who is on her feet much of the day should sacrifice some smartness for comfort and choose a shoe that has a thick soft sole and gives her foot some support. A good suggestion, if feasible, is to keep an extra pair of shoes at your place of business, as a change in the middle of the day is very restful to the feet.

Shoes to be worn with more formal clothes should match or blend with the costume in color and be appropriate in material and style. You wouldn't, for example, wear alligator pumps with a satin dress, even though they might both be brown. Generally speaking, leather shoes such as alligator or kid, in dark colors, are correct for daytime in the winter. Black shoes go well with almost every winter costume. Suede or satin shoes in a color matching your dress are worn for more formal occasions or in the evening. Pumps in gold, silver, or a color matching your dress, or gold or silver sandals, are worn with a formal evening dress. During the summer months, shoes of any color of the rainbow are attractive as long as they complement the rest of the outfit, but if you do not wish to buy a variety of colors, a pair of "spectators" (white pumps trimmed with black, brown, or navy) for daylight occasions and white linen or cotton pumps for after dark will go happily with almost any summer ensemble.

HANDBAGS

Styles in handbags have changed as much as those of any accessory or clothing. The result is that over the years the best features of many types have been retained, and bags can now be found in a literally unlimited variety of colors, styles, and materials. There is little to be said about color—you simply decide on one that will go with a special outfit or will blend with all of your costumes, depending on your need. Your own taste will be your guide in selecting your purse, but there are a few suggestions that may be helpful. A good quality black leather one, large enough to contain all the items you may need for a whole day, will last for years and pay for itself many times over in usefulness, durability, and beauty. A straw handbag for daytime use in the summer will go with all cottons and sport clothes, and on some the decorations may be changed to match a special costume. Small linen fold-over bags are so inexpensive that two or three in different colors will not strain your budget.

One of the most practical innovations of recent years is the bag with changeable covers. These are not inexpensive, but the cost is more than made up for by the versatility, and one bag may make up your entire pocketbook wardrobe. For a winter bag of this type, the basic purse might be black leather, and the covers (which are cleverly designed to snap on so that the result appears to be an ordinary purse) might be of brown kid, black lizard, or possibly, for dressier occasions, suede. The summer bags are less expensive as the covers may be of cotton or linen, and they have the added advantage of being washable!

Evening bags come in many materials and colors, and they can add greatly to your costume. Gold metallic bags, sometimes adorned with artificial (or very occasionally, real) jewels are popular; and for older people, embroidered black velvet, silk, or satin is a good choice. For cocktail time, small suede or satin bags come in a variety of pretty colors and shapes.

CORSAGES

There is no rule in existence about how a woman wears a corsage. She pins it wherever and however she thinks most becoming to her dress, to herself, and to the flowers themselves. In short, she stands in front of her mirror, holds the flowers against her dress in different places until she finds where they are most pleasing, and that is where she pins them. If the dress is so designed that a corsage does not go well on it, or if the wearer is afraid of crushing the flowers while dancing, they also may be pinned on a cloth evening bag.

MAKE-UP AND HAIR STYLES

To the modern generation, it must seem fantastic that not so very long ago all make-up was considered wicked. Today the only restraint in the use of every item in the cosmetic catalog lies in the answer to the question: Are you sure you are not exchanging a face for a mask?

Except for special occasions, a little powder to dull the shine on your nose, a touch of rouge sparingly applied if you are pale, lipstick of a color becoming to your complexion, a touch of eye make-up if you live in the city, and a neatly combed hair-do are sufficient to make every woman appear well groomed. A good powder base, which contains nutrients for the skin, is an excellent idea for older women. The powder should be applied lightly and evenly over the base, and when properly done, the two together will cover the natural blemishes and wrinkles that come inevitably with the years. This, however, is not necessary for a young girl whose skin is loveliness itself.

Eye make-up, if used, should also be applied with discretion. A heavy outline intended to enlarge the eye can, in reality, destroy the natural line and appear nothing short of grotesque.

Lipstick should follow the line of the lips. An attempt to enlarge or change the shape of the mouth by running the lipstick over the natural outline of the lips generally gives the appearance that your hand has slipped.

Hair-dos should be chosen to flatter your face—not to follow the latest fad. Of course, if you are young and pretty, many styles will be becoming, and it is great fun to attempt different effects and to experiment with current fashions. It is not worth doing, however, if the latest thing could be harmful to the hair—such as spraying with excessively drying lacquers. The well-groomed woman finds a style that is pleasing to her and not difficult to maintain, and while she may vary her coiffure on special occasions, she returns to the simple, becoming style for ordinary dress.

And always remember that a mask can never take the place of a face. The face of a clown is grotesque, for it is meant to be. If cosmetics are to add to beauty, they must be the allies, not the enemies, of nature.

BUDGET BUYING

The woman of means has little problem in buying clothes, for she may have an outfit for every occasion and a set of accessories for each outfit. But the vast majority of us must plan our wardrobes carefully and take advantage of all the available means of stretching our pennies.

To begin with, sales can be of great help to the budget-conscious woman, but only if taken advantage of with thought and planning. End-of-season sales are generally limited to left-over odd sizes and the less attractive styles, but if you happen to fit those sizes or suit a rather un-usual color, you can sometimes find a wonderful bargain for the follow-ing year. Beware, however, of buying anything "high style" at these sales—the dress will probably be "out-of-style" in a year's time.

In buying at one of the "cut-rate" stores, you may also find fabulous bargains, but again, take care! These stores get their merchandise from the stocks of more expensive houses for several reasons. The clothes may be defective in workmanship, faulty in cut, or out of style. Or (and you are in luck if you happen to go in on the day this shipment arrives) they may be bargains simply because too many of one design were or-dered. If you are knowledgeable about clothes and able to recognize good design and workmanship, as a penny-wise shopper you will do well to frequent these stores.

Wherever you decide to do your shopping, you must plan your needs in advance. If you wish to be able to use the same accessories with all your clothes, your color scheme must be in harmony. For example, for fall wear, you might choose dresses and suits in olive greens, golds, browns, and beige. With all these colors, you may use the same pair of brown alligator or kid pumps, brown or dull green leather "flats," a brown purse, and a brown or beige coat. A camel's hair polo coat would be a good choice in the country, but you would probably want some-thing a little dressier in the city.

Outfits that can be changed to fit different occasions are helpful. Skirts are most versatile—with a sweater they are practical for every day use, but if not too "tweedy" they can be dressed up by a silk blouse or a decorated sweater for informal evenings with friends or at home. A short-sleeved or sleeveless wool or silk dress with a little jacket is a good choice. Without the jacket, it may be worn for a dinner party or an eve-ning of theater and night clubs. By putting on the jacket, you are ready for a luncheon, movie, or informal cocktail party.

To make your budget wardrobe truly adequate, you should try to choose two or three basic dresses—one for afternoon and two for eve-ning—of good quality. The higher cost of these will be amply repaid in durability and excellent fit. They should not be conspicuous in color or style, but rather, becoming to you, so that you can wear them time and time again without feeling that your friends are saying "There comes Janey in her polkadot dress again!"

Coats are a problem to the budget-minded. Not only are they the most costly item to buy, but no one coat can cover all your needs. A polo coat or a lined gabardine is most practical for country wear, and both go well with all daytime clothes from slacks to afternoon dresses. But for winter evenings it is essential to have a second coat—a well-cut black wool will fit any occasion, but best of all, if your budget allows, or if you have a generous mother or husband, a fur coat. A three-quarter or full-length fur coat, cut in a simple style, will last for years, and of all coats it provides the greatest warmth and beauty. In choosing a fur coat, you will do well to follow the recommendations of a reputable furrier.

Spring and summer coats are less expensive and more versatile. A light-weight wool in white, beige, or red (strangely enough, red goes well with most summer colors) can serve for daytime or evening, although a small fur cape or stole, if one can afford it, is a comfort when sitting near the ocean on a cool summer night. Raincoats come in such attractive fabrics now that they can also serve as your summer coat even when the sun is shining.

DAYTIME CLOTHES

There are so many wonderful synthetic fabrics on the market today that it would be impossible to list them by name each time that a specific fabric is mentioned. The drip-dry materials or blends are in many ways preferable to plain cotton, as they need no ironing. There are various forms of synthetic linen, silk, and cotton which do not wrinkle, making them ideal for traveling. Therefore, each time that a material is specifically mentioned here, the reader must assume that any of the newer (and often improved) fabrics having the same visual effect, are in equally good taste, and are, in many cases, more attractive and practical.

By the same token, it is impossible to list the best clothing material for each climate in all parts of the United States or for traveling all over the world, so we have chosen to speak in terms of the four seasons as represented in a temperate climate. The reader who lives the year round in southern Florida or in the desert of the Southwest must realize that even in the so-called "winter" months, she may never need the basic wool dress or suit, nor will she often wear very dark colors, even in the city, because they simply are not appropriate in very hot weather. One must use one's own judgment and consider her own circumstances, but the material and colors mentioned in connection with a certain season are the most comfortable and in the best taste over the largest area of the country.

MORNING

The housewife busily doing her chores in her house or apartment should certainly wear whatever clothes are, for her, most comfortable. In the country, this often means shorts or slacks for all morning activities, and in the city, these are certainly proper in her own apartment, or if she is hurrying out for a moment to a shop in her block or to walk the dog to the corner. No matter how informal the outfit, if it is neat and clean (of course, you may have dirt from the garden on your hands or smudges from cleaning the oven on your face, but if your chores for the day have been of this sort, do them first and wash and change before going on to something of a less demanding nature), you need make no apology when a salesman comes to the door or your friendly neighbor drops in.

Two cardinal rules must be mentioned: *Never* go shopping or to any public place with your hair in curlers, unless they are so skillfully concealed with a scarf or hat as to be completely invisible. *Never* wear short shorts or a bathing suit on the street. In many communities it is actually illegal to appear in these costumes, so if you don't wish to change into other clothes to do your errands, you must cover your *lack* of clothing with a skirt, a beach coat, or a shift.

AFTERNOON

Dresses for luncheons, card parties, teas, or other afternoon parties vary so widely in different sections of the country that it would be impossible to recommend any one type. One must generalize and say that during the cool months women wear wool dresses or suits (not "tweedy" country-type suits, but preferably something in a solid color or with tiny checks or stripes) to luncheons and that hats are usually worn, although they are not essential. In the summer, cottons are the most popular choice, with darker colors being chosen for the city. Clothing for other afternoon parties, perhaps for bridge, is the same; but at a formal tea one would choose a somewhat more elaborate wool or a silk in a solid color or print. These same daytime dresses are worn for informal cocktail parties, but at larger parties or cocktail buffets, the cocktail dress or suit appears. These are usually of silk or satin, they are always short (as opposed to a dinner dress), but they may be quite sleeveless and have a very low neckline. The sleeveless ones generally have a jacket, which is kept on at a cocktail party unless the buffet is followed by dancing, in which case the jacket may be removed.

CLOTHES FOR THE EVENING

For evenings at home, either with your family or good friends, nothing is more comfortable than a smartly tailored pair of evening slacks, velvet or satin in the winter, and cotton or silk in the summer. Equaling these in popularity are the "hostess skirts" that come in enchanting colors and fabrics and are often matched by gay blouses.

But for evenings away from home, you must have a separate wardrobe. For cocktail and dinner parties, the winter wool (not too tailored) or the gay summer cotton is the most common costume. For more formal parties, a silk or satin cocktail dress is almost a necessity, as, without a jacket, it serves as a dinner dress. A true dinner dress is long (unless current fashion dictates that all dinner and evening dresses are short), but is not made of as dressy a material or cut as low as an evening gown. It may be of wool or velvet in winter, or cotton or silk for summer. It is worn at formal dinners and may be worn to informal dinners and dances, the opera or theater, and to any party that is "black tie." An evening dress, worn only at balls, the opera, opening nights at the theater, and on a few other very special occasions is sleeveless, sometimes strapless, cut low in back and usually in front, and made of the most elegant materials—satins, brocades—and with endless variations in decoration and embroidery. Hats and veils are never worn with dinner or evening dresses.

In deciding what to wear to any function, afternoon or evening, when the invitation has not made it clear, there is one rule that is fairly safe. If you have no way of finding out what the correct attire is, wear the plainer dress. If you must decide between a ball dress and a dinner dress, wear the dinner dress, or between velvet and wool, choose the wool.

IN A RESTAURANT

Afternoon dresses or suits are worn to restaurants for both lunch and dinner. If you are going to a dinner party given at a restaurant, you would wear the somewhat more elaborate cocktail dress or, if formal, a dinner dress. Hats may be worn with the daytime dress, but rarely with the cocktail dress and never with the dinner dress.

CLOTHES FOR THE BUSINESS WOMAN

The first requirement is neatness. The unfailing directions for clothes worn in an office are that they be tailored, smart, in good taste, but in no way conspicuous. Above all, avoid wearing clothes that need constant arranging. If you have to keep fussing at your belt or your neckline or your wrists, if anything dangling drips into things or catches on knobs or typewriter keys, discard the distracting detail quickly. It is not necessary to sacrifice prettiness to exaggerated sleekness, but do avoid everything that interferes or catches or keeps getting out of place.

Also wear clothes that properly cover you. Scant attire may be very alluring in a musical revue, but men do not look for or want to find that allure in their offices. In hot weather, very short sleeves are permissible.

Mourning clothes are not suitable in an office, but you may wear black and white or gray. » *For details, see Chapter 42*.

One important accessory for beautiful business clothes is a pair of plain sensible shoes of best quality. High-heeled, fancy sandals and heelless slippers are not only inappropriate and extravagant but ruinous to any foot that must be much stood upon. A well-shod foot is much to be prized—and noticed.

Your hair should be neat and carefully done by all means, but do avoid that little-girl effect of hair hanging loose.

YOUR TRAVELING WARDROBE

When you plan a wardrobe for a trip, whether it be by airplane, car, train, or boat, there are two considerations—space and weight. Air travel is not the only means of transportation where weight is a factor. Have you ever tried to carry your own fifty-pound suitcase through the train station when no porter can be found, as is so often the case nowadays? Or seen your host take your bag from your car trunk and stagger gasping up his steps because the days of the butler and houseman have passed?

Even more consideration should be given your travel wardrobe than your regular outfits, because of the need for traveling with as few accessories as possible. Nothing takes up more space or weighs more than handbags and shoes. If you can plan your costumes so that one pair of the most comfortable, sturdy shoes available for sightseeing can be exchanged in the evening for a pump of the same color, your packing and overweight problems will be almost solved. The handbags with changeable covers mentioned earlier in this chapter are ideal for traveling. You may carry the bag itself onto the boat or plane and pack only the lightweight covers. For evening, a small flat silk or satin bag will look well with any costume and add little to the weight of your suitcase.

Dresses of wrinkle-proof material are a "must," and they can now be found in all styles and weights for summer or winter travel. Do take along a little package of cleaning powders, put up specially for travelers —a spot on a dress that forms an important part of your clothing scheme can be a disaster.

Think again of the versatility of your clothes. Sweaters should be chosen because they go well with *all* your skirts, shorts, and dresses. A skirt with a matching coat makes a stunning costume for cruise or country wear and is better than dress and coat, because with a change of blouses, the skirt can give the appearance of several outfits. One rarely needs an evening dress when traveling, but a sleeveless cocktail dress with a jacket may be worn in any restaurant or theater or at any party to which you are invited.

Shorts and slacks, incidentally, are never worn by foreign women except at such resorts as the Riviera, and therefore American women should "in Rome, do as the Romans" or they will appear conspicuous and typically "tourist." So if you are traveling on the continent rather than on a cruise ship (where the same clothes are appropriate as those worn in any resort at home), save space by not taking more shorts than you will need for the day or two you plan to spend in Cannes. But don't forget a bathing suit—even a wayside stream can provide a refreshing relief from the heat of southern France, Italy, or Spain in summer, and swimming pools and lakes are found near resort hotels all over the world.

» *For clothes appropriate to special occasions, please consult the Index.*

74

Men's clothes

Let us say at the start that, although the clothes a man wears (especially his evening ones) are certain to reveal his background, fashion is not as important or as changeable as is the case with a woman's clothes. How old a suit may be doesn't matter a bit. The right kind of clothes, the clothes that follow the accepted conventions, are very important. The wrong kind, whether new or old, are an indication that the wearer has either little education or poor taste.

Fashions in men's clothes have changed very little in recent years. A well-made suit bought ten years ago should still be perfectly wearable today, although its age would be noticeable in some details. Lapels have become narrower, trouser legs slimmer, and neckties, too, are much narrower than they used to be. Padded, square shoulders, which were very popular a few years ago, have been replaced by the natural sloping line. Padding is now used only to correct a difference in shoulder level or something of that kind. A particular style may come and go, and the well-dressed man may choose to follow these styles if they are not overly flamboyant and if they are becoming to him. Certain colors have a temporary vogue, in shirts, for instance. One year yellow shirts may appear with gray or brown suits; the next year they will be replaced by blue. Bow ties, for example, are popular in some years; in others one sees only the four-in-hands. And with the emergence of so many new synthetic fabrics, styles in sports clothes have become almost unlimited.

But whatever the fashion of the moment, if a man's suit fits him well, is appropriate to whatever he may be doing, and is not conspicuous in style or color, he may rest assured that he will be labeled "well-dressed" in any community.

THE IMPORTANCE OF FIT AND GOOD CARE

Whether you buy your clothes at a men's store or a department store or have them custom made by a tailor, the most important consideration is excellent fitting. Although you may be on a strict budget and are buying your clothing as inexpensively as possible, be sure to spend the extra time required to have any necessary alterations made. Any suit appears more costly than it is if it hangs well and does not sag or stretch.

Another means of adding years to the life of your clothes and adding immeasurably to their appearance, whether they were the best bargains you could find or the most expensive suits you could have made, is the care that you give them. Suits and sport jackets should be pressed, brushed, and spot-cleaned after two or three wearings. But if it is important to you to lengthen the life of your clothes, they should only be sent for general cleaning when they are soiled all over, as from dust or smoke, or have a stain which cannot be removed at home. Trousers should be pressed each time they are worn if the crease is gone or they are very wrinkled at the seat or knee. But if you invest in a good "silent valet" (a stand over which you hang the trousers, which are then pressed by another hinged board that is clamped tight against the hanging legs) a suit, because the jacket does not show signs of use to the extent that the trousers do, may be worn many more times before either pressing or a trip to the cleaners is necessary.

The immediate replacement of a missing button or hook is a "must." Not only does it ruin the appearance of the clothing, but it can actually cause the material of the suit or jacket to lose shape if it is left unrepaired for a long period of time.

Another worthwhile investment is a pair of shoe trees for each pair of shoes. Nothing increases the life of the shoes so much as being properly stretched on trees each time they are removed, and nothing improves the appearance or preserves the leather so much as proper shining.

THE MAN ON A BUDGET

The man on a budget is more fortunate than the woman in the same situation. A man does not need so many complete changes of outfit as a woman, because the same suit with different shirts, ties, and socks may be used for almost every day and for any occasion. But the budget-minded man must consider the same things as his female counterpart. If a limited supply of ties, shirts, socks, and shoes must go with all his suits and jackets, then he must restrict himself to one or two colors. A gray suit for business, a dark blue suit for evening, and a sports jacket in a gray-blue tweed could be worn, for example, with blue and red neckties, white, blue or yellow shirts, and blue, maroon, or black socks. Since a white shirt is more formal than a colored one, it is always correct with the blue suit in the evening and may also be worn at any other time. Dark brown shoes could be worn with all three, although most well-dressed men prefer black with a blue suit. A good solution for a two-pair wardrobe would be a black pair to wear with the two suits, and a pair of brown loafers or other casual shoes to wear with the sports jacket.

Because of its versatility, a dark gray flannel suit is an invaluable asset to the man on a limited clothes budget. It may appear anywhere in the daytime and yet go to the theater, a restaurant, or any informal gathering in the evening. In addition, the trousers may be worn separately with a sports shirt or jacket. Some stores sell "two-pants" suits, and in the case of gray flannel, whether bought in a store or made to order, the extra pair is a very practical idea, because it will double the useful years of the jacket.

INFORMAL DAYTIME WEAR

Rules for daytime clothes are less rigid than they used to be, but the man who works in an office in the city must dress according to a set pattern if he wishes to impress his clients and his employers or superiors favorably. Sport jackets, open-necked shirts, and loud plaids are worn in the city only on weekends (for a picnic in the park, for instance) or in your own home. For weekday wear during office hours, a suit is the proper attire.

THE BUSINESS SUIT

The business suit is supposed to be an inconspicuous garment and should be. Today's suit usually consists of trousers and a single-breasted coat. Some men do wear double-breasted suits, but the jackets must be very well fitted, and they tend to look a little old-fashioned. Vests may be worn, but seldom are. A few rules to follow:

Don't choose striking patterns or materials, although a quiet plaid or muted stripe or herring-bone pattern can be very handsome. Suitable woolens come in endless variety, and any that look inconspicuous at a short distance are safe.

Dark gray (charcoal), dark blue, and brown are first color choices, although olive greens and lighter grays are also correct. But don't get too light a blue, too bright a green, or anything suggesting a horse blanket.

Trousers may be and generally are made with a cuff; they should not be wide or "bell-bottomed," nor as narrow as the "continental" cut. Lapels are moderately small. Padded shoulders are an abomination. If you must be eccentric, save your efforts for the next fancy-dress party, where you may wear what you please. But in your business clothing be reasonable.

It is better taste not to wear silk socks in winter, except in the evening, but lisle or cotton are correct for those who are not comfortable in wool. Above everything, don't wear white socks in the city. Don't cover yourself with chains, fobs, lodge emblems, etc.; and don't wear plaid shirts and neckties. You will only make a bad impression on everyone you meet. The clothes of a gentleman are always conservative; and it is safe to avoid everything that can possibly come under the heading of novelty. If a salesman offers you anything that has "never been seen before," the safest rule is to shun it unless your judgment is very experienced.

Summer suits are lighter in color as well as weight, and their accessories can be much less conservative. Socks are entirely proper not only in browns and grays, but in other colors as well. Ties of printed silk or any of the new synthetic fabrics can be gaily colored, but patterns should be small, and stripes should not be too wild.

A tan, gray, blue, or olive green suit in the new lightweight, crease-resistant summer fabrics has the advantage of being correct for the city and not looking out of place in the country.

Some of the new materials are so cool and light that the wearer is comfortable in even the hottest weather, and the necessity of removing the coat has been almost eliminated.

THE COUNTRY OFFICE

Many men who work in offices in the country prefer to wear a sport jacket rather than a suit. Some companies require their employees, even in small towns, to wear suits, however, because they feel it is more dignified and makes a better impression on clients or customers. Unless the company specifies the color, suits worn in the suburbs or country may be lighter in color or a little gayer in pattern than those worn in the city. While a suit is always correct for business wear, if your work is such that you do not have to meet outsiders—as does, for instance, a salesman—it is certainly not incorrect to wear a comfortable sports jacket in your office.

WHEN NOT AT WORK

It would not be possible to go into all the types of clothing that may be worn out of working hours. But there are certain general observations that may be made.

Clothing should be appropriate to the occasion. If you have been asked to spend a weekend at a fishing camp, you would be foolish to take light-colored, easily spotted linen slacks rather than dungarees or khakis. Nor would you be wise to appear at an exclusive beach club in clothing appropriate for a weekend on a farm. Don't wear loafers on board a boat. Not only might you slip and fall overboard, but most owners will shudder at the marks that the hard soles may make on their polished decks. In other words, choose your vacationtime clothes with an eye toward what your activities will be, and if you don't know, ask! No one has ever been criticized for wanting to have the appropriate clothes, but many a friendship has been dampened by the need to outfit or loan clothing to some one who didn't take the trouble to find out what might be needed. » *See also Chapters 37, 68, and 75.*

In general, men in the city wear the same clothes in their own homes as do their brothers in the country. But when they appear in public, they should put on jacket and tie, and for most social activities, suits are usually worn.

The country dweller need not be so formal. Open-necked polo shirts and slacks are standard attire in any warm climate, and in the cooler months, flannel shirts and sweaters are seen all over the country. But even the suburbanite or farmer puts on his sports jacket and tie when going to any sort of social gathering, from a friendly brunch to a morning meeting of the "Little League" fathers. Men attending weddings, cocktail parties, luncheons, or any other daytime function, unless it is specified as "formal," wear the same dark suit, white shirt, and conservative tie and socks that they would wear to informal evening affairs.

FORMAL DAYTIME WEAR

When it is necessary to dress more formally, the cutaway or a black sack coat and striped trousers are worn at any affair that takes place before six o'clock in the evening. They are often worn at government or diplomatic receptions, but they appear most frequently on the principals in a formal afternoon wedding or when they are worn by pallbearers in a large funeral.

THE CUTAWAY

The cutaway is the most formal afternoon attire, and it is rarely seen except on participants in large afternoon weddings or at official teas or receptions. For this reason, few men not in the diplomatic corps or in high government positions have cutaways, but they can always be rented.

When renting *any* formal attire, make your arrangements well ahead of the date on which it is to be worn if you possibly can, so that it may be perfectly fitted to you. This is particularly true of cutaways and tailcoats. *The cutaway (sometimes called morning) coat*—Black or oxford gray worsted or cheviot, with peaked lapels. Edges may be bound, but generally plain edges are preferred. Buttons are bone or self-covered.

Waistcoat—Double-breasted. In winter, black wool to match the coat or pearl-gray fine wool. In summer, white or fawn linen or white piqué.

Trousers—Black and gray striped worsted or cheviot. Cuffless.

Shirt—White, with starched bosom and starched cuffs.

Collar—Detachable wing or starched fold collar.

Tie—For weddings, ascot, in gray, silver-gray or black silk, plain, figured, or striped. Worn with wing collar. For funerals, black four-in-hand, worn with fold collar. Other occasions, a four-in-hand or bow tie may be worn with either wing or fold collar.

Socks—Black or dark gray. Any material except very heavy wool.

Shoes—Black calf oxfords.

Hat—Black silk hat. Less appropriate, a black Homburg.

Topcoat—Black, dark gray, or dark blue.

Gloves—Gray, any material of good quality.

Accessories—Jewelry, pearl pin with ascot, gold cuff links. With stiff shirt with bow tie, single stud should be gold. Boutonnière, white or red carnation. Boutonnières are not worn at funerals. At a wedding, the groom may wear a small sprig from his bride's bouquet. Handkerchief (white linen) and white or gray silk scarf. Handkerchief should be initialed in white, with all initials, or that of last name only. It is folded square and shows no more than ½ inch to inch above pocket.

THE SACK COAT

The sack coat is a less formal version of the cutaway. It is worn by the participants in morning weddings, afternoon weddings, large funerals, and on any daytime occasion when the formality of the cutaway is not essential.

Sack Coat—Black or oxford gray worsted, single breasted.

Waistcoat—Double-breasted. Black or oxford gray, same as the sack coat, or pearl-gray fine wool.

Trousers—Same as for cutaway.

Shirt—White, soft bosom, starched French cuffs. Starched fold collar.

Tie—Black or gray-and-black pattern, silk. Four-in-hand style.

Hat—Black Homburg or soft black felt.

All other clothing and accessories are the same as for a cutaway.

EVENING CLOTHES

For all informal evening wear, the dark (preferably blue) suit, with white shirt, dark tie, and dark socks, is the accepted outfit. For formal evenings, either full evening dress, called "white tie" or "tails" (sometimes "white tie and tails") or a dinner jacket, called "black tie" or "tuxedo," is worn.

If ever in doubt what to wear, the best rule is to err on the side of informality. Thus, if you are not sure whether to put on your full dress suit or your tuxedo, wear the latter.

On the other hand, when an occasion is important, and a man wants to make sure that his clothes will be correct, it is entirely proper for him to call his host or his hostess on the telephone and ask, "Do I wear a black tie tonight, or a white one?" or the question may be: "Day clothes or tuxedos?"

BLACK TIE

To go out for the evening dressed in "black tie" means that you are wearing a dinner jacket or tuxedo. The term "tuxedo" appeared in the early nineties when the dinner jacket was introduced in the Tuxedo Club to provide something less formal to wear than the "swallowtail" or full evening dress. Nowadays, black tie is accepted as correct on almost every formal occasion, and few men have any need to dress often in a more formal manner. Therefore, while it is more practical for most to rent a "set of tails" when the occasion demands, it is advisable for those who can to invest in a good quality, well-fitted tuxedo, which will last for many years. It consists of:

Jacket—In winter or summer, black or midnight blue is always correct, and the material is usually tropical worsted or, if it is not shiny, one of the new blended materials. The lapels are faced with satin. In hot weather, white linen is worn for formal affairs, but for less formal parties, plaid (madras) or a solid-color cotton, dacron, or other blend is appropriate, attractive, and gay. On all jackets the lapels may be rolled or peaked and of whatever width current fashion demands. Dinner jackets are usually single-breasted, but a few men still prefer the double-breasted form, which requires neither waistcoat nor cummerbund.

Trousers—When a dark jacket (black or midnight blue) is worn, the trousers are always of the same material. If a colored jacket is worn, they are of a good quality black material, usually the same pair that is worn with a black jacket. In either case, they do not have cuffs and do have a single stripe of black braid or satin.

Waistcoat or Cummerbund—The waistcoat is of white piqué or plain or patterned black silk. Nowadays, instead of a waistcoat, a cummerbund is frequently worn. It is usually (and most formally) black or maroon silk, but it may also be plaid or figured, especially in the summertime.

Shirt—A daytime white shirt with fold collar may be worn, but for a formal occasion, a piqué or pleated bosom makes a better appearance.

Tie—Black silk bow with waistcoat or black cummerbund. If cummerbund other than black is worn, the tie should be of matching color and material.

Socks—Black silk or lisle.

Shoes—Black patent leather.

Hat—A black Homburg or black or gray soft-brimmed fedora in the winter, gray fedora in the spring or fall, and a Panama in the summer. However, if the weather does not necessitate the wearing of a hat, many men prefer not to do so.

Gloves—Gray chamois or buck.

Topcoat—Black, dark gray, or navy coat, with or without velvet collar.

Accessories—Jewelry, pearl or mother-of-pearl or black onyx studs. Cuff links may be gold or mother-of-pearl to match the studs. White linen handkerchief, with or without initials. White silk scarf. Boutonnière, white or red carnation.

WHITE TIE

Full evening dress, nowadays, is required only occasionally for some men, and never for most. Therefore, relatively few men own their "tails" and the great majority rent them for those special occasions. This is perfectly correct, as long as they are rented from a reputable establishment that has excellent tailors to do alterations, because there is no outfit whose appearance is so ruined by poor fitting as the tail coat.

A tail coat *must* be worn by the fathers and escorts of debutantes at their coming-out parties. It *must* be worn to any affair when the invitation reads "white tie." Otherwise, it *may* be worn to formal dinners or balls, or to official or diplomatic parties, or when sitting in a box at the opera. It is often worn by the principals involved in an opening night at the theater, or by those in charge of benefits or charity affairs.

Tail coat—Black worsted or tropical worsted. Lapels are peaked and faced in grosgrain or satin. The tails should hang to the break at the back of the knees.

Waistcoat—White piqué. Usually single-breasted, but may be double-breasted.

Trousers—Match the coat. Single stripe of satin or braid; no cuffs.

Shirt—White, made to wear with detachable wing collar. Piqué or plain linen bosom, stiffly starched. Cuffs are single, starched. Shirt may have either one or two buttonholes for studs.

Tie—White piqué bow. Current fashion favors straight ends rather than "butterfly" shape.

Socks—Black silk or nylon.

Shoes—Black patent leather pumps or oxfords.

Hat—High silk or opera hat is most formal, but a black Homburg is
more frequently worn. Many men prefer not to wear a hat with tails.
Topcoat—Black, or dark gray or blue.
Gloves—White chamois or doeskin.
Accessories—Jewelry, pearl or mother-of-pearl studs for shirt, mother-of-
pearl for the waistcoat and cuff links, or of platinum or white gold.
White linen handkerchief and white silk scarf. Boutonnière, white
carnation or small white gardenia.

COATS AND HATS

Men's topcoats come in an infinite variety of colors and materials.
For the man who lives a very active social life and frequently wears evening clothes, a solid black, navy, or dark gray coat is a necessity. For daytime wear, he must also have a less formal coat in the color that goes best
with his suits.

The dress coat may or may not be double-breasted—the daytime
sports coat, never.

For the average man, and especially the young man who is starting
his wardrobe, a coat that will look well in any circumstance is preferable to the very dressy or very sporty one. For the city dweller, a dark gray
herringbone tweed is most practical. Brown tweed is handsome, but
should not be worn with formal evening dress. For either city or country
wear, a polo coat for the cold months and a straight gabardine (or one
of the newer waterproof materials) to double as a topcoat in the summer
are ideal solutions.

Some men, in both city and country, prefer not to wear hats unless
it is absolutely necessary. For these men, or for anyone whose wardrobe
is limited, a gray felt fedora is the best choice. It can be worn with any
color, and in any circumstance, except with full evening dress. Those
who wear white tie frequently should certainly have a black Homburg or
silk hat to go with it. Derbies, which used to be worn with business suits,
are rarely seen, and the high silk hat has almost disappeared.

Men who live in the country may choose a fedora in a rougher
material than the regular felt. They may have special bands of braid or
cloth other than black silk, and occasionally they have a feather or other
ornament tucked into the band at the side. This type of hat should not
be worn with a tuxedo, however.

In the summertime, coconut straw hats are handsome and cool. The
bands may be of any solid color, or figured or plaid. These are accepted
for all daytime wear, even in the city, but with evening clothes the conservative Panama hat is correct.

LIFTING OR TIPPING THE HAT

Lifting or tipping the hat is a conventional gesture of politeness shown to strangers or mere acquaintances only. In lifting his hat, a gentleman merely lifts it slightly off his forehead—by the brim of a stiff hat or by the crown of a soft one—and replaces it. Hats are generally tipped in the following circumstances:

When walking with a friend who greets a woman who is a stranger to him, a man lifts his hat without either bowing or staring at her.

If a lady who is a stranger drops a glove or other article, a man should pick it up, hurry after her, offer the glove to her, and say, "I think you dropped this." The lady replies, "Thank you." The man should then lift his hat and turn away.

If he passes a lady in a narrow space, so that he blocks her way or in any manner obstructs her, he lifts his hat as he passes.

If he gets on a bus and the bus gives a lurch and throws him against another passenger, he exclaims, "I'm sorry!" or "Excuse me!" If the passenger is a woman, he lifts his hat as soon as he regains his balance. When a man has to ask someone to let him pass by to enter or leave the bus, he merely says, "Excuse me," without lifting his hat.

We all know that a gentleman does not take a seat ahead of a woman, but if he is seated and women enter, should they be young, he may keep his seat. If an older woman or a young one carrying a baby or heavy packages enters the bus, a gentleman rises, lifts his hat slightly as he indicates the proffered seat, and lifts his hat again when she thanks him.

If he is in the company of a woman anywhere in public, he lifts his hat to a man who offers her a seat, or who picks up something she has dropped, or shows her any other civility. He lifts his hat if he asks a woman a question, and always if, when walking on the street with a lady, she greets another person.

In other words, a man lifts his hat whenever he says, "Excuse me," "Thank you," or speaks to or is spoken to by a lady. He always takes his pipe, cigar, or cigarette out of his mouth as he lifts his hat, takes it off, or bows.

WHEN TO REMOVE A HAT AND GLOVES

A gentleman takes off his hat and holds it in his hand when a lady enters the elevator in an apartment house or hotel—any building which can be classified as a dwelling. He puts it on again in the corridor. A public corridor is like the street, but an elevator in a hotel or apartment house has the character of a room in a house and there a man does not keep his hat on in the presence of women.

But in public buildings, such as offices or stores or buildings that contain neither apartments nor assembly rooms, the elevator is considered as public a place as a bus or train. What is more, the elevators in such business structures are usually so crowded that the only room for a man's hat is on his head!

A situation requiring some dexterity faces a man who stops on a city street to speak to a woman of his acquaintance, in taking his hat and glove off, and (should he be smoking) in getting his cigarette out of the way. First he transfers the cigarette or pipe to his left hand, then he removes his hat and transfers it to his left hand, at the same time gripping the fingers of his right glove and pulling it off. He then offers his glove-less right hand to the lady. If they walk on together, he puts his hat on, but while he is standing in the street talking to her, he should remain hatless no matter how cold the wind or how torrid the sun, unless, of course, she thoughtfully says, "Please put your hat on—you'll catch pneumonia in this freezing wind." In the country, he may very well be bare-headed and also be smoking; but in a city street, it would be in very poor taste for a man to stand talking to a lady with his hat on, and a cigar, pipe, or cigarette in his mouth.

I hope that it is not necessary to add that, out of doors, every American citizen stands with his hat off at the passing of the flag, and both indoors and outdoors when the national anthem is played. Also, every man should take his hat off in the presence of a funeral and in all Christian churches.

A gentleman wearing *outdoor* gloves never shakes hands with a lady without first removing his right-hand glove. But at a formal ball, or when he is usher at a wedding, he does *not* remove his glove, which is intended to be worn indoors. If in the street he cannot free his left hand to pull his right glove off, he may say, "Excuse my glove," but he does not ask that an indoor glove be excused.

SHOES AND SOCKS

Shoes, like all men's clothing, should be conservative in style and color. Dark brown, cordovan, and black are the best choices and go well with all business or sport clothes. If you have evening clothes, you must have black patent leather shoes to go with them.

The better quality shoes you buy, the more wear they will give you. Good leather, properly cared for with wax polish, will last for many years. Good shoes are well worth resoling, and you should have it done before they become too worn. The more expensive shoes will also fit your foot better, and the added cost is quite justified, especially if your work requires many hours of standing.

As to style, plain leather (like "cordovan"), perforated insteps and toes, or "capped" toes are chosen according to your taste. It is well to avoid pointed toes, higher-than-average heels, and such fancy innovations as buckles in place of laces. Loafers are fine for country wear, but tend to look too casual during business hours in the city. Open-work, suede, and novelty leathers may ruin an otherwise well-chosen outfit.

Socks are selected according to the color of your suit. Black and navy are best with blue suits; black, gray, green, or maroon with gray; and brown or green with brown. They may be solid color, ribbed or plain knit, with or without clock, and they may have a small stripe or a tiny pattern.

When you are selecting socks, remember that there is nothing attractive about an expanse of bare masculine leg below the trouser cuff. Unless you sit primly with both feet on the floor at all times—as is not likely—you will do well to avoid anklets, especially with a business suit, and should invest in a good pair of garters unless you prefer a style of sock that has built-in support.

NECKTIES

Neckties should, of course, go well with the color of your suit, and often they match the socks as well, but ties that match shirts—white on white, for example—are not in good taste. Solid colors, muted paisleys, narrow stripes, or small patterns go well with business suits. They may be of foulard (silk), knit, or smooth wool in winter, or cotton or silk in summer.

Choosing a tie to go with a sports jacket can be difficult. With a loud plaid, you must avoid stripes or a bold pattern. A solid-color knit or wool is the safest choice with a wool jacket, and the color should match one of the tones in the plaid. A tie with a very sparse pattern—perhaps two or three flying birds, or a single emblem of some sort—also can be worn with a sports jacket. Cotton or silk ties are worn with madras or patterned light-weight jackets.

The four-in-hand is by far the most popular style, but the bow tie is very becoming to some men and provides a good way of giving your outfits a little variety. When choosing a bow tie, try several lengths and shapes, as certain styles are definitely better suited to one shape of face than others. And practice tying the bow until you are truly adept—if you can't avoid a flying end or a sagging loop, stick to the four-in-hand!

VESTS OR WAISTCOATS

The vest, or waistcoat (those worn with evening clothes are always called "waistcoats"), is not seen so frequently as it used to be. There are many men, however, who do wear them for added warmth and extra pockets, as well as for the appearance.

When worn with a business suit, the vest is of the same material as the suit. With a sports jacket, it may be of gaily colored flannel, a check or plaid wool (often called "tattersall"), or other pattern. Many wives enjoy embroidering vests with the emblems of their husbands' schools or with designs derived from a favorite sport or hobby. Vests such as these make wonderful "conversation pieces" and add a distinctive note to a man's sports clothes.

One warning, however: if you are wearing a vest, remember to remove it if you take off your jacket for any reason. Vests were never meant to be seen uncovered from the rear.

JEWELRY

The two most important requisites for men's jewelry are first, that it be of good quality, and second, that it be inconspicuous.

Naturally everyone cannot go out and buy solid gold or platinum tie clips or cuff links. So until one can buy expensive jewelry, he must exercise great care in choosing what he can afford. The best rule is to choose the simplest design that can be found—it invariably gives the appearance of being more costly than does ornate or gaudy jewelry. There is a great deal of imitation jewelry available that is handsomely designed and well made. The problem is to choose something that not only looks very smart, but will not tarnish, lose its finish, or otherwise fall apart.

Cuff links for wear with a business suit should be made of solid metal—usually gold or silver—and should be of moderate size. They may be initialed, have a personal or other crest, or a raised or etched design. Flashing stones in the daytime are never in good taste.

For evening wear, mother-of-pearl cuff links are usually accompanied by matching studs. They may or may not have a circle of tiny diamonds around the edge. Darker pearl and black onyx are handsome with a tuxedo, and white gold or platinum may be worn. But other colored stones are to be avoided, as they cannot but look conspicuous.

Collar pins are made of gold and tie clips may be of almost any metal or combination of metals. The width of the clip depends on the taste of the wearer, and its length, on the width of the tie. Tie pins to hold ascots or scarves in place may be set with a pearl, diamond, or other stones.

The most attractive man's ring, in my opinion, is one of gold, with initials or crest, worn on the little finger. Rings may also be set with a single stone. Onyx, opals, moonstones, star sapphires, or rough-cut stones are more masculine than other gems. Seal rings, from school, college, or military service, are popular and handsome. These are often worn on the fourth finger of either hand rather than the little finger. Wedding rings are almost always of plain gold, although occasionally they have a pattern or design. They are usually chosen to match the ring of the bride.

Other than the articles mentioned above, accessories for men are of a practical, rather than an ornamental, nature. Money clips, cigarette lighters, and watches are all utilitarian, but although they may not, in the strictest sense of the word, be *jewelry*, they may be *jewelled*. A ciga-rette case or lighter used in the evening may bear a design or initials done in precious stones, and a watch may be so beautiful and have such a fine gold band as to be as decorative as a bracelet. But all these things, and the many more like key chains or gold pencils, that have not been discussed, must be carefully chosen to suit the taste of the wearer and the purse of the buyer.

» *For clothes appropriate to special occasions, please consult the Index.*

Clothing for various sports

Although there are no "do's and don'ts" at all about the proper dress for certain sports, others require considerable knowledge of the right clothing if you do not wish to appear a rank amateur. To those about to go on a trout fishing trip, it is hardly necessary to say that you need waterproof waders or hip boots, or to a hunter, that you wear a red hat or shirt in order not to be shot at by other hunters. Except for this sort of essential clothing, there are no rules as to what one wears—it is simply a matter of most practical and most comfortable.

And this actually is the basis for the choice of clothing that, over a period of time, has come to be considered correct for a number of other sports. Some of these rules for dress have become so much a part of the game that one is required to dress in a prescribed style in order to be allowed to participate.

TENNIS

Tennis provides an example of the practicality of the standard garb. As more and more people became tennis players, it was evident that in the heat of the summer, white clothes were the coolest (white actually does not absorb heat as do darker colors) and the freshest looking on the court. It is true that nowadays many clubs and organizations will not allow players to play in colored clothes at any time, and almost all others require white on weekends or for tournaments.

MEN'S CLOTHES

Shorts and polo shirts are standard attire for the men. The flannel "Bermuda" short is the smartest for spring and fall, but too hot for the summer months or in a Southern climate. Shirts may be open collared or round neck, and they may have a narrow band of color at the neck or a shield on the pocket, often the colors of the club, school, or team that the player represents. Plain white socks and sneakers and a visor or cap complete the outfit. For after the game, a heavy ribbed or cabled v-neck sweater with or without a stripe of color at the neck will mark you as a well-dressed tennis player.

WOMEN'S CLOTHES

Women play in either shorts or short skirts, depending on their age and figure. The short (above the knee) tennis dress with full or pleated skirt and matching "short shorts" underneath is so becoming that even very young girls are wearing it instead of shorts. There is no rule as to style or material—round neck, shirtwaist, or any other design that is comfortable and attractive—but, unless the wearer has lovely slim legs, it must not be *too* short. If shorts are worn, they should be of medium or "Bermuda" length—not brief as a bathing suit.

Women, unless their hair is worn very short or smoothly knotted or pinned, should wear a cap, net, or band. It is untidy and distracting to any player to have hair flying wildly over the face in the middle of a fast rally. In any case, it is safer for older women to wear a hat when playing in the hot sun.

GOLF

SHORTS AND SLACKS

There are few golf clubs left that do not allow members of both sexes to play in shorts and permit women to wear slacks in cool weather. Fortunately, most clubs also now specify that they be long shorts or "Bermudas." As long as this rule is followed, and if you have reasonably presentable legs and at least a "medium" figure, shorts are certainly the most comfortable costume for hot weather. There is no limit to color combinations for both men and women. Solid color shorts with blending, printed shirts or blouses are a popular style, but the scheme may be reversed. Solid colors are attractive as well. Plaid or madras shorts are favored by many men.

The male golfer may prefer slacks to shorts and has his choice of linen, cotton, or any other light-weight material. In cool weather, flannel is the most popular choice, and although gray or brown are the most prevalent colors, gray blue, green, and many other shades are often seen.

Slacks should be cut reasonably full for ease in bending and walking, and shirts should be generously cut to allow free movement of the arms. When it is chilly, the men may prefer a flannel or wool shirt so that they need not wear a sweater or jacket.

SKIRTS AND DRESSES

Women who feel that their figures are not suited to shorts—or whose clubs do not allow them—should choose dresses or skirts of a comfortable, simple design. Any color is acceptable, and dresses are sometime sold with a matching sweater. Skirts should be A-shaped or flared—not pleated or gathered, as these kinds will blow in the wind and may distract the most avid golfer just as she is about to sink a putt. Short skirts, ending above the knee, and knee-length socks are another costume popular with many women. In cool weather, slacks, if becoming, are the warmest and most comfortable clothing, but if they do not look well, or are not allowed, flannel or wool skirts and high socks or wool stockings will ward off the chill.

JACKETS

Golf jackets for both men and women come in all colors and styles. They may be open-down or pull-over, long or short, but they must be windproof, waterproof, light-weight, and loose fitting.

SHOES

Shoes should be chosen for comfort, waterproofing, and durability, and therefore they must be of good quality. Men's shoes should be brown, black, or a combination of either of these with white. They should *not* be yellow or any other light color. They may have a flap over the laces or not, as the wearer chooses.

Women's shoes are much the same as men's, with the addition of navy blue to the list of colors.

HATS

The poor frustrated male who must restrict himself to conservative business clothes may indulge himself and go "all out" in his choice of a golf hat. Be it straw, felt, or cloth, he may pick any style or color that will keep the sun out of his eyes and the rain from his head. He may decorate it with golf insignia, feathers, colored bands, or anything else he likes, and as long as it stays on when it should and suits him well, the wilder it is the more admiration it will arouse in his foursome.

SKIING

The newest sport to reach the zenith of popularity is skiing, and styles in ski clothes have changed, and are changing, so fast that is hard to keep up with them. But in spite of this, certain types of clothing have proved to be most practical as well as attractive to look at, and the best features of these have been retained, although such details as color, belts, and hats may vary from year to year.

The main differences between men's and women's ski outfits are the colors, the use of fur or fancy trimming, and hat styles.

TROUSERS AND SHIRTS

"Stretch" pants have proved to be most flattering to almost every sort of figure, as well as the most practical, because they do not buckle, flap, or sag out of shape with hard use or dampness. While they must fit snugly, without fullness or wrinkles, there must also be enough "give" so that the seams do not split with the first fall. They come in every color of the rainbow, but the best men skiers stick to the more masculine colors —browns, olives, dark blues, blacks, and the like.

Knickers are popular with many young people, but at best are not as flattering to boys *or* girls as stretch pants.

Any type of shirt that is comfortable and goes well with your outfit is perfectly correct—cotton, flannel, turtleneck, man-tailored, whatever becomes you best.

PARKAS

Parkas come in an infinite variety of colors and should be chosen to match or blend with the pants. Girls—especially those who are seen around the base lodge more than than on the slopes—usually choose wildly printed, fur-trimmed, or solid fur (I have even seen mink on occasion!) parkas. The more serious lady skiers tend to choose more conservative patterns or solid colors in the same style as those worn by the men.

The light-weight quilted parka is standard for both men and women—it is waterproof, windproof, and warm. Many are reversible, a good idea for those who ski frequently and cannot afford more than one outfit. The tendency now is toward longer parkas, a fine idea as they protect the upper legs and seat from bitter winds (especially while you stand in the ever-present line for the lifts) and from the wet or freezing seat of the chair lift. The parka may be belted or not, according to your own taste, but it should have a hood, which usually rolls up under the collar when not in use.

SKI BOOTS

The heavy ski boot, with inner and outer laces or, more recently, adjustable clips for ease in doing up the outside boot, are the most important item of your ski clothing. Before buying your boots, wear them for several hours with the socks you plan to use when skiing. Many, many pairs of boots have been bought without taking this precaution, only to be exchanged after the first ski trip, because blisters have appeared on the skier's heel, ankle, or toe after the first hour's skiing. Boots should be bought from a reputable ski shop, and it is wise to seek the advice of a knowledgeable salesman who can tell you which is the best boot for the price you can pay. This will be your most expensive clothing investment, so it is well to choose carefully, remembering that the better quality boot, though more costly, will give you many more years of wear.

Ski boots must be well cared for to keep the leather pliant and waterproof. They must be put on racks made for the purpose immediately on removal, and from time to time they should be treated with a leather conditioner and waterproofer. These supplies are sold at all ski shops.

UNDERWEAR

Ski underwear is especially designed to give the greatest warmth possible. It is usually double-layered wool or a wool and synthetic or cotton blend. Long pants and long-sleeved round-necked or turtle-necked shirts are standard equipment. Red is the usual color, but pants and shirts can be bought in other colors as well as stripes.

SOCKS

Two pair of socks are recommended—one light-weight pair of silk, nylon, or thin wool, and a heavy wool pair of the new "duotherm" socks, which are double-layered.

GLOVES

Gloves may be self-lined or worn with a thin nylon, cotton, or silk liner underneath. Mittens are warmer than gloves and are preferred by the average skier. They also may be self-lined, but an outer "shell" with a wool mitten inside is more practical because the inner one can be changed for a dry pair when soaked by melting snow.

HATS

No particular style of hat is correct or incorrect for the skier. Whatever the style, it should be chosen for warmth, comfort, a fit that will not let it fly off, and, especially for the girls, appearance. Fur and make-believe fur hats are very popular with the ladies and are attractive as well as warm. Wool hats in all colors, knits, and shapes can be found to match any parka, and the men are often seen in caps with flaps that come down to cover the ears.

SNOW BUNNIES

As I have said all through this chapter on sports clothing, the most important thing of all is appropriateness. And one of the least appropriate sights I know is a "snow bunny"—a girl dressed in lavender stretch pants so tight that they appear to have been painted on, a pink and purple fur-trimmed parka, an enormous white fur hat, and a face made up for a night club act in New York City—struggling miserably down the beginner's slope on Skiball Mountain. Or worse yet, sitting at the bar in the lodge attempting to look as if she had just come in from the expert trail! These women are not there to ski, and their outfits announce the fact by their very conspicuousness. The true enthusiast, be he an earnest novice or an ardent expert, dresses in a well-matched, good-looking outfit, chosen as much for comfort and wear as appearance. He—or she—makes no attempt to catch the eye of all the members of the opposite sex on the slope.

BOWLING

A full skirt or slacks, worn with a loosely cut cotton or cotton knit blouse, is the standard outfit for women who bowl. If you are blessed with a figure that looks well in slacks, they are the most practical choice, as they combine complete freedom of movement with modesty. A skirt must be flared to allow for a full stride, and long enough not to ride up too high in the back when you bend over. A box-pleat skirt is ideal, as it hangs smoothly and yet allows freedom of movement. The short-sleeved blouses may be of any style most comfortable and becoming to the wearer, with either slacks or a skirt.

A man wears slacks and any open-necked sport shirt or whatever shirt is worn by his team or club.

Most bowlers have their own shoes, but if you don't, you must rent them. Almost all alleys have shoes available, because they require them for the protection of their alleys. If there is no such regulation, sneakers will do, but never hard-soled shoes.

Except by young children, shorts are not worn at the bowling alley.

RIDING

A riding habit, no matter what the fashion happens to be, is che counterpart of an officer's uniform; it must be beautifully fitted, smart, and utterly conventional. Don't wear loud plaids, pockets, or eccentric cuffs or lapels. The best choice for the coat is a plain dark color, but small checks, herringbone tweed, or muted plaids can be handsome, too. A medium-weight closely woven material holds its shape better than a light loose weave. The trousers are solid color, usually fawn or gray.

There are two accepted types of riding habits for women—the jodhpur and the high boot, but men are more correctly dressed in the high boot.

Jodhpurs are breeches that are wide in the lower leg, so that they fit *over* a low boot rather inside a high one. For both men and women, the rest of the outfit is the same as that worn with high boots.

The boots should be low heeled and have a straight line from heel to top of back. The tops should be no wider than absolutely necessary to get the boots on and off, and they should not be curved or fancy in shape. Be sure that there is no elbow sticking out like a horse's hock at the back.

Low boots for wear with jodhpurs should be of plain leather. The ornamental Western boots that are available in some sections of the country are suitable only with Western riding pants or blue jeans.

Hats must fit the head well, and the shape must be conventional. The peaked velvet cap is most often worn, but derbies are correct, especially for show riding. Hats are worn straight—never on the back of the head or tipped over the nose.

Gloves should be leather.

Neckties or stocks should be tied so as to make them as flat and neat as possible and anchored so securely that nothing can possibly come loose.

If you are asked to ride with a hunt, you wear your most formal riding clothes, with collarless shirt and stock, and a derby if you have one.

Members of a hunt, on special occasions, wear the red (but called pink) coats peculiar to the sport, white or fawn breeches, high black boots, and a black derby. The style is rigidly prescribed, although some details may be varied to identify a particular hunt.

The riding habit is proper for riding in city parks or in horse shows. Riding clothes for the country are completely casual, and shirts, sweaters, or jackets may be chosen according to the weather. Open-necked cotton or flannel shirts, turtleneck or polo shirts are all comfortable and attractive, and sweaters may be worn instead of jackets. Jodhpur boots are easier to care for than the highly polished boots, and therefore jodhpurs are often worn in the country by those who ride a great deal.

IN GENERAL

There are many other sports that we could discuss in this chapter, but most of them either need no particular costume or require clothing so prescribed that those taking part know what they are to wear without having to read a book. The fancy skater, for instance, knows without being told that she wears a short flared skirt and tights to keep her legs warm.

If you are taking up a new sport, make a point of observing those who are old hands—they will know what is correct. Then you can choose the features that will be most becoming to you and most suited to your degree of skill. The rank beginner need not choose the very expensive equipment that the expert requires, but remember, as in choosing all clothes, quality, simplicity, and appropriateness are the most important requisites of dressing well.

Part FOURTEEN

THE WELL-APPOINTED HOUSE

76

The personality of the house

Every house has an exterior to be made as presentable as possible, and an interior continually to be set in order and cleaned. There are meals to be prepared and served, clothes to be laundered and mended, and perhaps children to be cared for. The devices or appliances essential to these needs must be provided to the best of the ability of the head of the household.

Beyond these fundamental necessities, luxuries can be added indefinitely. A little house cannot be a splendid mansion any more than a diamond weighing but half a carat can compare with a stone weighing fifty times as much. But this is a good simile, nevertheless, because the perfect little house may be like a corner cut from precisely the same stone and differing therefrom merely in size, whereas the house in bad taste and improperly run may be like a diamond that is off color and full of flaws or a mere piece of glass that can suggest a valuable gem only to those as ignorant as its owner.

A gem of a house may be no size at all, but its lines must be honest and its painting and furnishing in good taste. As for its upkeep, its path or sidewalk is beautifully neat, steps scrubbed, brasses polished, and its bell answered promptly by a tidy maid or by the mistress herself

—all these things contribute unmistakably to the impression of quality and refinement.

But the mansion of bastard architecture and crude detail, with its brass indifferently clean, with coarse lace behind the plate glass of its golden-oak door, and the bell answered at eleven in the morning by a sloppy and disinterested servant might as well be placarded, "Here lives a vulgarian who has never had an opportunity to approach the outermost edges of cultivation." As a matter of fact, the knowledge of how to make a house distinguished both in appearance and in service is harder to learn than how to present a distinguished appearance oneself and to acquire presentable manners.

The personality of a house is indefinable, but there never lived a woman of great charm whose home, whether a mansion or a tiny apartment, did not reflect the charm of its owner. Houses without personality are a series of walled enclosures with furniture standing about in them. Sometimes their lack of charm is baffling; every article is correct and perhaps even beautiful, but one has the feeling that the decorator made chalk marks indicating the exact spot on which each piece of furniture is to stand. Other houses are filled with things of little intrinsic value, often with much that is shabby, and yet they have that inviting atmosphere, that air of unmistakable rightness, which is an unfailing indication of people of excellent taste.

"BECOMING" FURNITURE

Suitability is a test of good taste always—the dress to the occasion, the article to the place, the furniture to the background. And yet to combine many periods in one and commit no anachronism—to put something French, something Spanish, something Italian, and something English into an American house and have the result the perfection of American taste—is a feat that has been accomplished time and again —by those who know how!

A woman of great taste follows fashion in house furnishing, just as she follows fashion in dress, in general principles only. She wears what is becoming to her own type and personality, and she puts into her house only such articles as are becoming to it.

That a quaint old-fashioned house should be filled with quaint old-fashioned pieces of furniture, in size proportioned to the size of the rooms, and that rush-bottomed chairs and rag rugs have no place in a marble hall, need not be pointed out. But to an amazing number of persons, proportion seems to mean nothing at all. They will put a huge piece of furniture in a tiny room so that the effect is one of painful indigestion; or they will spoil a really good room by the addition of senseless and inappropriately cluttering objects in the belief that because they are valuable they must be beautiful, regardless of suitability.

Sometimes a room is marred by "treasures" clung to for reasons of sentiment. If you happen to collect old glass, it should be kept in one room, easily accessible so that it can be shown to other people who are interested, but not scattered over table tops everywhere so that your house has the appearance of a museum or antique shop.

THE BLINDNESS OF SENTIMENT

It is almost impossible for any of us to judge accurately about things to which we have been accustomed throughout a lifetime. A chair that was Grandmother's, a painting Father bought, the silver that has always been on the dining-room table—all are so much a part of ourselves that we are sentiment-blind to their defects and incongruity in new surroundings.

For instance, the portrait of a Colonial officer, among others, had always hung in Mrs. Oldname's dining-room. One day an art critic whose knowledge was better than his manners blurted out, "Will you please tell me why you have that dreadful thing in this otherwise perfect room?" Mrs. Oldname, somewhat taken aback, answered rather wonderingly, "Is it dreadful? Really? I have a feeling of affection for him and his dog!"

The critic was merciless. "If you call a cotton-flannel effigy a dog! And as for the figure, it is equally false and lifeless! It is amazing how anyone with your taste can bear looking at it!" In spite of his rudeness, Mrs. Oldname saw then that what he said was quite true—when the fact was pointed out to her. Gradually she grew to dislike the poor officer so much that he was finally relegated to the attic. In the same way, most of us have possessions that have "always been there" or perhaps "treasures" that we love for some association, rather than their appearance. But habit has blinded us, though we would not have to be told of their hideousness were they seen by us in the house of another. Or perhaps they are not bad in themselves. Perhaps they are quite beautiful, but unsuitable in the place in which they are and to the objects surrounding them.

It is not to be expected that all people can throw away every esthetically unpleasing possession; but those whose pocketbook and sentiment will permit would add greatly to the beauty of their houses by throwing out the bad. Far better have stoneware plates that are good in design than costly porcelain that is bad in decoration. Expensiveness, in other words, is never a criterion of taste.

The only way to determine what is good and what is horrible is to study and try to understand the principles underlying what is good—from books, in museums, in art classes at the universities, and in the magazines devoted to the decorative arts.

Be very careful, though. Do not mistake modern eccentricities for "art." There are, quite literally, frightful things in vogue at times—flamboyant and discordant colors, grotesque deformities, designs that cannot possibly be other than bad, because aside from striking novelty there is nothing good about them.

The vocation of a servant

Before going into the various details of service, it may be well to speak of the unreasoning indignity cast upon the honorable vocation of a servant. There is an inexplicable tendency, in this country certainly, for working people in general to look upon domestic service as an unworthy if not altogether degrading vocation. The cause may perhaps be found in the fact that this same scornful public, having for the most part little opportunity to know first-class servants, takes it for granted that inefficient "servant girls" and "hired men" are representative of their kind. Therefore, they put all servants in the same category—regardless of whether they are uncouth and ill-trained or experts in their own special field who in most instances have also had the great advantages of many cultivating environments.

And yet so insistently has this down-grading of the word "servant" spread that everyone sensitive to the feelings of others avoids using it exactly as one avoids using the word "cripple" when speaking to one who is slightly lame. Yet are not the best of us "servants" of the church? And the highest among us "servants" of the people and the state?

To be a slattern in a vulgar household is scarcely an elevated employment, but neither is belonging to the lower and incompetent ranks of any other calling.

COMPLETE SERVICE

In these days of "do-it-yourself" housekeeping, a large household staff is rare indeed. A moderate number of households have one maid living in, but the most that a great majority of the women of today expect is to have help with the housecleaning chores once or twice a week. Beyond that, they may hire a combination cook-waitress to assist on a special occasion.

But for the comparative few who lead a life different from the average, the problems of a household staff, although on a reduced scale, are the same as they have been for many years. Those women who must run official establishments (embassies, for example), or possibly women who must turn the running of a large house over to a competent staff because of the demands of a career, have much to learn. Even though the staff of such an establishment does all of the actual physical labor, it is still the job of the mistress to direct and coordinate the work, exactly as a general leads his army.

For what one might call complete service (meaning service that is adequate at all times), the minimum number is three: a cook, a butler or waitress, and a housemaid. If there are children, a nurse must be added to the list. This number is necessary because the waitress (or butler) and the housemaid are on alternate shifts in staying in and going out, the waitress being on duty to answer bell and telephone one afternoon, and the housemaid taking his or her place the next and also serving dinner (or supper) one evening in the week and every other Sunday. One of them also takes the place of the cook on her evening out. When the schedule has been established, their days off should not be shifted around unless it is really necessary. If it is, try to give them sufficient notice so that they can rearrange their plans for their time off.

It stands to reason that one may expect more nearly perfect service from a "specialist" than from one whose functions are multiple. But when there are two—each of whom is capable of taking over for the other on her time off—the house can be run perfectly as far as essentials go. Service could be handicapped if, when the waitress goes out, the cook does not substitute for her and still further if, when the cook goes out, there is no one to prepare the meal.

Whether you have one servant or many, consideration for them— for their feelings as well as their working conditions—is essential. » *See also Chapter 78 on this important point.*

THE STAFF OF A LARGE ESTABLISHMENT

The management of a house of great size is usually divided into several distinct departments, each under its separate head. The housekeeper, if there is one—otherwise the lady of the house—has charge of the appearance of the house and of its contents, the manners and appearance of the maids, as well as their work in cleaning walls, floors, furniture, pictures, ornaments, and books; taking care of linen is also her responsibility.

The butler has charge of the pantry and dining room. He engages footmen, even though they are only hired on a temporary basis for special occasions, apportions their work, and is responsible for their appearance, manners, and efficiency. He is also responsible for silver and wines.

The cook is in charge of the kitchen and the kitchen maids, if any.

The nurse, the personal maid, and the cook are under the direction of the lady of the house. The butler and the valet as well as the chauffeur and gardener are usually engaged by the gentleman of the house. When garage or garden requires more than one, the head chauffeur usually engages his own assistants, and the head gardener always does so.

THE HOUSEKEEPER

In a very big house, the housekeeper usually lives in the house. Smaller establishments often have a visiting housekeeper who comes for as long as she is needed each morning. The resident housekeeper has her own bedroom, bath, and sitting room. Her meals are brought to her room by a kitchen maid if there is one, or by the waitress or parlor maid if there is not.

In an occasional house, all the servants, the gardener as well as the cook and butler and nurses, come under the housekeeper's authority; in other words, she superintends the entire household exactly as a very conscientious and skilled lady of the house would do herself if she gave her whole time and attention to it. The housekeeper is always called "Mrs. Hart," never by her given name.

THE BUTLER

The butler is not only the most important servant in every big establishment, but it is by no means unheard for him to be both steward and housekeeper. However, although he perhaps supervises the cook's orders or even goes to market, the cook is not otherwise under his supervision, and neither, of course, is the children's nurse or the lady's maid.

Where there is no housekeeper and the butler takes her place, he engages not only the menservants but the housemaids, parlor maids, and even on occasion the cook. But normally in the house of lesser size, the butler has charge of the dining room and pantry or possibly the whole ground floor. In all smaller establishments, and in many great ones, he is valet to his employer. In a small house, the butler works a great deal with his hands and not so much with his head. In a great establishment, the butler works very much with his head and with his hands very little.

At Golden Hall, when guests used to come in dozens at a time, his stewardship—even though there was a housekeeper—was not a job that a man of small ability could fill. He had perhaps twenty men under him at big dinners, ten who belonged under him in the house always; he had the keys to the wine cellar and the combination of the silver safe. He also chose the china and glass and linen as well as the silver to be used each day, and he oversaw the setting of the table and the serving of food.

At all meals, he stood behind the chair of the lady of the house so that at the slightest turn of her head he need only take a step to be within reach of her voice. The husband, by the way, is "head of the house," but the wife is "head of his table."

In the smaller house of today, the butler also takes charge of the wines and silver and does very much the same as the butler in the larger house, except that he has less overseeing of others and more work to do himself. Where he is alone, he does all the work—naturally. Where he has a parlor maid or waitress, he always cleans the silver and answers the front door and telephone and passes the main courses at the table. The assistant passes the secondary dishes and also washes dishes and cleans the dining room and pantry. Every other afternoon they take turns in anwering the door and serving tea. The butler is also valet not only for the gentleman of the house but for any gentlemen guests as well.

The butler never wears the livery of a footman. In the early morning he wears sack suit—black single-breasted jacket and gray and black striped trousers, with a dark inconspicuous tie. For formal luncheons, he wears black trousers with gray stripes, a double-breasted, high-cut black waistcoat, and black swallow-tailed coat like a cutaway but without silk on the lapels, a white stiff-bosomed shirt with standing collar, and a black four-in-hand tie. At informal or family luncheons, he may serve in his sack suit.

In fashionable houses, the butler does not put on his dress suit until six o'clock. The butler's evening dress differs from that of his employer in a few details only: he has no braid on his trousers, and the silk on his lapels (if any) is narrower; but the most distinctive difference is that a butler wears a black waistcoat and a white lawn tie, and a gentleman always wears a white waistcoat with a white tie, or a white waistcoat and a black tie with a dinner coat, but never the reverse. In hot weather, except on the most formal occasion, the butler may wear a soft shirt with black tie, and a white linen single-breasted jacket to serve luncheon, and the same white jacket with a standing stiff collar to serve dinner.

A butler does not wear a mustache, and to allow him to open the door collarless and in shirt sleeves is in the worst possible taste. He never wears gloves or a flower in his buttonhole. He sometimes wears a very thin watch chain in the daytime, but none at night. He never wears a scarf pin or any jewelry that is for ornament alone. His cuff links should be as plain as possible, and his shirt studs white enamel ones that look like linen.

The butler's clothes are usually provided by his employer, but in some communities he is expected to provide his own.

FOOTMEN

The position of footman, sometimes called "second man," is almost nonexistent today, and when the butler needs extra help for a special occasion like a very large dinner or ball, the footmen are hired from a caterer or an agency that provides temporary help. They are provided by the agency with regulation "liveries" consisting of trousers and tail coat to match, buttons of either brass or silver, stiff-starched collar and shirt, white lawn tie, striped waistcoat, and white cotton gloves. Usually there are three buttons on each side of the front of the coat in addition to two linked together on each side of the front edge to hold the coat nearly closed over the waistcoat. There are also twelve buttons on the tails of the coat.

In the rare establishment large enough to require a permanent assistant to the butler, his duties are the following: Cleaning the dining room, pantry, lower hall, entrance vestibule and sidewalk, attending to the furnace, carrying wood to any open fireplaces in the house, cleaning the windows, cleaning brasses, cleaning all shoes and boots, carrying everything that is too heavy for the maids or moving furniture so they can clean behind it, valeting all gentlemen who are guests in the house, assisting the butler in setting and waiting on table, attending the front door, answering the telephone and writing down messages, and cleaning and polishing silver.

The butler himself usually answers the telephone; if not, it is answered by the footman. The footman is deputy butler and takes his place whenever the butler is off duty.

THE CHAUFFEUR

The position of chauffeur differs from that of the other domestic employees in two respects. The first is that he usually has no regular days off. Second, he usually finds and pays for his own board and lodging. Sometimes a single man may eat with the servants in the kitchen, but this is not common. Sometimes, too, there may be a room over the garage—or perhaps a whole apartment—in which he and his family may live. Although he seemingly gets higher wages than any of the other servants, it must be remembered that his hours are difficult, and living expenses have to come out of his wages, whereas the pay of other servants includes their room and board.

When traveling, the employer always pays for the chauffeur's room and meals as long as they are away from home.

His uniforms are furnished him by his employer.

His duties are irregular, sometimes extremely so. In a large family, particularly where there are half-grown sons or daughters, a chauffeur's life can be inhumanly strenuous. He can, for example, be expected to take the younger children to school, come back and take the lady shopping, go back to school for the children, drive various members of the family during the afternoon, come back and take his employers out to dinner, go back later to fetch them, and perhaps take a debutante daughter to a night club or ball. Or, if his employers are entertaining that evening, he may perhaps have to stand on the sidewalk to open the car doors of the arriving guests, and then do so again when they depart.

On the other hand, there are places in which the chauffeur is almost a man of leisure; his employer is an old lady, perhaps, who goes to church on Sunday morning from eleven to half-past twelve, who likes to drive from three to five every afternoon, and who goes out to dinner or to a concert or to the theater not oftener than once a week. Both of these extremes can be encountered in almost every city. The typical schedule is midway between the two. Perhaps he has long driving days interspersed with short ones. But every considerate employer tells his chauffeur that he is not going to want the car as far in advance as he can, because it is only in these circumstances that the chauffeur may himself make any personal engagements.

When the car is in a private garage, the chauffeur must of course wash it and take care of it himself. In a public garage, the washing may be done for him and the interior of the car is also brushed out by the garage attendant.

A chauffeur never carries a robe on his arm when waiting at the car door for his employer. Properly, the lap robe is laid in deep full-length folds on the far side of the seat. As soon as the occupants have taken their places, the chauffeur reaches across and, holding the edge of the fold, draws it toward him across their laps. Upon arriving at a destination, if a doorman or a chauffeur is stationed on the sidewalk, he remains seated; otherwise he leaves his seat and holds open the door for the occupants to alight. In assisting a lady or possibly a gentleman who is elderly, the chauffeur presents his forearm held horizontally so that the person alighting puts her or his hand upon his sleeve as though it were a balustrade.

He touches·his hat at the close of any order given him, unless the car is in motion, when he merely nods his acknowledgment.

It is unnecessary to add that a chauffeur may never smoke when driving his employer. If he smokes when alone in the car, he must see that it is completely aired out and the ash tray is clean afterward.

THE COOK AND KITCHEN MAID

The cook is always in charge in the kitchen. In a small house or in an apartment, she has all the cooking and all the cleaning of the kitchen and pantry to do, the back door bell to answer, and the servants' table to set and their dishes as well as her kitchen utensils to wash.

In a larger house, the kitchen maid prepares vegetables, does all cleaning of the kitchen and pots and pans, answers the bell, sets the servants' table and washes the servants' table dishes. She also carries the houekeeper's meals to her.

In most houses, the cook does all the marketing, usually by telephone. She sees the lady of the house every morning and submits the day's menus for her to approve or change. The butler always goes into the kitchen shortly after the cook has had the menus checked and copies the day's menus on a pad of his own. From this he knows what table utensils will be needed.

The cook always wears a white dress and usually a high apron with pockets, stockings (often white), and white shoes. She is expected to furnish her clothes herself, but her aprons and uniforms (and her hair coverings if she wears them) are laundered for her. A few fastidious cooks wear small white kerchief-shaped caps or hair nets when they are preparing food. It is to be hoped that this custom may become universal, since the thought that a sudden breeze is quite likely to blow a hair into the food is most unattractive.

The kitchen maid most often wears a colored cotton dress to match that of the other maids in the house, but she wears a heavier, larger apron and short sleeves. Her dress is given to her. Sometimes she wears white. It is better that she wear color all the time or white all the time, since to dress her in white in the afternoon and color in the morning really means a double supply of clothes.

THE PARLOR MAID-WAITRESS AND CHAMBERMAID

The parlor maid or waitress keeps the drawing room and library in order and lays the fire. In some houses, she takes up the breakfast trays; in other houses, the butler does this himself and then hands them to the lady's maid or the chambermaid, who takes them into the bedrooms. She cleans the windows and the brasses if there is no utility man.

The parlor maid-waitress assists the butler in waiting at table and washing dishes and takes turns with him in answering the door and the telephone.

The chambermaid does all the bedrooms, cleans all silver on dressing tables, polishes fixtures in the bathroom—in other words takes care of the bedroom floors. She also takes care of the rooms of the other servants.

In a larger house, the head housemaid has charge of the linen and does the bedrooms of the lady and gentleman of the house and a few of the guest rooms. The second housemaid does the children's rooms, extra guest rooms, and the servants' floors. The larger the establishment, the more housemaids, and the more the work is further divided.

In the more typical house in which the bedrooms are taken care of by one person who is possibly waitress too, she is called the chambermaid or chambermaid-waitress.

The waitress or parlor maid and the housemaid are dressed alike. Their work dresses are of plain cotton or drip-dry material, in whatever color the lady of the house prefers, and have just-above-elbow sleeves that are edged with a turn-back attached white cuff. The dresses are finished at the neck with a matching turned-down collar. With them are worn large white aprons with high bibs.

In a formal house, at mealtime, the waitress and anyone who assists her in the dining room change to long-sleeved dresses of taffeta, or silk, or synthetic, either in black or dark colors, with embroidered white collars, cuffs, and matching white aprons. In summer or in hot climates, these dresses are often of light-colored dimity or dotted muslin, with the same accessories as for silk, and they may have short sleeves.

A maid's hair must be smooth and neat. Anything suggesting a faddist hair style or curls flying long and loose would be in almost as bad taste as a butler wearing a mustache.

THE LADY'S MAID

A first-class lady's maid, often called a "personal maid," is required to be a hairdresser, a good packer, and an expert needlewoman. Her duty is to keep her employer's clothes in perfect order and to help her dress and undress. She draws the bath, lays out underclothes, dresses the lady's hair, and gets out the dress to be worn, as well as the stockings, shoes, hat, gloves, handbag, or whatever accessories go with the dress selected.

As soon as her lady is dressed for the day, everything that has been worn is gone over carefully. Everything mussed is pressed, everything suspected of not being immaculate is washed or cleaned and, when in perfect order, is placed where it belongs. Stockings are looked over for threatening runs or holes and mended if possible. Fine stockings and fragile underwear, as well as washable gloves, are always washed by the maid. In many cases, the meticulous maid refuses to let anyone but herself launder items of special fineness. This is more reasonable than it perhaps appears, since mending these fragile items is her very special task.

The majority of ladies' maids are never asked to wait up for their employer beyond a reasonably early hour. Those who sit up late are permitted to sleep comparatively late in the morning.

On duty, a lady's maid wears a dark skirt, a white blouse, and either a small white apron, the band of which buttons in the back, or else a small, round-cornered, black taffeta apron with a narrow self ruffle. This is either tied or buttoned at the back. Her aprons are supplied by her employer; otherwise she always wears her own clothes. These, however, must be very quiet in color and of shirtwaist plainness. She never wears a cap.

Usually, she changes her white blouse and black shirt of the morning for an afternoon and evening dress of black taffeta or silk or synthetic with a small soft white or cream collar, and a small, black apron.

Certain ladies give their maids more than lavish supplies from a scarcely worn wardrobe. Others give them things of small account or nothing. This is especially true of those employers who have many relatives or friends or organizations to whom they feel obliged to give everything.

THE VALET AND HOUSEMAN

The valet (pronounced VAL-et, not valLAY) is what Beau Brummell called a gentleman's gentleman. He keeps his employer's clothes in perfect order, brushes, cleans, and presses everything as soon as it has been worn, lays out the clothes to be put on, and puts away everything that is a personal belonging. Some gentlemen, particularly those who are very old, like their valets to help them dress, run the bath, shave them, and hold each article in readiness as it is to be put on. But most merely require that their clothes be laid out for them in good order.

The valet also unpacks the bags of any gentlemen guests when they arrive, valets them while there, and packs again when they go. He always packs for his own gentleman, buys tickets, looks after the luggage, and makes himself generally useful as a personal attendant, whether at home or when traveling.

At all hours of the day or evening, the valet wears an ordinary business suit, dark and inconspicuous in color, with a black tie.

In this present day, a valet is usually a "visiting one" who goes each day to a number of employers to keep the clothes of each in order.

In a bachelor's quarters, however, a valet is often general factotum, not only valeting but performing the service of cook, butler, and even housemaid. He is more frequently know as a "houseman." When serving meals, he wears a jacket like that of a steward or, for very formal occasions, the dress suit of a butler. The bachelor employer usually feels that the jacket of a steward is less pretentious and therefore in best taste for a simple house or apartment.

A serious problem for the valet who cooks is preventing spatters of grease from getting on his sleeves and cuffs. For this, a thin, washable, seersucker gown, put on with the opening in the back, like a surgeon's apron, is practical when he broils or fries or takes the roast out of the oven. It is much easier to put a thin, long-sleeved gown with elastic bands at wrists over what he wears than to take off coat, undo cuff links, roll up sleeves, and then have to reverse this process—just to handle one roast or frying pan.

THE CHILDREN'S NURSE

Everybody knows the children's nurse is either the comfort or the torment of the house. Many an excellent cook has left an otherwise satisfactory job because the nurse was upsetting the kitchen routine. Everyone also knows innumerable young mothers who put up with inexcusable crankiness from a crotchety middle-aged woman because she was "so wonderful" to the baby. And here let it be emphasized that she usually turns out to have been not so wonderful to the baby at all. Devotion must always be unselfish; the nurse who is really wonderful to the baby is pretty sure to be a person who is kind generally. In ninety-nine cases out of a hundred, the sooner a domineering nurse—old or young—is let go, the better. Many a mother has had life made perfectly miserable by her belief that if she were to dismiss the tyrant, the baby would suffer, only to find that in the end—and there always is an end—the child was quite as relieved as the rest of the family when the right sort of kindly and humane person took the tyrant's place. It must never be forgotten that a young child is inescapably imprisoned in the atmosphere created by the disposition of the person in charge of him and that sunlight is not more essential to a plant than an atmosphere of sympathetic lightheartedness is to a child.

It is hardly necessary to add that one cannot be too particular in asking for a nurse's reference and in never failing to talk on the telephone personally with the lady she is leaving. Not only is it important to have a sweet-tempered, competent, and clean person. Her moral character is of utmost concern, for she is to be the constant and inseparable companion of children whose whole lives are influenced by her example, especially if busy parents can give only a small portion of time to their children.

When the mother of the children cares very much about appearances, their nurse is always dressed in white in the house. With the wonderful wash-and-wear fabrics, it is possible for every nurse to dress at all times—even when traveling—in spotless white, since it is entirely possible to rinse out each uniform and hang it above a bathtub to dry very quickly, and it needs no ironing. On the street she may wear a simple suit or dress and hat. To dress any nurse in the cloak and cap of the English nurse is suitable only if she actually is British.

OTHER HOUSEHOLD ASSISTANTS

In addition to those regularly employed on the staff of any large establishment, there are others whose assistance may be required from time to time or on special occasions—the tutor, the registered nurse, and so forth. Then, too, there are the baby-sitters and the daily maids who, more than the butlers and the valets, are familiar and necessary parts of many present-day households. The companion may be a permanent member of any staff, or she may be employed on a temporary basis in a home with no staff at all. In the same way, one household may require the services of a social secretary at all times, whereas another family employs her for only a few months, to handle the details of their daughter's elaborate wedding, for example. Less can be said specifically about the duties involved in these other categories of employment, for so often they are dependent on very special circumstances. But perhaps the suggestions given here may make life more comfortable for employer and employee alike, in spite of their necessarily general nature.

THE COMPANION

A companion's position is always one of social equality with her employer. The object of her care may be an invalid, a very elderly person, or a young girl. In the last case, the companion is a chaperon. In the majority of cases, the companion is a relative or friend who becomes a permanent member of her employing relative's or friend's household on a salaried basis.

Her duties cannot very well be set down, because they vary with individual requirements. One lady likes to travel continually and merely wants an agreeable companion to go with her or to accompany her for a drive in the car in pleasant weather. Another will want the papers, her favorite magazines, or the new books read to her.

Another is a semi-invalid who never leaves her room, and the duties of her companion are almost those of a practical nurse—quite possibly she may have been one and was persuaded to make the house of her ex-patient her permanent home. The average requirement is being personally agreeable, tactful, intelligent, and—companionable!

A companion dresses as any other lady does, according to the occasion, her personal taste, her age, and her means. If she is expected to go out to public places or to be constantly dressed for company at home, she should be given a definite dress allowance. This means that if an employer wants her companion to travel with her or go out with her socially, she should make it possible for her to be suitably and becomingly dressed for each of these occasions, by paying extra for this very considerable personal expense.

THE TUTOR AND THE GOVERNESS

The social position of a tutor is similar to that of the companion. For reasons that are in many ways unfair, the tutor's social acceptance is much more enthusiastic than that of the governess. In all probability, he is an attractive and intelligent young man still in or just out of college and therefore welcome as an extra man. The governess, on the other hand, is a usually not-so-young additional woman.

A tutor is expected to be present when wanted and absent when not, to be at all times agreeable and at the same time impersonal, and to remember that as far as his character and behavior are concerned, his job carries on through the hours when he is off duty as well as when he is on.

The position of governess varies greatly according to her own accomplishments, the ages of the children, and the mode of each family's life. If the house is a large one, she has a sitting room of her own. Otherwise her room should be furnished as an attractive and transformable sitting room, with a day bed, a desk instead of a bureau, easy chairs, and good reading light. This is not an excessive amount of luxury, but a very plain necessity, because otherwise she has nowhere to sit except in the discomfort of a bedroom or else with the family—a situation that is at times as trying for them as for her.

A governess usually comes to the family breakfast and lunch table and, if her pupils do, to dinner as well. But when her charges are half-grown, it is often arranged that they shall dine with their parents while the governess is served in her own sitting room or in the dining room at an hour earlier than that of the family. Arrangement is always made whereby the children and the governess are served elsewhere when formal company is expected. When friends of the family come for lunch or dinner and the governess is to be present, she shows herself ready to be agreeable to anyone inclined to talk to her, but she should rarely lead the conversation. After a luncheon she withdraws to her own quarters, goes out for a walk, or occupies herself as she wishes until late afternoon, unless she is especially asked to stay.

According to best taste, a governess should not wear unsuitably conspicuous clothes—which does not mean that she cannot wear the latest fashion of the day, but that fashion should be whispered rather than shouted out loud.

CONFIDENTIAL SECRETARY

The most important secretarial position and one that comes into immediate contact with an employer's home and social, as well as public, life is that of resident confidential secretary. The employer of such a person is most often someone of so much importance in public life—perhaps as a diplomat or a governor or the President's wife—that he needs an assistant who is always on hand. In many ways, this type of secretary is considered a member of the family. He is always present at business meetings and often at social ones as well. He usually has a secretary of his own and perhaps several stenographers. In other words, he is a deputy who serves as extra eyes and hands and supplementary brains for his chief. A position of this sort is rare, hard to find, and still harder to fill.

THE SOCIAL SECRETARY

The social secretary very rarely lives in the house of her employer; more often than not, she goes to two or three or more houses, since there is seldom work enough in one to require her whole time.

The duties of a social secretary are to attend to all correspondence, file papers and documents, telephone personal messages, arrange appointments, and also serve as extra hands and eyes and intelligence for her employer. She writes all impersonal notes, of course, takes longer letters in shorthand, and writes others herself after being told their purpose. She also audits all bills and draws the checks for them; the checks are filled in and then presented to her employer to be signed, after which she puts them in their envelopes and seals and sends them. When the receipted bills are returned, the secretary files them according to her own method, where they can at any time be found by her if needed for reference. In many cases it is she, though it may equally well be the butler or waitress or personal maid, who telephones invitations and other messages. If there are children in the house of boarding-school age, she may have to attend to details of their tuition, arrivals and departures, etc.

She may also be a social manager who devises entertainments and arranges all such details as the decorations of the house for a dance or the program of entertainment following a large dinner.

Her dress is that of any business woman. Extremes of fashion that border on the eccentric are out of keeping, as they would be out of keeping in an office.

THE REGISTERED NURSE

The social position of a registered hospital nurse is, of course, that of a deputy physician and, if on a long case, the closest of the family's friends. She always eats her meals with the family or has them served to her on a tray in a sitting room. She never eats in the kitchen unless that is where the family also eats.

When on duty in her patient's room or anywhere in a private house, she wears her uniform. But when going into the street, going downstairs in a hotel, or traveling with her patient, she dresses as does any other lady.

COUPLES

A satisfactory solution to the problem of household help for many families who have large houses but cannot or do not wish to employ many servants is the married couple who are hired together. The work is divided according to the abilities of the man and wife, but the most usual arrangement is for the woman to do the cooking and to clean the bedroom floor, while the man waits on table, cleans the living rooms, dining room, halls, etc., and also does some driving and takes care of the cars. They share the work of cleaning up after meals, and he may also help with their preparation, especially if the employer is entertaining.

The couple must have an apartment of at least two rooms, preferably with a private entrance, perhaps over a garage. Some employers do not object if a child lives with the parents, but it must be understood in advance that he or she will not be disturbing in any way and will not be allowed the run of the house except when playing with the children of the employer.

THE BABY-SITTER

With smaller family houses and small-apartment living, the shortage of a "live-in" staff has, especially for young people, created a special demand—and baby-sitters have achieved both amateur and professional standing. Age of sitters may range from the early teens, if he or she is a responsible youngster and fond of children, up to elderly ladies. In the intermediate group, many high school and college boys and girls and young business women are glad to supplement their allowances or salaries by baby-sitting a few times a week.

In many large cities, girls who live in residential clubs post their names to indicate their availability for baby-sitting, and mothers in the neighborhood may avail themselves of this service. In some communities, there are agencies that provide approved sitters at standard rates.

The rate of payment varies in different localities, and no set schedule can be fixed. But the customary rate of the community should be observed, and the sitter should be paid at the end of the evening. The sitter should be told that after the children are asleep he or she may use the television set or play the radio, read, or do homework. In other words, it should be clearly understood what he is expected to do and what he may not do. It is thoughtful to leave a snack in the refrigerator—the hours can become long and tiresome. Be specific about where you are going—leave address and telephone number, as well as the name, address, and telephone number of the children's doctor. Always tell the sitter when you expect to be back—and try to be on time.

Adequate transportation must be provided for the sitter's safe return home, and this applies for sitters of any age.

PART-TIME HELP

The maid, or "cleaning woman," who comes by the hour or day should be treated with the same courtesy that is expected by the permanent servant. She should be paid promptly, daily, weekly, or in any other way agreed upon.

If the house is far from public transportation, the employer must see that she is transported to bus or train or, if she is not, that her pay is augmented to cover taxi fare.

If the lady of the house wishes her to wear uniforms, she naturally provides them for her. The part-time cleaning woman often prefers to wear her own clothes, covered by a large apron, but if she wishes to wear a uniform in order to save her clothes, she may ask her employer to buy one or two.

The maid's duties should be carefully outlined in advance. Will there be cooking to do? Are washing and ironing expected, and what about heavy cleaning like waxing floors and washing windows? All these points should be clearly understood on both sides, and if she is asked to do any unusual work or stay on late, to help with a dinner party, for example, her hourly rate for this extra service should be agreed upon beforehand.

78

The employer-servant relationship

Everyone who employs a servant is at some point faced with the problem of doing so for the first time. Even the young woman who has grown up in a household with a large staff is confronted by a new situation when she begins to look for her own maid for her own new establishment. Far too many people give too little thought to what is involved in the employer-servant relationship, not only when they interview applicants, but throughout the months and years that follow.

THE NEW EMPLOYER

If you have never kept house before and do not know what a maid should be able to do, it is best to go to a reliable employment office where the personnel will be glad to tell you about hours and wages and an average working plan. On the other hand, if you advertise in the paper, then you could perhaps ask a friend whose own house is run very nearly the way you would like your own to be to give you advice on making a fair and practical schedule.

INTERVIEWING AN APPLICANT

The first thing the applicant does when you see her is to hand you her written references from her last employer. If she has several, she shows you the last two or three. A good reference should say that she is honest, sober, capable, trustworthy, and of good disposition. If one of these items is missing in each of the references shown you, then you should take this shortcoming into consideration. They should also give the telephone numbers and addresses so that you may talk to or write the previous employer if you wish to check the reference personally.

Let us say, however, that the references of a certain applicant are good and that the wages you can pay meet her expectations. Let us say, too, that you find her personality pleasing. (Perhaps this feeling is not always reliable, but it is a point to consider.)

The next move is to give her briefly but accurately the schedule of both working and time-off hours. Accuracy is emphasized because careless misrepresentation of facts or intentions is unfair. It is unfair, for example, to assure the maid that she is to have no care of the baby and then gradually ask that she do just about everything that would be expected of a special nurse—as well as her other work.

Another important point is to try to visualize what you offer her as well as what you expect of her. Don't say that you are always prompt when you are not; don't say that your meals will be very simple and then expect her to be an expert chef. Don't say that the house is easy to take care of when it couldn't be more inconvenient. Don't say that her work will take a certain number of hours a day without having the vaguest notion of how much work can be reasonably expected in this length of time. At the other extreme, it isn't necessary to exaggerate whatever inconveniences there may perhaps be, particularly when there will be much compensating pleasantness that could make her quite happy with you— more so, in fact, than in a house whose shortcomings might be fewer.

HOW MUCH WORK?

The details of just how much, and just what, one maid should do constitute a subject of importance to tens of thousands, but it is a subject that is almost impossible to treat in a general statement because her work must be adjusted not only to the needs of the particular family by whom she is employed, but also to her own capability.

Out of every twenty-four hours, every normal human being should have at least nine hours for sleeping, dressing, and undressing, in addition to plenty of time for eating three meals. During the rest of the day, she must find the time for rest and recreation as well as for work. It is impossible to establish a fixed schedule that can apply to time in and time out, because these are in many cases subject to personal requirements and agreements. But her days off should be clearly stated and respected. If it is absolutely necessary to change a day off, she must be given ample warning so that she may change her own plans.

The maid's food and lodging, her uniforms and aprons are part of her pay; and when one considers that the greater part of the average businessman's or businesswoman's earnings goes for food and clothes and rent, it is not unreasonable that her hours for housework would—at least on occasions—run longer than ordinary business hours.

MAY SERVANTS ENTERTAIN FRIENDS?

Certainly they may! Whoever in remote ages thought it was better to forbid their men friends the house and have Marie and Bridget and Selma slip out of doors to meet them in the dark had very distorted notions, to say the least. And today she probably would not be able to keep a maid!

In every very large house, there is always a sitting room furnished with comfortable chairs and a sofa if possible, a radio, usually a television set, good lights to read by, and always magazines. In other words, the employees have an inviting room to use as their own exactly as though they were living at home.

In a smaller house where no sitting room is possible, the kitchen table has an attractive cover put on it, and a droplight and a few restful chairs are provided. Or the maid's room, especially one on the ground floor, may be furnished as a sitting room.

In homes with one servant, the relationship is sometimes on such a friendly basis that the use of the living room is offered the maid when the family is not at home. Naturally, she and her friends would not abuse this privilege by helping themselves to cigarettes or liquor. If he wishes, the man of the house may suggest that her caller will find a beer or soft drink in the refrigerator. The maid, of course, will make the room immaculate when her caller leaves.

UNIFORMS

All maids' uniforms as well as aprons and collars and cuffs are furnished by the employer, with the exception of the dresses worn by a lady's maid and those worn by a cook, for whom the employer furnishes only the aprons.

AN ATTRACTIVE ROOM

Now let us go to the day of your new maid's arrival. Try to imagine yourself in her place and take pains to make her room as attractive as possible. Surely nothing could be more dispiriting to any normal young woman—or to an older one, for that matter—than to arrive in a strange place, which is to be her "home," and be taken into a drab and comfortless room that all too plainly shows that you have not given so much as a thought to what these surroundings must mean to her happiness.

After all, a comfortable bed, attractively painted furniture, and a little becoming chintz are not very difficult to supply, especially in this day when smooth-flowing paints or enamels in beautiful colors can be put on by the merest amateur, by anyone, in fact, who has the slightest manual dexterity. In other words, dingy brown and buff are really inexcusable. The same attention to attractiveness and convenience should be evident in the kitchen—in which she is not only to work and to take her meals, but in which she is also to spend many of her hours of leisure.

COURTESY ON BOTH SIDES

In a formal household, a servant is never spoken to as Jim, Maisie, or Katie, but always as James, Margaret, or Katherine, and a butler should be called by his last name. The Worldlys' butler, for instance, is called Hastings, not John. The housekeeper is Mrs. Jones and the nurse may be called by her name or a nickname such as "Nanny." In a less formal household, the maid may be called by a nickname, or if she is an older woman, she may be called Mrs. Helper.

Every courteous person says "please" in asking that something be brought her or him. "Would you mail these letters, please" or "Some bread, please." One can, of course, put a smile into one's tone and say, "A little more bread!" But usually one who is well mannered instinctively adds "please." No lady or gentleman barks, "Mail this letter!" or "Give me the bread!" So too, in refusing a dish at the table one says, "No, thank you" or "No, thanks."

Any who may think they appear superior by being rude to others who happen to have been less fortunately placed might as well know that on the contrary they are proclaiming to all who hear their rudeness that they themselves have never had any of the early advantages.

ON THE OTHER SIDE

The well-trained servant is faultlessly neat in appearance, reticent in manner, speaks in a low voice, and moves silently. In answering a bell, she asks, "Did you ring, Madam?" or possibly she asks, "Did Madam ring?"

A courteous maid answers her employer, "Yes, Madam," or "Very good, Sir." Possibly she may say, "Yes, Sir," but never "Yes," "No," "All right," or "Sure."

In a very formal house, grown sons and daughters are called "Miss Katherine" or "Mr. Oliver"; half-grown children are generally called by their familiar names with the prefix of Miss or Mr. (Miss Kitty, Mr. Ollie), but never by the nurse, who calls them by their first names until they are grown and if she has been with them since their babyhood—always.

In the smaller house with one maid, all the young children are called by their first names or nicknames.

SUCCESS IN HOUSEHOLD MANAGEMENT

Those who have servant trouble might do well to remember a basic rule that is often overlooked: Justice must be the foundation upon which every tranquil household is constructed. Work must be as evenly divided as possible; one servant should not be allowed liberties not accorded to all.

This, perhaps, explains why some people are always having a trouble—finding servants difficult to get, more difficult to keep, and most difficult to get efficient work from. It is a question whether the servant problem is not more often an employer problem. I'm sure it is! Because, if you notice, those who have woes and complaints invariably have them continually, just as others never have any trouble at all. It does not depend on the size of the house; the Lovejoys never have any trouble, and yet their one maid-of-all-work has a far from easy place. A vacancy at Brookmeadows is always sought after, although the Oldnames entertain a great deal.

It is not just to be too lenient, any more than it is just to be unreasonably demanding. To allow impertinence or sloppy work is inexcusable, but it is equally inexcusable to show causeless irritability or to be overbearing or rude. And there is no greater example of injustice than to reprimand those about you because you happen to be in a bad humor and then at another time to overlook offenses that are greater, because you are in an amiable mood. There is also no excuse ever for correcting either an employee or a child in front of anyone else.

If we attempt to analyze the spirit pervading happy houses, I think it will be found in the understanding and fairness that is shown by both sides. Proper pride on the part of every high-minded employee exacts that she give fair value for wages received. On the other side, the obligation of the lady of the house and the other members of the family is to show human understanding and fairness in what they exact. If they are just in their point of view, and if, being themselves kind and trustworthy, they naturally believe that those serving them have the same traits, they are very unlikely ever to have any housekeeping difficulties.

Serving the family meals

In the household staffed by two or more servants who prepare and serve every meal, the table is set, the places arranged, and the food served to the family alone exactly as they are when guests are present. Therefore, the mistress of such a household should consult, not this chapter, but Chapters 29 and 31.

In the average home, however, the lady of the house (or possibly one maid) prepares, serves, and cleans up after the meals, and as a result, the number of courses, dishes, and implements is necessarily greatly reduced. But simplification should not mean sloppiness, and the following suggestions are important in the most informal of households.

THE TABLE

In many of today's houses and apartments, the pressures of space and expense have caused the large, formal dining room to disappear. The dining table appears in any one of a number of other places—in an ell or an alcove off the living room, for example, in the end of the living room nearest the kitchen, or sometimes in a large foyer or a wide hall. The location of the table does not affect its use, however, and even though it may not have the formal surroundings that it did in Grandmother's day, it should be thought of as a pleasant center of family gatherings.

The table itself should be large enough to accommodate the entire family comfortably, for young children especially need plenty of room to eat properly and crowding only 'encourages jostling and other unsuitable behavior.

A pretty cloth or attractive place mats (in any material that is easily wiped clean or laundered) should always be used, not only to protect the table top, but also to lend an air of graciousness to even the simplest meal. Although not necessary, a centerpiece is pleasing. With a little help, children can pick and arrange a few flowers or make a simple table decoration for some particular holiday or special occasion. Such contributions add to the family's enjoyment of mealtime and help the children recognize the importance of household appointments as well.

Seating arrangements at table depend entirely on the convenience of the family. Most often, when there is no maid, mother sits nearest the kitchen door with the youngest, who may still need help from time to time, next to her. The place opposite hers is where father sits. Some families make a tradition of seating a birthday child as the guest of honor would be seated at a formal dinner, a custom that is flattering to the child and at the same time provides practice in the behavior that will be expected of him when he is older.

If there is a maid in the house, the family always eats at the dining table, where they are served simply, in whatever way best fits their preference and the capabilities of the maid.

KITCHEN-DINING

If space permits, it is most desirable to have an end or corner of the kitchen set apart, furnished and decorated in such a way that children growing up in the home feel the importance of good manners at any table, just as they would if they were being served in a beautifully appointed dining room. When there is no such space, the ordinary kitchen table must do, but an extra effort should be made to make the room attractive and to make sure that the table is uncluttered and immaculately clean.

Even a kitchen table should be charmingly set for dinner, with place mats (even though they may be paper doilies), spotless utensils (although they may be stainless steel), and pretty plates and glasses, attractive in color and pattern (no matter if they were bought at the local "five and ten").

THE PLACE SETTINGS

The main difference in setting a table for guests and setting a table for the family is that a minimum number of utensils is put at each place

—only those absolutely necessary for each course. Very often there may be no more than two or three pieces of silver: a fork, a knife, and a spoon or fork for dessert. At a family dinner, it is certainly not necessary to have a separate fork for salad, but a salad plate is another matter. Who could wish to have the meat gravy and salad dressing run together into an unsavory soup?

Butter plates and knives are often omitted, and the bread and butter are placed on the edge of the dinner plate, but with the convenience of an electric dishwasher, it is far nicer to have a separate plate. This is especially true if the dinner plates are, as they should be, heated, so that butter put on them melts at once. Or sometimes the butter might be put on the side of the salad plate to reduce the number of dishes.

The table settings described below indicate only the correct positions of whatever articles might be used. No china or silver that will not actually be used needs to be put on the table—no salad forks if you are not serving salad, no bread and butter plate if you have no bread.

BREAKFAST

More often than at other meals, there is a wide difference in the tastes of breakfast-eaters. Some people, teen-age girls especially, prefer to eat no breakfast at all—or perhaps a piece of toast and a glass of milk. Many women take only a cup of coffee and a glass of juice, while others eat a hearty morning meal and watch their calories at lunch time. Men and boys generally like a more substantial meal, sometimes two or three courses, including fruit, cereal, pancakes, and eggs. Unlike other meals, breakfast may, and should, be prepared "to order." That is, if daughter Susie truly dislikes eggs, she may be given a dish of cold cereal, but Father should not therefore be deprived of his scrambled eggs and bacon.

In setting the breakfast table herself, Mother may put out just those utensils which will be needed by each person.

In the informal household, a variety of cold cereals, milk, cream, sugar, salt and pepper, and jams or jellies are in the center of the table or on a convenient side table, but whoever is doing the cooking serves the hot food directly onto the plates and places them in front of those sitting at the table. If your table is large enough, a "lazy susan" or turntable is most convenient and makes each item easily accessible to all.

If breakfast is served by a maid in the dining room, the setting is as follows:

Fork at left of plate.

Knife at right of plate.

Spoon for cereal at right of knife.

Teaspoon for fruit (but not for coffee) at right of cereal spoon.

Butter knife across bread and butter plate, which is to the left and above fork.

Napkins at left of plates if cut-up fruit compote or fruit juice is at places; otherwise, napkins at the center of each place.

Coffee cups with spoons lying at right of saucers, at the right of each plate if coffee is served from the kitchen (or, if served by the lady of the house at the table, cups and saucers near tea or coffee pot at her place).

Glass for milk or water, to the right and above spoons.

LUNCH

For the busy woman of today, lunch usually consists of a sandwich, a bowl of soup, or a salad. It may be served at the dining-room table if there is a maid, or it may be brought to the living room or patio on a tray. When children are home for lunch, it can be served either at the dining table or in the kitchen, according to the preference of the family. If the man of the house has lunch at home, he will probably want a more substantial meal, and the table is set in accordance with the food to be served. In the simple household, unless the main meal is eaten at midday, in which case the table is set as for dinner, no more than three courses are ever served for lunch, and even that number is most unusual. The setting is as follows:

Salad fork at left, next to plate, if salad is to be served after meat.

Meat fork at left of salad fork.

On the right, a meat knife; and at the right of this knife, a bouillon or fruit spoon, if necessary.

Butter plate and knife above forks at left.

Because dessert, if served, is brought in after the main course, the dessert fork or spoon may be brought in with the dessert plate.

DINNER

The dinner plates are at each place on the table when the family sits down if the food is to be passed, or in front of the head of the household if he is to serve. However, many women prefer to serve the plates directly from the stove in order to avoid the use of extra platters and serving dishes. If there is a maid in the home, she may pass the plates around as they are served by the man of the house, or, if the family is small, she may pass the dishes to each person. The table setting for dinner is similar to that for lunch:

At left of plate, salad fork (if necessary), then dinner fork.

At right, the dinner knife next to plate, then the soup spoon or the oyster fork or fruit spoon on the outside (if necessary).

Glass or goblet for beverage at right above knife.

Butter plate with butter knife laid on it diagonally from upper left to lower right.

In every case, the implements necessary for each course are arranged in order of their use. The one to be used first goes on the outside; that to be used last is put nearest the plate. Dessert spoon and fork may be brought in on the dessert plate after the table is cleared; otherwise the fork goes next to the plate on the left, and the spoon immediately to the right of the knife.

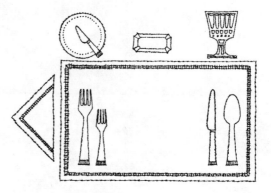

THE MEALTIME TRAY

Although few women in a simple household are served breakfast on a tray, there are many occasions when a member of the family is ill and must remain in bed for his meals. An attractive tray with a flower in a little vase or a gay napkin and tray cloth can do much to aid a lagging appetite and a sagging spirit.

For all meals, the tray is covered with a tray cloth or, if you do not have special tray linen, a doily of any sort. The setting is the same as the individual place setting at the table insofar as space permits. The dessert plate and the coffee cup and saucer are usually brought when the main meal is finished because of lack of room. The dinner plate should be heated and covered if the meal is hot, to insure that it will stay warm while being carried to its destination. If you do not have a regular domed plate cover, a piece of foil laid over the food will keep it warm for several minutes.

Individual breakfast sets for trays are available and often given as wedding presents. They generally include an egg cup, a cereal bowl, two or three plates, and a cover, coffee cup and saucer, sugar bowl, cream pitcher, and a small coffee pot. They come in gay patterns or lovely solid colors and, by the very charm of their appearance, make the morning more cheerful.

Part FIFTEEN

FAMILY LIFE

The young child

I have often been asked how best to teach rules of etiquette to young people—children or teen-agers—and whether there are special rules which they should be taught. The most important thing for all of us to realize is that etiquette applies to everyone, old or young, and that the best way to teach etiquette to children is the best way to teach any-thing—by precept, consistency, firmness, and example. Children are people—indeed they are, and parents and teachers will do well to re-member it.

Children who are spoken to in baby talk and treated as if they were adorable idiots are inclined to act like babies or idiots. But children who are treated as interesting individuals with minds of their own will re-act by trying to prove that they *are* intelligent and they *are* individuals.

Children can scarcely be too young to be taught the rudiments of etiquette, nor can the teaching be too patiently or too conscientiously carried out. Any child can be taught to be well behaved with no effort greater than patience and perseverance, whereas to break bad habits once they are acquired is a herculean task.

FAIR PLAY

Quite young children are able to understand the principles of justice, and they should be taught, even before they go to school, to "play fair," to respect each other's property and rights, to give credit to others, and not to take too much credit to themselves. They must be taught to share their playthings and to take good care of toys that belong to other children. A bright, observing child should never be encouraged to brag about his own achievements or to tell his or her mother how inferior other children are. If he wins a medal at school or is praised, the family naturally rejoices, and it is proper that they should, but a wise mother teaches her child that selfishness and conceit can win him no place worth having in the world.

"BECAUSE EVERYONE ELSE DOES"

All young people feel a need for conformity with the activities of others of their age. This they express in their speech, their play, their choice of clothing, and their relationships to each other. This conformity is quite normal and is to be respected as part of the development of individual personality as well as social responsibility. Adults, after all, conform to their world too. Young people in time learn that through conformity with most of the social customs of the adult world they will be able to take their place in that world.

Children should be permitted to follow the customs of their community, so as not to differ too radically from the other children in the neighborhood. However, there are necessary and obvious qualifications to this advice. It is possible for children to be well brought up even though the community where the family lives may seem to have accepted lower standards of behavior than the family's own. The phrase one hears so often from children—"Everyone else does thus-and-so"—is not sufficient excuse for lowering standards. Surely, to take an extreme example, no one could condone cheating at games or on examinations just "because everyone else does."

Of course, parents sometimes must make a decision at the risk of having their children a little different in some particular from their friends. Certainly there are times when children should be required to set an example for others to follow, rather than be just like all the rest. There is a certain element of risk involved in this position, but there is also an element of discipline that is far more important.

Parents and teachers must never underestimate the problems that a child has in adapting himself to a world full of contradiction that can only be explained by experience. Precepts and lectures are never a substitute for understanding and sympathetic guidance.

EATING HABITS

The first requirement in table manners is neatness. When children are a year and a half to two years old, they will begin to learn to feed themselves, and while they are too little to be taught the refinements of truly good manners, it is never too soon to start them in the right direction. From the very first, they can be encouraged to keep the food on the plate, taught how to hold a cup so that it will not spill, and shown the use of a bib or napkin. These skills do not come naturally, but with patient repetition and gentle insistence, they can be acquired.

As soon as the child has learned to eat well enough so that his presence at the table is not offensive, he should be allowed to eat with adults, occasionally at first, and more often as his manners improve. When he becomes a member of the family group at meals, there are more advanced lessons to be learned.

He must be clean and neat when he comes to the table.

He must chew quietly, with his mouth closed.

He must not overload his spoon or fork.

He must not interrupt the adults, but at the same time, he should be included in the conversation. If it is beyond his understanding, his mother or father should from time to time introduce a subject that is within his range of interests.

He must not fidget or play with his food or the implements at his place.

He must use his fork and spoon properly and never leave the spoon in his cup or bowl.

If he finishes before the others, he must ask, "May I please be excused?" and wait for permission before leaving the table. Very young children should be given this privilege, because if they are forced to remain at the table when their food is gone, they are sure to resort to wriggling, fiddling, and noise-making to pass the time.

If he refuses to be good, the best course is to say nothing but lead him as quietly as possible from the table. The child will learn much more quickly to be well behaved if he understands that good behavior is the price of admission to grown-up society.

There are many ways in which the little one's mother can help to pave the way for him. His plate should be brought to the table ready for him to eat. The portions should be of small or moderate size—never a heaping plateful. Meat should be cut in small bite-size pieces, as should vegetables such as asparagus and string beans. To avoid accidents, his glass or cup should have a broad base and be of plastic or pottery. If he is very small, his fork and spoon should be of appropriate size. He should wear a bib large enough so that an accidental spill will not ruin his clothes. And he should either sit in his high chair or have cushions on a regular chair that will raise him to the proper height. If you think this is unimportant, try sometime to eat neatly while kneeling at a table that comes approximately to the level of your chin.

All these small aids put together help to make the child look forward to his meal as a time of pleasure, rather than a time of strain. Mealtime should, above all, be pleasant. The child who sees his family enjoying their food and enjoying each others' company cannot help but follow their example. Constant nagging and correction are as detrimental as a total lack of instruction. If older children are allowed to complain about the food, if Father refuses to eat anything but steak and potatoes, and if there are continuous arguments at the table, the young child will come to dread the dinner hour, and the unhappy associations will result in antagonism to food and to good manners in eating.

MONEY MATTERS

From the time a child is old enough to buy a candy bar or an ice cream cone for himself, he should be given a small, regular allowance. In return, he should be expected to perform certain chores, such as helping with the dishes or keeping his room neat. But extra duties—washing the dog or running an errand—deserve special consideration and are paid for separately if the parents feel that they merit a reward. Only by having money of their own can children begin to appreciate its value, and they should be permitted to use an allowance as they wish. The amount must be decided upon by considering what uses the money will be put to and the approximate amount small friends are given. It is as bad for a child to have twice as much as the neighborhood children (even though his parents can well afford it) as it is to have him always saying, "I can't go to the movies with you—I don't have enough money." Some parents give the child more allowance but insist that a part be set aside for the weekly church contribution or that a certain sum be put in a piggy bank or otherwise saved for birthday presents or a special hobby or treat. This seems to me to be a wise system, as the child acquires a sense of the value of money that he cannot have if the parents simply put his quarter in the plate each Sunday or pay for the birthday presents as the dates arrive.

As the child grows, so must his allowance, and so must the expenses he is expected to pay for himself. As he approaches his teens, he may be expected to pay for movies, for cosmetics, for presents, or for extra pieces of clothing or jewelry that are not actually necessary. To pay for such items, he may well have to plan ahead and give up other smaller pleasures until he has saved a sufficient sum, and this is excellent training. If he is working toward something worthwhile that he really cares about, his parents will be wise to encourage him by giving him extra chores which they may pay for at an hourly rate and by adding to his fund with a small check for Christmas or birthday.

A CHILD'S APPEARANCE

Speaking of children who wish to buy a bit of extra clothing with their allowance brings up the subject of clothes. As soon as a child shows any interest in what he is wearing, he should be allowed a voice in choosing his clothes. Naturally, his mother must make the final decision, as a little child will not consider cost, practicality, or suitability, but within the limits of these requirements, the child can be given a choice of garments. He will thus absorb some principles of dressing well, and he will also be happy to wear the clothes that are bought for him.

There are several offenses committed by doting mothers that should be avoided.

Don't overdress your child. If he or she is invited to a party, ask the mother of the host or hostess what type of clothing will be appropriate. Nothing could make a little girl more miserable than to wear a frilly organdy dress to a party that turns out to be an outdoor barbecue. Even school clothes should conform to those of the other children. If wearing ties is not required of the small boys, let your son go in a sport shirt, and if the girls all wear brown loafers, don't insist on patent-leather slippers.

Never dress your child in clothes that are too old for him. Your three-year-old dressed in long gray flannels and a sport jacket may look, to you, too "cute" for words, but it is as inappropriate as his father going to business in shorts and an Eton jacket.

Little girls should never wear high heels, even moderately high, before they reach their teens.

Don't let little girls wear make-up or dress their hair elaborately. Of course they want to imitate Mommy, but let them play at being grown up in the privacy of their rooms or at a costume party, but never in public. This is not to say that their hair should not be arranged in an attractive, simple style and neatly combed. They have many years ahead when they will need make-up to enhance their looks, but until then, the natural fresh glow of youth is the most attractive sight in the world.

CHILDREN'S PARTIES

A child's party that has been well planned can be a joy to everyone. Parties for very young children, under six, let us say, should be quite short, preferably not more than two hours long. The span of attention of tiny children is very limited, and they also tire quickly, which leads to crankiness and naughtiness. Refreshments should be simple to allow the mother and her assistants more time for supervision and less time in the kitchen. Also, a large amount of rich food can upset little stomachs that are already in a turmoil with excitement. Finally, to avoid confusion and permit better organization, the guest list should be short. Five or six guests would be ample for a second birthday party, and ten or twelve should be the limit for a six- to eight-year-old. The formula for a successful party for the very young is as follows:

Guests arrive at four. One half hour is allowed for opening presents and letting off steam. One hour of organized games or entertainment follows. A magician is always popular, and comedy movies, if you have a projector or can borrow one, are invariably a great success. Treasure hunts, "pin-the-tail-on-the-donkey," musical chairs for tiny children, and guessing games, a "three-legged" race, or other contests for older ones, all help to make the hour fly. At 5:30 refreshments are served. A sandwich (peanut butter and jelly cannot be surpassed for popularity), ice cream, and the birthday cake are all that are necessary. If the weather is warm, a fruit punch, soda, or ice-cold milk may be served, and in the winter, hot chocolate is always welcome.

Parties for older children can be extended to two and a half or three hours if enough entertainment is planned. Games can be more complicated, thus taking more time, and a short feature movie could be shown rather than "shorts." A scavenger hunt is always popular outside the city, or if you have the use of a swimming pool, that may be all that is necessary to have a successful summer party. As children reach the age of 10 or 11 or even older, hay rides, sleigh rides, trips to baseball or football games, or circuses or rodeos become more fun than the "game party" at home. When a group is taken to this sort of entertainment, the invitation should make it clear whether or not lunch or supper will be provided and whether the guests should take money of their own for snacks or souvenirs. Remember, when planning a trip to the ball park or anywhere, a small group will be easier to chaperon, it will be less expensive, and your child will enjoy it every bit as much as a large rambunctious crowd.

If the birthday child is old enough, he may help in deciding on the guest list, sending out invitations, and setting the table. A girl may even help prepare the refreshments—mixing the cake batter or making sandwiches.

Whether they are 3 or 10, the essential manners for party guests are identical. They must say "Hello" to their host and the host's mother when they arrive, and they must shake hands and say "Good-by, and thank you for a wonderful time" when they leave. The young host or hostess must, in turn, greet them when they come and, in answer to their farewell, say "Good-by, and thanks again for the present" or "Good-by. Thank you for coming."

PARENTS AND CHILDREN

First and foremost, every parent must realize that each child is an individual, and, as such, must be treated with respect. There are thousands of books and articles in print on the subject of bringing up children, and many of them offer valuable advice, but their suggestions must be tempered to suit the personality and the specific problems of your child.

THE PARENT'S ATTITUDE

The first outward sign of respect you can show your toddler is not to talk *down* to him. Of course you must use simple words and sentences or he will not understand you at all, but "baby talk" is an insult to the intelligence of a normal child and does nothing to encourage him to increase his vocabulary or to speak as fluently as possible.

This same attitude of treating a child as an individual carries through to your judgment of what he can or cannot do. I have found that most children are far more capable than their elders can believe. If you expect good behavior or assume that your child will react to a situation in a reasonable way, you will generally find that he will live up to your expectations. If, however, you start out by saying to Johnny, "I'll cut your meat for you, dear—you're too little," he will certainly not be encouraged to make the effort to learn to do it himself. One word of warning, however: This can be overdone, and nothing will frustrate Johnny more than being required to do things that he simply is not capable of handling. To scold him for not being able to do up his snaps or buttons will quickly cause him to rebel against all attempts to teach him to dress himself.

Study your child as an interesting person, increase his responsibilities as he seems able to cope with them, reprove him when he falls short, and praise him when he takes a step forward. Include him in your conversation, correcting his mistakes and teaching him new words, and share as many family activities with him as you can. Don't laugh at his mistakes or ridicule him, but at the same time, try to appreciate his developing sense of humor, and laugh *with* him. Encouragement, appreciation, and lots of love are the most essential elements in a baby's happy environment.

OBEYING THE RULES

Little children must be taught from their earliest years that there are certain rules that have to be obeyed. You may be one of the many parents who believe in self-regulating schedules for small children (I happen to believe that a certain amount of regulation is better for both children and their parents), but this does not mean that they cannot be taught the rules that govern the relationship between themselves and other people. I firmly believe that the increased amount of delinquency today is the result of overly permissive parents, who either think that they should not ("Oh, I wouldn't stunt Harvey's independent development for anything in the world!) or are afraid to discipline their children ("But Sally won't love me if I don't let her eat her ice cream before dinner"). Young people, no matter what they may say aloud, want and need direction and correction, and the more honest ones will even admit it. I have actually heard a young girl say, "I wish my mother would say 'No'—then I wouldn't have to make up my mind."

PUNISHMENT

The single most important thing about disciplining a child is to make your point and stick to it. If you say "No" to an extra half hour at bedtime, and then say "Yes" when Susie says "But Mommy, this is my favorite TV program," how will Susie ever know whether you mean what you say or not? Nor will she have much respect for your decisions.

The severity of the punishment should be directly related to the seriousness of the misdeed. If it is a minor infraction, it should not result in a major penalty, or you will have nowhere to go when a more serious crime is committed, and the child will have no way of differentiating between an important and an unimportant offense. If possible, the punishment should be related to the error. If Judy, who loves cherries, insists on throwing her cherry pits on the floor, she might be deprived of her favorite fruit for several meals. Or if Johnny refuses to remove his muddy rubbers time after time, he might be forbidden to go out and play in the mud puddles the next time his best friend calls him.

Unless you know that you will be able to hold to them, don't make threats. When you have broken a threat once, your child will pay little attention when you make another. A simple one such as "Bobby, if you don't stop throwing the wrappers on the floor, I will have to take away the rest of your chewing gum" is all right, because it is simple and easily carried out, but to say "Karen, if you don't go to bed at once, I won't let you go to kindergarten for a week," when you know perfectly well (and so does Karen) that she will be there the next morning, carries no weight at all and only makes you appear ridiculous in her eyes.

When a child has committed a serious misdeed, especially if he has repeated it after being corrected, take the time and trouble to explain the reason for the rule. The most obvious example of this, and unfortunately one of the commonest, is lighting matches and setting fires. I am not quite of the school that believes you should burn the child to prove your point, but for an offense as dangerous as this, punishment should be quick and severe. First show him, with paper or kerosene or however you can make it the most impressive, how quickly a fire can spread and explain the consequences from his point of view—his favorite toy would be burned up, his dog might be killed, etc. And then decide on the punishment that you think will make the deepest impression. It might be deprivation of certain privileges like watching television, or the cancellation of a longed-for treat, or something equally important. In extreme cases, where repeated admonitions and punishments have not brought any results, I believe there is no substitute for a good hard—not brutal—spanking, with the palm of Daddy's hand!

RESPECT

In the relation between children and their parents today, the quality that is most lacking is respect. In a large part, this is the result of the atmosphere that modern psychologists advocated when they went overboard in recommending that parents be "pals" with their children rather than continuing the normal relationship that has existed for centuries. If children are taught that their parents should have no authority over them and are simply their equals, regardless of age, education, and experience, how will respect arise? This trend, which fortunately has been somewhat modified and even reversed, showed itself in families whose children called their parents by their first names, where they were never required to rise when older people entered the room nor adhere to any other special conventions. This resulted in a directionless youth, and rather than being mature, independent people, these children grew up as lazy, confused individuals, lacking respect not only for their parents, but for all society. If you as parents lead your youngsters to believe that your experience, your education, and your attitudes are worth emulating, respect will follow of its own accord. This, in turn, will be expanded, as your children grow up, to include relatives, friends, and, finally, more mature people of every sort.

81

The teen-ager

Boys and girls who have reached their teens have a whole new set of problems to face. This is the time when they really begin to emerge from the constant supervision of their parents and develop independence and a social life of their own choosing. Because they are well on their way to becoming adults, they are expected to act in an adult manner, and they must make the adjustment from childhood, with its complete dependence on parental care, to adulthood, which brings not only the joys of independence but the trials as well.

Parents of teen-agers must try to recognize this transition, and the wise mother and father will, from the very early teen years when the child is still "in between" and under a good deal of supervision, encourage him to make his own decisions, with guidance and help, rather than with a domineering attitude.

THE EARLY TEENS

If parents have had a loving, intelligent relationship with their sons and daughters during childhood, with confidence and respect growing on both sides, the problems will be greatly modified. Even though the emotional make-up of a teen-ager is vastly more complicated and often more high-strung than that of younger children, the same characteristics of patience, give-and-take, and restraint will tide the family over what can be difficult years.

But this is not a book designed to discuss the psychological aspects of the young, but rather to discuss their manners and what they should or should not do. Just remember, when making a rule or saying "No" to a teen-ager, to consider the importance of the decision to him (Does it really *matter* if Bob stays out a half hour longer?), the customs of his friends and classmates, and whether it will actually help him, either from his own point of view or in the eyes of others. The last reason in the world for making a regulation is "Well, I always had to wash the dishes when I was your age!"

APPEARANCE

Teen-agers from thirteen to nineteen have one thing in common. They apparently *like* to be sloppy. This applies not only to themselves but to their rooms and possessions. It doesn't seem to do much good to remind them that they will be more popular with the opposite sex if they have their hair combed and their clothes clean, nor are they interested in keeping warm in cold weather if no one else is wearing a coat. Shoes seem to be a forgotten item of clothing in the summer everywhere except in the largest cities. My feeling about this general attitude is that they be allowed to dress as sloppily as they please during vacations, in their own homes, on the beach, or at picnics. But at school (fortunately most schools set certain standards, which the pupils must adhere to), at meals, on any excursion with adults, on all public conveyances, and at all social functions, they must be properly and neatly dressed. This does not mean that they should not go to an informal gathering without a tie and jacket. Of course they may wear a sport shirt, shorts, and sweater, or whatever the favorite local costume is, but the sweater and shirt should be clean, the hair combed, and shoes ON.

Young boys must be constantly reminded to wash and to shave. Nothing looks dirtier or messier than a stubble of whiskers on a young face, but many boys who are not accustomed to regular shaving habits simply do not realize that their beard is becoming heavier each year. The only way to achieve this is to keep after them day in and day out until it becomes a habit.

Teen-age girls need less urging to fix their hair—in fact most of them spend interminable hours under a hair dryer. What they do need is guidance as to style, length, becomingness, and good hygiene. Extreme styles should be avoided in the younger teen years—the simplest hair-do currently popular is generally the most becoming. As they get older, they will want to experiment with more complicated arrangements, and the only restriction should be that they refrain from becoming too extreme, for such styles invariably make a young girl look "cheap."

The same suggestions apply to make-up. A thirteen or fourteen year old may wear lipstick to a party, but it should be light in color and application. As she gets older, she may use a more vivid shade, and by the time she is sixteen or seventeen, she may choose any shade that goes well with her complexion as well as powder, a *very light* rouge if she is pale, and inconspicuous eye make-up. Heavily made up eyes belong only on the stage or in the chorus line.

CLOTHING

Styles in clothing change so that it is impossible to make hard and fast rules, but there are certain ones that are, and always have been, important. Again, avoid extremes. The shortest skirt, the lowest neckline, the barest bathing suit, the tightest trousers, or the longest boy's haircut are all conspicuous attention-getters. And, as always, those people, young or old, who have the most delightful manners and the greatest charm are those who do not go out of their way to attract unfavorable attention.

TABLE MANNERS

Slouching, tipping the chair back, and fiddling all seem to be within the special province of the teen-ager. To be sure, many of them are growing so fast that they hardly know how to manage their arms and legs, but not even the gangliest sixteen-year-old should be incapable of sitting still and upright in his chair. It is up to the parents to instill in him the importance of good posture. Teen-agers' appetites are generally tremendous, and they must be constantly reminded not to bolt their food and to wait for the others at the table. Their faults are more likely to be errors committed than good habits omitted, and because they can hardly be sent to eat in another room like a child, their mothers and fathers must improve their manners with firm, patient, repeated corrections. In many cases, it is not willful disregard of directions—they simply do not absorb them. Their minds are on a thousand other more interesting matters—girls, boys, parties, school, sports, ad infinitum, and the only hope of penetrating the screen is repetition, in the hope that eventually your words will "sink in." By the tone of your voice and the way you say it, repeated correction can avoid the undesirable effect of "nagging."

ALLOWANCES

As children advance into their teens, allowances may become a question of what the parents can afford and how much responsibility the youngster himself wants to assume. Teen-age boys have more expenses than girls of the same age, and therefore their allowances may be raised sooner. They have to pay for their dates, they are likely to have the use of a car at a younger age than girls, and they generally wish to attain economic independence much sooner than their female counterparts.

The question of a "clothes allowance" usually arises in the middle teens. Some youngsters can't wait to be given enough money to dress themselves and pay all their own expenses, while others cling to the security of letting their parents pay for their clothes and receiving a small weekly or monthly "daily expenses" allowance. As a general rule, the year a boy or girl enters college, or becomes of college age, is the time to give him or her financial independence.

But there is no set rule—the time might come a year or two earlier for a boy who is responsible and understands the value of money and the danger of wasting it, while the girl who has had little experience in shopping or managing a checking account might better wait longer.

A system that seems to me to be excellent is practiced by one of my neighbors. Her daughter of fourteen, a sensible, intelligent girl, was most anxious to be given a clothes allowance. Rather than telling her that she was just too young or putting her on a large allowance all at once, the parents started her out with a monthly sum that was to cover school clothes—blouses, skirts, shoes, socks, underwear, etc.—but no expensive ones such as party dresses or overcoats. In this way she is learning to shop carefully and to understand the handling of money, but she does not have a large sum at her disposal, which might prove to be a temptation to spend irresponsibly. They plan to increase the sum and the variety of clothing she is expected to buy each year so that by the time she finishes high school, she will be completely responsible for her clothes and incidental expenses.

Most parents pay as much of their children's tuition at school and college as they can, but if it is too severe a strain on the family budget, teen-agers should certainly help as much as possible by applying for scholarships, working part-time at one of the jobs (in the cafeteria, dormitories, or library) that most colleges provide, or taking an evening job, preferably one like baby-sitting that will allow the student to study during those hours. Parents should never be ashamed to discuss the need for financial assistance of this sort with their children. Young men and women, if they really care about a good education, are more than willing to do what they can to attain it. If they have been brought up with love and respect for their families, they will never criticize parents who may not have amassed great wealth, but rather will take pride in what has been achieved.

As to the actual amounts for suitable allowances, it is impossible to say, because the requirements vary so in different areas. A city child needs more—every time he takes a bus or subway it costs him something, while his country cousin is riding the same distance on a bicycle. Prices are higher, too, in the city. Movies, food, and entertainment are much bigger budget items than the equivalent items in the country. The country boy might take his date to a square dance at the local grange for fifty cents or so, while the city boy, if he wishes to dance, must go to a night club or dance hall where the admission, or cover charge, may be as high as several dollars.

A possible scale for a weekly allowance, necessarily subject to change to fit the circumstances, might run something like this:

13-14 years	$1.00-2.00
15-17 years	4.00-5.00

When the teen-ager is older and it seems advisable to add a clothing allowance to his pocket money, he might receive a monthly amount something like this:

16-18 years	$25.00-35.00
18 and over	75.00-100.00

Naturally, a boy or girl receiving as much as $100.00 a month would be expected to pay all expenses such as school books, cleaning bills, etc.—everything, in other words, except tuition and doctors' bills.

College years

Young men and girls during their four years in college not only are receiving an academic education, but also are taking part in the social life of their school. Etiquette on the campus must cover some rather specialized situations, but there is one basic consideration that always applies: Whatever constitutes proper and decent behavior for young men and girls anywhere is correct in any college situation.

PERSONAL POPULARITY

Your decision to attend college is a very serious one, of course, and should be made chiefly because of your wish to further your general education or to study for a particular career. As is true of everything, you may expect to gain from your studies in proportion to the time and interest you devote to them. But surely you do not want or expect your years in college to be a "grind," devoted solely to the acquisition of book-learning. To be able to make people like you, to get on easily with those who are thrown into close and continued contact with you, and to make friends is of vital importance to you now, as it will be all the rest of your life.

The best way to make yourself liked and to make friends is to like people enough to become interested in what interests them and to be outgoing and friendly. Don't overlook this rule! The truly interested and outgoing person is very rare. Most of us go through life mentally wrapped in the cotton wool of our own affairs. We go about thinking of what we are going to do, what we hope or fear is going to happen to us, instead of thinking or caring about what happens to those about us.

Sensitive awareness of the reactions of others is a priceless gift. There are far too many of us who never note the effect that our unthinking speech or behavior is quite plainly having upon the feelings of others. If you would be liked by those with whom you come in contact, you should cultivate sensitiveness of perception.

Attractive looks are an asset, certainly, but a bright, responsive personality is far more friend-making than great beauty—even for a girl. True, the great beauty may get easily what others have to work for. On the other hand, these others know that what they get is more likely to be securely theirs. Men, too, will find that the possession of a charming personality will be of more value than any movie-star appearance. Good grooming, however, is the one aspect of good looks that always counts. You should always make a neat, clean appearance. Campus clothing should be casual and comfortable, suited to the informal activities of the college day.

THE FRESHMAN ARRIVES AT COLLEGE

Granted, your first days in college will be harried and hurried, but they'll also be a lot of fun. You'll be learning new things, meeting new people, and adapting to a whole new life. Orientation or Welcome Week is included in the first-of-the-semester activities at many colleges. It is a time devoted exclusively to the freshman, for in this week there are group meetings to explain such matters as study programs, registration routine, the faculty-advisor system, and other facts of campus life. Faculty members are available for the new students to meet and talk with. There are also meetings devoted to a presentation of extracurricular activities, with representatives from each student group describing its program and membership qualifications.

Orientation Week is a busy procession of events, all devoted to helping the new student feel at home in his new environment. If you will welcome the Welcoming Committee with interest and cordiality, you will receive the full benefits from this special time—in addition to acquiring many first-of-the-year friends that will be yours for four years and possibly for life.

DORMITORY LIFE

Consideration is the key to successful dormitory living, whether it be for a roommate, your hall mates, the dormitory personnel, or the maintenance staff. The facilities of the dormitory are yours, but they're also your roommate's. This means sharing the mirror, the shower, the desk, the lounge; it means preserving the life of all dormitory property; it means keeping "your side" in order. It also means being considerate of your roommate's sleeping and studying habits and observing the quiet hours that the dormitory imposes.

Obeying the regulations that every dormitory must enforce will not make you a "goody-goody." It is merely showing thoughtfulness to those among whom you must live, for dormitory rules are designed only to make the lives of many strangers living together run more smoothly.

A custom much to be deplored, but not likely to disappear, is that of borrowing among dormitory mates. Avoid borrowing like the plague, but you must of course respond graciously when asked to lend an article of yours, whether you accept or refuse the request. If you must borrow, don't do so at the last minute, and always take better care of borrowed property than of your own. Whether you borrow a book or a sweater, its prompt return to the owner as soon as you have finished with it is essential.

The house mother is there to guide you, not to guard you. Treat her with the respect you would show any older person, but also with friendliness. Dropping into her apartment now and then with a few friends for a chat before dinner is a gesture that takes little time, but will be appreciated for its thoughtfulness. Never, of course, allow yourself to impose on her time or otherwise become a nuisance.

Christmas gifts to the house mother and tips to the staff are certainly in order. The manner of presentation depends on campus custom. Usually a box is passed, with a sum being collected for those on the household staff, and a gift from all presented to the house mother; otherwise, a small remembrance can be given individually.

IN CLASS AND AFTER

The professor or lecturer in a college classroom may be more remote than was the teacher in your high school classroom, but you nevertheless owe him quiet, attention, and your fully alert mental powers.

In college, the responsibility for handing in assignments on time is yours, even though you may not be pressured and reminded to do so.

When you recite in class, speak so that you can be heard by the professor as well as your fellow students. But talk only if you have something to contribute, or if you really don't understand a point. Killing time in the classroom is a trick of many pseudo scholars, but such vocal antics will fool nobody but the student himself!

The student encounters faculty members not only in the classroom, but also at joint student-faculty committee meetings, departmental teas, extracurricular activities, and on the campus. A professor should never be addressed as "Doc" or "Prof." If a graduate assistant himself requests it, it is all right to call him by his first name, but in general faculty members should be treated with the respect due to their position and age.

With a host of extracurricular activities confronting him, the student must selectively determine which ones interest him the most. He may choose among those that supplement academic interests, such as a history, education, or a foreign-affairs club that offers opportunities to speak the language of his major, or among those that provide a contrast to them, such as religious organizations, student government, and any kind of athletic club.

You will miss a lot if you don't join in any of these activities during your years in college. On the other hand, if you're inclined to be an "organization man," remember that moderation is always the wisest course. Consider Joe College, for example: he is an officer of the Men's Athletic Association, a member of the Dramatic Club, the basketball team, and a fraternity, and he writes for the humor magazine. Always busy, Joe has no time for his studies. Even worse, he has made too many acquaintances and too few friends.

Every club, no matter how informal, functions through some degree of parliamentary procedure. Respect for the rights and opinions of other members and the chair is essential. *Robert's Rules of Order* may not be followed to the letter, but being able to conduct a meeting is one of the responsibilities of a club officer.

Participating in extracurricular activities is an excellent way to make new friends. You will encounter fellow students whose leisure interests are similar to your own, but whom you might not meet during your regular academic hours.

Fraternities and sororities are an integral feature of most campuses throughout the country, but it would be a mistake to believe they are essential to a collegiate social life. Whatever the fraternity picture on your campus may be, follow your own individual tastes and needs in deciding whether to affiliate with one or remain an Independent.

You should remember that the homecoming or reunion weekend is in honor of the alumni. Members of the class of '27, having their reunion, may seem pretty far removed from your college situation. They may even be "old fogies"! But they are loyal alumni, giving financial and moral support to your school, and they should be given respect and consideration. A little out-goingness from your group can do much to make these returning alumni enjoy their visit to your campus.

THE BIG COLLEGE WEEKEND

To the students at a college, one of the most important events of the year is their special annual weekend. It may take place in the fall or in the spring, and—at a men's college—it may bring an influx of girls to the campus. There may be a Friday-night informal party at the fraternity houses, on Saturday, a picnic or a game to watch, or perhaps a ski excursion in mid-winter. Saturday night is the formal dance, often preceded by a sit-down dinner. Sunday, students and their dates may go to church together and organize an excursion or informal party. After Sunday dinner, the weekend closes.

Though the girl pays for her own transportation to and from the campus, the man should, as soon as she has accepted his written invitation, inform her of the train or bus schedules. If it is impossible for him to meet her, he should arrange for a friend to be there or see that a taxi will be available.

The girl may stay in the college's chapter house of her sorority, in a dormitory made ready for the visitors, or at a local hotel, perhaps sharing a room with another "import." The man should make all the arrangements, and far enough in advance to enable his date to have the most comfortable and convenient accommodations available. He, of course, assumes the financial obligations.

He also pays for all her meals and for all transportation after she arrives at the local railroad depot. He would be well advised to inspect his wardrobe more than one week in advance of the weekend and make sure his evening clothes, dress shirt, and the other garments he intends to wear are ready for use.

Whether the man's date is from his campus or from out of town, he owes her all the courtesies due a guest. He shouldn't leave her alone while he hobnobs with his pals and fraternity brothers. Though he is in his element, she may not be in hers, and his thoughtful attentiveness to her will enhance the enjoyment of the weekend for all.

DON'TS FOR ALL HOUSE PARTY VISITORS

To begin with packing: DON'T put off looking at your bag until the last moment, unless it is new or you know it is in perfect condition. Don't arrive with a shabby, down-at-heel suitcase with handle half off or lock broken, or packed with straps carelessly hanging out. Neat, compact, good-looking luggage will please a man much more than you might suspect.

DON'T forget to dress mentally as you pack. Stockings? Now, shoes? Slip? Dress? What goes with it? Belt, clips or other accessories, bag, etc. No one is less likely to be pleasing than the girl who begins to borrow from the other girls or sends a boy on repeated trips to the drugstore for the comb or toothpaste or whatever else she forgot. And yet: DON'T make your luggage one inch bigger or one ounce heavier than necessary, unless you are driving your own car! Any girl who brings more than one moderate-sized bag will not add to her popularity either with the others who are going in the same car or with her host who meets her at the station and perhaps has to carry this extra weight up a steep hill to the house where she is to stay. Don't forget that on holiday occasions in small college towns there may not be taxis or cars for more than about one out of ten. Therefore DON'T count on being that one.

Upon your arrival at the house, DON'T greet the house mother and other chaperons as though they were inanimate objects upon whom you need waste no attention. DON'T show an alive and interested manner toward the boys and total indifference toward the girls. When you are shown to the room which you are to share with another girl, DON'T claim the bed you like best by throwing your bag on it. At least make the gesture of asking the other girl if she cares which she takes.

DON'T take up more than exactly your share of the closet space and drawer space. If you have brought too many things for the space that is yours, you must leave some of them packed in your bag and leave the bag neatly closed.

DON'T monopolize the bathroom; remember that others are waiting. If you have a bathroom to yourself at home, all the more reason for remembering this. DON'T leave your personal belongings around on all the bedroom furniture. DON'T leave powder scattered over everything. Later, when you pack to leave, DON'T leave powder or smears of lipstick, or bobby pins in the bureau drawer. Also, open dresser drawers wide to be sure you have not left panties or other personal items behind. DON'T leave rubbish behind you, either. Remember that the regular occupant of the room may have to move back in before there is time to have the rooms cleaned. DON'T forget, throughout your stay, to respect the wishes of the house mother and other chaperons. Be sure to say good-by to her and to the others, and to thank them for their kindness.

But now, to turn back to the evening of your arrival—at the time, let us say, when you all congregate before dinner and introductions are made. In a fraternity house with no outsiders except each brother's best girl, the introductions would very likely be not only by first names but by nicknames: "Sally, this is Slim," or Babs, and so on.

DON'T, however, wait for introductions under the house roof. Friendliness should be your natural inclination. It would be too bad to be thought a snob when you are really only shy. If you are afraid you won't make friends, don't forget that nearly every other girl is feeling exactly the same!

If you don't know anything about the boy seated beside you at dinner, ask your own date, who should be seated at your left, about him first so as to know what to talk to him about. It is cynical advice, but it is as true today as it was in the day of Cleopatra that a man is rarely bored if you talk—but with some intelligence—about him. DON'T, however, get his abilities confused with those of someone else, and DON'T in any case lay flattery on with a trowel!

At the dances, greet the chaperons as though you liked them. The moment of enthusiastic attention that courtesy demands is one of the easiest and most rewarding social investments you can make.

DON'T refuse to dance with anyone who cuts in, unless he is drunk or objectionable.

Throughout the days of your visit, DON'T think only of what you like to do; that is, DON'T insist on playing ping-pong if your host would like you to make a fourth at bridge—unless your ping-pong is expert and your bridge is very bad indeed. In this case tell him you would be delighted to play, only you know how sorry everyone else will be if you do. But in general, to do whatever the majority suggest is no more than what is expected of you everywhere—unless what is suggested is something you think is wrong. For instance, there is no obligation to drink anywhere at any time—unless you choose to.

DON'T be jealous of every attention your best boy friend pays to another girl. The more you show your dislike for this interest, the more jealous he is likely to try to make you. DON'T show that you hate to be teased, or you'll be a target for even those who never thought of teasing until you showed how badly you take it.

DON'T show chagrin or disappointment. The fundamental secret of the popular house guest is to show delight in everything pleasing, and to be blind, deaf, and insensible to annoyance or disappointment. Above all, DON'T do anything that can seem unappreciative of the efforts made for your pleasure by the man who is your host. It is not playing the part of a fascinating woman of the world to try to impress him with your powers by attracting one of his classmates; on the contrary, it is the maneuver of an extremely stupid as well as vain young woman, whose lack of loyalty to a friend is resented by every member of his crowd.

Above all, DON'T forget that the friendship of other girls is the crown of your own success. Popularity with girls may not make you popular with men, but earning their dislike by treating them with contempt and by trying to take their boy friends will end in ostracism of yourself. The really popular girl is popular with girls as well as boys.

In short, DON'T try to be the house party coquette in an attempt to see how many of the men you can add to your chain of admirers! It is natural that every man wants the girl he asks to this big social event to be liked by all his friends. But you must not confuse the friendliness shown you in these circumstances with that which might otherwise be given to you for yourself alone.

Chaperons and dates

It is hard for the present generation to understand the position of the chaperon of yesteryear. We are likely to think of a chaperon as having been a kind of policewoman professionally employed to look after the morals, as well as the manners, of a young girl. Although the chaperon has largely become a lost convention, there are still a few situations in which a genuine chaperon is required. Today, however, parental training has largely taken the place of the chaperon's protection.

MODERN CHAPERONAGE

From an ethical standpoint, the only chaperon worth having in the present day is a young girl's own efficiency in chaperoning herself. The girl who has been trained to appraise every person and situation she meets needs no one to sit beside her and tell her what to do. She must develop expertness in handling situations herself, because the modern girl is allowed to go without protection. She must be able to gauge the reactions of various types of persons, particularly men, in varying circumstances. She must learn to judge which man has the instincts of a gentleman and which is likely, if given the opportunity, to exhibit traits quite different. The girl who, in addition to trained judgment, has the right attributes of proper pride and character needs no chaperon—ever. But if she lacks these qualities, not even Argus could watch over her!

Apart, however, from the consideration of ethics, which is concerned with what the girl herself thinks or feels or the motives behind what she says or does, there still remain the appearances to be considered. Many young people today are foolishly inclined to ignore them; they feel they can act independently of public opinion.

It is necessary to act with propriety in the eye of the world for the same reason that one does not shout in the street: if you would keep your affairs private, you should never let yourself become a subject for public discussion. There are too many people like Mrs. Grundy even in this modern day, whose gossip still influences a world that seldom takes the trouble to sift appearance from fact.

To be sure, Mrs. Grundy is a disagreeable old woman who has nothing to do but meddle in affairs that do not concern her. Her business in life is to track down and destroy the good name of every woman who comes within range. The pretty young woman living alone is her special quarry. The news of her every going out and coming in, of everyone whom she receives, when they come, how long they stay, and at what hour they go, is checked with a stopwatch and is spread posthaste. But a young woman who behaves with natural propriety is not likely to excite the gossip of Mrs. Grundy, who is looking for the juiciest morsels she can find.

Many parents, unfortunately, become overprotective of their teenaged children, restricting their activities and friendships unreasonably. Perhaps they are afraid that more lenient guidance would give the impression that they are indifferent to their daughter's well-being. They should realize that overzealous guarding will hamper their child's development of responsibility and judgment and that unnecessary restriction may separate her from her friends. It is admittedly difficult to achieve the middle road of reasonable supervision, but it is important to the child's social development to receive freedom as well as guidance during these years of adolescence.

THE NECESSARY PROPRIETIES

If a young girl's family is not at home, she must not, on returning from a party, invite or allow any man to "come in for a while." If he persists, she should answer casually but firmly, "Sorry, another time," and bid him "good night." However, if her parents are home and have been notified, it is perfectly all right to invite her friend in for a snack. He should not overstay his welcome, and when he sees that his date is tired and the hour late, he should leave.

Some families insist on a practice that is quite sensible—merely that their daughter telephone home just before leaving a dance if she plans to go on to someone's house or bring friends to her own. This is not unreasonable from the daughter's point of view. If she has poise and loyalty and is sure of herself, she can make her practice of telephoning an evidence of respect for her mother, and there will be no more question about her going to the telephone than about going to get her coat! Moreover, if she has these attributes of character, she will agree that the type of man who might resent her mother's insistence on knowing her daughter's whereabouts is not one of the type that she hopes to marry.

An unmarried girl should not go on overnight trips with any young man, even with her fiancé, because convention still decrees that she may not stop in a hotel with a young man unchaperoned. However, a girl of eighteen may perfectly well go on a weekend trip with several couples to a ski resort or a beach resort. In this case, the presence of a few other girls in the party is sufficient protection from idle and malicious gossip.

THE CHAPERON AT THE SCHOOL DANCE

Chaperons for a school dance may be recruited from among the faculty, the parents of the students, or other townspeople; they may be single persons or married couples. Chaperons are the ringside participants at the dance, responsible for the general discipline and order of those dancing. A school dance should be fun, and the chaperons should never put a damper on it, but should rather enhance the party by their own enjoyment of it. While a chaperon is not expected to serve as a "bouncer," he or she should be prepared to put down the firm foot of authority when some young person gets too boisterous.

A committee of one or a few may be in charge of securing the chaperons for the gala evening. The committee should select two or three chaperons who will be congenial to one another and whatever the event is to be. It is thoughtful to invite chaperons at least two weeks in advance so they can obtain baby-sitters or make any other necessary arrangements. If you are asking single persons, you must tell them that they may bring escorts. The same committee is responsible for writing thank-you notes to each chaperon after the dance.

And, of course, everyone must bid the chaperons good night and thank them for having come to the dance.

THE HOUSE MOTHER AS RESIDENT CHAPERON

The most usual chaperon today is the house mother, who, as her title implies, is a substitute mother for the girls or young women in her charge. She is to be found in preparatory boarding schools, college dormitories, or metropolitan women's residence hotels.

The house mother should be neither inquisitive nor interfering, except for seriously considered, valid reasons, since she must serve as an advisor to the young girls. Charm is a necessary quality, because she will be meeting and greeting the parents, girl friends, and beaux of her charges. She'll also be asked to serve at teas, be at the head of reception lines, and preside at luncheons, dinners, and other social occasions.

Genuine friendliness and kindness are at least as important as being charmingly gracious when a visiting V.I.P. is on hand. A house mother must offer friendship to all the girls under her wing, and not show favoritism to the few to whom she may feel partial.

A YOUNG GIRL IN HER PARENTS' HOME

It is perfectly proper, not only for a college girl but also for her little sister of thirteen or so, to invite friends to a party without the necessity of chaperonage other than that of her parents' presence in some part of the house. They should, however, arrange to be present at some time during the party. Perhaps they could say "Hello" when their daughter's guests arrive and then leave the young people alone, returning to serve the refreshments or, at the younger girl's party, bid the guests good-by.

A girl of sixteen could invite a boy she knows well to have dinner with her in her parents' home on an evening when they are dining out, as long as they are returning shortly after dinner. She also might invite a group in under the same circumstances, but she must be responsible for seeing that the kitchen is left clean so that her mother does not return to a stack of dirty dishes in the sink. After all parties are over, the teen-age host or hostess should empty ash trays, dispose of empty bottles, wash glasses, dispose of paper plates or other trash, and generally "pick up." If they do this faithfully, parents will rarely object to another party in their home.

WHEN A BACHELOR ENTERTAINS

The bachelor-about-town may occasionally entertain in his apartment, perhaps for a large group at a cocktail party or for a few friends at dinner. Propriety decrees that four is a better number than two for a small dinner party. A young woman visiting a man's apartment alone is still frowned upon and talked about by Mrs. Grundy, and a wise girl avoids a tête-à-tête in a bachelor's apartment. A hard and fast rule, however, cannot be made, since the answer will always be determined by the girl herself. Her character is her chaperon and will provide the ethical standard in each situation.

Young men who live out of the metropolitan area or who have a country house may give weekend house parties to which both men and women are invited. As mentioned above, the presence of several girls in the party is sufficient chaperonage.

The bachelor as weekend host should be sure that sleeping accommodations for his guests are adequate and comfortable. If conditions are somewhat primitive at his country house, he should see to it that the women have precedence in using the bathroom. He should arrange for transportation into town for any guests who may wish to go to church.

The male guests may offer to share some of the expenses of such a weekend, and their host may accept this offer if he chooses. But any bachelor who undertakes to entertain for a weekend must expect to pay all the expenses himself, unless when his guests are intimate friends, he asks them to contribute to the expenses when he invites them, as he properly may.

With domestic help becoming more and more a thing of the past, the bachelor may with all ease of conscience ask his female guests to help in preparing some or all of the meals. This is not only allowed; it can add greatly to the fun of the party.

DATES

The age at which a girl may go out alone with a boy in the evening, and how late she may stay out, will vary according to the responsibility of the girl herself and the custom of the community. Only a parent can make the exact decision. A girl of fourteen might go out with a boy as part of a group of four or more to an early movie, dinner, sports event, or some other special occasion. Most of the parties she goes to will, however, be those at the homes of friends or dances organized by her school. Her parents should at all times know where and with whom she is and at what time she will be home. As she grows in age and experience, her dates will naturally include many more activities, she will go out more frequently alone with a boy, and her hours will be later.

HOME-COMING HOURS

The hour at which a teen-ager must be home is one of the most difficult problems to be settled between children and their parents. The customs of the community, the hours kept by friends, the amount of sleep the individual child needs, and the confidence of the parents in a girl's escort, all are important factors. During the early teen years, when children do not have the wisdom to recognize their own needs, the parents must set time limits on dates and see that they are kept, even though it may mean waiting up to greet the returning son or daughter. This is a simple matter of good health, as well as setting a high standard of behavior. It is wise to discuss home-coming hours with other parents and try to arrive at an hour to which everyone, including the children, agree. If this is impossible, try to choose a time you think sensible—not the earliest, for this will only cause resentment and disobedience, or the latest, which may cause criticism, as well as being detrimental to the child's health.

Dates should be absolutely restricted to weekends and vacations.

Even high school students who are "going steady" should not be permitted to date during the week, even to study together. The only exceptions might be very special occasions, such as if a boy were given theater tickets to an excellent difficult-to-see show, or a league-winning game, or some other extraordinary event. In these cases, they should study especially hard in advance to be sure that their work is ready for the next day and get extra sleep the nights before and after the date.

As a general rule, 10:30 or 11:00 is a reasonable time for a thirteen- or fourteen-year-old to be home. On occasion, he or she may attend a school or club dance, or other special party until 12:00. The hours should be made a little later each year so that sixteen- or seventeen-year-olds might stay at parties until 12:30 or 1:00. For an ordinary movie date, this age group should still return by 11:00 or thereabouts. If they plan to go to a friend's house or a snack bar afterward, their parents should know in advance or be called on the telephone, so that they may know the whereabouts of the child and readjust the hour when he must be home. When a youngster reaches his late teens, his hour should be regulated only by his or her own need for sleep, or if he is away at college, the rules of the university. Parents of a child living at home should realize that, were he away at college, he would be making his own rules as to hours, and allow him the same privilege. They may, of course, point out that he is not getting enough sleep, or suggest that he needs a "health night," as my teen-agers call an early-to-bed evening. But many eighteen-year-olds live away from home, they work, they are in the armed forces, and they are even married, so it seems a little ridiculous for parents, simply because they are fortunate enough to have their youngster at home, to attempt to treat him as a child, rather than an intelligent, if young, adult.

ASKING FOR A DATE

The cartoon depicting a girl confiding to her friend, "We met in the strangest way—we were formally introduced!" is not too far removed from the realities of today's casual way of life. Young people in high school or college are likely to begin friendships on the school steps, in the student room, or in the classroom. Acquaintances formed in this way are not "pick-ups," a derogatory term referring to a much more public kind of encounter that is never correct.

A young man may properly ask any girl to whom he has been introduced for a date, at any time. Usually he uses the telephone, but there is no reason why he should not ask her in person when he sees her.

When telephoning, make sure your identity is established immediately and definitely: "This is Jim Brown. We met at Mrs. Worldly's." Then a minute or two of "small talk"—"How are you? Hasn't it been a freezing week?"—and then state your purpose. Here, too, you must be specific; never say, "What are you doing Saturday night?" and leave her wondering whether you are or are not asking for a definite date. If you say, "I've managed to get two tickets for *Romeo and Juliet* for Saturday night. I hope you can come with me," she will know what and when—as well as what to wear—and she can give you a definite answer. If she says she'd love to go with you on Saturday, you can say, "Good," or, "How about dinner first?" Decide on the time, say something like, "I'm looking forward to seeing you," and end the conversation.

Some young people do not know how far in advance a date should be made. Many men are too negligent to make their weekend plans before Thursday, and they are likely to discover that the more popular young women have already made their plans well before then. A woman would like to have at least four or five days ahead for an invitation to an informal evening on a weekend, two or three days ahead for a weekday date, and a week or two ahead for a formal dance or dinner or a house party. This is not as unreasonable as it sounds because she may need the time to buy a new dress or arrange an appointment with the hairdresser. In any case she should be given as much time as possible.

REFUSING A DATE

If she is really busy and really sorry, the young woman should refuse in such a way that the man will be encouraged to try again. This requires diplomacy and charm. Keeping her apology brief, general, and sincere—"I'm so sorry. I've already made other plans"—is better than going into detail about her aunt who has come to town. She can encourage him to call again by suggesting another night ("I'm so sorry I can't make it Friday. I wish you'd call again"), or she can ask for a "rain-check."

Refusing because she does not care enough for the young man's company to want to spend a whole evening with him is also a problem in diplomacy. She should not be rudely blunt; neither should she be coy enough to encourage him to try again. "I'm so sorry, but I've already made plans for Saturday" is sufficient. Remember that, having refused a date because you simply do not wish to go with that person, you may *never* appear at the same party, movie, or any other function with someone else who asked you later.

The man who is refused may try again, if he thinks the refusal was of the first type. However, if he receives three refusals in a row, he may assume she's not interested, and forget her and her telephone number.

BREAKING A DATE

Illness, business, family ties—there are a variety of legitimate reasons that may cause a date to be broken. The receipt of a more desirable invitation is *never* sufficient reason for canceling an appointment. Should it be necessary, for a valid reason, to break a date, you should notify the person concerned immediately, explaining as briefly as possible why you cannot keep the appointment and perhaps trying at that time to make another.

The practice of willfully not keeping an appointment, known as "standing up," is inexcusable and is practiced only by a boor. A well-bred person will not plan an appointment with someone he does not care to spend time with; but if he is trapped into making such a date he will feel in honor bound to keep it.

DURING THE DATE

The man must call for his date at her home. Only if he knows her well and if there is good and sufficient reason (such as an early dinner appointment in the city) may he meet her at some other convenient place. It is the man's responsibility to plan and to pay for everything they do that evening—transportation, entertainment, and food.

The woman is sometimes able to make things easier for a man's financially strained situation. For instance, if the young man has asked her to the movies, and she knows this is really all he can afford, she may offer to extend the evening by suggesting, "How about having dinner at our apartment first?" In a restaurant she should not order the most expensive item on the menu, unless the man indicates what he expects her to order by saying, "Their sirloin is wonderful. Would you like some?" If his budget is too low for steak, he can recommend the fried chicken—and perhaps choose a more modest restaurant the next time.

The man should arrive on time, and the woman must be ready promptly; there is no truth in the old saw about "keeping him waiting." She should be dressed suitably, assuming the young man has told her what they are going to do; if he has been vague, a simple dress will be in the best taste. It is always better to be under- than over-dressed. Should she discover that her date is dressed for bowling while she thought they were going to a cocktail party, she should excuse herself for ten minutes—no more!—while she hastily changes into something more casual.

When the young man arrives, the girl should introduce him to her parents or roommates. The man who takes a few minutes to chat with her parents makes a good impression. She should join in the conversation briefly before saying, "Shall we go now?" and then get her coat, and handbag, and bid her parents good night.

During the evening, she participates with enthusiasm in whatever activities have been planned. At the end of the evening it is she who suggests that it is time to go home.

At her door, he thanks her for the pleasure of her company; she thanks him for an enjoyable evening. He may say, "I'll call you next week," or even make another date then and there. But if he is not interested in seeing her again, he says nothing but "Good night."

THE BLIND DATE

The "blind date" is a peculiarly American variation of the formal introduction, which in this case is made indirectly and for the express purpose of arranging a date. It is sometimes arranged by a third person such as Mrs. Towne, who thinks that Gloria Gorgeous and Harry Handsome would enjoy each other's company. She first makes sure that Harry would be interested in calling Gloria; then she asks Gloria if she would like to meet an attractive man. Only after both parties have indicated that they are willing to be so introduced should Mrs. Towne give Gloria's telephone number to Harry.

The date may also be arranged by a girl who is asked for a date by a boy she does not know well or does not wish to go out with alone. She might say, "Jane Ratsey is spending the night with me, so I would love to go out with you if you have a friend who would like to take her out, and we'll make it a foursome."

The most frequent type of blind date, however, occurs when a host or hostess arranges a date for his or her overnight guest. A girl may call a good friend and say, "Tom, Sally, who is my roommate at college, is spending the weekend with me, and I think you would like her, so how about taking her to a movie with Jim and me on Saturday night?"

Dates arranged in any of these ways should not be expected to result in anything more than a pleasant evening. Even close friends do not always agree on whom they like or dislike, and while Cindy may think Charley is divine, her friend Jane may well be bored to death in his company. So make the best of a blind date, and no matter what you may think to yourself, act as if you were enjoying every minute. After all, it is probably better than sitting at home with a book, and whether he is enchanting or not, you may meet more attractive men through your new acquaintance.

"GOING STEADY" AND "PINNING"

The dating habits of young people today include some customs that were unknown a short generation ago. To the chagrin of many parents and teachers, "going steady" has become a fact of American teen-age life. Gone is the traditional stag line at the high school dance; today a girl usually dances only with her escort. When a boy and girl date each other consistently, they are considered by their contemporaries to be "going steady." Usually they have an agreement that neither is to date anyone else, and this may even be formalized by an exchange of friendship rings or identification bracelets.

For several reasons, this is an unfortunate practice, and it is the wise young person who widens rather than narrows his circle of friends. Many girls fear not having a date for Saturday night, and some boys are afraid to be told "no" when they call a girl for a date. But these young people are putting limits on the development of their own social personalities when they limit their dating friendships. Only by meeting many other young people of varied backgrounds and interests can a boy or girl broaden his or her own experience and gain enough insight to be capable of making a good choice of a marriage partner when the time comes.

The presentation of a fraternity badge by a college man to his girl, known as "pinning," may be merely another type of "going steady," or it may mean that the couple are "engaged to be engaged," depending on the customs of that particular college. Generally the couple intends marriage but in the somewhat distant future, and this relationship allows them to examine their compatibility without committing themselves formally to an engagement. It is not considered proper for a girl to give a man her sorority pin or to collect fraternity pins as trophies of her dates. If the "pinned" couple "breaks up," the girl is expected to return the pin to the young man. In many cases, "pinning" does lead to a formal engagement and then to marriage.

After leaving college, of course, unmarried young men and women do not follow these customs, which seem to have significance only in the high school or college community. Although a couple in their late twenties or thirties may be dating each other exclusively, there will usually be no formalizing of their relationship until they decide to become engaged.

DON'T NEGLECT YOUR GIRL FRIENDS!

Many girls make the mistake of boasting of boredom when compelled to be with girls alone, as though this boredom were an asset. The girl who tells other girls that she understands men—implying that the others, poor things, are lacking in sense as well as charm—is not instilling feelings of envy and admiration in the hearts of her hearers, but feelings of resentment against her conceit and contempt for her stupidity.

The mistake, of course, is in boasting, and not in preferring the companionship of men to girls. Girls who enjoy great popularity are most likely to be those who recognize the necessity of having friendships with girls as well as men. The girl who really has a capacity for friendship with men rarely boasts of it.

A happy marriage

There are no two people in the world, no matter how much in love they are when they get married, who do not have to make adjustments to each other. There is simply no way of getting to know each other completely when still living apart, and the first months, and even years, of married life are an exciting, stimulating time of discovery and deepening affection. If, that is, each partner is willing to make concessions to the habits of his mate that annoy him and to look for and enjoy the traits that please. The wife who starts nagging soon after marriage because her husband does not hang up his suit every night or the husband who can't stand her stockings drying in the bathroom will have a difficult period of adjustment. Of course, he should try to improve his bachelor habits in order to make his wife's housecleaning easier, and she should do her wash early enough so that her stockings can be put away before he gets home, but this type of irritation should never be allowed to become so important that the happy times are forgotten in a constant stream of recriminations.

HINTS FOR THE NEWLYWEDS

I don't know why people should feel that because they have married, they may give up all pretense of good manners and treat their partner as an "old shoe." During courtship, both men and women put their best foot forward, and rather than being a trap to catch their mate, this should set the pattern for their marriage. But it does not always work that way, and many a marriage has failed because one or both of the partners allowed their attitude toward the other to become careless, ill-mannered, or just plain bored. It takes effort to keep a good marriage going, and the close proximity of home life makes the constant presence of good manners more important than in any relationship with those outside the family.

THE WIFE'S PART

How many times has one heard someone say, "No one is coming in. That old dress will do!" Old clothes! Sloppy manners! And what is the result? One wife more wonders why her husband neglects her! Curious how the habit of careless manners and the habit of old clothes go together. And how many women, really lovely and good—especially good—commit esthetic suicide by letting themselves slide down to where they feel natural in an old housecoat, not only physically but mentally.

She who changes her dress and fixes her hair for her husband's homecoming is sure to greet him with greater charm than she who thinks whatever she happens to have on is good enough. The very fact of *looking* more attractive makes one feel less tired and therefore more charming and better company.

So many people save up all their troubles to pour on the one they most love, the idea being, seemingly, that no reserves are necessary between lovers. Nor need there be, really. But why, when the roses burst into bloom this morning, does she never show them to him instead of insisting that he look at the hole dug in his garden by the neighbor's dog?

She who complains incessantly that this is wrong or that hurts or that some other thing worries or vexes her, so that his inevitable answer to her greeting is "I'm so sorry, dear," or "That's too bad," is getting very decidedly into an old housecoat! If something is seriously wrong, if she is really ill, that is different. But of the petty things that are only remembered in order to be told to gain sympathy—beware! There is a big deposit of sympathy in the bank of love, but don't draw out little sums every hour or two—so that by and by, when perhaps you need it badly, it is all drawn out and you yourself don't know how or on what it was spent.

The wife who smears her face with cream and rolls her hair in curlers before going to bed is not a sight that many husbands can endure. With a handy portable drier, there is no reason that hair cannot be dried while doing chores, feeding the baby, or paying the bills or during any other household duties in the morning. And the wife who prepares and sees her husband off to work in a dirty bathrobe, with hair uncombed and face unwashed, sends him off with a thoroughly unflattering picture of her in his mind. No wonder many a man has found his neat, efficient, pretty secretary more appealing than his unkempt, uncaring wife!

The intelligent woman will listen as if she cared to her husband's problems at the office. Many wives complain after being married for some years that their husbands never talk to them when they come home. This may be because at the beginning of their married life, John eagerly started out, "Guess what, darling, I have an appointment with the President of the Fix Corporation, and he may give me their account . . ." but Joan, not fully understanding the importance of the meeting to him, interrupted, "Oh really? But you must come and see Junior's new tooth, and then please repair the stopper in the sink, and . . ." John soon gave up trying to discuss his business with Joan, and a rift was started that was never quite healed with talk of babies, sitters, etc.

Even though a girl may loathe cooking, she should make an effort to cater to her husband's likes and dislikes and to make meals appetizing and interesting. If he hates liver, she should not serve it once a week because "it's good for the blood." If she is on a diet, she must not feed her husband a dinner of one lamb chop and a small green salad. And no matter how noble he may be about claiming he likes it, she never feeds him frozen dinners more than once a week! A little surprise now and then—something he especially likes, such as a homemade apple pie or a special cut of steak ordinarily beyond her budget—will do wonders toward making her seem a marvelous cook and clever wife.

A considerate wife doesn't make plans without consulting her husband, unless she knows the event is something he will enjoy. If he is working very hard, it is terribly thoughtless of her to plan a dinner party for Friday, to accept an invitation for a dance on Saturday, and to organize an all-day picnic with the children on Sunday. Of course, a girl who has been tied down to babies and household chores all week looks forward to a little gaiety on the weekend, but here again there must be compromise and she must remember that her husband, while he also enjoys a little diversion, may need some extra rest.

If her husband is the type who enjoys an evening of poker with his friends, the smart wife will cheer him on his way and even offer to provide refreshments for his gang at home when it is his turn to invite them there. She leaves everything in readiness and disappears—completely! But if he is bringing a business acquaintance home, she must be a gracious hostess until after dinner, when she excuses herself, washes up quietly, and goes to her room to leave them to their business discussion.

THE HUSBAND'S PART

For some reason, it seems that the bride generally has to make more effort to achieve a successful marriage than the groom, but it is certainly a two-sided partnership, and she cannot do it alone. The man who rushed to open the car door or light her cigarette when they were engaged is still the same man, but he will soon fall far short of her expectations if he drops these little politenesses as soon as they are married.

It is just as true that a husband must show some interest in his wife's daily happenings as that she should listen to his business news. The worst of evenings begins when the husband—whose wife has had no one but the baby to talk to all day long—grunts and buries his nose in the newspaper when she tries to carry on a conversation.

He may have been accustomed to living alone or in a bachelor apartment where no one cared or at home where his mother picked up for him, but the new husband must learn that trousers dropped in the middle of the floor, a sink spattered with shaving soap, and soggy towels on the bathroom rug can be an unpleasant shock to his bride.

Many men do not care too much for babies until they are old enough to respond or even to show interest in things about which Daddy cares. But this can be a very sore point with a young mother who firmly believes that every move her baby makes is without equal, and her husband's lack of interest seems callous and cruel. If Daddy will take the time really to observe and play with, as well as discipline, his children when he comes home, it will not only please his wife, but he will find himself more interested in the babies than he thought possible.

The husband who will keep his wife company in the kitchen while she is finishing the dinner preparations, rather than retire to the TV set or his newspaper, will find himself more than repaid by his appreciative wife. A girl who has been alone all day doing household chores is desperately anxious to have someone to talk to, and a comfortable chair where her husband may sit and chat with her is well worth the expense. A helping hand with the dishes after dinner is never amiss, although many men, and some wives too, feel that this is the woman's department.

A considerate husband never brings home unexpected guests without giving his wife some warning. He and the guests can hardly wish to walk in on her in her negligee and with her hair in curlers, any more than she could welcome their arrival. And he certainly cannot expect, without advance notice, that she produce a succulent meal for four, when she has chopped meat for two hamburgers.

It has been said many times before, but it is still true, that it is important to women that their husbands remember special occasions. If the budget is limited, the remembrance need only be a card for Mother's Day, a single rose for an anniversary, or a simple little gift for a birthday. It is the thought that counts, and women, generally more sentimental than men, attach tremendous importance to these little gestures.

Unless he has come to an agreement with his wife, it is very selfish of a man to spend all his free time pursuing a sport or hobby that does not interest her. Of course, he should follow his interest within reason, but the husband who spends all weekend on the golf course, making his wife into a "golf widow," may find that she will look for interests other than his, which may include a man who has tastes more similar to hers. A Saturday golf game with his friends, and a Sunday picnic with his family, plus, perhaps, an hour's workout at the driving range one evening or two during the week can be a happy solution for the whole family.

One of the most important things a man can do to please his wife is to plan occasional entertainments that will appeal to her—especially a dinner at a restaurant if he can afford it. He may surprise her, or they may plan it together, but a trip to the theater, an overnight jaunt to some favorite spot, or even an evening at the movies can be a wonderful treat to a girl who spends much of her time at home. If a man's budget simply cannot stretch this far, he can still make his wife very happy by offering to plan and cook the dinner occasionally, or by taking her on a picnic at a beach or lake, or to a free concert or museum or lecture, depending on her interests. In any case, she will appreciate the effort he has made to plan something for her, and it will give her something to look forward to and, afterward, a happy memory to share.

AIRING THE PROBLEMS

There are endless other suggestions that might well be considered by the newlyweds, but the above seem to be the principle bones of contention in many marriages. There are lesser ones—interrupting each other, making fun of idiosyncracies, not laughing at his or her jokes, never being on time, the wife using the husband's razor, and a thousand others that can build up a huge wall of resentment. And there are greater ones—basic differences of opinion on bringing up children, how to spend vacations, watching television in the bedroom, and so on—that can undermine an otherwise sound marriage. But great or small, the only way to handle these problems is by bringing them into the open and keeping the lines of communication free between husband and wife. The moment that one or the other feels he cannot discuss a problem and it is left to fester and grow inside is the moment the marriage begins to dissolve. The couple who agrees not only to listen to each other's problems, but to make an effort to see the other side and to DO something to correct the situation is one hundred percent certain to stay out of the divorce courts.

IN-LAW SITUATIONS

One is likely to overlook the fact that when John Jones marries Mary Smith, a number of Smiths and Joneses are suddenly forced into the closeness of family relationships. Even when a bride or bridegroom has no family, he or she becomes son or daughter, sister or brother, to those who may have hitherto been total strangers.

The two most difficult situations to meet happily and successfully are those between the husband and his father-in-law and between the wife and her mother-in-law. The other positions are easy and there is little reason for failure. In any case, the very first rule that every father-in-law—and especially every mother-in-law—must learn is DON'T IN-TERFERE. Never mind what small blunders your daughter or daughter-in-law or your son or son-in-law may make; remember that it is their right to live and do and think as they please. If you are asked what you think, answer truthfully, of course; but don't, upon being given one opening, cram in every item of good advice that you've been storing up for just this chance—or you will risk never being asked again.

LIVING WITH RELATIVES

When a young wife, for any one of many reasons, goes to live with her husband's people, she must in this difficult situation adapt herself not only to their mode of living, but also to the dispositions of the various members of the family. In this way alone can she herself be happy. On the other hand, it is essential that the mother-in-law encourage the younger woman's efforts to become adjusted to completely new surroundings instead of showing irritation over the shortcomings, of which she will certainly have at least a few.

When a mother or father must live with a married child, the situation demands the wisdom of a Solomon, the tact of a Recamier, and the self-control of a stoic. Moreover, she or he must conscientiously practice the art of "invisibility" at frequent and lengthy intervals. This does not mean that the mother, for example, must scuttle out of sight like a frightened mouse, but that she shall have or make occupations of her own that keep her from being idly, plaintively, or forcefully present—particularly when special friends of her daughter-in-law or even old friends of her son are present. Perhaps she can find some friends and play bridge or canasta one or two evenings every week. Her room should be equipped with radio and television so that she can always be free to enjoy her own favorite programs. She should assist with household chores or caring for the children as much as she easily can, but she should not be imposed upon or made to feel like a built-in baby-sitter.

On the other hand there is no excuse for the ruthless unkindness that certain wives show when they are obliged to have a parent-in-law live in their house. This attitude, did they but know it, is not only distressing to the helpless victim of their cruelty, but is certainly resented by all who see it.

IN-LAW RELATIONSHIP AT ITS BEST

An in-law relationship should be unhampering, uninterfering, uncriticizing.

Whether we be mother or father, bride or groom, the safe rule for our own happiness is to take things as we find them, take pleasure in the assets, not go searching for flaws, and not ever for a single second permit ourselves the happiness-destroying weakness of feeling sorry for ourselves. Nothing is harder to build than this impersonality of mind, and one moment's relaxed indulgence in self-pity can bring it all crashing down. The first step in the achievement of impersonality is keeping our thoughts away from every trend that is sentimentally focused upon ourselves by thinking of something else—never mind what.

If it is physically possible, it is far better for parents to live apart from their married children. The young people should, if necessary, help to support the older ones, especially a widow, but the parents should be allowed to feel that they are handling their own affairs and managing their own lives until they are no longer capable or do not wish to do so. Love and affection will flourish in an atmosphere of independence, supplemented by close family ties. But people of different generations living together are bound to find some friction even though they may feel great affection for each other.

SEPARATION AND DIVORCE

Unfortunately, there has been such an epidemic of divorce raging in this country for the past fifty years that it must be rated as a catastrophe along with floods, dust bowls, and tornadoes. There are cases, of course, where divorce is the best—sometimes the only—solution for everyone concerned. If two persons are truly mismated, they certainly and perhaps their children too are better off if they part. The only consideration of vital importance is that they shall not part because of a love-for-another attack that might prove to be transient.

Sometimes a period of separation can solve the problem of too-hasty divorce, for separation and divorce are different not only in terms of the law, but to some extent in terms of the behavior expected of the people involved.

A separation may be legal or it may simply be arranged by unwritten consent of both parties. It may be a "trial" separation, or it may be viewed from the beginning as permanent. This is often true if the faith of the couple forbids divorce, as does Catholicism.

A trial separation is exactly what it sounds like. Two people have found it increasingly difficult to live together and wish to find out if they can readjust, and be happier, living alone. But for one reason or another, because of children, finances, or any number of other situations, they want time to consider before taking the final steps toward divorce. If they find they are better off apart, and if they are not interested in remarriage or are forbidden by their church to remarry, they may make the separation legal, and papers making property settlements, arrangements for children, financial support, and so on, will be drawn up by their lawyers.

When a couple separates, it is never publicly announced, although the news generally spreads quickly. Because they are still legally married, the woman continues to use her husband's name and wears her wedding ring. He quietly moves out of their home, possibly on an extended "business trip," or she may take her children for a "visit" to her family. They refuse invitations that come to "Mr. and Mrs.," although if they accidentally meet, they should act as friendly and normal as possible. Friends, of course, should respect the situation and never invite them both to the same party without their knowledge and consent.

If they decide that life together was better than life apart, they simply move back together and make as little of the separation as they can. For this reason, it is wise for the wife, or husband, whichever has remained there, to keep the home and other property intact, rather than selling or renting in a moment of bitterness.

When a divorce is finally and irrevocably decided upon, both parties must accept the fact that their marriage no longer exists. The husband who insists on "dropping in" to see the children or the wife who keeps calling his office to ask his advice on this or that is only prolonging the agony and achieving nothing but more unhappiness. People who have made the decision to part should have done so with enough serious thought so that once accomplished, all ties are severed, and they can start to make new lives for themselves and leave their ex-partner to do the same.

A divorce is almost always a tragic experience for at least one of the couple. Therefore, it should not be announced publicly and certainly never, even in private, treated as a matter for celebration. The fact that a woman discards her wedding ring and substitutes her maiden name for her husband's first name (Mrs. McCallum Ford) is sufficient announcement in itself. In the happy event that the couple resolve their difficulties after the divorce is final, they should remarry quietly, with only their families or closest friends as witnesses. The divorced couple's friends should extend their sympathetic friendship—never criticism or censure—but at the same time respect their privacy, and avoid prying or questioning the reasons for or mechanics of the divorce.

There is no longer any stigma attached to divorce in this country, but neither should anyone approach it lightly. There could never be any argument with the fact that if there is any chance of maintaining a civil relationship, if not a deeply loving one, it is far better to do so, not only for the couple, but most especially for their children.

In the thousands of cases where children are involved, it is far, far better that the divorced parents make every effort to remain on friendly terms. Nothing in all the world is so devastating in its destruction of character and of soul as living in an atmosphere infused with hatred. Anything is better for children than that!

One wonders what part divorce has played in the point of view of many of a now-grown "younger" generation. Their hardness, their lack of consideration, and their indifference toward family obligations! How many of the thousands of children who have lived through this experience have suffered spiritual injury, and to what degree? No one can know for certain. Nor can one know to what degree other children, who have been witnesses to the broken homes of their playmates, live in fear of the same things happening to them.

At present the breaking up of homes is so widespread it may be that those who grow up never having known the completeness of home will find it unessential. Or will it be the other way around? Perhaps the children of today's divided houses will be twice as earnest in their efforts to provide their own children with the priceless security of a father and mother together in one place called HOME!

INDEX

"going steady," 668–669
golf, 554–556, 603–604
"Good afternoon," use of, 13
good-by, saying. *See* leaving
governess, 624
government officials. *See* public officials
governors of states:
 addressing and introducing, 5–6, 60–
  61, 64–65, 478
 announcing, 168
 name for residence of, 72
 place card for, 479–480
 and precedence, 168, 173, 477
 visiting card of, 462
 writing paper of, 51
grace before meals, 520
"gracious," use of, 27
graduation, 296–299
 clothes for, 297–298
 and gifts, 298
 invitations to, 440–441
grapefruit spoons, 179
gravy, 522, 526
green beans, serving, 191
greeting cards, 89–92
greetings:
 in business, 13
 in church, 14, 410
 to guests. *See* receiving guests
 "Hello," use of, 13
 in public places, 13–14
 in restaurants, 108–109
 See also forms of address; shaking
  hands; standing
groom. *See* bridegroom
guest of honor:
 bride as, 173
 celebrity as, 564
 at formal dinner, 173, 194
 at formal luncheon, 199
 at informal dinner, 224
 and introductions, 6
 at official dinner, 167
 seating of, 95–96
guest rooms, 276–279
guest speaker. *See* public speaking
guests:
 announcing. *See* announcing guests
 at balls, 211, 212–213
 at buffet dinner, 241–242
 cars of, ordering, 194
 in club, 216, 516–518
 at cocktail parties, 220–221
 at college weekend, 656–659
 at dances, 212–213
 at formal dinner, 172–175, 195–197
 at formal luncheon, 198
 gifts from, 285

guests, *contd.*
 greeting. *See* receiving guests
 of honor. *See* guest of honor
 house. *See* overnight guests
 at informal dinner, 231–232
 introducing. *See* introductions
 inviting. *See* invitations
 and lateness. *See* punctuality
 and leaving. *See* leaving
 meeting at station or airport, 276
 offering to help hostess, 229, 230, 232
 at official dinner, 166
 overnight. *See* overnight guests
 and pets, 572–574
 at picnic, 253
 in restaurant, 101–107
 and returning hospitality, 215–216,
  468
 seating. *See* seating
 and smoking, 508–509
 at tea, 207
 and telephone charges, 497
 at wedding, 409–410
 at wedding reception, 410–412
 for weekend. *See* overnight guests
 at White House, 482–483
 See also visits

H

hair styles, 562, 576–577, 649–650
handbags, 196, 581
handicapped people, courtesy to, 567–
 570
hand, kissing, 11, 163–164
handshaking. *See* shaking hands
handwriting:
 for acceptances and regrets, 450–455
 appearance of, 45–46
 and formal invitations, 177, 198–199,
  441–442
 and informal invitations, 223, 275–
  276, 445–446
 versus typewriting, 46–47
hats:
 of bridegroom, 362
 of men, 596–598
  removing, 597–598
  tipping to women, 13, 597
 and social visits, 470
 for sports, 603, 604, 606, 608
 of women, 579
  at restaurants, 586
  at theater, 114
  at wedding reception, 411
  when required, 100–101
heads of state, introducing, 2
headwaiters, tipping, 105–107, 138